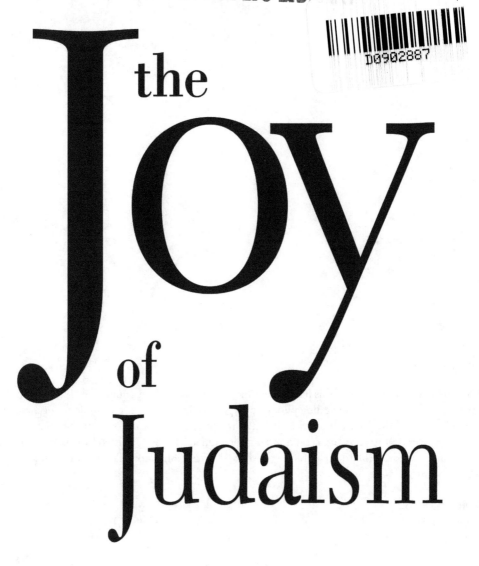

the JOY of Judaism

A practical guide to spiritual living using Judaism's timeless teachings

SAM GLASER

Shefa Press
1941 Livonia Ave
Los Angeles, CA 90034
www.shefapress.com

Printed in the United States of America

Ordering Information:
Quantity sales. Special discounts are available on quantity purchases by corporations, associations, and others. For details, contact the publisher at the address above.
Orders by U.S. trade bookstores and wholesalers. Please contact Shefa Press: Tel: (800) 972-6694; Fax: (310) 204-6222 or visit www.shefapress.com.

Publisher's Cataloging-in-Publication data Glaser, Sam. The Joy of Judaism: A Practical Guide to Spiritual Living Using Judaism's Timeless Teachings / Sam Glaser. p. cm. ISBN 978-1-7329506-0-3
1. Spirituality—Judaism 2. Music—Travel. 3. More categories —
II. Title. HF0000.A0 A00 2010 299.000 00–dc22 2010999999

First Edition May 2019
14 13 12 11 10 / 10 9 8 7 6 5 4 3 2 1

ISBN 978-1-7329506-0-3

Praise for
The Joy of Judaism

"The Joy of Judaism is the remarkable result of Sam's twenty-five years of globetrotting to spiritual communities of all shapes and sizes. Sam lives his Torah and speaks from the heart. His stories entertain with wisdom and humor and serve to clarify the potential for energized spiritual living and 24/7 mindfulness."
–RABBI DAVID AARON, author of *Living a Joyous Life* and *The God Powered Life*

"Sam Glaser is a very talented guy. I have spent many a Shabbat in his company and enjoy all his albums—he embodies the joyful Judaism that he teaches. This book brings life to to a world thirsty for spirituality."
–KIRK DOUGLAS

"It's about time Sam Glaser wrote this book. Tens of thousands who have enjoyed his songs and spirit over the years have awaited a publication like this. I read it and wept with joy. I had trouble putting it down and felt blessed by its message; its easy reading, engaging style gripped me from the get go. It is one of the best introductions to the world of Judaism in print. I wish every young Jew (and non Jew, in fact) would read it. I promise—you'll thank me."
–RABBI YECHIEL ECKSTEIN, founder and president of the International Fellowship of Christians and Jews

"Everyone wants more joy in life, and anyone who knows Sam Glaser knows that his joyousness is deep, real, and rooted in his Judaism. This beautifully written book is nothing less than his buoyant personality distilled into words. Treat yourself to The Joy of Judaism *and feast on the ways that Judaism can set your soul dancing."*
–RABBI BRADLEY SHAVIT ARTSON, Dean of Ziegler School of Rabbinic Studies, American Jewish University

"I rarely get on an airplane without Sam Glaser's gorgeous music, his Torah, playing in my ears, connecting me, reminding me, bringing me peace. I rely on it. Sam and I have been sharing this road for decades, woven together in friendship by our love for Judaism and music. He is a true model of K'lal Yisrael. His lessons on the Joy of Judaism inspire students and teachers and build bridges between communities. Just like his deeply connected music, this collection of stories will elevate your Jewish experience no matter where you are on your journey."
–JULIE SILVER, celebrated performer of contemporary Jewish music

"The same joy that Sam's music brings to listeners, his book brings to readers. The Joy of Judaism is a loving celebration of our tradition."
–RABBI DAVID WOLPE, author and rabbi of Sinai Temple, Los Angeles

"Sam Glaser is the Energizer Bunny of the Jewish world. He seems to be everywhere, joyfully celebrating Jewish identity and connecting his audiences with Jewish tradition. Sam's prolific recordings, thought-provoking workshops and hectic travel schedule are a testament to his love for the Jewish people. We are so excited to share The Joy of Judaism *with our community."*
–**RABBI DANIEL FREELANDER**, President, World Union for Progressive Judaism

*"*The Joy of Judaism *is an overview of the opportunities for supercharged spiritual living. The ever upbeat Sam Glaser is a wonderful guide for this journey. Spiritual seekers will gain significant insight from the essence of Judaism that he vividly shares on each page."*
–**RABBI SHMULEY BOTEACH**, author of *Judaism for Everyone*, host TLC's *Shalom in the Home*

"Sam Glaser is my teacher, my guide, my backbone, my inspiration and guiding light. I owe much of who I am today to my brother and best friend, Sam. He is a rare breed: vastly creative and industrious, a musician's musician, an artful wordsmith who has condensed decades of his Torah experience into this manifesto. The Joy of Judaism *is yet another Sam Glaser adventure into the world of the spirit, one that is not to be missed."*
–**RABBI YOM TOV GLASER**, Senior Lecturer, Aish HaTorah, Founder of The Possible You seminar

"Sam Glaser brings passion and joy to every endeavor. The Joy of Judaism *is a fount of inspiration in which he describes Jewish tradition as the source of that joy—in his life, and potentially in yours."*
–**MICHAEL MEDVED**, nationally syndicated radio host and author of *The American Miracle*

"Chabad Houses worldwide can attest to Sam Glaser's enthusiasm for Yiddishkeit and love for fellow Jews. His songs are beloved, his ability to lead davening is sublime and his concerts are engaging for all ages and backgrounds. Now with the release of The Joy of Judaism, *Sam shares his own journey in order to encourage students and scholars alike to deepen connections with Hashem. This book is thought provoking, well researched and offers jewels on every page."*
–**RABBI TZVI FREEMAN**, senior editor of Chabad.org, author of *Bringing Heaven Down to Earth*

"I have watched Sam blossom over the course of our thirty-year friendship. He has become a leader in the L.A. Jewish community and a shining light in the greater worldwide community. He is one of the busiest performers and producers of Jewish music and yet found the time to author this encyclopedic guide, The Joy of Judaism, *a detailed yet utterly readable overview of enthusiastic Jewish living. This text will be a cherished part of any Jewish library and will have a profound influence on anyone who has the merit to read it."*
–**RICHARD HOROWITZ**, president Aish HaTorah International

"Sam is the most dynamic and positive influence on the Jewish scene today. His ability to show people the spirit and hip-ness of Judaism makes him the best candidate to bring Jews back to their roots, and The Joy of Judaism *adds immeasurably to his arsenal."*
–**RABBI BEN ZION KRAVITZ**, founder of Jews for Judaism Crisis Intervention Center

"All the joy, exuberance and love of Sam Glaser's music fill the pages of this marvelous book. This is much more than a guide to living a Jewish life—Sam offers us a heartfelt celebration and a soulful interpretation of Judaism's genius. Each page invites us to taste the ineffable sweetness of a life lived in God's presence. Sam's The Joy of Judaism *is a gift to us all.*"
—RABBI ED FEINSTEIN, Senior Rabbi, Valley Beth Shalom, Encino, CA

"Sam Glaser is the most prolific and consistently excellent composer of Jewish music alive. I have worked with him on recordings and in concert around the US for over 25 years. His songs are some of the most inspiring I've heard, encouraging Jews at all levels of awareness to embrace their heritage. I have a respect for Sam's feel for harmony that I reserve for the hippest composers like Steely Dan, Joni Mitchell and Stevie Wonder. Most don't realize Sam wakes up in the middle of the night and downloads the full arrangement of new songs from his dreams. He then brings the best players in L.A. to his studio to capture this vision. In the hundreds of sessions I have done with Sam, he has drawn out some of the best work of my career. He has a staggering work ethic—how many artists alive can say they have composed, produced and engineered the dozens of albums they've released? What a gift that his insights are in print for the world to enjoy."
—MAT GURMAN, guitarist with The Beach Boys, The Backstreet Boys and k.d. lang

"Sam Glaser is a Jewish national treasure and his writings and videos are highly valued at Aish. com. I have all his recordings—his incredible music makes me get up and dance! We are so excited to learn from The Joy of Judaism."
—RABBI SHRAGA SIMMONS, founder of Aish.com and HonestReporting.com

"To say Sam is a kind and generous person is an understatement. Sam loves his Jewish brethren, but his humanity is truly revealed by his work with all humankind. Sam's music is a candid expression of his love for God. It has already left an eternal mark on this world. Now, this incredible book will be an invaluable resource for all truth-seeking individuals. Sam is a hero among Noahides: he created the first ever joint Noahide/Jewish unity CD for our global community. He composed and recorded the "Nations of the World" song specifically for our cause. His performance at our World Conference in Dallas had our members and rabbinic faculty dancing in the aisles. Sam is a blessed messenger of joy and this book is a blessing for all."
—RAYMOND L PETTERSEN III, founder and president, Noahide Nations

"The story is told about the Chofetz Chaim, then an unknown, when seeking approbations for his book on the laws of speaking negatively about others. He was at first refused by the great rabbis since they wanted to confirm that the subject was offered by one who personified the sanctity inherent in observance of these fundamental laws. They sent people to engage the Chofetz Chaim to confirm he embodied that which he wrote. These people returned with glowing reports of his holy personality, and the Rabbis wrote glowing approbations. The Joy of Judaism *is offered by someone who embodies all the wisdom and joy that is so expressively articulated in every paragraph. Reb Sam, as I call him, rejoices when studying and sharing Torah. He then shares that joy in his beautiful music. Reb Sam doesn't sing to make prayer a better experience. His soul reverberates with the joy of prayer, and expresses itself in song. It is no exaggeration to say that when Reb Sam sings Hallel, you can hear the author of Psalms singing along with him.*"
—RABBI SIMCHA WEINBERG, founder of The Foundation Stone virtual beit midrash

This Book is Dedicated By
THE COLIN FAMILY

Sam, you have touched the world with your lifelong devotion to creating music, imparting wisdom and seeking adventure. The Joy of Judaism is the result of your tireless drive to share your spiritual journey. May you be blessed to bring light to every corner of the earth. We are so grateful for our abiding friendship.

Pesach • Tefillin • Shabbat • Community • Torah • Prophets • Niggun • Pesach • Teshuva • Wardin
Spirituality • Holiness • Emunah • Diaspora • Bar Mitah • Simcha • Halacha • Bitachon • Holidays
Tzvele • Tallit • Israel • Mitzah • Avira • Nusshach • Tefillin • Shabbat • Community • Torah • Prop
Niggun • Pesach • Teshuva • Wedding • Spirituality • Holiness • Emunah • Diaspora • Bar Mit
Simcha • Halacha • Bitachon • Holidays • Bar Mitzah • Tallit • Israel • Mitzah • Avira • Moshia
Tallit • Shabbat • Community • Torah • Prophets • Niggun • Pesach • Teshuva • Wedding • Spiritus

Acknowledgements

This book is dedicated to my wife, Shira. Thank you for loving me, sacrificing so much to raise our children, tolerating my craziness and sharing your ever-flowing wisdom. Thank you for allowing me to complete this colossal endeavor.

Max, Jesse and Sarah, my beautiful children, you are the lights in my life and my constant source of inspiration. Words cannot describe the love I feel for you. Thank you for allowing me to share our adventures in this book. Yes, I expect you to read the whole thing.

Thanks to God for the gift of life.

I am grateful for the air that I breathe. I am grateful for family. I am grateful to be Jewish. I am grateful for oceans, mountains, active vacations and national parks. I am grateful for challenges to overcome. I am grateful for the gift of music.

Thanks to my incredible parents, Manny and Harriet Glaser, who give me so much love and make me feel "super." Thanks to my beloved brothers Aharon, Yom Tov and Joey and their awesome wives and kids. Thanks to the extended Glaser-Berman-Fassino-Vigil clan for the gift of family.

Thanks to my dear friends around the globe. Thanks to the fans of my music who support my dreams. Thanks to my gifted musicians who spoil me with their talent. Thanks to my amazing staff, past and present. Thanks to those who trust me to create meaningful, memorable programming for their communities.

Thanks to all the rabbis and teachers who inform my writing and my being—I started to make a list of names and when I got to fifty, I realized that I couldn't mention everyone. I'm grateful to all and mention specific individuals in the Suggested Reading List. Those I learn with on a regular basis are a continuous source of inspiration: David Sacks, Howard Witkin, Rabbi Tzvi Freeman, Rabbi Yonah Bookstein, Rabbi Dov Newman and my *Rav*, Rabbi Moshe Cohen. Thanks to the community of Pico-Robertson in Los Angeles for spoiling me with friendship, food and wisdom.

Thanks to Azriela Jaffe for carefully editing this book and Sandra Lilienthal for eagle-eye proofreading and furnishing the "Four Questions" in each chapter. Thanks to my mom for a <u>lifetime</u> of proofreading help and to Liza Wiemer for the editing master class. Thanks to my awesome sister-in-law Leah Glaser and Karin Conn for the invaluable feedback. Thanks to the various publishers for the use of the graphs in the appendix. Thanks to Ramiro Fauve for the cover design and designing ALL twenty-five of my albums to date. I'm grateful to Ramiro, Chuck Sparks and Nissan Mosapor for a lifetime of the best times.

I am forever grateful to those who helped sponsor this book's publication:

Jeff and Shawni Astrof
Shmuel and Lynn Bar-Lev
Brad and Julia Berger
Daniel Berman
Dennis and Debra Berman
Theo and Deborah Brandt-Sarif
Merle Carrus
Jeff and Kate Colin
Hal Crane
Michael and Valerie Deitch
Herb and Sharon Glaser
Jonathan and Nancy Glaser
Jerry Glaser
Manny and Harriet Glaser
Richard Glaser

Noreen Green and Ian Drew
Dana Gluckstein and Michael Dieden
Richard and Beverly Horowitz
Doron Jacobius
Ezra and Lauren Kest
Brian and Robin Kettler
Mitch and Karen Kuflik
Norman and Nancy Lipoff
Nissan and Gillian Mosapor
Cheston and Lara Mizel
Steve Romick
Edward Slatkin
Diane and Phil Stein
Rabbi Simcha Weinberg

In 2009, I was working out at a hotel gym, taking a break from teaching at a Jewish conference. My friend Michael Monheit, then publisher of Moment Magazine, was on the elliptical trainer next to me. He noted my connection with Jewish educators and clergy across denominational lines and suggested that I include ideas in my monthly newsletter to inspire their students and congregants. From then on, I enhanced my Living Inspired newsletter with 2500-word essays, with the long term goal of piecing them together as an overview of ecstatic Jewish living. Thanks Michael, for getting me to write.

Thanks to my dear readers for choosing to share this journey. Enjoy the ride!

Contents

Acknowledgements vii
Introduction xiii

Part One — Judaism 101: Simchas, Nachas and All That Jazz 1
   Hineni: Just Do It! 4
   Kedusha: The Imperative of Holiness 9
   Simcha: The Joy Inside My Tears 14
   The Science of Struggle 19
   Nachas: What Everybody Needs 24
   Shefa: The Jewish "Secret" 30

Part Two — Judaism 202: The Artform of Jewish Living 35
   Can't Beat Bitachon 37
   B'chira: Lessons in Free Will from a Talking Donkey 43
   Middot: The Measure of a Mensch 49
   Halacha: The Chok's on You 54
   Eretz Yisrael: The Gift of the Promised Land 60
   Redemption Song 66

Part Three — We Got to Pray Just to Make it Today 71
   Be a Blessing 73
   The Amidah: United We Stand 79
   Surviving Shacharit: Kabbalistic Insights into the Morning Service 84
   Mincha, Mincha 90
   Ma'ariv: Shuckling on the Dock of the Bay 94

Part Four — Sacred Stuff: Putting the "Rich" in Rituals 99
   Mezuzah: Knockin' on Heaven's Door 101
   Kippah: Skullcandy 105
   Tallit: Life on the Fringe 110
   Tefillin: Strapping Up 114
   More Precious Than Pearls: An Inside View of "Women's" Rituals 119

Part Five — The Joy of Jewish Holidays: Spring and Summer Festivals 127
   Shabbat: TGIF 129
   Shabbat: Get Unplugged 136
   Pesach: War of Worldcraft 139

Pesach: Unbreakable Soul 144

Minor League Holidays...149

A Shavuot Revelation...155

The Three Weeks: My Family Vacation..159

Tisha B'Av: Jews and Aspens...163

Part Six — The Joy of Jewish Holidays: Fall and Winter Festivals.........169

Elul: T'shuva—Masters of Return 171

Rosh Hashana: The Parade of Tears 177

The High Holidays: Why Are We Here?...180

Sukkah's On Fire...186

Sukkot vs. Halloween 191

Chanukah: I Have a Dream 195

Purim: From Exodus to Esther 200

Part Seven — Transitions and Celebrations: Jewish Lifecycle Events.........206

Brit Milah: A Cut Above the Rest..209

Bar/Bat Mitzvah: Great Expectations 214

Marriage: Lucky Seven...218

Bumps Along the Road: The Other Lifecycle Events 223

Epilogue: Engage the Dying of the Light...226

Part Eight — Organized Religion: Navigating Jewish Institutions.........233

Toward Loving-kindness: The Holiest Shul in Town 235

Finding a Rabbi: Asey L'cha Rav 239

In Search of Jewish Unity: The Family Portrait.................................246

Can I Get a Witness? A Tachlis Twelve-Step Program 251

Jews in the Pews: Hillel and Holy Chutzpah.....................................258

Chabad: The Closest Thing to Judaism 264

The Biennial: The Good, the Bad and the Plenary 267

Nurturing Jewish Educators: NewCAJE OutRAJE 271

Self-Hating Jews: Terror at the GA 274

Jewish in America: The United States of Israel..................................278

Part Nine — Raising Jewish Kids.........281

Love and Marriage 283

Early Childhood: Telescope Parenting 286

Day School: The Key to Continuity..291

Reward and Punishment: The Gift of a Reprimand............................295

The Teenage Years: Better Run Away 299

Keeping Consistency Constant..304

Kids on Meds: Mood-Altering Drugs 308

A Love Letter to my College-Bound Son 311

Dear YULA Graduates: A Commencement Speech 316

The Baby and the Bathwater 319

Part Ten — Music of the Soul..**323**

    Music in Judaism: In Search of the Tenth Song................................325

    The Making of a Musician 330

    Deepening the Experience: Ode to the 8-Track................................336

    Legacy: The Yellow Violin 339

    Mentors: Losing Debbie 342

    Music Festivals: The Treasure of the High Sierra 347

    The Jewish Music Manifesto 354

    Coda: The Secret of Six..358

Appendix **365**

    Dedications...366

    Hebrew Alphabet and Gematria..372

    Biblical Chronology..373

    Holiday Calendar..374

    Reading List/Sources...375

    Music that Moves Me 377

    Discography..380

    Tour Schedules 389

    Glossary 396

    About the Author..406

Introduction

Who am I anyway, where am I going to
How did I get here, what do I need to know
What am I supposed to do with my life
Can I start living
If I don't know which way to go
I heard somebody say
In the quiet of the night
If you close your eyes, you'll hear the answer

I just want to find my letter in the Torah
I know it's somewhere out there

If I could only see
I just want to find my letter in the Torah
The one that's written just for me

So many words, so many pages
I keep finding more every time I look
Sometimes I need to take a little break
Sometimes I can't wait to open a book
I heard somebody say
If you listen to your heart
You were born with all the answers

The *Joy of Judaism* is a chronicle of encounters with the Jewish heritage from twenty-five years of performing in over a thousand venues around the world. Each time I leave my home, through music, humor, sermons and stories, I share my belief that being Jewish is a priceless gift. I get tremendous satisfaction when I am able to connect my audiences to their faith, to their communities and to God.

Jews have been entrusted with the mission of nudging the world toward an appreciation of an omniscient, caring God and spreading such concepts as the value of life, equality under the law and loving-kindness. In the words of the prophet (Isaiah 42:6), we are steadily fulfilling our role as a "light unto nations." All of us generate light in our own unique way. Even with the scourge of persecution, assimilation and annihilation, Jews have outlasted empires that have vanished from earth. Miraculously, we stand on the shoulders of the hundred and twenty or so generations since Mount Sinai and continue to shine.

Our deep-seated drive to advertise ethical monotheism is a spiritual legacy from Avraham and Sarah, the first Jewish couple. In every generation, this sacred task is presented anew—the choice is ours to opt into this historic social experiment. The urgency of responding affirmatively transcends denominations and demographics. No matter where we find ourselves on the continuum of Jewish practice, we maximize life satisfaction when we contribute to *Tikkun Olam*, the healing of the universe. This book is a manual for joyfully enhancing Jewish commitment. It offers a macro view on our faith while encouraging future explorations into the microcosm. Its primary goal is exposing the majesty of God's everyday presence and sharing Judaism's tools to live with powerful purpose. If we're not living it, we can't be giving it.

Our sages insist that the *simcha* (joy) resulting from the performance of one mitzvah (commandment) leads inexorably to the next, satisfaction guaranteed. Even with today's distractions, we can make Judaism a priority. We are all Jews-by-choice. When we get involved, even with the smallest increment of commitment, we become an inspiration to others. All Jewish communities begin with a single individual taking a stand for his or her heritage. Each of us has something special to offer—I appreciate everyone's unique path, knowing we're all on this journey together.

Throughout my life I have grappled with understanding God's vehicle for transforming the world, the Jewish People. Our mission certainly hasn't been easy. Tevye in "Fiddler on the Roof" asked God, "Once in a while, can't You choose someone else?" This line may get a big laugh, but it's a serious question. Every kid called to the Torah recites: "Blessed are You God, our God, Master of the Universe, Who selected us from all peoples…" Our claim to chosenness sounds politically incorrect and sparks controversy. However, I'm convinced that deepening our unique relationship with God is the source of the greatest joy attainable for members of the tribe. It is this joy I hope to share with you.

Growing up in a Los Angeles-based Conservative Jewish family, we didn't dabble in theology but enjoyed our culture and peoplehood. We didn't keep kosher and rarely attended synagogue. In Hebrew school, our clergy and teachers presented everything other than *emunah* (belief in God), concentrating on The Four H's: Holyland, Hebrew, Holidays and Holocaust. There is plenty within these parameters to fill a Jew with meaning and substance, cradle to grave. During my theological jump-start in my twenties, I gained an awareness of a fifth "H," Holiness. I learned that spiritual growth requires including spirituality in the equation. Awareness is the first step toward integration…I began an odyssey that continues to this day.

Most of my youthful Jewish experiences were positive. I loved summers at Camp Ramah and to my relief, performed well at my Bar Mitzvah. I treasured our extended family lifecycle celebrations. I could appreciate an authentic deli sandwich. But on a seminal post-college trip to study at a yeshiva (Torah academy) in Jerusalem, I realized there was more to Judaism than pastrami on rye. Gracing one of the classroom walls was a photo of an overstuffed bagel with the caption, "Is this all there is after 3000 years of Jewish history?" During my Hebrew school years, I suspected I wasn't getting the whole picture—how could anyone in a mere two to four hours a week? My relationship with God was based on a sense of wonder for the natural world, with a side order of guilt. I possessed a moral tripwire allowing me to distinguish between good and evil. I knew I had to go to *shul* (synagogue) on Yom Kippur and knew Jews didn't get tattoos or eat shrimp. However, I was content to do it "My Way" and melt into my host culture, relegating religious stuff to recovering addicts and rabbis.

Try as I may, after that first yeshiva experience, I couldn't return to my comfortable "unexamined life." My routine back in Los Angeles didn't flow with the rigorous lifestyle of believers. Following a few years in limbo, I recognized I needed to take proactive steps to get back into holiness. I witnessed such simple, unfettered joy in Israel—the lure of Hollywood and stardom paled in comparison. The "fifth H," holiness, was easy to grasp in Jerusalem but in L.A., I would have to work for it.

I resonate with the parable of the miserable bird in the Garden of Eden. The bird complains to God that other animals have functional arms, while it has burdensome appendages at its sides. God explains that those strange limbs are actually wings and with them the bird can FLY! I once believed mitzvot were capricious demands of a distant diety; now I perceive them as engines of spiritual flight, enabling us to link with the will of a loving God. I took on one mitzvah at a time, sometimes tentatively, sometimes grudgingly, and stuck with it until I "got it." I joined the incredible community of Pico-Roberstson in L.A. and rode a wave of growth and connection. I'm ever grateful for my guides and teachers, especially since they let me find my own "wings," on my own timeline.

Years later, after I integrated Shabbat and keeping kosher into my life, I served as Musical Director at Brandeis-Bardin Collegiate Institute. Amongst the array of wonderful courses and activities, there was a weekly question/answer panel discussion on Jewish topics. I was the only observant member of the staff and felt like a dartboard as students fired controversial questions. One of them asked, "Sam, your lifestyle is so restrictive. Why would you undertake so many sacrifices, like giving up your secular music career and non-kosher restaurants?" I responded, "Imagine stopping in a 7-Eleven to buy a lottery ticket. The next day you are shocked to learn that you won the multimillion-dollar prize. The whole enchilada. That's how I feel everyday…like I won the lottery." Yes, I've made sacrifices, but it's like I spent a buck and made millions.

In this book, I intend to demonstrate that any sacrifices made to be involved in Jewish life will come back in spades. *The Joy of Judaism* is an adventure-filled journey in search of truth and meaning, suggesting multiple points of entry into sacred space. Enjoy this smorgasbord of opportunities in Jewish life and feel free to take home a doggy bag to share with a hungry friend.

Let's get started! Who wants to be a millionaire?

PART ONE

Judaism 101: Simchas, Nachas and All That Jazz

This section is dedicated by
HARRIET AND MANNY GLASER

We gave life to the author of this book. His writing began as a seven-year-old when attempting poetry inspired by the book "Hail Stones and Halibut Bones." When I tried to set one of his poems to music, he stopped me and said, "That's NOT how it goes." I was shocked and asked him how DID it go? He sang that song to me. I ran for my tape recorder and in the days that followed we recorded his melodies for all his other poems. Since then, Sam has composed thousands of powerful songs with inspiring messages about day-to-day life, humanity and the world. Sam treats life with great joy and shares his enthusiasm with everyone. We lovingly and proudly honor his latest accomplishment, "The Joy of Judaism." May he and Shira, Max, Jesse and Sarah continue to give us nachas.

IN THIS SECTION:

Hineni: Just Do It! 4

Kedusha: The Imperative of Holiness 9

Simcha: The Joy Inside My Tears 14

The Science of Struggle 19

Nachas: What Everybody Needs 24

Shefa: The Jewish "Secret" 30

OVERVIEW

J udaism offers an eye-opening lens to the world and our personal spiritual path. Finding our way gets easiser when we grasp key phrases and concepts. As the People of the Book, we live and breathe by the power of the word. Therefore, we begin with Judaism 101, an overview of fundamentals.

Let's start with God. Everyone has issues with God. Who is God? Where is God? As Rabbi David Aaron says, "The God you don't believe in, I don't believe in either."

God is infinite, beyond description and dimension, and yet I'm confident my readers will garner a definitive grasp of the Jewish angle on this unique relationship. While I frequently use the word God, one is welcome to substitute any euphemism, such as Universe, Creator or Mother Nature. Of course, my fellow Star Wars fans can use The Force. Please note: I choose to spell out God (rather than G-d) and strive to refer to God in gender-neutral form.

Hashem is the normative conversational Hebrew word for God, meaning The Name. Hashem is a substitute for the sacred term *Adonai* (my Master), which is reserved for prayer. *Adonai* is actually another substitute, this time for the unpronounceable *yud-hey-vav-hey*, the ineffable name, the tetragrammaton. I think you'll be glad to hear—I'm sticking with God.

While it is standard practice to italicize foreign words, certain Hebrew words aren't italicized due to their ubiquity. Examples are Shabbat, the names of the *Yamim Tovim* (holidays) and common terms like Talmud, Torah, Kabbalah and mitzvah. On the subject of mitzvah, I recommend translating it as "commandment," not "good deed." It's helpful to remember that the plural form typically adds *-ot* or *-im* to the end of any given Hebrew word, i.e., one mitzvah, two mitzvot.

There are many ways to transliterate Hebrew. I utilize my own subjective method of doing what looks right to me and best communicates the proper sound to an English reader. Some folks are "CH" challenged. "CH" in an expression like "chutzpah" is pronounced like the gentle gutteral scrape terminating the word "Bach." Want to sound like a local? Say Chumus, not Hummus!

I define each Hebrew word the first time it appears and offer a glossary for reminders. I heartily recommend neophytes compile a list of unfamiliar terms. While I'm an Ashkenazi Jew (of Eastern European descent), I typically use Sephardic (of Spanish descent) pronunciations for the sake of Jewish unity. Sephardic Hebrew is the common denominator default for Israelis and all but the Ashkenazi Orthodox. Bear with me: sometimes I go back and forth with words like Shabbat (Sephardi) and Shabbas (Ashkenazi). I try not to overwhelm the reader with too much vocabulary; any time I jump into the Holy Tongue, it's because that particular Hebrew term is common parlance for English speakers fully invested in the Joy of Judaism.

Each chapter begins with an abridged lyric and a link to an appropriate song in my catalog. This is an important part of the Joy of Judaism experience and I urge my readers to be listeners as well. Take a break before each chapter, put on a nice pair of headphones and hit the link. Each song/lyric was carefully chosen to deepen the message of the written material. Unless otherwise noted, I wrote the music and lyrics; Hebrew lyrics are typically from liturgy.

Throughout each section, I incorporate personal stories to express how I initially encountered these various concepts. I also describe a plethora of amazing "coincidences" that I believe serve as signposts of God's reassuring presence. Lastly, I end most chapters with a section called The Four Questions. No, not "*Ma Nishtanah*" from the Passover *Seder*. These Four Questions analyze the *tachlis* (bottom line) of the subject matter and are exclusively for those who want to personalize the reading experience. I recommend answering them using a pen and journal—the exercise of writing serves to integrate ideas and provides a cherished record of the journey.

When studying Torah, numbers represent both quantities and mystical qualities. The birth of this overview of ecstatic Jewish living took nine years of gestation, from Pesach 2009 through Pesach 2018. After my editor had her way with the text, I considered it complete only after thoroughly proofing it fifteen times. It is comprised of ten sections, seventy chapters and about 180,000 words, mystical numbers all. I hope you enjoy every one of them.

Vaiter! (Forward!)

Hineni: Just Do It!

♫ **HINENI** ♫

joyjud.com/m/hin

I wasn't there when God spoke to Abraham
I wasn't there when Moses freed the slaves
I would have walked
Right up to that burning bush
But I wasn't there, and Moses was

I wasn't there when Judah led the Maccabees
I wasn't there when Esther took a stand
In every age we get to make a choice
To rise up and take a stand
Or ignore the outstretched hand

But if I'm here, God
And if I can help
Let me be the one who is the first to say
Hineni

I wasn't there on the eve of Kristallnacht
I wasn't there when they packed the trains
Millions were crying
Could nobody hear a sound
I wasn't there
But I feel the pain

Upon graduating the University of Colorado, Boulder, I returned to Los Angeles highly enthusiastic and mostly clueless. I wanted it all, I wanted it now, and I had no idea how to begin. The first order of business was asserting my independence by moving out of my parents' home. This required cash flow and at age twenty-one, my Bar Mitzvah fund was running dangerously low. At this point, L.A. had a few free newspapers in circulation which I typically read cover to cover: the ecologically-oriented Santa Monica Bay News, the hipster L.A. Reader and the downtown-based L.A. News. I had never studied journalism but was able to transform my train of thought into decent prose and could spot a typo a mile away—perhaps I could work for the papers? As a tireless tree-hugger and avid outdoor sportsman, there were plenty of environmental exposés I was compelled to compose. I contacted the editors and was thrilled to parlay my first assignments into weekly columns, occasional cover stories and photography for all three publications.

Soon thereafter, I supplemented my writing stipend with income from my first recording studio, LAX Records, a masterfully soundproofed room adjacent to an airport runway. It was increasingly clear to me that journalism was the fastest way to poverty since the vast amount of time required for investigative journalism resulted in a pathetic hourly rate. Eventually, the proceeds from music production allowed me to move in to a simple bachelor pad with my studio partner and new best friend, Chuck Sparks. That year, I got an amazing gig doing TV music for various professional sports franchises and my dad got the *nachas* (satisfaction) of hearing my tracks every time the Dodgers, Angels or Clippers called time out. When I tried to parlay this success into writing for other shows, one name kept coming up: "You gotta meet Stuie Wax!"

My Hineni Moment

Stuie was a Deadhead and an Orthodox Jew, the only one I had ever met. He offered to see me at his fancy office at Lorimar Television. I was a nervous wreck for this big industry meeting but Stuie immediately put me at ease, laughing about his executive suite and claiming he had no idea what he was doing there. I told him about my big plans to break into film scoring and all he wanted to discuss was Torah and Rabbi Shlomo Carlebach. I kept trying to steer the conversation back to my career but it became evident he scheduled this meeting only to get me to come to his house for Shabbat dinner. He promised delicious free food, beer and musicians. I agreed to join him the next Friday night—what could it hurt?

I arrived at Stuie's diminutive apartment to find nearly forty creative types crammed around an array of folding tables. One had to walk on couches to get from one side of the room to the other. How could there be enough food for this horde? We drank shots, told stories and sang rowdy Jewish songs into the night, until the downstairs neighbors freaked out. I met several musicians who would become lifelong friends. It was like arriving at a Chassidic Woodstock revival and I felt right at home. Remarkably, there was enough food for everyone.

I became a regular at Stuie's table but never gave up on my quest to do music for Lorimar. I had new material composed for an upcoming Warren Miller ski movie, so I scheduled a meeting to show off my expanding demo reel. Once again, Stuie didn't have much to say about my music but was overflowing with *divrei Torah* (Torah thoughts). Finally, he mentioned Capitol Records was compiling an album to benefit Soviet Jewry. Would I consider writing a song for the collection?

That song, *"Hineni"* (Here I am, Genesis 22:7) became my point of entry in the Jewish music world. Throughout my childhood, I participated in rallies and manned phones to benefit *refuseniks* (those denied an exit visa from the U.S.S.R.). Of course I would be involved in Stuie's project! My inspiration for the song was the courage of our many biblical heroes who uttered *hineni* at crucial holy moments. The imminent dissolution of the Iron Curtain seemed like my generation's cue to stand up and say this sacred word. After I recorded *"Hineni,"* my teen choir leader at Sinai Temple, Craig Taubman, had success with a cover version of the song which he featured on his *Journey* album. Much thanks to Craig and Stuie, I discovered that Jewish music could be an ideal channel for my budding abilities and spirit. In a sense, the word *hineni* became my mantra.

Get Crackin' with Alacrity

Jews of all stripes are waiting to be called upon to make a difference, either by God, a community leader or a friend in need. We are hardwired to respond, "I'm ready and willing! I want to do something meaningful, something great." Master Torah commentator Rashi (Rabbi Shlomo Yitzchaki, 1040-1105) states that *hineni* implies *z'rizut*, or alacrity, an intense readiness to perform God's will. Whereas Jewish prayer is voiced in the plural, *hineni* is singular. We must start with ourselves—I am here. Avraham said *hineni* at the binding of his son Yitzchak (Isaac). Yosef (Joseph) said *hineni* when he was about to face his jealous brothers and get sold into slavery. Moshe (Moses) said *hineni* at the burning bush. Thanks to Google Maps, we can readily pinpoint our physical location. *Hineni* indicates our metaphysical GPS, where we are "holding" spiritually. It is a communal code word urging us to heighten self-awareness, to align with the Jewish mission, to maximize our limited time on this planet. Learning to say *hineni* is a primary takeaway of "The Joy of Judaism."

Nike nailed this concept with their "Just Do It" campaign. There's no such thing as "maybe next week" when it comes to working out. One can't delegate attending a yoga or Zumba class. We either carve out time in our busy schedule or it's never going to happen. We may intuit this for our physical fitness but fall short for our metaphysical fitness. We mistakenly assume we can leave the heavy lifting to clergy. Abraham Joshua Heschel said it best: "Judaism is not so much about a leap of faith as it is about a leap of action." Our spiritual priorities include incorporating prayer into our day, learning Torah, performing acts of loving-kindness and connecting in person with our social network. Joyful Judaism requires actively taking initiative, not passively pondering philosophies. A person with *Hineni* Consciousness schedules these "active-ities" on the "repeat" setting in order to remain spiritually lean and mean.

One of my *hineni* heroes was dear friend Lou Rudolph, a six-foot-three powerhouse Hollywood executive who produced the *Rich Man, Poor Man* and *Roots* miniseries. He was in his fifties when he found his "Letter in the Torah." Bitten by the *Yiddishkeit* (Judaism) bug, he filled his days with Torah learning, fundraising and reaching out to his peers. Singlehandedly, he mobilized our Pico-Robertson community to action. When Lou Rudolph phoned, you took the call. And when he described what he needed you to do, you answered, *"Hineni!"* I watched him encourage many of his Jewish friends in the industry to take on Torah study and give big to charity. Tragically, Lou had a heart attack in his car and couldn't call for help. Anytime I want to avoid doing what needs to be done, I hear his voice. I feel his presence in a palpable way—his wife gave me his wardrobe to remember him. Every time I don one of his suits, I aspire to honor his larger-than-life legacy.

As Henry David Thoreau says, "The mass of men lead lives of quiet desperation." We all want to answer the call to greatness. Don't wait! The mitzvah of daily prayer keeps us attuned to God's prayer <u>for us</u>: "Come join Me! I'm calling on you to transcend limitations, to look out for others, to avoid selfishness and maintain an open heart. Think big! Ask Me for anything you desire." God has tremendous expectations of us and summons us everyday. The call may not come in the form of a burning bush or splitting sea. Usually, the Almighty communicates via customized messengers we refer to as our friends and family. Often these people unknowingly deliver the exact information we need to hear—if we keep our antennae up and eyes open.

Crisis Management

Hineni is only three syllables. "Sing it strong and proud, Hee-nay-knee!" It's easy to pronounce but challenging to put into practice. Why is it so difficult? Many of us live on a treadmill, barely managing daily disasters. We are overburdened by the demands on our time and pocketbook. How can we be available for God's call? The solution is to get organized. We must transcend "crisis management mode." Only with loose ends buttoned up will we find the bandwidth to process signals beyond our personal needs. Then we can be on the lookout for *hineni* opportunities and eventually, learn to integrate a *hineni* outlook into everyday life.

Saying *hineni* requires a "big plate" perspective. One of my friends became a personal success coach and chose me as a guinea pig client. After one of our sessions, she gave me a homework assignment: I was to visit our local Color Me Mine pottery studio and decorate the biggest platter in their inventory. I did so, painting the most alluring design I could muster. As soon as it was fired, I presented it to my wife, Shira, to grace our Shabbas table. It went straight to the attic and I haven't seen it since. The lesson stuck with me, however. My coach insisted I possessed broader shoulders than I could ever imagine. Rather than complain I had "too much on my plate," she had me envision that my plate was enormous and could bear any load. I could handle my busy work schedule and family needs and still say *hineni*.

A few years into my stint as a journalist, my father lured me into his garment business. The initial incentive was the chance to travel internationally to inspect production. Travel the world with my camera? Twist my arm! I relocated my recording studio to our piece goods (fabric) warehouse and spent nine-to-five making deals alongside my dad. We had our own brands of men's and boy's sportswear and also were licensed by Jordache, Jag and Beverly Hills Polo Club. The stakes were high; at one point, we had factories in over a dozen Asian countries producing a variety of products for major department stores across North America. This meant juggling hundreds of purchase orders at any given time. We had computers on our desks to oversee the flow of production, except for my dad who somehow stored everything in his head. During the Reagan era, protectionism ended and imports started flowing freely into the U.S., making it impossible to keep our Arizona-based factory profitable. That's when we were forced overseas to compete, and that's when the business began to unravel. There were too many poor quality and late delivery emergencies and our thirty-year business model devolved into crisis management. We lost the ability to execute plans for the future while mired in chaos and the bank soon closed our doors.

My dad lost everything, his business, his factory, his home. On one hand, he could no longer say *hineni* due to a landslide of business disasters. But because he had always answered to *hineni* to his peers, his name was sterling. In our time of need, all our customers came through and paid what was owed, an unheard of collection rate for a bankrupt company. No one would stiff the highly respected Manny Glaser. This was one of my most powerful *hineni* lessons.

Have Mercy Baby

Once we transcend crisis management mode, we can aspire to the ultimate *hineni* possibility: performing acts of kindness for others. The prophet Michah (Micah) gives us a list of crucial spiritual goals: "What does God demand from you? Do justice, love mercy, walk humbly with your God (Michah 6:8)." The recepients of mercy cannot only be those in our immediate family. The Torah commands us repeatedly to love the stranger—thirty-six times, in fact. Looking out for those beyond our inner circle is a prerequisite for Torah leadership and is an opportunity available to all of us.

Our patriarchs and matriarchs laid the groundwork for an eternity of *hineni* accomplishments in the realm of compassion. They all had the same day job: they were shepherds maintaining the well-being of their flocks. The *Midrash* (classic text of rabbinic commentary) tells us Moshe also was chosen to lead due to his concern for his father-in-law Yitro's (Jethro's) livestock. Caring for animals is an indication of one's propensity to care for humans. Furthermore, shepherds have time on their hands to contemplate the Creator and extrapolate Godly behavior. The *Hagaddah* (Passover guide text) hints to the importance of altruism when it quotes the phrase from *Shmot* (Exodus 6:6), "I will redeem you with an outstretched arm." Perhaps what God is really saying is, "I will redeem YOU with the outstretched arm." In other words, only those of us with arms reaching toward others merit redemption. This generosity of spirit typically only happens when we are in "shepherd time." The *hineni* formula: maintain unscheduled space in our day to "dwell in the house of the God" (*Tehillim*/Psalms 27:4) and recognize the primacy of helping someone in need.

Rabbi Hillel stated in *Pirkei Avot* (Ethics of the Fathers 2:5), "In a place where there are no men, strive to be a man." *Hineni* is an invitation for all of us to take initiative toward greatness. Why do we think small? According to author Marianne Williamson, we are marooned in a societal "conspiracy for mediocrity." We make excuses for staying in jobs we hate, we're habitually late, we procrastinate, break diets and promises. These excuses keep us cemented in place. Why do others accept our excuses? Because they, too, don't want to be held accountable. Listen to President Truman: "The buck stops here!" The next time the opportunity presents itself, be the one to stand up and take responsibility, or as Mahatma Gandhi says, "Be the change that you wish to see in the world." Our sages implore us to do *t'shuva* (repent, return to God) one day before we die. Since we don't know when that will be, make this the day to thank God, love God, talk to God. And when you receive the call, say *hineni!*

THE FOUR QUESTIONS

1. What is your greatest *hineni* moment and how has this impacted your life?

2. What does it mean to be ready for spiritual heroism?

3. What "tiny step" can you take to deepen your spiritual and physical presence?

4. Look at your calendar. Schedule a regular five-minute learning experience. When is it going to be?

Shabbat • Community • Torah • Prophets • Niggun • Pesach • Teshuva • Wedding
Nullity • Holiness • Minyan • Diaspora • Bar Mitah • Simcha • Halacha • Brachot • Holidays
Tallis • Israel • Mikvah • Prayer • Moshiach • Tefillin • Shabbat • Community • Torah • Diaspora
Teshuva • Weddings • Spirituality • Holiness • Niggun • Diaspora • Bar Mitah
Teshuva • Brachot • Holidays • Bar Mitzvah • Tallis • Israel • Mikvah • Prayer • Moshiach
Niggun • Community • Torah • Teshuva • Weddings • Spirituality
Niggun • Diaspora • Bar Mitah • Holidays • Bar Mitzvah

Kedusha:
The Imperative of
Holiness

♫ PRESENCE ♫

joyjud.com/m/pre

Out of the darkness	*I feel a power guiding me*
Reaching for the light	*An open hand inviting me*
Keeping You in sight on the way	*Lighting up the pathway to Your Presence*
Moment by moment	*Every note a sacred sound*
Searching for what's right	*Every step on holy ground*
Holding back the night we seize the day	*Opening the doorway of Your Presence*

O ne winter weekend in 1991, I discovered that the spiritual realm could be as real as the physical. Scott, one of my first friends to get married, became Sabbath observant and moved to L.A.'s Pico-Robertson Jewish neighborhood. He was scheduled to attend a meatpacking convention at the Reno-Sparks Convention Center and asked me to join him. No, Scott isn't a butcher—he's a stockbroker. One of his mentors advised him to find a niche and become the money *maven* (authority) in that field. Therefore, Scott wrote a few financial management articles for Meat and Poultry magazine and soon became a monthly columnist. He parlayed his newfound status as the *fleishig* (meat) financial guru by taking a booth at the annual "meating" of the industry.

Scott invited me to keep him company during the Sabbath portion of this convention. I accepted the offer not only to spend time with my friend…this would be the perfect opportunity to ski at my beloved Squaw Valley prior to the conference. After a few days of dropping into the alpine chutes in search of untracked powder, I unpacked my bags in Scott's casino hotel room. I was nearing *shomer Shabbas* (Sabbath observant) status at this point and knew the game plan for a typical Friday Night. We *davened* (prayed) the evening service and recited the blessings over the delicious meal judiciously packed by his wife, Lisa. We then studied the Torah portion, sang a few songs and after dessert, decided to take a Shabbat stroll around the hotel.

I will never forget the feeling I had upon leaving our room and seeing the garish décor of the hallway. Something happened in that hotel suite. That "something" disappeared when we opened the door, breaking the vacuum seal of our sacred space. We had generated holiness. It dissipated silently into the smoke-filled air of the cavernous casino. I felt a palpable sense of *yerida* (going down) from our spiritual bubble as we wandered the legions of gamers staring into their slot machines. I recognized for the first time that I had the ability to sustain holiness in my life. The treasure of *kedusha* was elusive but attainable, regardless of my environment.

Defining Holiness

When one thinks about holiness, what usually comes to mind is the angelic realms or the High Priest performing the Temple service on Yom Kippur. Yet, the Kotzker Rebbe (Menachem Mendel of Kotzk, 1787-1859) emphasizes the phrase, "<u>People</u> of holiness shall you be" (*Sh'mot*/Exodus 22:30). In other words, holiness isn't just for priests and angels. Within the context of our messy, error-prone human nature, we are coaxed to emulate our Creator. The commandment, *"Kedoshim t'hiyu"* (You shall be holy, *Vayikra*/Leviticus 19:1) wasn't delivered via the standard channel of Moshe to Aharon and then to the elders, but from Moshe directly to the entire assembly. Holiness is for all of us: men, women and children, Reform, Conservative and Orthodox. For those choosing to actively celebrate our heritage, aspiring to holiness is the first priority.

The term *kodesh* (holy) implies separation and can be seen in the root of other words with the same integral meaning. *Kaddish*, for example, serves to divide our prayer services and *Kedushin* is the word for marriage wherein two people separate themselves from all others. The first time holiness is mentioned in the Torah is right at the beginning, with the distinction of the light from dark and the day of rest from the "profane" days of the week. We declare this primordial separation with the *Kiddush* (blessing over wine) on Shabbat and holidays. History demonstrates that when God's beloved nation loses its holiness/separation, we quietly disappear into our host culture. That's why the most stringent rules in Jewish law involve those activities subjecting us to the melting pot, namely 'Eat Pray Love.'

The key to separation is abstention. According to our tradition, there are certain things we can and cannot do. Abstention sounds like a bummer—who wants to be a party pooper? It's clear, however, that the greatest rewards in life are gained through abstention. God urges us to steer clear of bacon cheeseburgers and lobster bisque. We aren't told why, and we still don't know. Marital bliss and the resulting gift of holy children are germinated in cohesive households where partners abstain from extramarital affairs. Accessing the potential of the Sabbath and holidays require a long list of abstentions. Interestingly, the laws of Shabbat are largely framed in the negative, delineating the things we cannot do. We then fill the empty space with nurturing activities like prayer and delicious meals and quality time with family and friends.

God teaches us an invaluable lesson: most worthwhile endeavors involve postponing immediate gratification for a brighter future. For example, no matter how hungry we are, we pause to make sure the food is kosher and make the appropriate blessing. The long term effect of postponement of gratification is highlighted in a 1960 Stanford research study wherein children were tempted with tasty marshmallows. Each received one treat and were told they could either eat it now or wait a few minutes and enjoy two later. Researchers followed the kids throughout their lives and those who delayed gratification demonstrated higher SAT scores and educational achievement. Attaining holiness requires learning key distinctions and developing the self-control to maintain an exalted path.

Three Classic Views of Holiness

Rashi claims that a state of holiness results from avoiding the illicit sexual acts enumerated in the *Kedoshim parasha* (chapter). However, Ramban (Rabbi Moses ben Nachman, also known as Nachmanides, 1194-1270) argues that holiness is the result of abstaining from those things which <u>are</u> permitted to us. He points out one can keep kosher and still be a slovenly glutton. Holiness requires balance. Learn Torah, but don't be a snob. Make a fortune, but give *tzedakah* (charity). We may be a separate nation that "dwells apart," but we are loving and tolerant to all.

In the search for holiness, it's tempting to go to extremes or attempt asceticism. Rambam (Rabbi Moses ben Maimon, also known as Maimonides, 1135-1138) explains that the key to joyful living is remaining integrated with one's community and walking on the *shvil hazahav* (path of gold) or golden mean. An excellent example regarding the importance of maintaining balance can be found in the biblical laws of becoming a *Nazir* (one who feels the need to get super-religious for a period of time). One might think undertaking extra commandments is commendable but remarkably, it can actually be deleterious: upon completion of the Nazirite period, the *Nazir* had to bring a sin offering to the Temple. Some assume growth in Torah engenders extremetism. Rambam would argue that it is the ultimate self-help guide for balanced living.

Mitzvot—The Engine of Holiness

The mitzvot sum up God's aspirations for our Holy Nation. They are neatly divided into positive and negative, thou shalt vs. thou shalt not. The "shalt" category is a list of 248 gateways of connection to the Infinite. The 365 "shalt-nots" are activities that clog up those pathways. The grand total enumerated in the Five Books of Moses is 613. These 613 commandments (not suggestions!) are our most invaluable inheritance. FYI: since we no longer have a *Beit Hamikdash* (Temple) in Jerusalem, only about half the mitzvot are applicable.

Stop for a moment and ponder your next mitzvah. Perhaps it will be giving a buck to a beggar or lighting Shabbat candles. What may seem like a simple act actually creates an opening to *kedusha*. According to Rabbi Shlomo Carlebach, every mitzvah performed has "angels doing backflips." Some claim the system of mitzvot is archaic, valid only in ancient times or that today's Judaism is a vestigial rabbinic construct. No! These principles are more important than ever in these fast-paced times. Mitzvot are the best hope for igniting our imperiled national spark.

The Reward of Holy Living

When I got serious about my Judaism and initiated a sincere effort to strive for holiness, it led to nothing short of a Matrix-style "red pill" revelation. I entered a new realm, a powerful, palpable parallel universe. A realm filled with joy and tranquility, even when everything seemed to be going crazy. This transformation is the inevitable result of aligning with the God's destiny for the Chosen People. Just like planets and atoms follow orbits, we, too, have a path. As Jews, we call our unique path *halacha* (the walk), the term used to describe Jewish law. From this perspective, law isn't confining or strict. It's liberating…we're on the move! Taking on *halacha* with intention, understanding and balance launches us on a trajectory where we soar with God. We learn to intuit heavenly messages. Human interaction becomes refined and enlightened. Prayer becomes a mind-blowing tool of sweet partnership and dialog.

When we walk with God, we can better perceive when we are off track. We feel the disconnection in our bones. I used to arrive at synagogue on the High Holidays and wonder what I was doing there. I'm a good person after all! Why put on a woolen suit in the late summer heat and stand for hours with other Jews who also show up once a year? When I transitioned to a mitzvah-focused life, I became spiritually sensitized to when I had strayed. No longer was I riddled with guilt or participating to please my parents. Now I was in *shul* on the holiest day of the year with twenty-five precious hours to set things straight with my beloved Creator and best friend.

King David summarizes the formula for entry into a holy space: "*Sur meyrah v'asey tov*" (Run from evil and do good, Psalm 34:15). That's it. We must distance ourselves from negative commandments and actively do the positive ones. Part of running from evil requires understanding what is evil. Only then can we remain vigilant against the allure of the "dark side" and choose the highest good. That's right, we have to study! Ever wonder what those yeshiva guys in black suits do all day? Our job as Jews is to integrate these positive and negative commandments into our being. That way, in every situation, we are primed for optimal choices. According to Rabbi David Aaron, "We learn Torah to know what God wants, we pray to want what God wants and we do mitzvot to live what God wants." Inculcating these divine distinctions allow us to fine tune our internal compass—clearing the muck that clouds the glass and resetting our magnetic north.

An L.A. actor friend, Benson Simmonds, visited my studio to record his upbeat song, "Holy Jew." This song reflects his mission to help Jews tap into the incendiary holiness in our *neshamot* (souls.) Once in touch with this innate gift, when confronted by a spiritual challenge, we can simply ask, "Is this what a holy Jew does?" and then act accordingly.

The biggest obstacle we must overcome is ourselves. Everyone has fears, everyone has excuses: "I can't read Hebrew," "I'm broke," "I'm too busy," "I'm too far from a synagogue," "it's great for others, but not for me." I understand—been there, done that! My friends, holiness is everpresent. There are so many mitzvot. Start with one and make it your own. Do it for the wrong reason—guilt, shame, because I told you to, to make money, so God won't strike you down. Eventually, that mitzvah will become part of your life for the right reason. It's as simple as putting a penny in a *pushke* (charity box). Join a synagogue, take a stand for Shabbat, avoid Dodger Dogs, reach out to a friend in need.

One of my favorite Torah passages is, "It is not hidden from you and it is not distant. It is not in heaven…nor is it over the sea…rather, the matter is very near to you, in your mouth and in your heart." (*D'varim*/Deuteronomy 30:12-14) Taking on mitzvot isn't brain surgery. Our job is to access the information while making a concerted effort to open our spiritual channels to perceive holiness. Trust God to fill the vacuum.

Even the smallest step toward holiness impacts the individual, the Jewish People and the entire world. We are seeing the cumulative effect of millennia of mitzvot coming to fruition in our own times. Remarkable lifesaving technologies emanate from our Promised Land. The Internet has made Torah ubiquitous. Jewish Harvard professors teach the world about happiness. Hipster TV rabbis enlighten non-Jewish families about *shalom bayit* (peace in the home). Rock stars quote Kabbalah. Can the Messiah be far off?

Kedoshim t'hiyu—<u>you</u> shall be holy. That's the mission statement. The rest is commentary.

THE FOUR QUESTIONS

1. What is your earliest memory of a holy experience?

2. How do you bring holiness into your life?

3. What takes you out of the realm of holiness and what can you do to avoid it?

4. Which new mitzvah can you integrate into your practice?

shirach • Father • Shabbat • Continuity • Torah • Prophets • Nigun • Pesach • Teshuva • Wedding
irituality • Holiness • Emunah • Diaspora • Bar Mitah • Simcha • Halachi • Birachot • Holiday
ewish • Tallit • Israel • Mitzvah • Prayer • Moshiach • Tefillin • Shabbat • Continuity • Torah • Prop
Nigun • Pesach • Teshuva • Weddings • Spirituality • Holiness • Emunah • Diaspora • Bar Mi
Simcha • Halachi • Birachot • Holiday • Jewish • Tallit • Israel • Mitzvah • Prayer • Mosh
Tefillin • Shabbat • Continuity • Israel • Prophets • Nigun • Pesach • Teshuva • Weddings • Spiritu
Holiness • Emunah • Diaspora • Bar Mitah • Simcha • Halachi • Birachot • Holiday • Jewish • Mitz
Israel • Mitzvah • Prayer

Simcha:
The Joy Inside
My Tears

♫ SHEHECHEYANU ♫

joyjud.com/m/she

Count all the blessings	*Lighting the candles, drinking the wine*
That we witness each day	*Feeling the embrace of Your love*
Every moment is a gift from above	*Just as the day turns into night*
Reaching this perfect place in time	*The seasons measure*
We touch forever	*Our greatest pleasure*
When we're all together celebrating	*Shehecheyanu v'kiy'manu...*

Judaism defines *simcha* (joy) as anticipating a bright future. The key is optimism and a confident connection to the Source of All Things. While we can mow over each other in our personal quest for happiness, joy requires a communal state of flow with the Universe. J.D. Salinger's take: "Happiness is a solid and joy a liquid." Seeing a great movie makes you happy, doing a great mitzvah brings joy. Shabbat emphasizes *oneg* (enjoyment) whereas *simcha* is the goal of Jewish holidays. In other words, *Oneg* is here and now happiness, as opposed to the future tense joy of holidays. The Jewish recipe for *simcha*? Give *tzedakah*, dance at a Bat Mitzvah, fully celebrate holidays, appreciate the gift of friends and family. Do things you love with those you care about. As a proud father, my most joyful moments have been my everyday interactions with Shira and our kids, Max, Jesse and Sarah. Even when they were teenagers.

At least most of my dealings with my teens were joyful. One evening, I hoped to surprise my family with gourmet Chinese food from a favorite restaurant. I maneuvered through rush hour traffic, waited for a parking spot, spent a fortune and then was rebuked by my daughter for buying dishes she didn't like. In her angst, she castigated me for not "knowing" her and marched to her bedroom without eating a bite. Not even a dumpling! This ungrateful behavior left me with little motivation to surprise her again…let her eat cereal.

I mention this altercation to clarify that a prerequisite for *simcha* is verbally acknowledging the good in our lives. God wants to give us the maximum joy possible. The responsibility of responding joyfully to the miracle of our lives is mentioned eighty-eight times in the *Tanach* (Bible). Conversely, the Torah lists an array of terrible *k'lalot* (curses) visited on the Israelites because they neglect to "serve their God with joy." It's up to us to manage our personal joy reservoir. Anytime we feel sad or anxious, it's a cue we need to restore our partnership with God. The resulting burst of positive energy dispels *k'lalot* and invites *b'rachot* (blessings). Just like I wanted to delight my daughter with fortune cookies, God yearns to deliver our deepest dreams.

Simcha is the natural state of being alive. Just look at toddlers who are playful, ebullient, and bounce back quickly after a tantrum. They are content playing hide and seek, building a sand castle or eating ice cream. They haven't yet learned to be morose or pessimistic. As we mature, we accumulate years of hurt and disappointment, rendering us defensive and callous. We erect filters to avoid life's barbs and prevent further emotional injuries. With the constant stream of disturbing news, fact-filled gossip and snarky criticism in the media, we withdraw further into a stoic shell. As a result, we grow cynical, harder to impress and lose our sense of wonder. The Hebrew word for baby, *tinok*, has the same letters as *tikkun*. Healing ourselves and by extension, the world, requires carving away stoicism, reclaiming vulnerability and accessing our joyful inner child.

Joy doesn't result from entertainment or good news. Rather, it springs from having a positive attitude, knowing every moment presents a growth opportunity. When we expend negative energy over life's little problems, what we <u>don't</u> have becomes our focus. My *Rosh Yeshiva* (Head of School) at Aish HaTorah, Rabbi Noah Weinberg, zt"l (an acronym for *zecher tzadik livracha*, may the memory of the holy one be a blessing) said that joyous people are problem solvers, not problem sufferers. It's a glass-half-full thing. Our patriarchs and matriarchs led difficult lives, yet, they minted the currency of Jewish joy for time immemorial. Jewish tradition teaches that the divine communication mastered by our biblical heroes was a byproduct of a joyful outlook. No joy = no prophecy. A joy connoisseur mines adversity for opportunity and learns to celebrate in the heart of darkness. Kierkegaard sums up this distinction eloquently: "It takes moral courage to grieve; it takes religious courage to rejoice."

Permission to Cry

Speaking of grieving, our tears are just as essential as our smiles. In Psalm 23, King David says to God, "Your rod and your staff comfort me." Whether we're cruising in the fast lane or broken down on the side of the road, God is with us. We can lean on God's staff, or take a blow from the rod…either way, God's involvement in our lives is an eternal source of consolation. The key is feeling the impact of the blow, acknowledging the source and not suppressing the resulting emotion.

I inherited my father's ability to cry. Joyful moments cause him to stroke his tear-soaked face with both hands. Any mention of his late father, whom he lost when he was only thirty-two, elicits the same reflex. He usually claims there is smoke in the air.

Some of my band's gigs are for weddings, often for couples I didn't previously know. Nevertheless, I cry at every *badeken* (when the groom veils his bride) and during the *chuppah* (ceremony under a canopy). I'm so moved at the creation of a new "*bayis ne'eman b'Yisrael*" (faithful home among the Jewish People) and relive the memory of my own nuptials.

My kids can't handle seeing me cry. They have to grapple with their own sympathetic tear response and typically resist with all their might. Despite their discomfort, at least they have learned from their emotional dad that big boys do indeed cry. Robert Frost said, "No tears in the writer, no tears in the reader."

Our family had a beloved elderly neighbor who was like a grandmother to our children. Evelyn frequented our Shabbas table and often called me to reset clocks or install new gadgets. She was strong and sensible until she succumbed to congestive heart failure at age ninety-two. Shira and I decided her *levaya* (funeral) would be the first our kids would attend. At the service, Evelyn's offspring recounted humorous anecdotes and her accomplishments in the community. Then I was asked to sing *Keyl Maley Rachamim*, the prayer for the soul of the departed. Even though Evelyn lived a full life, I was broken because she was no longer with us. I couldn't help but weep as I described how I missed her, setting off a chain reaction of tears throughout the mortuary. Perhaps the mourners needed permission to cry. Maybe we all did. I can still see my children sobbing in the pews, suddenly in touch with their own grief. A key aspect of Jewish lifecycle *halacha* is the permission to express our deepest emotions.

Reclaiming Joy Through Tears

The crying reflex has much in common with intimate relations. With tears, most adults train themselves to stifle the flow, to catch the feeling before it gets out of hand. To reclaim joy, we have to overcome that tendency. When we're in the bedroom with our beloved, we have to remain present to sustain intimacy. If we worry about performance or are otherwise preoccupied, we wreck the moment. And trying to get the groove back once it is gone isn't easy. It's the same with tears. Once we squelch the emotion, we have missed the opportunity for the catharsis that comes only after a good crying jag.

Humans are hard-wired for connection and tears are the ultimate connector. As Rabbi Stephen Baars explains, tears are both glue and solvent. They bond us together and wash away barriers. Think about the impact of videos of sobbing, malnourished kids in Africa. We cannot "stand idly by" while someone is crying. How about spontaneous tears when acts on America's Got Talent get the Golden Buzzer? I cry right along with the triumphant contestants. It may seem counterintuitive, but the ability to cry is on the same side of the continuum as the ability to feel great joy. This is the crux of Stevie Wonder's song, "The Joy Inside My Tears." The LIFE side of the aliveness spectrum features deeply felt emotions, allowing our sensitivity pendulum to swing to the apex. The other end of the continuum is the DEATH side, typified by aloof behavior, wearing a poker face, keeping it cool. Reaching the brass ring in the Joy of Judaism requires valiant effort to remain present and fully expressed. Choose life!

Once, on a trip to Israel, I received a powerful reminder of the close connection between tears of pain and tears of joy. Israel has always been the land of contrasts: adamantly secular vs. ultra-religious, arid desert vs. verdant swampland, right wing hawks vs. left wing doves. On this trip, the people of shalom (peace) were in the midst of what was known as the "Knife Intifada." I arrived in the country to perform, shoot a music video and enjoy my nephew Moshie's Bar Mitzvah. What a gift to celebrate a *simcha* (joyous event) in Israel with my extended family. Just breathing the springtime air was enough to fill my soul with delirious joy. But then every day there was another horrifying incident, often on the same streets I had recently walked. The sobering news reminded me of the precariousness of living as a Jew surrounded by those who deny our right to exist.

Over the course of my two-week trip, I made several visits to the *Kotel*. Although my prayers were sincere, I never truly absorbed the devastation of the current events. I knew I should be crying, but no tears came. This emotional paralysis left me deeply unsettled.

On the last weekend, my brother and nephew guided me on a pre-Shabbat mountain bike ride in the Jerusalem Forest. After the sweaty adventure, we returned to their neighborhood to immerse in the *mikvah* (ritual bath) just before it closed. Using the *mikvah* on *Erev Shabbat* (pre-Friday Night) is a cherished *minhag* (custom) of mine. I love the sensation of sweltering water relaxing my muscles and easing my mind. I dunk seven times, each for an extended period, testing the limits of my breath while enjoying the stillness underwater. This time, as soon as I plunged in, something inside me shifted. It was a tear welling up, perhaps a hint of the emotion I hoped would come while praying at the Wall.

Immediately, the visceral need to reclaim my "manliness" choked the impulse to cry. This failsafe measure is a vestige from when I burst into tears as a second grader when teased and chased through the schoolyard. Or from when I wept through my first and only fistfight in third grade. I won that fight but lost the battle; my peers would always remind me how I cried like a baby while I was swinging.

I dunked again and the urge to cry returned. I noticed how as soon as I resurfaced, my mind wandered to happier, more normal thoughts. The third time, I let it flow. The tears came hard. Soon I was sobbing underwater. To my knowledge, it wasn't audible in the *mikvah* chamber but when I came up for air, some Chassidim looked at me like I was *meshuga* (crazy). It didn't deter me. I went back under and screamed. Raw, primal, agonized screams. I screamed for the victims. I screamed at the senselessness of the violence. I screamed for the legions of brainwashed souls who believe murdering innocents is commendable. I screamed for the children who had lost their father that afternoon. They will never see him at the Shabbat table, never get his praise, never share a lifecycle event, never enjoy his loving embrace. I cried for the widows, for the bereaved communities, for the entire Jewish People.

I emerged purified and mellow, ready to enter the holiness of Shabbat. Only then could I walk to the *Kotel* and fully unite with the international assortment of my beautiful fellow Jews as I led the Friday night prayers for the Carlebach Minyan. Thanks to the power of tears, I regained a childlike vulnerability, carving away the barriers preventing my experience of the holiness of my surroundings.

Connoisseurs of Joy

My friends, I urge you to become connoisseurs of joy. Be the person who always thinks the weather is great, no matter how hot, humid or freezing it may be. Have you ever set out on an adventure with a complainer? Oy vey! It's easy to be a critic, to point out the things that "suck." Rabbi Shimon Green says we are commanded to love every Jew, but those who tend to rain on the parade, we love from afar. The fire of joyous wonderment and enthusiasm is easy to extinguish. Embrace the current temperature or situation as perfect. Of course, it's perfect, because that's how God made it. Can't embrace it? OK, but don't rock the joy boat with a snarky remark. Silence can be a mitzvah. We can be rays of sunshine rather than harbingers of doom.

Reclaim the ability to cry. Feel life deeply. Avoid retreating in cynicism or self-medication. Reclaim the inner child by recognizing the filters we erect to keep us safe.

Embrace activities that bring joy. Participate fully in lifecycle events and increase communal commitment. Banish the grouch by getting plenty of sleep. Learn about our heritage in order to feel great *simcha* for the gift of being part of God's master plan for the world.

THE FOUR QUESTIONS

1. How do you distinguish between happiness and joy?

2. Do you cry easily? If not, how can you regain access to deep emotions?

3. How do you handle those people in your life who take you away from joy?

4. What activities can you add to your life that will bring you joy?

The Science of Struggle

♫ YISRAEL SHELANU ♫

joyjud.com/m/yis

And when we pray
We set our sights to face her walls of golden
stone
The words we say
Reflect a love that grows each time
We're whispering her ancient name
Yisrael shelanu l'olam...

Two thousand years
Without a piece of land that we could call
our own
We never feared
Secure within the promise
Of a distant day that we'd come home
Yisrael shelanu l'olam...

O ne day, a boy found a fuzzy caterpillar and put it in a cage as a new pet. Soon, he observed the fascinating metamorphosis as the caterpillar disappeared within a cocoon. He checked the crusty shell daily and eventually noticed a small opening. As he hoped, a butterfly was trying to emerge. The boy waited impatiently and feared it was stuck. He took a scissors and gently opened the hole so the creature could escape. Sure enough, the butterfly inched out with a large swollen body and small, misshapen wings. Sadly, those wings never grew properly and the malformed insect spent its last days haplessly crawling around the cage. The boy learned that wings only develop when butterflies mount a tenacious struggle to escape their cocoons. His misguided act of kindness led to the creature's doom.

Like the butterfly, Judaism teaches that life's struggles strengthen us and give us the ability to fly. A theological maxim dictates God only gives us tests we can pass. Ideally, we accept our trials as proof of God's love for us, proof God wants us to maximize our potential. In the words of Leonard Cohen, "Forget your perfect offering. There is a crack in everything. That's how the light gets in." Tests aren't an interruption of your life—they are your life.

So, too, with parenting. Parents present a series of gradual, age-appropriate tests over the course of a child's lifetime. Good parents inspire development by encouraging children to walk, speak, go to bed and use the toilet. Later in life, kids must learn altruism, how to drive, cook and clean for themselves, how to say no to society's vices. The opposite of good parenting isn't dispensing punishment—it's ignoring a child. Similarly, tests from the Almighty are not penalties, but instead, prods to inspire leaps in our spiritual journey.

Parkour is a great example of the value of challenges. It is the growing sport of moving rapidly through an urban environment, negotiating obstacles by running and jumping. I often engage in parkour on hikes when I'm in rowdy mood, challenging my aerial dexterity bouncing off boulders, tree trunks and ledges. Since I was a kid, in any given cityscape, I am more likely to walk on walls or the edge of the curb rather than the sidewalk. Overcoming barriers can be fun! Parkour athlete Caelan Huntress explains, "In parkour, we do not see the obstacle as an impairment to movement. Indeed, it is the obstacles that make the movements worthwhile."

The word *Yisrael* (Israel) means "struggling with God." Yaakov (Jacob) receives his new name Yisrael when he victoriously wrestles with an angel. He establishes the essence of Jewish meritocracy: to grapple with God and faith and emerge stronger for the effort. We are *B'nai Yisrael* (Children of Israel), inheritors of this legacy of spiritual pugilism. Avraham, Yaakov's grandfather, starts this trend. He argues with God to refrain from destroying the evil city of Sodom. He stands in stark contrast to his predecessor, ark-builder Noach, who didn't consider wrangling with his Creator. Ten generations later, Avraham has the temerity to "go to the mat" with the Creator of the Universe. Hence, he is the first Jew. We share his innate chutzpah and feel comfortable calling God to task. Interestingly, Islam means submission, a fundamentally opposite paradigm to Jewish theology. The Torah pulls no punches when it refers to Jews as a "stiff-necked people" (*Sh'mot*/Exodus 32:9). We lead, we speak our mind, we persevere. A case in point: Israel's Prime Minister Golda Meir famously insisted her job was more difficult than that of President Richard Nixon. "You may be the president of 250 million people," she said, "but I'm the prime minister of five million prime ministers."

Perhaps the best example of the value of struggle is to witness any given yeshiva study hall. The din of disputation between impassioned students can be deafening. They battle *l'sheim Shamayim*, for the sake of Heaven, to better extrapolate the will of God. Like grapes that must be crushed to produce wine, students seek the most skilled sparring partners, valiantly parsing the text in the quest for truth.

Permission to dispute is our divine right as partners in a covenant with the Creator of Heaven and Earth. We confront God for allowing human suffering, for natural disasters, for the Holocaust. Our blessings are voiced using the familiar version of the word "you," *Atah,* as in *Baruch Atah.* God is our debate partner, our peer. According to Dennis Prager, this precept of struggle with the divine has "enabled Jews to believe in the importance of reason—God could be challenged on the basis of reason and morality; one does not have to suspend reason to be a believing Jew." Chassidic master Rabbi Tzadok HaCohen (1823-1900) argues that humankind ranks above the angels because we are the only creatures in existence sanctifying God through struggle. Angels have it easy! Mastering the Science of Struggle is essential skill in the pursuit of the Joy of Judaism. It is a crucial prerequisite to forging a meaningful relationship with a living God.

The Trap of Victimhood

One of the most difficult times to embrace our partnership with God is when we are wounded. When we are depressed, our *yetzer harah* (evil inclination) convinces us we are worthless, that God doesn't care. Of course, the opposite is true. The malady from which we suffer is evidence of God's gentle presence. According to Rabbi David Aaron, "When life gets rough, ask not WHY this is happening but WHAT this happening is asking of me." The Creator of the Universe roots for our healing, *davens* to connect with us and exults in our spiritual victories.

My brother, Rabbi Yom Tov, used to recommend the GO-NAD method to enable his students to survive emotional troughs. The acronym stands for GO into a "Non-Analysis Day" when plunging into a low state. Avoiding analysis paralysis means postponing big decisions and not giving the state a name like sadness or depression. Just coast. Resist self-pity, acknowledge the source of the *tzuris* (pain) and a natural upswing will follow. Another technique is to consciously focus on the good stuff in one's life. We have to give ourselves sufficient credit for making it out of bed, for getting dressed, for surviving yet another day. Life isn't easy for anyone, even those who seem like they lead a gilded existence. I've heard it said, "The only people without problems are people you don't know very well." All of us have multiple accomplishments…list them! Every human is a masterpiece—a piece of the Master.

I learned the value of setbacks the hard way. Is there any other way? Sometimes injury is the best teacher. I am often accused of getting too rowdy with the youngsters at our synagogue. I'm a big kid at heart and am referred to as a Pied Piper. One time, during the *Kiddush* at our synagogue, I pursued the kids as the monster Grendel, threatening to toss my prey into my lair. Later on, I had a line of riled-up pint-size children waiting to be swung by Sam the Human Swing. All went well until later that evening when I felt a funky twinge in my neck that sent tingles to my thumb and forefinger. The next day, I couldn't sit without excruciating pain. I couldn't work, I couldn't drive and I became an ornery grouch. A massage and chiropractic treatment offered relief, until I tried to sit down at the piano. Weeks went by. I believed my career was over, I'd never be able to ski or bike and without yoga, my body would plunge into a downward spiral of dis-ease. No one could convince me otherwise.

The next month I was scheduled to perform at a casino in Reno and the High Sierra Music Festival in Quincy. I considered cancelling due to the incessant ache. This was a trip I eagerly anticipated and the disappointment added to my malaise. Rather than continuing to sulk, I recognized I needed to take action and couldn't wait for anyone to do it for me. My first step was to verbally acknowledge that God did not abandon me. I created a mantra: *God loves me and is always with me and this challenge is a gift for my own good*. Next, I made *hishtadlus* (effort) by purchasing an airplane ticket. While it seemed ill-advised to spend the money if I was unable to perform, I knew these gigs, like all gigs, were a gift from God and God would be with me.

The morning of the trip I awoke in utter discomfort. Even with the help of Advil, I had difficulty lugging my suitcase and sitting in the airplane seat. Remarkably, the pain dissipated when I landed in Reno. I continued to rally throughout the trip. I felt triumphant pulling off my show in a posh casino ballroom for the local Jewish congregations and performing at the top of my game at the music festival. Perhaps it was because I spent five days on the road instead of sitting in my studio or negotiating L.A. traffic. Perhaps it was the magic of the soul-enriching Sierras. I'd like to believe my cure came as a result of accepting the pain as a heavenly message to slow down and take a leap of faith, rather than remaining in a place of anger which distanced me from the Almighty. I emerged from this test with a "no piggyback ride" policy for the kids and a reminder that ultimately, the only thing I could rely on was my relationship with God.

Easy Street is Not the Jewish Goal

One mid-summer afternoon, my brother Yom Tov and I hiked a favorite L.A. trail. The path hugs a mostly dry riverbed as it ascends through stands of sycamore and oak. It then departs the shade of the riparian zone with switchbacks leading to panoramic views from three rocks we have named Shipwreck, Hawk and Eagle. As we gingerly avoided the poison oak arching towards our exposed legs, we discussed the typical struggle of the artist. Is a life filled with obstacles a prerequisite for great art? In the wonderful autobiographies by rock stars Sting and Joe Jackson, their early years were fraught with financial and familial turmoil. Both ended their books with their first taste of stardom, perhaps because their most compelling challenges came before they were superstars.

As Yom Tov and I crested the apex of Hawk Rock, we pondered why the two of us have been on a financial precipice during much of our adult lives. Though we have been blessed with financial salvations, this situation engenders stress and worry, especially for our wives. Over the years, I have discovered that the more I "go for it" in my career, the more I reap such salvation. Month-to-month we somehow manage our financial commitments, providing the clarity that we can live abundantly with joy and *bitachon* (trust in God), regardless of our bank balance.

My brother reminded me of a teaching of Rabbi Noah Weinberg: God keeps the emissaries who do God's work hungry. Would one satiated with riches choose retirement on the beach or a life of hard work? I had to pause for thought: *would I shlep to fifty cities a year singing my songs if I didn't need the income? Or would I just book gigs in Aspen and Maui? Is my passion for outreach truly all the reward I need?* Without the need to support my family, I would not have the the joy from my travels and this book would never have been written.

When Aish was in dire financial straits, the aging Rosh Yeshiva launched a final multi-year tour of the Diaspora to teach and fundraise. Upon his return to Jerusalem, he explained to his frustrated acolytes that without the cash flow issues, he would not have had the privilege of meeting so many awesome people around the world.

Indeed, life disconnected from life's vicissitudes does not make for great art. We feel angst in every canvas by Van Gogh, who only sold one painting in his lifetime. We taste darkness in every phrase of Edgar Allen Poe, who lost nearly every member of his family and died penniless in a Baltimore gutter. How many entitled children of celebrities are humiliated as tabloids chronicle their demise? How many great musicians never top their hit debut album? Their early repertoire typically chronicles adventures in the trenches as artists claw for recognition. They have years of pathos and poverty during which they compile and perfect their material. Typically, a hastily recorded sophomore release fails to recreate the emotional intensity of the first album. Without radical reinvention, the performer joins the heap of "one hit wonders."

Great artists take us on a ride as they chase a personal vision, never satisfied with the status quo. We marvel as Picasso transitions from Blue to Rose, from Cubism to Surrealism. David Bowie morphed between theatrical personas from his youth until his last project, released right before his death. Miles Davis pushed the boundaries of jazz regardless of critics' disdain. Miles lambasted those who imitate others or who "ape" themselves at the sunset of their careers. Having nothing novel to offer, they simply perform an endless greatest hits package into their retirement. Miles stated, "if you're trying to ape...you don't have anything to give the world, you might as well be dead."

Rabbi Nathan Lopes Cardozo named his venerable Jerusalem-based institution "Beth Midrash of Avraham Avinu" (Study Hall of Abraham our Forefather). Avraham's quintessential trait wasn't necessarily *chesed* (kindness)—it was his utter refusal to accept a substandard status quo. Only when he accepted the role of rebel, regardless of his family or society's reaction, was he able to follow his unfettered logic and reach the revolutionary conclusion of Ethical Monotheism (belief in a caring, singular God). Rabbi Cardozo insists our heritage is based on rebellion: we keep kosher as an act of disobedience against eating like an animal, we join a community in prayer rebelling against the tendency to think one can do it alone, we use the *mikvah* to protest our society's obsession with sex. We do not commit to mitzvot to fit into religious society or please a wrathful deity. Instead, we perfect the Science of Struggle in order to continuously evolve in our personal power and strive for excellence.

Most Jewish day schools present only 90% of the breadth of Torah. What's the missing 10%? It's the "why" of Judaism: why we do mitzvot, why we serve God, why we are different from the other nations of the world, why we merit redemption. Without emphasis placed on communicating this first 10%, observance can become rote and meaningless. Asking fundamental questions should not be seen as heretical; ignoring the "why" of Judaism imperils the Jewish future. Struggle with God isn't optional! Picture that butterfly without the chance to fight its way out of the cocoon. A butterfly that didn't struggle is not a butterfly! I treasure my post-college period of grappling with tradition; my engagement with foundational issues only strengthened my relationship with God.

The answer to our collective salvation lies in offering each individual the full gamut of opportunities in Jewish life and then granting permission to struggle, to question, to personally engage. Jews are experts at making lemonade out of lemons. Until the day we leave this earth, we must strive for greatness. We are not merely human beings, we are human becomings. Struggle is life. Keep struggling, or else! Like the butterfly, we are writhing and striving and competing, building and breaking and building again. While it is hard to perceive the merit of setbacks, the challenges we face create the most powerful, beautiful wings, wings allowing us to soar in this dramatic quest of ultimate holiness and humanity.

THE FOUR QUESTIONS

1. When you are dealing with a challenge, what can you do to perceive it as a gift from God?

2. Analyze past challenges—were there positive outcomes?

3. What status quo situations in your life do you want to change? How are you going to make those changes?

4. What are your "why" questions? Who can you turn to for answers?

Nachas: What Everybody Needs

Always in a hurry and you don't know why
Always running late and you never got time
Still on a roll and the world is a blur
Why you're in the race you are no longer sure

Buried in email, you can't take calls
Too busy climbing the same four walls
Worry and pressure are taking their toll
Can you remember the last time you fed your soul

Take a deep breath, that's a good start

Say a few words that come from the heart
Feel the wind, watch the sun rise
It's a beautiful world
When you open your eyes

Whisper a prayer, say an amen
See how much you have and say it again
Let your song fill the skies
It's a beautiful world
When you open your eyes
Thank God for this beautiful world

Jewish survival depends on maximizing *nachas*. *Nachas* (or *nachat* in the Sephardic pronunciation) is the feeling of soul satisfaction when connecting Jewishly. It is a uniquely Jewish sensation and is therefore tough to define for those outside the tribe. All Jews have experienced *nachas*. We get it at lifecycle events when we perceive all will be well for the Jewish future. Brises, baby-namings, Bar/Bat mitzvahs and Jewish weddings are the headquarters of *nachas*. It isn't quite pride, although that's a big part of it. Parents swell with pride when their kids achieve significant accomplishments. A pride moment is your child getting an A on a math test or passing the Bar Exam. A *nachas* moment is seeing your offspring called to the Torah. Or when a bride circles her groom under a chuppah. *Nachas* involves continuity. When Jewish organizations worry about connecting with the next generation, what they are really saying is they are concerned about nurturing *nachas*.

My *rav*, Rabbi Moshe Cohen of Aish L.A., offered the following etymology of *nachas*. Because Hebrew is the divine tongue, word roots communicate the essence of a concept. The root of *nachas* is *nach*, just like the name of ark builder Noach. Related terms are *menucha* (rest) and *nechama* (comfort). *Nachas* implies having peace of mind, knowing God's well-managed world is running smoothly. When the angels praise God, they do so *b'nachat ruach* (with tranquility). *L'haniach* comes from the same root and is mentioned in the blessing when we put on arm *tefillin*. *Nachas* is about "placing" or setting a firm foundation for our Jewish destiny, just like we place our *tefillin* on our bicep. *Nachas* indicates one can <u>rest</u> assured about the long-term spiritual health of the Jewish People.

Nachas isn't only for parents and children. Siblings can have *nachas* for one another. So can dear friends and even strangers. You don't even need kids of your own. I'm a veteran of the Jewish Big Brothers program and have immense *nachas* from the accomplishments of my "little" bro. Unselfish gestures on another's behalf inspire *nachas* for all who hear about them, like the profound self-sacrifice of a daughter of a dear friend who donated a kidney to her ailing mother. Organizations like Jewish World Watch and American Jewish World Service advocating on behalf of international humanitarian concerns bring *nachas* to our benevolent tribe. Established Jewish neighborhoods like Pico, the Five Towns and West Rogers Park are *nachas* factories. Each boasts a robust, all-volunteer Jewish paramedic service called *Hatzolah* (rescue). They have *gemachs* (free loan societies) for just about everything: strollers, high chairs, wedding dresses and shtick, children's clothing, shoes, *tefillin*, even free loans of cash! My wife Shira founded a L.A.-based gemach for table centerpieces and party decorations. Big *nachas*! Great Jewish leaders who publicly acknowledge their Jewish roots and stay out of trouble inspire *nachas*. Elie Wiesel: *nachas*. Jewish gangsters: not so much.

While performing for a concierge tour of Israel, I met a certain well-heeled American philantropist. He possessed immaculate poise and understated confidence, intimating he had the best of everything. He had recently divorced his non-Jewish wife and was rediscovering his heritage. I sensed there was an emptiness he was trying to fill during this short visit to the Holy Land. My rabbi brother turned to me and said, "He has everything, except *nachas*."

Money can't buy *nachas*. It's a human pleasure on a higher plateau, up there with love, power and divine connection. *Nachas* takes investment, sacrifice and wisdom. In Jewish life, it's not "he who dies with the most toys wins." We don't do roasts or talk about real estate acquisitions at Jewish funerals. Those properly delivering *hespedim* (eulogies) discuss *nachas* moments, such as meaningful acts of charity and loving-kindness.

My parents mentioned *nachas* frequently. By doing so, they ingrained in their four boys that worldly success is worthless without it. Very few of my friends picked up this message from their folks. What happened to my generation? Many of us had grandparents who preferred the country club to the *kiddush* club. In the rush to appear American, *nachas* was thrown overboard. Connecting with *nachas* is enhanced by *yichus* (family connection) with our Jewishly-enlightened ancestry. That's why we get nostalgic when we think of *bubbies* (grandmothers), Yiddish and chicken soup. Unfortunately, Mr. Seinfeld and Mrs. Maisel cannot replace the influence of a flesh and blood mentor. When we lose the link with those who lived and died for *nachas*, we lose our awareness of what is truly important. Those without living Jewish mentors face the formidable task of finding their own inspiration. Barring radical anti-Semitism, without Judaic inspiration, it is inevitable they melt into the greater culture.

My parents modeled their belief that the best shot at *nachas* is an intact family with a Jewish spouse, with children on a clear path to a fulfilling Jewish life. As kids, my dad told us we were out of the will if we married out of the faith. He wasn't joking. And this was in a home without *kashrut* or Sabbath observance. I mention this to demonstrate that one does not have to keep all 613 mitzvot to pass on Jewish values to the next generation. That said, we can't just "phone it in." Turning kids into enthusiastic Jews means teaching them about *nachas*, serving as their role model. We can also resource role models in the community, exposing our kids to tireless heroes who are building the Jewish People. We can all be Jewish heroes! Regardless of one's family circumstances, we create *nachas* by conscientiously contributing to the world around us. *Nachas* is one of those things we can grab hold of at any time in our lives, in any circumstance.

With our own children, Shira and I have prioritized *nachas* at the expense of luxury and even fiscal responsibility. Nurturing our three kids through Jewish day school K-12 and beyond has required a monumental financial commitment. For us, this is tremendously important. Shira wears yesterday's fashions and there is a reason Sony Music refers to me "the hardest working musician in the business." The sacrifices we make are a small price to pay for the rewards of nurturing Jewishly active offspring. We are striving to pay it forward, planting the seeds of spirituality so our kids can receive *nachas* from their own Jewish grandchildren, God willing.

A *nachas* moment: thanks to my prodigious frequent flyer miles, our family took a two-week vacation in Israel to visit our oldest son Max. After high school he spent a year and a half learning in yeshiva and we missed him terribly. He showed up at Ben Gurion airport to pick us up on a Friday afternoon, already decked out in his form-fitting Shabbas suit, in top shape thanks to the yeshiva gym and with *tzitzit* dangling. Imagine the overwhelming rush of *nachas*. It was worth every ounce of sacrifice.

Nachas comes one mitzvah at a time. The subtle pleasure from one holy act multiplies exponentially and illuminates a Godly pathway. Building one's *nachas* reservoir requires patience. There's no rushing this stuff—quality over quantity. No need to blame or point fingers for previous intransience, no need for regret or panic. The *Ba'al T'shuva* (return to tradition) movement shows it's possible to reclaim *nachas* even without direct contact with *bubbies* and *zaydies* (grandparents). Start now with simple, positive steps. Celebrate Shabbat. Read a Jewish book. Get involved with your community. Consider synagogue-based adult education and adult Bar/Bat Mitzvah programs. As described in previous chapters, helping those in need is the nursery where *nachas* flourishes. Every step we take broadcasts the message that increasing *nachas* is a priority above career accomplishment and material acquisition.

Jewish parents are waking up and realizing: we want *nachas*! We want to inspire our kids to love Judaism, to marry Jews. The future of the Jewish People is in our hands. Don't assume kids get this message through osmosis. Drop lots of hints and actually have a discussion! Our kids DO care what we think. I heard about a proud Cohen (from the lineage of Aharon, the high priest) from a Midwest synagogue who never told his kids how he felt about intermarriage. When his only son became engaged to a non-Jew, it hit him: 3,000 years of the priestly line dies with me.

There were times I criticized my brother Yom Tov's affiliation with the Chassidic *veldt* (world) in Jerusalem. I felt he was losing touch with Western culture due to his reticence to go to movies, mixed gender beaches or ball games. As much as I tried to convince him of the importance of remaining connected with the world at large, he insisted that recoiling from "culture" was necessary to regain a sense of purity. I retorted that there are many valuable things in modern society and he could filter the good from the bad. In response, he said he didn't want to have any filters. He hoped for an open heart and the ability to hear God's voice without distractions.

Ultimately, I lost these arguments. My brother got *s'micha* (rabbinic ordination), moved near the *Charedi* (ultra-religious) neighborhood of Meah She'arim, married a like-minded woman and is raising eight beautiful blonde hair, blue eyed Chassidic kids who wear matching outfits. His oldest daughter was engaged at the age of seventeen and married at eighteen. I now see that my brother is laughing all the way to the "*nachas* bank." His kids will likely marry young, live close by, raise huge families and give him exponential *nachas*.

I get *nachas* from all seventeen of my remarkable nieces and nephews from my three brothers and sister-in-laws. The following saga describes an experience with Yom Tov and Leah's brood to illustrate the opportunities for *nachas* outside of one's immediate family and to highlight our big surprise at the end of the trip. One of the great gifts in life is getting "winks" from God. We often call them coincidences or say, "It's a small world!" Whenever they happen, I exclaim, "Large world, well managed!" in order to keep gratitude flowing.

One spring night, my brother called me from Jerusalem. The time was nearing for his once-every-five-year trip to the States to visit grandparents. Since the airfare for his whole *mishpacha* (family) is prohibitive, he wanted to maximize the impact of this rare excursion. Yom Tov had a lifelong dream of introducing his offspring to the wonder of Southern Utah's magnificent national parks. I turned him on to these treasures when I was a student at University of Colorado. Five years my junior, Yom Tov joined me on many of my cross-country drives from L.A. and we'd explore, hike, and four-wheel drive our way across this magnificent red rock wilderness. Yom Tov was worried he couldn't adequately plan the itinerary, transportation and lodging, all within a tight budget. I relished in the opportunity to help out since I have so much experience navigating these environs.

I assembled a ten-day whirlwind tour of Zion, Bryce, Antelope and Grand Canyons for the family plus the new son-in-law and baby. At the request of the kids, I arranged for the trip to culminate in a day of skiing at the nearby red rock resort of Brian Head. I secured a massive, centrally located home on the outskirts of Zion National Park and rented a twelve-passenger van. I planned age-appropriate hikes and all-terrain-vehicle, zipline and horseback riding activities. By the time I was finished, I realized that this was a trip I could not miss. With a few phone calls I cleared my studio schedule so I could serve as driver, tour guide, photographer and crazy uncle.

I learned early on just how difficult it could be to get twelve people motivated. Just packing up the car was a painful ordeal, not to mention the frequent rest stops and a three-hour delay at the St. George, Utah Walmart. You'd think these Israelis had never seen a big box store. Somehow we found room for four carts of groceries in a van that already was packed to the brim, thanks to the willingness of the *menschy* kids to be tightly packed in and have little ones on laps. We finally arrived at our mountaintop palace and everyone scrambled to find beds.

The next morning was utterly hectic. We were going to explore the phenomenally photogenic Checkerboard Mesa region but once again, I couldn't get the family in the car. Breakfast and the sandwich assembly line took over an hour. Each time we were about to roll away and sing our traditional family song, "We're Off on the Morning Train," someone else needed to pee or forgot a sweater. When we finally hit the trail, everyone was in great spirits and the four and six-year-olds were just as gung ho as their older siblings. After lunch, I led the big kids and Yom Tov on an advanced exploration of a prominent peak and we then angled down through a daunting slickrock canyon to meet the rest of the group back at the car. Later that afternoon, we visited the main junction of the spectacular park and Uncle Sam (me!) gave every child a budget to buy shiny rocks and geodes in a rustic rock shop. I was impressed that several of the kids opted to use their allotment to buy gifts for friends rather than their own bookshelves. Now that's *nachas*!

Thankfully the weather cooperated grandly and our week was filled with once-in-a-lifetime adventures. One highlight was our hike along the Queen's Garden loop of Bryce Canyon. At one point, the group split up, leaving me to pick up the rear with Sruli, the adorable four-year-old. What goes down must come up—at the base of the canyon we had to walk a few miles back to the ridge and this poor kid was exhausted. I had the pleasure to walk slowly with him and share his sense of wonder, perceiving the pinecones, squirrels and puffy clouds through his innocent eyes. We made it to the end of the trail hours after everyone had finished. When his big brother Avrami saw him struggling to walk the last quarter mile, he galloped down the trail and put lucky Sruli up on his shoulders. Another hike took us from a trailhead at the apex of Zion Park along three ambling miles to Inspiration Point. The view was dizzying as we peered down the two thousand-foot magenta, orange and yellow cliffs into the verdant Virgin River gorge. Our day on ATVs (all-terrain vehicles) featured a rollicking tour of backcountry canyons and ridgelines. While the adults and teens each had their own vehicle, I took the youngest three kids on a four-passenger Polaris. What fun to drive like a lunatic and make them scream with delight and terror.

Here is the "large world, well managed" moment: after packing up the van on the final morning, we headed an hour north to the Brian Head ski area. I had never visited this resort, preferring to travel to "real" ski areas like Park City and Snowbird a few hours further. On the way to the slopes, I expressed my desire to find an apres-ski Jacuzzi before enduring the eight-hour ride back home. I then called my parents in L.A. to give them an update on our adventures. My mom said, "Did you know your brother Joey took his family to a ski area called Brian Head for a few days? They arrived last night." *Our brother is at the same ski area? On the same day? A place that none of us had ever been before? Without knowing that we were going there? Really?* Sure enough, we spent the day with Joey and his wife Jennifer and their three adorable kids, Jacob, Josh and Julia. The cousins had a blast together. I loved initiating my Israeli family to winter sports and dashing about to keep everyone's skis attached. Best of all, at the end of the day, fifteen of us crammed into Joey's outdoor Jacuzzi for a hot soak and cold Coronas.

As we were about to leave, Jennifer received a distressing call: her dear stepfather was on his last legs. He had been suffering for the past year and prognosis was dismal. She panicked, sobbed and told Joey he would have to drive her several hours back to the Las Vegas airport. Well, that was exactly the direction we were going. We were able to do the mitzvah of rushing her to her stepfather and comforting her on the way. We also got to salvage Joey and the kids' vacation. We said our goodbyes, stuffed into the van and got Jennifer to the airport just in time for the flight, allowing her to share her stepdad's final hours, may his memory be for a blessing.

At my own wedding, one of my rabbi friends settled my nerves by giving me a simple prayer to say under the *chuppah* (marriage canopy): over the course of my life I should always give Hashem *nachas*. That sums it up. We give God *nachas* by being the best versions of ourselves. In the immortal words of Sting, "Be yourself, no matter what they say."

May we all have lives filled with sweet song and abundant *nachas*. May we serve God with joy and merit a speedy redemption for our beautiful world.

THE FOUR QUESTIONS

1. What is the difference between nachas and pride?

2. What have you done to give your parents nachas?

3. Who has given you nachas? How did it impact you?

4. What barriers do you have to nachas? How can you break them down?

Shefa:
The Jewish "Secret"

♫ MA ASHIV ♫

joyjud.com/m/mas

How can I repay You for all that You give
How can I request even one day to live
How can I seem grateful when words aren't
enough
Just let me walk in Your ways

I'll be Your canvas, I'll be the paint
I'll be Your soldier without a complaint
I'll be Your servant, I'll be a saint
For You have released my bonds

Ana Hashem ki ani avdecha
Ani avd'cha beyn amatecha
Ani avd'cha beyn amatecha
Pitachta l'moseyrai

Sometimes when I call You seem so far away
Sometimes I cry out and no one's there
But lately I recall things I cherish most of all
Like the hand of my baby clutching mine

Shira shops for the smallest packages of food in order to conserve space in our three-shelf pantry. When I find one of those ten-ounce boxes of Cheerios, I cringe and dream of buying supersize at Costco. I prefer a plethora of cereal options to mix and match my breakfast. Shira retaliates by purchasing mini jars of peanut butter. My closet full of clothes is another issue of contention. I have more than she does and she calls me a pack rat. I like having choices and as long as they still fit, see no reason to dispose of my favorites. So, too, with my CD collection, the gear in my music studio and my extensive library.

Am I too attached to material things? Yes! But I prefer to give my obsession another name: *Shefa.*

Shefa (abundance) is one of my favorite Hebrew words. On the basic level it means having plenty of money in the bank account. *Shefa* is a full take of gas, robust health, a beloved job, satisfying hobbies, ample time for family and friends. Having an array of cereal and T-shirt choices serves as my subconscious method of living in the world of *shefa*, for at least some of my day. We add *shefa* to our lives by celebrating Shabbat and holidays like royalty, entertaining guests in grand style, holding court as the monarchs of Livonia Avenue.

I resonate with living large. I love my king size bed. I love skiing big mountains, eating overstuffed burritos and sitting on an enormous Relax-the-Back chair at a sixty-four input mixing console in my recording studio. I love epic movies on big screens and multi-day music festivals. Big things give me big joy. I recognize that conspicuous consumption flies in the face of political correctness. This is a time when conscientious Americans reduce carbon footprints by bringing canvas bags to the supermarket, driving hybrids and recycling. We must not abandon these astute practices—I am simply suggesting we distinguish between minimizing our consumption and maximizing our joy.

Some believe the drive to accumulate material wealth is at odds with Judaism or a liberal agenda. In fact, all of our patriarchs and matriarchs were loaded! Their illustrious sagas are enshrined in our national consciousness to demonstrate that financial abundance isn't just tolerated, it's encouraged. Capitalism is great as long as we use our capital to heal the world and strive to be a *mensch* (a person of integrity). For example, when Avraham left Egypt with the gift of livestock, he ensured his vast flocks didn't graze on anyone else's property. Yitzchak (Isaac) managed his prodigious holdings with a low profile. When neighbors maliciously tampered with his wells, he reached out with overtures of peace. After Yaakov made his fortune, he radically transitioned from determined businessman into the spiritual father of the Jewish People. Great wealth brings great responsibility.

The popular new-age film *The Secret* echoes a truth that Jews have espoused for time immemorial: words have tremendous impact. We bring abundance into being by harnessing this under-appreciated source of power. The incantation *abracadabra* comes from the Aramaic "I will create as I have spoken." Prayer is simply speaking our deepest desires into being. Be careful not to radiate what you don't want. Use words that express what you <u>do</u> want! Cry out to the Almighty, "help me gain financial freedom," instead of exclaiming, "I'm sick of being broke." God is continuously creating the world in alignment with humanity's deepest desires. Envision your success. Express yourself. We are God's partners in creating the world we want. A world of peace and harmony, a world of unfettered joy, loving relationships and monetary success. Ask for your life to be filled with *shefa*.

Giving *tzedakah* (charity) is the ultimate *shefa* "magnet." If we respond to those in need with with our hard earned cash, clearly God can trust us with abundance. *Tzedakah* is the quintessential key to the gate of righteousness. The root of *tzedakah* is *tzedek*, justice. We don't give our mandated 10% because we feel guilty or sorry for someone. We give because it's the right thing to do. I differentiate between macro and micro *tzedakah*. The macro level is supporting the Jewish Federation, Israel, disaster relief and the homeless. In our bustling neighborhood we support local day schools and several synagogues. The micro level involves *tzedakah* in person, always having cash on hand to dispense on the streets, in the *minyan* (synagogue services), to aging veterans at freeway exits. Micro *tzedakah* involves the transfer of cash <u>and</u> love in the form of consideration and words of comfort. Holy generosity demonstrates we are aware of God's presence, thankful for our gifts and excited to share the bounty. God aches to give us more, but we must avoid arrogance and selfishness.

In order to attract *shefa,* we must fashion ourselves into vessels primed for ever-increasing blessing. A sixteen-year-old praying for a red Ferrari is most likely not ready for such a vehicle. The answer to his prayer, regardless of how earnestly he asks, is going to be no. Over our lifetimes, God gives us challenges to determine how much *shefa* we can sustain. Too much *shefa* can destroy us. We don't dare sip water from a fire hose. The tests we get on a daily basis build us into people who can deal with ever-greater gifts. Only God knows how much we can handle, even better than we know ourselves. We must trust God to know what is best and dispense our blessings with tenderness. Remember my "big plate?" Our attitude influences how much God places on our shoulders.

Building vessels for *shefa* is not only a spiritual call to action. Maimonides, the epic scholar and physician, insists we are fully responsible for maintaining our health so we are able to carry out God's will. "As long as a person exercises and exerts himself, takes care not to eat to the point of being completely full, and keeps his bowels soft, illness will not come upon him and his strength will increase." To maximize our Joy of Judaism, we must stay in shape and avoid blemishing our bodies with excess weight or otherwise abusing our health. On the other hand, we are not to overly obsess about the "body beautiful" or we risk emulating the behavior of our former Hellenistic oppressors. Once, on a chairlift at Vail, an Orthopedic surgeon next to me asked what I do to stay in shape. I mentioned surfing, biking and skiing. He responded, "No, that's what you do to your body! What do you do for your body?" The right answer would have been yoga, walking, stretching and cardio machines. I took his advice to heart and eventually, thanks to the prodding of my friend Rob Steinberg, finally showed up for a yoga class. I've been a yogi for over a decade and find it crucial for remaining sufficiently limber to withstand life's shocks and spills. Staying in shape enables the flow of *shefa* and by extension, benefits our family, our community and the Jewish People.

Just as we need mentors to guide us spiritually, so, too, do we need coaches in the physical realm. Shira and I encourage each other in our athletic achievements. My boys lift weights with workout partners who push them to maximize gains. Weight Watchers and Jenny Craig are successful because many benefit from guidance in reaching dietary goals. There is not a professional team in the world without a "trainer who trains." Our physical fitness *chevrusa* (partner) is the best guarantee we will actually "Just Do It!" Rambam prescribes playing ball games—when we engage with others in our exercise regimen, we increase laughter amidst the exertion, "deriving enjoyment while stimulating our breath." That's 900-year-old workout advice!

Speaking of breathing, I have a "breath *chevrusa*" who reminds me to breathe. Yes, breathe! I'm sure I'm not alone in losing touch with the need for deep, cleansing breath. At a post-concert meet and greet in Milwaukee, when the last of the guests were leaving, this friend asked me to take a deep breath. When I did, she looked dissatisfied and said, "That was a really shallow breath." I responded, "No, I'm a singer…I know how to breathe!" She then changed the subject, asking me about my dreams and goals and before long, got me to admit I had placed a self-imposed moratorium on making future albums. I explained how the expense of recording was prohibitive and I already had plenty of albums and songbooks to sell after my concerts. Diminishing creative output is not optimal for a creator! She asked me to repeat a mantra several times: "I will return to L.A., start a new project and it will be easy and fun." By the tenth repetition, I took my first deep breath in years! I couldn't believe it. How could I have held my breath for so long? That's what happens when we deny our own essence. I was killing myself! After this experience, I returned to L.A. and initiated production of the "Kol Bamidbar/A Voice in the Desert" musical, a program which was a tremendous success for me. Basking in *shefa* requires following our hearts. Just thinking about this Milwaukee milestone gets me breathing again.

One of my co-presenters at a Jewish conference in Burlington, Vermont was a Chassidic maple syrup farmer named Rabbi Shmuel Simenowitz. He lectures on the subject of eco-farming, getting back to the land and working with one's hands. He explained when to be thrifty versus when to aim for abundance. We must tread lightly on our planet, but with God we must ask for the moon. Rabbi Shmuel brought a diminutive, two-handled cup for the ritual hand washing before eating bread. It was given to him by a Jewish ecological organization to minimize the water used in the washing ceremony. He lambasted this assault of *shefa* in no uncertain terms. Indeed, according to the rabbi, we bring abundance into our lives when we wash with <u>lots</u> of water. In other words, don't hold back with your performance of mitzvot. Do them with alacrity and dedication. Give big charity, make loud blessings over your food and learn Torah with fervor. Take shorter showers but pour it on when you wash.

Kabbalah describes a higher meaning of *shefa*: our God is essentially good and created the universe to extend goodness in every direction. *Shefa* isn't just material abundance. It refers to the <u>flow</u> of God's beneficence in all forms. Imagine a brilliant beam emanating from a spotlight toward a performer on stage. This is like the divine light highlighting all creation. Spotlight operators have a choice of filters to dim the light down to near darkness. The *Zohar* (chief text of Kabbalah) emphasizes that we are in control of these filters; we can open or close our personal apertures based on our actions and attitudes.

In troubled times we tend to self-limit the flow of God's light in our lives. We allow economic woes to diminish our outlook. We feel beaten down at work, have less time to do the things we enjoy, feel hopeless trying to pay stacks of bills with shrinking salaries and struggle with health issues. Life can be scary. Living in fear takes us out of the flow of *shefa*. The million-dollar question is, how can we pursue our dreams full throttle, without trepidation, attracting blessing in our income, health and happiness? Learning to ski requires pointing one's skis downhill and letting them rip! Maximizing *shefa* means taking calculated risks, bravely committing to a particular outcome. Courage doesn't mean the absence of fear—it means, "I'm afraid but I'm committed." Tony Robbins says, "Stop being afraid of what could go wrong, and start being excited of what could go right."

Another factor dimming God's light is feelings of inferiority. We can be our own worst enemy. We might label ourselves bad Jews or sinners, distancing ourselves from community and becoming paralyzed with depression and doubt. Our inner voice tells us we've gone too far, we're beyond redemption. Only God knows our status—it's chutzpah to second guess. God never stops loving us. There is no such thing as a perfect person. *Mishlei* (Proverbs 24:16) says, "A righteous person falls seven times and rises again." This implies that even the *tzadik* falls…and what makes them *tzadikim* is they get back up. Sometimes we need a helping hand to get out of "the rough." We must dust ourselves off, pound our chest and start a new day. God is infinite and therefore infinitely forgiving. God has tremendous gifts in store for all of us—if we can get out of our own way.

Shira loves me so much. A few months after the cereal argument, she recognized that having variety is an important ingredient in my personal quest for *shefa*. Now, she not only provides it lovingly, she actively shops for brands I like. Our relationship with our Creator is much like a marriage: success is based on expressing heartfelt gratitude, being sensitive to what makes the relationship flow and rectifying what doesn't. God is continuously showering us with *shefa*. Only we can choose whether to acknowledge it. *Shefa* surrounds us in the form of every breath we take, our miraculous bodily functions, intelligence, loving relationships, self-awareness and inner peace. And of course, in plenty of cereal in the cupboard, landing a great gig or the holy grail: a perfect parking spot. Living a life of *shefa* is the Jewish "secret," one we can share with all humanity.

THE FOUR QUESTIONS

1. How do you distinguish between shefa and conspicuous consumption?

2. What can you do to bring shefa into your life?

3. What are the things you do that limit shefa? How can you overcome them?

4. How can you spread shefa to others?

PART TWO

Judaism 202:
The Artform of
Jewish Living

This section is dedicated by
DR. DANIEL S. BERMAN, MD

Sam, what an accomplishment! I have marveled watching you grow into the accomplished man you are—musician, composer, performer, educator, and now author. We are all so proud of you. The world is a better place because you are here. Best of luck with the first of many books to come!

IN THIS SECTION:

Can't Beat Bitachon 37

B'chira: Lessons in Free Will from a Talking Donkey 43

Middot: The Measure of a Mensch 49

Halacha: The Chok's on You 54

Eretz Yisrael: The Gift of The Promised Land 60

Redemption Song 66

OVERVIEW

Now that we have the Joy of Judaism basics, in other words, we say *hineni* to *kedusha* and extract every ounce of *simcha, shefa* and *nachas* out of life, it's time to delve into Judaism 202: The Artform of Jewish Living. We transition from simple *emunah* (belief in God) to manifesting that belief in day-to-day activities. We will be maximizing our most powerful human asset: the gift of free choice. Through the lens of Torah study, the oldest self-help seminar in existence, we will examine our character traits. Then, in a vocabulary challenge of biblical proportions, we will forge a path in the realm of *halacha*, the system of Jewish law that keeps us on the straight and narrow. Lastly, we will explore the unbreakable bond between Israel and her People and dissect the human drive toward a world perfected.

Judaism isn't big on getting comfortable. We never quite "arrive." The Hebrew word for a wise person is *talmid chacham*, a student of wisdom, one who is always growing. Just when our patriarch Yaakov was ready for retirement, the "ship" hit the fan. Daughter Dinah was raped, sons Levi and Shimon went on a murder spree and Yosef was kidnapped. Yaakov spent years concerned that neighboring tribes or his twin brother Esav's army might attack. Then he had to descend to exile in Egypt. This illustrates that life can be extremely challenging, even for our leaders, even when we think we merit living on easy street. The upcoming chapters will illustrate techniques to establish and maintain spiritual momentum, emerging triumphant in the face of adversity.

In the final statement of the original five chapters of *Pirkei Avot* (5:23), Rabbi Ben Hei Hei concludes with, "According to the effort is the reward." The more exertion we expend, the greater our fulfillment. Comfort <u>isn't</u> synonymous with pleasure, it's the opposite! Comfort is for vacations, not real life. Ask parents what is their greatest pleasure: their kids. And their greatest pain? Their kids! The more pain, in terms of effort and self sacrifice, the more joy. Our Jewish commitment is not merely theoretical—it's time to ramp up to Judaism 202: The Artform of Jewish Living.

Can't Beat Bitachon

♫ BITACHON ♫

joyjud.com/m/bac

Everyone thinks you got it made
But life can be tough when you're in fourth grade
You know that tomorrow's a spelling test
But you're way behind and you're totally stressed
Only one thing's gonna save you now
Bitachon, bitachon (and you gotta study)

Finally it's time to drive a car
So you're out on the road and you feel like a star

Just as your life is getting on track
You smash up your dad's new Cadillac
Only one thing's gonna save you now
Bitachon (and a lot of money)

Close your eyes and rest assured
He listens to your every word
There's a reason why you're in this situation
At times it's hard to understand
That when He opens up His hand
He's giving you exactly what you need

Emunah is defined as belief in God. According to Rambam, it is the <u>knowledge</u> that Hashem created and continues to maintain all creation. Jews are not Pantheists, those who share a sense of wonder for God's universe but eschew an immanent deity. Our legacy is the radical concept that there are no random occurrences. God is intricately involved in every detail of life. Acts of God are not only famine, disease and disaster. Acts of God are also dolphins, babies and snowflakes. With *emunah*, we know God is present with every individual 24/7, loving us, hearing our prayers and decreeing our fate.

Bitachon (trust) is the Judaism 202 level of connection. With *bitachon*, we take our relationship with God onto the test track. We are proactive in life but acknowledge God is in charge of the results. It's possible to have great *emunah* in God's existence, but not trust God to have our back. According to a 2016 Gallup poll, nine out of ten American adults say they believe in God. The Jewish goal is to go beyond belief. The ideal is to live every day manifesting belief, or as I like to put it, walking the talk.

At Ben Gurion airport in Tel Aviv, the *Bitachon* counter is where charming young Israelis ask if we've packed everything ourselves. It's the modern Hebrew word for security. As faithful Jews, we place God at the helm of our security team. Yes, we make efforts to secure the flight by screening passengers and luggage. But we do so knowing our ultimate security remains in the hands of the Almighty. Our goal is to become *ba'alei* (masters of) *bitachon,* with unflinching confidence that the Creator of all reality is doing what is best for all creation, for all time.

Bitachon and Gam Zu L'tovah

True *bitachon* goes beyond thinking, *although things aren't great right now, it's all for the best.* A higher form is perceiving that everything is good <u>right now</u>, even though on the surface, circumstances may seem nightmarish. God isn't out to punish. Rather, God systematically tests and tempts in order to enable us to grow. *"Gam zu l'tovah"* (this is also for the good) is the *bitachon* slogan. We must be patient with ourselves—*tzadikim* (righteous individuals) who are able to thank God for their adversity are a rare breed.

Regardless of how advanced our *bitachon,* we don't ask for tests or leap in front of speeding trains, hoping for miracles. A person with *bitachon* is grateful God has created a world with predictable physical and spiritual laws of cause and effect. And yet, within these limitations, the *ba'al bitachon* recognizes that no challenge is insurmountable with God's assistance. Rabbi Noah Weinberg implored his students to remember their strength to pursue outreach comes from the Almighty, especially when doing the urgent work of inspiring God's children. Masters of *bitachon* see their paychecks coming not from their employers, but rather from God through their employers. Similarly, a disease is cured not by a doctor, but instead, the doctor or drug is a vehicle for God's healing power. Those with *bitachon* are less prone to jealousy since they know God always gives them exactly what they need.

It's easy to tell when one in the company of *ba'alei bitachon.* They are not fazed by life's vicissitudes, but rather, focus on what's important and slough off what is not. *Ba'alei bitachon* are typically humble and since they don't have unrealistic expectations, avoid disappointment and rarely lose their temper. In fact, anger is considered equivalent to *avodah zarah* (idol worship), one of the ultimate transgressions. The literal translation of *avodah zarah* is "strange worship." In other words, someone with *bitachon* sees an anger-inducing situation for what it is: a test. Losing our temper means we temporarily lose sight of God's omnipresence and master plan. Therefore, in that moment, we must be "worshipping" something other than God.

Ba'alei bitachon never brag about their level of trust in God. That is akin to asking for a test, and one need only look at biblical figures like Job or King David to realize such requests can be perilous. Sharing one's *emunah* helps others solidify their own faith. *Bitachon* is more personal and is best kept to oneself. One might ask why a *ba'al bitachon* doesn't just retire. After all, one can sit and learn Torah all day. God will provide, right? On the contrary, say the sages. Hashem blesses us in everything we <u>do</u>. We invoke God's blessing with our own passion, drive and courageous effort.

The term for this mandatory exertion is *hishtadlut* (or *hishtadlus* in the Ashkenaz pronunciation). Choose a goal, do *hishtadlus* and know God will help finish the job one way or another. The key is to balance exertion with our trust in God. Making any effort without spiritual aspirations is at odds with *bitachon.* Likewise, having spiritual aspirations without making any effort won't get results. There is no preset formula. Each one of us has a unique *tafkid* (task) in this world, requiring variable ratios of *hishtadlus* and *bitachon.* Establishing this crucial balance is a key to the Joy of Judaism and finding the point of equilibrium is best achieved with the help of an insightful rabbi.

As we grow in *bitachon*, our tests evolve commensurately. That's why taking baby steps is a good idea. The Hebrew word for a test is *nisayon,* from the word *nes* (a miracle or a banner). A miracle is where the *Shechina* (Hashem's presence) interrupts the natural order, bursting out of hiding, waving like a banner. Similarly, tests are markers, flagging turning points in our lives. They often indicate a change in direction is needed. Avraham faced ten epic tests, beginning with his rebellion during the reign of Nimrod, through the *Akeidah* when he brought his son Yitzchak to be sacrificed. In hindsight, we can look back on formative tests we have endured and appreciate them as divine banners soliciting our waning attention. Each test is therefore a profound revelation of God's Presence, an entry point into the realm of the miraculous, bolstering our *bitachon* reservoir.

Perhaps the best Torah example of *bitachon* is Nachshon ben Aminadav. According to the *Midrash*, while everyone was panicking and/or praying at the Red Sea, Nachshon intuited God would not redeem the Jews only for them to perish at the hand of the Egyptians in a bloody, beachside massacre. Hashem said, "Why are you all crying out to me? Get moving!" (*Sh'mot*/Exodus 14:15) Nachshon was the first to take the historic leap of faith by walking into the sea—only when the water reached his nose did the sea split. God parts waters in our lives and helps us overcome obstacles. But first we have to get wet.

One of the benefits of frequent worldwide travel with exacting schedules is the opportunity to flex my personal *bitachon* muscle. The more I live on the edge, the more I must rely on God to get me out of harrowing situations. If I don't break through barriers, I never get out of the box. Life is exciting outside the box!

Adventures in Bitachon #1

I had the good fortune of getting booked to perform at a prestigious Saturday night wedding at the King David Hotel in Jerusalem. Any opportunity to travel to Israel is a gift—especially when helping with a mitzvah. Due to a Wednesday gig in L.A., I had to take a Thursday morning flight, the only flight that would get me to Israel before the start of Shabbat. Shira drove me to the airport, kissed me goodbye and as she was about to drive away, I realized that my passport was on our kitchen counter. Oy vey! Thankfully, we live close to the airport. Shira beelined home for what should have been a forty-minute round trip. Meanwhile, I attempted to drop off my suitcase, but the attendant wouldn't take my bag without my passport. I told her my tale and begged for clemency. Taking pity on me, she contacted her supervisor and was given permission to take my bag, but only after she inscribed, "No boarding without passport" on my boarding pass. I returned to the curb and waited patiently for my wife. Patiently, that is, until it was clear she wasn't going to make it back in time.

Twenty minutes before the door closed, I decided to take my chances without my travel document. I had to sprint to the very last gate in the terminal. There were still a few people in line, so I surreptitiously used the space behind the woman taking boarding passes to sneak onto the jet bridge. Thank God, I got on the flight! I thought, *better to deal with Israeli authorities than American ones*. One problem. We had a stopover at JFK and had to disembark and then reboard a few hours later. Would I receive another miracle?

I sat in the JFK boarding area and prayed fervently, asking God to allow me to make the bride and groom joyous with celebratory music and of course, earn *parnasa* (income) to support my family. Thanks to my fledgling *bitachon* I was able to minimize panic. I waited until the attendant was distracted and slid past her as she scanned someone else's boarding pass. No Jedi mind trick needed. Heart pounding, I took my assigned seat toward the rear of the plane. Just before takeoff, my name was called over the PA system. The jig is up! I bid farewell to my new friend seated next to me, gathered my belongings and walked to the front of the plane to meet my fate.

I approached the flight attendant at the boarding door. Sheepishly, I said, "I'm Mr. Glaser." She scrutinized me and responded, "Oh, great. A seat opened up in business class. Would you like to move up?" I closed my gaping mouth and graciously accepted her gallant offer. As soon as the jitters subsided, I fell asleep for the duration of the flight, only awakening when we reached Israeli airspace. At Ben Gurion airport's passport control I headed straight into the co-located security office and presented my California driver's license. After a one-minute interrogation, the staff waved me through and bid me Shabbat Shalom.

Adventures in Bitachon #2

My beloved cardiologist uncle, Dr. Dan Berman, bought a new car for his big sister, my mother. He is so enamored of his Tesla that he wanted my septuagenarian mom to have the same electric thrill zooming down Sunset Boulevard. She had been making the most of this gas-free lifestyle and wanted to try the Tesla Superchargers dotting the US countryside. She decided the perfect week for this adventure would be when I had a series of concerts scheduled in Northern California.

My first stop was Sacramento, which happens to be where my mom and her brother grew up. She volunteered to drive me—we would have a lovely day together in her "0-60 mph in three seconds" racecar and then she would drive back alone the next day. She invited all her McClatchy High School friends and a few of our relatives to attend my performance at Mosaic Law Synagogue. We even rehearsed her cheerleading fight songs so I could add them to my setlist. She brought the tuna sandwiches and I assembled a selection of our favorite songs on my iPhone to enable us to harmonize throughout the drive.

The day before our trip, my mom called to let me know we would have to leave at least nine hours before my 5:30 pm sound check. "What?" I responded. "This drive should only take five hours!" Evidently the Tesla computer indicated we had to stop at three superchargers. Recharging would add about three hours to our trip. "But don't worry," mom said, "they are located in nice places to take a break." Suddenly my leisurely day with my mother sounded a bit too leisurely. I prodded her into leaving a little later, promising her all would be well. After all, I had *bitachon* that God wanted me to reach my gig on time. She didn't buy it. There is no arguing with my mom when she makes up her mind. I would sacrifice sleep for the sake of shalom.

The next morning arrived too soon. After working until 4:00 am and getting only a few hours of sleep, my mother arrived right on time, bright eyed and raring to go. We loaded my gear in the surprisingly roomy car and set off on our adventure. A mere hour later we hit the Grapevine, an extensive mountain pass that sucks heavily on electricity. I didn't realize the range indicated on the odometer would be sharply reduced by excess speed and climbing. For this reason, the Tesla Corporation situated the first supercharger outside of L.A. in Lebec, a truck-stop town at the end of the Grapevine. Fortunately, it's located next to a delicious do-it-yourself, kosher-certified Yogurtland.

We enjoyed our treats in the air-conditioned shop while the car recharged in the sweltering ninety-five-degree heat. We returned to the vehicle to discover my mom hadn't properly inserted the recharging cable. That's right, it didn't get any charge whatsoever. She plugged it in securely and we returned to Yogurtland to escape the stifling Central Valley haze. After another half-hour, we returned to the car. Mom screamed, "Oh %#$!!!, I locked the keys in the car!" Somehow I managed to keep my cool, confident that Elon Musk had a brilliant solution for such emergencies. After calming my mother down, I called the Tesla dealer. Eventually, a service person was able to unlock our car remotely. Victory! I did a quick calculation and to my relief, we would still be on time, but we had to get moving.

When we set off, I could no longer keep my eyes open. I apologized to my mom for being lousy company, reclined my seat and passed out. A half hour later I awoke with a horrible sense of dread. As the street signs came into focus, I noticed we were driving SOUTH on the 5 Freeway. *Nooooooooo!* I struggled to maintain composure and growled, "Mom, what happened?" She responded that twenty miles out of Lebec the computer flashed a warning indicating she had to return to the previous supercharger—the car would be dead on the side of the road if she didn't turn around. My well-developed *bitachon* eroded like a California mudslide.

Back to the same charger, back to the same Yogurtland. The lady behind the counter giggled when she saw us return. Evidently this behavior is not uncommon for supercharging customers. As we waited for the charge we called the dealership to assess the problem. They told us that the only way to make it from one charger to the next is to go between 55 and 60 miles per hour. On a freeway. Where the speed limit is 70 and most drive 85! How ironic that our speed had to be slower than the eighteen-wheelers and yet, we were in a revolutionary sports car.

Clearly this celebrated automobile is not quite ready for prime time. Before my Sacramento concert, I would be breaking in a new drummer and rehearsing with a local kids choir. Showing up late was not an option. I have built my reputation on being reliable and prompt. In over twenty years have never missed a downbeat (the start of a show), thank God! Now what was I going to do? Even at a lethargic 55 miles per hour, the onboard computer kept sounding the alarm that we wouldn't make it. Who wants a car that keeps the driver paralyzed with fear that it is going to die at any moment?

Despite this predicament, I somehow kept it together, consciously converting my agitation to a placid complacency. I repeated, *all will be well. God wants me to get to my show and will help one way or another.* I called the cantor at the synagogue to advise him of our situation, assuring him I would make it but might be a bit late. I couldn't get upset with my mom—she was already freaking out. As we limped along in the slow lane, I realized at the next stop I was going to have to hitchhike with someone who had a very fast car. Electric vehicles need not apply! It was time to double down on my *hishtadlus*.

At the halfway point in the trip, the sprawling Western-themed Harris Ranch restaurant is equipped with a dozen superchargers. I entered the main dining room, summoned my chutzpah and loudly asked if anyone was traveling to Sacramento. Tourists from all nations stopped their meals and shot me icy glares as if I were a homicidal maniac. Me! I tried the next dining room, to no avail. I then braved the outside heat to wait for any travelers who might sympathize with my plight. Letting the families and non-English speakers pass, I eventually set my sights on a middle-aged couple who appeared to be good-natured Christians. When they replied that yes, they were Sacramento-bound, I walked with them to their car and explained my strange saga. They saw my mom and her ill-fated Tesla and opened their hearts, allowing me to stuff my luggage, keyboard and stand into the back seat of their brand new Mercedes C300 Turbo Coupe. My new friends Ron and Christine were even kind enough to let me ride shotgun!

Yes, I abandoned my mom at the rest stop. She would have to wait a full hour for the charge and, quite frankly, she was thrilled to be rid of me and my urgent deadline. As the Mercedes flew down the road at 85 miles per hour, my "saviors" and I conversed about Judaism, overseas travel and Ron's life in the navy. We had a scary moment when Ron narrowly avoided a multiple car fender bender. Upon arriving in Sacramento mid-rush hour, I deferred to Waze to find the most expeditious route. At long last, we pulled into the synagogue's driveway. It was EXACTLY 5:30 pm, my promised arrival time.

Cantor Ben radiated relief as he welcomed me at the door. I did the sound check and rehearsal and performed a spirited concert for three hundred enthusiastic congregants. My mom arrived just in time for the show, nearly twelve hours after leaving her home. In the end, she was elated to survive the experience and share the evening with her friends and family.

Transforming Emunah into Bitachon

The best technique to acquire *bitachon* is to attempt something new, something fundamentally challenging. Otherwise the need for heavenly assistance is minimal. Pick a new hobby, take on a side job, learn to play a musical instrument, go back to school. Don't be afraid to ask someone for something you need or want in fear of rejection. Ask anyway! Note that in the previous story, I got a lot of nos before I got to yes. Over and over I have been amazed by how the Universe conspires to answer yes. Sometimes nos steer us to the yes we need. Having *bitachon* plays a huge part. I rely on Rabbi Jagger: "You can't always get what you want, but if you try sometimes you just might find…you get what you need."

The best trust-building technique is becoming one who is "*la'asok b'divrei* Torah," engaged in Torah and occupied with daily mitzvot. Mitzvot are actually "*bitachon* bites"— small doses of divine serum inoculating us from triviality. One who says *hineni* to each mitzvah opportunity lives in the realm of action and affirms the Commander-in-Chief is doing an outstanding job running the world.

Because we're human, we usually don't have the whole picture. Acquiring *bitachon* requires discerning that our perspective is subjective and only God knows why things are the way they are. Gaining *bitachon* requires time, patience and daring. It's a state of being we strive to achieve every day. Some days are easier than others. With practice, despite stormy seas, we can navigate smoothly by filling our sails with the wind of God's providential love.

THE FOUR QUESTIONS

1. How would you describe the difference between emunah and bitachon in your life?

2. How do you balance hishtadlut and bitachon when you face a challenge?

3. What situation did you overcome with bitachon?

4. When you experience adverse circumstances, what steps can you take to remind yourself of God's love?

B'chira: Lessons in Free Will from a Talking Donkey

♫ LO BASHAMAYIM ♫

joyjud.com/m/lbs

How did I ever find my way back home
What did I do to deserve this prize
Searching the world to find the secrets
That were hiding right before my eyes

It isn't in the heavens
It's not over the sea
The answer's soundly sleeping in my heart

Is there a home for me in history
Is there a purpose to my wanderings
When will I realize the reason
I was cast inside this destiny

It isn't in the heavens, it's not over the sea
You and I are never far apart
Lo bashamayim…

The key to Creation is *b'chira* (free will). Without *b'chira* we'd behave like programmed robots, and there would be no one with whom God could have a real relationship. Free will is how Hashem made life exciting! The steering wheel of life is in our hands. When we want something with all our hearts, God opens doors to facilitate our dream. Paradoxically, God runs the Universe, <u>and</u> we have the ability to choose. We can even choose whether or not to have a relationship with God. Remember the poignant scene at the end of "Bruce Almighty?" Even though Jim Carrey has divine powers, he is powerless to make his girlfriend love him because she has free will. Judaism 202 requires that we appreciate this immense power in our grasp. Our free will is both empowering and frightening. God will be with us whether we choose the road of darkness or light. The high road or the low road—it's totally our call.

Free will is on a continuum. Too much and we crave boundaries, too little and we feel imprisoned. The Torah offers priceless wisdom to help us maintain this balance and stay focused on our *tafkid* (life task), confident we are doing so in God's good graces. Torah boundaries may seem restrictive, but actually give us the ability to maximize free will as fully expressed, unique individuals. Growth in free will mastery results in the reward of more freedom. We must teach street safety to kids, for example, so they learn to explore their neighborhood without getting hit by cars. Instead of locking our kids in the house, we give them clear, step-by-step parameters of proper behavior. So, too, God imposes restrictions not to stifle us, but to liberate our potential.

Our Creator has given each of us the gift of an internal moral compass known as the *yetzer hatov*, the good inclination. We commonly refer to this as our conscience. The evil inclination (*yetzer harah*) "crouches at our door" (*B'reishit*/Genesis 4:7) ready to sabotage our dreams, but only so we rise to the occasion and vanquish it, thereby experiencing the holy pleasure of choosing life. Whether we realize it or not, we are always making choices. In *D'varim* (Deuteronomy 30:19), the Torah bluntly states: "I place before you life and death...choose life!" When we seek escapes of the Internet or chemical variety, for example, we denigrate the gift of life. Eating an extra cupcake, succumbing to binge TV or obsessing over professional sports—these are "death" experiences. However, using those exact same indulgences as rewards for reaching goals are what I call "choose life victories." This is the fine art of employing the *yetzer harah* in service of the *yetzer hatov*, throwing a bone to our everpresent evil inclination in order to achieve greatness.

God created humans "in God's image" (*B'reishit*/Genesis 1:27). Of course, God has no physical image—our claim to Godliness lies within this miracle of independence we enjoy, differentiating us from the rest of creation. Our lives are designed not to be effortless, but to make us great. Greatness is the result of acting Godly, "choosing life" one decision at a time. As shocking as it sounds, the opposite of choosing life is suicide. Most of us commit suicide on an installment plan. Little increments of wasting precious minutes add up to years flushed down the drain. Like everyone, I need work breaks, but I try to make them beneficial, for example, writing a chapter of this book or practicing the piano. Steve Jobs studied calligraphy in his spare time. Einstein played the violin. I heard of a rabbi who completed the entire Talmud while in carpool and grocery store lines. Rather than waiting until we're on our deathbed, every day we can, in the words of Dylan Thomas, "rage, rage against the dying of the light."

I face the choose life/death dilemma daily. As a freelance musician, I struggle with abundant freedom and little structure. My daily routine is anything but routine. Many of my deadlines are self-imposed. The craft of making music is vastly time consuming, goals are difficult to quantify and the quality of the final product is subjective. Musicians typically survive from gig to gig and operate without mission statements or business plans. All of my kids are becoming musicians in their own right and while I am gushing with pride over their accomplishments, I am not pushing them into the field. It is too easy to flake, to get distracted, to start projects and never finish. If, by some miracle, recording artists get their masterpiece shrink-wrapped, then they have to put on a businessman's hat to bring the product to market. Most musicians don't like switching hats. They believe it isn't part of the job description.

My parents wonder where I got my propensity to choose life. As a child, I intuited the importance of postponing gratification and programming my days with specific goals until they were all checked off. I kept a balance sheet of my cash flow in elementary school. I'd even eat one candy bar methodically over a period of weeks. Yes, I'm weird. I spent my high school and collegiate summers participating in a plethora of nurturing adventures designed to enhance my every waking minute.

Perhaps it's this efficient, meticulous quality that keeps my record production clients coming back for subsequent albums. I had an insight about this ability while conversing with my father. As I've mentioned, he was a sportswear manufacturer and I love hearing his stories about the "old days" in the business. He inherited the company from his father, my namesake, Sam Glaser. For most of my life, I believed my grandfather was in sales. I asked about his tactics to woo buyers and my father retorted, "Grandpa Sam didn't sell, he was too busy with production." "Oh," I responded, "how did I not know this?!" I never realized my grandpa was the disciplined mastermind behind the mass production of the clothing. He started with a pushcart on the Lower East Side of Manhattan and became one of the founders of the garment industry in Los Angeles. Perhaps I inherited my namesake's ability to see the big picture and intuit the steps to get there. No wonder Production Management was my favorite class in business school. No wonder I'm able to produce music and stay on task. Thanks, Grandpa Sam, for the propensity to use my *b'chira* effectively.

Once I get on a "choose life" roll, it gets easier to maintain positive momentum. Unfortunately, the converse is also true. "Choose death" decisions beget more wasted moments, more opportunities to crash and wallow in a low state. We start to rationalize poor decisions and allow them to morph into an "inevitable" lifestyle. According to the classic Cherokee story of the two wolves inside each of us (representing the *yetzer hatov* and *yetzer harah*), the one that wins is the one we feed. Once momentum is established, it's easier to keep the wheels rolling in the right direction. Feed the good wolf and starve the interloper.

Shira sometimes questions why I must work such long hours at the peril of my health. I set goals with deadlines that are very real for me, even though to an outsider they appear arbitrary. When I get on the ball, I tend to binge in order to maximize productivity. If I get to Shabbat without reaching my self-imposed quota, I feel unfulfilled, whereas I feel like a rock star when I maintain consistent *b'chira* victories. Like everyone, I dig myself into seemingly inescapable ruts. The escape path is usually illuminated with a single, simple choose life decision. Judaism scatters these pellets of salvation throughout our every day. Soon, my "choose death" disposition recedes in the background with each small faith-building triumph.

Famous last words:
I'll feel good about myself when _____.
I'll take that great vacation when _____.
I'm saving this outfit for _____.

The nemesis of efforts to enhance *b'chira* is the word "eventually." Don't wait for the big break! Carpe diem! I love visiting the High Sierras, one of the most beautiful spots on the planet. For a few precious days, I relish in seeing snow-capped peaks, horses grazing on endless meadows and azure skies punctuated by billowing clouds. I choose vacations in natural settings because I know my *neshama* needs wilderness moments to thrive. I schedule "food for the soul" retreats like I would anything else in my calendar. I don't have "time" for these excursions, but I'm confident these trips are why God gave me the gift of time in the first place.

One great way to prioritize life goals is to make an account of which needs are most perishable. Ski while there's snow, hit the beach when it's hot. Can't afford a vacation? Don't miss the opportunity to nourish your soul—go camping or take a day trip. Have a favorite suit or dress hanging in the closet? Wear it, even if it's only around the house. Don't save that expensive bottle of wine—it just turns to vinegar. I, the master of delayed gratification, grant permission to live it up. Have a l'chaim, slip on that outfit, crank up the stereo and dance around the house!

Ephemeral item number one: our children will not be excited to hang out with us forever. Cherish them now! We never regret the quality time we spend with them. I feel blessed I was able to get my kids on the road quarterly. My annual work trips became family vacations during the weeks of Passover, High Holidays, summer and winter breaks. I also took them on solo trips even if it meant they had to miss a few days of school. The additional expense might have sabotaged my profits but I go proudly into empty-nest mode knowing I seized every opportunity to spoil my *mishpacha*.

One guy I was shmoozing with on the way to *shul* was venting regarding his lack of sleep, thanks to his multiple children age five and under. He told me he saw no light at the end of the tunnel; he'd be suffering for the next eighteen years. I gave him the advice I wish someone had given me: we think parenting young children will last forever. It only seems that way! They lose interest in us well before they leave for college. At best, we have their rapt attention until fourteen or fifteen. Another friend, an attorney, had been entirely self-sacrificing to the firm where he was head counsel. He had grandiose schemes regarding how to use the decade of vacation time he had accumulated. Eventually. Then the tides of fortune turned and the firm declared bankruptcy. All that time—gone—when he could have relaxed and enchanted his family. Ouch!

Another *b'chira*-streamlining tool, morbid as it may seem, is to retain a daily awareness of one's mortality. When saying *Modeh Ani* (the first prayer said upon waking), be aware that <u>today</u> God has returned your soul. There will be a day when God doesn't. We have a commandment to visit the sick so we remain other-focused rather than me-centered, and also to stimulate gratitude for our own vitality. We don't avoid end-of-life matters, but instead attend funerals and *shiva minyanim* (post funeral prayer gatherings) to comfort the bereaved and appreciate the value of our own lives.

Rabbi Aryeh Kaplan offers an unconventional description of hell in his book, "If You Were God." According to our sages, we are constantly measured on how we maximize our potential. We are not judged against our peers. Instead, at the end of one hundred and twenty years (the ideal human life span based on that of Moshe Rabbeinu, Moses our teacher), we are faced with the discrepancy between our potential and actual selves. The degree of difference between them is a source of tremendous humiliation, the "fires of hell." Were we the best that we could be? By nailing our free will decisions, we have a better chance of finishing the game in alignment with our greatest potential. According to author Leo Buscaglia, "What you are is God's gift to you, what you do with yourself is your gift to God."

Becoming aware of the power of free will forces one to contemplate, *whose life is this anyway?* When we confront mortality and place every activity on the "choose life/death" continuum, we are more likely to take ownership of our choices. Our forefather Avraham was commanded, *"Lech L'cha*—go for <u>yourself</u> to a land that I will show you."* During my first yeshiva experience I was forced to confront the big questions: *Am I Jewish for my parents? For my ancestors? For my teachers? For me? What theological baggage am I carrying? How did society, my upbringing, synagogue and community shape me? Is my career path just a rut in which I'm stuck? Why am I running from making a commitment to Judaism? What do I need to accomplish before I leave the world?* These questions may not have been answered during my first months in yeshiva, but that period engendered a life of introspection, encouraging me to continuously assess my goals. I strive to remind myself that each day is a new day, a fresh creation. I am not a prisoner of my past decisions. I have free choice. My time is my own, my life is mine to live. Cue Bon Jovi: "It's my life, it's now or never, I ain't gonna live forever…"

A famous chapter of the Torah describes the saga of Bilaam (*Bamidbar*/Numbers 22), the non-Jewish prophet who was driven to destroy the Jewish people. Maybe take a moment to read it now. Our sages tell us Bilaam was an extraordinarily gifted figure who chose the dark side. He tried to use his powerful *b'chira* to outsmart his Creator in order to make a few bucks cursing the Jews. Bad idea. Within these passages, God teaches crucial lessons regarding the use of free will for "choose life" moments and methods to avoid Bilaam's pitfalls.

1. Bilaam was a prophet for profit. Even though he was an enlightened leader, he was beguiled by greed. Something about dollar signs makes us do dumb things. For example: *I know God is watching me, but there is no way I'm going to declare all that cash on my taxes.* Or, *I'll just work like an animal and ignore my family to build up a nest egg.* How about: *Bruno Mars won't notice I ripped his new album from YouTube.* Yeah, I know. We all do it. King Balak knew the Jews were marching to the Promised Land and taking no prisoners. He contracted Bilaam to curse his enemy and Bilaam was so excited to make some dough that he awoke early to personally saddle his own donkey. Even the donkey could see the folly of Bilaam's ways. God miraculously "opened" the animal's mouth so she could castigate her owner. We all have a personal "talking donkey." As mentioned before, that's our *yetzer hatov*, our conscience. Listen to it!

2. Misdirected sexual energies are another stumbling block. The *Midrash* teaches us that Bilaam "lived" with his donkey. He was driven by his passions regardless of consequences. At the end of the saga, he couldn't curse the Jews but he sure could tempt us with seductive Moabite women. How many of our sports, music and political heroes get tripped up by their passions? How easy is it for us to commit career suicide or end our marriages by exchanging tawdry banter with an old flame on Facebook or in text messages? How many of us have sacrificed a lifetime of good decisions to a golden calf at the height of our personal triumph?

3. God let Bilaam go on his Jew-cursing mission even though it was a ridiculous idea. Be careful what you ask for! God will allow you to take any road you choose—choice is real! Have the humility to start personal prayers with *yehi ratzon* (if it is your will). Ask, "if it is your will, God, then _____ is what I want."

4. Bilaam lived to the extreme. He crushed boundaries. All or nothing. As I mentioned in the holiness chapter, Rambam urges us to walk the *shvil hazahav*, the golden path of life. Not the high road or low road. Our enduring quest as Jews is to bring balance to the world and banish fanaticism. Bilaam's

parting words in the Torah are featured in the daily "*Ma Tovu*" prayer of our siddur, in which he salutes the inherent modesty of the Children of Israel. As he looked down from above, he noticed the multitudes had positioned their tents facing away from one another. We were cohabitating in those tents, but doing so in an appropriate, private manner. The Jewish way to celebrate the gift of free will is not to gorge on food, sex, money and power, but instead, to express ourselves prudently and respectfully.

Four invaluable life lessons. That's a lot to learn from a talking donkey. We have an all-knowing Creator Who gives us the freedom to make choices. We can listen to the lure of the crafty evil inclination or allow our pure soul to guide us on a path of integrity and balance. We can be driven to distraction by our technological tools or empowered by them. We can succumb to temptation or use those same vices to reward our "choose life" triumphs. The "dark side" exists only to sweeten the thrill of successful free will choices. Let us recall the downfall of Bilaam and learn from his mistakes. Ask yourself, *what would Bilaam do?* Then do the opposite.

THE FOUR QUESTIONS

1. What are your primary "choose life" and "choose death" moments?

2. How do you balance goals and deadlines with healthy "taking a break" opportunities?

3. What is keeping you from maximizing b'chira in your life?

4. How can you channel your yetzer harah? How can you strengthen your yetzer hatov?

Middot:
The Measure of
a Mensch

♫ I ALWAYS COME AROUND ♫

joyjud.com/m/aca

I could be lonely for the rest of my life
If you really meant the words you said to me
I wish that I could read your mind
I'd never let you hold inside
All the tears you never cry
All the closets that you're stuffing full of
secrets

There are things that I'll never understand
about your love
Certain things were meant to be a mystery
So when the bottom's fallin' out
And my spirit hits the ground
I remember those words you said:
"I always come around"

The Jewish Nation has contributed profoundly to the sciences, politics and arts, but perhaps our most crucial gift is disseminating methods of building character. Judaism is the original self-help seminar. We've been offering personal growth secrets long before Andrew Carnegie, EST and Tony Robbins. One of my studio clients, Rabbi David Geffen, is producing the musical soundtrack for his UK-based educational program, Loving Classroom. Rabbi Geffen realized that Judaism's teachings regarding improving character traits and interpersonal relationships must be shared with the world. He helps public school teachers recognize the importance of refining students' character traits as a prerequisite to improving scholastic performance. By adopting the program, client schools have documented marked results in the reduction of bullying, cliques and vandalism. The eight core lessons discuss the basic *middot* (character traits) of respect, compassion, listening, kindness, gratitude, love, care and friendship. When students endeavor to reach mastery in these areas, the result is a "loving classroom" and as they graduate, a loving world.

Middot comes from the word "measure." We are measured by our *middot*. Alternatively, each of our character traits must be "measured" or balanced, within limits. For example, if we are too charitable, we may neglect our own needs. If we are too compassionate in justice, murderers may go free. If we are too strict with children, we stifle their natural curiosity. Any given *middah* isn't good or bad until it gets extreme. When we notice one side getting off kilter, we have to emphasize the other side of the continuum to restore equilibrium. Piece of cake, right? Actually, Rabbi Yisrael Salanter (1810-1883), the founder of the *Mussar* Movement (concerned with enhancing moral and ethical conduct), states that repairing one bad trait is harder than learning the entire Talmud—but that shouldn't stop us from trying— our Joy of Judaism is at stake! Rambam maintains that imbalanced character traits create a veil blocking holiness in our lives. Achieving holiness is our foundational mission statement and our channel to true joy. Yes, we have a lot of work to do.

According to Rashi, the Torah should have begun with the first laws given to the Jews in the book of Exodus, at the cusp of our liberation from Egypt. So then why does God include the adventures of the *avot* and *imahot* (patriarchs and matriarchs) in Genesis? Rashi's response: so that we can learn about their *middot*. Learning how to be a *mensch* comes <u>before</u> appreciating our liberation from Egypt and the gift of the Torah. The Talmud echoes this priority, stating "*derech eretz kadma Torah*" (common decency comes before Torah wisdom). Our brilliant laws are irrelevant if they don't result in creating a just, compassionate society. The Vilna Gaon (Rabbi Eliyahu ben Shlomo Zalman, 1720-1797) states: the purpose of our lives is to break bad traits and inculcate good ones. This is the field we work "by the sweat of our brow" (*B'reishit* 3:17-19). Judaism rejects "I am who I am" thinking. All of us are works in progress. We are born narcissistic and egocentric and must evolve into altruistic behavior as we age. Perfecting *middot* is another way of saying growing up.

Examples of character development in *B'reishit* are plentiful. Avraham becomes an icon of kindness and radical hospitality, coming closer to the One True God by emulating Godly acts. His servant, Eliezer, when searching for a potential mate for Yitzchak, constructs a complicated scenario to ascertain which prospective girl will be the one. The test consists of finding someone who will not only show kindness to him, but also to his animals. Rivkah passes the test in spades and her superlative *middot* make her a perfect candidate to fill Sarah's shoes. The legacy of greatness is set in stone with the addition of matriarchs Rachel and Leah, whose generosity and compassion inspire all who follow. As each subsequent generation in the Torah is challenged with the mantle of leadership, the quality of *middot* determines who carries the torch.

Anyone studying Torah sees repeating patterns from one generation to the next. Our sages teach the principle, "*Ma'asei avot, siman l'banim*," what happens to the forefathers is a sign to the children. Often the same circumstances that tested our parents are visited upon us. Another way to understand this precept is to appreciate that the actions of the *avot* and *imahot* are a sign of what we are <u>able</u> to do. We have inherited the genetic predisposition to accomplish the same remarkable level of excellence. The Jewish term for such an individual is a *mensch*. In his ninetieth birthday speech, my Uncle Herb Glaser, a big *mensch*, mentioned the following qualifications for the "Glaser Mensch-o-meter" test: kindness to all, no bragging, integrity, helping those less fortunate, good citizenship, always learning and the willingness to pass good *middot* down to the next generation. It's an honor to be part of such a *menschy* family.

Ask any *shadchan* (matchmaker) to list the three most important characteristics of a potential spouse, and the answer will be *middot, middot, middot* (OK, maybe it's *middot, middot*, net worth). In our community, the first question asked by parents regarding a child's choice of friends is, "How are his/her *middot*?" Ultimate *nachas* (Jewish pride) results from hearing one's offspring instigated an act of compassion. With our own children, Shira and I have marveled at these special accomplishments. Max, our very social eldest child, had large groups of friends "kicking back" at our home every Shabbat afternoon. We were happy the gang chose to chill under our roof, but that was because Max was so careful to monitor their activities. They never damaged the house, raided the refrigerator or disturbed my beloved Shabbas nap. Jesse was fiercely loyal to his friends and had no patience for the antics of class bullies. When he saw someone getting picked on, he would rally for the victim at the expense of his own health and popularity. Sarah noticed that when birthdays were announced in the morning *davening*, some girls got enthusiastic cheers and gifts and others were barely applauded. She took it upon herself to bake gourmet cupcakes for EVERY member of the class so no one would feel left out. Yes, we were thrilled to hear our kids were on the dean's list. But it's these *middot* victories that are carved in our consciousness and earned our greatest praise.

Our children's day school curricula promoted proper *middot* not only for interpersonal harmony. Our sages teach that God operates *middah k'neged middah*, measure for measure, or trait for trait. God deals with us in the precise manner that we deal with others. When we are compassionate, we are rewarded with compassion. When we are judgmental of others, strict judgment results. So, too, with cruelty, impatience, aggression and bitterness. Our sages urge, *"Dan l'chaf s'chut"* (judge to the side of merit). Go easy on friends and family! Some call this universal law of "what goes around comes around" karma. As Jews, we call it God's love.

The importance of nurturing good *middot* is a primary reason to moderate the intrusion of popular culture in our lives. The media thrives on sensationalism, gossip, violence, criticism and extremism. It's a business thing—producers need eyeballs glued to the screen, the more controversial, the merrier. Currently, Big Data (Amazon, Netflix, Google, etc.) has made us the product. We think we're the ones doing the consuming, but they are consuming us—and selling details of our every move to the highest bidder. The industry thrives when we gaze and glaze. Judaism wants us checked in, not checked out! Torah frees us from The Matrix. One may choose to stay current on the latest movies, TV shows and songs. But ideally, for every input glorifying negative *middot*, we need one emphasizing positive *middot*. Hence, the existence of the *mussar vaad*.

A *mussar vaad* is a group meeting or class systematically analyzing and applying specific character traits. Some spend a few weeks on a given *middah*, some over a year. Many *vaadim* are "locked in," meaning, once the group is established it cannot be joined by others, thereby allowing the unit to bond without outside distraction. Usually, men and women have separate groups, allowing for the unique needs of each gender to be addressed. Text study is selected to reinforce the importance and application of the specific *middah* and the passages are exhaustively reviewed to inculcate the message. The goal is to settle for nothing less than heroic character, to emulate the patriarchs and matriarchs in the quest for ultimate human nobility.

I have watched my friends in *mussar vaadim* reach great heights in their personal growth. For those of us who cannot fulfill New Year's Resolutions and are frustrated with the "same old, same old" each Rosh Hashana, perhaps joining a *mussar vaad* is worth investigating. If one doesn't have time to dedicate to a *vaad*, what's the next best option? Work independently on one *middah* at a time. The best way to figure out where to start is to contemplate which *middah* is the hardest to keep in balance. That's your soul *tikkun* (healing). Once you deduce whether it's impatience, laziness, selfishness, callousness or anger, learn to focus on the appropriate counterpart, for example, patience, industry, generosity, compassion or composure. The next step is appreciating we can and must control our responses. The repetitious exhibition of negative traits is destructive to all in our midst and invites hardship and misery. Pay attention to *middah k'neged middah* cycles. These patterns are a wake up call. If unchecked, poor *middot* can destroy everything of value. Improving *middot* saves lives.

As a personal example, I used to be baited into arguments and would lose my temper, saying things I regretted. I hated feeling out of control and I knew this had to change. So, when saying *Modeh Ani* each morning, I contemplated how joy, patience, selflessness and compassion would fill my day. I trained myself to do the diametric opposite of getting irate: I would go into serenity mode when getting sucked into an argument. Rather than retorting with a snappy comeback, I would offer the gift of silence, removing myself from the altercation and waiting for my blood to stop boiling. Like a benevolent king, I would only respond when I cooled down and regained my composure. And often, my response would be in the form of an email so that I could write and live with it overnight, to be sure I carefully chose my words. Rather than a reaction, I took positive action. When only one party is getting angry, it makes for a much shorter argument.

Here are some further techniques for transformation: keep written track on a calendar of the times you blow it, when you are humiliated or disappointed with yourself. Then you will have a running list where you need to focus and you can visualize the patterns of your emotional output. Rabbi Zelig Pliskin recommends "reframing." Imagine someone you respect entering your room. Certainly, you would not act rashly in their presence. If you are prone to lose your temper when you are hungry, eat an apple or granola bar before you get home and face the family. If you cuss out everyone on the highway, it works wonders to leave an extra fifteen minutes for the trip. Always have your favorite music available to soothe you in a traffic jam. If you struggle with miserliness, make sure to leave the house with twenty dollars in singles in your pocket for the sole purpose of sharing. Force yourself to overtip, sponsor a Kickstarter campaign and put an extra ten bucks in the pot when splitting a check.

This may come as a surprise, but we are on a multiple lifetime odyssey of *tikkun middot* (character healing). Yes, Jews believe in reincarnation. Our healthy *middot* were already fixed in past *gilgulim* (lifetimes). Those challenging us now are the ones on which we have to concentrate. Start today—this is our life's work! As I've heard my friend David Sacks say, "Are we living life or is life living us?" Let's get the most out of this lifetime. Imagine how empowered and exalted we could feel mastering weak links in our personalities. Think of the inestimable gift we can bestow on those in our sphere of influence. We are not helpless. We are not robots. We can grow. We can transform our behavior. Perhaps the most important technique is earnest prayer. We must ask for God's help in the task since, as Rabbi Leib Kelemen, Director of the International Organization of Mussar Vaadim suggests, it's impossible to change without a miracle taking place. When we have a sustained *middah* victory, it propels us into a realm of heroism where anything is possible.

Can't decide where to begin your *tikkun middot?* There are multiple *middot* lists available. Perhaps the most famous is the "Forty-Eight Ways to Wisdom" enumerated in *Pirkei Avot* (Ethics of the Fathers 6:5). This is the fount from which Rabbi Noah Weinberg drew so much inspiration. The ethical program influencing Founding Father Benjamin Franklin is Rabbi Mendel of Satanov's Cheshbon Hanefesh (moral accounting). Incorporating these lists in our efforts is praiseworthy, but as mentioned earlier, our main task is in mastering those areas posing the most formidable challenges.

One of my brother Yom Tov's crowning achievements is creating "The Possible You" seminar. He has trained me to lead it and I have personally witnessed the efficacy of this five-day intensive program with many of the thousands of students who have invested the time to reclaim personal greatness. I'm honored Yom Tov chose to incorporate many of my songs in the curriculum. One of the critical steps in the seminar is acknowledging positive *middot* we have learned to emphasize habitually, simply to survive childhood. We may have become overly generous because we felt deprived of attention as kids. Now, without realizing it, we are on a constant quest to be loved. We may be the brave, overachieving warrior-type because we felt scared or helpless in grade school. The detailed work of this seminar involves exposing the origin of these behaviors, shedding light on these *middot* we have learned to emphasize. Once we understand why we do what we do, we can then continue to excel in that area with "license" to do so. We are not following an intangible, automatic life script, but, instead, functioning with full awareness. We cater to our strengths with deliberation, not as insecure children but as noble adults.

Tikkun Hamiddot is hard work. Yet, it is the very task we were placed on this planet to accomplish. We all want to be experts at life. No expert gets credentials overnight. We sweat out four years in college to gain cognitive intelligence. We study Torah and engage with family and community to become emotionally intelligent. Judaism offers profound techniques to realize our goals of self-control and personal power. We just have to make the effort. Hillel the Sage asserts that the primary mitzvah of the Torah is "Love your neighbor as yourself." One way to understand this precept is that love of self is the prerequisite to loving others. When we master our shortcomings, we gain self-respect. When we gain self-respect, we are more likely to gain the respect of others. We become less self-absorbed and are able to truly radiate love.

Rabbi Yisrael Salanter said, "I wanted to change the world but it was too hard, so I tried to change my city. I couldn't do that so I tried to change my family. I finally realized I could only change myself." Michael Jackson sang a similar refrain for our generation: "I'm starting with the man in the mirror, I'm asking him to change his ways. No message could have been any clearer: if you want to make the world a better place, take a look at yourself and then make a change."

THE FOUR QUESTIONS

1. What are three middot in which you excel?

2. What are three middot needing balance in your life?

3. How are your shortcomings affecting others in sphere of influence?

4. What techniques can you use to remain in a place of peace and balance?

Halacha • Tehillim • Shabbat • Community • Torah • Prophets • Nigun • Pesach • Teshuva • Weddi
uality • Holiness • Emunah • Diaspora • Brit Milah • Simcha • Halacha • Brachon • Holidays
vah • Tefila • Israel • Mitzvah • Prayer • Moshiach • Tehillim • Shabbat • Community • Torah • Prop
ligun • Pesach • Teshuva • Weddings • Spirituality • Holiness • Emunah • Diaspora • Bri
ilah • Halacha • Brachon • Holidays • Bar Mitzvah • Tefila • Israel • Mitzvah • Prayer • Moshi
ehillim • Shabbat • Community • Torah • Prophets • Nigun • Pesach • Teshuva • Weddings • Spir
uality • Holiness • Emunah • Diaspora • Brit Milah • Simcha • Halacha • Brachon • Holid

Halacha:
The Chok's on You!

♫ V'HA'ER EYNEYNU ♫

joyjud.com/m/ven

Enlighten our eyes to Torah
Never to be apart
Bind us to Your commandments
To fulfill them with all our heart

Make us worthy of so great a gift
Give us a place to stand without shame
Help us try to unify
Our passions to love and fear Your Name
V'ha'er eyneynu b'toratecha...

Joanne Atkinson was everything a young student could want in a piano teacher. She was humble, upbeat and encouraging. Never harsh, never demanding. If she gave me a piece that didn't resonate with me or was too intricate, she allowed me to move on, no problem. She also instituted a separate music theory class for her advanced students, enlightening us with such concepts as harmony, counterpoint and transcription. I loved her style and felt nurtured and respected.

Then my Bar Mitzvah tutor, Aryell Cohen, offered his perspective on my musical education. He told my mom, "Sammy has something special and needs a REAL teacher." My five-year love affair with Joanne ceased and I now faced the tyranny of Aryell's German instructor. She-who-must-not-be-named was a stern, elderly woman living in the Hollywood Hills with a pair of Dobermans and Bosendorfers. If I didn't perfect my repertoire or flubbed my dexterity exercises, she chastised me. She never hesitated to remind that I wouldn't "make it" as a pianist. Her creaky turn-of-the-century home felt eerily haunted and reeked of the food she cooked for her pampered pets. I had to wash my hands before stroking her beloved 88s and God forbid I ever touch my shoes and then her keyboard. She even denied my mother entry, making her sit in our family station wagon, shivering in the dark as she waited for me to finish each lesson. Talk about dedication—thanks, Mom!

In spite of the horrors of this caustic spinster, I learned to take my art more seriously. I still use the practice techniques she taught me. Although it was shocking not to be coddled, thanks to her unremitting tutelage, I tackled pieces I would not have entertained had I remained with the effervescent Mrs. Atkinson. After a year of this torture, I rebelled. As a man (of 13!), I told my parents I was quitting piano and taking up guitar. Of course, I still used the piano for songwriting. It wasn't long before I found great piano teachers in David Kaminer, who taught me how to rock like Jerry Lee Lewis, and Dick Fister, who enlightened me on the finer points of jazz. While it was liberating to learn to jam and improvise, I never worked on my craft with the same degree of discipline as my year with the tyrant.

In hindsight, I realize my cantankerous teacher gave me the gift of learning how to harness my creative energy. My innate ability was meaningless without imposed structure. This revelation helped me understand the value of the "harness" that Jews have used to thrive through the millennia. The *Sh'ma* emphasizes the importance of taking on *Ol Malchut Shamayim* (the Yoke of Heaven.) This yoke is commonly referred to as *halacha* (Jewish law, literally, the path one walks). The multitude of constraints on our freedom actually serve to give us direction and purpose, to coordinate our human efforts toward *Tikkun Olam*.

Wearing the "Yoke of Heaven" sounds like a burden no one would want. Why would anyone want to wear a yoke? Especially this beach loving, quasi-hippie California kid. Save that stuff for religious fanatics or masochists! But a yoke allows oxen to plow and bring *shefa* into the world. These rules and regulations give us freedom, true success, a wellspring of joy. Rules are tools. Mastering *halacha* might seem like a dry, empty endeavor, but incorporating it into one's life transforms mundane acts like getting dressed, eating and interacting with others into profound portraits of spiritual significance. Our sages teach that our relationship with God is predicated not on what we want from God but, instead, what God wants from us. Therefore, to advance to Judaism 202, we must ascertain God's demands by exploring the basic structure of Jewish law.

The Written and Oral Law

We begin with a primary distinction, the Written and the Oral Law. The Torah *Shebichtav* (Written Law) is based on the legal sections of the *Chumash* (Five Books of Moses) while the Torah *Sheba'al Peh* (Oral Law) is based on the teaching of Moses and subsequent commentators. Although there is disagreement on the exact numbering, our sages agree that there are 613 official mitzvot in the written text. These are divided into 248 positive (Thou Shalt) and 365 negative (Thou Shalt Not) commandments. The "Oral Torah" elaborates on how we do these 613. Clearly there is more to the divinely inspired script than one can find in print; several passages of the Torah indicate that Moses perceived celestial diagrams and was not just taking dictation. Around the year 217 CE (Common Era, a more ecumenical way to denote the period AD) Rabbi Yehudah Hanassi committed this orally transmitted tradition to writing in order to preserve it for posterity. His masterpiece is a terse six-book set called the *Mishnah*. Over the next 400 years, the commentaries on the *Mishnah* were compiled in the expansive sixty-three-volume *Gemara*. Together the *Mishnah* and *Gemara* form the Talmud. Got it?

As an example, let's assume that you need to know the rules to build a *sukkah*. The Written Law succinctly states that all citizens of Israel must dwell in booths for seven days. That's all the detail we get. Thankfully, the Oral Law elucidates exactly what the parameters of such a booth should look like, who is obligated, what to do if it rains, what activities comprise "dwelling" in the *sukkah*, etc. Yes, every last detail has been covered! Our sages maintain that both Written and Oral Law are binding, and that the inspiration for all the legalese as espoused by the commentators stems from the original revelation at Mt. Sinai.

Next we have a further distinction in our legal code: these biblical written laws and their interpretations are called *D'oraita*, and laws introduced by the sages are called rabbinic or *D'rabbanan*. Examples of rabbinic laws are the mitzvot to light Shabbat candles and to celebrate Purim. These are not part of the original 613 mitzvot but we refer to them as mitzvot nonetheless. Just like the logo on the side of L.A. police cruisers states, "To protect and serve," our concerned rabbis instituted multifarious *gezerot* (fences) to keep us from trampling on the *D'oraita* commandments. They also established *takanot* (decrees) for the public welfare. Even though we may feel that we already have plenty, these "extra" laws are for our own good. Furthermore, each community has *minhagim* (customs) that can acquire the force of law when the majority adopts them. Wearing a *kippah* is one of these *minhagim*.

These days, without a Temple and sacrifices, there are only 369 of the original 613 mitzvot available to us. Of these, some only apply to men, some to women, some to firstborns, some to *kohanim* (priests). Not to worry: the rabbis have given us plenty more *takanot* to keep us busy!

The Three Categories of Mitzvot

Within the Written Law there are three categories of mitzvot. The first is *mishpatim*, from the word *mishpat* (judgment). These are the rational laws, the social ordinances any functioning society might require. Just remember *mishpatim* are the laws that you could figure out using your own "judgment." Do not murder or steal are two of the *mishpatim*, for example. The next category is called *chukim* (*chok* in singular). A *chok* is a superrational law, one that cannot be understood using human reason.

Observing *chukim* is an act of love, a trusting surrender to a Creator Who has the ultimate perspective, Who gave these laws for reasons we may never grasp. In spite of the fact that we don't understand them, we observe *chukim* because we trust the Lawgiver. This is the secret of the powerful formula, "*Na'aseh v'nishmah*" ("We will do and then we will understand") uttered collectively by the Jewish People at Sinai (*Shmot*/Exodus 24:7). We recognized that performing only the mitzvot we understood would undermine the relationship, signifying a lack of *emunah* by second guessing God's ability to nurture us. Scrupulous performance of *chukim* is the spiritual equivalent of PAC-MAN munching those yellow dots: they are holy *emunah* pellets rendering one invincible! When focused on the details of observing *chukim*, a subliminal transformation takes place: our concern with seemingly trivial laws makes us more likely to be reliable with the common sense regulations and the law of the land. We are anchored, attached to something bigger, trustworthy and directed.

The laws of *kashrut* are some of the best examples of *chukim*. Yes, we can analyze why certain foods are off limits, but we are left with a best guess and will never truly know. I'm sorry to be the bearer of bad news—even though USDA-certified ham will not give us trichinosis at this juncture of history, it is still *verboten*! Assuming that we know better than the Master of the Universe is naïve and even foolhardy.

A short story: once, an intimidating 6'6 cowboy was following me through the shadowy streets of downtown Nashville. I sensed his presence and took a few turns to lose him…but he persisted. When I ducked into a gift shop, he followed. I spun around and asked, "May I help you?" "Yes," he quietly replied. "I see that you are a Jewish man. There's something I must tell you…I don't eat pork." He waited for my response. Puzzled, I said, "Well, you're not Jewish, right? So you can eat pork!" "NO," he replied, "I read the Bible and I know it's not OK." I thanked him for his admission, glad he wasn't interested in my wallet. If this Bible Belt Christian gets it, hopefully the Jewish People will too.

Finally, there is a category called *eidot*, or mitzvot that are testimonial in nature, declaring God's guidance of history, reminding us of our mission in life. These are the laws like the observance of Shabbat and our major holidays, wrapping *tefillin* and affixing a *mezuzah*. *Eidot* comes from the word *eid*, or witness. As we will learn in subsequent chapters, serving as witnesses to God's eternal Presence is at the top of our Jewish job detail.

The minutia of performing *mishpatim*, *chukim* and *eidot* are bandied about in animated conversations recorded in the Talmud, the intimidating Aramaic text requiring seven and a half years to complete by reading both sides of one oversized page per day. Thankfully we have a number of compilations that summarize the *tachlis* (bottom line) of Jewish law so that we don't have to spend a decade looking up the proper blessing for a banana.

The Shulchan Aruch

The primary *halachic* text with universal hegemony is the *Shulchan Aruch* (Set Table), compiled in 1555 by Talmudic genius Yosef Caro while he lived in the holy city of Tsfat in northern Israel. Caro had the misfortune of being born in Toledo, Spain in 1488; he and his family were victims of the infamous expulsion of 1492. They immigrated to Portugal only to be sent packing in the Portuguese expulsion of 1497. Like Maimonides, he had to study and teach while on the run. Remarkably, his exposition of Jewish law still stands to this day; there is scarcely a home without a copy of the *Kitzur Shulchan Aruch*, an abridged version of his code. Ashkenazim get their specific angle on observance through the Chofetz Chaim's (Rabbi Yisrael Meir Kagan, 1839-1933) *Mishnah B'rura* (The Clarified Teaching), a text that I have taken great joy in studying over the years. Sephardim get their unique insights from kabbalist Rabbi Yosef Hayim's (1832-1909) masterpiece, *Ben Ish Chai* (The Son of the Living Man). Both of these *seforim* (holy books) appeared in the 1800s and remain the trusted references in the Jewish world.

With the advent of the Internet and quality English books like Artscroll's new *Kitzur Shulchan Aruch* (which includes the commentary of the *Mishnah B'rura*), it's tempting to avoid bothering one's rabbi with a *shyla* (question). Just know that most rabbis enjoy this dialogue with their congregants and typically agree that it's the questions they <u>don't</u> get that bother them the most. Ideally, your rabbi knows you well and can advise you based on your unique circumstances and idiosyncrasies. Jewish law is not monolithic. It is highly flexible and your skilled rabbi will know just what you are ready for…or not. Furthermore, there is far greater leniency in the enforcement of *D'rabbanan* as opposed to *D'oraita*. Any time I ask my *rav* a *shyla,* I see him pause to reflect on the origin of the commandment and commentaries and guide me accordingly. The interpretation of *halacha* is also geographically dependent. A case in point: when my younger brother Aharon moved from our community to the other side of town (the Hancock Park area), he was told to find another *posek* (a rabbi who specializes in *halachic* issues) in his new domain. Indeed, every locale has its own nuanced framework that only a qualified local rabbi can know. The Torah empowers our rabbis to serve not only as arbiters in legal disputes but also originators of the standards within their fiefdom. After all, the aforementioned verse from *D'varim*, "It's not in heaven..." indicates God entrusts the interpretation of divine will to the sages.

Pirkei Avot opens with a description of the exacting chain of transmission of Torah law from Sinai to the present day. We can trust this immense quantity of Jewish "how-tos" is not the invention of some crafty revisionist rabbis along the way. Illustrating the veracity of our canon is beyond the scope of this text but the information is readily available. While it may appear the Talmud is rife with disagreements, it is important to note the rabbis of the Talmud agree on nearly all the major precepts handed down in that chain of transmission. They are simply arguing the finer points, the seemingly insignificant "hairsplitting" details shedding light on the ultimate truth of any given matter. God refers to us as "stiff-necked." We get especially stubborn in our search for truth and we do not budge from our time-tested beliefs. I believe this is the reason why we have over fifty synagogues within a one-mile radius of our home in Pico-Robertson. It's not that we don't get along, but rather, each subset of our multinational nation has an abiding love for specific *minhagim* and whenever possible, prefers not to compromise.

Observing Jewish law offers access to the highest realms of spirituality. Far beyond personal benefit, our devotion to understanding and carrying out of God's truth affects reality in ways we cannot fathom. Just like a smile is contagious, so, too, there is a celestial ripple effect from each mitzvah contemplated and performed.

A caveat: it's important not to confuse *halacha* with God. We worship God, not *halacha!* I like to think of Jewish law as a window through which we can see the grandeur of Creation. Some of my peers are so obsessed with the minutia of the dos and don'ts that they can't see the forest for the trees. The goal is to appreciate the view, not the pane of glass in the window.

In the end, all laws are mysterious *chukim*. We will never understand the inner workings of God's great plans for humanity. *Halacha* seems daunting, but only when studied from a distance. Put that analytical, college-trained logic aside for a while and try on a *chok* for size. Go ahead and do the research...but you will never fully understand the reason for any given mitzvah. You may feel foolish or worry that you are entertaining antiquated superstitions. But then something clicks inside and you feel a sense of connection with your heritage. Then you try another mitzvah and that leads to another. Soon you are using your power of choice to choose God. You are experiencing a fundamental, inexplicable sense of joy. Now you realize you want to soak up every mitzvah opportunity and you have a lot to learn. At last, the *chok's* on you!

We only have so much time allotted in our mortal days to do mitzvot. A euphemism for someone who has died is *niftar*, literally meaning "relieved from duty," one no longer obligated in commandments. This teaches that we have to maximize mitzvah opportunities in this lifetime. My friend David Sacks compares this to the TV game show "Supermarket Sweep." Within a short period, contestants scramble to fill the shopping cart with as much high-ticket merchandise as possible. Most go straight for the caviar, Patron and champagne. Why waste time deliberating which flavor of Snapple to grab? Go for the good stuff! Fill the cart with the best bang for the buck in this life and next! Mitzvot are our eternity—the only currency transcending lifetimes.

By studying the "owner's manual," we become acquainted with the Creator and our ideal path. When we align our will with God's will, we are "dreaming God's dreams." Yes, there are eternal rewards for each mitzvah we perform. But there is also profound payoff in the here and now: living with deep meaning, optimal relationships with all those we encounter, emotional and physical well-being and most importantly, a sweet song of joy and holiness accompanying our daily dance with the Almighty.

Early in my life I learned that true art requires the imposition of order upon chaos, transforming a palette of oil paints or a collection of random notes into a masterpiece. All of us can develop the expertise to master the instrument of our soul, playing our unique role with diligence and passion, capably contributing to the sublime symphony of creation.

THE FOUR QUESTIONS

1. When, in your life, do you find that you most benefit from structure and boundaries?

2. Can you think of a chok that you find meaningful? How does it enhance your love of God?

3. What is the next mitzvah that you would like to master?

4. How can you incorporate rabbinic wisdom in your life?

Eretz Yisrael: The Gift of the Promised Land

♫ IN ISRAEL ♫

joyjud.com/m/isl

Open my lips to sing Your praise	*Let me fall in love in Israel*
My heart to feel the joy	
Let me have the gift for which I'm yearning	*Wherever you go, I will go*
Another night in Israel	*Having to follow my heart*
	Riding the wings that will carry me home
Desert flowers blooming in the spring	*Wherever you live, I will live*
The grapes upon the vine	*If just to breathe in the air*
Let me walk the beaches in the moonlight	*You'll find me in Israel*

Any discussion of Judaism must mention Israel. Israel is part of an unbreakable, interdependent triad that includes God and Torah. All Jews are the Children of Israel. We are united as the offspring of Jacob/Israel, whose children formed the twelve tribes, the progenitors of our extended family. Furthermore, we are all connected with *Eretz Yisrael*, the geographic entity of the Land of Israel. This tiny country is not just another global travel destination for Jews; most feel a palpable sense of holiness and an awareness they are "home." As sophisticated sophomores, Judaism 202 requires that we explore the deeper aspects of the strip of earth we call The Promised Land. Grab your passport and let's go!

A Vision of Israel

I feel exuberance in every footstep as I walk Israel on my annual trips. I must suppress the drive to hug everyone I see, Arab and Jew alike. I am energized and focused. I have felt this on every trip starting with my Bar Mitzvah at the Western Wall. It's an indescribable feeling of oneness with People and place. It's not uncommon for seemingly casual trips to the Promised Land to result in radical spiritual transformation for unsuspecting Jewish tourists. This phenomenon is the source of the efficacy of programs like Birthright, Gap Year and Aish HaTorah. This is why folks like my younger brothers, Andy/Aharon, a busy real estate capitalist and Johnny/Yom Tov, a surfer dude just out of University of California, Santa Barbara, started learning in Jerusalem for the first time and were hooked for life.

That year, Yom Tov was planning a post-grad around-the-world surf safari. The itinerary sounded amazing, but I wanted him to have the same high-octane Israel experience that ignited my *neshama* when I was his age. I filled out a yeshiva scholarship form and wrote an essay portraying him as the greatest leader since Maimonides. He got chosen for the program and I promised to ship his surfboards to Southern Spain when he tired of the Promised Land. I never did send those boards. The weekend before he left, we bonded on a farewell trip pedaling around the rocky circumference of Catalina Island to raise funds for the American Lung Association. We set up our tents with hundreds of new friends in an enormous field and when the sun went down, initiated a jam session around some picnic tables. Well after dark, two lost-looking women approached—they had arrived on a later ship and couldn't find their tent mates in the pitch darkness. I didn't realize it, but a drunken guy in our group turned to one of them and said, "Hey baby, I don't remember seeing you on the boat...why don't you lose your fat friend and join us?" Needless to say, they condemned all assembled as inconsiderate inebriates and continued their search. Over the course of the three-day mountain bike ride, I kept noticing one of these young women and tried to make conversation. She rebuffed me each time and finally, on the last day of the ride, I cut in the lunch line behind her and awkwardly initiated small talk. That lady would become my wife.

Our conversation centered on favorite bands and Southern California musicians we both knew. We marveled that we had never met in spite of all these common connections. On the two-hour ship ride returning to L.A., I felt a subtle but fundamental shift in the light as we schmoozed on the top deck. The sunset's twenty-four-karat glow ignited Shira's eyes and I was convinced we were surrounded by some sort of supernatural brightness. Others gathered around and corroborated that something strange was happening. That night, her uber-spiritual roommate, Karen, dreamed of two brilliant orbs joining together. She believed these orbs represented the future union of Shira and this wacky Jewish musician she had just met.

A year later, I had the opportunity to spend a month in the Holy Land to study, perform, and most importantly, to verify Yom Tov wasn't brainwashed. He had been sending fire and brimstone missives that were making our parents nervous and they blamed me for his fundamentalist jag. Once again, upon arriving in this arid land ten thousand miles from my apartment, I felt a deep knowing I was home. I was recently engaged to Shira and used the opportunity to bone up on "*chassan* classes" (workshops with the *Rosh Yeshiva* for neophyte grooms). Thankfully, I found my brother in excellent shape, enthusiastic and quite resolved to pursue a path of holiness. He was anything but brainwashed. We spent many a night on the rooftop of his Old City dormitory discussing the meaning of life while watching otherworldly clouds streaming in perpetual motion over the Temple Mount.

Yom Tov was excited to introduce me to his peers and favorite rabbis. Among the personalities he wanted me to meet was a Chabad rabbi named Guru Gil. Yom Tov was hopeful that he might allow me to play the biblical instruments he had hand crafted. I found Gil (Rabbi Gutman Locks) at the *Kotel*, joyfully wrapping *tefillin* on any willing tourist. I told him of my musical predilection and he offered to serenade me on his handmade harps and lyres right after Shabbat. I wound up getting a concert and a vision I will never forget.

Gil acquired the guru moniker because he followed his spiritual muse to India where he acquired both enlightenment and a cadre of devoted acolytes. After coming to an intellectual and spiritual dead end with capitalism, Hinduism and Christianity, Gil was faced with his unexplored heritage while visiting the Holy Land. He discovered that countless hours of meditation didn't hold a candle to touching the hearts of his fellow Jews with acts of kindness. Eventually he became a giant in Torah.

That *Motza'ei* Shabbat (Saturday night) I found my way to Gil's Old City apartment and took a seat in his spacious living room with a few other guests. He served a booze-enhanced concoction, dimmed the lights and asked us to relax as we turned our chairs to face the Temple complex. As he prepared to pluck his ten-string harp designed to emulate that of King David, I felt serene and buzzed and ready for whatever insight the music might summon. He told us to direct our attention to the fount of holiness springing from the foundation stone of the Holy of Holies, the emanation from Zion as described by the prophet Isaiah (2:3), "*Ki miTziyon tetzei Torah.*"

At first, I focused on the simple pentatonic tuning of the finely crafted instrument. Soon, I was able to venture beyond the physics of note interactions and allow the sustaining strings to evoke a palette of iridescent grandeur. No, he didn't feed us hallucinogens! I envisioned a black and white tornado spinning up from a singular vortex, black fire on white fire, culminating in two heavenly orbs. These swirling orbs became fiery crimson and the deepest indigo and at one point, the two separate spheres combined in an explosion of incendiary, regal violet. I knew in my heart these colliding circumferences represented the imminent joining of the souls of my fiancé and me, just like Karen's dream a year before. I believed divine intention guided our consolidated mission. We would work together to direct the attention of *K'lal Yisrael*, the Jewish Nation, to this wellspring of spirituality originating in Jerusalem. It was clear to me that this glimpse of inner Israel, the spark of temporal, geographic Godliness, is accessible to all. Like an incandescent Tesla coil, it lies dormant until the circuit is completed when one's *neshama* touches down on Israel's sacred soil.

Holy Land History

Avraham's initial journey to the Promised Land starts with elements of surprise, challenge and mystery. The first commandment he receives is "*Lech L'cha...*" or "go for/to yourself to a land that I will show you." Within that initial call to action is the requirement of trust, coupled with a reassurance that all will go well. This simple lesson can inspire every Jewish journey—we go forth into the unknown with faith God is by our side. Furthermore, every journey we take is a revelation both of the external world and our own personal topography. *Lech L'cha* is paradox of opposites. This alliterative seesaw requires that Avraham go out (*lech*) while coming back to himself (*l'cha*). The Chidushei HaRim (Rabbi Yitzchak Meir Alter, 1799-1866) states that all Jews share Avraham's commandment: we thrive within this virtuous cycle of spreading our wings in the world, brimming with light, then retreating back to ourselves until our energy is restored.

As discussed in the Science of Struggle chapter, the land is only subdued through heroic effort. Soon after reaching the land, further tests challenge the first Jewish couple. Famine strikes, requiring that Avraham seek refuge in Egypt, Sarah is kidnapped and then Avraham is told that his progeny will serve as slaves in a strange land. Yitzchak, who is forbidden by God to leave Israel under any circumstances, must struggle with the locals at every turn. Avraham's grandson Yaakov acquires the name Israel at the breaking point of his wrestling match with an angel. Retaining the Land of Milk and Honey requires optimism, diligence and faith in the face of adversity. These are the crucial ingredients for any meaningful conquest. Our patriarchs and matriarchs ably transmitted the tenacity required for possession of this spiritual terrain.

The last verses of the Torah finish with a cliffhanger—the aquisition of Israel is still in question. Our redeemer Moshe dies on the border and the Israelites look to his successor Yehoshua (Joshua) to engage in the conquest of the Land. One must delve into the Torah's sequel, known as *Nevi'im*, or the prophetic writings, to get the full picture of our journey. From Yeshoshua's invasion (1272 BCE—Before the Common Era, a more ecumenical way to denote the period BC) until the Babylonian exile (422 BCE), Jewish history appears like a grand sine wave, with the apex of peace, faith and invincibility leading to a nadir of self indulgence, decadence and defeat and then back again. We possess the Land, but much like our turbulent wanderings in the desert, we go from dutiful service to complaints and dissension, repeatedly testing God's patience until destruction ensues. Our possession of this holy space is conditional. Each time around this hopefully finite cycle, the Children of Israel gain insight into what it might take to stay on top, but then sadly, the process begins yet again.

With the devastating invasion of the Romans and destruction of the Second Temple (63 BCE), it appears the jig is up. The Torah's prophecies of the Jew's utter despair, remaining few in number and serving a protracted sentence wandering the nations, is tragically fulfilled. It seems all is lost; our mission has failed and we are now orphans of history without a homeland or hope. However, we receive certain guarantees in this ultimate exile in which we are still entrenched. We are assured God will be with us, the Torah will always be accessible and at some distant time we will come home. The ember of hope remains alive as we leave our nest to spread our message to all the nations. Finally, after two thousand years of remarkable influence in every corner of the globe, we return to our homeland with great signs and wonders. History continues to unfold in the information age with Israel at the forefront of current events in each day's news broadcast. Unfortunately, world opinion of this remarkable, tiny country is not as upbeat as we may wish.

Israel Today

Even in the Diaspora, the daily life of the Observant Jew revolves around Israel. Every meal, every prayer service, we dwell on the Land. The quest of *aliyah* (emigration to Israel) is the persistent theme of each of our festive occasions. The Shabbat liturgy repeatedly mentions the importance of remembering our origin story, namely, the formation of our nation in Egypt and subsequent journey toward Israel. With all this textual emphasis on where we began, it begs the question, "Where are we going?" Israelis are striving for more than eating *shakshuka* or surviving yet another Arab attack. Why are we anchored to this resource-restricted real estate in the hostile Middle-East? Why are the nations that surround us taking up arms in every generation? What do they want from us? What do we want for ourselves?

Israel serves as the punching bag for a planet possessed by a malevolent obsession with Jewish exceptionalism. Our detractors seethe with envy and struggle to knock us down from our supernatural, unprecedented eternity. It drives them crazy that a persecuted nation without a land should survive the millennia and still ask the "Four Questions" at the *Seder* table and celebrate joyfully in fragile *sukkot*. These "disgraced" Hebrews then commit the ultimate chutzpah: returning to their homeland to create a flourishing first-world country amidst violent, tribal monarchies! Who can tolerate such brazen behavior from these obstinate Jews?

Once, while enjoying my bagel in a Vail ski lodge, I engaged a group of seasoned German skiers in conversation. When they learned I was Jewish, they professed a desire to visit the Holy Land so they could see the sights and learn about the Jewish People. I challenged them to guess the size of the total Jewish population. They estimated a few hundred million.

My assertion that there are at best fourteen million left them in a state of disbelief. We make a great deal of noise for a people numbering less than .2% of humankind!

When searching for Israel on a globe it becomes immediately apparent that in spite of the excess of press received, it is truly miniscule and vulnerable. Smaller than the state of New Jersey, there isn't sufficient space on the map to indicate the name of the country, so "Israel" floats in the Mediterranean with an arrow pointing to a small, shapeless chip of paint. This geographic perspective also clarifies the logic behind God's choice of a homeland for God's treasured nation. If the goal of the Jewish People is to merely survive intact, we could have been stashed away in the Amazon. But if our mission is to influence the world with the truth of ethical monotheism, it makes sense to locate our capital at the crossroads of civilization. Indeed, Israel is directly in the trade route of both North to South and East to West movement between Eurasia and Africa. Israel's centrality is not only geopolitical, it is geological: before the Suez Canal was dug, a raindrop falling in the Israeli hills would eventually flow to either the Pacific or the Atlantic Ocean.

There is also logic to God choosing a land without abundant natural resources. With no land-based oil reserves, limited mining opportunities and an inadequate water supply, the residents are forced to innovate and thereby apply those innovations to all areas of life, the very engine of the "start-up nation." Whereas the Nile was an ever-flowing body of water for the boastful Pharaohs, the settlers of Israel could never rely on grandiose self-satisfaction. The trickle that is the Jordan River left us perpetually dependent on God's compassion in the form of rain to survive. We must pray, we must beseech, we must connect. This beneficent dependence is the crux of the fundamental spiritual message we broadcast while dwelling at the nexus of humanity.

The Dalai Lama studied the resolve of the Jewish people as a primer for surviving exile. He learned that our holidays center on the relationship with Israel and witnessed us facing Jerusalem whenever we pray. As a result of the destruction of our Holy Temple, we leave a part of a new house incomplete, we symbolically break a glass and sing the psalm "*Im Eshkacheich Yerushalayim*" (If I forget thee, Jerusalem) at a wedding. Every Tisha B'av, we sit on the floor in shoddy clothes crying fresh tears for our vanquished kingdom. As Napoleon famously said, "A nation that cries for its Temple for two thousand years surely will see it rebuilt." Upon learning about our customs, the Dalai Lama stated, "This is what I call the Jewish secret—to keep your tradition. In every important aspect of human life, something is there to remind you: we have to return, to take responsibility."

Fighting for the Future

To travel to the Promised Land today is to personally invest in the cosmic miracle of our homecoming. I implore my audiences around the world to make THIS the year they venture on the same steps of our forefathers and four mothers. We take ownership of the land not by talking about it but by walking about it. In my concerts, I emphasize the unprecedented feat of Israel's successful absorption of the various waves of immigrants from around the globe. We are all Dancing in Jerusalem! Today, the majority of the world's Jews live in Israel—amazing! Even if one can't make the trip, it's possible to advocate for Israel. As it says regarding the Jewish People (*B'reishit* 12:3): "I will bless those who bless you, and whoever curses you I will curse; and all peoples on earth will be blessed through you." Jew and gentile alike can be part of the winning team by taking a stand for the Holy Land.

Our troubled Mideast neighbors are coming to the table not because they have a sudden love of Jews but because they are witnessing the birth of an economic powerhouse with resources to share. Israel's $100 billion economy is larger than the sum of all its Arab neighbors. Israel has more listings on NASDAQ than high tech rivals Japan, Korea and India combined. Our seventy-year-old homeland has more technology companies and venture capital funds than any country other than the US. Remember the 11th commandment, "Thou Shalt Go to College?" A quarter of Israelis have university degrees, a statistic only exceeded by the US and Holland. Israel has the highest rate of scientists and technicians in the workforce in the world. More scientific papers, more new books published, more home computers and more female entrepreneurs per capita. Israel boasts a higher average income than our former landlord, the UK. The entire world takes for granted the daily use of Israel's spectacular advances in hi-tech, medicine, biotech, physics and chemistry. Jews hold 22% of Nobel Prizes. Israeli innovations in agriculture, alternative energy and desalinization are rays of hope on this ever-crowded, ever-hungry, warming planet.

Unfortunately, Jews are still wandering the desert, the desert of ignorance and brutality. We witness the denigration of our Land even while we readily share its assets and sow the seeds of loving-kindness, justice and charity. There are over 400 million Arabs in twenty-two Arab states versus the six million in the one Jewish state. The United Nations has issued over five-hundred condemnations of Israel and none for Hamas or Hezbollah. The Arabs enjoying the most freedom in the Middle East live in Israel's flourishing democracy. Yes, Israel's government must be called to task for shortcomings but the overwhelming sound from the Diaspora sidelines should be enthusiastic cheering. Who else is going to root for us?

The forces of evil in the form of Islamic fundamentalism, anti-Semitism, Boycott, Divestment and Sanctions, Holocaust denial and terror are no match for the vast power of the Jewish spirit. We are engaged in a millennia-old program of world redemption, influencing society in a patient, loving manner while attempting to maintain our unique identity. When we are plugged into our source, our Joy of Judaism renders us untouchable. The trials of each generation are one and the same, largely because they are eternal: to cling to our Land, to hold on to the dream of freedom, to keep the faith and keep our focus, to teach, touch and entertain, to find laughter amidst tears and in times of defeat, pick ourselves up and strive once again. This is the mission of the Jewish People for the benefit of all humankind, the true gift of the Promised Land.

THE FOUR QUESTIONS

1. Have you ever been to Israel? If so, describe your spiritual connection to the land? If not, can you imagine how you would feel being in Israel for the first time?

2. What can you do to bless Israel?

3. How are you kept updated on what is going on in Israel?

4. Can you describe your personal Lech L'cha, your unique drive towards holiness?

Redemption Song

♫ AL KEYN ♫

joyjud.com/m/akn

Give us the power to imagine　　　　*Give us the gift of Your splendor*
The whole world united eternally　　　*Regal, exalted, invincible*
Jealousy, hatred abandoned　　　　　*May it be soon that all people*
In Your Name　　　　　　　　　　*Know Your Name*
Al keyn n'kaveh l'cha...　　　　　　*Al keyn n'kaveh l'cha...*

One year, my family enjoyed a wonderful week of travel while I was leading High Holidays for Beth El, Yardley, a suburb of Philadelphia. We returned to L.A. just in time for Shabbat and Sukkot started that Sunday night. Needless to say, holiday preparations were rushed. Thankfully, our boys rallied to help set up the *sukkah* and Sarah and Shira attended to the decorations and edibles. The L.A. weather was relentlessly hot and yet our beautiful *sukkah* was the coolest spot in town. Each night, I fell asleep under the *schach* (organic *sukkah* roof material) surrounded by my sleeping kids while watching the full moon slowly arc across the Southern California sky. I had a powerful revelation: we Jews are still living in *sukkot*, on a panoramic journey from exile to redemption. Every holiday cycle we get a bit closer. Our sages explain that the intense happiness we experience over this holiday is a taste of the joy we will feel in the time of *Mashiach* (Messiah). The *Yamim Noraim* (High Holidays) serve as an annual resecutation of the Jewish soul, offering a glimpse of the actualization of *Tikkun Olam*.

When the Jewish People departed Egypt, we made forty-two stops over the course of our forty-year march to the Promised Land. We enjoyed protection from the elements thanks to our humble *sukkot* and the *Ananei Hakavod* (supernatural clouds) shielding us from all dangers. According to Kabbalah, we all are reincarnated from those same brave, wandering Jews. These days we are sojourning in modern cities around the globe instead of encampments in the desert, sharing our spiritual gifts throughout the Diaspora. The Baal Shem Tov enumerates forty-two personal spiritual levels to be attained throughout our lives. Simultaneously, the Jewish People is in the midst of forty-two stop journey through exile as we move toward redemption. I counted the number of major national expulsions/destructions of Jewish communities on Wikipedia—it hovers right around this forty-two mark. We see this pattern of forty-two daily: there are forty-two words in the *V'ahavta* paragraph of the *Sh'ma* and then forty-two words in the opening paragraph of the *Sh'moneh Esrei*. According to our sages, this number signifies our humble origins and fabulous destination.

Like it or not, Judaism is a messianic religion. Currently, the phrase Messianic Judaism has a negative connotation, largely due to the association with the Christian missionizing of unsuspecting Jews. However, messianism is an integral component of our theology and harkens back to Avraham's inspired prophecies, Bilaam's attempted curses and the drama of Deuteronomy.

For many, the subject of the Messiah provides an insurmountable stumbling block. I tend to avoid any mention of eschatology (matters pertaining to the end of days) for fear of offending my audiences. Once, on a flight en route to a Shabbaton (Sabbath program) I was leading in Knoxville, TN, I was pouring over *Farbrengen*, a hip Chabad publication that used to arrive on my doorstep several times a year. An article by Rabbi Heschel Greenberg entitled, "The Mysterious Logic of Mashiach" particularly interested me. The *Mashiach* word had always given me the willies. I felt a human being ushering in a "golden age" sounded like an L. Ron Hubbard novel. Any talk of sudden transformation filled me with foreboding. I grew up in a politically correct world and inherited the value of moral relativism: nothing is absolute, no one really has the truth, no one can tell anyone what to do…especially some fanatic who calls himself *Mashiach*!

This article took the reader on a step-by-step explanation of why the belief in a messianic age is absolutely normal, spans all cultures and bridges the religious and secular divide. Christians pray for Jesus to return, Muslims wait for the *Mahdi*, Capitalists place their faith in science to perfect the world and Communists attempt to create an atheist worker's utopia. Why <u>shouldn't</u> it be an individual who ushers in this messianic age? After all, history honors enterprising upstarts who choose to enlighten the populace rather than accept the status quo. Intrepid individuals have launched every revolution in human history.

The article provided such a paradigm shift that I spent the rest of the flight preparing a talk on the Jewish concept of the messianic age for my Knoxville fans. I even peppered my Saturday night concert with songs inspired by eschatological themes. I thought the presentation was important and interesting and no, I never got invited back. I find that no one wants to discuss the Messiah except for Chassidim, who end every *d'var* Torah with "and *Mashiach* should come speedily in our days." Even many Modern Orthodox avoid the subject, as if the announcement of *Mashiach* might affect their real estate holdings or require that they wear *shtreimels* (the fur hats worn by certain Chassidim). The Conservative movement is officially undecided on the topic and Reform has confidently avoided mention of a messiah in its principles and liturgy. And yet, Maimonides, the great rationalist, considered the belief in the coming of *Mashiach* to be one of the thirteen core principles of our faith. Judaism teaches that mitzvot are cumulative; every act of kindness and love reverberates through the universe and leaves an indelible imprint. Whereas evil dissipates and is forgotten, goodness is rooted in eternity. Given all the acts of kindness over the millennia, we should be outraged that the messianic age isn't here yet. As one sweaty, slightly inebriated friend said to me amidst the revelry on Simchat Torah, "We're such nice people! What is God waiting for?"

The era of the messianic redemption will come speedily, much like how our Exodus from Egypt transpired with such haste that we couldn't even wait for our bread to bake. But it will only seem sudden. The roots of this transformation go back to the survival of

Avraham's nephew Lot, the heroism of Ruth and the birth of King David. Our third and final exile is ending in the miraculous homecoming party that is the modern State of Israel. The seeds of Torah have now been sown worldwide with more people studying in more locations than ever in history. Jewish parlance is the lingua franca of Western Civilization. Maimonides views the advent of Christianity as an integral vehicle to spread awareness of monotheism and messianism to all nations. Miraculous leaps in technology have given us PCs, the Internet and iPhones; we realize more than ever we are one, connected and interdependent. Whereas it seemed the former Soviet Union collapsed overnight, its demise had been festering over decades. So, too, will this "new age" seemingly spring upon us, leaving us shocked and surprised and even laughing at the intensity of the transition. Only in the aftermath will we be able look back and perceive the steady progression towards our yet unimaginable destiny.

The advent of *Mashiach* isn't a fairy tale or a crutch but is our raison d'être as a nation. Working towards redemption gives our lives direction and meaning. It assuages Jewish suffering over the millennia when seen as a function of an ultimate goal. Even agnostics among us possess God-given messianic inclinations. Just like we know we have a pulse, we know we are driven toward making the world better, to fostering the triumph of good over evil. We entertain this phenomenon every time we see a movie where the hero is victorious. Humans possess an irresistible drive for *Tikkun Olam*…and we are willing to sacrifice our lives to make it happen. Ask a Darwinian evolutionist to explain that adaptation! This passion is universal and is particularly active in the Jewish *neshama*. God instilled it within us so that we will not accept mediocrity, we won't stand idly by our neighbor's blood, we can't rest until we accomplish something monumental in our lives. Jews believe in evolution more fervently than Darwin: the evolution of the entire world toward perfection.

So yes, we ought to discuss our redemption destiny, pray for it and in the words of Maimonides, wait daily for its coming. The Talmud echoes this sentiment; it states that one of the first questions with which we are challenged when we leave this mortal coil is, "Did you yearn for the arrival of the Messiah?" *Mashiach* awareness is programmed into our everyday worship, namely the *Adon Olam, Yigdal, Aleynu* and *Sh'moneh Esrei* prayers. We can consciously utilize these passages to keep our yearning for a perfected world alive. Waiting for *Mashiach* can get frustrating and actually damage one's *emunah*. The best attitude is serene confidence that God knows best and has the power to bring Mashiach at any time. It could be today!

Thanks to the gift of free choice, a prerequisite for redemption is that we desire redemption. Unfortunately, we have been in exile so long that we have lost the yearning to flourish in our own land. We get so comfortable in our suburban refugee camps that we forget we're only "passing through." The price of immersion in the Diaspora is a gradual disconnect with our essential mission statement. Many Israelis I know have also lost focus of our Jewish destiny and pray instead to reach the Promised Land of Hollywood or the Golden Medina of New York. After years of striving to live in our own land, Israeli *yerida* (leaving the land) is particularly ironic. Some search for elusive riches, some claim that they feel safer outside the Middle East. Tragically, reaching a state of peace and tranquility with our Arab cousins in the region is an ever-distant goal. Perhaps God is trying to nudge Israelis to an awareness that *davening* for *Mashiach* is the only way; in the words of Rabbi Adin Steinsaltz, "We are stuck in a very unfortunate position, we try to move to right, left, forward, retreat and the way is blocked…we are surrounded on every side…there is one direction, however, that is not closed: upward."

What should we expect from this imminent spiritual revolution? According to the Lubavitcher (Chabad) Rebbe, "The age of *Mashiach* is not something separate from our times. It is pieced together from everything we do now, and all that we know of shall remain. Only the negativity will vanish, and the Godliness within each thing will be obvious to see." The Torah promises our heart will be circumcised. Yes, our heart has a foreskin and no, we won't need a *Mohel* (one who performs a *bris*). This impediment to spirituality is the voice that tells us *maybe there is no God,* or, *prayer is a waste of breath*. This negative voice is what we are going to lose. We will be less narcissistic and miserly. In the wake of total clarity of God's presence, denominational strife will vanish and unity will prevail. (Of course, there will still be that synagogue in which we won't set foot!) *Mashiach* will be a charismatic, brilliant, world-famous leader who becomes the undisputed king of Israel. Hard to imagine the Knesset unanimous about anything, but that's the idea. As an example of the Messiah's power, war will cease to exist AND Israel's borders will expand. According to Rabbi Manis Friedman, we will be continuously head over heels in love with our Creator, as well as our spouse, children and fellow humans, seeing only an interconnected state of reality and the deepest inner beauty in all creatures. Sounds a lot like a summer music festival, but without the drugs.

And that brings us full circle back to my revelation over Sukkot. While we are inspired to reinstate our ultimate destiny during Rosh Hashana and Yom Kippur, it's during Sukkot that we act on this awareness by leaving our fortified homes to live in divinely protected huts. According to the Talmud, Passover corresponds with the First Temple, Shavuot with the Second and Sukkot with the Third Temple, the one that will be built by *Mashiach*. Sukkot is also known as *Chag Ha'asif*, the gathering holiday, when we collect the bounty of our harvest in gratitude to our Heavenly Provider. *Asif* also refers to the joyful gathering of Jews during the holiday and the ultimate gathering when we are all brought on "wings of eagles" (El Al?) at the time of our redemption.

Over Sukkot, we read the prophet Zechariah's prediction of wars preceding this age of everlasting peace. He describes the seventy nations that will gather to judge Jerusalem at this propitious time. Jewish texts consistently describe a total of seventy root gentile nations. Imagine my shock when reading the 2017 Reuters headline, "Seventy nations gather in Paris to discuss the future of Israel." Zechariah describes the archenemy as Gog, which can be translated as roof. It's the "roof people," those who put their faith in buildings, technology and material wealth, versus us, the *s'chach* (the vegetation that forms a *sukkah* roof) people, those who know that ultimately God is the true source of security. The prophet tells us that the remnants of the nations surviving this cataclysmic battle will join the Jewish People in Israel to rejoice and give thanks every Sukkot. Some folks don't want to wait for *Mashiach;* one of the highlights of spending the week of Sukkot in the Holy Land is witnessing the hundred thousand gentile pilgrims on their annual Jerusalem March.

Let me conclude with a sweet story I heard from the Happy Minyan's effervescent Rabbi Tzvi Freeman. Right before candlelighting on Sh'mini Atzeret/Simchat Torah, the holidays that cap off the celebratory week of Sukkot, the rabbi's son was in the lobby of our local Marriott. He overheard a discussion between a family from Israel and the clerk at the front desk. They had a reservation but no credit card and the clerk was adamant they could not check in without it. The rabbi's son seized the opportunity to do an amazing mitzvah: he approached the panicked couple and offered to get a credit card so they could check in. He sprinted home and asked his dad for the car keys so that he could hurry back and save the day. Rabbi Freeman told his son he would take care of it…he wanted the mitzvah for himself! But his son insisted and followed through with this benevolent act. In the aftermath, the rabbi realized having his son involved made it it a far superior deed. After all, his son learned such sacred behavior from his loving parents, and what *nachas* for the parents to see that he went beyond the minimum and elaborated on the mitzvah of *chesed* (kindness).

The rabbi then reflected on the incredible pride God must feel for his treasured nation on the holiday of Simchat Torah. After the celebratory week of Sukkot, we take our beloved Torah out of the ark and dance with it for hours in interwoven, chaotic circles of joyful abandon. That's right…we dance with a book! What other nation dances with books? We have never been commanded to do so. It's "just a custom." But what a custom! The Torah ends with the letter *lamed* and starts with a *beit*. On Simchat Torah, we finish the scroll and immediately begin again, thereby bringing the *lamed* together with the *beit*. This spells the word, *lev* (heart). Torah is the heartbeat of the world. When we beautify mitzvot, putting our heart into them, we invigorate the global circulatory system. Like the rabbi's son took divine service to a new, innovative level so, too, do God's children on this most blissful of holidays. We speed redemption when we go beyond the letter of the law and bring our utmost to our holy service.

So don't be afraid of *Mashiach*. Call it *Tikkun Olam*, utopia or the New World Order. We can choose to have a role in hastening it. What can you do to heal the world? Think globally (pray) and act locally (with loving-kindness). Take a few minutes in your daily *Sh'moneh Esrei*, after you ask for all the "me" stuff like health and livelihood, and pour your heart out to the Almighty. Pray with chutzpah! Master of the Universe, there has been ENOUGH suffering in the world. Please, don't make us wait any more. Let no one else go hungry, let no one else become a victim of senseless violence, no more wars, no more refugees. Please uplift the fallen, protect the weak, protect our planet. Help us now—heal us now. Please, God. Amen.

THE FOUR QUESTIONS

1. Have you ever yearned for the arrival of the Messiah? Why?

2. What is your vision of a perfected world?

3. Do you have any personal "hang ups" with the concept of Mashiach?

4. What is your personal prayer to help hasten the arrival of redemption?

PART THREE

We Got to Pray Just to Make it Today

This section is dedicated by
JULIA AND BRAD BERGER

Congratulations to Sam Glaser and the entire Glaser family on the publication of Sam's first book. May this and all of Sam's work be a source of ongoing inspiration to the Jewish people and the world. This section is dedicated in loving memory of Martin S. Berger (Moshe ben Shlomo) and Terry R. Berger (Tova bas George).

IN THIS SECTION:

Be a Blessing 73

The Amidah: United We Stand... 79

Surviving Shacharit: Kabbalistic Insights into the
Morning Service... 84

Mincha, Mincha 90

Ma'ariv: Shuckling on the Dock of the Bay......................... 94

OVERVIEW

The most concise prayer uttered in the Bible is Moses' urgent plea that God heal his sister, Miriam. He cries out, *"El na, refa na la!"* (God please heal her!) We also learn that he prayed for forty days on behalf of the Jewish People after they worshiped the golden calf. Thus, we have two types of prayer we must undertake: spontaneous/heartfelt vs. canonized/encyclopedic.

God understands all languages and it's crucial to comprehend the words one is saying. That said, there is an indescribable power to praying in Hebrew, the *Lashon Hakodesh* (Holy Tongue). Regardless of our age or upbringing, this skill merits due dilligence. Until we grasp the basics, we may feel like an outsider in the synagogue, and typically that's where Judaism happens. But perhaps even more important is acquiring a sense of comfort and normalcy with speaking with God on a casual basis, in one's own words.

At this point, we have refined our Judaic outlook from the 101 and 202 levels to an enlightened upperclassman worldview. This section is designed to emphasize the power of *tefillah* (prayer) for personal transformation, suggesting methodologies to make the thrice-daily Jewish prayer opportunities meaningful. Each service has its own character and role to play in a busy Jew's life. It may seem *chutzpadik* (with chutzpah, nerve) to pray for one's own needs but our sages teach that God waits for us to enunciate our desires and then acts accordingly. While animals live on the level of survival, humans thrive when they frequently beseech the Almighty and subsequently recognize that everything they receive is a gift.

In the *siddur*, even our personal requests are made in the plural form. While we must petition for our own needs, the genius of the *siddur* emphasizes the welfare of the collective. For example, we don't say, "Give me healing," but rather, we pray that we are among those who are granted health. It's a subtle distinction indicating that even when we don't feel like *davening*, we must remember our prayer benefits the greater community.

Prayer is an extraordinarily powerful weapon in our spiritual arsenal. But like any weapon, it requires mastery, and mastery requires patience and the ability to humbly accept help, as embarrassing as that might be. To some degree, we are all unskilled apprentices in need of a mentor. Even the expert *davener* retains apprentice status since prayer is all about acknowledging servitude to the Almighty. That's why *tefillah* is related to the word *tofel* or secondary—we are making God #1. With God in charge, anything is possible! Jewish prayer is a precious inheritance, its efficacy is well documented and mastery is a key element in our sacred goal of achieving The Joy of Judaism. Don't wait…try talking to God right now. As Reb MC Hammer says, "We got to pray just to make it today!"

Be a Blessing

♫ A DAY IN THE LIFE ♫

joyjud.com/m/adl

Awake, arise
Livin' a day in the life
React, review
Remind us why we're alive

One more chance
To understand Your Name
One more day
To contemplate Your beautiful design

We laugh, we cry
We're livin' a day in the life
Repair, renew
Return to paradise

One more chance
To make somebody smile
One more day
To celebrate the precious gift of time

My oldest son Max's Bar Mitzvah was a true peak experience for this doting father. During the year of preparation, I watched him master a formidable mountain of Torah, liturgy and speeches. We celebrated first in L.A. and then in Jerusalem amidst tears of joy and a tidal wave of *nachas*. Belated gifts were still rolling in when it was his brother Jesse's turn to start practicing. I helped both of them prepare, giving us plenty of quality time and challenging me to dust off my Torah chanting skills. Jesse's *simcha* included a beautiful lunch replete with sushi, the Glaser family flag ceremony and my Kol Sason a cappella group leading the singing. He raked in a pile of gifts and donated 10% to the scholarship fund at his beloved Camp Moshava in Wisconsin. Like Max, he got a brand-new pair of first-class tefillin to don in the morning services at his day school.

The big question is: what happens to our B'nai Mitzvah the day after? Will they embrace their Jewish obligations or see mitzvot as burdensome? Will they pray with *kavanah* (spirit and focus) or just go through the motions?

Once in a while I would join my kids' *minyan* at their yeshiva. While it was sweet to see most students participating in the self-led service, some stood there like zombies. I was pained to see them catatonic with boredom, turning pages absentmindedly and whispering jokes to one another. The rabbis tried hard to make the service meaningful, but clearly some of the boys were thinking, *what am I doing here? I'm exhausted! Why are we saying this again? How can I text my friends and not get caught?* How many adults sit in services thinking the same thing? The key to deriving enjoyment from this most prominent Jewish practice is better understanding the structure of prayer.

Steps in Prayer

Our sages describe three elements in effective prayer: praise, petition and thanks.

Step one is praise for God, a technique to get in a grateful place. Truly, prayer begins and ends with gratitude. The Hebrew word for Jews is *Yehudim*, which means "those who thank." By declaring God's virtues, our lengthy morning blessings and Psalms of Praise remind us of the wonder of life and restore our sense of amazement at God's constant creation of our world. For those who awaken with prayer on their lips, everyday is Thanksgiving! Step two is to ask for something specific, be it health, wealth, an asset, an idea. Nothing we request is outside of God's ability to deliver. Finally, we must enunciate our gratitude with confidence, knowing our gracious God, Who thirsts for our prayer, will answer us. We need the presence of mind to tune in to our heavenly messages over the course of the day, to be aware when Hashem is trying to get our attention with any responses.

Daily prayer forces us to ask tough questions and figure out what we want out of life. Our ultimate dreams are possible. We just have to desire them with unremitting intensity, to be willing to "march into hell for a heavenly cause." Effective prayer requires recognizing Hashem's proximity. So many times after a concert or workshop, members of the audience approach me and state they wish they could have a deeper connection with God. My friends, God is everywhere! Surrounding us like molecules of oxygen, sending us love and blessings 24/7. Transformation is in our hands and we have the Master of the Universe as our life partner, ready to assist.

All we have to do is ask.

In the prayer workshops I lead, I emphasize the key to powerful prayer is daily awareness of Hashem's immanence—to see sunlight, cereal, sisters, cars or buildings as miraculous. One of the best cinematic parables of God's maintenance of our everyday life interactions is the movie, "The Truman Show." Just like Truman is surrounded by props and sets that are only for his benefit, so, too, are we surrounded by people and situations precisely positioned to teach us what we need to learn. All of us are Truman. And what an amazing God we have, able to perfectly orchestrate our deeply meaningful, interconnected paths.

The most accesible yet deepest *tefillot* are spontaneous, heart-to-heart chats with Hashem, in one's native language. Take a moment right now. Tell God what makes you happy, what you most want out of life, what you fear, where you need help. That's prayer. And when you get a response in any form, be it a new friend or an annoying person, a work opportunity or a stubbed toe, treat it as the divine communication that it is.

According to the Rambam, we can know God exists if we investigate with an open mind. Living with this "knowing" is a constant mitzvah and is one of the ways we can fulfill the first of the Ten Commandments. Jewish composer Avraham Idelsohn said, "We don't pray because we believe in God, we believe in God because we pray." Exercising our *emunah* (faithfulness) is a primary reason for regular prayer. It's aligning our will with God's will for us. We learn to perceive God's loving hand supporting, guiding and comforting us. Prayer is not about appeasing a distant deity. It's a chance to check in with our "personal coach" Who only wants for us to reach our full potential.

A Successful Prayer

I'm typically blessed with new songs several times a week. While we were first dating, Shira asked how I would support myself if music didn't pan out. I sat there for a moment and admitted I had no fallback position. I got emotional when I explained how these songs just pour out of me, how I feel inexplicably compelled to bring them to life. Thankfully, she married me anyway. I rarely sit down at the piano to write. Songs come to me as the soundtrack of dreams; they arrive in the middle of the night and I must force myself out of bed to get them recorded before I can go back to sleep.

Once in a while, a few weeks will go by with no new material. During one of these dry periods, I made a simple request of God before saying the bedtime *Sh'ma*. I said, "God, You are awesome! I need a new song for this project I'm producing. Thank You for the all the gifts in my life." Praise, petition and thanks. Like clockwork, sometime around dawn I received the exact aural offering I needed. What a feeling! I hear songs in a finished state—the flash of inspiration is usually orchestrated, containing the introduction, verse, chorus and bridge, the instrumental arrangement and a vague idea of what the lyrics should be. The tough part is finishing these new creations, actually sitting down to work out the lyrics and arrangements, and then producing the track in the studio with my musicians so it matches that initial vision.

Typically, my new songs go into a vast file of unfinished work, joining melodies easily in the thousands on my computer hard drive (and formerly on legions of cassette tapes). Unfortunately, my neglecting to finish songs negates an element of the third step of effective prayer: expressing gratitude for one's gifts <u>and</u> acting on heavenly messages. Why should God send me new material if I just put it in cold storage? A new song should open doors, awaken unconscious yearnings, create possibilities, make it to the market.

The next night I prayed again for inspiration, but this time, I committed to spending an hour at the piano when I was in the moment, to at least get the song to a point where it could be performed. In response to the nightly repetition of this prayer, I was given the gift of new songs all week—wildly varied tunes, some with a Jewish flavor, a ballad for a friend who just lost his wife, a musical theater piece, a kids' tune. Each time, I resisted the temptation to go back to sleep until I recorded the idea. Each morning, I forced myself to the piano to flesh out the lyrics. Just like I had my request answered affirmatively, I am confident God is working behind the scenes to process all my prayers.

The Formula of Blessings

One of the best ways to initiate conversation with God is to master the system of reciting blessings. Until one is ready for a full prayer service, single-sentence blessings smooth the entry into divine correspondence. Most begin with a six-word formula meaning: "You are the source of blessing, merciful and powerful, sovereign of the universe." Here's an analysis of the six Hebrew words:

1. *Baruch:* blessed, from the same root *berech*, knee. Blessings are humbling, lowering us just enough to ascribe any benefits we receive to God. The same root forms *b'reicha*, a pool. Blessings begin with a recognition that God is the reservoir of all sustenance.

2. *Atah:* the informal word for You. There are four mentions of God's name in any given blessing. Atah is the most intimate, expressing God's essence. It's a bit of a chutzpah to address God using the familiar form of "You," but that's the whole idea. Our own essence/soul connects with the Great Soul more readily since we already nullified the ego when saying the word *baruch*.

3. *Adonai:* the unpronounceable *yud-heh-vav-heh* word, representing the feminine, compassionate aspect of Godliness. This word can be read as a verb, expressing

God's "God-ing" the world into being from a vantage point outside time and space.

4. *Eloheinu:* the non-gods claimed by other nations are referred to as *elohim. Eloheinu* means Our God, the One God. This term implies the masculine, exacting God of Creation, Source of the phenomena we are experiencing or substance we are about to eat.

5. *Melech:* king or sovereign; an absolute ruler Who is in a relationship with all humanity, responsible and concerned. Think benevolent monarch, not despot.

6. *HaOlam:* the universe, from the root *elem* or concealed. God is hidden in the fabric of our physical world, but is continuously running the show.

Blessings Over Food

Now, put these six words forming the prefix of any given blessing together with the relevant suffix and we are tweaking the fabric of the universe. The easiest blessings to begin with are those for food. These simple utterances allow us to pause before gorging in order to express gratitude for our sustenance. Here's a breakdown of these essential blessings to help jumpstart the process.

The blessing thanking God for bread, the *motzi,* is well known to anyone who has been to a Shabbat meal. But it's only for bread! What happens when you just want to eat an apple? Then you say the same prefix, *Baruch Atah Adonai, Eloheynu Melech HaOlam…* and add the suffix, *borey p'ri ha'etz* (Who creates the fruit of the tree). For a vegetable we add, *borei p'ri ha'adama* (Who creates the fruit of the earth). Easy, right? For pastry or cereal, *borei minei m'zonot* (Who creates various kinds of sustenance). Wine and grape juice have their own blessing: *borei p'ri hagafen* (Who creates the fruit of the vine). The catch-all blessing for everything else (candy, meat, beer, tofu) is, *shehakol nihiyei bidvaro* (by Whose word all things came to be). That's about it! Yes, there are also specific blessings for <u>after</u> you eat…but why not start with the basic *b'rachot* (blessings) beforehand? Learning to say them in Hebrew is best. This exercise may sound complicated, but an hour of memorization and one is off to a lifetime of holy consumption and the benefit of frequent prayer.

When I was first taking on this discipline, one of my rabbis insisted that nothing enter my mouth without a blessing. Nothing? That was a tall order but I discovered it was feasible. I kept a pocket sized *b'racha* book handy (nowadays we have smartphones) and endeavored to try it for a week. Remarkably, that's all it took to get fluent with the Hebrew and recognize the benefits. Some musician friends worried I was losing my grip on reality as I was frequently talking to myself. Now that I wasn't taking my food for granted, I explained, I was even more appreciative of <u>all</u> the gifts in my life. Eventually I made the effort to integrate the various "after blessings" into my practice, and if I had eaten bread, I'd seek out two others so I could say the *Birkat Hamazon* (grace after meals) with the proper introductory verses. I learned that the importance of saying the blessing <u>after</u> the act of eating takes priority. Whereas the rabbis instituted the mitzvah of blessing our food beforehand, the obligation to thank God after the meal comes directly from Torah, "And you shall eat and be satisfied and bless Hashem your God" (*D'varim*/Deuteronomy 8:10).

There are also blessings for observing various phenomena like thunder and lightning, the ocean or a rainbow. Even witnessing exotic animals, unusual people or extraordinary beauty calls for a *b'racha*. Seeing great leaders, Torah scholars, huge multitudes or old friends or relatives after a long hiatus…more blessings! There are specific blessings for pleasant fragrances, depending if they are from trees, spices, fruits or shrubs. All these can be found in the Artscroll Siddur or online. Knowing what situations requires a *b'racha* is important. Even if the atypical blessings aren't memorized, it's good to recognize when they are appropriate. Essentially, moments of wonder and sensation are opportunities for connection. Credit must be given where credit is due.

Can I Get an Amen?

The Talmud says responding "amen" to a *b'racha* is even more praiseworthy than making the *b'racha*. "The gates of Heaven are opened for whomever answers amen with all his might." My wife and I nudged our kids to make loud *b'rachot* so that we were empowered to say amen (and of course, so that we could hear if they were getting it right). Amen is a simple two-syllable ratification of God's praise in any given blessing. Saying a blessing aloud gives everyone within earshot the opportunity to declare, "I second the motion!" Amen is an acronym for "El Melech Ne'eman," God, trustworthy Ruler." Ne'eman (trustworthy) has within it the word amen—it hints to an infinite cycle of angelic praise, and also has the same root as *emunah*, belief. Amen isn't just for formal *b'rachot*. Anytime someone says, "Good luck on that test" or "I hope your job interview goes smoothly," a hearty amen is the best response, even if the speakers don't realize they are making a blessing. Needless to say, it's easy to tell when one is in a Jewish neighborhood (or the Bible Belt): people are saying "amen" all the time.

Sefer Chassidim reminds that the reason we make *b'rachot* is to bring Hashem into our lives. Mumbling incoherent words doesn't quite accomplish this task. Don't just ramble out of habit—focus! Learning the mechanics of blessings is step one. The *ikar* (central point) is focusing on gratitude to the Almighty for that one precious moment before taking benefit from our amazing world. Here's the passage emphasizing this point: several years after his passing, a man appeared in one of his relative's dreams. The relative asked him, "How are you doing in the other world?" The deceased replied, "Every day I am judged for not having been careful to think about Hashem when making *b'rachot*…and though many years have passed, I am still being cleansed of this fault." Let's get those blessings memorized <u>and</u> remember to say them with *kavanah*.

Livin' on a Prayer

My friend, Rabbi David Baum, compiled a list of prerequisites for effective prayer, paraphrased below. Before we *daven*, it's important to understand the nature of our relationship with the Creator of the Universe.

- God loves us more than any human
- God is aware of everything; our thoughts, desires and goals
- God has the power to give us everything, there are no other powers
- God does more for us than we can imagine, and has done so since our birth, without being asked
- God gives to us unconditionally, no strings attached
- God knows what is best for us

These points clarify that God doesn't need our prayers. God can't be bribed. *L'hitpalel,* to pray, is a reflexive verb, something we do to ourselves. By praying, we bring about a transformation in our being. We sort out our role in our most important relationship. We feel overwhelming gratitude when we realize we are showered with undeserved gifts 24/7. God may not need our prayers, but God loves them. Prayer is why we were created in the first place.

The Jewish people have been *davening* with fervor for millennia. From the lengthy *Amidah* to simple, one-line blessings, our collective prayers have transformed humankind. The world has progressed from barbarism to one where basic Jewish precepts have become the standard for civil society. We have withstood attempts of great empires to dismantle our dreams. Our generation has the unique merit of witnessing the fulfillment of our yearning for return to the Jewish homeland. Don't be stingy with prayer…anything is possible! In the immortal words of Jon Bon Jovi, "We're halfway there, whoa, livin' on a prayer."

THE FOUR QUESTIONS

1. How can you show appreciation for what God has given you in your own words, your own prayer?

2. What are the needs in your personal, communal and global reality for which you can pray?

3. Is there a time in your life when you felt your prayers were answered?

4. How can you incorporate making meaningful blessings into your daily life?

ach • Tehilla • Shabbat • Community • Torah • Prophets • Nigun • Pesach • Teshuva • Wedding
lality • Holmes • Emunah • Diaspora • Bar Mitah • Simcha • Halacha • Birachot • Holiday
h • Eilat • Israel • Mikvah • Flavor • Mishnah • Tehila • Shabbat • Community • Torah • Proph
• Pesach • Tehilla • Wedding • Spirituality • Holmes • Emunah • Diaspora • Bar Mitah
• Halacha Birachon • Holidays • Bar Mitzvah • acher • Israel Mikvah • flavor • Mishnah
lity Shabbat • Community • Torah • Prophets • Nigun • Pesach • teshuva • weddings • spiritua
mes • Eilat • Israel Mikvah flavor • Mishnah • Tehila • Shabbat • Community • Be

The Amidah: United We Stand

♫ KAH RIBON ♫

joyjud.com/m/krb

My God, Creator of all life
Can I hope to understand Your ways
My God, Master of the world
Open up my lips to sing Your praise

Shelter me, protect me from myself
Help me choose a pathway that You favor
Take my hand, wrap me in Your love
Kah ribon olam v'almaya

My God, King of kings
How can I be worthy in Your eyes
My God, Designer of all things
Who made me so that I would realize

Everyday, every single breath
Is mine because You want me to be breathing
Take my words, make of them a prayer
Kah ribon olam v'almaya...

My cherished custom every time I land in South Florida is to head straight to the beach and jump in the glassy, warm water. The shock of the Pacific chill is absent—no wetsuit required—and the soft, white sand unfolds to the north for hundreds of miles. Upon arriving in Boca Raton with a fellow Jewish singer who was joining me on this tour, I dropped my bags at our beachfront hotel, *davened* a peaceful *mincha* (afternoon prayer) and then cavorted into the shallow blue-green playground. As we pondered the pelicans and sandpipers, my friend asked why one would want to say the same *Amidah* (standing prayer) three times a day. He was curious what I get out of it. Am I focusing on saying the words or am I actually thinking about meanings? Where do I add my own thoughts? Isn't it a chutzpah to ask for all this stuff? Is anyone listening?

This conversation got me thinking about why I am so obsessed about not missing a service. Is it for God or me? Why do the words have to be just right? Have I been brainwashed? Isn't repeating the same behavior while expecting a different result the definition of insanity? I know…lots of questions. On the most fundamental level, prayer keeps my God-focus intact. Just like a marathon runner would never start a race without extensive training, saying the *Amidah* three times a day keeps me spiritually limber. I recommend neophytes tackle the *siddur* in bite size chunks, little by little. Adding a few miles each week makes the runner a success. I don't wait for a burst of inspiration, which may or may not come. *Davening* regularly makes God your best friend, your coach with whom you train daily.

When facing the thousand-plus pages of a typical siddur, one might think: *Do we have to deal with this ancient liturgy? Can't we stick with prayer from the heart?* Over the past twenty years, I have found that respecting Jewish tradition is a safe road. Generations of righteous people have rallied around the established prayers of our people. The specific wording of each paragraph, especially the primary prayer, the *Amidah*, is the secret to our unique and unprecedented survival. The *Anshe K'nesset Hag'dolah* (Men of the Great Assembly) codified the *Amidah* nearly 2500 years ago, and it was clearly already in use when they did so. Among the ranks of the one hundred twenty elders were scores of prophets. Interestingly, Israel's modern K'nesset also has one hundred twenty MKs (Members of Knesset). This ancient body boiled down God's will for the Jewish People in eighteen (later nineteen) crucial categories. Don't mess with the formula! My *rav*, Rabbi Moshe Cohen describes the first paragraph of the *Amidah* as the web address. This opening salvo is THE place to deeply focus on the precise phrases that have served us for millennia.

When we repeat this menu of our deepest needs, we work in partnership with God to bring them to fruition. So central is this prayer to our existence that the Talmud simply refers to it as *tefillah*. The *Sh'ma* and Psalms are important, but the *Amidah* is IT. We utter nineteen dreams for humanity and those dreams become part of us, defining our aspirations and clarifying our mission.

Anytime we want to understand the origin of a Hebrew term, it's informative to find the first place it appears in the *Tanach* (Bible). The English word "prayer" comes from the Latin root "to beg" and perhaps is not the ideal definition of what Jews do three times a day. As we discussed, *L'hitpalel*, to pray, is a reflexive verb meaning to assess oneself. This term makes its debut in the moving scene in *B'reishit* (Genesis 48:11) when Yaakov is about to bless Yosef's sons. The patriarch says, "I dared not <u>pray</u> that I would see your face again and here God has shown me even your offspring!" Rashi tells us that the use of the word *"pilalti"* can be translated as imagine or dream, to think ultimate thoughts. That's what we are doing when we pray.

When my brother and I were getting more involved in our heritage, we strived to "Holocaust Proof" the *Amidah*. Over the years, with minimal effort, we were able to internalize the morning, afternoon and evening services so that if we were to find ourselves without a prayer book or, God forbid, in an adverse situation, we would always have these precious words on our lips. Interestingly, we both worked towards this goal on our own and only later shared it with one another. The structure of the *siddur* is set up for memorization due to the repetitive nature of the prayer experience. The natural byproduct of an investment in regular *davening* is confident ownership.

In my personal practice, I frequently pray without a book, with my eyes closed, to deepen the experience and avoid losing the accumulated knowledge. One of the keys to this technique is mouthing the words silently, a custom we learn from our prophetess Hannah when she so ardently prayed for a child. Just scanning the words doesn't seem to be as effective as quietly pronouncing every last one. Not only does silently speaking these sacred phrases better establish the words in one's memory, it also serves to bring these spiritual concepts off of the page and into the physical world. A caveat: as fluency with prayer improves, it's easy to unwittingly mumble nonsense. Every now and then, I must dissect standard *t'filot* like the *Ashrei* and *Aleynu* and "unmumble them," re-teaching myself to enunciate clearly and slowly before ramping up to speed once again.

Sometimes it's good to just get the words out, even if we're not really "feeling it." A recently divorced friend was appalled that the rabbi writing her *get* (divorce document) didn't have any special *kavanah* (spiritual intent) as he wrote each letter. She kept suggesting he infuse the document with spiritual meaning and the frustrated rabbi retorted, "My *kavanah* is that I'm writing a *get*, period!" Even for *davening* veterans, the emotional connection to prayer isn't always so passionate. It's the exercise that counts.

Anytime Rabbi Nathan Lopes Cardozo comes to L.A., I try to corner him to get questions answered and enjoy his phenomenal accent, even if it's just giving him a ride to the next gig. After one class, I offered to take him to the Rembrandt exhibition at the Getty Museum. Remarkably, he agreed! I got to witness a Dutch master with a Dutch master. During our walk around the spectacular grounds, I asked him about my propensity to say memorized words habitually, devoid of passion. He remarked that even if one is thinking about the stock market, engaging in daily prayers is a triumph. Taking time out from one's busy schedule to stand with God is a profound step that cannot be underestimated. When using the *siddur*, one who prays "intuitively knows there is a vast landscape of deep content behind these prayers. He no longer lives there, but he bathes in its light. And so he says words that transcend him, because he's aware that they have great meaning." I find that my personal *Amidah* is on a continuum, from an express *Mincha* at an airport gate to an awe-inspiring, tear-filled expression session. I'm convinced these radical moments of sublime unity happen because I subscribe to the "Just Do It" day-to-day practice.

Even a single minute of concentration is hard to achieve when one's head is filled with worry and deadlines. That's why we begin the *Amidah* with a sentence asking God to open our mouths for us. Interestingly, the word for lips, *s'fata'im*, is the same for the banks of a river. We want our prayer to overflow the banks, to supersede our human limitations in order to enter the realm of the spirit. My friend David Sacks notes how first we pray to have the ability to pray, and then we actually pray—our prayer is already answered! I take three small steps back and breathe deeply, clearing my mind for the awe-inspiring approach into God's proverbial throne room. Then I take three steps forward and ask the Master of the Universe, Who chose to create me, to enable me to open my lips so I can speak words of praise. Sometimes I imagine I'm standing on a promontory overlooking all of creation, much like Pride Rock in The Lion King. Only when I feel rooted in my personal power, confident and clear minded, do I proceed with the sacred words.

A great technique to stay focused is to isolate the last words of each blessing during the recitation of the relevant paragraph. The Artscroll *Siddur* helps in this effort by offering a heading for each section upon which one can ponder. I increase my concentration with a multi-tasking exercise in which I focus on each individual word AND keep in mind the last words of the paragraph throughout. As a mental aid, sometimes I envision entering an eighteen-story building with a single, enormous room on each floor. I walk in on the ground floor and utter the foundational first paragraph in which we offer appreciation for the legacy of the first Jewish families. While I say these words, I envision the paragraph's subject emblazoned across the ceiling. I wander across a cavernous space that is ornately decorated in the appropriate style and then, in the back of the room, say *Baruch Ata Adonai* and the relevant suffix as I press the button for the elevator. On the next floor, I'm overwhelmed by

God's power, then regal holiness, then the gift of knowledge, and so on, until I'm standing on the rooftop proclaiming peace in every direction.

There are many places in the weekday *Amidah* in which we can personalize our needs and wants. A crucial place to pause is the prayer for healing, *Refa-eynu*. Here we earnestly say the names of those in urgent need of a revitalization of body and spirit. Our tradition teaches that healing is generated from our maternal bond, so we utilize the sick person's mother's name. For example, if I was ever in need of healing, God forbid, someone praying on my behalf would use the name Shmuel ben Chaya Lieba. When I ask God to bless the year in the *Barech Aleinu* paragraph, I ponder my progress from the previous *Tishrei* and think of any friends in need of an income boost. I ensure I'm focused on Jerusalem during the paragraph blessing the holy city. It's not enough that I'm facing east; I try to envision God's Presence spreading from site of the Temple to wherever I'm standing. To facilitate this, I placed a panoramic photo of snow-covered Jerusalem on the eastern side of my favorite backyard *Mincha* perch. During *Sh'ma Koleynu* I insert any of my concerns in my own words, silently speaking in plain English exactly what I need. At this point I typically pray for my children's well-being, success with my music, *shalom bayit* (peace in the house) and peace in the world. Then I make sure that my *Modim* (prayer of thanks) is real, exuding gratitude like a vulnerable defendant who just received a positive verdict.

One might ask how to navigate personal prayers on Shabbat. The middle thirteen weekday petitionary blessings are not part of the Sabbath liturgy. This omission heightens our sensitivity to the glory of the day—since we are tasting *Olam Habah* (the next world), we are in a realm where our desires are already met. Crying about our physical needs on Shabbat indicates a sense of lack and even bitterness, clearly counterproductive in our attempt to establish a sacred island in time. We do pray for communal imperatives like healing and peace. Praying for a soulmate is considered a spiritual need. What happens for those who only pray on the Sabbath? When do they get to ask for their personal needs if not on the day when they do show up to the synagogue? The solution? Pray on weekdays too!

Since the practice of reciting the *Amidah* involves engaging and understanding the Hebrew text, it's important to find a good *siddur*. The book I prefer is the Artscroll Interlinear Ashkenazi edition since its painstakingly accurate English is printed in a clever way underneath each word. It also has the prayer "aerobics" instructions for when to stand, bow and say amen. If reading Hebrew is a roadblock, perhaps begin with the standard Artscroll, Metsudah or Koren *siddur* since the well-written English follows the Hebrew on the other side of the page, in close proximity to each paragraph. One of my issues with Sim Shalom, Siddur Hadash and Mishkan T'filah *siddurim* is that the English is often a poetic interpretation and not the *tachlis* (bottom line) translation. One can pray in English until reaching a comfort level with Hebrew—just don't let the crutch of reading English prevent engagement with the holy tongue. Eventually, one can move over to the Hebrew side, at least for the blessings at the end of each paragraph. It's fine to use one's synagogue prayer books supplied for communal *davening*, but I recommend keeping an Artscroll in one's *tallis* bag for personal *tefillah*.

Here's the rest of the opening saga in Boca Raton: following our community-wide concert in a beautiful park, I urged my cohort to join me back on the beach for a seaside *Ma'ariv* (evening prayer) before returning to our hotel. After *davening*, I plunged into the jet-black ocean. My friend looked at me like I had lost my mind. I said, "Brother, there is nothing better than laying on your back in the liquid wonderland of the night sea while pondering the moon and stars." He was unconvinced and used the shark argument. "Sharks?" I replied. "Do you know the chances of getting killed are way less than getting hit by lightning? C'mon!" He eventually succumbed when I reminded him that he was going right back to land-locked Phoenix and this was his last chance to enjoy the ocean. When we got to waist deep water, my friend looked very uncomfortable. I urged him to go a bit deeper to have the full experience. Again, he dug in his heels. "No way am I going out there!" Again I cajoled him into swimming out to the depths where we could peacefully float away from the surf and seaweed and appreciate the heavenly firmament above.

As soon as he got back to Arizona, he forwarded me a clip from that night's Miami TV news. The video shot from a helicopter revealed the migration of hundreds of thousands of blacktip sharks swimming immediately offshore. Google "Shark Migration Miami." Yikes! I guess all that beachside prayer paid off. Prayer affects worlds beyond our grasp. It connects, corrects, consoles, propels, heals and inspires. The *Amidah* is one of the best tools to unite us in the common dreams of our nation. When we stand together, anything is possible.

THE FOUR QUESTIONS

1. Do you have a vision of what you want to pray for?

2. What circumstances (place, time, etc.) make prayer the most meaningful to you?

3. How can you improve your experience with the Amidah?

4. How can you make time for regular prayer in your busy life?

Surviving Shacharit: Kabbalistic Insights into the Morning Service

♫ THE LADDER ♫

joyjud.com/m/tld

Up in the morning, start my routine
Say the words I always say
I try to remember the feeling I had
When I realized one day

If our souls are eternal then Avraham
Could be praying right beside me
Who with all of the ancestors
I never knew
Keep reminding me I'm not alone

All my grandmother's grandfathers
Smiling inside
As their merit patiently guides me
Stretching to the beginning of time
On a ladder uniquely my own

Let me celebrate each new day
As if it were my first
Always allow me to praise Your Name
But not like a script that I've rehearsed

A certain fan learned several of my songs on the piano so that he could share them with his synagogue prayer team. He eventually became a dear friend and at one point invited me to share my music with his summertime *chevra* (group of friends) in the High Country of North Carolina. During the days before and after my concert we hiked, biked and zip-lined and the nights were spent enjoying the company of his fellow South Florida sunbirds who welcomed us in their posh mountain homes. Since this was the week of my wedding anniversary, a second airfare was offered so that I could bring Shira on the adventure—our first vacation without the kids in as long as we could remember. We were grateful for the gift of verdant forests painted with a rainbow of wildflowers and azure skies punctuated with cotton-ball clouds. My friend marveled that even though I was making a vacation out of this Beech Mountain and Asheville concert tour, I still managed to keep up with my prayer ritual and don my *kippah* wherever I went. I explained that especially when

I'm on the road, I rely on my Jewish daily practices to keep me grounded.

One morning, I brought him out to the deck behind the house to enjoy the imperial view and try on my *tefillin*. I strapped him up, coached him through an abbreviated service and left him alone to ponder his possibilities. When he finished, he looked unsatisfied, as if he was expecting pyrotechnics. "Is that it?" he asked. I sat him down to explain the following kabbalistic take on the Jewish morning rituals. Sometimes you just get through it. But other times it gets through you!

I carve out time for my various rituals no matter if I'm sore, sleep deprived or rushed. Inevitably, as soon as I am finished with my prayers, I feel ready to face the day. The repetitive rigor of morning mitzvot offer a sense of accomplishment even when I wake up feeling brain-dead. At the sound of the alarm, I resist the urge to push snooze, (who invented this perennial challenge?) and sit on the edge of my bed while saying *Modeh Ani*, the prayer of gratitude to God for faithfully returning our soul to our body each day. My screenwriter neighbor David Weiss told me that he repeatedly sings my *Modeh Ani* song "until he gets it." First thing in the morning, I'm not quite on that level. I lumber to the bathroom where I do the traditional washing as soon as I'm done with the toilet, pouring copious amounts of water on my hands from the wrists on down, using a special two-handled pitcher, right-left-right-left-right-left. This practice is reminiscent of the washing by the priests when the Temple stood and is likely the reason that Jews survived the various plagues afflicting the unwashed ancient world. For me, it makes a statement that I am on a distinctive *derech* (path) of purpose and purity, starting first thing in the morning. I then wash my face, brush my teeth and shave with an electric razor (since the acoustic version is proscribed by the rabbis).

Even the manner in which one puts on clothing is mandated by Jewish law; for example, I put on the right shoe, then the left shoe, then tie the left one and then the right one. This teaches subtle lessons in the primacy of the right (representing *chesed*, kindness) over the left, which represents *g'vura*, judgment. FYI: lefties do things the opposite way. Some may laugh at this level of requisite detail and when they do, I tell the story about a friend who realized that he wasn't ready to be Sabbath observant but at least he could put on his shoes in a kosher way. This small mitzvah got him started on a profound path into Torah life.

When I'm not headed to a *minyan*, I go straight to my living room, even if I'm really hungry, and "strap up" in my *tallis* and *tefillin* in the nook of my grand piano. Our sages recommend we pray before eating a meal or starting our workday. I resonate strongly with making the connection with God before I stuff my face. Having an empty stomach gives my prayer a bit more urgency and ensures I do my *davening* without getting carried away with my agenda. I step out on our verdant front porch and find being outside is enough to enliven my senses and fill me with joy (unless the gardeners are mowing)! Even though some neighbors don't *daven* themselves, they have expressed that seeing me veiled behind the jasmine vines in my prayer garb is enough to give them a spiritual boost.

The morning prayers are extensive, involve vast fields of Hebrew on the printed page and contain some seemingly redundant parts. On my own, the *Shacharit* service takes about a half hour, start to finish. In a *minyan* it's about twice that amount of time. If I'm in a rush, I still do the whole service but only hit the highlights of the *P'sukei D'zimra* (Verses of Praise) portion. As I have said, I worked my way up to negotiating the full service in baby-step fashion. I recommend that prayer neophytes start with the morning blessings and then the *Sh'ma* with the *V'ahavta*, eventually adding the other two *Sh'ma* paragraphs. Once those are wired, one can tackle the *Sh'moneh Esrei,* one paragraph at a time. The main three prayers of the *P'sukei D'zimra (Baruch She'amar, Ashrei* and *Yishtabach)* are next. Take your time—there's no need to try to eat the whole enchilada in one sitting.

The four sections of the *Shacharit* service can be compared with a hike up a mountain, much like the verdant five-mile loop we just explored on this North Carolina tour. The *Birkot Hashachar* (Morning Blessings) can be compared to the parking lot at the trailhead where we are gathering up our gear, the *P'sukei D'zimra* are like the first set of switchbacks on the trail, the prayers before and after the *Sh'ma* demarcate the end of the ascent when we are really sweating, and the *Sh'moneh Esrei* is the glorious view at the top. Then we return to the trailhead, step by step. Understanding this level-by-level ascension can be facilitated by consulting the Jewish mystical tradition. But to get the insights, it's necessary to explain a few essential Kabbalistic concepts.

Kabbalah

Kabbalah is our "origin story," the science of how God interacts with creation. According to our family friend and Kabbalah expert, Rav Simcha Ashlag, it isn't out of reach of laymen or reserved for those over forty—it is readily accessible for those with open hearts and a patient teacher. Some say Kabbalah is like whiskey and *Gemara* is like bread. We need bread in our stomach or the whiskey will make us sick. In other words, it's good to get the basics before endeavoring into the mystical. Hopefully the first few sections of this book will serve as an ample appetizer and we are ready for some shots!

We believe before the "big bang" there was only the infinite light of God, known as the *Or Ein Sof*. Within this all-encompassing divinity there was no possibility for anything "other" to exist. Therefore, God had to constrict God's own light to allow for the formation of finite, limited physicality. The expanding universe in its entirety exists within this space. Yes, God is great! We call the progressive constriction of Godliness *Tzimtzum* and we can best understand the process in the Kabbalistic description of four levels of reality, just like the four aspects of our hike.

All matter is on a continuum from pure spirituality to raw physicality, even inanimate objects like a chair or a rock. That rock isn't a-spiritual—it's just on the physical edge of the continuum. We can decode the physics of the metaphysical thanks to the genius of Rabbi Shimon Bar Yochai, author of the Zohar. Our daily prayer experience takes us through these levels, from our opaque, dimly lit world until we stand at the pinnacle of unadulterated spiritual clarity.

According to Judaism, holy sparks of divinity animate everything, with the Almighty serving as Creator and Maintainer of all matter. Hopefully we live with a sense of awe for God's Presence in all of nature—how much more so in every human being! We inhabit the lowest of the four Kabbalistic worlds, known as *Asiya*. The word for the universe or world is *olam*, as in *Melech HaOlam*, Ruler of the Universe. As we discussed, *Olam* is from the root of *elem*, meaning hiddenness, in that God's presence is hidden within nature. Remarkably, at our mundane level, Godliness is concealed to the degree that even brilliant human beings, the apex of God's creation, can deny God's existence. Regardless of the platitudes of atheists, even our "opaque" world is infused with spirituality. Our job as Jews is to reveal God's handiwork to the masses.

The essence of the world of *Asiya* is action. *Asiya* is related to the word *"la'asot,"* or "to do." *La'asot* is the final word of the passage that describes the seventh day of the Creation saga in Genesis. We say this passage every week in the *"Vay'chulu"* paragraph of the

Friday Night *Kiddush*. Humankind was created "to do," to complete an incomplete world, to engage in *Tikkun Olam*. Our mission is to serve as God's eyes and hands, to seek out what is lacking and make it whole. The Talmudic statement, "For me the world was created" is less an ego boost than a prescription detailing our responsibility to rectify humankind's lack of awareness. *Asiya* is the only realm where the 613 mitzvot are necessary. In the other worlds, Godliness is obvious, unquestionable. Therefore, it should make sense that the morning blessings with which the *Shacharit* service begins reflect this world of *Asiya*, outlining our physical needs and actions. The *Asyia* section of the *siddur* contains the blessing over washing hands, the blessing for the gift of our bodies, the blessing for Torah study and for our unique gifts as human beings. Human fragility and temptation to the "dark side" is addressed, as is the system of sacrifices in the Temple for which our prayers are designed to substitute.

The next level is referred to as *Yetzira* (Formation), the realm of feelings and emotions. Time and space are part of the realm of *Asiya* whereas in *Yetzira*, these dimensions do not exist. *Yetzira* yields a clearer manifestation of the infinite light of Godliness. In our holiest moments, we get brief glimpses of this light. This is the loving presence toward which many who have had a Near Death Experience are drawn. *Yetzira* is dimension itself, beyond the physical, and is detailed in Kabbalah as the ten *S'firot*. The second section of the *Shacharit* prayers, the *P'sukei D'zimra*, is primarily composed of *Tehillim* (Psalms) describing the greatness of God. It opens with the description of God speaking the world into being and goes on to extol God's myriad attributes. All God's creations praise God! It finishes with a verbatim recitation of *Az Yashir* (*Sh'mot* 15:1-18), the song we sang prophetically at the splitting of the sea. These paragraphs are intended to awaken an emotional attachment to God and inspire gratitude.

Sadly, in most Ashkenazi *minyanim*, *P'sukei D'zimra* goes by with stunning speed. I can still hear the voice of my late mother-in-law, Rosie, may her *neshama* have an *aliyah* (may her soul have an elevation), telling me to slow down when she heard me *davening* too fast. She intuited that an auctioneer's pace was a disservice to proper service. *Zimra* comes from the root of *zemer* or holy song. These passages are laden with musical cadence and were likely sung in their entirety back in a more leisurely era. Many Sephardic congregations still sing every word. Whereas the morning blessings are simple statements of awareness of God's gifts, the *P'sukei D'zimra* section fosters emotional, *Yetzira*-engagement with the *Or Ein Sof*. This is an opportunity we do not want to miss.

The third of the four realms is that of divine intellect, known as *B'riya* (Creation). In the *Shacharit* service it corresponds with the *Bar'chu*, the two blessings before the *Sh'ma*, the *Sh'ma* itself and the two blessings afterwards. *B'riya* is the penultimate level before unlimited Godliness. Therefore, it implies a nearly unlimited reality, the concept of being, the highest level of the *Tzimtzum*. In this world, divine light is still somewhat obscured and allows for differentiation. *B'riya* is the location of the *Kisei Hakavod*, God's throne. It is also houses the repository of holy Jewish souls. This is the higher angelic realm described by our prophets, starring Uriel, Gavriel and Rafael and company. A close look at the third part of the *Shacharit* service reveals an exploration of the workings of the angels, including their secret formulas, "*Kadosh, kadosh, kadosh*" (Holy, holy, holy) and "*Baruch kevod Adonai mim'komo*" (Blessed is the glory of Hashem from God's place). Angels are creations of God, emanations of heavenly energy directed towards a certain, singular goal. While we can't emulate these perfect beings, we can use the power of Torah and mitzvot to keep us on an angelic path. At this point in *Shacharit*, we exclaim our *B'riya*-level awareness of God's uniqueness by loving God with all our heart, soul and might. *Sh'ma* is also the last prayer we say before we go to sleep at night, and if we can muster the strength, the last six words we say before we die.

Each phase of our service is divided by the *Kaddish*, an Aramaic prayer praising God. Mourners say *Kaddish* during the mourning period for loved ones and on the anniversary of death, called the *Yahrzeit*. Other points in the service feature a *Kaddish* led by the cantor. Interestingly, the *Kaddish* makes no mention of death, rather, it affirms God's justice and upholds the value of life. This is the crucial message the mourner must integrate, and by doing this prayer, the mourner also sets up the whole community to "second the motion" in unison. The refrain, *"Y'hei sh'mei raba m'varach l'olam ul'al'mei al'maya"* (May God's great Name be blessed forever and ever) hints to the lower three worlds we are discussing: *l'olam* is *Asiya*, *ul'ol'mei* is *Yetzira* and *al'maya* is *B'riya*. We ask that God's great name be blessed in these three realms. Think of the *Kaddish* as the ramp leading the *davener* from level to level. Please note there is no *Kaddish* between the *Sh'ma* and *Sh'moneh Esrei*; instead we have a silent launch from *B'riya* into the realm of pure spirituality.

Finally, we arrive at the highest world, the realm of *Atzilut* (emanation), the primordial, unrestricted light before *Tzimtzum*. What a gift to ascend this ladder of existential thought three times a day, culminating in the *Amidah*, when we stand in unity with the Creator of the Universe. Clearly this is not a time to make haste! Thankfully, in synagogues that speed through the other sections, there is at last a sense of peace for the *Amidah*. Bustling *shuls* go silent as the community enters *Atzilut*, beyond even the metaphysical. When in this deep communion, I try to imagine God's conversations with our patriarchs and matriarchs. This is the legacy of ultimate connection they made available to their progeny. It may seem like chutzpah for us to bask in God's glory and then make the various requests in our weekday *Sh'moneh Esrei*, but just like a parent is happy to give to a grateful child, so, too, is our Parent in Heaven delighted to give when we make requests and express heartfelt gratitude.

Back to our hiking analogy: after a delicious sandwich while enjoying the expansive view at the top of the mountain, now we have to go back down. Similarly, our *siddur* offers a gradual level-by-level descent to conclude the morning service, also featuring a *Kaddish* dividing each step. On most weekdays, we delve into the *Tachanun* service where we pray for forgiveness, like a mini-Yom Kippur to keep the soul whitewashed. Then, corresponding to the *P'sukei D'zimra* on the way up the hill, we have a second recitation of the *Ashrei* and the *Uva L'tziyon*. By saying the *Ashrei* twice in *Shacharit* and then once at the beginning of *Mincha,* we are able to fulfill the three-time daily requirement suggested by the Talmud to guarantee us a spot in *Olam Habah*, the World to Come. Finally, corresponding with the morning blessings back at the trailhead, we say the *Aleynu* and the Psalm of the Day, restating our *Asiya* action-based mission statement to use our efforts to bring our incomplete planet to a place of perfection. And then the next morning we do it again!

I finished writing this chapter on that scenic North Carolina deck while watching the setting sun ignite the distant hills of seven Southern states. Too soon my wife and I would leave this blessed Beech Mountain paradise and head to Ashville and Denver for the next leg of my tour. Back in L.A., I strived to retain a vision of that bucolic view, the clarity of the sapphire sky and the gift of dear, generous friends. At my humble home on Livonia Avenue, I may not have the magnificent mountains or extensive leisure time but God willing, thanks to my quaint morning ritual, I can still soar to dizzying heights in my daily ascent to the realms of *Atzilut* and beyond.

THE FOUR QUESTIONS

1. How can you make prayer a part of your morning routine?

2. What aspects of your life belong in the world of Asiyah (action) versus Yetzira (feeling/emotion)?

3. How can you better direct yourself to awareness of God's majestic Creation and to a deep communion with the divine in your personal prayer?

4. Describe breakthrough moments in prayer. How can you get back to that place of access?

Mincha, Mincha

♫ THROWIN' ME A LIFELINE ♫

joyjud.com/m/tml

You sent me on a journey through this world
To see what I might learn along the way
And You sent me down some darkened roads
To see if I could find the light of day

You kept Yourself from view
To see what conclusions
That a drowning person just might come to

Oh Lord, You're throwin' me a lifeline
Oh Lord, throwin' me a lifeline

Just when I was goin' under
And I thought I had no hope
You held out Your hand

You sent me all the riches in this world
To see how I might spend 'em on the way
And You sent me folks in desperate need
Whom I wouldn't give the time of day
You kept Yourself from view
To check on the memory
Of someone who thought they didn't need You

As a teenager, I remember exploring Ben Yehudah and Kikar Tziyon (Zion Square) in Jerusalem. Amidst the shops selling jewel-toned Bedouin clothing, shawarma and Judaica, the call of "*Mincha, Mincha*," rang out from the entrance of a small storefront *shul*. I would do my best to avoid the squat, elderly man with a thick Sephardic accent who beckoned in the doorway. God forbid I have my afternoon fun interrupted with fifteen minutes of boredom while pretending to pray. At that point in my life, I was aware of *Shacharit*, the morning service, which I avoided since I saw it as far too long and inconvenient. I was familiar with *Ma'ariv*, the evening service, from summers at Camp Ramah and occasional Friday nights at Sinai Temple. But *Mincha*? No, doing *Mincha* (the afternoon service) was a foreign concept to me, lost in the same wasteland that claimed Shavuot, *S'firat Ha'omer* and the "Three Weeks." If it was left out of our Conservative Hebrew school practice, it couldn't be something I needed to worry about.

Fast forward to my twenties. I hungered for more connection, as long as the rituals didn't take too long. I was careful to manage my balance of You-ish and Jew-ish: too much Judaism might make me a freak, but a short minimum daily requirement promised to hedge my bets, just in case this God thing was real. Over the next several years, wrapping *tefillin* in the mornings became a cherished habit that gave me the discipline to chew on those thorny Hebrew paragraphs until they were smooth like the worn black leather on my arm.

Mincha followed later. Much later. After all, who has the time mid-afternoon to stop the action to pray? Didn't we just say those same words in the morning? I'm a busy recording professional with clients and deadlines. I owe it to my customers to be focused on their music and not *shuckling* (swaying during prayer) in some hiding place.

Two factors inspired me to make *Mincha* a highlight of my day. The first is my limited attention span. Even an express *Shacharit* takes a long time whereas *Mincha* fits perfectly in a five to ten-minute window of opportunity. The other factor is the opportunity to consciously unplug from my work to plug into my relationship with God. After I received my BS in Business from the University of Colorado, I pondered continuing my education with a MBA. Several peers recommended I should get some work experience in my father's garment business and only then go back for an advanced degree. While the MBA curriculum wouldn't change, I would change, becoming better equipped to know what real world business challenges I might face. *Mincha* works the same way. We are already out on the test track of life. In the morning our day is theoretical, whereas by *Mincha*, we know exactly what we are up against. For me, this awareness creates more intense, deeply felt prayer.

Interrupting the workflow has its own celestial merit. *Pirkei Avot* (2:21) states we can't desist from the work at hand but we should not feel compelled to <u>finish</u> it. As Rabbi Joe Black sings, we must "leave a little bit undone." At our core, we are spiritual people who flourish when we include God in all endeavors. Taking a break before the sun goes down on our workday allows us to share our burden, invoking God's blessings with specific requests based on whatever we're going through.

When I have a Jewish client in the studio, if they are interested, I strive to make the *Mincha* service a teaching moment rather than a distraction. I set them up with a *kavanah* that includes seeking blessings for their families as well as the great success of their musical endeavors. I'm often told these holy breaks in the recording process are among the highlights of their overall experience.

Our daily prayer ritual reflects the contributions of each of our three forefathers. Avraham gave us the custom of *Shacharit* due to his early morning divine service. Yaakov gave us *Ma'ariv* thanks to the dramatic midnight revelation of a ladder stretching up to heaven. We have Yitzchak to thank for *Mincha*. He is described as *lasuach baderech* (meditating in the field) just before sunset when his *bashert* (destined one) Rivkah gets a glimpse of him for the first time. Likely, this thirty-something young man was *davening* passionately to merit a good wife. It's no wonder that we too are "in the field" when we daven *Mincha*, either in the agricultural sense toiling the ground by the "sweat of our brow" (*B'reishit* 3:19) or in whatever "field" we are engaged.

Yitzchak's quintessential quality was *gevurah* (strength/discipline). This helps to explain his connection with *Mincha* since it requires supernal commitment to break away from one's workday. Once we get the ball rolling it's hard to stop. *Halacha* demands we do *Shacharit* before we eat breakfast, which I believe is a great tactic to make sure we "wrap up" before we get wrapped up in our day. Once we get started in our eating-commuting-working routine, it's easy to forget matters of the spirit. *Mincha*, on the other hand typically interrupts the daily flow since we must do it before the sky gets dark. Hopefully that interruption isn't so stark as we transition from conducting a holy business life into holy prayer. Ideally we find a *minyan* of like-minded people, but if that's not possible, all one needs is a quiet place and a *siddur*.

Mincha has three primary facets: *Ashrei,* a prayer where we get in touch with gratitude, the *Amidah,* where we ask for whatever we need, and then the *Aleynu,* where we conclude by praying for God's oneness and the redemption of the world. For the advanced *davener,* a short *Tachanun* is also included before the *Aleynu*. One might think we have already praised God so much in the morning that no more praise is needed, but as we discussed, praise is an essential appetizer to the prayer experience. The Artscroll prayer book asks the reader to "concentrate intently" during one particular line of the *Ashrei*: "*Poteyach et yadecha…*" This single sentence sets us up for an "aha moment." God's "open hand satisfies the desire of every living thing." When I'm hustling midday for gigs, when I'm feeling jealous of peers, worried about cash flow, I read this passage and feel comfort. My portion is my portion; God gives me exactly what I need. That realization, my friends, is reason enough to pray *Mincha*.

Another feature of "*Poteyach et yadecha*" is the idea God satisfies the desire of those with "*chai ratzon*," a will that is <u>alive</u>. So much of our day is spent in repetitive tasks and drudgery. We take the same way to work, eat the same lunch and see the same faces. Our fire is slowly extinguished by the repetition of the "daily grind," our ennui evolves into hopelessness. This passage teaches we must take responsibility for keeping our will alive. Only <u>we</u> can turn things around and attract *shefa* (abundance) into our lives. Take a different way to work, get together with old friends, rediscover activities you enjoy, do something physical rather than remaining passive in front of a TV screen or a Facebook feed. Being truly alive requires more than food, work and an occasional jaunt on a treadmill.

While writing this chapter, I had a pair of powerful moments I'd like to share. One instance occurred while skiing with my boys in Vail, CO. After my gig in Denver, we drove two hours to enjoy a few days in this unparalleled ski paradise. On our last day on the hill, I was hopeful to meet up with one of my college buddies, Brian, who had just moved to the area. Unfortunately, my iPhone kept freezing up and we were unable to get in touch. Mid-afternoon, I was doing laps with my kids on one of our favorite runs, Grand Review, in the remote Blue Sky Basin of Vail's famed Back Bowls. My son Max is quite the kamikaze and was flying right behind me when he caught air off of a lip. He didn't notice the diminutive middle-aged woman cruising next to him. He inadvertently tackled her midair and they tumbled together several times. I slammed on the brakes, kicked off my skis and ran up the hill in a panic. The woman's friend screamed at me to call ski patrol and alert her ski partners back at the chairlift. When I confirmed Max was OK, I had him wait with her and exchange information. Jesse and I rushed down in search of the woman's compatriots. We didn't find them but by the time we returned, ski patrol was already loading the poor pummeled woman in a toboggan. Thankfully, she was only shaken up but decided to get checked out as a precaution. Who was waiting with Max? My college friend Brian, the guy I was looking for. Remarkably, it was Brian's ski partner who my son mowed down. This was not how we hoped to connect—but this "large world, well managed" moment gave us all a serious jolt of wonderment. Thank God, the woman was fine and Max escaped with a bruised leg and an important lesson to look before he leaps.

Soon thereafter, following a Shabbaton and youth concert for the largest Conservative synagogue in North America, Beth Tzedec, Toronto, I flew directly to Cabo San Lucas to deliver a Tu Bish'vat jam for Chabad of Cabo. Yes, it was a decadent week! My wife and daughter flew down from L.A. to join me for some fun in the sun and thankfully, Chabad kept us well fed with delicious kosher meals delivered to our hotel. The last day, I opted to dive in the nearby city of La Paz so I could experience a rare, seasonal treat: swimming with the largest fish in the sea, the whale shark. Jacques Cousteau calls the Gulf of California "the world's aquarium." Local dive boats charge around $200 a person for this trip but if one is equipped with gear, panga (small fishing boat) captains will do it for $20.

I expected the Sea of Cortez to be more placid than the Pacific side of the peninsula, but once past the breakwater, we were tossed about by whitecap-ridden swells. After about forty minutes of turbulent travel, the panga captain announced to the dozen Mexican tourists onboard that it was time to suit up. I noticed I was the only one getting ready. "What?" I stammered, "You folks aren't getting in?" "*Estas loco?*" they replied. They weren't about to jump in the water with thirty-foot plus creatures lurking about the depths. When a vast grey shadow longer than our boat cruised by, the captain yelled, "Now!" I plunged into the sea and swam towards the white polka-dotted hide of the leviathan. The enormous shark was ambling by at the exact pace of my panicked strokes. I travelled alongside for nearly twenty minutes, only a few feet away from this beautiful beast. I steered clear of both the mouth, which could have swallowed a Smart Car and the tail, which could have smacked me unconscious. When I was out of steam, I flagged down the vessel to rescue me. This exhilarating experiment was repeated another three times as we trolled the area.

My fourth dive was utterly transformative. I was now more relaxed, as relaxed as one could be swimming alone with a sea monster. At least now I was calm enough to film the adventure with my GoPro camera, whereas previously I was too freaked out to remember to breathe. At one point, the shark I was chasing met up with a fellow giant and they affectionately rubbed heads against one another. For the first time, I was able to just enjoy the scene without having to frantically keep up. I felt an uncanny sense of union with these peaceful creatures and immense gratitude to Hashem for the opportunity. When I flipped onto the safety of the deck, I looked back to bid farewell to my new friend. Just then, the larger shark surfaced, rolled on its side and WAVED its six-foot long pectoral fin at us. And not just once—repeatedly! I'm confident this was a deliberate wink from the Creator of the Universe, Who *sheps nachas* when we get a kick out of Creation. My response was to *daven* a misty-eyed *Mincha* upon returning to shore. How can I not concretize "large world, well managed" moments with definitive thanks?

I often hear friends complain that organized religion turns them off. They are disheartened by synagogue dues and politics, can't relate to clergy or don't feel the need to affiliate. Well, *Mincha* offers a spiritual high and requires only a quiet place to concentrate. Could there be a better way of spending a short afternoon break than connecting with our Creator, analyzing our lives, expressing thanks and keeping our precious will alive? Now, whenever I see the setting sun, I hear that clarion call of "*Mincha, Mincha*" and joyfully respond with gratitude for another chance to dance with my Partner in Heaven.

THE FOUR QUESTIONS

1. How might your personal needs vary from morning to afternoon?

2. How can you fit in a break during work to connect to God?

3. Do you have a sacred space in your home or work environment to pray?

4. What are specific areas you need God's help?

Ma'ariv: Shuckling on the Dock of the Bay

♫ LIFT MY EYES ♫

joyjud.com/m/lme

It's been a long time since I've said I love You
It's been a while since I've said anything at all
Captive in a fortress of my choosing
And it's time that I tore down the wall

Lift my eyes to see the light within the darkness
Lift my spirit to appreciate Your hand
Lift my eyes to see the answers to the questions
I don't understand

It's been a long time since I've kept a promise
It's been a while since I have had a single goal
All my dreams are being held for ransom
Cause I cannot find the self-control

Lift my eyes to see the truth for the illusion
Lift my heart to see the good inside the pain
Lift my eyes to see the reason for Your wishes
That I can't explain

For four years I led the High Holiday services for a wonderful beachside congregation, Temple Emanuel of Virginia Beach. Each time, I brought my family and we used the period between Rosh Hashana and Yom Kippur to explore the region, particularly a special aquatic retreat, Lake Anna. Lake Anna was formed in the early 1970s to cool a nuclear power plant. Nearly 13,000 acres were flooded, creating hundreds of miles of lakefront property in the middle of an old growth forest.

The silver lining on this ecological stormcloud was the creation of a ski lake of unprecedented access and "glass." We are lucky to have incredibly generous friends with a beautiful home boasting its own dock equipped with a ski boat and jet ski. They live at the far end of one of the fingers of the vast lake, in a setting of sublime peace and stillness. Just arriving at this slice of paradise is enough to get me breathing again. I make every effort to spend as much time outside as possible, enjoying the camaraderie of my athletic family during motorized water sports, reading on the dock's cabana and listening to the cadences of songbirds in the forest canopy.

Allow me to describe a memorable *Ma'ariv* (evening prayer) in this special place, an experience I will reference the rest of my life.

Ma'ariv was the last service added to my daily regimen. I used the excuse that the Talmud classifies the evening prayer as optional. Sure, there are opinions that it's mandatory, but for years I took the easy way out. Eventually I learned to tame my own *yetzer harah* (evil inclination) with a specific technique: usually, just after dinner with my family, I change into my PJ's and well-worn Acorn slippers. If I slip into something more comfortable before I pray the evening prayer, well, it's likely that it's not going to happen. Jewish law stipulates one must wear honorable clothing when *davening* and not threadbare nightwear. Therefore, my technique to ensure I commit to *Ma'ariv* is to do it <u>before</u> I get too comfortable. Of course, finding a *minyan* is always the best way to go.

Ma'ariv is a fairly simple service. It features a few short blessings before and after the *Sh'ma*, the *Amidah* and then *Aleynu*. In the evening service, the *Amidah* isn't repeated by the cantor, so it streamlines the experience. *Ma'ariv* can be easily memorized and takes less than ten minutes. Reflecting a time before twenty-four-hour productivity and incandescent light, the prayers describe trepidation in the face of darkness, God's guiding the passage of day into night and supervising the changing of seasons. Built into the siddur is the opportunity to consciously fulfill two nightly Torah mitzvot, namely, the evening recitation of the *Sh'ma* and remembrance of the Exodus. We get a chance to assess the day gone by and infuse the coming day with the blessings of the *Amidah*.

After an active afternoon on the lake, my family was relaxing in the living room discussing waterski triumphs and mishaps. We sang spontaneously while playing Canasta and Settlers of Catan and then, much to my family's chagrin, I repeatedly rehearsed the Yom Kippur services. When everyone went to sleep, I ventured down the uneven steps to the water's edge to ponder the stars and pray the evening service. On this particular night, a sliver of the new *Tishrei* moon appeared and disappeared amidst the stratus clouds high above. The motionless ink-black water stretched to the horizon. I was enveloped in the clamorous cacophony of countless crickets and surprised by the occasional splash of leaping lake trout. I closed my eyes and quietly recited the passages before and after the *Sh'ma*, then walked to the edge of the dock to engage in the *Sh'moneh Esrei*. As I whispered the sacred words, I searched the outlines of the gently swaying trees and felt them beckoning me upward. Suddenly, a warm gust of wind welled up behind me and jostled the baritone tubular bells of the dockside wind chime. A chill rose from my feet to the top of my head and I felt like I was about to lift off the dock. Strange as it may sound, I was ready to fly, to accept the gift of Heavenly wings.

I realized at that moment I was no longer "just praying." The words silently ushering from my lips were actually transforming the world. These were not idle recitations of the official thirteen paragraphs of weekday requests. Instead, I felt with certainty I was acting as God's partner in the establishment of these realities. I was creating health and healing. I was contributing to a year of blessing. I was ushering those in exile to the Promised Land, rebuilding Jerusalem and assisting with the birth of the Messianic Age. There was no distinction between my efforts and God's efforts to shape history. My will was inseparable from the divine will; I felt enormously powerful and yet pragmatically humble. By the time I got to the concluding prayer, *Aleynu*, I was actively creating the possibility of a world where all nations proclaim God's unified name.

At that moment, maybe for the first time, prayer made perfect sense…finally!

The gift of Jewish prayer is a vehicle for radical transformation with an impact on a global scale. It is not just an ancient rabbinic wish list we repeat to badger God into action. Prayer is the very instigator of Heavenly action in our material realm. The transformative power of the human soul is unlimited by space and time. Even though I am surrounded by darkness in the vast forest of Central Virginia or wherever I am, I can participate fully in the formation of a peaceful, loving planet, impacting my family, America, Israel, the entire world. Just as God is everywhere, I am everywhere. My pure soul, my *b'tzelem Elokim* (in God's image) spark of divinity makes me immortal and omnipresent, at least for those few minutes a day I choose to connect.

After *davening* I sprawled out on the papa-san chair to ponder the implications of this experience. All the pieces of our vast heritage were falling into place. I could perceive the priceless value of walking the path of *halacha*, studying Torah, observing the commandments, keeping kosher, committing acts of loving-kindness. Powerful prayer requires the unification of our physical being with the ephemeral, utilizing the eternal tool of the mitzvot. Only with this material-spiritual connection are we able to stand with God in the Heights and impact world history.

As I stared out into the vastness of the Milky Way, I silently wondered, *how can I ascend to this exalted place again? How can I launch spiritually when I'm not relaxed on vacation but instead burdened with worry and deadlines in cement-laden Los Angeles? How can I exude this passion when I'm leading a congregation or conducting a Shabbaton? How can I share this insight with my children?*

On that magical night, I believe I was able to soar due to a rare combination of events: the sensational setting satiated my senses, allowing for unabashed humility within God's breathtaking natural world. Spending quality time with my family gave me that degree of pleasure best described as *nachas*. I was entirely mindful, with no deadlines or agendas. Most importantly, I was able to surpass feelings of inferiority or insignificance and stand erect, confident and fulfilled. Big city life can beat us down. We succumb to a subliminal mantra: *I'm not good enough, I'm an imposter, I'm terrified of failing.* How can we serve as God's heroic partners when we are exhausted, demoralized and anxious most of our waking hours? After we bend our knees when saying *Baruch* and bow at *Atah*, the sages advise us to <u>stand upright</u> in our full potential when we utter the word, "*Adonai.*" The Almighty is desperate for us to perceive our own power, to claim our vast birthright and launch into action. Once we find our own "Letter in the Torah," we are truly invincible.

This prayer victory transpired during the period between Rosh Hashana and Yom Kippur known as *Aseret Y'mei T'shuva*, the ten days of return. That night I closed my eyes and whispered each delicious word of the *Amidah* with special care, taking my time so I wouldn't skip the unique seasonal insertions. These amendments force us to ramp up the *kavanah* (focus) so we don't miss any of them. The penalty for omitting certain passages is repeating the whole lengthy prayer! There is something innately purifying about the High Holiday period, especially when entering it with the right intentions and an open heart. Perhaps I lifted off the dock spiritually because I was riding this ten-day free gift of enhanced holiness and was taking the time to enjoy its fruits.

Living in the present is not just for vacations. It is difficult for temporally marooned mortals to contemplate God's timeless realm. Our only access point is the here and now. Transformative prayer cannot occur when mired in the past or obsessing about an uncertain future. God's real "present" to us is the opportunity to live passionately in the moment.

For most of us, this requires slowing WAY down. Patience, patience! For that half hour in the morning or the ten minutes each for *Mincha* and *Ma'ariv*, one must start with deep breathing, meditation or whatever it takes to bring the maddening internal dialogue to a halt. Certain Chassidic masters would meditate for an hour before opening the *siddur*. The High Holidays allow us to initiate our year with added opportunties to pray and feel inspiration from clergy. Hopefully we can capture enough of this holy energy to bring here-and-now intention into our entire year.

I have gained profound appreciation for *Ma'ariv*. The potential of true *avodah* (divine service) like that night on the lake has given me renewed enthusiasm for this highly repetitive act and the impetus to share my discovery with others. Each time I pray, I challenge myself to bring a little more joy, a little more focus to the enormous task at hand. I'm incentivized to better understand every nuance of the Hebrew and the genius of the *siddur's* composition.

When I take my three steps back for the *Amidah*, I pause to silence my inner maelstrom and create a space for God's Presence. And then, when ready, I take three humble steps forward and stand in *Tadasana*, mountain pose, self-assured of my personal power. I enter a realm of timelessness and bask in Technicolor divinity. When my *tefillah* is complete, I bow in sincere gratitude and retreat three steps back to my earthly plane.

Back in L.A., I catch myself rushing through my prayers and consciously pause to breathe in the memory of *shuckling* on the dock of the bay, under the canopy of stars above the Virginia forest. I shift from "lip service" to mindfulness, from passivity to impassioned action. King Solomon states in *Mishley* (Proverbs 20:27), "The soul of man is a lamp of God." Like a flame strains heavenward, our soul aches for *d'veykut* (connection) with God, and our light shines brightest in the depth of night. We are God's candlelight! The founder of Chabad, Rabbi Schneur Zalman of Liadi (1745-1812) said, "A little bit of light dispels a lot of darkness." *Ma'ariv* gives each of us the opportunity to end our day with joy and illuminate the universe.

THE FOUR QUESTIONS

1. How can you make the time to review the day that just ended?

2. Why is the evening an ideal time to intertwine your will with God's will?

3. How do you think it would feel if you instituted a thrice-daily practice of thanking God, praising God, and asking God for what you and the world need?

4. What can you do bring more enthusiasm to your prayers, especially when you're tired at night?

PART FOUR

Sacred Stuff: Putting the "Rich" in Rituals and Ritual Objects

This section is dedicated by
BRIAN AND ROBIN KETTLER

Thank you, Sam, for your friendship. We are awed by the boundless energy and light you bring to our faith and the multitude of lives you touch. You help all of us "Keep the Dream Alive." It's a blessing and privilege to have you in our lives.

IN THIS SECTION:

Mezuzah: Knockin' on Heaven's Door 101

Kippah: Skullcandy 105

Tallit: Life on the Fringe...110

Tefillin: Strapping Up 114

More Precious Than Pearls: An Inside View of "Womens'"
Rituals... 119

OVERVIEW

Jewish ritual objects are lightning rods, earthbound terminals for heavenly inspiration. Whereas our prayers often address global concerns, ritual objects highlight the fine details of our Joy of Judaism. Anyone who has visited a Jewish museum with a priceless Judaica collection can testify to the vast array of wildly creative Torah crowns, spiceboxes, *menorahs*, *etrog* holders and candlesticks. We give glory to the Creator and sanctify our lives by enhancing our simple observance with sublime aesthetic beauty. *Hidur* mitzvah, or beautifying a commandment, is the legacy of Betzalel, the biblical artisan who expertly fashioned the Temple implements. We extend this tradition to our homes and houses of worship. From the spectacular old-world *shuls* of Eastern Europe to ultramodern architectural masterpieces in North America, a beautiful prayer space uplifts the congregation and is a source of tremendous pride for the community.

One year I performed a concert in the only synagogue ever designed by Frank Lloyd Wright, in Elkins Park, PA. This massive pyramidal "ritual object" was Wright's attempt to emulate both "a luminous Mount Sinai" and the original *Mishkan*, the Tent of Meeting. It is perhaps the ultimate example of *hidur* mitzvah; the cavernous acoustics combine with eye-candy angles, textures and light to create a sense of humility and transcendence. What a gift to fill this room with music! An amusing footnote to my exploration of this legendary edifice: no expense was spared in the construction and yet, upon completion, the roof leaked and then in warmer weather, chaos ensued when the glue binding the ceiling panels melted. I realized that the foibles of this building prove my theory: the beauty of ritual objects is inversely proportional to their practicality.

This section is by no means exhaustive; it focuses on those ritual objects with which I personally interact on a daily basis. Since *kippah, tallit* and *tefillin* are traditionally the realm of men, I opted to conclude with a chapter featuring rituals commonly associated with women. And since I'm not the ideal gender to pontificate on those particular mitzvot, I took the initiative to interview my wise and capable wife, Shira. I hope you will learn to see sacred objects in a new light and perhaps incorporate them into your own life.

Pesach • Tefillin • Shabbat • Community • Torah • Prophets • Sigun • Pesach • Teshuva • Wedding
Sanctity • Holiness • Emunah • Diaspora • Brit Milah • Simcha • Halacha • Birkhon • Holiday
...Tallit • Israel • Mikvah • Prayer • Mishan for Tefillin • Shabbat • Community • Torah • Prophets
...• Pesach • Teshuva • Wedding • Spirituality • Holiness • Emunah • Diaspora • Brit Milah
...• Halacha • Diaspora • Birkhon • Mikvah • Bar Mitzvah • Israel • Mikvah • Sigun • Wedding
...• Shabbat • Community • Torah • Prophets • Sigun • Pesach • Teshuva • Wedding • Spirituality

Mezuzah:
Knockin' on
Heaven's Door

♬ MEZUZAH ♬

joyjud.com/m/mzz

Fifteenth night of Nissan	Armies of our enemies
Not a sound could be heard	Marching door to door
At the stroke of midnight God fulfilled his word	Knew the simple symbol they were looking for
Blood on the doorpost	But unafraid and undeterred
Soon parchment would replace	We set that holy scroll
Making clear this home's a holy space	On the doorpost we reveal our soul
Mezuzah, mezuzah	I reach for you in times of joy
Greets me on the wall	When my cup is full
Protecting and connecting all the family	When laughter fills my soul
Mezuzah, mezuzah	I reach for you when I can't go on
I hear your silent call	You give me hope, help me cope
Waiting patiently for the next time I reach for you	When all my strength is gone

J uly 8th was a deliciously brisk, sunny day in Vancouver, Canada. Our family
commemorated Shira's birthday with a mountain bike adventure through one of the
most gorgeous urban refuges on the globe, Stanley Park. As we careened down the
bike paths, I did my best to capture the highlights with my handy Canon pocket camera.
Regretfully, I attempted the "stupid dad trick" of shooting video while riding. At considerable
speed. In the process, I just barely grabbed the front brake lever by accident and my finely
tuned hybrid bike stopped on a dime, flipping me over the handlebars and onto the pavement.
I broke the fall with my hands and cut up one of my palms pretty badly. Embarrassed by all
the attention, I quickly dusted myself off and got back on the bike, soon catching up to my
kids who were oblivious to my aerial dexterity.

Thankfully, a nearby lifeguard patched up my wound and I was able to complete
this dream ride with my family. Later that afternoon we embarked on a six-mile hike into
the Canadian Rockies beginning with the crossing of the famous Lynn Canyon suspension

bridge. This well-worn trail accessed a majestic coniferous forest of the deepest green and a jewel-like chain of pristine, cobalt-blue lakes. My wrist started to throb a few miles into the wilderness. I figured I was letting too much blood get to the area because I was hiking with my arms hanging down. I relieved much of the discomfort by fashioning a sling out of one of my kids' sweatshirts. Evidently I had injured myself worse than I had initially suspected.

Back in Downtown Vancouver, my wrist was now double the size and super sensitive to touch. Not a good thing for this piano player. My kids accompanied me to an emergency room where we waited with a sad variety of patients with problems much worse than mine. At one point I grew exasperated and walked over to the window to get an update. The cheery attendant reported that I would have at least a three-hour wait, longer than that to get an x-ray, and be charged a minimum of $800 that may or may not be covered by my U.S. insurance. All this and Shabbat was coming in an hour. I opted to bail on the emergency idea, bought a sling and a wrist brace at a drug store and returned to our well-appointed 33rd floor rental penthouse (yeah Craigslist!).

We enjoyed an elegant Shabbat/birthday dinner over the lights of Vancouver. I was able to ignore my swollen wrist thanks to three Advils and fine Canadian ale. The next morning, we strolled over to the local Chabad where a standing-room-only crowd gathered for services. I led a spirited *Mussaf* (the additional service on Sabbath and holidays) followed by a hearty lunch, during which I had the chance to shmooze with a few local doctors. All of them told me to get an x-ray. Several others told me to check my *mezuzot* (parchment affixed to the doorways of Jewish homes). The x-ray I understood. But check my *mezuzot*? That seems to be textbook Chassidic advice for preventing mishaps.

After returning from our inspiring Canada/Alaska cruise adventure I kept thinking, *maybe I should check those mezuzot.* Then I'd reason, *what could have gone wrong with them? They are just hanging there and no one is messing with them!* In the meantime, our local hand and wrist specialist fashioned a removable cast to immobilize the hairline fracture where the wrist bone meets the thumb. This allowed me to play my gigs over the month but isolate the area the rest of the time. I was well on the mend but couldn't shake that superstitious *mezuzah* mantra. One morning, I couldn't stand it anymore. I counted twenty *mezuzot* in our house, including my recording studio, and asked one of my neighborhood *sofrim* (scribes) for an estimate to check them. He replied that I could expect a $200 house call plus $7 per mezuzah, plus repairs if needed, plus new parchments if there were irreparable issues. Thankfully, the new rabbi at the *shteibl* (small *shul*) down the street is also a *sofer* and was willing to do it without the house call fee. OK…you got a deal!

The whole exercise of putting up *mezuzot* in our home came into question. Why do we bother affixing parchment with ancient hieroglyphics to our every entrance (other than closets or bathrooms)? What has motivated Jews over the course of history to do so at their peril, knowing anti-Semites are on the prowl? Why would God command such a strange thing? Why do we mention the mitzvah to affix a *mezuzah* when we say the *Sh'ma* twice a day? What does that little scroll have to do with freedom? First I'll tell you what happened and then I'll share the answers I discovered.

This gentle, unassuming rabbi gingerly took down every single *mezuzah* in our home, ensuring he kept the *batim* (housing) and the *klafim* (scrolls) together. He sat at a desk in my studio and scrutinized every detail with a powerful magnifying glass. Seven of the twenty were *posul* (not fit for use). The two on our front and back doors had weathered to the point where they were unreadable. Many of the others had worn out or were improperly formed in the first place, rendering them useless. Some were reparable—he was able to scrape away ink where letters were touching so that they could be put back into service. One might think: *this guy just wants to sell more mezuzot!* But he went to great pains to demonstrate why each was deficient and explained the particular *halachot* (laws) specifying which flaws couldn't be repaired. Let the buyer beware…only buy scrolls from a certified scribe or reputable store.

The total bill came to $450. Ouch. Seven new scrolls, the inspection fee and some new waterproof *batim* for the outside doors. It was money well spent, however, because as soon as he hung the final *mezuzah,* I felt a surreal sense of light and healing pervade our home. I just knew everything was going to be OK. Kosher *mezuzot* are an intangible but invaluable asset to any home. Doing this mitzvah right really does make a difference. A further sign I did the right thing: I booked three gigs that week!

Our sages insist a *mezuzah* is not an amulet. The magic of hanging this parchment is the same as fulfilling any mitzvah—the power of enhancing one's connection with the Commander-in-Chief. However, some textual sources elucidate the concept of divine protection. King David writes, "God will guard your going and coming for all time," a hint towards the efficacy of the *mezuzah.* The Talmud mentions that the *mezuzah* serves as a conduit for blessings for the home and its inhabitants. I believe *mezuzot* heighten our awareness that a home has the capacity for holiness. It's more than just a place to hang our hat. The simple act of reaching to kiss a *mezuzah* when passing through a gateway has a powerful effect on one's consciousness. It's like our dwellings wear *tefillin.*

All this doorpost drama was unfolding during the Torah portion of *Shoftim.* It opens with the famous line, "Judges and officers shall you appoint in your gates (*D'varim* 16:18)." Emphasizing the establishment of judicial systems is one of the great contributions of the Jewish People to the world. However, a certain grammatical anomaly begs inspection: "YOUR gates" is in the singular, not plural. In other words, we have to appoint judges and officers in our <u>personal</u> gates. Renowned kabbalist Rabbi Chaim Vital (1543-1620) suggests these gates refer to our sensory organs: sight, hearing, taste, touch, smell. Just like a *mezuzah* offers protection at the entrance to any given room, we must establish spiritual guardians at the sources of input into our lives. We live in an age of 24/7 bombardment of the senses—it is more relevant than ever to monitor the input. How much news do I need to hear? Do I need to see every blockbuster movie? What dosage of violence, sex, gossip is appropriate? Is this something I should eat? Is this someone I should touch? Clearly, this passage in *Shoftim* is sending us a much-needed prescription for spiritual living.

A Chassidic story comes to mind: A troubled chassid approached his rabbi, stating he couldn't keep sexual thoughts off his mind. He felt helpless and despondent, unable to focus on his learning and prayer. The rabbi recommended he visit a certain home at the edge of the town and ask to speak to the owner. The chassid dutifully walked the distance and knocked on the door several times. When no one answered, he sat down and waited. Eventually he fell asleep and was awakened the next morning when the man inside finally opened the door. The chassid inquired, "How could you have left me out here all night?" The man replied, "I chose not to let you in." The chassid was furious and reported the incident to his rabbi who replied, "The power is in our hands to decide what or who comes in or out."

One further insight: The Torah dictates we must free slaves in the *sh'mitah* (sabbatical) year. A slave preferring to stay with his host family is taken to a doorpost and his ear is pierced with an awl. This symbolizes his having relinquished his right to autonomy, wounding him in the very organ that heard the imperative for liberty at Mt. Sinai. Interestingly, it was the doorpost on which we were commanded to sprinkle lamb's blood so the angel of death would "pass over" our homes during the final plague in Egypt. Affixing parchment on our doorpost alludes to the gift of freedom. By electing to fulfill God's will and display a *mezuzah*, regardless of what the neighbors think about our strange customs, we are walking in the shoes of generations who made the choice to cling to the Almighty.

Therefore, our communal love of this mitzvah in spite of possible danger makes sense. Yes, the *mezuzah* on the door reveals our faith to our enemies. Rather than serve as our undoing, however, it is the very reason we have freedom, the essence of our survival, the source of our protection over the millennia. No wonder we are commanded to repeat this *mezuzah* mitzvah orally twice a day in the *Sh'ma*. We stand as proud witnesses to God's presence in history. Responding to the divine imperative to guard and sanctify our physical and spiritual gates is the key to our success as individuals and as a nation. Appropriating the precious gift of freedom to the kindness of our Creator is the ideal *kavanah* (focus) each time that we kiss a *mezuzah*.

When my brothers and I became observant, we convinced our parents to affix *mezuzot* in all the rooms of their house, not just the front door. They did so at great expense—they had a rustic, ranch-style home they eventually sold to actor Dustin Hoffman. We also had to convince them to leave the *mezuzot* up when they moved out. *Halacha* dictates if one is selling to a Jew, any *mezuzot* must be left on the doorposts. My folks weren't terribly happy about leaving this small fortune in parchment for Mr. Hoffman, but were committed to doing the right thing. I'm confident their reward in *Shamayim* (Heaven) far exceeds the money they spent for new scrolls.

I'm not sure if it was due to our new certified-kosher *mezuzot,* but God slowly but surely returned my wrist to full function. I marveled at the clean new skin where an open wound once festered. Before long, I was back to hammering my left hand octaves and carrying my suitcases. I even got back on my bike and yes, I avoid the temptation to film as I ride.

THE FOUR QUESTIONS

1. Do you have *mezuzot* on all your doorposts? Why or why not?

2. How does seeing a *mezuzah* in your home bring holiness into your life?

3. What input do you need to prevent from entering your "personal gates?"

4. How are you maximizing your God-given freedom?

Tefillin • Shabbat • Community • Torah • Prophets • Nigun • Pesach • Teshuva • Wedding
tuality • Holiness • Emunah • Diaspora • Brit Milah • Simcha • Halacha • Brachot • Holidays •
ah • Tefila • Israel • Mikvah • Prayer • Moshiach • Tefillin • Shabbat • Community • Torah • Prophe
gun • Health • Teshuva • Weddings • Spirituality • Holiness • Emunah • Diaspora • Brit Milah
• Pesach • Brachot • all Rides • Bar Mitzvah • Tefila • Israel • Mikvah • Prayer • Moshiach
Shabbat • Community • Torah • Prophets • Nigun • Pesach • Teshuva • Wedding • Spiritu

Kippah:
Skullcandy

♫ LEARNIN' MACHINE ♫

joyjud.com/m/lnm

God only knows if I will ever get my fill
I just keep comin' back for more
Just the other night when everybody was asleep
I was goin' till a quarter to four

I can't get enough
I've been working on my attitude
This is heavy stuff, but I'm ready
'Cause I'm a learnin', a learnin' machine

A pasuk of the Torah or three blats of Gemara

You can have it your own way
Singin' out Tehillim while layin' your tefillin
It is guaranteed to make your day

Try the trope of the Megillah
Or the nusach of tefillah
You will never know it all

Till you're ready for Kabbalah
You can learn to make Havdalah
All g'dolim started out small

Someone once asked how my skullcap stays put on my head. I jokingly replied, "Peer pressure." Wearing a *yarmulke* (pronounced ya-ma-keh, otherwise known as a skullcap or *kippah*) 24/7 is something I said I would never do. My brother Yom Tov started wearing a *kippah* full time before I did. He returned from his first year in yeshiva with long, curly hair and a funky, oversized knit *kippah* on his head. I remember our conversation clearly: we were riding mountain bikes in the Southern California desert and as we flew down the sandy trail, we managed to converse while avoiding the cacti lurking around every bend. I recall shouting, "I will NEVER wear a *yarmulke* all the time!"

I should have known better than to use the word "never." During my month as a student at Brandeis Collegiate Institute, Dennis Prager quoted German philosopher Franz Rosenzweig as preferring the phrase, "Not yet." I repeat this advice whenever I hear a fellow Jew say, "I will never _____!" (Fill in the blank: keep Shabbat, keep kosher, set foot in that synagogue, etc.). "Not yet" implies an openness to growth, to new possibilities, for example, "I don't keep kosher, <u>yet</u>." At that point, I had no interest in being identified as a Jew everywhere I went. While I was proud to divulge my Jewish identity, to be singled out or even targeted before someone even knew my name…no way!

All that changed when I discovered a community in L.A. where I could celebrate Judaism on a full-time basis. It's like the Dr. Seuss's beloved book about the Sneetches who had "stars upon thars." Upon moving to Pico-Robertson, our beloved *shtetl* in the middle of town, I was surrounded by skullcap-festooned men of all stripes. Not that I took on the custom to fit in; now I had living examples of young guys like me who were proud of their heritage and ready to take on whatever challenges the rabbis sent their way. I was learning to perceive the world through spiritual lenses and for the first time I discerned the "Yids with the lids" were the real players.

Wearing this six-inch circle on my head has fringe benefits. It serves as a unique conversation starter. I can't go long without someone approaching me and "outing" himself as a member of the tribe, often telling me about every Jewish experience since his Bar Mitzvah. I patiently field rounds of "twenty questions" by Jew-loving gentiles. I get grabbed for a *minyan* in places like the airport, Disneyland and movie theaters. Germans have approached me to apologize for their people's actions during the Holocaust. Some folks are reverent, some stare. Most importantly, a *yarmulke* forces full-time *menschy* behavior. God forbid someone see a *Yid* cut in line, utter a curse word or order *treif* food. I even drive more nicely now. Tempting as it may be, I can't flip someone off and risk desecrating God's name when it's obvious I'm a Jew.

The origins of the *kippah* are ancient and convoluted. I always thought Jews adopted the custom from Roman slaves because they, too, wanted to demonstrate servitude to a Master. According to Rambam, one must wear a head covering when praying, but he doesn't mention a full-time requirement. By the seventeenth century it became *halachically* mandated as a way to distinguish Jews from non-Jews and to serve as a *Kiddush Hashem*, bringing honor to God's name. The Talmud clarifies that single men of the era didn't wear *kippot*. I will refrain from learning this passage with my unmarried sons.

Nowadays the general opinion in Orthodox circles is that guys aren't supposed to walk more than *daled amot* (six feet) without a skullcap. It should be wide enough to cover one's fist. That's right, bigger hands mean a bigger *kippah*…size does matter. One's *kippah* of choice reveals something about political leanings and levels of observance. Those uncomfortable wearing it at work or reluctant to display religious trappings have *heterim* (rabbinic leniencies) on which they can rely. The Vilna Gaon even permits making a *b'racha* (blessing) without one. When Conservative Jews put one on it's usually for prayer, study and eating, and Reform Jews tend to wear them only in the synagogue, if at all. Wearing a *kippah* is a beautiful, brave custom to take on but there's plenty of wiggle room while figuring out how it fits into one's life.

I've never pushed wearing a *kippah* full time on anyone but my children. These days, I'm becoming more vocal in my advocacy. Increasingly, Jews are villified both on the right and the left. To be perceived as an upstanding Member of the Tribe is more important than ever. It's harder to hate when one has personal interaction with the hated. Being conspicuous defuses the situation, creating connections with both Jews and gentiles. I've been to concerts or other social events where I've gotten a stinkeye from racists. My reaction is to get in their face, introduce myself, tell a joke or buy them a drink. No matter how scary they look. I may not make Jew-lovers out of them, but I am one less Hebrew they hate and hopefully, a living example of peacefulness and generosity. A friend wrote about the Jews of South Africa during the end of Apartheid; she realized we were hated by black revolutionaries <u>and</u> the white Afrikaners. I was grateful to be ten thousand miles away from that nightmare. Now I fear this irrational, ancient scourge is reawakening in global society—surely in the Arab world but also in Europe and beyond. The United States may be founded on principles of religious freedom, but when leaders of the both Women's March <u>and</u> the Aryan Nations want the world *Judenrein*, I say, let's speak up, show up and be counted.

My oldest son's Bar Mitzvah portion was *Tetzaveh* (*Sh'mot* 27:30-30:10), which goes into great depths describing the accouterments of the priests. It was a perfect match for young Max who has been concerned about his style since he was two years old. From our study together, I gleaned that our external appearance is of tremendous import; just like the priests' clothes represent honor and glory, both on the inside and outside, so, too, does our modern wardrobe. As members of upright society, we know that we must keep our body parts clothed in properly fitting, laundered apparel. God forbid my wife find me in a ripped-up T-shirt! A *kippah* tops off our wardrobe and serves as a constant reminder that we are in a battle to make good choices, with our internal qualities matching our outside appearances. We have to maintain "balance" to keep it on our head, literally and figuratively. Just like we put on a good suit for an interview and feel like a million bucks, a *kippah* can make us feel like God's most trusted teammate.

The following stories from the road transpired for no reason other than the ubiquitous presence of a *yarlmuke* on my head. The first occurred when my flight to Youngstown, Ohio was forced to land in Pittsburgh due to freezing rain. We sat at the gate for over an hour watching the storm grow increasingly hostile. Eventually, I saw the pilot pick up and leave. I approached the uniformed attendant and stated, "I'm an Observant Jew and must get to Youngstown to lead a Sabbath program. Would you consider putting all of us on a bus?" She replied that she didn't have the seniority to make such a decision, so I quickly found someone who did. The plan was established that we were to form groups of three or four and take cabs paid for by the airline. I noticed there was an elderly couple on our flight shuffling along at a glacial pace. I must admit I avoided them so I wouldn't be hindered on the long walk through the airport. Sure enough, they purposefully stood next to me so they would be chosen to share my cab. I later learned they saw my *kippah* and felt confident I would look after them.

As I pushed their Smarte Carte through the airport at .5 miles per hour, I managed my stress level by reframing. I started to relax as I pondered *perhaps the whole reason God put me in this mess was to help out these nice people*. Once we boarded the cab, I introduced myself. The man replied with a thick Yiddish accent, "Oh, I used to be a Glaser...I was in the glass business!" Then his diminutive wife added, "I was a Glaser too." "Oh really," I said, "You were in the glass business?" "No," she responded, "Glaser is my maiden name." I learned she was from Glod, the hamlet in Transylvania from which my ancestors hail. That's right...we're cousins. And my Uncle Max, for whom my son is named, helped them emigrate from Cuba to the States after the war. Rose and Jack were honored guests at my concert in Youngstown the following evening and I visit them every time I perform in South Florida.

Another incident occurred at a check-in counter at LAX. I was on my way to perform a Christmas day Chanukah concert for Chabad of Scottsdale. The youthful Hispanic guy weighing my luggage saw my *kippah* and asked if I had seen the movie "Ushpizin" (an Israeli film I highly recommend). He was confused by a few scenes and was seeking clarification. Like, why was the protagonist screaming at God in the forest, and why was the old man doing a careful accounting before giving away his money. I explained to the best of my ability and then remarked that this guy, Raul, seemed to know a lot about Judaism. He responded that he had learned much from aish.com. I asked him which columnists he liked best and he said, "Well, I bought the mp3 player." I asked, "How many of the lectures have you listened to (the Aish mp3 player came with countless hours of lectures)?" He replied, "All of them, of course, many times!" I responded that he has learned more Torah than most Jews alive.

By now, the line had grown behind me and I realized we needed to end this conversation (remember that I'm the guy with the *kippah* and want people to get the impression Jews are courteous). But Raul was in no hurry. He had many more questions and wasn't going to let a live Jew out of his grasp so easily. I suggested that Raul sit in on my weekly Seasons of Joy class to get more answers. I handed him my card and a copy of my Kol Bamidbar CD. His eyes brimmed with tears as he said, "Oh my God, you are the Sam Glaser! I listen to your music all the time with my daughter! You are the reason I started studying!"

A final *kippah* tale: My boys and I played hooky for a day to do some local skiing. Upon our arrival at the windswept parking lot of Mountain High, while donning my ski pants, I felt a sudden twinge of pain in my low back. Sadly, on my first run, I was seized by a crippling spasm. I hadn't felt pain like this since my twenties and I knew immediately my ski day had just ended. I limped down the slopes and spent the day on a gurney in the ski patrol office, barely able to move. Now I had a dilemma. I was two hours away from home and couldn't operate my vehicle. Neither of my boys were of driving age—I needed a volunteer to drive us in my car. I waited until lunchtime when I knew there would be a crowd in the lodge. After dining with my concerned kids, I limped around the lodge with a makeshift sign that read, "Need a driver to take me to LA." People looked at me like an alien and Max sneered, "Dad, you look homeless…this is never going to work!" I said, "Watch kid, we're going to find an angel."

I abandoned the sign and strategically explained my situation only at tables where there were several adults. I asked each group if they were from L.A., a simple yes or no question to get a conversation started. I had a good feeling at one particular table. I assured them I was a nice guy and had a decent car for one of them to drive…no monkey business. They seemed unmoved by my story and dismissed me by saying, "We'll think about it." At this point I was really hurting and couldn't stand anymore. I gave them my cell phone number and hobbled to a nearby bench. Just as my kids walked over to commiserate, one of these individuals approached us and said, "I'll drive you home. I noticed your *kippah*. How could I turn down a fellow member of the tribe?" To make our angel story even sweeter, this unaffiliated Russian Jew moved to the States when he was two and is in the business of helping people with back injuries find ergonomic solutions for their offices. On the way home we schmoozed about techniques to heal issues like mine but unfortunately, all the lumbar support in the world wouldn't help. A few months later, the skilled hands of a Cedars-Sinai surgeon nipped the offending disc material and I was able to get on with my life.

I'll close with a compelling reason to consider a *kippah*. Our daily prayers remind us that we were miraculously redeemed from Egypt and are still awaiting the final redemption. These prayers elicit an important question about the present state of the Jewish People: do we merit delivery from our extended sojourn in the Diaspora? Do we deserve to be rescued from worldwide terrorism, from the renewed threat from the Persian Empire, from festering anti-Semitism? According to the *Midrash*, we were saved from Egypt for four reasons: we didn't completely assimilate into their hedonistic culture and maintained our Hebrew names, language and clothing. With this in mind, I have appointed a few friends to call me Shmuel to keep my soul name alive. I work on my Hebrew, both Biblical and Modern so I can navigate our texts in the original tongue and attempt conversations with Israelis. Lastly, I fly my *kippah* and *tzitzit* for all to see. Thanks to this simple mitzvah, every interaction became an opportunity for spiritual connection, and I transitioned from saying "never" to "bring it on!"

THE FOUR QUESTIONS

1. How do you feel about being publicly identified as a Jew? Why?

2. How do you behave differently when you are aware that people know you are Jewish?

3. Do you have a personal miracle story that transpired because someone found out that you were Jewish?

4. Do you know your Hebrew name? What is the spiritual significance of this name to you? What about your parents' and grandparents' Hebrew names?

Tallit:
Life on the Fringe

♫ MA YAKAR ♫

joyjud.com/m/myk

Ma yakar chasd'cha Elokim	*Clothing me in the shadow of Your wings*
Uv'nei adam b'tzeyl k'nafecha yechesayun	*Shelter me in the comfort of Your home*
Ma yakar chasd'cha Elokim	*Light of life, surrounding me with love*
Uv'nei adam b'tzeyl k'nafecha yechesayun	*In Your arms I'll never be alone*

I experienced my first taste of yeshiva learning when I was a twenty-something wanna-be rock star. My band had just broken up and I was in between recording clients. After perusing an attractive brochure that appeared in the mail, I applied for the all-expenses-paid scholarship to study in Jerusalem. I interviewed with Richard Horowitz, a businessman who I later learned covered the cost of my flight. Aish HaTorah provided an incredible curriculum with a dozen brilliant rabbis teaching us hour by hour in an Ottoman Empire study hall perched atop the Old City walls. I considered the millennia-old alleyways my personal playground and had the Western Wall in my front yard. Religious expectations of us new students were nil; we filled our days with Judaic studies and travel, and nights were spent out on the town or in deep conversations until dawn. The neophytes didn't have to attend the yeshiva prayer services, but since I had a fair grasp of the basics from Hebrew school, I would occasionally don the *tallis* (or *tallit*, prayer shawl) given to me for my Bar Mitzvah and join the *minyan*.

Once, after *Shacharit,* a peer announced, "Sam, you don't need to wear that *tallis* here." "Why not?" I responded, "I feel more comfortable praying with it." He then sat me down and gently explained that according to Ashkenazi tradition, men don't wear a *tallis* until they are married. I looked around the *minyan* and saw he was right. "But what about the last paragraph of the Sh'ma? I need a *tallis* to kiss the *tzitztit*, right?" "Look, Sam," he replied, "Just go with it. This way the single ladies on the other side of the *mechitza* (room divider) know who the single men are." That was all I needed to hear…I never wore a *tallis* again until I was married.

I enjoyed four months of intense learning and growth on that formative trip. I was on fire! Loving Torah study, loving Jerusalem, perceiving God's presence from one end of the universe to the other. Then Passover arrived. I celebrated my first *Seder* with one of my favorite rabbis and it lasted until 4:00 am. I learned so many new Pesach songs, some of which I still sing today. All the study in preparation for the big night allowed me to connect to the *Haggadah* (Passover guide text) in the deepest way. While I adored the Reform-style *Seders* at my Grandpa Bill and Grandma Zetta's home in Sacramento, I never experienced an intellectual-spiritual marathon like this. After dinner, my fellow yeshiva *bochers* (students) and I passed out on couches for a few hours and then got lost returning to the Old City.

Since I am a resident of the Diaspora, I had to scramble to find a second *Seder* the next night (Israelis only have to do one). I remember shlepping all over the *Rova* (Jewish Quarter) in search of a certain visiting American family. Thankfully, I found the place and the gracious host treated us royally. Mid-*Seder* he shared an eye-opening overview of the Jewish calendar, explaining rabbinic insights into the seven weeks of *S'firat Ha'omer* (the Counting of the Omer) and the juxtaposition of Pesach with the holiday of Shavuot. One of my fellow students turned to me and said, "Sam, did you realize no one is going to want to hear your music for the next month and a half?" Of course, I didn't believe him. Judaism without music…how could that be? The next day I verified with the *Rosh Yeshiva* that music was out during this upcoming period of semi-mourning. Evidently, the time had arrived to go back to my L.A. recording studio and sports car.

My last Shabbat in Jerusalem was bittersweet. I prayed an abbreviated service at the Wall in a state of torment. How could I leave this magical place, this medieval "Jewish Disneyland?" I felt I had learned more in those four months than in four years at my university. But there was also an undercurrent of homesickness, missing my extended family and my beachside apartment. One by one, the rabbis pulled me aside to discourage me from going back to L.A. so soon. Particularly Rabbi Weinberg, my beloved *Rosh Yeshiva*. "C'mon Sam, give us a year," he implored, looking at me with that trademark gleam in his eye.

I felt so vulnerable next to the massive Herodian stones as I stood at the base of the *Kotel*. I thought to myself, *it's been so good getting to know You, God. I am so grateful for this chance to learn and celebrate my Judaism in this incredible country. I love You. Thank You.* Tears streamed down my face. I realized I had been touched for life, that this knowledge of the truth and power of Torah was now a part of me. There would be no going back. I recited a few passages in the *P'sukei D'zimra* (Psalms of Praise) and then the *Sh'ma*. *I really wish I had my tallis on right now*, I silently prayed. *I feel naked without it.* Just then I heard footsteps behind me. Before I could turn around, a man with an intimidating beard tapped my shoulder and motioned that I should come over and join a *minyan* at the back of the Western Wall plaza.

I reluctantly followed, still not sure what he wanted from me. He led me to Rabbi Scheinberger, a kabbalist and famous *Kotel* personality, who indicated I should be the one to serve as *hagbah* (one honored with lifting the Torah at the end of the public reading). I had no idea why he picked me but I stepped right up and grasped the worn wooden handles. I unrolled the scroll a bit and thrust it as high as my 6'3 frame would allow. Suddenly, as I spun around to allow those present to see the carefully crafted letters, an oversized *tallis* was draped over my shoulders. Shaking with emotion, I recalled Rav Noah's statement: "Here in Jerusalem, reaching God is a "local call!"

My next connection with a *tallis* would be at my wedding seven years later. I sent my Israel-bound mom on a mission to purchase a perfect *tallis*. She returned with a black and white striped, super lightweight, extra large garment and "sold" it to my fiancé Shira (the custom is for the wife to give the sacred shawl to her new husband). That sunny August afternoon, we stretched it atop four poles and gathered underneath as a cavalcade of seven illustrious rabbis gave us our blessings. Now, whenever I wear it, I think of that day and feel the hug of my wife as well as the comfort of God's "wings" holding me close.

Each morning, we recite a short prayer called *Ma Yakar* when donning the *tallis*. Since I find it difficult to hold a book while surrounding myself in the flowing fabric, I wrote the text into a song to aid in the memorization of the words. I resonate with the sentiment of standing in the "shadow of God's wings" and I intentionally linger in this space. Later in the service, before saying the *Sh'ma*, the custom is to collect the fringes from the four corners of the garment together in one hand. The words we say while gathering them is an impassioned request, "*v'havi'eynu l'shalom*," for God to assemble Jews from the four corners of the earth to Zion. Rabbi Shlomo Carlebach told me he collects the *tzitzit* deliberately and lovingly as if he's holding all the Children of Israel in a warm embrace. So I do it the same way. During the last paragraph of the *Sh'ma*, we delicately kiss the fringes every time we mention the word *tzitzit*. This intimate act has been performed by legions of brutish, sleepy men every morning for millennia.

The "forget me knot" fringes tell a story of their own: the *gematria* (numerical value) of the word *tzitzit* is 600. Add that to the eight strings and five knots in each corner and you get the mystical number of 613, the sum total of commandments enumerated in the Torah. Furthermore, one of the strings is dyed blue with the ink of a certain snail (although today most people don't have this blue thread). The idea is to see the beautiful aqua blue and think of the sea, which reminds us of the sky, which then conjures up a vision of the *Kisei Hakavod*, God's Heavenly Throne. By observing our breathtaking natural world we can extrapolate the presence of the Creator and concretize that relationship with the observance of the 613 commandments. A *"tzitz"* in Hebrew is a spark. This foundational mitzvah can ignite our spiritual connection much like a sparkplug keeps a car engine humming.

Since the *tallis* is typically worn only during the morning service, there is a way to stay connected to the mitzvah all day: I wear a *tallit katan*, a small t-shirt-style cotton garment under my shirt. Some tuck in the fringes to maintain a low profile. I say, let them hang out—I celebrate my *tzitzit!* After all, the mitzvah is based on <u>seeing</u> the fringes and then connecting to God and the commandments.

The *tallit katan* is a covert badge of honor. A Torah lifestyle offers impeccable integrity training. Those wearing this simple undergarment are typically super-sensitized to "choosing life" and distancing from the voice of the *yetzer harah* (evil inclination). They are on a path of learning, scrupulous with mitzvot and committed to family and community. Most are honest to a fault and pursue heroic acts of loving-kindness. This degree of integrity is based on morals clarified in a relationship with a Living God. I've heard it said, "If you lose an object, make sure to do it in a Jewish neighborhood." Of course, there are those wearing the garb who fall from grace or are agents of destruction in society. They represent an infinitesimally small percentage of the *k'lal* (group) and their infractions are often surprising enough to make headlines. Some of my friends claim they have no interest in spiritual growth since they have heard about such miscreants. I urge them not to throw the baby out with the bathwater, saying, "Don't confuse Jews with Judaism!"

I must admit it was a profound challenge for this surf-short-wearing California kid to add another layer of clothing. As I have mentioned before, quoting *Pirkei Avot*, "According to the effort is the reward." Sometimes I sweat and yes, it's worth it. Since I'm always on the move, I'm pretty tough on my fringes. Therefore, I learned to weave my own replacement *tzitzit*, a skill I practice on long airplane flights. The people sitting next to me think I'm doing some sort of bizarre crochet. I try to weave with mindfulness and carefully follow the tradition of winding the string in between the knots 7, 8, 11 and 13 times, hinting towards the metaphysical values of those numbers (to be discussed in subsequent chapters). I tell my curious seatmates that wearing fringes is an optional commandment—we only have to place them on four-cornered garments. Unless you are living in Mexico and wear a poncho, it's pretty rare to find such angular clothing. Therefore, by actively seeking out a garment with distinct corners, we are making the powerful statement we desire to be close with the Almighty all day long.

There is an amusing coda to the aforementioned story at the Western Wall: during a recent concert tour in Israel, I wound up at Rabbi Scheinberger's Friday night service at the *Kotel*. After the *davening*, I asked the rabbi if he remembered the incident when he called a young stranger from across the *Kotel* plaza to be *hagbah*. He didn't recall the day but looked me up and down and remarked, "That makes sense…I like giving *hagbah* to tall guys."

My relationship with my prayer shawl and *tallit katan* is a loving one, as long as the temperature doesn't get too hot! I have fond memories of playing with the fringes of my dad's *tallis* at our synagogue. Now it is my turn to cherish this mitzvah. Whereas once I felt I had to be undercover with my Judaism, displaying this round-the-clock four-cornered garment has become a celebrated part of my life. Believe it or not, I have some wonderful fans in the Jewish deaf community who have shared with me the sign language gesture for Sam Glaser: two hands at the waist with fluttering fingers pointing down, imitating my fringes. Keep your eyes open next time you're at an airport. You may see me at one of the gates wearing my black and white superhero cape, doing my part to save humanity.

Try on a *tallis*. Savor that moment, the secluded, private space shared only with God. May we all reap the benefits of life on the fringe.

THE FOUR QUESTIONS

1. What is your earliest memory of interacting with a *tallis*?

2. Do you have other symbols in your life that "spark" up your connection with God?

3. Have you had a mentor that has suddenly entered your life and touched you deeply?

4. Have you ever considered wearing a *tallit katan*? Why or why not?

Tefillin: Strapping Up

♫ V'ERASTICH LI ♫

joyjud.com/m/vsl

I will betroth You forever　　　　　　*I betroth You forever*
I will betroth You with righteousness　　*I betroth You with righteousness*
And with justice, kindness and mercy　　*I betroth You faithfully*
And with justice, kindness and mercy　　*And we will be as one*

My first exposure to *tefillin* was in a basement workshop of a holy *sofer* (scribe) in Jerusalem. I was in Israel for my Bar Mitzvah; a lucky Brentwood, CA boy whose parents opted not only for an L.A. celebration but also for a meaningful few weeks touring the Promised Land. The culmination of the experience was a second Bar Mitzvah service at the Western Wall, surrounded by Israeli friends, relatives and curious Chassidim. I got to *lein* (read Torah) at the spiritual "ground zero" of our planet and forge an unbreakable bond with Israel and the Jewish People. I remember my new *tefillin* straps feeling sharp and rough—it would be months before the leather would soften and become comfortable on my skin. After this trip, my father made a point of praying with me in his crepuscular, walnut-lined study in the mornings before school, allowing for quality father-son time and ensuring my *tefillin* would actually get some use.

Unfortunately, I fell into the pattern of most of my Conservative peers and my thirteenth year would be the last I'd have any shred of active affiliation. Yes, I partially attended Confirmation, Hebrew High and youth group activities, but Judaism as I saw it was for nerds without a social life. My priorities were fitting in at public school, skiing, biking, bodyboarding and playing in bands. I was proud to be Jewish and enjoyed family Friday

Night dinners, but my *tefillin* were relegated to an obscure closet never to see the light of day.

Fast forward to my twenties when I was operating my recording studio and working as a full-time composer. I was chasing TV and movie score work, producing albums for clients and trying to get a record deal with my band. At this point, I had experienced a few bouts of learning in yeshiva and loved it, but the regular wrapping of *tefillin* never factored into the equation. When I was twenty-nine, my newfound interest in writing Jewish music brought me to the Center for Jewish Culture and Creativity. I yearned for inspiration to compose more Jewish tunes, so I applied and got accepted to their all-expenses-paid Arts Institute in Jerusalem.

Imagine the thrill of living in the elegant creative conference center, Mishkenot Sha'ananim, where artists of all stripes performed, collaborated and workshopped late into the nights. I wrote another three songs that would become part of my first Jewish album and bonded tightly with the international group of composers assembled from the four corners of the earth. On the final night of the program, one of our mentors made a point of engaging me in a one-on-one conversation. Phillip said, "Sam, I've noticed you are a deeply religious guy." I laughed, waiting for the punch line. "No, I'm serious," he insisted. He had overheard me in dialogue with the Israelis on our program and noticed I always took the reverent side of theological arguments. From his observations, I seemed to be a big proponent of God.

Phillip recommended I further investigate this side of my personality to see if it would bear fruit. When I asked how I might do that, he suggested that I choose a mitzvah and make it my own. As we pondered alternatives, he asked if I had ever wrapped *tefillin*. "Yes," I replied, "I received a pair for my Bar Mitzvah." Phillip told me to try wearing them again as a daily way to remember the connection I felt in Israel. Upon returning to L.A., weeks went by before I made it over to my parents' house to find the aged leather in the exact place where it had been abandoned sixteen years earlier. Eventually, I felt guilty enough to actually try them on. I had little recollection of how to tie the straps or utter the appropriate blessings but I gave it my best shot. I did know enough to say the *Sh'ma* and *V'ahavta* and thank God for the gifts in my life.

Midway through my prayers the phone rang. As I reached for the receiver, it dawned on me, *this is my time to pray and the moment shouldn't be interrupted with a call.* I returned to laboring over the unfamiliar Hebrew, but I paused to listen to my answering machine as it picked up the call. It was my friend Jymm Adams from the Sports Channel of L.A. asking me to serve as in-house composer for their professional sports broadcasts. I reached my strapped-up hands to the heavens and said, "Thank you, God...let's try this tefillin thing again tomorrow!"

This daily exercise of faith gave me something much more compelling than a new gig: a palpable relationship with the Creator of the Universe. Once I started setting aside a few minutes each day to pray, I slowly navigated the challenging waters of the long winded *P'sukei D'zimra* (Psalms of Praise) and the central prayer, the *Sh'moneh Esrei*. I added paragraph by paragraph onto my personal ritual, not wanting to bog myself down with too long a service but hoping to increase the fluidity of my reading. I became grateful for the years of religious school, Camp Ramah's Hebrew immersion and practice with my Bar Mitzvah tutor. Thanks to those with the thankless task of teaching this class clown, I could awkwardly negotiate the Holy Tongue and with time, flowed through the *siddur*. Soon, I tackled the majority of the *Shacharit* (morning) service and learned to put on my *tefillin* like a champ. Eventually, I managed to focus on the meanings rather than just the pronunciations of the words and learned to close my eyes and simply dwell in God's presence.

At first, I saw this binding exercise as a masochistic reenactment of the *Akeidah* (the binding of Yitzchak), a sublimation of my will to that of the Almighty. I surmised that *tefillin* are a physical expression of being "bound" in a servant/Master contract with God. While contracts and covenants both bind parties to their duties, there's a distinction between them. In a contractual dispute, the parties sue. In a covenant, one attempts to resuscitate the ailing cohort. God is not out to sue! We are in a covenantal relationship with God, our most supportive ally. *Tefillin* commemorate a degree of intimacy much like the covenant of marriage: When we wind them around our fingers we utter a betrothal passage (*Hoshea* 2:21) often recited at marriage ceremonies. For me, *tefillin* represent a daily *chuppah* (marriage canopy) moment where I get the opportunity to renew my vows with my Partner in Creation. Smart wives nudge their husbands to wear *tefillin*. The daily lesson in fidelity to God and self subliminally transfers to all critical relationships.

The commandment to wear *Tefillin* is mentioned four times in the *Chumash* (Five Books of Moses), two of which occur in the paragraphs of the *Shma*. It is these four passages that are meticulously transcribed on parchment, both in the head and arm boxes, with the same care as a *mezuzah* or Torah scroll. In the *Shma,* our love affair with God is described as one involving all of our heart, soul and might. So, too, do we wear the *tefillin* on the arm (close to the heart), on the head (the seat of the soul/intellect), and might (the realm of action, on our bicep). Also, the head straps hang unevenly down toward our genitalia. Essentially, we are employing a very physical system of checks and balances, a uniting of our spiritual and material existence, our *yetzer hatov* and *yetzer harah* (good and evil inclinations), all within the realm of love. *Tefillin* offer us the chance to navigate the elusive middle path in our service to God, keeping our intellect, emotions and physical being in peaceful coexistence.

Another virtue of this practice is acknowledging the fast connection between the Written and Oral Law. The *Chumash* advises us to place a sign on our arms and between our eyes, but does not tell us where that place is, what the "sign" looks like or even to employ leather and parchment. Yet, for millennia Jews have worn the same black boxes in more or less the same way. I remember hiking Masada at sunrise on my Bar Mitzvah trip and learning that the 2000-year-old *tefillin* discovered by the archaeologists were indistinguishable from those of today. Clearly, while on Mount Sinai, Moshe was shown diagrams and visions in addition to taking dictation. These revelations described in the Oral Law give us the "meat" on the bones of our written record of God's will. Also, the rabbis debate extensively whether one or two blessings are necessary when donning *tefillin*. Ashkenaz *siddurim* include two blessings but add a sentence ("Baruch Shem Kavod ...") just in case that conclusion is mistaken. In other words, the cornerstone of Jewish tradition as we know it is based on rabbinic <u>compromise</u> elaborated upon in the Talmud. By wearing *tefillin* every day, we deepen our understanding of the interdependence of Written and Oral Law and take our place in the chain of transmission.

I recommend Aryeh Kaplan's book aptly titled "Tefillin" for anyone curious about the role of gender and the deeper mystical aspects of this mitzvah.

These days I pack my *tefillin* wherever I wander. I find I am often in gardens or on the rooftops of hotels looking for a quiet, aesthetic space to strap up and say my morning prayers. I know it appears strange to onlookers, but laying *tefillin* makes a definitive statement: "I'm Jewish, this is what we do, thanks for respecting our differences." I welcome the questions that ensue. With my own kids, I was relaxed about pushing them to get to a *minyan* on

Shabbat mornings, but considered *tefillin* every weekday inviolate. Their willingness to do this mitzvah was a prerequisite to participating in our family vacations or other activities. Hopefully it's more than guilt that motivates them—they have their own relationship with God—why mess that up? As Woody Allen says, "80% of life is showing up." I believe faithful behavior like a daily appointment with *tefillin* elevates one's faith into the realm of knowledge.

How about a few *tefillin* stories? Everyone I know who wraps on a daily basis has a good *tefillin* story, usually about their quest never to miss a day under any circumstances. The first saga occurred between gigs in Virginia. I had a few days of downtime and opted to head for the spectacular Shenandoah Mountains for some chairlift-assisted downhill mountain biking and kayaking down the famous river. I found a great deal on a motel in one of the local hamlets. The property was adjacent to miles of peaceful cornfields, a perfect place for my prayers in a sea of maize and emerald green stretching toward the horizon, with purple mountain majesty just beyond. On one of the mornings, while enshrouded in my *tallis* and *tefillin* in the field, I enjoyed a particularly relaxed *davening* session. Upon finishing, I walked back to my room, blew my handy travel *shofar* (since it was during the month of *Elul*), and then placed my prayer articles back in their monogrammed velvet bags.

As soon as I zipped up the case, there was a stern knock at the door. I found myself face to face with an imposing Virginia policeman who carefully checked me out while looking nervously around my room. "Can I help you, officer?" I've learned to be REALLY polite when addressing members of law enforcement. He asked, "Is there a problem?" "No sir, no problem here." "Well," he responded, "I think there is a problem." "OK, what is that?" "I just got a report that people saw you bound in duct tape and then heard you screaming." I stifled a giggle, showed him my *yarmulke* and told him I was Jewish. That didn't impress him. Then I slowly opened my bags to show him the leather straps inside. "Really, officer, this is what Jews wear when they pray." After searching my room and calling in my ID, he departed with the knowledge that not only do Jews own all the banks, they're crazy too.

Here's another memorable story that inspires me every time I think about it. During a concert tour/family vacation on the North Shore of Kauai, I *davened* at dawn on Waioli beach overlooking a perfect double-overhead swell at Hanalei Bay. After my prayers, I stashed my *tallis* and *tefillin* in the car and paddled out to have one of the most exciting surf sessions of my life. I was surprised that the usually territorial locals were helping me get into position to drop into some of the smoothest bowls of bright green glass of my aquatic career. After a few hours of breathless exertion, I returned to my rental car, surprised the interior smelled of cigarette smoke. *That's funny*, I thought. *I don't remember this car smelling like smoke.* I slowly realized someone else had been inside. I checked under the seat and discovered my phone, camera and *tallis-tefillin* bag were gone.

I searched the area, interviewed onlookers and filed a report with the police, to no avail. How would I *daven* the following day, the last weekday of our trip? I didn't know of anyone else on the North Shore who might be observant. It dawned on me that the Brant-Sarifs, friends of ours from L.A., were vacationing on the South Shore. Thankfully Shira had their number—perhaps we could arrange a get together and I might borrow their *tefillin*? I had another problem...how would I reach the guy with whom I was supposed to be jamming that evening? After my concert for the Jewish community the night before, some audience members were inspired to get me to sit in with a local percussionist at his dinner club show. But now, without my precious iPhone, I didn't have their contact information.

The Brant-Sarif family agreed to meet us for a hike and wrapping party. We met on the edge of a certain condo complex where a treacherous trail leads to a system of ocean-side sea caves inhabited by giant sea turtles. After viewing these affable creatures in a series of shadowy caverns, we scaled the muddy cliff up to the parking lot where my son and I donned our friend's *tefillin*. Time was of the essence since we had to get back to our respective hotels before Shabbat candlelighting. Just as I strapped up, a warm Hawaiian drizzle started to fall. To avoid getting my friend's *tefillin* wet, we dashed into the alcove of one of the nearby condos and shared an animated communal *Mincha*.

Right in the middle of our *davening,* the owner of this particular condo walked down the stairs and shouted, "What the "#^+..." Upon closer inspection he exclaimed, "My *mishpacha!*" Sure enough, he was a Jewish guy from the mainland who had recently made Hawaii his home. He demurred when we offered for him to try on the *tefillin* but he invited us into his condo for a drink. When I introduced myself as a visiting musician from L.A., he responded, "You're Sam Glaser? We were supposed to jam last night!" Yes, this condo where we were huddled, trying to sneak in our mitzvah before Shabbat began, was the home of the percussionist I needed to reach. 60,000 souls on the island and I found the one I was looking for...*baruch* Hashem!

Wearing *tefillin* on a daily basis offers a lens through which I can perceive miracles in my life. Some mornings it's opaque. On others, I enjoy a spotless view of the inner workings of Creation. Thanks to this discipline, I have a regular rendezvous with the Almighty that is nurturing and unshakeable. Ensuring I never miss this appointment has created some truly memorable moments. I'm also reminded of the power of an encouraging word: just like my mentor on the Israel program gave me the idea of *tefillin* as a way to connect my trip to further spiritual growth, so, too, do I offer similar suggestions to those with open hearts.

Tefillin offer access to the deepest realms of the soul: a connection of mind, body and heart, a binding of servant to Master and a daily reenactment of our sacred marriage with the Creator of the Universe.

THE FOUR QUESTIONS

1. Is there anything that makes you feel that you are bound to God in a very concrete way?

2. Can you describe ways that other mitzvot unite the Written and Oral tradition?

3. Do you think it's appropriate to wrap *tefillin* in public?

4. Do you know any good *tefillin* stories?

More Precious Than Pearls: An Inside View of Women's Rituals

So beautiful to me
I guess I've lost my objectivity
But you are the loveliest I've ever seen
I've traveled miles from home
I never really minded being alone
Till you made me realize how lonely I had been

Oh, why am I compelled to be so close
So close to you
I've done so much dreaming
By now my heart is screaming
Darling, I give my life to you

So magical the scene
Lace and pearls and diamonds like a queen
Slowly revolve around my fragile heart
We drink a cup of wine
I say I'll love you till the end of time
Solemnly swear that we will never part

Oh, I cannot describe the way I feel
So close to you
Can't you feel me shaking
How my heart is aching
Darling, I give my life to you

At the risk of sounding sexist (too late!), certain Jewish rituals are considered the dominion of women. Rather than pontificating from this man's point of view, I interviewed my wife, Shira to obtain her enlightened perspective. Shira and I took the journey of mitzvah observance together beginning in 1991. She runs a joyful, well-managed, kosher household and is adored by her grateful husband and three kids. Shira is intuitive, high functioning, athletic, maternal and giving. She is the type of guest who will bring half the meal and won't leave until she cleans your kitchen. She is a reliable resource and pillar of strength for those lucky enough to know her. I should add that she has an MBA, spent years in finance and marketing for major corporations and makes incredible chumus. Who better to interview on the subject of women's rituals than my well-qualified wife?

Shira, can you describe your weekly Shabbat candlelighting ritual?

"OK. The panic and rush of Friday comes to a shrieking halt. I set up five candles (two plus one for each of my three kids) on the silver candlesticks I received for our wedding. I light, cover my eyes, sing the blessing and *daven*. Shabbas candlelighting is a special time of focus for me. First I recognize God as my Creator and Provider, then I request the things I need and hope for. I pray for you, for our kids one by one, for our extended family, friends and the Jewish People. I take an extra moment to cover specific family and friends needing *refuah* (healing), *parnasa* (income) or a *shidduch* (match).

"I enter a totally new space after I light. All distractions are gone. It's very freeing. No matter how much is going on, I can't worry about whatever didn't get done. It's nice just to let it go. I try to light at the eighteen-minute mark (the mandated candlelighting time before the sun sets) so I'm taking on Shabbas with the whole community. Sometimes I'm not quite ready, so I keep in mind that I'm not taking on the laws of Shabbat for another few minutes while I finish the details.

"It takes discipline to be present for candlelighting. Some of the time, especially when we have a big table (lots of guests), I'm panicked. Over the years, the Shabbas hustle (a tense period the hour before Shabbas comes in) has become more manageable. I pace myself and feel it's disrespectful to Shabbas to rush it. Of course there are unforeseen circumstances, so it's not always so smooth. The *yetzer harah* is very powerful before Shabbas—we all have be careful to not lose our cool.

"Candlelighting is one of my main prayer moments of the week. The fact is I'm praying most of the day. One thing making candlelighting so sweet is that since her Bat Mitzvah, I share it with our daughter Sarah. She lights two candles of her own and we sing the *b'racha* together using the Glaser family melody, written by Max Helfman at Brandeis Camp. When Bubbie (grandma) and any extended family members are lighting with us, it's an amazing scene. Bubbie lights over twenty-five candles...for her sixteen grandkids, all her kids and siblings. Quite a sight!"

Why do you suppose candlelighting is considered a woman's mitzvah?

"According to our tradition, our matriarch Sarah was the first to light candles and her candles stayed lit miraculously the whole week. They brought peace into her tent and weren't extinguished until she died. When Rivkah took on the custom and the miracle reoccurred, it was clear she was Sarah's righteous successor. Women bring light into the household. It's the woman's domain, especially the kitchen! I'm pretty traditional in that I like to have my hands in every aspect of the house. I maintain order, keep things stocked, cook and do the laundry.

"Obviously, the traditional roles aren't for everybody. They work for me. I think women have a more inward focus...just look at our bodies. The way we were created is inside-oriented, loving and nurturing. I'll be the first to admit I am a homebody. For example, I like doing laundry because touching your clothes lets me learn about you...what you did that day, if you worked out, what you ate. I impart love into the laundry. Having clean clothes lets you worry about other things because the fundamentals are taken care of. I think kids need a sturdy platform from which they can spring. Our kids don't stress about what they are going to eat or wear, and that builds security, gives them a sense of confidence. It's important they can trust us to be reliable, to always provide the essentials. When they can count on us, I think they will be able to trust others and have intimate relationships in their own lives.

There are many languages of love, and cooking and cleaning are how I love you."

Speaking of cooking, doesn't it get old always having meals ready for your hungry family?

"Yes it gets old. But I get sincere pleasure when my family eats with gusto. I strive to make things that everyone likes, the common denominator dishes. There's something intimate about feeding my family. People feel love toward the one feeding them. It's an intimate bond our kids have had with me since they were babies. It's connective...that's just my gut feeling. Also, I'm using recipes passed down from grandmothers. The food we make ties all us moms together—it's so deep—beyond lifetimes! If we relied on take out meals, I feel that something maternal and sentimental would be missing. And if we relied on you to cook, we would all starve."

Thanks. That brings us to another famous "woman's" mitzvah, baking challah. Any thoughts?

"I can't seem to get organized enough to make it and I've had too many disasters in the past. Making challah makes me feel A.D.D....I just can't get it right. We're lucky to live in a place where there are lots of bakeries making delicious challot. Someday I hope to do it myself.

"In the challah baking workshops I've attended, I've learned it's a special, spiritual food, one requiring significant human interaction in partnership with God. Apples, bananas, veggies, meat...those things don't require so much partnership. But going from seed to plant to harvest to threshing to grinding to kneading and baking—these are awesome symbols of human effort combined with God's gifts. The word challah actually refers to the small portion taken from the big batch of dough to be gifted to the *kohanim* (priests). In the absence of the Temple, we make a blessing and burn it in the oven. The simple action of baking challah unites us with our ancient sisters who were empowered with this mitzvah. In the desert, our people were dependent on *manna* from heaven, whereas the *motzi* thanks God for bread from the earth. Evidently, upon arriving in *Eretz Yisrael,* it amazed the Israelites that bread didn't originate in the heavens but instead came from the ground—wow! The *motzi* allows us to rekindle this sense of amazement, teaching us that all our achievements are never really our own; everything happens only with God's help.

"Every ingredient of challah is symbolic. When adding the oil I feel I'm anointing every member of my family like royalty. Let the sugar overflow so goodness and sweetness overflows for all of us. I'm sparing with salt since it connotes judgment. Eggs represent the human lifecycle and the preciousness of time. When we go to a friend's home where the challah is homemade, I can sense the blessing these women have invested. I watch you guys consuming it in glutinous ecstasy. Without a doubt, our favorite is Bubbie's onion challah. The taste is indescribable."

Especially with chumus! How do you avoid feeling burdened by all the entertaining for Shabbat and holidays?

"Some of the women in our community set the bar so high that even my best effort is going to fail in comparison. I realized I have to make Shabbat <u>my</u> best, not their best. If you're Martha Stewart, then great, go for it. It's important not to get trapped into thinking that festive meals have to be high level or not at all. My Shabbas and Yom Tov (holiday) meals are my expression, my creativity. I like things clean and simple, so I keep things simple. Light and healthy—that's my style. We don't stuff ourselves or eat fried and processed food during the week, so we're not going to do it on Shabbat.

"My meals usually have sumptuous, fresh appetizers and great, homemade desserts. I like to start and end with a bang. One thing that I'm obsessed about is making dessert. I don't bake challah but I make everything else. Once, when invited to a neighbor's home for lunch, our daughter Sarah innocently asked, "Excuse me, do you have anything homemade?" Yes, our kids are spoiled."

Do you feel compelled to have guests most of the time?

"We do our best outreach at our table. You run the proceedings, keeping everyone engaged in conversation, words of Torah and music. I keep the food and drink flowing. Our tables have become so popular that they are the places people want to send first-timers or bring their parents when they come to town. I love sharing our family's unique gifts. I think we make Judaism look good and we give singles something to emulate in their future households. Yes, I get burned out. Everybody does. I have to pace myself. Sometimes it's just our family and it's more casual. Still, Shabbas is a big step up from weekdays. We always eat multiple courses in the dining room, with fresh flowers, tablecloths and the fancy glassware.

"Our kids have grown up seeing that having guests is an important mitzvah. I know they will want this for themselves. I do a lot of meals for community members who are sick or have just given birth. When our kids were younger I got them to help in the preparation or delivery so they shared the mitzvah had a learning experience. I realized our children must always be the focus at meals. With our outreach-oriented tables, it was tempting to put the kids at the "kids' table" and concentrate on the guests. Whenever possible, I included them in the proceedings, sitting them next to you, making them part of the adult conversation. They loved telling our guests jokes and often initiated the games we played and the songs we sang. They grew up enjoying the company and didn't feel excluded when others were invited. And for our guests who didn't typically have kids around, they relished in joining the mischief of rowdy games like "Anger Bottle" and "Ghost in the Graveyard."

"I've been acutely aware of the brevity of the childrearing years. As we approach "empty nest," we have become reluctant to share the attention of our kids. Shabbas is the time they are not distracted by media and cell phones—we have them to ourselves and they really open up and express themselves. Therefore, when they are around, I'm not compelled to be entertaining as much."

Since you keep track of the finances in our family, that puts you in charge of *tzedakah* (charity), making sure we always give at least ten percent. Any comments on this mitzvah?

"*Tzedakah* is not just about giving money. It's also about giving time and attention to the needy. *Tzedakah* is justice. God gives us our income as a test to see what we're going to do with it. I want to live in a world where people look out for one another. So I start with me.

"There are many charities competing for our attention. I think of them as balls flying through the air that need catching. We can't juggle all of them and must remember that only certain ones have our name on them. Catch that ball and make it personal and meaningful. We have friends and relatives who have burned out on *tzedakah*. I've heard it said, "If yes to them means no to you, then the answer is no." Part of the giving process is knowing when to say no...I know you have a hard time saying no to anyone! As it stands, we pay dues to four synagogues, and by now we should be partial owners of two Jewish day schools. We give above the mandated 10% to a variety of organizations we choose. By the way, *halacha* also states one shouldn't give more than 20%. Jewish law recognizes the giver must retain the ability to donate in the future.

"For me, the big priority is Jewish day school education. As we are witnessing in our rapidly assimilating country, there is no Jewish continuity without it. This is my mission: to have substantial subsidies available for any parent in the Diaspora wanting to give their kids a day school education. Middle class families should not have to place themselves in dire straits to raise Jewish kids. That said, I think it's one of the worthiest sacrifices."

Can you comment on using the *mikvah* and what it has done for our relationship?

"The experience has evolved. At first I was nervous and self-conscious, worried I'd do something wrong. Then, as I grew more confident, I learned to love it. I have always enjoyed the preparation. When I'm in the bath, I feel just like a regal Queen Esther. Who wouldn't want a monthly spa treatment, to spend such concentrated time on oneself? I return in an elevated state, having accomplished something sacred.

"Of course the best part of the anticipation and preparation is that it makes our relations so special. I think it's natural to separate for a period of time. It's probably harder for you than me to be apart. During those twelve days (five days of menstruation plus seven clean days), we manage to build up a sweet tension and it makes the monthly honeymoon passionate. We relish the time we are able to be together, knowing it's not forever. Absence really does make the heart grow fonder. The more careful we are with details of *taharat mishpacha* (family purity), the more intense the reunion. Part of the joy of our reunion is the knowledge we are doing the right thing in God's eyes, living holy lives and sanctifying the family. Hopefully it creates a holy environment for our kids...so far, so good.

"Immersing in the *mikvah* implies sex is a crucial aspect of marriage. Participation in the relationship means participating in sex. I heard Dennis Prager say twice a week is the bare minimum. A loving couple makes time for relations. They should never be rushed. It's a chance to focus on each other's needs, to light candles, relax, to fall asleep in each other's arms. When couples lose their desire for one another, they are in trouble. When only one member wants abstention for any given period of time it can cause feelings of abandonment. This ritual maintains attraction by building mutual abstention into the fabric of the relationship. It's genius."

What are you thinking about in the *mikvah*?

"Here's how it works: after preparing at home, I do the final touches at the *mikvah*. Then, when it's my turn, I enter the soothing water and submerge completely, making sure every strand of hair is underwater. I keep my eyes and mouth loosely closed. If all looks good when I come up, the *mikvah* lady says "kosher" and hands me a washcloth to cover my hair and make the "*al hatevilah*" b'racha (the blessing over the *mikvah* mitzvah). Then I give back the washcloth and dunk two more times. My *kavanah* (focus) when I'm underwater is very intense: the first time I dunk, I *daven* for specific friends I hope will meet their *bashert* (soulmate). I pray they too will have the opportunity to use this ritual to sanctify their relationship. The next dunk I *daven* for all my needs and then the third time I *daven* for you and the kids. For the record, this is my custom. What one does and how many times they submerge could be different based on what was taught during their *kallah* (bridal) classes or what was handed down from mother to daughter.

"Going to the *mikvah* is such a private, personal opportunity for prayer. Friends of mine who no longer use the *mikvah* have empowered me to *daven* on behalf of people who are childless or in need of healing. Nowadays I never know if it's my last time at the *mikvah*. Many of my peers have been through menopause and I know my turn is coming. That makes me appreciate the whole process even more.

"I know some women think it's sexist to be considered *niddah* or impure, but I prefer the idea that my period makes me <u>unavailable</u> for relations, not dirty or tainted, God forbid. It gives us a chance to learn to function in a non-sexual manner. *Taharat mishpacha* isn't pejorative; it's simply appreciating the monthly gift of the ability to create new life and the conscious awareness of when that opportunity departs."

Speaking of separating, how do you feel about *davening* with a *mechitza?*

"I don't mind the *mechitza* (the barrier that separates men and women during prayer), as long as it's practical and not a huge barrier. It's OK for us to see the men. I like those *shuls* that have one-way glass or fabric. I'm in *shul* to *daven*, not to socialize or hold your hand. I politely tell women who can't stop schmoozing that maybe they should just come to the *Kiddush*. A *mechitza* clarifies what we are supposed to be doing; our attention shouldn't be directed horizontally, it should be going vertically!

"There's a feeling of sisterhood just having women together. It's good to be in a "girl zone" once in a while. It's so rare that genders are separated in our society and there's certainly a place for it. I just read about research demonstrating that guys need nights out with the guys. Certainly women create powerful camaraderie when they are with other women.

"Separation during prayer teaches that separating in society is beneficial. Our *shul Kiddush* is very social. But there is an underlying understanding in our community that physical contact between genders is reserved for marriage. We aren't quite *shomer negiah* (guarding touch) like your brothers. We will hug our friends and relatives as a greeting because that's what people do in society. But in our community, I don't touch the husbands, and you don't touch the wives. At least you better not!

"I remember hearing Rabbi David Wolpe remark that he respects his Orthodox peers who don't touch the opposite sex…there is never any confusion from a lingering hug or handshake, especially with starry-eyed congregants or friend's attractive wives. These days, in order to avoid harassment suits, corporate America has mainstreamed the Jewish customs of *tzniut* (modesty or privacy), *negiah* and *yichud* (prohibition of seclusion with a member of the opposite sex).

Do you ever wish you could be called to the Torah for an *aliyah?*

"I personally don't have a desire to be called to the Torah. But I can certainly understand there are women who would want to do that. It's a modesty issue in traditional Judaism. We have *shuls* in the neighborhood with women's services, it's just not my thing. I do like to dance with the Torah on Simchat Torah so I go to the places where that's the custom. In Orthodox circles, the home is more the center of Jewish life than the *shul*. Those feeling excluded in non-egalitarian settings might only have the synagogue to express their Judaism. In all these years I have never heard any of my community friends complain, probably because our Jewish expression isn't centered around the synagogue. Once again, I'm a traditionalist on these women/men separation issues.

"I think egalitarianism as a sacred value is a slippery slope. One compromise leads to others and eventually that movement is so far from tradition. The fact is that women can do everything. We are the pinnacle of creation, the final being created in the book of *B'reishit* and the most God-like in our ability to give life. If women are so involved with the prayer leadership that men get pushed aside, it's not a good thing. In some of the synagogues I've visited on your concert tours, I've observed that many men have opted out. It's like they are saying, "Oh great, you women have this handled! I'll just watch a ball game or get more work done." Men clearly need to have their participation compulsory, to be wrapped up in leather and bound to synagogue leadership and mitzvot. Women are connected to God more naturally. Most men won't show up unless they feel that it's up to them to keep Judaism going. I vote we not take their job away."

How do you feel about the emphasis of separate roles for men and women?

"I believe that the genders are very different and efforts to blend them are foolhardy. There are God-given realities we shouldn't mess with. Not accepting the differences in genders is not accepting who we truly are. Equality in society is crucial in terms of civil rights, wages, education and opportunity. But in terms of Jewish practice, the Torah distinguishes the strengths of each gender and optimizes them for the well being of the couple, their children and the community.

In a marriage, men want to be head of the household and get respect from their wives and children. Women want to feel they are their husband's number one priority. If their husbands are busy with their buddies, obsessing over hobbies or up all night with porn, it's sending the message "you are not enough for me." I'm sure our forefather Jacob loved both Leah and Rachel. But because he loved Rachel more, the Torah tells us Leah felt hated.

"I'm comfortable with femininity and support your masculinity. I like that you take initiative in guiding our family's destiny, plan our vacations or that you get the guys to go out on the town for your "Pico Men's Club" outings. I've learned not to criticize you in front of others or to gossip about you. I like that you take a leadership role when we entertain on Shabbat. I'm careful never to undermine you with our kids or say, "Who cares what dad says" when making decisions. I see friends roll their eyes when their husbands make dumb comments. It's all about body language. I'm not perfect but I know you flourish when you feel respected. And you do a great job in complimenting me, expressing desire for me and making me feel loved. And you take out the trash, as long as I remind you.

Yes, dear.

OK, friends. Sam here. Much thanks to Shira for sharing her wisdom. I want to give credit where credit is due: many of the ideas in this book were developed in our conversations. Because my recording studio is behind our home, I am able to share most of my meals with her and get feedback on any issues on which I'm cogitating. She always has an opinion and whether I like it or not, she is usually right. We feel blessed that our marriage has been bolstered by the brilliance of Torah, the sagacity of our rabbis and the support of our community.

Darling Shira, thanks for being my partner in this adventure. May our love always continue to blossom.

THE FOUR QUESTIONS

1. Do you feel there are certain differences between men and women that can be celebrated without being sexist?

2. What is your most powerful candlelighting experience?

3. How do you feel about men and women having some different commandments to observe?

4. Are you comfortable with Judaism's view on gender differences?

PART FIVE

The Joy of Jewish Holidays: Spring and Summer Festivals

This section is dedicated by
HERB AND SHARON GLASER

We always marveled at the inventive songs you wrote and performed when you were a boy. Now, as Mr. Jewish Music, the world is uplifted by your wealth of knowledge and the enthusiasm you share at your Shabbatons, concerts and workshops. May you continue to keep everyone learning, singing and swaying for many years to come. We are proud to be your Auntie and Uncle. Kol Hakavod!

IN THIS SECTION:

Shabbat: TGIF 129

Shabbat: Get Unplugged.. 136

Pesach: War of Worldcraft 139

Pesach: Unbreakable Soul.. 144

Minor League Holidays.. 149

A Shavuot Revelation 155

The Three Weeks: My Family Vacation 159

Tisha B'Av: Jews and Aspens 163

OVERVIEW

Jewish holidays are the times when all good things come together: The Jewish People, Torah study, prayer, family, community and of course, a plethora of culinary delights. The holiday cycle serves to enhance our Joy of Judaism throughout the year. In this section, you'll find musings on nearly all the important milestones, starting with our weekly "taste of the world to come" (Shabbat) and then onward chronologically with the first holiday on the biblical calendar, Passover. You won't find any kugel or *charoset* recipes—that's Shira's area of expertise. But you will find recipes for tapping into the unique spirituality of each period and methods to make them meaningful for the whole family.

I opted to divide the holidays by season. This section is about the sunny side of the biblical year. The *siddur* makes a similar designation; spring and summer are the seasons when Asheknazi prayer books omit the phrase, "*mashiv haruach u'morid hagashem*" (God makes the wind blow and rain fall) in the *Amidah* prayer. Spring serves us Passover, the period of *S'firat Ha'omer* which culminates in Shavuot, and then a long, dry summer dominated by the time of "lessened joy" known as the Three Weeks.

Holidays in Western parlance signify a recreational break from the typical work or school routine, but for Jews, holidays are truly holy days. They are called *mo'adim* in Hebrew, from the root *mo'ed*, or encounter. For example, the *Ohel Mo'ed* was the "tent of meeting" we built while wandering the desert. Hence, a holiday is really a meeting with God, an encounter with the special energy of the season. The Jewish view of time isn't linear, rather, we see it as an ascending spiral where each holiday is layered on top of the preceding holidays. When we celebrate the first night of Pesach, for example, we hold our *Seder* at a moment in time anchored in the original Exodus from Egypt. Therefore, if you really dig in, you can feel the essence of the original impetus for the day AND the power of cumulative celebrations throughout history.

For six years, I taught a weekly class called Seasons of Joy. This course satisfied the educational requirements for those seeking Orthodox conversion to Judaism through the L.A. *Beit Din*. My challenge to attendees was to spend the first-year learning about the holidays in depth, and then solidifying that knowledge with a sophomore year of "living" those holidays with all of their *halachic* requirements. I offer the same challenge to my readers. Consider committing yourself to experiencing the annual cycle with all its particulars. I'm confident you will enhance connection with God and community. Careful: you may also gain some weight!

Shabbat: TGIF

Working so hard, I keep on wondering
If there is a chance I will ever be through
Coming so far, but just as I'm finishing
It seems there is always some more work
to do

I need a day to collect my thoughts
To spend some time with You

Here comes Shabbas, Shabbas, Shabbas

Come Friday Eve,
The beggar and the billionaire
Will each have a feast that will last
through the night
Who could believe that families
everywhere
Are singing the songs by the same
candlelight

Taking the time to appreciate
The wonderful things that You do

As you may have guessed by now, I am who I am thanks to Shabbat. Due to this biblically mandated institution, I have peace of mind, a flourishing community, a great relationship with my family and a career where I traverse the country singing its praises. All this benefit for just taking a day off! I always enjoyed Shabbat as a kid. Our Friday night dinners were filled with singing, home-cooked food and extended family. But the real magic of Shabbat was revealed only when I dove into the supernal pool of this twenty-five-hour weekly oasis in time with absolute commitment, no turning back.

The crucial step was leaving my beachside townhouse to move into the urban Jewish community, thanks to the example of friends who had already made the jump. Living close to a synagogue (or in my case, fifty of them) was essential for me to maintain a God-focused consciousness. Perhaps this is why God invented peer pressure. Relocating required the protracted suspension of disbelief; I had to learn to trust the insights of the local rabbis and see where their advice would lead me.

The Torah emphasizes Shabbat more than any other ritual because it provides the most profound physical, financial and emotional evidence that one is serious about a relationship with God. I discovered prioritizing Shabbat is the benchmark, the golden ticket, the minimum deposit required to open a high yield spiritual bank account. In my new neighborhood, Shabbat was joyous, intellectually invigorating and united all age groups. Did I mention the regally served gourmet meals?

I keenly remember my last gig on the Sabbath. I was touring California as the soloist for composer Jose Bowen's Jazz Shabbat Service with big band and choir. During the curtain call at our final stop in the palatial sanctuary of Wilshire Boulevard Temple, I knew I was done. It was clear to me that the Sabbath-infused spiritual growth I was experiencing didn't jive with driving, shlepping gear, plugging in and getting a paycheck. Thanks to the infernal power of real commitment, just like my marriage has bloomed beyond my wildest expectations, so, too, has my love affair with the Creator of the Universe and my perception of the omnipresent realm of holiness.

I was advised early on not to tell anyone I was *Shomer Shabbat* (fully Sabbath observant) until I was all the way there. Otherwise I might get caught weaseling out of a family function I didn't want to attend based on the platitude of my newfound religiosity, but then making an exception to see a favorite rock band. It took me six years after I began the process of learning about the intricacies of Shabbat to actually take it on 100%. I'm glad I did the baby-step routine; it made every hour added to the sacred day a personal triumph.

I strongly encourage "closing the loop," creating a new reality by taking on Shabbat in all of its facets regardless of extenuating circumstances. In my workshops, I describe this level of commitment as the difference between inflating a perforated balloon versus one that is intact. Fill a hole-ridden balloon with helium and it won't stay aloft. But when you close up that last hatch for the gas to escape, you now possess a craft that can fly to the highest atmosphere. I didn't really understand this until I was "in." Ask any *Ba'alei T'shuva* (those who take on Jewish tradition) if they can imagine life without Shabbat. I guarantee they wouldn't trade this taste of paradise for the world.

Every week, our home is whitewashed: sheets changed, floors scrubbed and fresh flowers festoon even the bathrooms. We wear our best clothes, enjoy a multi-course feast in the dining room with our fine glassware and polished silver, sing songs both sacred and secular and offer words of Torah. We also laugh together, play board games, card games and tell stories. Of course, when we have guests, we take the meal up a notch, drink *l'chaims* and go around the table so guests can introduce themselves and mention something special from the past week for which they are grateful. I offer a *d'var Torah* (a Torah thought), usually explaining nuances in the weekly portion and how they might be relevant in our lives. Thanks to my incredible wife's cooking, obtaining an invite to our Shabbas table is considered an "E-Ticket" opportunity.

We are members of several synagogues in our unusual neighborhood and I do my best to "*shul*-hop" based on my mood, a sudden intuition or whichever among the fifty within walking distance has a special speaker or *simcha*. Wherever I show up, I am often coaxed into leading the *davening*. I generally say yes regardless of my level of exhaustion and rarely regret the decision. I feel that my singing ability and spirit is a gift I can give to my community, and the sound of the congregation joining me in song is all the compensation I need. While there are a lot of things one can't do on Shabbat, we are fully occupied doing what's permitted: eating, drinking, praying, schmoozing, spending time with family and maybe even taking a luxurious nap on Saturday afternoon.

Our family has no physical record of any Shabbat or Holiday celebration for the past few decades. No photos of my wife's beautifully set tables, videos of our raucous *zmirot* (songs) or transcriptions of the many scintillating discussions. Shabbat is truly an island in time, a dimension that cannot be grasped with cameras or recorders. The emotional and spiritual sensations of the day are engraved on our hearts and souls in a manner digital technology cannot capture. Shabbat moments are the stuff of ephemera and it would make little sense to attempt to document these experiences to be enjoyed later on. We don't stop the action to try to hold onto it, thanks to the detailed laws of Shabbat regarding turning on and off electronic devices. These holy days are ineffable, transient and yet are the most real experiences in our lives.

Thanks to the extensive preparation required, Shabbat is something we celebrate all week. Shira saves her best recipes for the festive meals and spends days planning the guest list and visiting various markets and bakeries for ingredients. I read the weekly Torah portion with a plethora of commentaries to remain in sync with the entire Jewish world and have something novel to share at my Shabbat meals. I make sure the dry cleaning is picked up by Friday so that we all have our Shabbat clothes pressed and ready. When our kids were in elementary school, they were primed with excitement to share new insights at the table. Now they just look at me funny when I request a *d'var Torah*. As we prepare, we remember these weekday activities are done *lichvod Shabbas* (to honor Shabbat). I must admit I binge on my work on Wednesday and Thursday nights knowing I have Shabbat coming to catch up on my sleep. Before leaving for the synagogue *Erev Shabbat,* there's a custom to check one's pockets to ensure they are empty. I do this both physically and spiritually, consciously emptying the worries from my cranial hard drive.

Becoming *shomer Shabbat* (Sabbath observant) requires a temporal shift in the perspective of one's week. This is hinted at in the laws regarding *Havdalah*, the ceremony with which we commemorate the Sabbath's departure on Saturday night. One can say *Havdalah* until sunset on Tuesday. That's because Sunday, Monday and Tuesday are considered to be in the "shadow" of the previous Shabbat. From Tuesday night and on we are in the zone of the upcoming Shabbat. The day of rest is not the "end" of the week, like a finish line where we break the tape and then collapse. Instead, it is the centerpiece, the pinnacle, the raison d'être. The *Havdalah Kiddush* doesn't just separate the sacred from the secular...it injects the secular with the sacred. Perhaps the best symbol of this concept is the golden menorah in the Temple, with its primary central branch and the three on either side angling toward it. When Shabbat and a God-focused life is the center of our week, we float on an exalted raft of blessing upon the raging river of life. We recognize the energy of the previous Shabbat is only three days behind us and another nurturing, faith-building day is imminent.

The prayers on Shabbat are longer and hopefully more musical than their weekday counterpart. Shabbat is the time when a mourner's *chiyuv* (*halachic* priority) to lead the service is superseded by the importance of having a trained chazzan with natural musical leadership ability. The celebration starts with a final weekday *Mincha* (afternoon) service and segues into the special *Kabbalat Shabbat* ceremony to welcome the Sabbath bride. Then *Ma'ariv* (evening prayers) are followed by a festive meal. On Saturday morning we have extra prayers in both the *Psukei D'zimra* (Psalms of Praise) and *Shma* sections of *Shacharit*. Following the Shabbat *Amidah* we hear the full-length Torah reading and *Haftorah* (passages from Prophets). Then we add the *Mussaf* (additional) service to commemorate the special sacrifice offered on Shabbat in Temple times. Tack on the concluding prayers and multiple repetitions of *Kaddish* and the service can last three hours.

I recommend newcomers take their time endeavoring this acquired taste. In other words, optimally we should be in the synagogue for all the prayers, but not if it makes us miserable. A good indication of our frustration level is when we start counting how many pages are left in the *siddur*. By coming a bit later to services, we can incorporate our public prayer quotient in measured doses and then schmooze at the *kiddush*. One caveat: each section of the service unlocks the gate to the following one. Our formal prayers are like a video game where each level must be passed to access the next. The *siddur*, like the Passover *Seder*, has order as its root. When arriving late, one must get through the parts that were missed before joining the group prayer. For example, one can do morning blessings at home and then squeeze in the highlights of *P'zeukei D'zimra* and *Sh'ma* in between *aliyot* of the Torah reading, then say the personal *Amidah* during the *Haftorah*. That way, by *Mussaf*, one has fully caught up with the congregation. If this sounds too confusing, just get there on time! It's a big mitzvah to be among the first ten assembled, thereby "making the *minyan*."

It's hard to imagine there was a time when there was no *Kabbalat Shabbat* ceremony on Friday night. The incorporation of this beautiful series of *Tehillim* (Psalms) ushering in our holy day was initiated in the holy city of *Tsfat*, only 600 years ago. That makes it a new service, compared to the rest of our 2500-year-old *siddur*. I think the *kabbalists* chose this specific set of *Tehillim* in order to fill us with a sense of wonder for God's power as revealed in nature. The passages vividly describe lofty mountains, rushing rivers, heaving oceans or thunderous storms, hopefully allowing us to recall intense personal experiences of the divine in natural surroundings. As we have discussed, what typically happens in a nature moment is that our ever-present ego takes a short break and a palpable awareness of God's presence fills the vacuum. Come Shabbat, manifesting this phenomenon is our ultimate goal.

Kabbalat Shabbat allows us to experience a degree of passion typically absent from the *Ma'ariv* service. The spoken word is our basic mode of communication, the next level is song, and when you just can't contain your joy another moment, spontaneous dance is the only appropriate outlet! When I'm leading a Sabbath program, I try to get even the most reluctant congregation on their feet and dancing around the sanctuary during the climax of the *Kabbalat Shabbat* prayers, the *L'cha Dodi*. These nine verses of romantic poetry celebrate the arrival of the Sabbath bride, the queen accompanying us throughout the festive day.

Sometimes I wonder where I get the discipline to be so *machmir* (strict) with my Sabbath and holiday observance. I certainly didn't start out life this way and I realize that for many, taking on such a seemingly inconvenient commitment seems out of reach. These days most can't fathom even an hour without checking their cell phone. I'm aided by a welcoming community dedicated to celebrating these holy days according to the letter of the law. It's also helpful to have my family unified in sharing the adventure. Perhaps there is a mystical force operating behind the scenes. I'd like to share a few stories illustrating the possibility that some ancestral merit is involved with keeping our family on this path of righteousness.

The first story involves my great grandmother Lena Barenfeld, for whom my daughter, Sarah Lena, is named. My brother Yom Tov was on an El Al flight waiting to depart when an attendant came down the aisle looking for a Rabbi Glaser. Yom Tov raised his hand and she told him there was a better seat closer to the front. Before he could leave his spot, a gentleman a few rows back said, "You're Rabbi Glaser?" This teacher in the Ponevezh Yeshiva had heard there were some *ba'al t'shuva* Glasers out there and wanted to verify a certain yeshiva legend. He motioned for Yom Tov to take the vacant seat next to him and told him this tale.

One auspicious evening in the late 1940s, the Ponevezher Rav, Rabbi Kahaneman visited Grandma Lena and Grandpa Abraham to raise funds for his new yeshiva. The Rav was attempting to restore the grandeur of his formidable Polish scholarly community which had been obliterated in the Holocaust. This new *Beis Midrash* (house of study) would be built in Israel, within the historic rabbinic stronghold of B'nei Brak. I imagine my great grandpa Abe had his fill of such *schnorrers* (charity emissaries) and sent the Rav away with a small donation. Before he left, however, my great grandma pulled Rabbi Kahaneman aside and cried, "My children have strayed so far from Torah and I am heartbroken. I don't have even one member of my extended family *shomer* Shabbas. If you can bless us that some of our progeny will become *shomer* Shabbas, we will dedicate the cornerstone of the *Beis Midrash*." The Rav gave her this exact blessing and the rest is history. I was honored to share this story and perform at the annual Ponevezh banquet. Remarkably, this yeshiva has now grown to become the leading *Litvak* (Lithuanian-style) institution in the Promised Land.

The next story occurred shortly after I started keeping Shabbat in 1992. My brother Yom Tov had just returned from his first year in yeshiva in Jerusalem. Our family was overjoyed to see how much he had grown spiritually and yet behind the scraggly beard was the charismatic Johnny we adored. Yom Tov and I have always bonded over action sports. We've never been able to sit still long enough to watch a ball game on TV; we much prefer to explore the backcountry on mountain bikes or hit the surf. That first weekend he was back we gathered a group of old friends for a few days of fun in Joshua Tree National Park. This magical moonscape lies in the high desert two hours from our home and it's perfect for climbing, biking and camping.

We set off that Friday morning in my trusty Toyota Supra laden with camping gear and our bikes strapped to the rack. A half hour down the road my car started to overheat. It clearly was not up for the drive and thankfully, when it broke down, we were able to locate a friend nearby with a loaner truck. He threw us the keys and said, "It's all yours, as soon as you unload the cord of firewood in the back." We frantically stacked the prodigious pile of lumber against his garage, transferred our gear and set off in his rickety 4×4. Unfortunately, an hour down the road, while doing eighty in the fast lane, we had an explosive tire blowout. No one was injured, but we were stuck on the wrong side of the freeway and it took an eternity for a cop to show up and radio for a tow truck. It's hard to imagine how we ever survived without mobile phones!

We waited for over an hour for a new tire to be installed at the repair shop. When we hit the road again, we realized it was unlikely we were going to make it to Joshua Tree by sundown. Still, we pressed ahead, hoping for a miracle. Shortly before candlelighting we had a tense dialog regarding the state of affairs. I was still at a point in my observance where I could rationalize that due to this emergency we should finish the drive and we would take on Shabbat as soon as we arrived (this is not a liberty I would take today). My brother, however, said, "I will not drive even a minute after Shabbas comes in, even if I have to spend the night on the shoulder of the freeway."

At that time in history, there was almost no civilization between L.A. and Palm Springs. Just a few "one horse" towns with gas stations and fast food joints—certainly not the continuous metropolis one finds today. We spotted a motel at the next exit and screeched off the interchange, only to find it was out of business. I saw a look of panic in my brother's eyes as he commandeered our friend's pickup back onto the freeway in search of another option. With sundown looming, we pulled off at the next exit and parked in the first motel we saw. As soon as we checked in, we started throwing our property inside the door of our unit. Just as the sun hit the horizon, we unloaded the last of our valuables and high-fived each other, thrilled we had a roof over our heads to celebrate this unusual Shabbat.

That night, we prayed with special intensity and enjoyed a delectable feast that my mother had lovingly prepared. We sang, danced and jumped on the beds until we were totally exhausted from the day's exploits. But now we had another problem. The lights were on in the room and turning them off would mean breaking Shabbas. I checked the front desk and found it uninhabited. I noticed a young couple in the room next door. I gingerly knocked on the door and a disconcerted, wide-eyed African American man peered through the crack. I explained we wanted to go to sleep but the light was on. (When asking a non-Jew to do an act forbidden to a Jew on Shabbat, one can't mention the exact thing action required—he has to intuit what's needed and do it on his own volition). He gave me an incredulous glare, so my brother stepped in to help, saying, "You see, we are really tired and it would be great if it were dark enough to sleep." With this, the man slammed the door shut, gathered his girlfriend and drove off into the night. Thank God for eyeshades.

The next morning, after we *davened* and ate lunch, we wandered the streets of this backwater town. It was called Banning and as we passed the few open stores, we joked that they were "banning liquor" and "banning police." We returned to the room for a nap and when darkness fell, promptly checked out and finished the last half hour up to Joshua Tree. We rejoiced around the campfire with our worried friends and toasted to our zany Shabbat experience. The next day, the whole gang scrambled the bodacious boulders of the park and enjoyed memorable mountain bike rides shredding the slippery single-track trails.

A few months later, I attended a Glaser holiday get together. I told my dear Uncle Charlie the saga of our Shabbas debacle when we got stuck in this hick town. As I finished the tale, Charlie blanched and didn't respond for a few moments. Then he said, "Sammy, are you telling me that you and your brother spent Shabbas in Banning?" "Yes, Uncle Charlie. What's the big deal?" He replied, "Do you know anything about Banning?" "Yes," I said with a grin. "They are banning police and liquor!" He looked at me sternly and said, "Sam, your grandfather, for whom you are named, founded the town of Banning. At that time in his life, as his garment business grew, Shabbas had to take a back seat to his need to supervise production in his new factory. Do you see that you and Johnny, his descendants, have done a *tikkun* (healing)? You kept Shabbas in Banning! What do you think of that?"

Most American Jews have great-great grandparents who were deeply connected to Shabbat and are pulling strings for us upstairs. Just imagine: since the time of Moses, the freight train of Jewish history has been thundering along the tracks, powered by the eternal combustion of Mount Sinai. Tragically, in our days, we see many of the cars have derailed. There's a supernatural reason our souls feel good when we affiliate, when we do a mitzvah, when we attend a Shabbas meal. Perhaps it's assuaging our Jewish guilt or a subliminal attraction to members of the tribe. Or maybe it's all those ancestors rallying for us behind the scenes shouting, "Go, go, go…just do it!"

You can be the one to get the train back on track.

THE FOUR QUESTIONS

1. How do you celebrate Shabbat at this point in your life?

2. How can you make Shabbat more meaningful to you and your family?

3. Would you be willing to give up one thing you currently do in order to try a new level of Shabbat observance?

4. What could you and your family accomplish together on a day without any other obligations or distractions?

Shabbat: Get Unplugged!

♫ KAD'SHEYNU ♫

joyjud.com/m/kds

Kad'sheynu b'mitzvotecha
V'teyn chelkeynu b'toratecha
Sab'eynu mituvecha
V'sam'cheynu biyshu'atecha

V'taheyr libeynu
L'ovdecha b'emet
V'hanchileynu Hashem Elokeynu
B'ahava uvratzon Shabbat kodshecha

Oh the greatest treasure of our lives
Unites the generations
Brings us closer
Makes us holy
Thank You for this taste of paradise

When we rest and relax, the burden off our backs
We remember the reason we're alive

The value of going "unplugged" was introduced shortly after MTV hit the airwaves. "MTV Unplugged" was supposed to last thirteen episodes when it debuted in November of 1989. It eventually topped a hundred shows, with a third of them released as soundtrack albums. Paul McCartney took the concept mainstream when he released his best-selling "Unplugged (The Official Bootleg)", recorded on the show in 1991. Clearly, fans love seeing the inner workings of music-making, without the distractions of producers, walls of vocals, electric guitars and drum loops. Real musicians making real music in real time. Without a net. Milli Vanilli types, whose careers survive with the help of studio magic or drummers who can't keep time, need not apply.

The collection of scintillating unplugged shows is now easily accessible thanks to YouTube. Some of my favorites are those where one can get a fly-on-the-wall perspective of how the songs might have been created. As much as I love playing with my band, there is something to be said for those piano/vocal only shows where intense intimacy can be established. Without the wall of sound, the crowd relaxes like they are in a living room, focusing on the messages with open hearts. Instead of performing to passive listeners, the unplugged realm creates a "playing with" the audience, like a concerto with the artist as soloist and the audience as orchestra.

Occasionally, sublime musical moments occur after my "official" concerts. After the crowd clears out, local musician friends gather on the stage to jam without the house P.A. system on. Or we have an after-party at a nearby home where everyone is surrounding a grand piano, with multiple guitars jangling and hand drums a-pounding. No electricity required! At CAJE (Coalition for Advancement in Jewish Education), the annual conference of Jewish educators for which I perform each year, I typically lead a sing-along on the last night. Insomniac attendees pack into a sweaty room and sing for three hours straight. One piano, one microphone and six hundred lead vocalists. I don't take breaks and have an assistant on hand to mop my brow and pour water down my throat. We segue from Israeli and camp songs to the best of R&B, Rock 'n Roll, Top 40 and a healthy smattering of Beatles.

Going unplugged is not a new concept to the Jewish people. We have been "unplugging" once a week for millennia. We call it Shabbat. Zionist leader Ahad Ha'am famously stated, "more than the Jews have kept Shabbat, Shabbat has kept the Jews." Without the help of our phones, computers and other "personality amplifiers," we reconnect with who we are and our place in the universe. It's as if God is saying: "Hey, get your mitts out of my creation!" The rest of the week, God gives us the illusion that we are making a living so we feel like partners in shaping the world. But on Shabbat, the illusion stops and we see the world through Godly eyes. We leave behind the great symphony of our lives and are left with simple song.

Unplugging is such an integral aspect of the Sabbath that it's ironic how many synagogues strive to increase membership by offering concert-style worship on Friday nights. Yes, it's true that churches have raised the spiritual bar by employing masterful ensembles to propel the prayers. But for the Jewish People, there is something to be said for sweet simplicity, at least on Shabbat. *Davening* in blissful, unamplified a cappella allows us to hear ourselves think while simultaneously connecting with the greater whole. Our community of fellow worshippers can express hopes and aspirations to the Almighty without enduring the lavalier mics, semi-tuned guitars and tribal drumming of overenthusiastic prayer leaders drowning us out. Concerts, jam sessions and *kumzitzes* have their place on the weekdays. But when the auspicious time of candlelighting hits on Friday afternoon, I'll take my Shabbat with shalom.

In my neighborhood, "Shabbat Shalom" is the operative greeting for the thousands of Jews walking the streets. These words mean more than "have a peaceful Sabbath." It's a wish that everyone shares our blissful Shabbas state of mind. John Lennon would have us imagine a world with peace between all races and creeds. On Shabbat we LIVE in that world. No imagination necessary. It's more than lip service or lofty dreams. It's <u>living</u> in a state of oneness with creation and when it's time to plug back in on Saturday night, we are grounded, connected and ready for the onslaught of our day-to-day.

Shabbat takes some effort to get used to. Initially one is consumed by the list of forbidden actions. But after a while, it's as natural as breathing. God is described by the prophets as communicating in a "still, small voice." When plugged in, it's impossible to hear it. God speaks to us in many voices and we are masters of methods to ignore them. These days we have more ways than ever to banish the precious commodity of silence. On Shabbat, we re-enter the quiet conversation and restore our relationship, shepherding our fragile faith into the realm of commitment, making our *bitachon* (trust in God) tangible.

Those who take on Sabbath observance make sacrifices that may seem daunting, but pale in comparison with the eternal rewards of true rest. I have turned down countless appearances because they require travel on Shabbat or holidays or because the client can't grasp the value of an a cappella prayer experience. My mother was recently offered passage from Europe to L.A. on a luxurious private jet but opted out because it departed on the Sabbath. One of my favorite singers, Michael Ian Elias, whose vocals decorate many of my albums, turned down a career-changing lead in JC Superstar in order to maintain his newfound religious commitment. I live in a neighborhood with scores of Hollywood writers who pass up major opportunities when their *shomer Shabbas* lifestyle cannot be accomodated. I'm convinced these heroic deeds ingnite the firmament and give our Creator untold *nachas*. Perhaps our Pico-Robertson community flourishes due to their merit.

The best way to get into Shabbat is to get into Shabbat. I have always said, "It's hard to learn to surf in Nebraska." Find friends who celebrate a full Sabbath and just have fun with it. Start with Friday night dinner, then add services, then try a Saturday lunch and eventually take the plunge and stay overnight in a nearby 'hood. During my first observant Shabbat, I didn't know if I was allowed to flush the toilet! One might ask dumb questions and even look like an idiot. Who cares? Give your hosts something to laugh about! Our sages tell us that we truly acquire a mitzvah when we do it three times in a row. Soon you will have attempted the twenty-five-hour lockdown thing three weeks in a row and you LOVE it. Then you're in. Simple as that.

Any object that isn't useful on Shabbat or could cause a violation is called *muktzeh*—steer clear of *muktzeh!* When Friday night hits, there are no iPhones or laptops. No Netflix or Xbox. We get our kids back, for one precious day a week. As a parent, I can relate to our supernal *Avinu Malkeinu* (Father in Heaven) Who eagerly anticipates getting us back for this weekly love fest.

Our media gets perpetually louder, racier and relentless. It's easy to be absorbed into the Matrix without even knowing it, to crave the world of OASIS more than our earth-bound reality. MTV has it right: a rockin' concert or state-of-the-art movie is great, but for a true classic, we've got to unplug.

THE FOUR QUESTIONS

1. From what in your life do you really need to unplug?

2. Do you feel there could be a stronger connection with the divine if you could disconnect from technology and work?

3. What is your favorite aspect of Shabbat?

4. What is holding you back from trying one full Shabbat unplugged?

Pesach: War of Worldcraft

♫ BARUCH HAMAKOM ♫

It's the time of year to remember
As if we ourselves were there
Recreate the scene with our families
We unite in song and prayer

Put your faith in Me
Safely through the desert will I lead you
I will set you free
And every year on this sacred night
You will say
Baruch Hamakom...

Drink four cups of wine while we're
leaning

And the afikoman we share
For this night to have any meaning
Children's questions must fill the air
Put your faith in Me
Safely through your lifetime will I lead you
I will set you free

And I will give you eyes to see
How to walk upon the way
At the midnight hour
You'll feel My outstretched arm
Right by your side so that you know
You are the precious child I long for
everyday

L ike most kids, ours spend a lot of time on their gadgets. We brought them into the world with the hope they might savor the gift of life. Or at least ride their bikes once in a while. As teens they saw the "real world" as the Snapchats, videos and TV shows they voraciously consumed. All the Jewish stuff they had to deal with in day school was a burden to be endured until they could get back online. Until ninth grade, our offspring grew up without television; we had a home theater for favorite movies, but nothing of the broadcast variety. This ended when they hit high school. Yeshiva University of L.A., our local day school, enacted a one laptop per child policy in order to enable students to compete in the 21st century. Enable is the operative word. Tech-saavy kids soon cracked the "net-nanny" software and all bets were off.

For young people, plugging in is a divine right. After all, they will live forever, have all of their needs met and perish the thought of enduring a vacant minute. They aren't in the game until owning the latest models of skinny screens of all sizes. God forbid the Internet is ever down.

At one point, a new enemy claimed our children's brains: online gaming. Sarah opened a Facebook account to shmooze with friends while playing addictive online games and posting her scores. During her one-hour TV allotment each day (ha ha!) she simultaneously played the games, watched a TV show and chatted with friends. I would leave for the evening and return to find her in the exact same position. She would practice the piano for ten minutes but as soon as she hit a tough passage she would give in to her palpable desperation to get back on the Net.

My boys succumbed to a game/drug even more potent, World of Warcraft. As in other role-playing games, W.O.W. allowed them to wander a remarkable alien world populated by characters manned by players from around the world. They got credits and booty for kills and strived valiantly to build their custom-designed creature to the highest level of power. While it was nice to see my boys cooperating in order to negotiate the adventure, I didn't appreciate that they were unwilling to leave the house. After all, we live in Southern California. They might as well have grown up in Anchorage.

The Jewish People are players in a grand scheme I call W.O.W.: "War of Worldcraft." We are in the midst of a 3500-year peer-to-peer networking phenomenon unrivaled in history. In every generation, we are engaged in a battle to the death against the monsters of ignorance, immorality and violence. With courage and unrivaled conviction, we cleave to our ancient texts and traditions, hoping to survive while influencing those around us. The Torah reveals the contradictory nature of our future as an eternal people: we will remain few in number and yet have vast impact on all of humankind as we wander the globe.

I would argue that God's farfetched "light unto nations" experiment is working rather well. Historian Thomas Cahill agrees: "The Jews started it all—and by "it" I mean so many of the things we care about, the underlying values that make all of us tick, Jew and Gentile, believer and atheist. Without the Jews, we would see the world with different eyes, hear with different ears, even feel with different feelings…the role of the Jews, the inventors of Western culture, is also singular: there is simply no one else remotely like them; theirs is a unique vocation. Indeed…the very idea of vocation, of a personal destiny, is a Jewish idea."

Pesach is a time to acknowledge our contribution to humanity and break free of those entities enslaving us. Each spring, the season of renewal, we begin by getting back on track with our national goal of worldcraft. Pharaoh may be gone from the stage of history, but servitude is still with us. We are trapped in a quest for wealth, status, career advancement and material acquisition. Bosses, teachers, parents, children and peers badger us. We are stuck in ruts of our own making, battling inner demons, bad habits and addictions. We come into this holiday well aware that the issues we complained about last year will likely be with us next year. How can we escape our chains during this *Z'man Cheruteinu*, the Passover season of freedom? How can we reclaim the gumption to accomplish our global mission?

Pesach is our national homecoming. We press reset, reconvene with our people, reprioritize. First we have to clear out the *chametz*. All that yummy challah, cream-filled *pareve* Oreos, glazed donuts—it's got to go. The rabbis tell us the *chametz* represents our ego. Big bread = big ego. EGO stands for Edge God Out! For the week of Passover we eat humble pie, otherwise known as matzah. Humility gets us on the playing field. As mentioned in the Judaism 101 section, when we override our sense of entitlement, we create a grateful space to rediscover our purpose, clearing our launch pad for explosive transformation. The custom is to search for *chametz* with a candle, not a torch. One might think we need the most powerful light to cleanse every crumb—but the search for *chametz* is spiritual as well, and too blinding a light into our psyche may make us feel depressed rather than empowered.

Humility doesn't require us to be pushovers. Moshe was the greatest prophet who ever lived and led us out of Egypt. The Five Books of Moses bear his name. Yet, he was the humblest man ever. Had you asked him if these accolades were accurate, he would have answered affirmatively. Humble people can be superstars! The secret is acknowledging the source of one's strength. Once, Rav Chatzkel Abramsky, zt"l, head of the London *Beit Din*, was called to testify in a secular London court. His attorney asked him to state his name and position and queried, "Is it true you are the greatest living *halachic* authority in Europe?" The Rav replied, "Yes, it is true." The judge interrupted, saying, "Rabbi, isn't that rather haughty on your part? Don't your laws teach you to be humble?" The Rav responded, "Yes, but I am under oath."

Only with our *chametz* destroyed can we endeavor the celebratory *Seder* meal with our families and tell our remarkable story. Anytime I'm teaching a workshop and see people drifting off, I launch into a story. We love stories! A capable *Seder* leader makes the Exodus real, for both adults and children. Act it out! Wear costumes! Even though I look ridiculous, I conduct the proceedings in my flowing white *kittel* robe and Legoland-designed Pharaoh hat. My typical audience is fifty to eighty members of the tribe who opt for the group family *Seder* on national Pesach programs. My family helps me reenact the plagues with marshmallow hail, rubber frogs, wild animal masks and we writhe on the floor for the Death of the Firstborn. As my friend Rabbi Nachum Braverman says, when kids are involved, the three most important ingredients for Shabbat and Yom Tov meals are fun, fun and fun. A corollary, at least in my book, is sing, sing and sing!

I love the *Haggadah* (The Telling, the written guide to the *Seder*). One of my favorite courses during my first four months in my Jerusalem yeshiva was a detailed analysis of this millennia old text with textual wizard Rabbi Tom Meyer. I opted to quote *"B'chol dor vador…"* from the *Haggadah* in my song *Hineni*: "In every generation we must see ourselves as if we came out of Egypt." *Seder* night is not a commemoration of something that happened to distant relatives. It's our story in perpetuity, in every age, with every enemy that seeks the destruction of our holy mission of *Tikkun Olam*. We are still travelers on a monumental journey, attending *Seders*, telling our origin story, eating sweet *charoset* mixed with bitter herbs, decrying anti-Semitism, taking our place in this historic march towards redemption.

Our hero Moshe isn't mentioned in the *Maggid* (story portion) of the *Haggadah*. This is God's night. Pesach recalls a time when we were in our infancy as a people. After womblike protection during the nine months of plagues, God lovingly led us through the harsh wilderness as if we were helpless newborns. Over the course of our forty years wandering the desert, our encounter with God and Torah coaxes us into our maturity as a holy people. On Passover, we relate to God as a protective, loving parent, Who is preparing us for the vicissitudes of "worldcraft." We affirm there is no other power than the Almighty, not even Moshe Rabbeinu! The famous hymn, "Let My People Go" omits the end of the biblical sentence, "that they may serve me" (*Shmot* 8:1). The secret to the *Seder* is emphasizing this essential choice: to serve our Creator or to serve humans. Cue my favorite line from Indiana Jones: "Choose wisely!" (Actually, "Never tell me the odds" is my real favorite.)

The classic *Seder* songs were chosen by our sages to express the essential messages of the day. The greatest hits in the Pesach Top 40 are as follows:

1. *Halach Ma'anya*: it's a great song and makes no sense. Let all who are hungry come eat? It's too late—the meal has begun! Actually, it's an invitation to everyone already at the table to perk up, to awaken their appetite for spirituality, to "Be Here Now."

2. *The Four Questions*: ask real questions! Inspire kids to ask their own questions and to become seekers of good answers. If they are not asking, it means they are not engaged. No kids at the table? Sing it anyway, allowing the familiar cadence to inspire our inner child.

3. *The Four Sons*: we have aspects of each son within us. These days, according to the Lubavitcher Rebbe, there is a fifth son—one who isn't even at the *Seder*. Deep insights can be unpacked when comparing the four questions, the four expressions of God's name, the four sons and the four cups of wine.

4. *Avadim Hayinu*: this night is about leaving *Mitzrayim* (Egypt). *Mitzrayim* can be translated as "from the narrow place." This is a night to regain our expansiveness, to acknowledge we are enslaved and freedom is imminent.

5. *Dayenu*: the fifteen verses of the song parallel the fifteen official steps of the *Seder*. Fifteen is the code number for completion; for example, the full moon is on the fifteenth of each lunar month. *Dayenu* parses our salvation saga into multiple elements in order to express gratitude for each cumulative miracle.

6. *Who Knows One: Seder* guests are guided through the sequence of fundamental numeric symbols in our belief system. (Ooh, ah, ooh, ah, ah!)

7. *Chad Gadya:* a mystical overview of the milestones in the grand arc of Jewish history.

The climax of the *Seder* is the recitation of *Hallel* (specific Psalms sung on Jewish holidays and Rosh Chodesh, the start of the new month). It's unlike any other *Hallel* the rest of the year. First of all, it's at night and it's interwoven into a festive meal. Secondly, we don't introduce it with the standard blessing. Why? Because we don't need to set up an intention for the mitzvah like we normally do. On *Seder* night, if we've done the work of clearing out our *chametz*, eating matzah, drinking four cups of wine and singing the aforementioned songs at the top of our lungs, we are in such an exalted state that *Hallel* is a spontaneous outpouring of praise.

If we don't get it right the first night, we get to try again the next! Outside the land of Israel, we give equal emphasis to the first two days of the holiday, *Seder* and all (in Israel they just do one). Living in exile means we have to work twice as hard to get the same inspiration. Holding on to this inspiration is challenging—so make the *Seder* a powerful memory. Be a ham (even if you can't eat it), drink liberally and stay up late. One year, we joined my Jerusalem-based brother's family for a night of music and laughter that lasted until dawn. Yom Tov and Leah served their eight children coffee in between each cup of wine. After the meal, we wandered the streets of his *shtetl*; I was dressed as an evil taskmaster, he was my Jewish slave and our kids followed closely as we searched for lazy Jews to beat with bulrushes. "You are lazy Jews!" we scolded. Yes, we actually whipped people (gently, of course)! None of us will ever forget it.

We usually go into the holiday overwhelmed by the cleaning and cooking, overburdened with the pace of our lives, never quite getting enough rest. Hopefully we finish this sacred week transformed and relaxed, with new focus and commitment. If we can survive such an austere diet, we can withstand any deprivation. Spiritual freedom is the acquisition of moral strength to avoid the shackles of poor decision making. This eight-day period requiring the meticulous avoidance of leaven initiates our calendar year with an invaluable metaphysical victory.

Pesach gets us back in touch with the big picture by appreciating the details: in small acts of kindness and observing seemingly small mitzvot like not over-baking matzah or dipping delicate greens in salt water. We emphasize how we were redeemed then and are continuously redeemed now, so that we may serve God with love. So crucial is the connection between the Exodus and and our Jewish mission statement that we are commanded to recall leaving Egypt every morning and night. Pesach may be the headquarters, but our freedom to stand with God is an everyday gift.

The *Seder* is a microcosm of Jewish history. After all the hard work, when all is said and done, we break out in joyous song from the depths of our hearts. Pesach serves to awaken our inner child, reprioritize our busy lives and restore our glorious goal of serving as soldiers in the War of Worldcraft.

THE FOUR QUESTIONS

1. When have you felt you served as a light unto those around you?

2. What are the things that currently enslave you?

3. What kind of internal *chametz* do you need to get rid of?

4. What can you do at your own *Seder* to reinforce the idea that we are serving as soldiers in the War of Worldcraft?

Pesach:
Unbreakable Soul

Work all day, dream all night
Turn the darkness into light
At the end of our rope
Keep the faith, don't lose hope
You can never break an unbreakable soul

Moshe went out, saw our plight
When no one was lookin' he picked a fight
He had a word with Paro (Pharaoh)
Said won't you let my people go

A hundred years of slavery
Forget what it means to be free
Steal our senses, smash our bones
Take our children from our homes

Eat our bread and drink our wine
Seize our future, waste our time
You may think you're in control, but
You can never break an unbreakable soul

One Rosh Chodesh *Nissan*, I had the pleasure of culminating my eight-day tour of Florida with a Shabbaton in Cooper City, just north of Miami. Before launching into *Kabbalat Shabbat* services I sang "Auld Lang Syne." After all, we just concluded *Adar*, the final month of year in terms of the biblical count. I explained to the surprised congregation that we were marking the transition into *Nissan,* the true New Year's Eve. Rosh Chodesh *Nissan* is the anniversary of the first commandment given to the Jews as a nation: establishing a calendar. Clearly, the foremost responsibility of freedom is maximizing our most valuable asset, time. On the first night of *Nissan,* we start the count until the moon is full on the fifteenth. This is *Seder* night, our annual birthday party as a nation. Some 3000 years ago we were an enslaved people yearning for liberation from a decadent tyrant. At the stroke of midnight on that initial Passover we emerged from the womb of Egypt to our destiny of "worldcraft." Thanks to the genius of the *Haggadah*, every year we gather to retell the saga of the birth of the unbreakable soul of our nation.

Pesach reminds us that we have a powerful, unique *neshama* (soul) as individuals and are also a part of the greater soul of the Jewish People. Every day we grapple with allegiance to self versus selflessness in regard to the whole. Pesach is the celebration of the power of peoplehood. We arrived in Egypt as seventy individuals within a family and became a nation, eternally unified in the "iron crucible" of slavery and suffering. Following the unprecedented miracles of the ten plagues, the splitting of the sea and revelation at Sinai, our collective soul then merges with the One True God, the Great Soul. Pesach is an ideal time to investigate the interaction of these three aspects of our metaphysical existence.

Chazal (our sages) teach that ideally our *neshama* is the rider while the body is the horse. Following this logic, our body is merely a meat-jacket maintained with food, water and exercise, honored with shlepping our precious, divine soul on its mission. Only when we connect with the needs of our soul can we stake our claim in our national destiny. Preparing for Pesach offers the chance for the spring cleaning of *chametz* and any *klipot* (shells) blocking our innermost expression.

Kabbalah offers a window into our unique soul, a user manual that establishes best practices and engenders pride in ownership. Our tradition teaches a Five Levels of the Soul paradigm clarifying the features of the ephemeral self. Imagine the pyramids Jewish slaves helped to build—these five levels can be visualized by picturing the broad base as level one, up to the topmost triangle for level five. In the interest of enhancing the Pesach experience, let's explore these five levels using the teachings of three of my favorite rabbis, David Aaron, Benjamin Blech and Tom Meyer.

The first level is known as *Nefesh*. This is an aspect of consciousness we share with the animal kingdom. It is the basic life force, our instinct, our autonomic survival functions. *Nefesh* allows us to read "The Joy of Judaism" while our bodies quietly digest and respirate. For humans it takes on a more elevated role than animals. When the Torah tells us we were created *b'tzelem Elokim* (in God's image), it refers to this elevated *nefesh* distinction. Nearly 6000 years ago, Homo sapiens achieved a fundamental shift in consciousness. The Torah teaches that God breathed a spark of divinity into our nostrils, animating us with those unique human traits of free will, speech and creativity. Archaeologists concur regarding the timing of the rise of the earliest monuments and cities, tributes to this Godly gift of humanity. Unlike all other creatures, humans don't rely on mere instinct; we also have a deep-seated feeling of nobility and awareness of right and wrong. For example, whereas a dog learns not to urinate on your Persian carpet in order to avoid a swat, we don't pee on the rug because it's just not the right thing to do.

Our *nefesh* is expressed when we hear the voice of the conscience, the fundamental, cross-cultural awareness of good and evil. We know it's inherently wrong to punch an elderly stranger in the street. Hollywood blockbusters with heroes and villains can be marketed internationally because all humans share certain internal ethics. That's our *nefesh* speaking. Another important aspect of *nefesh* is our craving for meaning. The worst form of torture during the Holocaust was repetitive, irrelevant manual labor. Without meaning, our lives become sheer agony. Darwinian evolutionists and physicists cannot adequately explain why the *nefesh* is present. But it is. And we know its voice like we know we have five fingers on our hand.

The next level is known in Kabbalah as *Ruach*, and is based on our quest for <u>truth</u>. It is a uniquely human attribute and words are the vehicle for its dissemination. *Ruach* is typically translated as wind or spirit—like the passage of wind from our lungs when we speak.

What do we mean by saying words "ring of truth?" It means that our soul can intuit truth from falsehood. It's the reason our society rewards honesty and punishes the liar. When we hear someone is badmouthing us with *lashon harah* (gossip), it's our *ruach* that is damaged. Having a good name means maintaining the integrity of one's *ruach*. When we feel damaged by our own personal shortcomings, it's our *ruach* reeling in pain. Great music endures forever because our *ruach* soul hears it as truth, a taste of eternity.

The third level is referred to as *Neshama*. *Neshama* is the generic Hebrew term for soul. But in this five level model, it refers to the power of our <u>thoughts</u>. We are affected by more than mere actions and words. We have ideals. We have a sense of mission, a belief we have a special purpose. Somehow each of us is unique, in spite of the fact that we are among billions of similarly entitled beings. It's our *neshama* speaking when we pursue happiness. I'm sure scientists have convincing theories about why we strive toward a *tafkid* (a personal mission), why we need to feel in sync, why we feel we are deserving of a happy life. But any true pleasure seeker does not need science to explain this universal drive. When we stop to think about it, it's clear we have a *neshama*, a divine force informing our every motivation.

The penultimate level of the soul is the reason that Passover is one of the most widely celebrated holidays. We love the traditions, songs and stories associated with our annual homecoming party. We love spending time with fellow members of the tribe, engrossed in the powerful mitzvah of the transmission of our heritage. That, my friends, is our *Chaya*. *Chaya* means life-force and that of every nation is distinctive. For the extended Jewish family, it's our *chaya* that makes Jewish summer camp so redeeming. *Chaya* gets us to services on Friday night even though the prayers will be the same as the previous week. We just love to shmooze with our fellow Jews and eat herring, *chrein* and rugelach. Germans have their own *chaya*. So do Nigerians and Japanese.

One of the best textual examples of the realm of *chaya* is the manner in which the Torah describes death. As described in the chapter discussing Eretz Yisrael, at the end of their days, our biblical heroes are "gathered to their people." We, too, will be escorted to this heavenly Jewish jam session at the end of our lives! Our *chaya* is the "*pintele yid*" (Jewish pilot light) that gets sparked up when we hear a great sermon, Chassidic story or Jewish song. That's our *chaya* igniting when we fall in love with Israel the first time we stroke the stones of the *Kotel* or stroll Dizengoff Street in Tel Aviv. This fourth level of the soul supercedes common sense in regards to the survival of the fittest; thanks to our *chaya* we are willing to lay down our lives for the love of country.

The top of this pyramid of the Five Levels of the Soul is known as *Yechida*. It's the identification with the ultimate universal soul, connecting with the omnipresent entity we call God. *Yechida* is related to the idea of being separate, alone with another. The "*yichud* room" at a traditional Jewish wedding is where the bride and groom complete their marriage with seclusion in an intimate space just after the ceremony. We've all felt *yechida* with the Almighty—those times when we are deeply connected and totally blown away. Most parents describe unbridled *yechida* at the birth of a child. Some get it while carving fresh tracks on a deep powder ski day. Some find *yechida* in the solitude of the box canyons of Southern Utah or when surfing glassy, barreling waves at dawn.

I have many friends who <u>know</u> they were saved from a potential accident by miraculous intervention. Another word for that "knowing" is *yechida*. *Yechida* is when we've finished the third cup of wine at a great *Seder* and we're singing *Hallel* with joyful abandon. We say the *Sh'ma* twice a day to remind ourselves of the possibility, just for that moment, to love God with all our heart, soul and might. Keep your eyes closed and relish in that *yechida* hug.

We can't stay in the realm of *yechida*. We get momentary glimpses and then our ego pulls us away. Try this at the next *Seder:* when mentioning how the Jews united at Mount Sinai, suggest that guests teleport to the base of the mountain and personally witness revelation amidst the fire and smoke, thunder and lightning. Over two million Jews were there—and our sages insist we were too! Connect with the power of Jewish unity, standing as "one people, with one heart." Of course, in the narrative we didn't stay in this lofty place… shortly afterwards we built a golden calf.

Even though *yechida* is fleeting, it is still of supreme value. Imagine getting lost in the countryside on a stormy, moonless night. Crushing darkness surrounds and the path disappears. Luckily, sporadic lightning illuminates the landscape. Just like we can use that flash to find the way, we can use moments of *"yechida* memory" to guide us through times of darkness. I think God gives us these comforting tastes of *yechida* so we become accustomed to this highest realm of joyful oneness our souls reach when we leave this world.

The Pesach *Seder* is a celebration of the Jewish soul. The experience of immersing in this week of freedom impacts us on all five levels. We emerge from the holiday able to maximize the expression of our *neshamot,* connect deeply with our *chaya* and hopefully taste *yechida* with the Great Soul. Humans are subject to wide ranging vicissitudes in every attribute, ability to perceive God's presence nonwithstanding. Pesach allows even the empirically minded the chance to connect. Some get so inspired by a great *Seder* that they feel compelled to share their glimpse of *yechida* with the world.

Don't be frustrated by those emotionally unavailable to hear the soul's voice. Don't give up on them either—we all have different paths and processes. Anytime I sit next to a self-professed atheist on an airplane, a short discussion of the Five Levels of the Soul yields new vistas into perceiving God's presence, or at least into the miracle of our human complexity. I like to explain how these unique metaphysical qualities of humanity are abstract and yet are the most real things we know. The universally respected paradigms of Mother Nature, human instinct, even quantum mechanics are forces Jews simply refer to as God. At the core, we are all speaking the same language.

If the analysis of the Five Levels can't convince diehard skeptics, I resort to the remarkable research in the field of Near Death Experience (NDE). The pioneer in NDE, Dr. Raymond Moody, interviewed thousands of individuals who "flat-lined" for over twenty minutes and then came back to life. Many report a multi-stage chain of events paralleling the description of death in Kabbalah. The *Zohar* (mystical text) describes these commonly experienced phenomena: seeing their body from above, hearing everything that was going on and enduring a rapid review of their lives (much like the James Brooks movie, "Defending Your Life"). Some are met by loved ones and sent back or feel they must return to their corporeal existence to complete a task. Many describe a comforting, loving, radiant light. Our rabbis tell us that this is the *"ziv hashechina,"* the light of the first day of Creation. The sun wasn't set into orbit until the fourth day…could this healing luminosity be the purely spiritual light created on the first day?

It's remarkable our Oral Torah has been discussing the secrets of life after life for thousands of years and it took humanity until the 1970s for NDE paradigms to be popularized. I may not make believers out of my unsuspecting flying companions, but it's not for lack of trying. Deep inside, I'm amused that legions of brilliant philosophers and physicists deny God—the God Who lovingly keeps them breathing as they think heretical thoughts.

A final thought: I have enjoyed the gift of years of peformances in the Berkshires. I hike and bike and revel in the historic Massachusettes hamlets. On one trip, I made a point of visiting the Norman Rockwell museum; I've always loved his vintage magazine covers and was excited to see my favorites on the full-size original canvases. After viewing the expansive collection, I noticed a docent was about to lead a group tour through the exhibits. I opted to make the rounds again with this well-informed woman and this time I had a completely novel experience. I saw features in those paintings I hadn't noticed and the characters came to life as I heard the background story of their creation.

Similarly, two people can sit side by side in a *Seder* and have vastly different perspectives, based on their enthusiasm, level of Jewish education and the ability of the leader to unpack the *Hagaddah*. Pesach is no time to be cynical and cavalier; we must endeavor to bravely dive into the adventure! Embrace the rollercoaster ride of unabashed *neshama* inebriation! Use the four cups of wine to get just a bit out of time and space in order to enter the story, a story that is still being written. Make this the year to experience the *Hagaddah* with a capable docent, taking the time to nurture each wrinkle in the canvas of our national tapestry. Remember the Five Levels of the Soul and how the realm of the spirit can be even more real than that of the material. Bask in the love of the the Great Soul Who has sustained us to reach yet another cycle of Jewish holidays.

THE FOUR QUESTIONS

1. Can you distinguish between *nefesh*, *ruach* and *neshama* in your own experience?

2. Can you think back to a moment in which your *chaya* was ignited?

3. Can you remember a moment of *yechida* in your life? What triggered it?

4. What can you do to allow your soul to experience Pesach in the deepest way?

Life After Pesach: The Minor League Holidays

An Insider's Guide to S'firat Ha'omer, Yom Hashoah, Rosh Chodesh, Yom Hazikaron, Yom Ha'atzma'ut, Lag B'omer and Yom Yerushalayim

♬ BORN TO REMEMBER ♬

joyjud.com/m/btr

Dreams, what are these dreams
Why are these images returning every night
Who is breathing life
Into these photographs of fading black
and white

Out of the depths
Of a darkness we can never hope to
understand
Somehow the voices still sing we survive

Born to remember
Born to remember our families
Born to remember
Cause all we have left are the memories

A lesson learned not very long ago
From generations we will never know
We tell their story to the world today
A world silent as they passed away

As soon as the Passover *Seders* have passed, many are content to NOT celebrate so much for a while. And yet, there are another six days of matzah munching plus a dozen holidays and commemorations in the space of a month and a half, leading up to the anniversary of receiving the Torah, Shavuot. Any description of the Jewish festive cycle must make mention of these milestones typically left out of the holiday hall of fame. Borscht-belt Comedian Alan King famously summarized all Jewish holidays: "They tried to kill us, we won, let's eat!" Therefore, I'm illuminating all of the lesser blips on the radar so we don't miss out on any of the fun.

These special dates are listed according to their placement on the lunar calendar.

To figure out their solar/Western counterpart, simply consult a current Jewish-Gregorian calendar. Hebcal.com is an indispensable online resource; it syncs with phones and desktops and includes the relevant Torah portion and candlelighting times by region.

The 15/16th of Nissan—Leil Seder

The Passover *Seder* nights...it's matzah time!

The 16th of Nissan—S'firat Ha'omer

As soon as the first day of Pesach is over, we start a unique period called *S'firat Ha'omer,* during which we count the forty-nine days until Shavuot. Forty-nine is a crucial number in Judaism; since the number seven runs throughout the fabric of reality (days of week, colors in rainbow, notes in a scale), logically, seven squared is significant.

In the days of the Temple, a certain measurement known as an *omer* (about ten cups) of barley was offered by the *Cohanim* (priests) beginning on the second day of Pesach. We would start the count of one a day, building up our anticipation of the new wheat harvest and the upcoming offering of whole bread loaves on Shavuot. This counting recreates our initial preparation for the undisputed climax of of human history, the Revelation at Mount Sinai in the year 2448. During the *S'firat Ha'omer* period we contemplate all the permutations of the lower seven kabbalistic *s'firot* (mystical emanations through which God interacts with the world). This daily roadmap of spiritual growth opportunities allows us to refine our character traits to prepare for the ultimate *kabbalah*, personally receiving the Torah.

Nowadays, we commemorate this ascension with a simple blessing and then a counting of our own each night. It's a tremendous challenge to remember every single day... if we miss even one, we can no longer make the blessing the rest of the nights! God forbid I miss out on a chance to make a blessing! I'm very grateful for technology to keep me in the mix: I get a daily email to remind me and my iPhone Siddur app concludes the *Ma'ariv* service with a listing of the proper day.

According to the Talmud, 12,000 pairs of Rabbi Akiva's students died during *S'firat Ha'omer* as a punishment for not treating each other with proper respect. Therefore, this period became associated with an awareness of the importance of *achdut* (Jewish unity) and a state of semi-mourning. Celebrations like weddings, Bar/Bat Mitzvah parties, concerts or even niceties like a shave or haircut are prohibited. Many businessmen and professionals shave in order to appear presentable at work. Ask your rabbi if you need a *heter* (leniency). The bottom line: what should have been a time of joyous anticipation is now subdued. I must admit these restrictions are somewhat of a bummer, especially for us musicians. With no parties or events in need of live music, many hunker down in the studio or take extended vacations, wondering how they will pay the rent come June. Since the one exception to this edict is singing without instruments, grateful a cappella groups do a lot of business this time of year.

The 17th of Nissan—Chol Hamo'ed

The *Chol Hamo'ed* (intermediate days) of Passover begin as soon as the second day (or the first day in Israel) of the holiday has ended. Yes, it's still officially Pesach! These four days retain a festive nature but most types of *melacha* (creative acts forbidden on holidays) can be done. Our prayers are of the weekday variety with special holiday insertions, plus the addition of a celebratory *Hallel*, Torah reading and *Mussaf.* That means one is spending a lot of time in *shul* all week! FYI: a *Chol Hamo'ed* period also takes place during the week of Sukkot in the fall. Many in the working world attempt to keep their jobs intact by showing up in the office normally, or as normal as one can appear when munching matzah at lunch break.

I think it is best (and the rabbis agree), if at all possible, to take the week off in order to relax and enjoy day trips with friends and family. Most amusement parks, hiking spots and beaches are empty, unless Passover coincides with Spring Break. There are certain restrictions in place to keep a sense of the sacred...check with your favorite rabbi for details. The Shabbat of *Chol Hamo'ed* is a unique collision of holiday joy and Sabbath sanctity. The services that day are particularly animated and in most synagogues, are enhanced with the public reading of the evocative love poetry of King Solomon's *Shir Hashirim*, the Song of Songs.

21st/22nd of Nissan—Sh'vi'i and Acharon of Pesach

These are the last two days of the week of Pesach. They have the same restrictions as any Jewish holiday, in other words, they are just like Shabbat, but cooking and carrying things from one place to another is permitted. There are no special observances other than the pleasure of hearing the Torah portion featuring the splitting of the Red Sea on the anniversary of our crossing. The eighth day of the holiday is one of the few formal times we pause to remember those loved ones who are *niftar* (passed away) in a short memorial ceremony called *Yizkor*. Since I'm typically leading Passover programs around the country, after a busy week of concerts for *Chol Hamo'ed* (yes, live music is permitted during Chol Hamo'ed), these two holy days offer much needed R & R. Sharing the final meal of the eighth day with Chassidim yields another four cups of wine and raucous *nigunim* (wordless melodies) during the annual *Mashiach Seudah*. This festive meal echoes themes of the *Haftorah* reading of the day, heralding the imminent arrival of the Messiah.

The 26th of Nissan—Yom Hashoah

The first of many commemorations on the heels of Pesach is Yom Hashoah (Holocaust Day). This date was chosen by the Israeli government to memorialize the Six Million since it is close to the anniversary of the Warsaw Ghetto uprising. Clearly, the authorities chose this famous revolt because it represents the indomitable Jewish spirit, even though it was doomed. Whereas some Orthodox pundits maintain that Tisha B'Av memorializes all maladies throughout history, I think it is appropriate that the Holocaust has its own milestone. We must remain present with the atrocities of our not so distant past, especially now that the last survivors are leaving this earth. While it is more of an event in the Holy Land, Diaspora organizations typically hold memorials featuring survivor testimonials, and it is also the day on which over 10,000 participants on the annual March of the Living meet in Auschwitz. I am often asked to perform songs like my "Born to Remember" or "One Hand, One Heart" at ceremonial gatherings and I appreciate the opportunity to help my fellow Jews connect both to the vast destruction and the miracle of our survival.

The 1st and 2nd of Iyar—Rosh Chodesh Iyar

The next special day is actually a holiday occuring every month. Rosh Chodesh (head of the month) is the celebration of the new moon. As we have discussed, this mitzvah is the very first given to the Jews as a free people right before leaving Egypt. Not only are we accountable for how we spend our time, but we also have the opportunity to sanctify it. Two weeks after the beginning of Pesach is the next Rosh Chodesh, this time for the month of *Iyar*.

Rosh Chodesh is formally announced during the Torah service on the prior Shabbat. Leading that *Shabbat Mevarchim* (Sabbath of Blessing) service is one of my favorite cantorial moments and is always a happy time for our community, not only for the optimism with which we greet the new month, but also because in many synagogues it means that there will be a sumptuous free lunch. Determining the precise day of the new moon used to be the job of the *Sanhedrin* (biblical Supreme Court). Remarkably, it is up to humankind to determine exactly when our sacred holidays take place. Unlike the Sabbath, which arrives every week like clockwork, the holidays represent our partnership in the destiny of the universe since we play a role in determining when they occur.

The Rosh Chodesh service includes *Hallel* and a special *Mussaf*. *Hallel* is a series of Psalms describing our national redemption, God's love for the Jewish People and how we reciprocate with dutiful partnership and gratitude. Yes, you should check out my *Hallel* album, which features the full text, in order to get the vibe and memorize the words! These poetic verses are typically sung with enthusiasm and have served as a beacon of hope in our long exile.

The primary theme of Rosh Chodesh is the miracle of the eternal Jewish People—like the moon we wax and wane but keep on shining. *Chodesh* (month) is also closely related to the word for newness, *chadash*. Following a lunar-based calendar demonstrates the importance of welcoming newness in our lives. New insights, fresh inspiration, renewed hope and of course, *shir chadash*, new music! Rosh Chodesh is also considered a feminine holiday, perhaps because of women's innate connection with cycles. According to the Talmud, it is a special day of the spirit given to women as a reward for their unwavering faith throughout the ages.

The 3rd of Iyar—Yom Hazikaron

Yom Hazikaron is Israel's official Memorial Day in remembrance of those who fell in war or acts of terrorism. Back in 1951, the Israeli government decided to separate the ecstatic celebration of Independence Day from mourning and memory, so Yom Hazikaron split off and shifted to the day before. One-minute sirens are sounded at the start of the day at 8:00 pm (our days start at night) and then again the following morning at 11:00 am when the official ceremonies begin. This practice of solemnity before jubilation heightens the awareness of the price paid for Jewish independence. Israelis stop in their tracks (even on the freeways) to pay respect to the fallen. Many visit the graves of loved ones. For Modern Orthodoxy in the Diaspora, the two days are juxtaposed at large scale public gatherings in most cities during the early evening of the third of Iyar. Typically, the events consist of an array of school choirs singing memorial dirges that segue into songs of victory. The requisite theme colors for Independence Day match the Israeli flag (royal blue and white), local dignitaries utter sound bites of support and then everyone sings an emotional *Hatikvah* (Israel's national anthem) together.

The 4th of Iyar—Yom Ha'atzma'ut

Yom Ha'atzma'ut, Independence Day is a serious party throughout the Land of Israel. Crowds gather for concerts and dancing and proudly display Israeli flags on their apartments, cars and bodies. Ad hoc BBQ's abound and an interesting custom of bashing strangers on the head with squeaky plastic hammers has evolved. Since we usually don't have this day off in the Diaspora, citywide outdoor concerts are scheduled on a proximal Sunday. Yom Ha'atzma'ut is an uplifting time of Jewish unity since affection for Israel is one thing upon which (nearly) all Jews can agree. I get tremendous *nachas* seeing my holy brothers and sisters from the four corners of the earth rejoicing together. This display of *achdut* is reason enough to brave the traffic and heat at the local events. Since my repertoire is Israel-focused, my band is frequently flown out to drive crowds into a falafel-fueled frenzy. Most synagogues have special *Shacharit* (morning) services to commemorate the day and include *Hallel* to acknowledge the miraculous nature of Israel's founding.

One Yom Ha'atzma'ut festival in Daytona Beach, FL was quite memorable due to a tornado touching down nearby, halfway through my set. I attempted to stand my ground but the wind went ballistic, the sky turned black and before long, the police came to the stage to announce the festival was over. My band panicked and packed up their gear as quickly as possible. Scores of vendors attempted to salvage their wares while I gathered my CDs and bid farewell to the event producers. I made it to the car just as the heavens opened with thunder, lightning and a spectacular deluge. I watched in awe as the now empty fairground was turned into a disaster zone—tents and booths airborne and balloon bouquets freed from their moorings. I did the logical thing: I drove a block east to witness the surging Atlantic Ocean, changed into shorts and bodysurfed the tumultuous shorebreak.

The 14th of Iyar—Pesach Sheini

Pesach Sheini is perhaps the dimmest blip on the annual holiday radar. Rabbi Shlomo Carlebach called it the "capital of second chances." It was initiated thanks to spiritually impure Israelites arguing to Moshe Rabbeinu that they too had a right to a Passover celebration. One month after the official *Seder*, God established the designated time when such individuals could bring the Pesach offering. Nowadays most forget about the holiday until it's time to utter the penitential *Tachanun* prayers in the morning service and the rabbi reminds everyone, to their immense relief, that thanks to *Pesach Sheini* they can be skipped.

The 18th of Iyar—Lag B'omer

Lag B'omer is an acronym of the Hebrew letters *lamed* and *gimel*, signifying the 33rd day of the counting of the *omer*. This day commemorates the *yahrzeit* (death anniversary) of Rabbi Shimon Bar Yochai, the great mystic who popularized the esoteric teachings of Kabbalah in his text, the *Zohar*. He commanded his disciples to rejoice on this day and therefore parties replete with bonfires, concerts and dancing erupt throughout the world in celebration of his life and the revelation of the hidden secrets of Torah. Also, according to tradition, the aforementioned tragedy with Rabbi Akiva's students ended on this day, so most welcome the end of the mourning aspect of the *S'firat Ha'omer* period.

My brother Yom Tov makes an annual pilgrimage to the site of Rabbi Shimon's grave in Meron where hundreds of thousands of Chassidim dance in an all night *achdut*-inspired frenzy. Many save the *upsherin* (third birthday first haircut) of their boys for this event. Here in the States I am often leading citywide jam sessions sponsored by Chabad, attended mostly by young adults. These outdoor, nighttime gigs are always rowdy and amusing. At one such gathering, the rabbi insisted my band play in the middle of a broad beach. He brushed off my concerns about sand in the equipment and lack of electricity. I marveled as he plugged in five consecutive hundred-foot lengths of extension cord to a nearby lifeguard office and stretched them over the bike path to our bonfire site. Within minutes of our first song, astonished lifeguards shut the party down, forcing us to finish the gig on acoustic guitars.

The 28th of Iyar—Yom Yerushalayim

Yom Yerushalayim commemorates the reunification of Jerusalem following the 1967 Six Day War. Many remember this milestone as the modern-day apex of international Jewish pride. For those of us who have visited the holy city and feel elated while wandering its golden pathways, we relish in this day to dwell upon her triumphs. Religious Zionists insist the recitation of *Hallel* is even more pertinent on this miraculous anniversary than on Israel Independence Day. While not widely celebrated outside of Israel, it is an occasion for public gatherings and concerts, especially on the milestone years.

The 1st of Sivan—Rosh Chodesh Sivan

Rosh Chodesh once again! That makes for a total of a dozen "holidays" for our enjoyment between the *Seders* and Shavuot on the 6th/7th of *Sivan*. Welcome to the Minor Leagues. Whoever said "it is hard to be a Jew" clearly missed the point; being Jewish is a PARTY! May we all celebrate together in Jerusalem.

THE FOUR QUESTIONS

1. In a month filled with so many holidays and commemorations, how do you keep the balance between the feeling of joy of the happy days and the feeling of sorrow on the difficult days?

2. How does the change from joy to sorrow and back to joy replicate in our lives?

3. What can you do to mark Rosh Chodesh each month?

4. In times when Israel is so criticized, what can you do to publicly celebrate Israel's existence and achievements, even when it's not Yom Ha'atzma'ut?

A Shavuot Revelation

Feel the wind blow, see the sunrise
Hear the music of a people singing in freedom
Anticipation, expectation
Seven weeks in preparation for a new life

With faith in our Creator
We entered the wilderness
Marched through the sea
And now we stand impatiently
At the foot of the mountain

A sacred wedding, a love eternal
Amidst the cry of the shofar we utter a vow
Kol asher diber Hashem
Na'aseh v'nishmah, na'aseh v'nishmah

Out of love for our Creator
We strive for holiness
To live in purity
And now the sound grows ever louder as we pray
Kol bamidbar...

Shavuot is a mysterious holiday. This commemoration of receiving the Torah at Mount Sinai isn't given a specific date for its celebration; instead we are told in *Sefer Sh'mot* (the Book of Exodus) to schedule it seven weeks from the second night of Passover. There are no particular mitzvot attached to the holiday, a flagrant non sequitur after mitzvah-drenched Pesach. While Shavuot is one of the big three *Shalosh Regalim* holidays (when the Israelites were commanded to travel to Jerusalem) and the anniversary of the seminal event in human history, I never heard about it as I grew up. It usually transpires after Hebrew School adjourns for the summer and other than serving Aunt Martha's blintzes without mentioning why, my folks never brought it up. The tradition is to enjoy four sumptuous meals over the two days of the holiday and ensure that at least a few of them feature dairy foods. Evidently, back at Mount Sinai we received the laws of *kashrut* (keeping kosher) but didn't have time to master proper slaughtering practices, so eating dairy was a safer bet. Another reason for cheesecake at this time of year: the *gematria* of the word *chalav* (milk) is forty, paralleling the number of days that Moshe spent on the mountain.

Shavuot offers a welcome respite after the semi-mourning of *S'firat Ha'omer*. One highlight is the custom of staying up all night to learn Torah, called *Tikkun L'eil Shavuot*, the healing of the night of Shavuot. Why a healing, one might ask? In the description of the morning of the Revelation at Sinai, the *Midrash* describes how the Israelites overslept and had to be awakened by Moshe. How could we have fallen asleep the night before? We should have been too excited to sleep a wink! Thanks to our exhausted ancestors, we now stay up all night to rectify this grievous error.

Shavuot is one of my favorite holidays. With no specific duties other learning, praying and eating as much as possible, it's a (cheese) cakewalk. One reason Shavuot has no set date is because the essence of Torah is outside of time and space. Whereas sanctifying food requires a new blessing with every meal, the blessing over Torah study need only happen once a day. We don't just study Torah. We live Torah. This blessing finishes with the words, "Who gives us Torah," stated in the present tense. Shavuot is less an anniversary than a celebration of the continuous flow of Revelation.

Some years, we have rented a cabin in the local mountains with a *minyan* of friends and a Torah scroll to reenact the Sinai experience. Most *shuls* in our 'hood keep java on tap and use the extended period to dive into titilating text study until dawn. When the horizon ignites at 5:00 am, all the bleary-eyed survivors slam dunk a festival *Shacharit* service and then walk home to pass out until lunchtime. The key to optimizing this learning opportunity is compiling a master schedule of all the presenters on an hour by hour basis and *shul*-hopping to hear the best of them. For years, the Happy Minyan sponsored a Torah Slam, allowing anyone to take the stage but limiting each speaker to exactly one minute to make a point. Intense creativity, humor and spontenaity were unleashed and best of all, it was easy to stay awake!

I have certain rabbis with whom I really connect—rare individuals who see the big picture, possess both academic and Torah backgrounds and live their learning. One year, one of those individuals was coming to town to lead the study and I didn't want to miss a word. Shavuot with Rabbi Simcha Weinberg featured almost continuous learning over the three-day weekend. The first night he spoke at services and then resumed teaching from 11:00 pm until 5:00 am. The topic, near and dear to my heart, was thorough text study of the *Hallel* service. After a sunrise *Shacharit* service, we slept until our festive lunch began and then did the Diaspora Groundhog Day routine for the second night of the holiday (much like the Bill Murray movie, Jewish folks outside of Israel are privileged with a duplicate day tagged onto our three primary holidays). That particular year, the extra day happened to be Shabbat. More inspired classes with the rabbi, celebratory meals and then a final class Sunday Night. I felt like I was opened up, firing on all cylinders, with new enthusiasm for the "same ole" prayers and new eyes to see the colors of life.

I was not only high from the Shavuot learning; the week before the holiday I enjoyed a soul and *parnasa* (income) boost from several unique concerts. I performed a few shows at synagogues in Northern California and then returned to L.A. to sing the "Star Spangled Banner" and "God Bless America" at the Dodger-Mets game. While it was quite exciting to sing for the nearly sold out crowd, my main focus was giving *nachas* to my season-ticket holder father who has occupied the same box seats behind home plate since the Dodgers moved from Brooklyn. The next night I regaled 1200 Aish banquet attendees at the Beverly Hilton and then drove to La Jolla to perform a Torah dedication concert at the San Diego Jewish Academy. I made it home with an hour to go before candlelighting, hugged my wife and kids and dashed off to *shul* for the *Erev* Shavuot services. Just like the glory of the revelation of Torah led to a cataclysm with the golden calf, so, too, did our communal holiday celebration end in disaster.

The day after this action-packed week, I opened up my studio, turned on the various racks of audio gear and started up my trusty Mac. My first move is to check my email and since I had been away, there were hundreds begging for attention. Two caught my eye, both with the heading *"Baruch Dayan HaEmet"* (Blessed is the True Judge). These are the emails I never want to read. These are the words Jews utter automatically when hearing shocking news, usually about someone's death. This stock phrase counters the tendency to respond, "Oh, it's not fair" or, "How could God let this happen?" Jewish tradition insists God knows exactly what is going on and even though we might not understand, this tragedy is also God's will.

Two of our close friends lost their wives. Both were young mothers, each with three grade-school children. Strikingly beautiful women, beacons of charity and kindness. Two agonizing funerals were followed by intense *shiva minyanim* (prayers during the first week of mourning). After the first funeral, I was asked to lead *Mincha* at the *shiva* house. I shouldn't have agreed: I sobbed throughout the service, starting and stopping and trying again. When visiting with their guests, the husbands would bravely tell anecdotes about their wives and then convulse again in misery. Speechless family and friends watched as prepubescent kids struggled with *Kaddish*.

These calamities occurred the day after we celebrated the giving of Torah. I struggled, as did many in our community, with this stark contrast—on one hand, the holiday emphasizes that everything happening to us is directed by God and like the Jews at Sinai, it's our job to respond with acceptance and allegiance. But I'm human, and I was grieving, and part of me struggled to accept the horrible events handed to people whom I really cared about.

To add to this schizophrenic contrast, the next night I went to a Laker game with my brother Joey. Yes, life is for the living. The energy was palpable as the crowd jumped to its feet with every heroic basket. We were awestruck by the player's miraculous coordination and perseverance. There was such a din, I had to resort to earplugs halfway through the game. After the final buzzer, I went to hear some of the greatest musicians in the world play at an L.A. nightclub. Keyboard wizard David Garfield led his septet through the brambles of some of the thorniest charts imaginable, bringing waves of unbridled pleasure to this music lover. I marveled as they spun spontaneous improvised melodies, flurries of notes soaring over the funkiest grooves, performed with seemingly impossible dexterity. Again I was brought to tears, but this time they were tears of joy.

I decided to drive home over the canyon, rather than the more expedient freeway. At the top of the pass, I pulled off at a beautiful wilderness area, the headquarters of the L.A.-based environmental group Tree People. With the aid of the ambient glow of the metropolis, I hiked a mile to the top of a hill and prayed *Ma'ariv* under a waxing moon. As I pondered the night sky against the shadows of towering pines, I had a realization: while dating my wife, the first party I saw her throw was a benefit for Tree People. I was astonished by her grace and efficiency as she made sure every detail was perfect and all her guests were cared for. I noted she shared her generous smile with everyone. That's when I knew she was the one. Shira is the light of my life, beloved in our extended family and treasured in our community. We also have three kids who are the same ages as the kids who just lost their mothers. The tragedies of the week hit too close to home. How did this figure in God's plan? Where is God's "beneficent kindness" amidst this daunting sorrow wracking our community?

I found comfort in the form of a "coincidence" the next day. My band frequently plays weddings at the finest westside hotels. Some are sweet and simple, some utterly ostentatious. Once, at a no-expense-spared event at the Beverly Wilshire hotel, my nine-piece ensemble propelled the five hundred guests into hours of rowdy dancing. Years later, I wanted to get a clip of that wedding video to enhance my recently redone Wedding Band page on my website. But how could I find the bride's new contact details? I started my research and tracked down her brother's email address. I contacted him and received the reply, "Which sister are you talking about?" The next day I responded and a few hours later the sister I was looking for sent me an email. She was contacting me to get the sheet music for one of the songs I had sung for the processional; I could tell from the context that she had no idea that I was trying to find her. When I called, I explained the situation and we both agreed this was indeed a "large world, well managed" moment.

The same God Who orchestrated this "coincidence" also arranged for these two women to pass on this week. This is the same God Who created the universe, Who gave us Avraham and Sarah, Who freed us from slavery in Egypt and gifted the Torah 3500 years ago on the very first Shavuot. This is the *Makom*, the Omnipresent, Who will help my now single-father friends cope and bring them and their children healing.

My friends, we are always receiving divine messages, heavenly love notes, holy whispers of Oral Torah. We may not always understand them. Shavuot is here to open our hearts to this communication and encourage us to keep the conversation alive. Perhaps Shavuot has no set date so we make every single day a celebration of receiving God's Instructions for Living. May the words of our beloved Torah always be sweet on our lips. May these two families feel the shelter of the wings of the True Judge; may the Omnipresent comfort them, together with all the mourners of Zion and Jerusalem.

THE FOUR QUESTIONS

1. Is there an all-night-learning in your area that you could join to celebrate Shavuot?

2. How do you reconcile God's infinite goodness with the sometimes harsh realities of life?

3. What does the idea of continuously receiving the Torah mean to you?

4. How can you celebrate the gift of Torah everyday?

The Three Weeks: My Family Vacation

♫ ACROSS THE RIVER ♫

joyjud.com/m/atr

Come with me across the river
Far across the great divide
Come with me across the river
To the other side

Pack up your things and go
To a land that I will show you
For no other reason than to join me on this journey
Into the great unknown
Where mysteries await you
You've got too much to give to live your life alone

Come with me across the river
Far across the great divide
Come with me across the river
To the other side

Open your heart and soul
And watch the magic happen
There's not a single thing your dreams cannot deliver
I am the pot of gold
That lies beyond your rainbow
I may be far away or right under your nose
It's up to you

For most of us, summer is a carefree time. As one Jew wrote: "Summertime, and the living is easy." We all have delightful memories of beach vacations, camp or family road trips. Thanks to our agrarian past, schools offered a few months off so the kids could help with the harvest. Nowadays our kids use that time to forget everything they learned the previous semester. For Jews, there's one wrinkle in the enjoyment of those long summer afternoons: just in case we are having too much fun, the spoilsport rabbis of yore gave us twenty-one days of semi-mourning smack dab in the middle of waterslide season.

The Three Weeks serve as an "Ice Bucket Challenge" to cool us off amidst our barefoot frolicking. There are six fast days in the Jewish calendar and two of them occur at the beginning and end of the Three Weeks. The others are scattered throughout the year: the Tenth of Tevet, the Fast of Esther, the Fast of Gedaliah and the famous one, Yom Kippur. While we are commanded to always serve God with joy, during the Three Weeks, we "lessen" our joy by refraining from such things as live music, weddings and haircuts, just like during *S'firat Ha'omer*. Minor inconveniences, but they make a subtle difference in our day-to-day, just enough so we acquire a sense of mourning. This period begins with the daybreak-until-darkness fast of the Seventeenth of *Tammuz*. It commemorates the day Moshe broke the tablets, daily offerings ceased in the First Temple and Romans breached the Second Temple -era walls of Jerusalem. Our sense of loss mounts over the three-week period, becoming especially intense from the first to the ninth of the month of *Av*. For these last nine days the restrictions multiply, including the abstention from meat and wine other than on Shabbat (yes, fowl is considered meat). To stave off bankruptcy, our neighborhood *fleishig* restaurants switch to pescatarian specials and veggie burgers. During this final countdown we also abstain from frivolous purchases, bathing or swimming for pleasure, doing non-essential laundry or wearing freshly laundered garments. Call us OCD: we actually try on and then immediately remove clothing before the Nine Days so it's not perfectly fresh when we eventually wear it.

At last, we arrive at the full twenty-five-hour fast on Tisha B'Av (the Ninth of Av), the saddest date on the Jewish calendar. This day of infamy commemorates the destruction of our Temples, the expulsion from Spain in 1492 and the start of World War One. We're not just mourning for the Jewish People; the annihilation of Jewish life has had a deleterious impact on the entire world. The Temple was the center of the universe, our oxygen source. Without it, we are on artificial respiration, clinging to life. If not for the dramatic steps in preparation for this traumatic re-enactment, the sense of loss would not be as pervasive. Whereas the intensity of mourning for a loved one wanes over the course of time, the opposite is true during the Three Weeks. By taking on these restrictions, the sense of foreboding is magnified each passing day until commemorating the absolute devastation of Tisha B'av.

The following saga illustrates the power of preparation as the key to acquiring this transformation, not only over the Three Weeks but also throughout all the holidays on the Jewish calendar.

As a child, I was fortunate to spend my summers backpacking in the Sierras. My soul has always been nurtured by exploring regions of unspoiled beauty, encountering the silence of the forest, fording rushing rivers and summiting peaks that pierce the clouds. My first album featured songs written from age seven to eleven with such titles as "Wilderness," "This World," "The Last Frontier" and "This Valley." I still can't get enough of my outdoor fix. To this day, when I'm on my concert tour and the opportunity arises in between shows, I try to fill my days with a walk to a waterfall, a ride on a mountain biking trail or a session at a local surf spot.

My kids used to run the other direction when I proposed we take a hike. I refrained from telling them where we were going and would hide their boots in the back of the van. That way I could get them out of the house without straitjackets. Once we hit the trail, however, they inevitably warmed to the experience. I would marvel as their personalities shifted from boredom to wonder, sarcasm to innocence, cynicism to curiosity.

Back when my sons were strapping adolescents, (Max, 14, and Jesse 12), I proposed that we go for a serious backpack trip, our first together, in the wilderness of Sedona, AZ. They had a week before camp was starting and I had gigs scheduled in Tucson. Surprisingly, they were excited about the idea and the itinerary occupied weeks of our conversation. Admittedly, using their pocketknives and building fires were the primary attractions. My daughter, Sarah Lena, then a nine-year-old diva in pink, would have to wait a few more years.

How could I remain sequestered in my recording studio knowing my boys were available for an adventure of this magnitude? I was growing ever aware of the fleeting nature of their precious childhood. What I didn't anticipate was the intensive preparation and expense. When leaving civilization, one can't run to 7-Eleven for a Slurpee. As a kid on those summer trips, all the hard work was done for me. Now I had to rent our packs, plan lightweight, kosher meals, deal with water purification, acquire sleeping bags and pads, a tent, first aid kit and plenty of sunscreen.

I inculcated my progeny with carefully curated classic rock for our seven-hour drive. To the strains of Boston, The Beatles, Kansas and AC/DC we jammed through the barren Southwest, arriving in Sedona just as the sun was setting. We stayed in a beautiful hillside home of friends in the area and that first evening, while I shared backcountry exploits in their Jacuzzi, we witnessed a spectacular meteorite, tail and everything, streaking across the star-stained sky. Our first hike involved climbing one of the famous red rock buttes surrounding the city. Within an hour, the sole of Jesse's boot fell off completely and he had to finish the hike in Crocs. After a dip in a spectacular Oak Creek swimming hole, we frantically searched all over town for new boots and after multiple stops, got lucky finding the only pair in his size.

Finally, after a few days of trial hikes, we had packs on our backs and set out on our fourteen-mile red rock canyon adventure. After the first three miles, we switched from hiking boots to water sandals. The canyon narrowed precipitously, the trail disappeared and we had to walk in the river the rest of the way. We gawked at bouquets of butterflies and walls of wildflowers clinging to weeping cliffs. The absolute solitude was broken only by soaring hawks and herons overhead, insidious spiders lurking in the shadows and sonorous mountain goats.

By the sixth mile, Jesse was at the breaking point. He couldn't go on. We needed a campsite immediately and there was nothing but red rock walls on either side of us. The final straw was a six-foot deep channel of water with no way to get through it other than swimming. Try swimming with a backpack! Max and I abandoned our packs and scaled the cliff wall to see if there was another way. Sure enough, we found a ledge with a fire ring. Someone else had gotten stuck here and made the best of it. But there was no room for a tent. Max noticed there was a route to get even higher up the cliff. Remarkably, we found a full-blown campsite about sixty feet above the river. A perfect, well-shaded hideout to enjoy for the duration of our trip, with flat ground for our tent and a fire ring with log benches all around it. Can you imagine our happy dance? That night we thanked Hashem for the providence of our discovery as we pondered the Milky Way and roasted salami on the open flame.

Why I am sharing this anecdote? It's all about the campsite. Our campsite was the sweetest campsite in the world. Better than any five-star hotel. Why? Because we worked so hard for it. Because we sweated out the intensive preparation required to survive half a week in the wilderness, because we drove so far, woke up at dawn and hiked miles with heavy backpacks. For us, that magical twenty square feet of dirt represented pushing beyond our perceived limitations and emerging triumphant.

This dynamic is the essence of Jewish holidays. The intensive pre-Pesach spring cleaning, cooking and *Seder* planning makes for a powerful Passover. The forty-nine-day *S'firat Ha'omer* countdown to Shavuot creates anticipation for the reenactment of the Sinai experience. There's nothing like the first night of Sukkot when sitting in the *sukkah* we shlepped from the storage room, built and decorated. And Rosh Hashana is as potent as the spiritual work we undertake during the preceding month of *Elul*. Preparation and persistence are the keys to any meaningful journey.

We carefully broke camp on the last day of our adventure, ensuring we didn't leave a trace of our visit. I emphasized "zero impact camping" to my young charges, quoting ecologist Chief Seattle: "Take only memories, leave only footprints." We stuffed down all our remaining food for lunch so we wouldn't have to carry it. In between mouthfuls of mashed potatoes, suddenly two brown beasts burst forth from the bushes. We screamed as we leapt up, ready to protect ourselves with our plastic sporks. These two energetic chocolate Labrador retrievers were exploring the canyon and must have smelled our kosher turkey MREs. Cocoa and Charlie became our dogs for the rest of the day. Their enthusiasm made the chore of hauling our packs a lot more fun. Towards sunset, as we neared the mouth of the canyon, we heard someone shouting, "Stop calling my dogs!" This poor guy hadn't seen his dogs all day. I scampered up a rock wall to the source of his voice and quickly explained to this lone backpacker that we weren't trying to steal his animals. As I spoke, he gave me a puzzled look. When I paused he said, "Are you Sam Glaser?" Can you imagine—it was Glen Good—a friend from high school! He had moved to Arizona in search of a tranquil place to build his brand of custom museum-quality furniture. The only other human that we had seen in days!

The Three Weeks commemorate the most painful events our nation has endured. Perhaps the impact of our profound loss is maximized when its observance is imposed on our carefree summer vacation. Without this three-week prelude, the torment of Tisha B'av would not be as acute. Our sages teach that proper mourning is the secret to our redemption. Those who weep for Jerusalem will merit seeing her rebuilt, God willing with uncontested borders and eternal peace. According to the prophet Zecharia, our days of sadness will become days of celebration. As my friend Rabbi Shlomo Seidenfeld says, "our mission is to put the *tish* (a joyous celebration) into Tisha B'av." The power to do so is in our hands. May it happen speedily in our day.

THE FOUR QUESTIONS

1. Do you feel that increasing the limitations in a three-week period helps to put us in the right mood for the day that commemorates so many tragedies in Jewish History?

2. What is an example of intense preparation making for a heightened experience in your life?

3. How do the changes required throughout the Three Week period affect your mood?

4. How can your Tisha B'Av be affected when you make an effort to observe the restrictions of the Three Weeks?

Tisha B'Av:
Jews and Aspens

♫ EICHA ♫

joyjud.com/m/eca

Like a widow the city sits alone
No more children
No more pilgrims on the road
Could this be the place called
The "joy of all the earth"
Perfect in her beauty she lies now
In ashes and dust, Eicha

No more laughter
No more cheer, no more song
We are strangers with no place to belong

Driven into darkness of desperate slavery
How long can the night carry on, Eicha

Yerushalayim, Ir Hakodesh
I can hear you weep
When you're broken
I am incomplete
How much longer will we wander
Chased by rustling leaves
God in heaven, lay me down to sleep

I am writing this on a long, lazy Tisha B'Av afternoon. The sky is brilliant blue and a gentle breeze is beckoning me to leave my air-conditioned studio and get on my bike. No, not today. I must conserve my energy and saliva. At my synagogue, we have undertaken a dramatic journey using prayer, compelling speakers and the chanting of *Kinnot*, the anguished, eyewitness poetry of Jewish suffering through the ages. We sit on the floor, wearing wrinkled clothing and simple, non-leather shoes. We are unshaven, unkempt and unconcerned about appearances. A particular challenge for this extrovert is the custom of not greeting friends. We acknowledge each other with a stare, recognizing this day is not about camaraderie, it's about alienation and exile, death and mourning, dashed hopes and bitter tears. Tisha B'Av was once a universally observed commemoration of disasters befalling the Jewish People. Nowadays the fast is undertaken by perhaps 10% of the tribe. That in itself is reason to mourn.

The Jewish People creates its own *simcha* (joy) and *tzuris* (pain). Our foes are often generated through karma of our own manufacture. The Talmud recounts the origin of our archenemy Amalek, who wreaked so much suffering on our nation throughout the ages. Our patriarch Yitzchak's eldest son was Esav, twin brother of Yaakov. Esav's son was Eliphaz, and Eliphaz's concubine Timna was a princess who wanted to convert to Judaism. She presented her case to a *beit din* (Jewish court) formed by the three patriarchs who all happened to be alive at the time. When they rejected her, she chose to remain with Eliphaz, stating, "Better to be a maidservant to this nation than a leader in another." Their offspring is Amalek, an individual who was hell-bent on avenging the disrespect shown to his mother. This hatred of the Jewish People was handed down through the generations, eventually leading to the tribe of Amalek's brazen attack on Israel when we left Egypt. Amalek surfaces again in the near genocide concocted by tribesman Haman in the Purim story.

The spiritual heir of Amalek is the force of weakness crippling our national resolve. It is the voice that chides us: *it's all random, God doesn't really care, God is too busy to hear our prayers.* The *gematria* of Amalek is the same as the word *safek*, doubt. When Moshe sends the spies to research the Land of Israel before the conquest, it is the influence of Amalek which erodes their confidence and instills panic. Thanks to this grievous error in judgment and lack of faith in God's ability to redeem us, God decrees that the generation will wander for forty years and die in the desert. Since we cried over nothing when the spies returned, God presents the anniversary of this incident as a day for tears throughout history. The impetus for tears becomes quite real in future generations: not only were our two Temples destroyed on this infamous date, but it also corresponds with a freakish collection of calamities befalling us throughout history. In other words, we created Tisha B'av, and we're still fasting three thousand years later.

My first Tisha B'Av memory took place at Camp Ramah in the summer after third grade. I was a precocious seven-year-old in *edah aleph* (group one, the youngest group of campers), enamored of my bunkmates and a natural at the Israeli ball game of *gaga*. One of my counselors had long hair and played the guitar—I thought he was the coolest guy in the world. I had my first crush on a young lady named Debbie and I remember inviting her on a walk so I could impress her by throwing rocks at a beehive. After a direct hit, one of the worker bees located the source of the disturbance and stung me on my earlobe. Although I screamed like a baby, I remember the nurse telling me, "You're so brave!" This wasn't much of a consolation since Debbie had seen me cry. Our *edah* worked together to fashion a beautiful outdoor *beit k'nesset* (synagogue) beneath a sprawling oak tree with custom painted benches and our artwork hanging from the *aron hakodesh* (holy ark for the Torah). One fateful morning we awoke to find that someone had upended our precious prayer space. The *aron* was on its side, benches strewn about, our works of art scattered on the ground. I was shocked to the core. Who could do such a thing? Then our counselors explained the destruction in Jerusalem transpiring three millennia earlier on that very day. This re-creation of the tragic events of the past created an indelible memory and allowed our bunk to bond during the rebuilding process.

In the summer of 2014, the war with Hamas in Gaza corresponded with the Three Weeks. It did wonders for Jewish unity. Among Israelis there was 95% agreement of the justice of our acts of self-defense, in a country that can't agree on anything. The same unanimity of purpose swept the Diaspora and created a sense of clarity so rare in a world shrouded in shades of grey. This galvanization of the Jewish spirit began when we were praying for the well-being of three kidnapped teenagers, Naftali Fraenkel, Gil-Ad Shaer and Eyal Yifrah. As the atrocity of their senseless death spiraled into war, Jews remained united in their revulsion of the unmitigated evil of Hamas and the need to be rid of the menace of their arsenal of rockets and terror tunnels. My Jerusalem-based brother Yom Tov told me that he waited twenty-three years to feel this degree of togetherness. As we went from ceasefire to ceasefire, we stood together in heartfelt prayer for a peaceful, lasting resolution. May we always remain in such a holy state of *achdut*, unity.

The Jewish People are connected more profoundly than any of us realize. In many ways we're like the aspen, one of the largest organisms on earth, famous for decorating mountain ranges with brilliant autumnal radiance. Aspen groves are not collections of disparate entities. They are typically distinct expressions of a single subterranean root system, sometimes stretching over a hundred feet from the parent tree. One such colony in Utah is estimated to be thousands of years old, having survived multiple forest fires because the roots survive beneath the heat of the fire. Deciduous aspens occupy a precarious niche in a coniferous forest, swelling their collective sunshine-yellow glory wherever the colony can obtain enough light. Similarly, the Jewish People is an interconnected family that has weathered the storms of history, shining the light of peace, love and innovation into the world whenever given the chance.

It took the kidnapping of three of our kids to remind us just how tight knit a family we are. Synagogues of all denominations worldwide were praying for their lives. Gentile friends of mine couldn't quite understand why I was so rattled by their abduction. We didn't know these kids or their families personally and yet we had their names on cards in our pockets and their images engraved in our minds. I wish I had the aspen analogy then to explain this connection. It's super-rational. Even weird. Why do we care so much about one another? Jewish individuals may appear like separate islands in an archipelago but drain the water and we clearly are attached. We are like fingers on a single hand. Cut one and we all bleed. The fires of the destruction of Jerusalem, European pogroms or the Holocaust may rage but they cannot extinguish the spark animating the collective Jewish soul. It is this very spark that Hitler, may his memory be obliterated, vowed to destroy.

We all feel the pain of our fellow Jew because in essence we are one entity. In our day-to-day we may not dwell on the miracle of eternal Jewish unity. But attack us, steal our children, murder the elderly who cannot make it to bomb shelters quickly enough...you have unleashed the fury of the Tribe. We will not be kicked around anymore. Now we are back in our land. Now we have the IDF (Israeli Defense Forces). We are interconnected both online and offline. We benefit the world with our scholarship and ingenuity. When we stand together we are invincible. The war in Gaza motivated my Jewish musician friends (most of whom hadn't been to the synagogue in decades) to take up arms. Even ardent leftists were taking a stand as militant members of God's Chosen People, rising to the defense of the *Am Kadosh* (Holy Nation) of the Creator of the Universe.

When the Chosen People succeed, a fascinating counter balance is unleashed. God stays carefully behind the scenes—this is humanity's drama to act out. Anytime we start hitting all the outside shots, a certain force goes insane with envy, filled with frustration and a maniacal desire for revenge. Anti-Semitism makes little sense. Hitler was willing to sacrifice trains carrying troops and ammunition to the front lines in order to send more Jews to Auschwitz. Haman offered his life savings for the chance to eradicate Persian Jewry. Give Jews some space and they will revolutionize technology, agriculture, medicine and the arts, for the whole world's benefit. We send humanitarian aid to the enemy and treat their wounded in our hospitals. When Hamas is neutralized, we will be the first on hand to rebuild Gaza.

Our enemy has had many names over the years: Radical Islamists, Nazis, Cossacks, Romans...it doesn't matter. Anti-Semitism is a force of evil that is backwards and irrational. But potent nonetheless. During the Gaza conflict there was little question which group held the moral high ground. But somehow this reality was lost on many of our Hollywood celebrities, the European Union, in fact pretty much every nation except for the US and Canada. In the face of anti-Semitism, Jews frustrate those taunting them by sending even more love and light into the world. When discussing Germany after World War II, Rabbi Shlomo Carlebach said, "I have only one heart, so I have to use it for loving." Israel's wars serve three primary purposes: to keep our enemies at bay, to unite the Jewish People in our holy mission and force everyone else to choose sides. Neutrality and evil are tight bedfellows.

For my concerned Christian friends, I have a suggestion when discussing distressing events in the Middle East. Should you find yourself in conversation with a Jew, don't dwell on Israeli military strategy, politics or who is right and wrong. Instead, consider offering words of condolence. After hearing of disastrous news affecting the Jewish People, I'm so moved by kind individuals who see my *kippah* and boldly approach me to offer comfort. A priest felt compelled to hug me at a Dodger Game. A young German rock and roll fan once made a point of telling me he was sorry about the atrocities delivered by his relatives. Our little nation is perpetually under siege. Our children are on the front lines. We are surrounded by bloodthirsty enemies with warped values, incomprehensible to those with a Judeo-Christian *weltanschauung* (worldview). I urge my gentile readers to share our pain and join us in prayer for a peaceful world. Stand with us in our time of need. Make sure to affiliate with a church that "gets it," in other words, an institution that isn't trying to divest from Israel, God forbid, but is bravely advancing the cause of the Jewish People.

For my Jewish friends, a fractured Middle East and the threat of terrorism should be a source of sincere reflection. We are in this boat, like it or not. Might as well like it! Events like the Gaza War can inspire us to rekindle a sense of wonder, to investigate our roots, to resource a teacher whose Torah is meaningful and eternal. Judaism is our most precious inheritance and the most important legacy for our offspring. Anti-Semites will hate us no matter how likeable we try to be. Nazis don't care whether we are Reform, Orthodox or never celebrated Bar/Bat Mitzvah. There is a spark of light lying dormant in even the most assimilated Jewish soul. Rabbi Noah Weinberg used to say, "If you don't know what you're willing to die for, you haven't begun to live." For what are we willing to lay down our lives? Our children, our country, the Jewish People? So then LIVE for them!

There is a silver lining to brighten this day of Tisha B'av dirges. The Talmud relates that *Mashiach* is born on Tisha B'Av. In the Messianic Era, rather than mourning and fasting, we will be celebrating a birthday bash—yum! We don't say the penitential *Tachanun* prayers on Tisha B'Av because it is indeed a holiday. On a deeper level, this teaching of *Mashiach's* unusual birthday demonstrates that the possibility for *geula* (redemption) begins only when we hit rock bottom, when our Holy Temple is destroyed and the entire nation yearns for God's salvation. Our sages teach the opportunity for redemption is present in every generation, as long as the generation merits it. Thus we have to work with all our might to lift not only ourselves but also our community and world. As the fast approaches, many state: "If *Mashiach* doesn't come, have an easy fast." Let's make this the year we no longer fast!

Tisha B'Av is hard on even the hardiest individuals. As it is said, "Society is only three meals away from anarchy." In the waning hours of the holiday, everyone is disheveled and drained. Jewish law stipulates we can't don *tallis* and *tefillin* until the sun is about to set, having been denied the glory of these crowns earlier in the day. We lumber into a minyan where we are comforted by the words of divine forgiveness in the Torah reading, which depicts the aftermath of the sin of the Golden Calf. Then in the *Haftorah*, the prophet Isaiah proclaims: "For you shall go out with joy, and be led forth with peace; the mountains and the hills shall break forth before you into singing, and all the trees of the field shall clap their hands." Even when all seems lost, God is with us, guiding us and giving us hope. Even on this most mournful day, we must serve God with joy! We then utter the *Amidah* and special insertions with an intensity only possible when one is ravenous and parched, poignantly aware of one's mortality.

Tisha B'Av is the saddest day of the year for those steeped in the Joy of Judaism. Our collective primal scream echoes throughout history like rolling thunder from the original lightning bolt of destruction, the obliteration of our faith by the spies in the desert. Even at the nadir or our joy continuum, there is a kernel of hope. By the end of the fast we teeter on shakey legs, ashen faced and cotton-mouthed. Finally, at the conclusion of *Ma'ariv* services we drink delicious gulps of water and step outside the synagogue to celebrate the end of the three-week mourning period with *Kiddush Levana* (Blessing the New Moon), dancing together in the darkness.

When I finished this chapter, I did an online search for "aspen tree poetry" and discovered a lovely poem by Monica Sharman. Can you imagine my shock when I saw the biblical passage she quoted was the aforementioned verse from the fast day reading? Another "large-world, well-managed moment!" Just when everything in the world seems so random, chaotic and confusing. Thank you, God.

Clapping Aspen

In the rising wind of a coming dust storm
a mini-stand of aspen planted between
the heron pond and the stucco home
made some noise; they say it's
"quaking." But that name makes one
think of timid fear. Listen like
a musician, with the psalter's ear,
and hear, instead, the sound of applause:

For you shall go out in joy
and be led forth in peace;
the mountains and the hills before you
shall break forth into singing,
and all the trees of the field
shall clap their hands.
(Isaiah 55:12)

May we continue to dance together like aspen trees shimmering in a gentle alpine breeze. May our unity be as self-evident as the aspen's subterranean inter-connectedness. May our miraculous survival mimic that of the age-old grove of this hearty species, with roots so deeply intertwined it can withstand the heat of any conflagration. May we adorn humanity with beauty like aspen stands flourishing on the fringes of majestic conifers. May we bring life, love, peace and the awareness of the Creator to all nations.

THE FOUR QUESTIONS

1. Is there anything that you could lose that might feel as if your entire world has been destroyed?

2. Think of a traumatic event in your past. How did you move forward after such destruction?

3. How can you promote *achdut* (unity) in your community?

4. Can you envision the Third Temple? Will there be sacrifices?

PART SIX

The Joy of
Jewish Holidays:
Fall and Winter Festivals

This section is dedicated by
NISSAN, GILLIAN, GG AND PEARL MOSAPOR

I am so lucky we were matched through Jewish Big Brothers when I was eleven, an age when I really needed guidance and a friend. Our friendship means more than I can describe. I'm a better man because of you and only hope I can be a role model to my kids the way you are with me. The world is lucky to have someone so passionate about making it a better place. You encourage everyone to see the beauty in the simple things like nature, only to demonstrate that what seems so simple is remarkably complicated. You excel in pulling people out of their comfort zones so they can experience life's magic. You are so gifted... your music is inspired, your words eloquent and I've seen you play just about every instrument! I love you, Sam. It's all about the ISH.

IN THIS SECTION:

Elul: T'shuva — Masters of Return 171

Rosh Hashana: The Parade of Tears.................................... 177

The High Holidays: Why Are We Here? 180

Sukkah's On Fire 186

Sukkot vs. Halloween..191

Chanukah: I Have a Dream..195

Purim: From Exodus To Esther 200

OVERVIEW

Fall and winter are the seasons when one must include the phrase *"mashiv haruach u'morid hagashem"* in our central prayer, the *Amidah*. Logically, we ask for wind and rain during the time that precipitation is more likely. I relish in this transition in the prayer service—the days may be growing shorter but ski season is imminent!

This section covers the High Holidays, Sukkot, Sh'mini Atzeret, Simchat Torah, Chanukah and Purim. Many synagogues "bet the farm" on the advent of the fall festivals. After all, the High Holidays are the times they see the other three quarters of their community and therefore feel compelled to hold fundraising drives and stack the calendar with enticing events. Members of clergy often get edgy this time of year; rabbis fret about writing sermons and cantors are frantically preparing choirs and rehearsing repertoire. Imagine their relief at the end of Yom Kippur! Tragically, many worshippers are all "prayed out" by the end of *Ne'ila* (the closing service of Yom Kippur) and miss out on the magical week of Sukkot. For this reason, I extend this charge to my loyal readers: hang in there! Find a place where Sukkot and Simchat Torah are celebrated with joyful abandon and make sure to resource a *sukkah, lulav* and *etrog*. Don't miss out on this headquarters of happiness, the profound payoff for all the effort expended over the months of *Elul and Tishrei*.

The Jewish year culminates with Chanukah and Purim, our rabbinic holidays. Even though they are not biblically mandated, they are among our most popular. While it's fun to eat *latkes* and *hamentashen*, I will share meaningful insights into these family-friendly commemorations—they are not just for kids! During Simchat Torah we finish the Torah scroll and begin again with Genesis immediately thereafter. So, too, with our holiday cycle: upon the completion of Purim, the last holiday of the Jewish year, the sages recommend we delve right into preparations for Pesach. Round and round we go! We only get a certain number of annual holiday cycles in our brief time on this planet. Make them count.

Tefillin • Shabbat • Community • Torah • Prophets • Nigun • Pesach • Teshuva • Weddings Holiness • Emunah • Diaspora • Bar Mitzah • Simcha • Halacha • Brachot • Holidays Edah • Israel • Mikvah • Prayer • Meshiach • Tefillin • Shabbat • Community • Torah • Prophets Pesach • Teshuva • Weddings • Spirituality • Holiness • Emunah • Diaspora • Bar Mitzah Halacha • Brachot • Holidays • Edah • Israel • Mikvah • Prayer • Meshiach • Tefillin • Shabbat Community • Torah • Prophets • Nigun • Pesach • Teshuva • Weddings • Spirituality • Holiness

Elul: T'shuva – Masters of Return

♫ TAKE ME AS I AM ♫

joyjud.com/m/tmi

A hundred times a day
I'm reminded I stand for something
Somehow on the way
You bring me to the light
Let the answer be
There's time for You and me to reconcile
Let the answer be
There's something that You see
That makes You smile

Take me as I am
Not for yesterday
Let me feel the sun on my face tomorrow

A hundred times a day
I whisper Your Name into the darkness
Sometimes You're far away
Sometimes I feel Your breath

Let the answer be
You'll be there for me until the end
Let the answer be
I've reason to believe You'll let me try again

Take me as I am
What I might become
Let me feel the sun on my face tomorrow

An executive with very little Jewish education started studying with a rabbi. He had been encouraged by one of his peers to give it a try and Torah study soon became a high point in his week. This encounter with his heritage boosted his Jewish self-esteem and gave him fodder to discuss with his family now that they started dining together on Friday nights. One thing that bothered him, however, was when the rabbi referred to their sessions as "learning together." The executive called the rabbi on this one day: "We're not learning together, rabbi. You are teaching me. Why not call a spade a spade?" "No, quite the opposite," said the rabbi. "I learn from your world of experience and you learn from mine." "What?" the executive replied, "Don't patronize me! I barely went to Hebrew school and you are a well-trained rabbi." The rabbi thought for a moment and responded: "Imagine you are racing Michael Phelps in an Olympic-sized swimming pool. Who would win?" "Well, of course Phelps would destroy me." said the executive. The rabbi stated, "Now picture the two of you dropped in the middle of the Pacific Ocean. Who would win in a race back to Los

Angeles? You see, we're both in the middle of the Pacific, you and I. In the vast world of God's Torah, the deepest ocean in the universe, we're even."

The month of *Elul*, before the High Holidays, is the beginning of the season of *t'shuva* (return). Introspection is challenging and it's easier to ignore issues. One is tempted to give up, to believe resolutions are futile and that next year will be just the same. We are all in the same boat: not quite *tzadikim* or *resha'im* (righteous or evil), all drifting in the great Pacific merely trying to survive.

The Imperative of T'shuva

Elul is the time to press reset, to clear the cache, reformat the hard drive. We blow the *shofar* every morning of the month in an attempt to awaken our souls from a tepid stupor of habit and mediocrity. We step out of our busy lives to figure out why we are living them. We can only set personal goals when we perceive the disparity between where we are and where we could be. Hopefully we do this crucial work <u>before</u> we show up in the synagogue on the first of *Tishrei* (the first day of Rosh Hashana). Get an early start on *t'shuva*—that way, there's still time for a rewrite if the first draft of our mission statement is lacking. Imagine hearing on a certain day in the future we can fill a basket with jewels from a king's treasury. How exciting! It would be dumb to show up with a basket already full of junk, leaving no room for the king's gifts. *Elul* is the time to get priorities straight, clearing our basket so we can fill it with God's light on Rosh Hashana.

Jews don't believe in original sin. We believe in original purity. *Elul* is like a spiritual car wash; we scrub off accumulated road grime and return to the candy-apple-red finish underneath. An important component of *t'shuva* is ownership. We try to figure out where we are falling short with God and take responsibility. The other ten months of the year we tend to pass the buck. Now we take the fall. Are we blaming our upbringing, family members or the rabbi for our issues? Just one more chocolate croissant? Just one more drink for the road? The dog ate your *tefillin*? Rosh Hashana is *Yom HaDin*, Judgment Day. This Judge knows our every secret. We anticipate the prosecuting attorney's arguments by analyzing our weaknesses and preparing a case explaining why we deserve another year.

I am part of the *Ba'al T'shuva* (Master of Return, or BT) movement. A small trickle of young Jews reclaimed their heritage in the 1960s and it turned into a flood in the next few decades. Countless neighborhoods nationwide have been transformed by yuppies looking to create modern day *shtetls* with *shuls*, bakeries, restaurants and bookstores all within walking distance. Jewish spirituality has been transformed by BT enthusiasm. During *Elul* we all become BTs. It doesn't matter where we are or where we came from. *Elul* is the time to analyze life goals and commit to a path to realize them. We seek new mitzvah opportunities <u>and</u> perform mitzvot we already do with alacrity.

There are a few pitfalls to avoid when becoming a BT, even if it's just for the months of *Elul* and *Tishrei*. As we've discussed, connecting with God requires humility in order to create the spiritual space for God's Presence. How ironic that some BTs feel that they themselves discovered God and Torah and now live in the smug triumph of their accomplishment. Anyone less observant is *treif*, anyone more observant is a fanatic. A self-righteous attitude leads to the next pitfall, harsh judgment of others. As discussed in the *Middot* chapter, we must judge others as we would want to be judged ourselves. This is particularly important advice in the weeks preceding the Day of Judgment!

The antidote to self-righteousness is gratitude, to scrutinize the gifts in our lives with laser-sharp focus and credit God for every detail. This is the foundation of our work during *Elul*. We must remember God doesn't owe us anything. Every moment of precious life is a gift. Genuine humility springs from this awareness of our indebtedness. There's an old BT joke about a yeshiva neophyte touting his newfound humility. "I am nothing," he repeats, trying to *mevatel* (nullify) his ego. The older students quip, "Look who thinks he's nothing!" Evolved BTs recognize they spend a lifetime as a "work in progress." Their upbringing may not have been 100% kosher, but it gave them tools to get where they needed to go, to launch on their own perfectly orchestrated, custom-made path. They remember to respect everyone's process and give credit where credit is due.

T'shuva was created before God initiated the Big Bang. According to the Talmud, seven things were created before the universe, the first of which was Torah. *T'shuva* is second! Torah is the blueprint for all reality and *t'shuva* is an imperative for God's highest creation, human beings, to have the chance to restore and maintain the relationship. So crucial is this relationship that the paragraph regarding *t'shuva* in the daily *Sh'moneh Esrei* is the only place God's "desire" is mentioned (Blessed are You, God, Who desires repentance). As we've discussed, God craves closeness with us and due to our precious gift of free will, it is up to us to decide to reciprocate.

Making Elul Personal

As my friend David Sacks said in the name of Rabbi David Aaron, God is a celestial sit-com writer hoping for feedback from us, the actors. David was a staff writer on Third Rock from the Sun and frequently asked actor John Lithgow for feedback on his lines. What do WE want for our character? What can we do to realize our goals, our potential? We share the co-producer credit in fashioning the script of our lives! If the actor tells the writer he wants to juggle in an upcoming scene, the logical question is, "Well, can you juggle?" God is prepared to fulfill our requests based on the vessel we have created. It's a partnership, not a magic show. When we are in the synagogue during the holidays, the most important dialog isn't in the *machzor* (holiday prayer book); it's in our hearts, helping God understand what we need in our lives. During *Elul* we formulate this answer, getting realistic in terms of our abilities, setting viable goals. Before we beg God for a better job, a raise or a spouse, we bolster our strengths, commit to repairing weaknesses and ask to have a starring role in the saga our lives.

I was out at a favorite L.A. jazz club hearing some absolute musical masters tearing it up. The volume was getting more intense with every song and I had to beseech the bartender for earplugs. At one point, I noticed the keyboard player's amplifier was on fire. Literally. No one seemed to notice. A timeless minute went by where my shock at the lack of response turned into action. In spite of having a broken foot parked in a knee-high Frankenstein boot, I abandoned my crutches and leapt to the stage to pull the flaming amp away from the thick red curtain on which it leaned. I yelled to the waiter to get a fire extinguisher. The owner of the club sprinted to the stage to tackle me...he assumed I was an overzealous fan. The fire was put out, the keyboards were patched through the PA system and the band didn't miss a beat, smoothly segueing into "Fire" by Jimi Hendrix.

After the excitement, I nursed my Corona and reflected: I cannot sit around and wait for someone else to help me. Yes, I must pray every day and endeavor to make God part of my team, but waiting for the big break or depending on anyone to make my life happen is folly. Which of my actions is postponing the fulfillment of my dreams? Am I looking for a free lunch? Am I going to live forever? I can't just wait for the phone to ring for the next gig or album client. I have to figure out what I want and get busy. The heat is on—it's *Elul!* Now is the time to compile an exhaustive list of life goals for myself and for the world before I meet the Master of the Universe on *Erev Rosh Hashana.*

By the time we get to Yom Kippur, we get the gift of a clean slate with our re-coronated King. Imagine we are kids coming back from a year abroad, running into the arms of a loving parent. Cleaning the slate with our fellow man is equally, if not more, important. All the prayer in the world won't substitute for a formal apology to a wronged friend. Don't let guilt and disgruntlement fester. During *Elul*, our rabbis urge us to break the ice with a simple "I'm sorry." When we clear the air of the pain and suffering we inflict on others, especially those closest to us, we create a more unified planet and show honor to our King, restoring the Joy of Judaism in our lives.

The Mechanics of the High Holiday Season

Here's the typical agenda for the months of *Elul* and *Tishrei*: from the second day of *Elul*, Sephardim begin a daily session of *S'lichot* (forgiveness prayers), usually just before the morning service. *S'lichot* consist of the *Ashrei*, the half *Kaddish* and a series of moving prayers expressing contrition for times we have fallen short of our potential. The highlight is the recitation of the *Shalosh Esrei Middot*, the Thirteen Attributes uttered by God right after the Jews were forgiven for the Golden Calf (*Sh'mot* 34:6-7). Ashkenazim say these prayers starting the Saturday night before Rosh Hashana. The joke in the community is that Sephardim get to eat rice on Pesach but are saddled with an extra three weeks of early *minyanim* for *S'lichot*. Typically, on the pre-High Holiday Ashkenazi *S'lichot* opening weekend, I get hired to offer a Shabbaton followed by a meaningful community concert. I then lead this unique midnight service which features a preview of seminal High Holiday melodies.

A Psalm known as *L'David* (*Tehillim* 27) is recited twice a day from *Elul* through the end of Sukkot. These words of King David are said right after the *shofar* is blown at the end of *Shacharit* services. They feature a line that sums up our goal for this holy period: "One thing I have asked of God: that I may dwell in the house of God all the days of my life." Interestingly, the *shofar* isn't blown the day before Rosh Hashana. On one hand, it makes it more special when we hear it on the official holiday. The deeper reason is to confuse Satan...it's a long story, but evidently Satan is hoping to sink our chances for a favorable judgement. When the *shofar* isn't sounded, it freaks him out. Or something like that. Also, for a similar reason, the typical *Shabbat M'varchim* (Sabbath of Blessing) announcement of Rosh Chodesh *Tishrei* is omitted before Rosh Hashana.

After *Shacharit* services *Erev* Rosh Hashana, we do a ceremony called *Hatarat Nedarim* in which we ask a panel of three ad hoc judges (formed from members of the community) to repeal any vows we've made in the past year. That's right...we get a jump start on Yom Kippur and start the new year with a clean slate.

Rosh Hashana is actually one of four "New Years" listed in the Mishnah. The first is *Rosh Chodesh Nissan*, the New Year for the numbering of months in the Jewish calendar, for the cycle of Jewish holidays and for counting the reign of kings in ancient Israel. Next is *Rosh Chodesh Elul*, the New Year for tithing one's animals, akin to our current mid-April national tax deadline. The first of *Tishrei*, the "regular" Rosh Hashana we know and love, is the New Year for seasons and the reign of foreign kings. It also demarcates the beginning of *Sh'mitah* (Sabbatical) and *Yovel* (Jubilee) years. Lastly, Tu Bish'vat (the fifteenth of Sh'vat), typically falling mid-January, is the New Year for trees. This ancient Jewish version of Arbor Day is the birthday for fruit trees, no matter what day they were planted. This is important to know since we are commanded to refrain from eating fruit from trees less than three years old. This date is when we make a Tu Bish'vat *Seder*, sampling new fruits with a *Shehecheyanu* prayer and expressing gratitude for nature's bounty. I resonate with the theme of ecological awareness, proud that my heritage emphasizes the commandment of *ba'al tashchit,* not wasting or destroying precious natural resources. Tu Bish'vat usually coincides with *Parashat Beshalach*, the Torah portion describing the Jew's miraculous crossing of the *Yam Suf* (Reed Sea). Since we prophetically sang *Shirat Hayam* (Song of the Sea) as a nation, most large synagogues worldwide ensure this Shabbat is especially musical, a boon for singers like me.

Interestingly, Rosh Hashana is the only holiday lasting for two days both in the Diaspora <u>and</u> in Israel. Our sages consider it one long forty-eight-hour day. There's a tradition not to nap on these days. After all, if we were being sentenced in a terrestrial court of law, we wouldn't be getting much sleep. We should approach the Days of Awe with similar trepidation. Since I lead the services and must stand for much of the five hours of *davening*, this *minhag* (custom) is particularly challenging for me. Some sages teach the first day is focused on matters of *ruchnius* (spirituality) and the second day, *gashmius* (material needs).

At the conclusion of Rosh Hashana, we are launched into what David Sacks calls the "Days of Wet Cement." Jewish tradition maintains that the *Aseret Y'mei T'shuva* (The Ten Days of Return from Rosh Hashana to Yom Kippur) are the times to do everything right. My *rav*, Moshe Cohen insists we shouldn't panic and get monastic. He recommends simply doing the mitzvot we already do, but doing them better, with more *kavanah* (focus) and love. This period is a sort of Jewish Lent. It's a good time to take on holy commitments, even if one lapses right after Yom Kippur. We believe we are judged "where we are at," knowing God sees our valiant efforts and seals the Book of Life accordingly. During this period, it's customary to visit the graves of loved ones, driving home the lesson of our fragility and fostering gratitude to those who gave us life.

The Shabbat in between Rosh Hashana and Yom Kippur is referred to as *Shabbat Shuva* (The Sabbath of Return). Yes, *t'shuva* is top of mind, but it got its name from the first word of the *Haftorah* of the day. Back in the old days, rabbis had it easy. They would only give a formal *drash* (sermon) on *Shabbat Hagadol* before Pesach and *Shabbat Shuva*. Nowadays they are expected to wax eloquent every week! In most communities, rather than speaking before the *Mussaf* service, rabbis offer an hour-plus lecture in the afternoon before *Mincha*. The big dilemma of living in a neighborhood with over fifty synagogues is deciding which of these talks to attend.

On *Erev* Yom Kippur, many communities do *Kaparot*. Even at this ecologically-aware juncture of history, some insist on the traditional spinning of a chicken above their heads, symbolizing that it could be their own necks on the line. The chicken is then immediately slaughtered by a *shochet* (kosher butcher) and donated to poor families. I suffered through one of these ceremonies with my brother in Jerusalem. I am totally into taking on everything Judaism has to offer...except this nauseating *minhag* (custom). I guess that means I may not be so comfortable should Temple sacrifices be reinstated. An alternative to using chickens is doing the same ceremony with a bundle of cash. I was so upset by the vision of those bleeding birds that I don't do this either. Another *Erev* Yom Kippur custom is taking a *mikvah*. After the morning *minyan*, I seek the largest body of water and spend the day soaking and pondering, mentally preparing for the upcoming spiritual and vocal marathon. Of course, if there are waves, I ensure they are properly ridden.

Before leaving for *Kol Nidrei* services, we eat a huge final meal and bless our children. Yom Kippur is the Sabbath of Sabbaths. As soon as the sun goes down, the laws of Shabbat are extant, as are the laws of a full fast day. These include no bathing, no food or drink, no anointing (lotions, perfumes, etc.) and no marital relations. You'll notice many wear light, white garments instead of dark suits. Even though we dress to impress, we are prohibited from wearing leather shoes. Make sure to resource vegan footwear before the holiday arrives! Better to be in socks than wearing leather. As ridiculous as they look, Crocs are perfect. As soon as there are three stars in the sky at the end of the *Ne'ila*, the final service of the day, a *t'ki'ah g'dola* (long *shofar* blast) is sounded and the community scatters to attend Break Fast parties.

The days between Yom Kippur and Sukkot are the closest thing Jews have to a "hall pass." We leave Yom Kippur in a state of purity and exaltation and retain this level while engaged in the holy work of preparing for Sukkot. Indeed, our sages recommend hammering the first nail of the sukkah right after Yom Kippur concludes. Our days are busy building and decorating our *sukkot*, inviting guests, preparing meals and purchasing *arba minim* (four species—palm, willow, myrtle and citron). *Chazal* teach that sins aren't reckoned until the first day of Sukkot. Of course, since Sukkot is a weeklong riot of festive meals, parties, concerts and fun, who has time to consider *aveirot* (sins)? Sukkot segues into the holiday of Sh'mini Atzeret and Simchat Torah, so we retain our untainted balance sheet until the twenty-fourth of *Tishrei*. If we can keep our act together from *Rosh Chodesh Elul* to *Rosh Chodesh Cheshvan*, we have enjoyed nearly sixty awesome days of deep communion with our Creator, hopefully enough to propel us on an ideal path the rest of the year.

We can utilize the power of these holy months to penetrate our essence, to bond with community, to demand the world become free from war, disease, disaster, cruelty and suffering. Take the time to tell the Director what you think of the script of your life. In actuality, we are not actors or puppets. We are God's children, God's chosen ones, God's partners. One of the amazing aspects of the High Holidays is having the opportunity to pray together. Using different styles of worship, in different buildings, in different countries, but still together. On a lifeboat in a vast ocean. We are the Jewish People. We are one. Connected, needing each other. Humbly travelling through history, accompanied by our loving Creator. Building a palace. Masters of return.

THE FOUR QUESTIONS

1. Where do you feel you are falling short and would like to make improvements in the year to come?

2. If you knew you had a half hour meeting with God, what would you ask for?

3. What are the life goals that you want to achieve this year?

4. Is there anyone you need to apologize to before Rosh Hashana?

Rosh Hashana:
The Parade of Tears

♫ HAVEYN YAKIR LI ♫

joyjud.com/m/hvl

Into the desert
Swooning in love
Without food and water
But with trust in God above

Marching towards a mountain
A celestial canopy
Betrothed to our Creator
Forever we will be
Haveyn yakir li Ephraim...

I just returned from my cousin Gene Samson's funeral. I left home frustrated I was losing half my day, begrudgingly donning a black suit on a ninety-degree L.A. scorcher. However, as soon as I entered the mortuary, I was immediately uplifted by seeing the faces of my extended family. There is a palpable soul-satisfaction when performing the ancient ritual of participating in the burial of a loved one.

Gene died at the ripe age of eighty-three and was beloved by all who knew him. He had a winning personality, a can-do attitude and was functioning on all cylinders until he left this world. Funerals for the elderly are bittersweet affairs combining mourning with humorous anecdotes and descriptions of the legacy of the deceased. We cried for Gene's widow, children and grandchildren who had clearly lost their patriarch. But our tears were tempered by the awareness that Gene's was a life fully lived and his departure, at least to me, was a celebration of life, more a bon voyage than a tragic ending.

Rabbi Mark Hyman eloquently led the service, mentioning that the timing of my cousin's passing coincided with the beginning of *Elul*. At that moment, I realized I had been too busy to experience *Elul*, too obsessed with my self-imposed deadlines to make a spiritual accounting. It's hard to smell the roses with your nose to the grindstone. Rather than hurry back to my studio, I took time to wander the cemetery with my parents and pay respects at the various graves of our loved ones. I got to witness my dear mom and dad hand in hand, a loving couple married for over fifty years, wearing white, exploring the verdant burial ground of our extended family. I wept at my grandparents' graves, an autonomic response whenever I see my dad getting misty-eyed. I love my parents so much. I miss the relatives that have left us. Perhaps I just needed to open my heart and have a "good cry."

As we have discussed, reacquainting oneself with the power of tears is the secret of unlocking the storehouse of *simcha*. Once, I attended a pre-High Holiday lecture in Israel which portrayed Rosh Hashana as the capital of tears. Every passage of Torah and *Nevi'im* (Prophets) read over the holiday depicts different categories of this uniquely human response to joy and pain. Perhaps the best exercise during *Elul* is to relearn how to cry by examining the inspiration for our biblical heroes' most poignant milestones. Allow me to present the various actors in the "Parade of Tears."

Our first tale comes from the Torah reading on the first day of Rosh Hashana, the expulsion of Hagar and Yishmael from the home of Sarah and Avraham. This is the famous *parasha* where Avraham is told "do whatever Sarah tells you" (*B'reishit* 21:12), the primal marital survival tactic of saying "yes, dear" to one's wife. Reluctantly, at Sarah's request, Avraham sends Hagar and Yishmael packin' into the arid desert. When the water runs out, Hagar leaves her son a bowshot away so she won't have to witness his misery. She cries her own tears of despondency and remarkably, God doesn't respond to her anguish but instead hears "the cry of the boy" and only then does salvation appear. The lesson here: We can and should cry out when we are in pain. But give up? Never.

Next we have the *Haftorah* describing Hannah as she weeps while beseeching God to grant her a child. Eli, the high priest, sees her mouthing words of prayer silently and assumes she's yet another Jerusalem madwoman. When Eli eventually consoles her, she feels confident her prayer has been heard and a year later gives birth to the infant who would become my namesake, the great prophet Shmuel/Samuel. We learn from Hannah how to pray fervently, with words silently on our lips, and from Eli, how to respond with compassion. Preparations for Rosh Hashana must include more than buying apples and honey. We can reach out to friends with an understanding ear and volunteer to help the needy. Our tears of empathy unlock the gates for the prayers of all humanity.

On the second day of Rosh Hashana, the Torah introduces the next player in the celestial dance: this time it is Yitzchak and the scene is the infamous *Akeidah*, his near sacrifice at the hand of his father Avraham on Mount Moriah. This is one of the most difficult passages in our canon to grasp. At the age of forty, Yitzchak seems to be complicit in his own demise. Avraham is asked to destroy the fruit of his life's labor. The *Midrash* tells us the angels were crying tears of disbelief and awe at their commitment. These tears fell into Yitzchak's eyes, leading eventually to his blindness. These angelic tears represent the tears of injury, tears from damaging wounds that stay with us forever. No one is immune from crises, trauma and tragedy. Our challenge is whether we let destruction sabotage our spirit or if we rise from the ashes stronger and more deeply connected to Hashem.

The final textual character can be found in the second day *Haftorah* with our matriarch Rachel. She is weeping for her exiled children and will not be comforted. Rachel is laid to rest not in the *Ma'arat HaMachpelah* (ancestral burial cave) with the extended family, but along the road, so that her *kever* (grave) remains a beacon for all those in exile as they return to Jerusalem. Hers are the tears of redemption, tears spilled over millennia of our wandering and persecution, tears that God carefully collects as we march slowly but surely toward a perfected world.

There's one more dancer in the Parade of Tears. Take a moment and try to figure it out…wait for it…it's the cry of the *shofar!* Our *shofar* blasts, the centerpiece of the holiday, are modeled after the mournful wailing of Sisera's mother. Sisera? I don't recall hearing about him in Hebrew school. In the period of Judges, Sisera was the Hitler of his day, a tyrannical Canaanite general with the blood of thousands of Jews on his sword. After the miraculous defeat of his army led by the prophetess Devorah, our heroine Yael cleverly waited at her tent for him to come by. She welcomed him with soothing milk and comfort and as he slept, drove a tent peg through his temple. The Talmud asks: how did Sisera's mother cry when her son neglected to return from battle? Long cries, short stuttering rasps or a combination? As usual for the Talmud, the rabbis are in complete disagreement. Hence we have the *t'ki'ah*, *sh'varim* and *t'ruah* blasts of the *shofar*, just to make sure we cover all the bases. Is that mind-blowing? The text never divulges Sisera's mother's name. She remains "the mother of Sisera" for eternity; in other words, her identity is entirely wrapped up in the accomplishments of her cherished, nefarious son.

The blasts of the *shofar* represent the tears of loss of identity. Reclaiming identity is a prerequisite to celebrating Rosh Hashana. Unless we stand on our own feet, we can never be counted, we are inauthentic, we are defying the very reason we were graciously given the gift of life. When we get in touch with our deepest selves, coronating God King becomes natural and effortless. The sounding of the *shofar* reenacts the soul being blown into the body, as Hashem did with Adam in the Garden of Eden. With every *t'ki'ah*, imagine God filling us with our essence, trumpeting our uniqueness.

On his deathbed, the Chassidic sage Rav Zusha explained he was crying not because he wasn't as great as Moses—he just wanted to be the best Rav Zusha he could be. Yes, we must look out for our families and our community, but in the end we must say *hineni*, taking ownership of our own destinies. Once we clean our personal slate and regain clarity on our *tafkid* (life mission), the cries of the *shofar* mainline straight to our hearts and shatter the walls of complacency.

I sang my song "Blessing" for the mourners assembled at my cousin Gene's graveside service. He died during *Ki Teitzei*, the Torah portion when we are introduced to this eternal priestly blessing of peace (Numbers/*Bamidbar* 6:24-26). I sang it for his *neshama* to have an *aliyah*, a heavenly escalation. I sang it for his adult children and teenage grandchildren when I saw none of them knew how to say *Kaddish*. I sang it for my kids for whom I wrote it in the first place. I sang it for my parents who gave me this blessing at the Friday night dinner table as I grew up and continue to bless my life. Most importantly, I sang it for myself, to connect to my personal destiny and to ingrain within myself that I can't run from opportunities to appreciate the kindness of our Parent in Heaven. Sometimes God's kindness comes in the form of a funeral, getting interrupted from one's work and having to wear a suit on a sweltering day.

THE FOUR QUESTIONS

1. How can you make yourself more open to your emotions?

2. Think of a time of crisis in your life — what helped you come out of it a stronger person?

3. What is your kavanah (focus) when you hear the shofar?

4. How would you describe your unique life mission?

The High Holidays: Why Are We Here?

♫ SHEYIBANEH BEIT HAMIKDASH ♫

joyjud.com/m/sbh

Take me to the Holy Temple
Let me walk on holy ground
Let me know Your essence
Let me feel Your presence
Let me be a blessing

Lift my eyes to see Your glory
Kings and prophets in our midst
Feel the mountains tremble
Watching us assemble
In the center of the universe

Y'hi ratzon milfanecha
May it be Your will, Hashem our God
Y'hi ratzon milfanecha
Sheyibaneh beit hamikdash
Bimheyra v'yameynu

Hear the cry of generations
Longing for Your open hand
How long can we bear it
Till we finally merit
Peace within our Promised Land

My favorite comic strip of the season is Bart Simpson at the blackboard scrawling repeatedly, "I won't count how many pages are left in the *Machzor* (High Holiday prayer book)." Formal prayer is an acquired taste, and its acquisition is best achieved with frequency. Hence the Jewish Catch 22: many of my fellow Jews only show up to pray on the two days a year when the prayers are by far the most long-winded and complicated. No wonder they are chomping at the bit to get out of there. Perhaps those planning to spend only two days a year in the synagogue should choose Purim and Simchat Torah!

Even with preparation and competent leadership, the High Holidays are still a lot to handle. How can clergy best communicate the essential themes of this period? Ideally, the chazzan keeps the congregation engaged in participatory melody rather than melismatic showboating. Hopefully the rabbi avoids politics and uses teaching moments to answer the elephant in the room question: "Why are we here?" The following is a multi-faceted answer to that fundamental question, inspired by my brilliant friend, Rabbi Simcha Weinberg. The five salient keywords are: first impressions, aspiration, desire, beauty and royalty.

First Impressions

Rosh Hashana and Yom Kippur are truly portals to newness. I've heard "you never get a second chance to make a first impression," but God gives us that very gift during these holidays. We are judged "where we are at," with a completely fresh opportunity to be the people we want to be. We learn by way of the aforementioned example of Hagar and Yishmael's expulsion from Avraham and Sarah's home, in the Torah portion read on the first day of Rosh Hashana. God judges Yishmael not for the mischief he caused with Yitzchak, nor for the trouble his offspring would create for Jews in future generations. Instead, Yishmael is judged as he is fighting for his life, dying of thirst in the harsh desert. God answers his heartfelt prayer with a miraculous rescue. Even Yishmael is a sweet child of the Almighty. The Talmud uses this example to explain that free will only exists in the present. We are judged where we stand at any given moment. On Rosh Hashana we can establish a radical new direction, regardless of previous transgressions. This opportunity to become new again isn't just semantics. Our cells are continuously regenerating. We are vastly different from the people we were ten years earlier. We know change is possible because we *have* changed as a result of our deepest experiences, both triumphant and traumatic.

I think of the *badeken* (veiling ceremony for the bride) at a Jewish wedding as the best example of creating an auspicious environment for first impressions. When my wife and I were contemplating the wedding of our dreams, we realized that the most profound events we had attended were the more traditional celebrations. We started learning about the various customs with a favorite rabbi and decided that while a full-blown *tish, badeken, kabbalat panim* and *yichud* might bewilder our secular friends, the spiritual rewards of these traditions were worth the inconvenience. Typically, the guys go to a *tish* where they offer toasts, sing and take care of the formal documents. The ladies surround the bride, a queen for the day seated elegantly during the *kabbalat panim*, where she receives her guests and dispenses blessings one by one. Then the male friends and family of the groom dance him into the bride's throne room for the *badeken*, a moment of indescribable joy. Guests witnessing this scene typically have chills up their spines and wide smiles on their faces as the groom gets to see his bride for the first time in a week, bedecked in all her majesty.

A dear friend who was my *chevrusa* during my first bout in yeshiva, Rabbi Aryeh Markman, suggested we not even speak during the week before our big day. "Not even speak? Isn't that severe? What about the last minute details? What about entertaining our out-of-town guests?" I asked in exasperation. He said, "On your wedding day, when you first see your beloved bride, the one you have chosen out of all others in the world, you don't want to think, *how could you have said that to me last night?*"

We wisely took the rabbi's advice. We created a most powerful first impression that will remain forever etched in our minds. Our capable photographer caught the crystalline tears cascading from my eyes while I veiled my bride in a timeless state of wonderment. According to the *Midrash,* the couple brings down the souls of their yet unborn children when the veil is lowered. Whoa! On the High Holidays, our principle task is to conjure such a first-time meeting when we stand in the synagogue. The new you. Totally separate from the person you were as you entered the sanctuary. Rosh Hashana is commonly known as the anniversary of the creation of the world. In actuality, it is the birthday of Adam and Eve, the anniversary of the sixth day, the one that really matters. Just like Adam stands alone in a nascent Garden of Eden, the very definition of a fresh start, so, too, can we on this first day of the year, and every day thereafter.

Aspiration

Adam's first prayer in the Garden of Eden was one of aspiration. He saw an incomplete world and according to Rashi, felt in his heart, "This could be so much more!" This theme should inform all our prayers during this High Holiday period. We're not *davening* for selfish reasons; instead, we see a world of potential and desperately want that potential realized. Interestingly, only when Adam prayed did the rain fall and bring forth the greenery of the garden (Rashi on *B'reishit* 2:5). In other words, the herbage God created on the third day waited in subterranean suspense until the sixth day when Adam aspired for more. Let us all be like Adam, truly wanting greatness for ourselves and for our world, and speaking these aspirations into being.

In my neighborhood, when people question my friend Rabbi Shlomo Seidenfeld's affiliation, he prefers "Aspiring Jew" to Orthodox Jew. He points out that one can be *halachic* but not aspiring—one must use *halacha* to bolster aspiration. Some of our brothers and sisters cocoon in cloistered communities due to the incessant persecution endured over the ages, or to ward off the siren song of modernity. When retreating from the secular world and *gashmius* (materialism), it's easy to lose aspiration for all humankind, for the pursuit of *Tikkun Olam* on a global scale. The challenge to the pious is to retain inner fortitude and outward focus.

In the book of *Bamidbar* (Numbers), the spies who rejected Israel weren't necessarily afraid of the conquest. Rather, they didn't want to leave the realm of perfection and protection God had provided in the desert. Rabbi Seidenfeld believes at a certain point in his growth, his rabbis should have tossed him out of yeshiva. The time had come to leave the womb of 24/7 *kedusha* and interact with society. Interacting is how we develop *bitachon*, compassion and leadership. The High Holiday season is the time to reawaken our aspirations for the planet, to reject our communal myopia. Think big thoughts! God will hear your prayer! We could be so much more.

Awakening Desire

God gives Adam a few jobs: take care of the garden, name the animals and avoid certain trees. Adam becomes a "yes-man," calmly awaiting God's next command. God perceives this is not ideal (*lo tov*) and in order to inspire Adam to take initiative and think outside the box, God gives him the gift of a wife. Eve ignites his passion and cajoles him to reach his potential. We see proof of Adam's complacency when God puts him in a "deep slumber" much like God did with Avraham and Daniel. Rather than seeing Technicolor prophetic visions like other biblical heroes, Adam sees nothing during his sleep. Adam's newfound desire with Eve is a good thing: although he eventually eats from the forbidden tree, at least he becomes an active partner with God, not just an employee. This time period, therefore, is the season for the rekindling of desire. We sing *Zochreynu L'chaim* in our prayers, acknowledging God wants us to desire life, to serve proactively as God's "hands" in the world, to fill our finite days with purpose and beauty.

Beauty

A popular *Midrash* from the book of Exodus describes how Jewish women made mirrors of copper to beautify themselves for their husbands. Most couples had given up on relations in the face of crushing Egyptian slavery and infanticide. We were redeemed in the merit of these exalted women who shared the mirrors with their exhausted husbands. The men could see the beauty not only of their wives—the wives would remind them that they too were beautiful. The women rekindled the men's self-esteem and appetite and thereby ensured the future of the Jewish people. In light of their "illicit" origins, Moshe was reluctant to follow the command to turn these mirrors into the *kiyor*, the washbasin the *kohanim* (priests) would use in the *Mishkan*. However, God knew the *kohanim* would see their reflection and be reminded just how magnificent they appeared to the Almighty. My friends, we are all God's children. We are stunningly beautiful to God, just like our own children are beautiful to us. We slide home at the end of a tough year of hard knocks and bruises to our ego. We may show up in stylish clothes on the High Holidays, but inside we feel like a mess. This is the season of connecting with our inner beauty and our legacy as precious children or our Creator.

Royalty

One of the crucial changes in the Rosh Hashana liturgy is the repeated emphasis of God as *Melech*, or King. The *Shacharit* service opens with the cantor's bold *Hamelech* fanfare and we make the "*Melech*" insertions in the *Amidah* or risk having to start the whole thing from the beginning. Does an omnipotent God need our flattery? Well, yes. Without loyal subjects, a king is either powerless or a despot. Having a king as our celestial Parent elevates us to the rank of prince or princess. Our sages tell us that we earned our regal pedigree as the offspring of our exemplary matriarchs and patriarchs. The *Akeidah*, the binding of Yitzchak, which we read about on the second day of Rosh Hashana, seals our royal status in the eyes of the angelic realms. Note that it's an angel who responds to Avraham's heroic act (*B'reishit* 22:12). The angels needed convincing that humankind was worthy of Torah and this episode sealed the deal. If we do our job over the High Holidays, we emerge whitewashed of sin, at parity with the angels, reunited with our Creator and our meritorious ancestors. We leave in royal robes, perceiving our inner beauty, filled with aspirations to make the world a proper kingdom for God.

It's not only Rosh Hashana where we see mention of God's kingship. An important part of our Yom Kippur service is the re-enactment of the procedures followed by the priests in the *Beit Hamikdash* (Holy Temple). The reason for this *Avodah* service is not only to commemorate what was. It's to remember we had a palace, God's palace, a national central address fit for our Monarch. When we sing about the rebuilding of Jerusalem, we're not talking about the Ben Yehuda shopping mall. The sound of the *shofar* is a coronation trumpet; the unforgettable major key cadence of the evening High Holiday prayers is the coronation suite. Thanks to the genius of the Ba'al Haturim (Rabbi Yaakov ben Asher, 1269-1343), we know the *gematria* of *Beit Hamikdash* equals 861. So, too, does the word Rosh Hashana. An integral connection binds both concepts, inspiring us to reclaim our regal heritage and turn our hearts towards Jerusalem.

Hooray for Judgment Day

Perhaps the best answer to the "why are we here?" question: we are being judged.

While it is serious business, we should be happy about it. Judgment Day sounds like an eschatological disaster movie. We live in a time of unparalleled political correctness where judging others is frowned upon. What works for you is fine for you just as long as you don't hurt anyone. *Shvitzing* in a synagogue for endless hours to be judged? I'll take the beach! But the reality is that we crave judgment. We're desperate to know we are on a true path. We spend millions on success coaches, consultants and seminars to realign our trajectories and reach our goals. The idea of God judging us should provide a sense of comfort that God cares.

The number one hit on the High Holiday Top 40 is *Avinu Malkeinu*, the moving prayer referring to Hashem as Father and King. This reference to God is the only gender specific term in this book. Why? Judgement is considered the masculine aspect of our Creator. While we hope for mercy and kindness, the feminine aspect of Godliness, Rosh Hashana requires welcoming God's unflinching assessment of our personal progress. As Yom Kippur transitions into Sukkot, we shift our conception of God from *Avinu Malkeinu* to spouse. In the end, our relationship is not about crime and punishment, it's about intimacy. I nurture the relationship with my wife by avoiding the things that upset her and doing the things that bring us close. When we build a home with God, we avoid *aveirot* (sins) not because we are afraid of the whip but because we can't imagine defacing the beautiful palace we have diligently constructed in loving partnership with the Almighty.

Who is God running against to become King? Us! The success of the coronation is in our hands. Yom Kippur is about begging forgiveness for the times that we didn't make God King. There is a cleansing power implicit in the day, absolving us of all our collective shortcomings, giving us a fresh start in the relationship. Once we learn the intricacies of *halacha*, it becomes clear how easy it is to transgress. What a gift that a single twenty-five-hour period of earnest prayer can wipe away every forgotten blessing, every vow, every illicit thought. The pageantry of *Kol Nidrei* opens the proceedings with a fanfare announcing the Heavenly Court. Over the course of the five services of the day we have multiple repetitions of the *Vidui* (Confession) to ensure we cover every possible transgression. To complete the experience, I highly recommend the evocative elucidation of the confessional in the back of the Artscroll *Machzor*. It's impossible to recite this extended translation and not see oneself on the pages. Just like the *Amidah*, the *Vidui* is in the plural, in other words, on this Day of Awe (or Awesome Day), seeking forgiveness is a team effort.

Chassidim frown upon saying the *Vidui* on Yom Kippur with a sad voice. In fact, the traditional *nigun* (song) is in a major key. Isn't trepidation the order of the day? How is it possible we can fix everything? Does God really forgive? Does God love humanity enough to care about each one of us? Remarkably, the answer is yes. A *chet* (sin) means "missing the mark;" in other words, there is no truly intentional sin. We are "off target" in life simply because we don't perceive the gravity of our actions. Any personal shortcomings serving as the impetus to repair our relationship can become mitzvot—in the long run, they get us closer to Hashem! Confession is a Torah mitzvah, and therefore, even when we confess, we can serve God with joy. I'm not recommending putting on a clown suit and parading around the *bimah* (pulpit) during *Kol Nidrei*. But rather than pounding one's chest for poor choices, may I suggest—do it gently, with a smile inside, knowing God judges us with compassion and is ALWAYS ready for us to come home.

The High Holidays are about restoring what we always have inside, which is a sweet, loving child. Our inner child is quick to recover from a hurt, is openly affectionate and sees the world with wide-eyed wonder. That child knows he is beautiful in his parents' eyes and since the world revolves around him, he can be a tyrant prince. When a toddler cries, a few moments later she may be laughing with joyous abandon. Rabbi Weinberg quotes the Zohar, stating that the *shofar* blast is really a lullaby. Imagine that the final *tekiyah gedolah* at the end of Yom Kippur is an extended lullaby from God, just for you. This is why we are here.

THE FOUR QUESTIONS

1. Why do you to attend High Holiday services?

2. How can you make High Holidays meaningful?

3. Do you have aspirations that need to be rekindled?

4. How can you retain an inner smile when reciting the *Vidui* (confession)?

Sukkot:
My Sukkah's on Fire

♫ MY SUKKAH'S ON FIRE (A PARODY) ♫

joyjud.com/m/msf

You shake my lulav and you rattle my fruit
This kind of etrog costs a lot of loot
Can't get my fill, oh, what a thrill
Goodness gracious, my sukkah's on fire

Let's make some food and send out invitations
Put up some walls and hang the decorations
We gonna roch, beneath the schach
Goodness gracious, my sukkah's on fire

Shake it baby, oh, you shake it real good
Let me shake it like a lulav should
You're fine and you're mine
Making my Kiddush on the fruit of the vine

East, South, West, North, up, down
Just take those branches and shake 'em all around
Shehecheyanu v'kiymanu
Goodness gracious, my sukkah's on fire

During the Sukkot holiday, the whole neighborhood of Pico-Robertson erupts in joyful celebration. Our forty-plus kosher restaurants all have *sukkot* attached. There's a *sukkah* on top of Ralph's supermarket. One could conceivably *sukkah* hop to a different hut every five minutes and not exhaust the inventory. Google "Sukkah's on Fire"—you'll find my video showcasing an assortment of local *sukkot*, accompanied by a wacky holiday parody of the Jerry Lee Lewis "Great Balls" classic. You'll also find a video of my brother Yom Tov's enormous Jerusalem-based *sukkah* going up in flames. A well-placed security camera caught the tragic conflagration and his kids mischievously added my song as a soundtrack. Little did I realize that this parody would prophetically chronicle our family misadventure.

For those driving down Pico Boulevard, it must look strange to see all the Jews happily parading with palm fronds. One time, a bewildered African American woman pulled her car over to ask me, "What are you people doing with those sticks?" Well, what are we doing with those sticks? Waving the *lulav* is perhaps our most primordial *chok*. We circulate the four species (willow, myrtle, palm and citron) in six directions during *Hallel* and then hold them aloft while marching around the *bimah*. It's really weird and a lot of fun. It's also expensive—a cheap set costs around fifty bucks! Some say we are unifying four types of Jews with varying degrees of knowledge and merits. Another theory is the species represent our spine, eyes, mouth and heart. When I've complained of back pain, I've been advised to set aside funds daily to purchase a *lulav*. Evidently it's a *segula* (protection) ensuring my spine is strong and straight like a quality palm frond. Some say waving in six directions plus the center acknowledges God's omnipresence. Others maintain it invokes a blessing for rain or favorably impacts the lower seven kabbalistic *s'firot*. We're not the only culture gesticulating with greenery: one friend experienced a guided, drug-induced South American Indian ritual—when he worried his visions were drifting toward the dark side, the shaman rushed over and shook some branches, effectively dispelling the negativity. Sensible Jews typically steer clear of superstitious practices, but even the most straightforward among us spends the week waving these expensive plants.

We have epic parties of our own in our twenty-foot squared *sukkah* and have a rich tradition of potlucks with neighboring families. We create a new decorative theme each year; past innovations have included Japanese Spa, Autumnal Splendor, Four Species Disco and my personal favorite, a Nacho Libré inspired *"Sukkah De Los Luchadores."* On most holidays, Shira does the hard work in the kitchen and I just show up. Not so on Sukkot. I labor with my kids to shlep and construct the *sukkah*, put up the lighting and decorations, scrutinize the local supply of *lulavim* and *etrogim* and lead the extended prayers for whatever *minyan* in which I find myself. More effort = more joy!

When Sukkot arrives, I feel a palpable rush of *simcha* during that first *Mincha-Ma'ariv* service at *shul*. I look around at my peers and can see in their expressions the exuberance of the season. The first *minyan* on any given holiday is about arrival. We made it—*Shehecheyanu!* Pardon the mixed-metaphor sports analogies but most of us barely slide into home plate after slam-dunking all the necessary preparations. Anything that hasn't been done by candlelighting won't be done, and believe me, we never finish everything. When it's time to cease from *melacha* (acts of creation), we really do stop. It's heavenly mandated and other than to save a life, there are no exceptions. No squeezing in one more errand, no sending another email or making a quick phone call. The feeling of letting go is intensely liberating, especially when plunging into the ultimate season of joy, Sukkot.

I strive to keep the joy flowing all eight days of the week. Typically, I rent out my musical services over *Chol Hamo'ed* (the middle section of the festive week when one can drive and play instruments, etc.) to propel revelers into previously unknown realms of ecstasy. I may do some studio work, but I go into a half-time mode so I can attend parties and chill in my own *sukkah*. I love my *sukkah!* My kids each get their own carefully selected *lulav* and *etrog* and we proudly march about every morning holding our *arba minim* (four species) aloft. This holiday is when the community really comes together. Everyone is on the same happy page, 24/7. We relish in the feeling of victory after our assumed favorable judgment on Rosh Hashana and whitewashing on Yom Kippur. Most of us have spent a month and a half of heightened scrutiny of our personal balance sheet. We reconnect with our true purpose; our elation is heartfelt and not manufactured.

Sukkot in Israel

I wish everyone could experience what it's like to be in Israel during the holiday of Sukkot. As much as I love celebrating in L.A., there is nothing like the unfettered joy of Sukkot in the Promised Land. Rashi suggests that mitzvot performed outside of the Land of Israel should be considered mere rehearsal. While I see this as a harsh view of the plethora of good and holy acts committed in the Diaspora, in one case I must agree: In Israel, the celebration of Sukkot is of another dimension.

I experienced my first Israeli Sukkot in 1994, just before my brother Yom Tov's wedding. I believe he planned his nuptials after this holy week to ensure his extended family would enjoy an experience making the deepest impression. At that point, I had been *shomer mitzvot* for a few years and thought I knew all about this harvest holiday. Wrong again. Enjoy the following highlights of our adventure.

My parents rented a perfectly situated four-bedroom apartment in the *Rova Yehudi* (Jewish Quarter) overlooking the *Kotel*. *Sukkot* could be spotted on every balcony, crammed in every courtyard, alongside every restaurant. Tens of thousands of Jews filed to and fro, armed with their four species in an assortment of rifle size cases. Each night, Yom Tov and I slept under the stars in our cozy *sukkah*. If we weren't praying, we were eating. I noticed a few quirks in the local libations: Israelis served coke and orange soda exclusively—no water was offered at any party that we attended. Plus all the cake, candy, challah and honey one could ever want. A dentist's dream come true!

We attended several midweek *Simchat Beit Hasho'eva* (Joy of the Water Drawing) celebrations in Meah She'arim *yeshivot*. One of the nights, we came armed with guitars and played in a central courtyard for anyone who would listen. Our raucous renditions of the most popular Sukkot melodies generated a spontaneous circle of dancers and singers. Curious boys surrounded us and gawked at close range. I assumed that they were fixated on my considerable mullet hairdo. A few of them were convinced I was a *Nazir* (in biblical times, one could avoid grape products and cutting hair in order to deeply connect with God). At one point, a chassid with a mangy *shtreimel* (fur hat), ragged beard and graying *peyot* (earlocks) circled me while scrutinizing my every square inch. He seemed to be fascinated by my beardless face and long hair and yet I knew all the Hebrew lyrics and was wearing *tzitzit*. He finally blurted out: *"Ata Yehudi!?"* (Are you a Jew?) I already felt out of place and struggled to maintain my composure. I stopped singing and replied, *"Ken, ani Yehudi!"* (Yes, I'm a Jew!) Before wandering off, he muttered, *"Bo nireh"* (Let's see).

By 10:00 pm we stashed our guitars and ventured to the largest *yeshivot* to dance. Each place was crammed with a clone army of Chassidic men marching like bearded penguins in lock step to bands playing reverb drenched, heavy metal klezmer. The lemming convention reached occasional climaxes when a favorite song would slow to half time, making everyone jump in place. We gleefully joined these human trains to nowhere and I was able to close my eyes and allow myself to be transported by the mob. Some were excited to include a clean-shaven guy in non-Chassidic garb, some weren't sure if they should touch me. My size 13 ½ feet were battered and my shoes were covered with muck. My ears were ringing since I couldn't plug them when passing the speaker stacks since the guys wouldn't let go of my hands. The sinks had been rigged to serve red Kool-Aid (yes, I'm serious). Occasionally a platter of greasy, black pepper-laced Jerusalem noodle kugel would appear and get decimated within seconds. I have never laughed harder, for longer. And yes, I was sober.

Around 2:00 am, after a four hours of dancing, Yom Tov and I sprawled out on a vacant picnic table in the cavernous, hundred-foot-long Toldos Aharon *sukkah*. When I half jokingly asked, "Now where do we go?" he replied with utter seriousness, "Well, there's only one place that's still happening, but it's in the middle of the Arab Quarter." I believe if Jews want ownership of Israel, they must walk the land, without fear. Yom Tov and I strolled the now eerily quiet, littered streets armed only with our guitars. After ambling down a mile of moonlit cobblestone steps, we arrived at Shuvu Bonim, the Old City *Breslov* yeshiva.

Shuvu Bonim is attended by formerly secular Israeli roughnecks who have found the Lord. Scary neighborhoods don't faze them for a minute. We found them sprinting around an imposing bookcase in the middle of the main *beit midrash* (study hall). We joined the throng for countless laps, running in time to the frenetic music until we encountered some of the guys who were waiting around the corner like the defensive line of a football team. Everyone went tumbling and then after finding their way free from the dog pile, resumed the jog/dance until the blockers set up their surprise line of defense again.

Amidst the festivities, I spied that skinny chassid out of the corner of my eye. The same guy who seven hours earlier asked if I was Jewish. I approached to wish him a *chag sameach* (happy holiday) and he immediately hugged me and laughed saying, *"Ken, ata Yehudi!"* (Yes, you <u>are</u> Jewish!) He then ripped off his long white coat and motioned that I should wear it. While I did so, he balanced his furry *shtreimel* on my head and lifted me up on his shoulders. Me! All 6'3 of me! And he was a skinny five-foot-something middle-aged yeshiva guy. Next thing I knew, I was at the vortex of the madcap dancing, crying tears of joy on this wiry chassid's shoulders, my arms outstretched heavenwards.

Just before 5:00 am, the band abruptly stopped and the whole group donned their *talleisim* (prayer shawls), facing the rising sun for *Shacharit*. Through the windows, I could see the interplay of pale orange light reflecting off the stones of the Temple Mount. I prayed with these holy men with my last ounce of strength, thanking Hashem for the gift of my zany brother and the chance to have an unforgettable Sukkot experience in the Promised Land.

The drama continued on the following evening, *Erev Shabbas*. This was the night before Yom Tov's *aufruf* (where the groom is called to the Torah on the Shabbat preceding his wedding day) and our entire family was enjoying a splendid meal in the *sukkah* of our friends, Bonnie and Alan Cohen. Their prime real estate home in David's Village overlooked the walls of the Old City. It featured a state of the art kitchen and an underground parking garage where Alan kept a shiny new Lexus. Halfway through our celebratory Friday Night dinner, Yom Tov turned to me and said he wasn't feeling well. He had an inflamed thumb from what appeared to be a spider bite, most likely acquired during one of our nights sleeping on the floor of my parents' *sukkah*. I asked to see the injured digit and sure enough the tip had inflated to about double the normal size. I then traced a thin red line up his arm and grew immediately concerned. We went to a side room and verified that this line had progressed nearly up to his underarm. We both looked at each other and realized Shabbas was over…we had to get to a hospital ASAP.

Alan reluctantly handed me the keys to his car and I pressed it into service as an ambulance. We roared through empty Jerusalem streets toward a local hospital near the Ben Yehuda mall which I remembered passing on previous trips. I pulled up to the front door and since it was Shabbat, left the engine running. I helped my now limping brother into the lobby and explained the situation in my best pidgin Hebrew. The ladies behind the desk were unimpressed and rattled off a rapid response that neither of us understood. I then raised my voice and supplemented my halting Hebrew with makeshift sign language indicating we needed help NOW! Finally, one of the ladies grumbled, "Dees ees a behrzink (birthing) center." We would have to drive all the way to Sha'arei Tzedek hospital.

Now Yom Tov could barely walk and implored me to hurry. I loaded him back in the Lexus and screeched through the streets toward our goal on the outskirts of the city. Thankfully, Sha'arei Tzedek retains Arab valets ready for Shabbat arrivals. Hospital personnel immediately admitted my brother and put him on a powerful antibiotic IV drip. I slept restlessly on a gurney next to him as I heard distant cries of pain in both Arabic and Hebrew throughout the night.

Thankfully, by the morning, Yom Tov's color was back. At 9:00 am, the doctor was willing to let him return to the Old City in the hospital shuttle so he could be called to the Torah. There is a special hospital shuttle for *shomer Shabbas* doctors and nurses; they assured me of a *heter* (leniency) allowing me to ride along since I was accompanying him.

I guided my beleaguered brother through the Old City alleys to the Aish HaTorah *beit midrash,* just in time for his *aliyah.* He slept through much of the elaborate Shabbat lunch but Baruch Hashem, the next day was back in form, promenading down the earthen aisle towards his rustic *chuppah* in the Jerusalem forest. Back at the wedding hall, the ecstatic dancing included our secular relatives, *ba'al t'shuva* Aish students, Chassidim of all stripes and a few major *rebbes.* Following this feast, just in case we hadn't danced enough, the festivities continued for seven nights of *sheva brachot* (post-wedding celebrations).

The Capital of Joy

Sukkot is indeed the capital of joy. Just sitting in a *sukkah* is a delightful mitzvah. The rest of the world relies on the permanence of structurally sound buildings and fine homes. Jews believe the only shelter we truly need is under the wings of our Creator, as represented by the fragile *sukkah.* This is where we feel totally secure and totally joyous. (Of course having the IDF doesn't hurt!) When our forefather Yaakov made it back to the Holy Land after dealing with his crooked father-in-law Lavan for twenty-two years, the first city he established was named after the temporary pens for his flocks, Sukkot. In the words of Chassidic master Rabbi Leibele Eiger, at that moment he made permanent the condition of impermanence. Our fragile human state of impermanence can be a source of consternation or celebration. As Jews we are commanded to celebrate! May we all merit to rejoice together in the ultimate *sukkah* in our Homeland, *bimheira b'yameinu* (speedily in our days).

THE FOUR QUESTIONS

1. How do you feel (or how do you think you will feel) when sitting inside a *sukkah*?

2. How does the *sukkah* enhance your appreciation for God?

3. What is your personal *midrash* (creative commentary) explaining the symbolism of the *arba minim*?

4. We are told to choose a beautiful *etrog.* How do you add beauty to your daily activities?

Sukkot vs. Halloween

♫ LULAV ♫

joyjud.com/m/llv

Prepare yourself to celebrate
The fact that we can congregate another year
Cause now you're in the Book of Life
It's time to let your worries disappear

Leave behind your heavy heart
Here's the chance for taking part
In putting it together
Regardless of the weather
A simple house where we can dwell
Drink some wine and sit a spell
Surrounded by the founders of our land

Oh, east, south, west, north, up and down
When I shake my etrog and my lulav
Nothing's quite the same as spelling out Your name
While stretching out my lulav to the sky

A week that's free from any stress
With so much joy and happiness
Your mood just keeps improving
Your feet just can't stop movin'
Dancing the whole night away
Then waking at the break of day again

The month of October unleashes a tension of sorts in our predominantly Jewish Pico-Robertson neighborhood. As one walks farther from Pico Boulevard, the ubiquitous *sukkot* on front lawns give way to macabre Halloween decorations festooning the facades of the local homes. Jewish kids must grapple with a continuum of responses to trick-or-treating: for the far right, it's as if the holiday doesn't exist. Modern Orthodox might allow their kids to make the rounds in search of kosher candy and haunted houses but downplay any outward signs of participation. Sadly, Jews of other denominations are more likely to be carrying a light saber than a *lulav*.

I grew up loving Halloween and scarcely knew Sukkot existed. For us Brentwood kids, Halloween had no religious connotation whatsoever. Instead, it was a night of after-hours fun when we normally would be stuck inside doing homework. We relished in a sense of mischief and mystery as we explored the darkened neighborhood streets, stopping at any given household when we needed another sugar fix. As we grew older, All Hallows Eve became an excuse to party. At the University of Colorado, Boulder or UC Santa Barbara, my brothers and I ensured Halloween was an epic night to remember. Since I garnered only positive associations with this American pastime, I allowed my kids to wander the neighborhood in search of candy. Shira and I would buy their treasure trove of sweets back from them so they wouldn't destroy their teeth. Better $10 for them than $1000 for the dentist. Neighbors knew I would happily accept a gift of a Corona when I arrived with my brood of Jedi warriors. Shira generally stayed home to supply trick-or-treaters with chocolate and ooh and aah at their costumes. Sukkot occupies such a primal place in our family life that I didn't worry about confusing priorities.

Some believe the two holidays occupy opposite ends of the spectrum. Whereas Halloween features themes of death and evil, Sukkot celebrates life, the bounty of the harvest and the joy of God's protective love. I have noticed, however, there are similarities between autumnal commemorations of all cultures. According to UK-based Rabbi Dr. Raphael Zarum, with whom I have had the pleasure to study on many occasions, the *Chumash* refers to Sukkot as *Chag Ha'asif*, the festival of the ingathering. This annual harvest tribute implies the last crops have been removed from the earth as it descends into the death-state of winter. We see this word *asif* (ingathering) several other times in the Torah. Remember how the Torah refers to the transition into death? That's right, we are "gathered to our people." Therefore, if we substitute the word death for ingathering, *Chag Ha'asif* becomes the Festival of Death. Whoa! Furthermore, each night of Sukkot we welcome our blessed (dead) ancestors as *Ushpizin* (honored guests) into our thatched hut. Spooky, right?

Aspects of our ancient Sukkot harvest/mortality celebration are echoed in festivals around the world. Samhain is of Gaelic origins and like Jewish holidays, it begins in the evening. This progenitor of Halloween arises from the ancient Irish belief that this period is one when the boundary between this world and the next is most easily crossed. Think of passageways between states of reality in the movie, "The Matrix," or as we learn in *Pirkei Avot* (Ethics of the Fathers 3:18), "This world is like a corridor before the world to come." Mexico's Day of the Dead is a multiday holiday around Halloween in which folks pray and remember deceased family and friends, blessing their spiritual journey. Our Sukkot celebration ends with the day of Sh'mini Atzeret, during which we offer a *Yizkor* service to allow the congregation to do pretty much the same thing. Pitru Paksha is a two-week holiday for Hindus that falls during the autumnal equinox. Much like our *Kaddish*, the ritual is regarded as compulsory to ensure the soul of the ancestor ascends heavenwards.

Perhaps the central connection with mortality on Sukkot is the *schach* that forms the sukkah's roof. It cannot be made from living vegetation; in other words, a leafy tree still anchored to its roots hovering over your *sukkah* renders it *posul* (invalid for use). *Schach* must be *adama* (vegetation), cut off from the ground, dead and disconnected. One lesson we learn from this use of refuse to complete our *sukkah*: just like true *t'shuva* can turn our mistakes into mitzvot, we take a waste product, put it on top of the walls of our *sukkah* and fulfill a mitzvah! *Adam*, or humankind, comes from the same root as vegetation, *adama*. Both terms indicate origins from the earth. Just like the *schach* must be dead, we will also die, returning to the earth, hopefully after one hundred-twenty joyful years. The vision of our *sukkah's schach* engenders humility and is a potent reminder of our fragility. *Halacha* states that the *schach* cannot be layered so heavily that it occludes the view of the stars above. In other words, while *schach* offers an awareness of our mortality, we keep our eyes on the stars, on our eternity, or as Rabbi Leibele Eiger says, on the aforementioned gift of our eternal soul in a state of permanent impermanence in this mortal world.

Further morbid connections with this holiday of joy are found in the *megillah* (sacred scroll) of this season, *Kohelet* (Ecclesiastes). Authored by Shlomo HaMelech (King Solomon) in his old age, this book suggests such cheery concepts as: it is "better to attend a house of mourning than one of feasting," "a time to be born, a time to die" and "the day of death is better than the day of birth." *Kohelet* is related to the word *k'hila*, or congregation, or a "gathering." Oy...there's that ingathering word again! For the *Haftorah* on Shabbat during

Sukkot we read about the bloody, apocalyptic battle of Gog and Magog and our duty to bury the dead in the aftermath. Feeling joyous yet? One might think that these reminders of our mortality would render the Jewish People despondent. No! It's quite the opposite. The Torah emphasizes three times that Sukkot is our ultimate season of joy, our *Z'man Simchateynu*. Real *simcha* requires facing reality. The end of life is part of life, and the cycle continues. Rather than despair, we are commanded to dwell in the *sukkah* with our best furnishings, singing songs, eating on our finest china, sleeping in comfort. We may be mortal, but as *Kohelet* concludes, we should "Enjoy life with a spouse who we love, eat and drink with a glad heart," in other words, just have fun with it!

Rabbi Shlomo Carlebach said spending time in the *sukkah* is like getting a divine hug. After all the *davening*, judgment, seeking forgiveness and fasting of the previous weeks, not to mention the effort cooking and getting the *sukkah* together, we really need a hug. A kosher *sukkah* can have two-and-a-half, three or four walls. One might think only a four-walled hut would do the trick, but just like the shape of the Hebrew letters spelling the word *sukkah* indicate (*Samech-Chaf-Hay*, see the Hebrew Alphabet page in the appendix), these three configurations are all acceptable. The message: we may not always feel the "hug" of God's presence. Sometimes it's overt—that's the four-wall version. But at other times when the hug seems absent, just like the missing walls, we know God is still there. Yom Kippur is commonly associated with fear/awe of God. Sukkot represents the flip side of the coin, love of God. Love of God wins! Is it any wonder so many Jews are estranged from their heritage? They may flock to the synagogue for the intensity of *Kol Nidrei* but miss out on the hug, the loving, reassuring holiday of Sukkot.

Yom Kippur is a Near Death Experience of sorts: we abstain from human needs like food, drink, relations and luxuries in the effort to become angelic for the day. We have just spent the ten days from Rosh Hashana to Yom Kippur in limbo, with the Book of Life open and our fate undecided. Perhaps we retain this angelic state during Sukkot, not quite in the land of the living throughout the week. Therefore, Sukkot can be seen as a week off from re-entering our day-to-day lives. Our old life is over, we are forgiven for any misdeeds and the book is sealed on Yom Kippur. Then we hover in this ethereal, angelic state between the old and new year, giving us time to comprehensively inculcate our refreshed relationship with the Eternal. Finally, on the last day we shake the *lulav* and *etrog*, known as Hoshana Raba, the sealed book of life is officially delivered to *shamayim* (heaven).

Sukkot teaches that the corridor between worlds is a joyful place. Hopefully we leave the month of *Tishrei* with a memory of accomplishment and elation sustaining us over the other eleven months of the calendar. After Sukkot ends, we finish the holiday-infused period with mad rejoicing with our Torah, dancing seven series of *hakafot* (circles) during the celebration of Sh'mini Atzeret-Simchat Torah. We complete the renewal of our cycle of life not with speeches but with our dancing feet.

A brief Sukkot-Halloween story: as a twenty-year-old, I had the incredible opportunity to travel around the world by sea. I had been appointed "ship rabbi" since I remembered the most about how to conduct a High Holiday service and celebrate Sukkot. I bravely led the shipboard MOTs (members of the tribe) through services, having very little idea what I was doing and without prayer books. Thanks to this ecumenical effort, this mischief maker got to sit at the captain's table! Semester at Sea visited some fifteen countries over the course of a hundred-day educational journey, hitting the verdant island of Sri Lanka just after our ill-equipped shipboard Sukkot celebration. After three days of surfing

Hikkaduwa and wandering the Kandy rainforest with my fellow students, a few of us opted to fly to Nepal for five days of Himalaya fun. The plan was to trek, river raft and explore Katmandu before we would fly down to New Dehli, see the Taj Mahal and then meet the ship in Bombay. One day, as we were lounging on the pillows of our incensed-filled Yin Yang hostel lobby, a parade came through the streets of downtown Katmandu. My friend June and I spontaneously joined the cavalcade, curious at the reason for the celebration. We soon learned we were in a funeral procession.

About a mile out of town, the marchers turned off into a forested enclave. This was the site of the final rites and cremation ceremony. The enshrouded body rested on a wooden palette covered with matching white flowers. The crowd gathered around the enormous pyre as loved ones approached with torches. The men remained stoic while women wailed. At twilight, as they ignited the wooden structure, a powerful baritone blast was sounded on ten-foot-long Tibetan horns, triggering the exodus of hundreds of vultures from the towering tree canopy. The mourners stood transfixed while the flames slowly consumed the lifeless body. I was shocked to witness the facial features melting amidst the inferno. As the moon rose over the thick, black smoke, June turned to me and silently mouthed the words, "It's Halloween!"

Halloween and Sukkot both commemorate the harvest and the cycle of life. The Jewish take on the season is one of uplift and renewal, celebrating our vibrant lifeforce amidst the inevitability of death. One year, at the conclusion of a seven-hour Simchat Torah marathon in Pico-Robertson, I joined my friend Saul Blinkoff and his family for lunch at the *shul* barbeque. We marveled at the pomp and pageantry of the event and agreed how much we had benefitted by investing fully in the month of *Tishrei*. We realized that only with such commitment to details does true catharsis take place. As we devoured our double burgers Saul said: "You don't need a huge crowd for this holiday. You just need to be with your family." We feel so blessed to be part of a connected, loving community. In fact, the entire Jewish People is truly our family. At this time of year, Halloween is a blast, but Jews deserve to take a step beyond trick-or-treating, zombies and hangovers. Our own *Chag Ha'asif* is the proven formula for celebrating realm of the spirit.

THE FOUR QUESTIONS

1. How does the idea of vulnerability of the sukkah help you face the vulnerability of life?

2. After the intensity of the High Holidays, do you find Sukkot to be a burden (*I want to go back to normal life*), or does it offer you a new window to perceive Godliness?

3. How do you reconcile the celebration of secular versus Jewish holidays?

4. Do you believe Simchat Torah is a good way to end the Tishrei cycle of holidays? Why?

Chanukah:
I Have a Dream!

♫ WE LIGHT THE LIGHTS ♫

joyjud.com/m/wll

On eight winter nights we light
The lights on the menorah
Together with millions of our people
everywhere
In spite of the darkness we light
The lights on the menorah
Knowing the dark doesn't hold a candle to our
prayers

We light the lights
Warming up the whole wide world all over
We light and we heal each broken heart

We light tonight
Singing out our favorite songs together
And for a moment we see
We're not so far apart

There have been times of danger
When we couldn't learn our Torah
When they tried to make our spirit disappear
So eight nights a year we light
The lights on the menorah
Showing the promise of our Torah perseveres

For eight nights, starting with the twenty-fifth of the month of *Kislev,* the Jewish People celebrate the victory of the Maccabees, a brave troop of warriors that vanquished the mighty Syrian-Greeks back in 165 BCE. As winter sweeps the Northern Hemisphere and the days grow shorter, we commemorate this military miracle by lighting the Chanukah candles, increasing the glow of spirituality in the world and saluting those who keep the dream of freedom alive. Interestingly, the Torah portions we read at this time of the year also highlight dreamers—we learn about the visions of our patriarch Yaakov and his son Yosef, followed by Pharaoh's butler and baker and then Pharaoh himself. The resounding theme of the power of dreams offers us hope amidst darkness, echoing the prophet Zecharia's motto, "not by might but by spirit" shall we all live in peace. Every single flame on every *chanukiah* (Chanukah *menorah*) is a small victory, a reminder of the of the triumph of good over evil throughout history. This chapter recalls those dreamers, from biblical times to the present, who were committed to the transformation of a barbaric world into one of liberty and justice for all.

Yaakov and Yosef's dreams signify points of profound transformation in their respective lives. Yaakov's first dream is the famous ladder stretching to heaven, which revealed the inner workings of God's glorious angelic realms. His second dream, twenty years later, is of spotted and speckled sheep, in other words, the "stock market." Lavan, Yaakov's father-in-law, has nearly derailed Yaakov's mission of serving as the progenitor of the eternal force that would become the Jewish People. Yaakov's transformation crystallizes when he realizes it's time to extricate himself from material concerns and return to the Holy Land. He wrestles with an angel and receives the name Yisrael (which means "to struggle with God"), demonstrating he has regained his stewardship of the Chosen Nation.

Yaakov's beloved son Yosef is a self-absorbed teen, all too focused on his external beauty. He has been spoiled by the attention (and colorful clothing) lavished upon him by his doting parents. Yosef dreams he is being bowed down to and then enthusiastically shares the visions with those who might do the bowing. The stage is set for fratricide at the hands of his jealous brothers. They throw him into a pit and sell him into slavery where he faces hard labor, carnal temptation and lengthy imprisonment. Yosef's profound transformation from narcissist to altruist is described in one easily missed scene when he notices the forlorn expressions of a few of his fellow prisoners.

Chances are no one was jumping for joy in Pharaoh's dungeons. In spite of the degree of degradation, Yosef is sensitive enough to perceive a change in the demeanor of Pharaoh's recently imprisoned butler and baker. When he comes to their aid by interpreting their dreams, Yosef sets the forces of redemption in motion. Soon thereafter, Pharaoh has his pair of nightmares and the butler recalls the young man who eloquently interpreted his own dream. Yosef is referred for the gig and the next instant, he is running the country. Yaakov recaptures the mantle of the ephemeral during his exile and Yosef perfects altruism in his. These historic events contribute to the formation of the unique spiritual DNA of our nascent nation, ensuring its success in subsequent journeys. Moreover, we are reassured of the efficacy of the secret weapon in our arsenal, the power of dreams.

In concert, I typically introduce my "Unbreakable Soul" song by asking the audience a question: "Everyone knows from the Passover story that God redeemed the Jewish People from slavery with great miracles. But why would our loving God also orchestrate the events to send the Jews into slavery in the first place?" What aspect of enduring torture, bondage and infanticide was necessary in the molding of this eternal people?

Jewish survival requires toughness and fortitude, an indefatigable resolve to stick together and stand up for truth and freedom. As a once enslaved people, the concept of bondage is so odious that we instinctively rally against injustice inflicted on any group. Chanukah further refines the Passover message of freedom, emphasizing that enslavement can also be spiritual. Our endurance is predicated upon our ability to learn God's word, to remain separate, to worship as we choose. The Greeks prohibited the three things they perceived crucial to maintaining the Jewish covenantal claim: observing the Sabbath, commemorating Rosh Chodesh and circumcision. Of course, these fundamental mitzvot are not optional for sustained Joy of Judaism and the Maccabees were compelled to take up arms. As we see in our current exile, the loss of enthusiasm for these Jewish non-negotiables can smother our spark just as readily as the threat of physical annihilation.

Jews are humankind's canary in the coalmine. The rise of anti-Semitism is the first warning of the nefarious plots of diabolical individuals or regimes. To paraphrase anti-Nazi pastor Martin Niemoller, "First they came for the Socialists, and I did not speak out, because I was not a Socialist…then they came for the Jews, and I did not speak out, because I was not a Jew. Then they came for me—and there was no one left to speak for me." God has dispersed us to the four corners of the earth to function as a global, spiritual tsunami-warning system. Lately it has been sounding with increasing regularity. On a positive note, while we're sojourning in far-flung places, we are gathering "holy sparks" of *kedusha* scattered among the nations. Ideally, we survive intact and simultaneously uplift our gentile neighbors with our example of loving-kindness and Godly connection. Chanukah is the week we become especially aware of this delicate give and take with our host culture.

I'm inspired by organizations of Righteous Gentiles like Noahide Nations and CUFI (Christians United for Israel). While some members have ulterior motives, most serve as modern day Maccabees, taking a stand to protect Israel from her enemies. Enlightened citizens of the civilized world grasp this eternal lesson: those who bless Israel are blessed, and vice versa. The enemies of the Jewish People are the enemies of freedom. We can look back on the great issues of history and find Jews standing on the side of peace and truth. During Chanukah we feel a sense of victory not only in the plight of the Maccabees and the restoration of our Temple, but in the continued triumph of good over evil in modern times. The powerful themes of *Kislev* are also loudly echoing in my personal life.

Winter is typically the busiest quarter in my career. It is not unusual for me to visit a dizzying thirty or so cities in this span, offering performances, workshops and Shabbatons for the full array of denominations and age groups. One of the highlights of a recent Chanukah tour was a week in the Southern U.S. where I visited Baton Rouge, New Orleans, Birmingham, Nashville and Chattanooga. This eight-day journey in the welcoming realm of Southern hospitality reassured my faith in humanity. It also gave me an insider's glimpse into a racially charged region where one still sees Confederate flags aloft.

The musical, mystical melting pot of New Orleans has always captured my imagination. Each night after my own concerts, I wandered Frenchmen Street to audition the auditory expressions of local artists and didn't hear a bad player in the bunch. New Orleans is a place where music lovers gather from all corners of the earth to dine on its unique cuisine and ingest its inimitable sounds. I can't eat the gumbo but I make up for it with nights feasting on the rich musical smorgasbord. And yet, not everything is so joie-ful. The aftermath of Hurricane Katrina revealed a deeply scarred city divided on racial lines. Shortly after the disaster, I had the privilege of performing for the tens of thousands of refugees who were living in immense storage warehouses in Texas. Nearly all of those who had to rely on the massive public rescue effort were African American. Clearly the upper class had resources and were already back in business—the Lower Ninth Ward, not so much.

One interesting New Orleans connection I discovered: Famed jazz trumpeter Louis Armstrong's job as a young man was hauling junk for my Karnofsky relatives. They gave him his very first instrument, a cornet, and the rest is history. The great Satchmo wore a Star of David pendant for the rest of his life as a tribute to this Jewish family, my *mishpacha*, who offered love and guidance and taught him "how to live with real life and determination."

A few days later, I arrived in Birmingham to find a city still grappling with the stain of segregation. It's apropos that the Museum of Civil Rights is located in this town that was so notoriously divided throughout the sixties. After a jubilant concert for my ski buddy Rabbi Jonathan Miller's congregation, Temple Emanu-El, I wandered the downtown area with local friends where we saw many disoriented homeless men wandering the streets. As unwise as it might have been to break out my wallet, I couldn't help but offer a few bucks to whomever asked. Needless to say, I was very popular. We strolled by several unofficially segregated African American clubs and then arrived at a sparkling new concert venue with a standing-room-only crowd enjoying a Pink Floyd-style band called Washed Out. Here the white youth of the city swayed in unison to the slow grooves enhanced by a tantalizing light show. Old habits die hard in Alabama, and it's not just country club seniors who reminisce about the glory days. While relaxing in a local coffee emporium, I learned from students how the University of Alabama's popular Greek system remains entirely segregated.

Dr. Martin Luther King worked tirelessly in Birmingham by the side of local organizer Fred Shuttlesworth to rally the African-American community in non-violent protest. My family resonated strongly with the urgency of Dr. King's mission and appreciated his eloquence and bravery. In fact, my parents named their third son John Martin Glaser in memory of this powerful leader (Yes, that's the name on Yom Tov's birth certificate). Growing up in Brentwood, CA, we were surrounded by neighbors with all the snobbery and WASP-y attitudes typical in pricey suburbs. Thankfully, our folks raised us to be comfortable with all strata of society and intolerant of intolerance. I remember feeling fearful of leaders like Malcolm X but wishing I could hug Dr. King who "looked forward to the time when blacks and whites would sit down at the table of brotherhood."

On my last day in Birmingham, I ventured with my local guides to the impressive Museum of Civil Rights. The builders tactfully situated the facility adjacent to the 16th Street Baptist Church which had been bombed at the height of the tension in the sixties. The design reminded me of L.A.'s Museum of Tolerance in its clever use of multimedia to tell the story and create a sense of catharsis. We wound through the maze of exhibits, gaining an understanding of the difficulties the region faced when transitioning from a reliance on slave labor after the Civil War. Blacks were freed from the shackles of slavery, but faced a resentful and pugilistic society that spared no expense to keep them in the underclass. This stain on our nation's past seems unthinkable today—I marvelled that this imposed segregation happened within my lifetime. Finally, with Dr. King's successful efforts, the tables turned on the supremacists and the antics of the racist mayor and governor were exposed to a nation no longer able to "stand idly by their neighbor's blood (*Vayikra*/Leviticus 19:16)."

At the end of our museum tour, we proceeded inexorably into a darkened chamber where the singular visual was a large screen showing Dr. King delivering the "I Have a Dream" speech. I was moved to tears by the reverend's biblically-inspired preaching. This event was clearly a modern-day Maccabee moment. I am proud Jewish leaders stood by Dr. King's side during this campaign and believe their efforts deserved more prominent mention in the museum's displays. Hopefully our persistent quest to uphold civil rights will be noted in the eyes of young African Americans when they investigate this painful chapter in U.S. history. As Jews celebrating Chanukah that week, we were especially sensitive to injustices depicted and felt a sense of unity with those afflicted throughout history and in the modern day.

I'm grateful to my parents for creating the paradigm of openness to all peoples for their four boys to emulate. They gave us the freedom and courage to explore the world with a sense of wonder and the discipline never to be "quitters." They raised us colorblind and ensured we had relationships with those of all races and religions. The highest-ranking executives in my father's garment company were Black, Hispanic, Asian and Irish. Straight and gay. This was totally normal for us brothers; we treated them like beloved aunts and uncles. We chose friends without regard to economic standing, sexual preference or age. Poor, rich, young, old, all were welcome in our household. I'm also grateful for the wide variety of musical influences in our environment. In our home and car stereos and singing around the piano, we enjoyed the full spectrum of music including jazz, Latin, Motown, rock, soul, classical and gospel. Our family road trips were accompanied by the best of R&B, our *Seders* concluded with Negro spirituals.

Chanukah is the time to remember that the battle of the Maccabees must be fought in every generation. Like Yaakov and Yosef, whose stories illuminate this season, we must reclaim our connection with the dreams of our people, but not at the expense of our connection with all humanity. Shira and I are doing our utmost to teach our own children to continue the work of my parents and grandparents, to fight for a distinct Jewish identity while making this world a better place for all nations. Let us realize Dr. Martin Luther King's dream of a "day when all of God's children, black men and white men, Jews and gentiles, Protestants and Catholics, will be able to join hands and sing in the words of the old folk song, "Free at last, free at last, great God Almighty, we are free at last."

THE FOUR QUESTIONS

1. Are there times when you feel spiritually enslaved?

2. How can you celebrate Chanukah authentically (in ways that are not reflective of assimilation)?

3. What messages can you give to your children/grandchildren about the relevance of the Chanukah story in our days?

4. What dreams do you have for our world and what steps can you take to make them come true?

Purim: From Exodus to Esther

♫ HANG THAT MAN UPON THE GALLOWS (A PARODY) ♫

joyjud.com/m/hmg

There was a man named Haman
Playin' in a rock and roll band
He only had one problem
Each time that Mordechai chose to stand
Soon everything around him
Got to start to feeling so low
So he decided quickly
That all the Jewish folks had to go

But they were dancin' and singin'
And movin' to the groovin'
We fasted and davened
And suddenly we all were shoutin'

Hang that man upon the gallows
Hang that rotten Haman high
Hang that man upon the gallows
Let's watch him boogie
And hang upon the gallows till he dies

At first it wasn't easy
Changin' Achashverosh's mind
But Esther was so clever
Got him to leave that edict behind
So now it's so much better (so much better)
We're funking out in every way
As long as we remember
Just how we learned our lesson that day

During a family dinner, Shira and I were discussing the concept of fiscal versus calendar years with our teenage kids. The times they are a-changing: my fourteen-year-old Jesse had recently opened his own E-Trade account so that he could play the market. He used to hunt bugs in the backyard, now he is studying corporate cash flow. Shira explained how most individuals in the U.S. follow the January to December calendar model, making January the "back to work" month following a holiday vacation and a drunken New Year's Eve. My dad's sportswear business year went summer to summer since we shipped everything by May and then had to figure out what to do the next season.

Many synagogues work on a fiscal year beginning with the High Holidays since that's when they put on the "big show" for the congregation and hold their capital campaigns. Since my gigs follow the ebb and flow of synagogue life, this schedule also holds true in my business. It would make sense to start the Jewish calendar year on Rosh Hashana, literally the "head of the year," the anniversary of the creation of humans, but that's not how it goes in the Bible. As mentioned in the Pesach chapter, just as we are about to leave Egypt with great signs and wonders, the first commandment given to the nation is to keep a calendar. Therefore, the Jewish year actually begins with *Nissan*, the month of Pesach, making the preceding month of *Adar* the last one of the year. *Adar* is both a time to party and a season of reckoning. I've heard many a rabbi comment on the evils of imbibing on the solar New Year's Eve, comparing that debauchery to the sanctity of our Rosh Hashana. However, if we acknowledge that Purim is the centerpiece of *Adar*, the last month of the year, then indeed our custom is to end the year with bacchanalian abandon!

The secret of *Adar* is concealed behind the "mask" of this beloved holiday. The scroll we read on Purim, *Megillat Esther,* is one of the closing entries in the Jewish biblical canon and interestingly, has no mention of God's name. We start the year with the Pesach *Haggadah* and its manifold recitations of gratitude to God for the miracles performed on our behalf. Missing from the *Haggadah* is mention of the story's hero, Moshe. By the end of the Jewish calendar year, God is out of the dialog and it's all about Mordechai and Queen Esther. What has changed? Over the Jewish year we transition from an emphasis on God's revealed hand in our redemption (Exodus) to a focus on the action of individuals while God operates behind the scenes (Esther). The message: God is always with us, even when God's presence is hidden. In order to retain our *b'chira* (free choice), God is precisely concealed, to the exact degree that we must strive to find God. This awareness defines spiritual maturity and is the engine of our enhanced joy during this special month.

Purim is a capstone in our evolution as an *Am Kadosh*, a Holy Nation. Over the course of our extended sojourn in Egypt, we morph from Avraham and Sarah's "*ganzeh mishpacha*" (extended family) into a vast, united civilization. Throughout the next millennium, the Bible describes our adolescence in the Promised Land, replete with rollercoaster spiritual ups and downs. Finally, by the time of *Megillat Esther*, we renew our covenant as adults. No more fear of Moshe's wrath, no more need to have Mount Sinai held over our heads (according to a *Midrash,* we were originally coerced to accept Torah). Now we accept the yoke of the commandments joyfully and willingly, knowing God's intimate Presence is with us wherever we wander. *Megillat Esther* can be translated as "revealing the hidden." This remarkable tome serves as a lesson plan for perceiving God's hand behind all events, for all time.

The month of *Adar* offers the opportunity to bask in the *emunah* (faith) we have crafted over the Jewish calendar year. Every holiday, beginning with our national homecoming (Pesach), receiving the Torah (Shavuot) and then the High Holidays and Sukkot, serves to bolster our perception of this invisible shield of divine love and protection. By Purim, we rejoice in a seemingly "God-less" story, knowing with *emunah p'shutah* (simple faith) that God's grace is behind all the triumphs and mishaps in our lives. In fact, the word *emunah* alludes to "craftsmanship," sharing the same root as *omanut*, the arts and crafts that Jewish kids do at camp. The subliminal effect of full immersion in the Jewish holiday cycle "crafts" a level of belief that is real, tactile, or as my *Rosh Yeshiva* used to say, offers "five finger clarity."

As discussed in the Redemption chapter, one of the central tenets of Judaism is the emphasis of a big-picture national destiny. We believe history is directed toward a goal and each of us have a crucial role in *Tikkun Olam*. When we are focused on our lofty objective, day-to-day mishaps become trivial. This eschatological awareness has kept the Jews on track through millennia of abuse and deprivation. As Monty Python's Black Knight might have said, "It's just a flesh wound." The Purim story emphasizes our celestial mission at the climax of the drama: when Queen Esther is given the chance to be the hero by Uncle Mordechai, he warns her, "If you remain silent at this time, relief and deliverance for the Jews will come from another place" (Esther 4:14). Thankfully, she says *hineni* and saves the day. All of us are faced with this fundamental challenge. We can opt in or relegate ourselves to the sidelines. God will get the job done regardless. I say: let's get on the playing field and go for it!

There's another aspect to this evolution from overt miracles to God's working subtly behind the scenes. Imagine a prisoner with a guard stationed right outside the cell. Obviously, with the watchful sentry present, he's on his best behavior. When the guard goes on rounds, however, he can do headstands, scrawl graffiti or return to the task of digging an escape hole with a spoon. The God of *Nissan* is an overwhelming presence limiting our personal freedom, whereas the God of *Adar* gives us the space to express the <u>fullness</u> of our unique gift of *b'chira* (choice). History follows this same principle; until recently, most folks were deeply religious due to social pressure or God's overt manifestation. Currently, we live in age where humans are stratified into believers vs. secular. The guard is on the rounds. God has created an environment where one can actually choose to <u>not</u> perceive God…what a triumphant example of God's might.

The Purim paradigm of individual empowerment is increasingly prevalent in the modern day. Humanity has witnessed a vast shift of power from a single leader into the hands of the masses. Judaism teaches that we are on a continuous *yeridah* (down-slope) of leadership quality since the revelation at Mt. Sinai. But there is a simultaneous elevation of the *k'lal* (group) as we move towards our ultimate redemption. The Internet is one of the best examples of this revolution of self-empowerment. Currently, the majority of citizens in the developed world have smartphones in their pockets. They have Google readily available for any question under the sun, Amazon will deliver any conceivable purchase in two days and millions of remarkable apps await deployment. Try as they may, it's challenging for leaders to control such an enabled populace.

Our foremost teacher and prophet, Moshe Rabbeinu, came down from Mt. Sinai with his face glowing. His light was so bright that he had to wear a mask just to deal with the regular folk. (Or was he just preparing for Purim?) Perhaps a great leader like Moshe had to die before the Jews went into the Land of Israel so they could stand on their own and become leaders in their own right. Hold up a candle in daylight and the glow is irrelevant—but in a darkened room it can light the way. Fast forward 3000 years and we have democracy, iPads and near total literacy. Our leaders lack the monumental stature as those of the Bible or even those of the preceding generation. We live at a time when we can truly sing, "This little light of mine, I'm gonna let it shine!"

Our goal during this season is to combine the energy of these proximal holidays, Purim and Pesach. Life satisfaction results from achieving spiritual equilibrium: full self expression <u>and</u> full connection with our Commander.

The sages mandate that this final month of the year should be one of celebration. *Adar* is the capital of joy, with Purim the headquarters. According to the *Midrash*, after the Messiah arrives, Purim will be one of the only holidays we celebrate. The Psalmist says (Psalm 126), "*Az yimalei s'chok pinu*," in the end "our mouths will be filled with laughter." Our historic saga is steadfastly culminating in a joyous conclusion, centered on the zeitgeist of Purim. We have discussed the edict to lessen our joy in the month of *Av* since we commemorate the loss of our beloved Temple and national sovereignty. When *Adar* comes in, we're told to increase *simcha*. All the disasters foretold in our Torah occur because we forget to serve God with joy. When our service becomes a burden…look out! The true goal of *Adar* is perceiving "bad" breaks as being for our good and accepting them without despair. As discussed in Judaism 202, our *bitachon* byline is "*Gam zu l'tova*," this is also for the good. It's meritorious to have acceptance for tribulations. The *Adar* challenge is to accept pain with joy.

Seven out of every nineteen years, the Jewish calendar includes a leap year to keep the lunar and solar calendars in sync. This is required because according to the Torah, *Nissan*, the first month and time of our redemption, must occur in the spring, the season of nature's renewal. Leap years are extended by adding a second month of *Adar* to the calendar, called *Adar Sheini*. Some argue that the rabbis chose the month of *Adar* to double because it is the last month of the year. I believe there's more to it. If one is choosing which month to repeat, make it the most joyous of months! Imagine a double *Av*…yuck! Furthermore, we deepen the experience with repetition. The added month of *Adar Sheini* can double our joyful *emunah*. The Talmud debates whether it is better to seize the day and celebrate Purim in the first *Adar* or wait for the second. The verdict? It is more important to celebrate in the second month in order to maintain Purim's thirty-day proximity to Pesach. That way our holidays of redemption at the end and beginning of our canonic saga are juxtaposed. Just like we finish the Torah on Simchat Torah and then start immediately with *B'reishit*, we flow from our spiritual maturity based on our awareness of God's hidden presence directly into renewed appreciation of God's manifest presence as we reenact the Exodus the *Seder*.

I love performing on Purim. Inevitably, I celebrate in a city or two where I concertize in conjunction with the evening *megillah* reading and then enhance the *ruach* (spirit) for the *se'udah* (festive meal) the next day. I can't quite drink with abandon since I have musical responsibilities but I can usually handle a few cold Coronas or shots of tequila. Ay-yai-yai-yai! I have appeared as a crazed hippie clown, a cowboy, archenemy Haman or the rotund giant Rubeus Hagrid from "Harry Potter." My latest getup is a treasured Mariachi outfit which allows me to channel Dusty Bottoms of the "Three Amigos," undoubtedly the greatest movie of all time.

Several years ago, I attempted a personal record: four full-length concerts in twenty-four hours. New Jersey friends caravanned with me for a zany day of levity and music at a series of Reform synagogues, culminating in a drunken moshpit jam while working with the Peh Dalid band at Aish HaTorah Philadelphia. Another year I got a call to lead a Purim Shabbaton in Hong Kong. I initially turned the rabbi down—I had already booked a gig in L.A. during Purim day. He told me he needed a few minutes and abruptly hung up the phone. When he called back, he stated, "Sam, I found a flight that will get you to L.A. in time…you're coming to Hong Kong!" Thanks to the time warp of the International Date Line, I was able to spend an amazing five days touring the colossal city, culminating in a Shabbaton and Purim concert for a fascinating collection of multinational businessmen and their families. I returned on a fifteen-hour flight that got me back just in time for my L.A. gig…the longest Purim of my career!

On another Purim in the holy city of Jerusalem, I joined my brother at his beloved Pinsk Carlin *shul* in Meah She'arim. The Chassidim were piled on risers reaching the ceiling. Surrounding the sixty-foot-long table were the gray-bearded elders of the community and at the head sat the *Rebbe* with his *gabbaim* (henchmen) on either side. The continuous *nigunim* were a cappella and at the climaxes, the *bachurim* (younger students) would jump in unison, making me fear for the integrity of the grandstands. At one point I had imbibed just enough wine to reason that my friend Adam and I should attempt a solo dance on top of the *Rebbe's* table. As you may have guessed, it wasn't long before the *gabbaim* tackled us and carried us out of the room. We laughed hysterically through the whole episode, eventually climbing back on the stands and trying again.

Once, I was hired to perform a Purim show for Chabad of Jacksonville. While I was checking the sound in the JCC auditorium, the rabbi approached the stage to ask if everything was to my liking. I responded, "The PA system is great…but where is the piano?" "Piano?" he said, "I thought you played the guitar!" I grumbled, "I do play guitar but I need a keyboard to perform!" Thankfully, I noticed a grand piano under wraps in a corner of the ballroom. He had his *bachurim* (young students) move all the banquet tables to make space for the piano in the center of the room. That way I could maximize connection with the audience using an "in the round" setup. Just before show time, the JCC director came running in stating, "You will NOT use this piano under any circumstances." This stubborn executive was not to be swayed by my assurances. Evidently he had seen first hand the level of intoxication and rowdiness at these Chabad events.

I reached deep into my reservoir of intuition, recalling that when I had previously performed in Jacksonville, there was a certain piano playing doctor in attendance. That year, I had invited the audience back to my hotel to have an après-concert jam session in the lobby and he was one of the musicians who joined us. I deduced his name and number and luckily he saved the day with a dinosaur of a keyboard delivered minutes before the rowdy gig. A full house of unsuspecting Chabad supporters gratefully accepted the pitchers of Everclear-spiked punch poured by the *bachurim* and soon, even the stodgy businessmen were jogging gleefully through the room.

In 2018, I started a full month on the road with a Purim gig in New Orleans. Right after Mardi Gras! One of my favorite New Orleans ensembles, Panorama Jazz, served as my backup band and helped me propel the dancing for two hundred supporters of the local Chabad in a (pork-free) Hawaiian luau. One of the key commandments of the holiday is distributing charity to any needy person who asks. Since I went straight to the French Quarter after the gig, I went through over a hundred dollars in singles over the course of the night. I asked the rabbi if there was a theoretical maximum to the length of the holiday. He responded that one can keep the afternoon meal going well beyond sunset, until one says the *Birkat Hamazon* (Grace After Meals). I didn't *bench* (say the blessing) until 3:00 am, and that was after auditioning over twenty talented ensembles. I stayed in town to do a Shabbaton for the Modern Orthodox *shul*, Beth Israel and then got the Panorama band into an eclectic local studio for a full day of recording a new album, "Sam Glaser's Kompletely Klezmer Shabbas." The celebration continued all month: I went on to Denver, Grand Rapids and Boca Raton, finishing up the trip with a week in Israel where I surprised my brother on his fiftieth birthday.

I urge my readers to choose a location where Purim is celebrated with heartfelt exuberance. At some point, try to check out the full-throttle rave of Shushan Purim in Jerusalem (in walled cities, Purim is celebrated the following day). In L.A., just walk Pico Boulevard. Take advantage of the transformative power of the four mitzvot on this special day: hear the *megillah* chanted both night and day, give substantially to the needy, offer neighbors packages of a few items of food as a token of friendship, and eat a hearty meal at the end of the day. For many of us, intoxication gets us to a place where the heart is opened, we can love more readily and tears of joy can flow. For some of us, getting intoxicated is a mistake. After a few *l'chaims,* my empathy muscle is stronger and charity becomes more natural. In fact, after a night on the town I can often be found outside a local 7-Eleven, nurturing the homeless with cash and conversation.

Let us apply the lessons of Purim year-round. Acknowledge the miracle of God's stewardship behind the scrim of our lives. Take a stand for a friend with a gift of food, the gift of time and a patient ear. Seek out opportunities to serve the needy. Be deeply grateful for the feeling of belongingness to this remarkable nation. Share words of Torah with a lighthearted song and a smile. May we always seek to emulate the courage of Queen Esther, not standing idly by the challenges facing our people and the entire world.

THE FOUR QUESTIONS

1. What helps you remind yourself that God is there even when God seems absent?

2. Do you see God behind the scenes in politics, the arts, history?

3. Do you feel that you have been put in this place and time for a purpose?

4. What can you do to increase your joy during the month of *Adar*?

PART SEVEN

Transitions and Celebrations: Jewish Lifecycle Events

This section is dedicated by
JONATHAN AND NANCY GLASER

What an amazing achievement. You have combined your love of music, education, family and Judaism into this impressive book that will inspire and bring joy to all who read it. Mazel Tov! We can't wait to see what comes next!

IN THIS SECTION:

Brit Milah: A Cut Above the Rest 209

Bar/Bat Mitzvah: Great Expectations.................................. 214

Marriage: Lucky Seven.. 218

Bumps Along the Road: The Other Lifecycle Events......223

Epilogue: Engage the Dying of the Light 226

OVERVIEW

I believe every family *simcha* (celebration) is a command performance. There are no second chances to attend the primary rites of passage. Sure, if you miss the event, videos and photos might be posted online, but they are two-dimensional and missing a key element: you! The best gift you can give to friends and relatives is your presence. Not as a wallflower, of course. If you can muster the courage, be the one to make the event memorable. Even if it's not your nature, pretend to be an extrovert. Stay on the dance floor until you're about to drop and then keep dancing anyway. Make a toast, connect with old friends, introduce yourself to new ones. True friends show up. Let's rally for each other's *simchas* and each other's lives. Ideally we commemorate the important "life" affairs and don't wait until funerals.

I relish in witnessing the grand spectrum of celebrations. Jewish tradition is rife with laws and customs contributing to the profundity of lifecycle events. *S'machot* (plural of *simcha*) range from simple to ostentatious, stoic to emotional. All are beautiful in their own way and every family has its own style of celebrating. I recommend going "old-school" in terms of sticking with established Jewish traditions…get "Jewy!" There's no need to try to reinvent the wheel.

Since live music is typically involved in the festivities, my band is often privileged to provide the soundtrack. Lifecycle events are moments in time when friends and family are spiritually available, sensitive and appreciative. I enjoy my role in perceiving these opportunities and bringing them to the forefront.

This section traverses the full gamut of Jewish life, from *bris* to burial. I added a chapter on those lifecycle events not typically on the radar, generated from the biased perspective of a middle-aged dad. While I don't recommend getting a second mortgage to throw a party, I do encourage friends to do whatever is necessary to make *simchas* uplifting, meaningful and deeply Jewish. I have noticed that peers are increasingly unlikely to celebrate birthdays. I say: throw a party! Every year is a gift. Be a big shot and spend a few bucks to get your buddies together. Enjoy life…that's the key to the Joy of Judaism. *L'chaim!*

Brit Milah:
A Cut Above
the Rest

♫ THE GREATEST GIFT ♫

joyjud.com/m/tgg

Looking at the world with brand new eyes
Confident and calm
Awaiting the next surprise
Somehow you know we're by your side
Since you came along
I've never seen such smiles
Everyone wants to meet you
They travel for miles and miles
Custom made to order, special delivery to me

Could this be the greatest gift

In this lifetime
How can I thank You
For this, the greatest gift

How was I to know
Who could have ever guessed
That I would see this miracle
That I would be so blessed
I can't believe that you are mine
From out of nowhere, best thing I ever done
I have a son, I have a son

The birth of our children was a wondrous experience. I trained with our lactation consultant to assist Shira in her breathing and liaise with the medical staff during our firstborn's delivery. The consultant was adamant I resist efforts by mercenary surgeons to pad the bill by rushing into surgery. Sure enough, by the fifty-second hour of labor, the doctor determined the Pitocin drip wasn't working and the time had come for a C-section. Although we had prepared for a natural childbirth, Shira's attitude shifted diametrically due to the protracted labor. "Cut me now!" she growled. I tried to restore calm and asked the obstetrician for another half hour. She responded that my wife had only dialated two centimeters and it was unlikely to change in such a short period. I said, "Never tell me the odds" and explained I needed a chance to pour my heart out to God. She granted me the half hour.

I immediately called my brother in Jerusalem and told him to get the entire yeshiva *davening* in Shira's merit. Then I climbed to the rooftop of Little Company of Mary Hospital and cried my eyes out, beseeching Hashem for a timely delivery and a healthy mother and child. When the stakes are high, one can make deals with God. I promised Hashem I'd make it to at least five *minyanim* a week. Then I did the *Sh'moneh Esrei* with desperate intensity. I rushed back downstairs to find Shira had dialated ten centimeters and was already pushing... miracles! Within minutes we had young Max in our arms, bald and bloody, the cutest baby I had ever seen.

Part of our incentive to go natural was the desire to have a *pidyon haben* ceremony. A *pidyon haben* (redemption of the first born on the thirtieth day) is a biblically-mandated mitzvah only necessary when the baby is male and comes into the world through "normal channels." We had beautiful *bris* at Aish L.A. which was catered by my folks who were elated to become grandparents. Then thirty days after Max's birth, we gathered all our friends and relatives once again to witness the spectacle of our first born displayed on a large silver tray, covered with jewelry, sugar cubes and garlic. Yes, this is the *minhag*. We paid our rabbi, Moshe Cohen, five silver dollars so Max wouldn't have to serve in the Temple. A bargain at any price.

One busy week in Pico-Robertson, Shira and I attended three *brit milah* ceremonies. There are two lifecycle occasions involving the whole community—while Bar/Bat Mitzvah and wedding celebrations typically limit the guest list, everyone is invited to a *bris* (or baby naming for a daughter) and funeral. It is a profound mitzvah to attend these events even when one doesn't know the family very well or at all, and is a rare opportunity to experience extended communal bonding. Besides, bagels, lox and cream cheese and fresh-squeezed OJ are on the house!

In Ashkenazi circles, baby boys receive a special welcome on their first Shabbat out of the womb as a prelude to the *bris*. All the neighbors gather at the family's home on Friday night for treats and *l'chayims* to toast the newborn. It's called *Shalom Zachar* (Welcome to the Son) and thanks to this bumper crop of babies, we had invites to three events in one night. This quaint custom involves dessert and singing and sometimes, young children will gather around the bassinet to sing songs of comfort. I'm sorry to report baby girls get no such accolades. Kabbalah teaches that the soul is reluctant to leave the realm of souls. It goes from basking in God's all encompassing love to enduring the vicissitudes of light and darkness in this world. The attendees comfort the nascent *neshama* by demonstrating the earthly realm isn't all bad. Here we can <u>add</u> light, an opportunity the soul didn't previously have. The *ikar* (main point) of the *Shalom Zachar* is just showing up; the simple kindness shown by this gesture moves mountains.

Before I describe these three ceremonies, some bris humor: what did the *mohel* (one who performs the *bris*) bring to the ceremony? A bris-kit! He reassured the crowd, "It won't be long now." We tried to pay him but he only works for tips. I think he's retiring soon...he just can't cut it anymore.

The first *bris* of that busy week involved a young couple that "*shul*-hops" amongst the myriad synagogues in the 'hood. They invited an equal representation of Ashkenazim and Sephardim, *Litvaks*, *Chabadniks* and a smattering of business associates and secular relatives who awkwardly wore the black satin *kippot* provided. The Lubavitch Rebbe's official letter was recited, a Sephardic cantor wailed the priestly blessing in an eastern mode, the Beth Jacob rabbi sang the *Kiddush* and the food was Persian. There was a definitive feeling of intense joy for these neophyte parents who were bringing their first child into the world.

Whereas daughters are welcomed in a naming ceremony in the synagogue on one of the first Shabbatot after birth, sons have to endure minor surgery before they get their moniker. After the hopefully brief operation with a *mohel*, *Kiddush* is recited and then the name is officially announced. According to my rabbi, the moment of the incision is the most powerful time to pray since intense *rachamim* (compassion) is raining down from above. That morning I was standing in a prime spot right by the *aron hakodesh* (ark holding the Torah scrolls). I hid my face in the red velvet curtain as tears welled up in my eyes. I prayed for the health of this child and the well being of my own children and extended family. I suddenly felt overwhelmed by the fragility of life and the ever-racing life-clock. I saw the face of my loving father who wants to give me so much love and spend time with my family and yet is in ever-increasing pain. I saw my oldest son who is wandering the globe as a life force independent of the nest in which we have nurtured him. It seemed like his *bris* and *pidyon haben* were YESTERDAY! People were looking at me quizzically…did I know this family so well that I was rendered a basket case over this rite of passage?

Two days later came the fancy *bris* of the week. All the neighborhood big shots were assembled and it was anyone's guess which bearded *rav* would be graced with the highest honor of *sandek*, the person who holds the baby in his lap during the ceremony. It was the parent's fourth child but they were as emotional as if it were their first. Amidst the pomp and circumstance of this first-class affair, there remained a simple presence of the *Shechina* (God's protective presence) and sure enough, I found myself getting misty-eyed once again. I was still wearing my *tallis* and *tefillin* from *Shacharit* and even though I had prayed in rote fashion, the power of the words I had just uttered finally registered, right when the baby started crying.

Our sages raise the question: why in the *V'ahavta* paragraph of the *Sh'ma* are we are told to "place these words <u>on</u> our heart?" Why not <u>in</u> our heart? The reason, sadly, is that most of the time our hearts aren't open. We have a God-given ego keeping us moving and motivated, usually in selfish survival modality. However, once in a while, our hearts open, just like mine did at this *bris*. At such moments, all those words placed <u>on</u> the heart can fall in. What a feeling!

One lesson for parents planning to spend a fortune on elaborate catering: it's not about the food. Most attendees come for the mitzvah and not the meal. That morning, stacks of ample delicacies were artfully displayed on food stations across the vaulted lobby of the Museum of Tolerance. Only about ten percent got eaten by the time everyone shuffled off to work.

The foreskin trifecta continued with a *bris* for a friend from the *shtiebl* (small synagogue) across the street from my house. Again, I was surprised by my potent reaction to this ancient ceremony. Perhaps it was the sight of the new dad surrounded by his five brothers saying *Kaddish* for their recently departed father. Maybe because the baby's name was keeping alive the name of the grandpa he would never know. I, too, was named for a grandfather who died right before I was born. Once again, I felt an involuntary emotional response to the bittersweet mixture of numbing sadness and palpable joy.

The survival of the *brit milah* ceremony is nothing short of miraculous. The newborn child is the next link in a chain of tradition passed down since the circumcision of Avraham. The Jewish People have maintained this controversial practice of "infant mutilation" in the face of admonishment and worse from the nations around us. This practice especially angered the Greeks who were unabashed advocates of the body beautiful. How dare this stubborn tribe do surgery on a perfect child? Jews insist we aren't perfect, but we're perfectable. We point to the mitzvah of *brit milah* as the best evidence that God created the world unfinished and empowered humanity to complete the task. We take matters into our own hands. There is pain and suffering because God stationed us in a construction zone, a world in progress where we must expend effort, summon compassion and respond with heroism. Also, a primary source of the disintegration of any civilization is in the misdirection of animal drives. Our charge is to channel our appetites, to elevate our instincts, to realize success through restraint. We inscribe the seal of the covenant on the organ that is typically the root of our undoing.

Right after the incision, the crowd responds in unison with an unusual statement found in the *siddur*, "Just as he has entered into the covenant, so may he enter into Torah, the marriage canopy and good deeds." Getting a *bris* hurts! I don't remember mine, thank God, but I've seen enough to know the baby isn't happy about it. We pray that all these blessings should also come with pain. What kind of blessing is that? Well, if you remember the Science of Struggle chapter, everything worthwhile takes effort. No pain, no gain, or in other words, no pain, no pleasure. The opposite of pain is comfort, and comfort is for wimps. We want our kids to have the greatest reward life has to offer. That doesn't come with a silver spoon—there is no free lunch. We don't wish for the newborn to win the lottery. Instead we pray that he taste the ultimate reward, which is the acquisition of both spiritual and material prizes through toil and sweat.

So why is the *bris* conducted on the eighth day? Our rabbis tell us the child should remain in good health for at least a week and experience at least one Shabbat. Also, the requisite coagulation factors peak on this day. This makes sense, considering that the ceremony was designed by the Designer of All Things! Of course, jaundice or other ailments postpone the ceremony. Futhermore, the number eight is associated with the infinite, the realm of miracles. Simply turn an eight on its side and you get the symbol for eternity. A *bris* reminds us that we are a miraculous, eternal people.

We look to King Solomon for further insights. He samples every lifestyle, every vice, every excess and then declares in his masterpiece *Kohelet* (Ecclesiastes), "There is nothing new under the sun." How true is this statement these days? How many episodes of James Bond or Star Wars will we pay to see? Are we doomed to a lifetime of spinning on a hamster wheel? During my first year in yeshiva, I remember how every time I came up with a novel question, I found the sages had been debating it for millennia. So where is there newness? King Solomon alludes to the only source of newness: it's <u>above</u> the sun, in the realm of the supernatural. And that is where the Jewish People reside—in a celestial space that is <u>beyond</u> the stars and astrology, represented by the number eight. From this zenith, we channel eternal holiness and Torah into the world, paving the way for redemption. The echo of eternity is the resounding melody of this seemingly dissonant rite of passage.

So when you attend a *bris*, know that you are celebrating a profound journey into the fundamentals of spirituality. Next time you hear that eight-day-old baby boy cry, ponder for a moment the preciousness of your place in history. You are part of this chain, an indispensable member of a miraculous nation, a partner with God in the creation of the universe. With joyous determination, we commit a strange act of elective surgery on a perfectly healthy baby. And when the enemies of the Jewish people (or even "enlightened" Jews that don't quite get it) try to stop this "barbaric practice," we stand proudly by the generations who have sacrificed their lives to keep our God-given customs alive.

Most importantly, at that moment of the circumcision, we can feel the presence of Eliyahu (the prophet Elijah), who attends every *bris* and will supervise our eventual redemption. The pain the baby is feeling, and the pain we have experienced as a people, is all for the good. Both *brit milah* and *simchat bat* (ceremonies welcoming daughters) offer moments of closeness with our empathetic Creator, Who loves us more than our parents, is in touch with our pain and partners with us in everything we accomplish. Now you know what to pack in your *bris*-kit.

THE FOUR QUESTIONS

1. Why do you think it is important to mark the entrance of a baby into a Covenant with God?

2. How do you feel about the fact that spiritual progress typically requires some pain?

3. Why is it important for the community to attend a bris even if they are not close to the family?

4. What is the significance of your name?

Bar/Bat Mitzvah: Great Expectations

♫ THE BAT MITZVAH SONG ♫

joyjud.com/m/bms

On this day of your Bat Mitzvah
We're so happy for you
Such an amazing lady and such a proud Jew
Your life is filled with Torah
And you hold in your heart
Just how much God loves you

Live each moment strong and unafraid
Set free that voice inside you
Let all those who meet you

Share in your smile
Their faith in the world renewed

On this day of your Bat Mitzvah
Take a look around this room
See the faces that have watched you
Everyday as you've bloomed
We all feel very lucky
To be part of your life
Always carry our love with you

I've seen it time and time again. A friend's kid, whom I've known since he was in diapers, is transformed into a young adult who can read hieroglypics from an ancient scroll, lead a prayer service and offer an eloquent speech in front of hundreds of people. Other cultures engage in body mutilation, the hunting of big game or mock combat. Jews train their youth to head a board of directors.

One doesn't need a fancy ceremony to become Bar/Bat Mitzvah. Traditionally, girls at twelve and boys at thirteen automatically transition into spiritual adulthood. Previously, any shortcomings in observance were the purview of the parents, whereas now the youngsters are liable for bearing the yoke of commandments. There is no formal prayer for the kid to say on the big day—only the father is mandated to say a public blessing stating that he is no longer responsible for his offspring's spiritual transgressions. That's it! One common custom is inviting up grandparents and even great-grandparents to the *bimah* (pulpit) so the congregation can witness the Torah actually handed down from generation to generation. Then there is the inevitable Bar or Bat Mitzvah speech. But all these things, even the kid getting called to the Torah, are optional.

Most parents use the pre-Bar/Bat Mitzvah period to nudge their child into prayer leadership. Some synagogues require attendance at Shabbat services. Ideally, kids get focused on their heritage and are primed for a future achievement by internalizing the value of disciplined effort toward a greater goal. My boys worked with me nightly during their Bar Mitzvah year to review their Torah portion, *Haftorah* and *chazzanut* (cantorial duties). They cried and moaned and quit and then tried again the next evening. Their Bar Mitzvah weeks included smaller celebrations at their day schools where they read Torah for their peers. Then, on Shabbat, they led the synagogue service like superstars and gave us all *nachas*. We were impressed they chose their beloved summer camp, Moshava Wild Rose, to be the recipient of ten percent of their gifts. All the suffering they endured in the preparation led to a personal triumph, witnessed by all their loved ones.

I realize our children were partially motivated by the party and the presents. We tried to give them tasteful events that would involve their friends and our extended family, without breaking the bank. Some parents feel compelled to take out loans to put on an event even more ostentatious than the neighbors'. I've heard it said that nowadays there tends to be more "bar" than "mitzvah" in the celebration. I will admit that our potentially awkward family reunions were eased with the generous flow of Glenlivet. Glasers love to party and it is not difficult to get us dancing. I ensured our sacred moments wouldn't be erased with the "blurred lines" of R-rated lyrics in the DJ set. We cleared the secular song list with the DJ and also provided a thirty-minute hora soundtrack that was pre-recorded by my band (released as The Songs We Sing, Volume 3). In retrospect, we had dignified events with fun for all age groups, with an emphasis on the importance of Torah, continuity and family.

My own Bar Mitzvah was a prototype for the event I wanted to give my own progeny. It was both customized and spiritualized. My mom hired a coordinator who allowed me to pick the color theme. My dad had the sheet music of one of my best songs, Wilderness, screen printed on all the tablecloths. I performed a short set of Jewish music as a duo with my mother, based on the programs we had offered at Hadassah conferences and senior homes. My dad sat in on trumpet with the band. The videographer accepted my idea that I open the commemorative video by appearing magically out of Sinai Temple's enormous, automated *aron hakodesh* (the ark that holds the Torah scrolls). When my cousin Richard heard I envied his brown velvet three-piece tux, he graciously handed it down to me, and my mom had it tailored to fit my much smaller frame. Since I was going to Israel a few weeks later for a repeat performance at the holy *Kotel* (Western Wall), we had a mockup wall constructed in which our honored guests inserted their own personal prayers. This replacement for the traditional candlelighting ceremony allowed us to deliver our loved ones' notes to the official Wall when we arrived in Jerusalem. In hindsight, I appreciate that our *frum* aunts and uncles from New York came to the occasion and never uttered a discouraging word about our comparatively lax Conservative customs.

The mechanics of transition from childhood to maturity are mysterious, and yet we witness this transformation with every Bar/Bat Mitzvah celebration. A so-called "man" of thirteen or "woman" at twelve is vastly more responsible, thoughtful and capable than the prior year. Some wow the congregation by reciting the entire Torah reading plus the Shabbat *Shacharit* and *Mussaf* services. It seems that something more than chronology is serving as the engine for this degree of acceleration. The key element propelling life transitions is <u>expectations</u>. As a species, we possess a propensity to rise up to the challenge, to make good and not disappoint. Whereas "kids can be kids" while they are preteen, high expectations from parents and peers create the space for the adolescent to flourish during the Bar/Bat Mitzvah year.

Another venue for the power of expectations is the fundamental life transition of marriage. With a few formulaic words guys leave bachelorhood behind and enter a committed, caring relationship, forever. These vows are usually accompanied by a tremendous expense for a catering hall, flowers and a band. On the basic level, those spending so much cash better be serious about the union. On a deeper plane, the expectations and prayers of all assembled help the marriage succeed, offering intangible but powerful support for the partners to get along, maintain fidelity and nurture their loving bond so it remains unbreakable.

One might think all of the well wishes and great expectations are of no empirical value. In "Supernature II," author Dr. Lyall Watson investigates phenomena beyond the scope of scientific research. One of his case studies involves the power of human will as observed at professional basketball games. Many factors are involved in creating the home court advantage (in the NBA it offers a 60% chance of winning) but according to Dr. Watson, the quantifiable force at play is the focused desire of fans that the ball drops into the hoop. Harvard researcher Ryan Boyko studied 5,000 soccer games in the UK to determine the formula that for every 10,000 people attending, the home team advantage increases by 0.1 goals. Is it the cheering and familiar locker room…or is it the collective will of thousands of devoted groupies?

In his popular lectures, my friend Charlie Harary describes the 1960s studies of Harvard psychology professor, Dr. Robert Rosenthal. Dr. Rosenthal administered an IQ test to a group of elementary school students and then chose a <u>random</u> sample as "academic bloomers." The kids learned to feel differently about themselves based on their teachers heightened expectations and indeed, when tested years later, had higher IQs than the control group. This "Pygmalion Effect" documents the power of beliefs shaping our reality. We can live in a world of high expectations for ourselves! The single thing uniting all acheivers is an inner belief that in the end, they will emerge triumphant.

One of my brother Yom Tov's buddies from his *Pinsk Carlin shul* became the official *Rebbe*, the head honcho. One day, he was just another chassid, the next, he was conducting *tishes* (ceremonial meals), answering *shylas* (questions) and performing miracles. Yes, miracles! I am convinced that this radical transformation came about because the community NEEDS him to be the *Rebbe*. They collectively invest a desire for his success, lifting him to great heights, giving him capabilities that even he didn't know that he possessed.

My career offers me momentary glimpses into the effect of high expectations, similar to what Bar/Bat Mitzvah kids or this newly crowned *Rebbe* experiences. When I show up in any given city for a successful Shabbaton or concert, the preparation is extensive. Ads and interviews grace local papers, my videos are playing in the synagogue or JCC lobby, the choir kids have been learning my songs and my albums are circulating in carpools. The producer needs the event to be a smash hit. The congregants come to services and/or the show hoping to be touched and uplifted. At meals during a Shabbaton, I am surrounded by those who want to share an anecdote, a musical memory involving my songs or a personal crisis. I truly feel uplifted by all this attention. It's not an ego thing. I call it empowerment. And with this empowerment I can sing higher and longer, my workshops are more profound, my delivery more lucid and I am able to look into a new friend's eyes and respond with the deepest knowing.

We can harness the power of expectations to accomplish anything in our lives. How can we make our own growth as transformative as the Bar/Bat Mitzvah year? How can we make our commitments as rock solid as our vows under the *chuppah*? Just as we honor our word while under the canopy, so, too, can we honor our commitment to anything to which we aspire. We can practice this skill by resolutely standing by our words, even in trivial matters. For me, this means refraining from stating, "I'll be right back," unless I mean it, or agreeing to send regards if it's likely I'll forget. In a "let's do lunch" culture like L.A. (the inside joke: the lunch never transpires), it takes formidable discipline to maintain an unshakable relationship between words and action.

Another "expectations booster" is enlisting others to stand behind us in our personal commitments. One reason Alcoholics Anonymous is successful is because the group with whom the addict meets is pulling for the individual. With "a little help from my friends" we can recover from setbacks, learn from mistakes and regain momentum. But another factor in AA's efficacy is connecting sobriety to spirituality. Our tradition teaches that God *davens* for each of us to actualize our potential. In *Pirkei Avot* (2:20) we learn that, "It's not up to us to finish the task, but neither are we free to desist." God is an awesome teammate, but as we discussed in the *bitachon* chapter, God waits for us to make the first move. The combination of personal action, great expectations and sincere prayer can launch us to any goal and ease us through any life transition.

Once, during a hectic morning driving around L.A., I did *Shacharit* in a park since I missed the *minyan*. A homeless guy living in his car saw me strapping up and exclaimed, "Hey, where's the Bar Mitzvah?" I laughed and replied, "There's no Bar Mitzvah, I just had to pray before it was too late." The more I thought about it, however, I realized that I am a Bar Mitzvah, every day. We are all B'nai Mitzvah. Children of mitzvot. We are raised by Hashem with love and guidance along the path of these 613 precious channels of connection. Like our Bar and Bat Mitzvah boys and girls, we allow God and community to share our celebrations as we endeavor the journey of life. Along the way, we nurture a core group of family and friends to serve as cheerleaders, hopefully offering praise with advice and constructive criticism.

Martin Luther King said, "Faith is taking the first step even when you don't see the whole staircase." Let us all reclaim the wide-eyed wonder of our Bar/Bat Mitzvah years, when everything was possible. Just like we survived adolescence, with so many challenges and frustrations, let us remember that our loving Creator is still pulling for us, praying for us and serving as the wind beneath our wings.

THE FOUR QUESTIONS

1. How can we convey to B'nai Mitzvah the idea that they are becoming Jewish adults when they go back to 6th or 7th grade the next day?

2. What is so special about being a Jewish adult? Should we be excited for increased responsibility?

3. What can we do to add a dimension of spirituality into our rites of passage?

4. What has been the effect of celebrating your milestones with community?

Marriage: Lucky Seven

♫ OD YISHAMA ♫

joyjud.com/m/oys

Let it be heard in the towns of Judea
Let it be heard in Jerusalem
The sound of joy and of celebration
Our voices raised together
Od yishama b'arey Yehuda...

As we dance in an endless circle
Touching hearts, holding hands
Sing a song heard by all the nations
Am Yisrael forever
Od yishama b'arey Yehuda...

One of my favorite Jewish traditions is the custom of seven days of partying after a wedding. I didn't quite understand the concept until I experienced it after my own nuptials. In secular culture, the bride and groom disappear on a honeymoon where they enjoy a luxurious vacation away from onlookers. Jews insist the couple isn't quite ready for such isolation. To mitigate the inevitable letdown after a bodacious *simcha*, seven nights of feasting follows the main event. For me, I was relieved I got to spend quality time with out-of-town relatives I barely saw at my wedding. At least a *minyan* must be present at each of these parties in order to repeat the *Sheva Brachot* (seven blessings) that were uttered under the *chuppah*. That means a good size crowd of dearest friends and relatives is partying every night. With plenty of *l'chaims!* The seven blessings are incorporated in the *Birkat Hamazon* (after-blessing for bread) at the end of the feast, each sung by a different guest while they hold a glass of wine to be consumed by the couple. A great *sheva bracha* is the very definition of communal joy.

Typically, dear friends and relatives throw the post-marital events. Shira and I felt blessed that we had enough offers to do the full measure of these extra celebrations. She asked, however, for me to schedule a night off so she could have a break from all the attention. We spent one of the evenings of our regal week enjoying a romantic dinner for two at our favorite date-night spot, Pat's Restaurant. I couldn't help myself—I surprised her by arranging a retinue of ten singing friends to join us for dessert. They quickly broke bread and serenaded us with wedding songs over a fine cabernet, in a cappella splendor...with the whole restaurant joining in!

The *Sheva Brachot* are rife with meaning. The first blessing hints at hidden qualities in one's personality revealed by the fruit of the vine. Hopefully the bride and groom enjoy not only the superficial but also the deepest aspects of their spouse. Also, the only way to produce wine is by crushing the grapes—there are going to be crushing, difficult moments, but overcoming them is how one vints the mellowest merlot. The next blessing reminds the couple that all is created for God's glory. They are now working toward a combined, holy destiny, beyond individual desires. The third and fourth blessings acknowledge God's miraculous creation of human beings, saluting our ability to perpetuate the species and acknowledging the original state of oneness to which the couple aspires. Next, we express the centrality of Jerusalem in Jewish life and recognize the gift of *nachas,* the inevitable result of a sweet, happy union.

These seven elements represent the possibility of ultimate life fulfillment awaiting the newlyweds. This bounty of goodwill bestowed on the couple by the honored guests is typically supplemented with tidbits of marital advice. Toasts are offered around the table and friends volunteer survival strategies and personalized prayers. Finally, by the end of the week, the newlyweds are spiritually elevated and ready to start their *shana rishona,* the first year of marriage during which they retain royal status. *Shana rishona* couples are discouraged from having Shabbas guests or traveling apart so they can "set the cement" of their eternal bond.

Surrounded by Sevens

You may notice a pattern of sevens surrounding a wedding: in addition to seven blessings and seven days of partying, upon reaching the *chuppah,* the *kallah* (bride) circles her *chassan* (groom) seven times, breaking down barriers between them and enveloping him with her protective love. Also, as a new groom I learned about the mystical aspects of the *mikvah,* offering us a honeymoon-like reunion each month after seven "clean" days.

The matrix of creation is suspended on a system of "sevens." While writing this chapter, I was helping make a *minyan* for a recent neighborhood *shiva* call each evening. *Shiva* (from the root *sheva,* or seven) is the week of intense mourning for a loved one and is typically shared by the whole community. Comrades gather around mourners for seven days of prayers, bringing them food and offering the solace of company and a listening ear. In this case, my late friend Jeff Mann didn't have many relatives. The community was his family and we all needed comforting. This particular *shiva* stood out because I went straight from these somber *minyans* to the *sheva brachot* for a friend's raucous wedding I had just played with my band. During this strange week, I danced a schizophrenic ballet from mourning at the *Mincha minyan* to table-pounding jubilation, nearly every night. Part of the joy and responsibility of living in a Jewish community is sharing lifecycle events, from birth to death. And all have that curious number seven at their core.

Judaism teaches that seven represents the natural world. Chemists will tell you that exactly seven diatomic (formed with two atoms) elements exist, like oxygen and hydrogen. I particularly like the acronyn by which we remember them: Have No Fear Of Ice Cold Beer. Physics counts seven fundamental units like length, mass and time describing all known matter. I got help from ROY G. BIV in grade school science to memorize the seven colors of the rainbow. Any musician will concur there are seven notes in the standard musical scale. Seven planets surround Earth in our solar system. I find it remarkable that the entire world is anchored to the seven-day week; although some societies have attempted to modify the length of this period, we find it resolutely remaining the universal standard of marking time.

Once, during a family vacation, I asked my kids to figure out all the appearances of the number seven in Judaism. We came up with over fifty! Yes, my daughter Sarah checked Google to help build our list. Among the septenary discoveries that day (cue the auctioneer): the first sentence of the Torah has seven words and therein begins the description of the seven days of creation. There are seven commandments associated with ark-builder Noach, before Judaism upped the ante to 613. The rabbis later codified another seven, like lighting Shabbat candles and making blessings over food. After the floodwaters parted, Noach released the raven and then the dove for seven days each. Our matriarch Leah had seven children. Yosef was freed from prison only after interpreting Pharaoh's dream of seven ears of corn and seven fat cows (came out of the Nile, ah, ha, ha). Moshe appeared on the scene seven generations after Avraham and was born and died on the seventh of Adar. The menorah he fashioned had seven branches. Yehoshua (Joshua) conquered seven nations in the ancient land of Cana'an and knocked down the walls of his first conquest after seven rotations. We wrap *tefillin* seven times around our forearm. We have seven major holidays and two of them last for seven days each. Shavuot (another "*sheva*" root) is the anniversary of the receiving of Torah, celebrated seven weeks from Pesach. *Tishrei* is the seventh month of the biblical year and is by far the most noteworthy and holiday-drenched. There are seven special agricultural products for which Israel is renown and are permissable as *bikurim* (first fruit offerings). Even in current times, we encounter the *Sh'mitah* (Sabbatical) year during which Jews in Israel let the land go fallow every seventh year. We count seven of these cycles to get to the *Yovel* (Jubilee) year. Whew!

My awareness of this magical number began when I attended Aish HaTorah in Jerusalem as a wide-eyed twenty-three-year-old traveler. A week into the program, we attended a five-day course called Discovery. Our small group journeyed to Maley Amos, a mobile home community in the wilderness of the West Bank, where our minds were blown with a formative version of this now popular seminar. The bottom line: modern computing has allowed mathematicians to analyze the entire text of the Five Books of Moses as a single string of letters (without the spaces in between). What did the researchers find? An awe-inspiring system of sevens and forty-nines stretching from one end of the book to the other. We learned about scores of these patterns spelling out relevant words and phrases—just enough to pry open our staunchly secular, science-fed minds to the possibility our Bible might actually have divine origins.

We remain anchored in God's original plan for the universe thanks to our weekly commemoration of the seventh day of creation, Shabbat. It's as if God is saying: "My children, I formed the world just for you in six days and the seventh, the Sabbath is your most valuable treasure." Observing the Sabbath is one of the best methods for enhancing one's marriage with both God and spouse. As soon as the sun hits the horizon on Fridays, busy couples have the first chance to engage with one another undistracted. I get down on one knee and look deeply into the eyes of my dedicated wife as I sing the *Ayshet Chayil* (Woman of Valor prayer). Of course there's the famous opportunity for a "double mitzvah," a custom with its roots in the Talmud. The Sabbath reminds us of this heptagonal matrix as the foundation of Creation. We see a seemingly self-generated natural world, but actually the watchful eye of the Grand Designer winks at us every time we notice the number seven throughout our lives. I'll say it again: "More than the Jews have kept Shabbat, Shabbat has kept the Jews."

Now it makes sense why Jewish lifecycle events gravitate to this number. During life transitions, we are more likely to stop and reflect, to perceive the great gifts God bestows upon us. Even my ardently agnostic friends can look back at their precious lifecycle milestones and perceive this repetitive digital theme, sensing the loving embrace of Hashem.

As discussed in the *Brit Milah* chapter, just beyond seven is the number eight, which signifies the realm of the supernatural. That's why we invite our baby boys into the eternal Jewish covenant on the eighth day of their lives. That's why we commemorate our miraculous survival over eight days of Chanukah. That's why the holiest member of the tribe, the *Kohen Gadol* (high priest), wears eight sacred garments when doing the service. Eight represents "one step beyond." Science is here to address the realm of seven. Rabbis help us grapple with eight. Our body is seven, our soul, eight. Judaism is obsessed with dragging the number eight into the realm of seven. Our task is to infuse our day-to-day "meatspace" with spiritual intention, navigating a perpetual tightrope between physical and metaphysical worlds. Or, as described by author Wilferd Peterson, we must aspire to "walk with the dreamers with their heads in the clouds and their feet on the ground."

In Defense of Marriage

Marriage is an ephemeral, ancient, God-given construct deserving of preservation. In the past thirty years, the worldwide marriage rate has plummeted by 50% while the mean age of first time marriage has gone up by five years. Europe leads the way to a mostly unmarried population and the result is a heartbreaking deficit of babies. Thankfully, Israel is among the few countries maintaining marriage as the partnership standard. Part of our role as a light unto nations is to protect this sacred institution. Mark Twain describes our "out of proportion contributions to literature, science, art, music, finance and medicine." Most important, however, is our contribution to the clarification of eternal values and methods to transmit morality to future generations, in other words, marriage.

One sunny afternoon, a man found a brass lantern on a deserted beach. He gave it a rub and out popped a genie who offered him any wish he desired. The man pondered for a minute and said, "It would be great to be able to get in my car and drive to Hawaii—how about you build me a highway across the Pacific?" The genie replied, "OK, I can do that, but isn't it a tremendous waste of resources?" The man saw his point and responded, "Fine, how about letting me understand how my wife thinks?" The genie replied, "How many lanes?"

Gentlemen, we may never unlock the code governing the opposite sex. No matter how long we've been hitched, we must continuously invest time and energy to figuring out how to light up our spouse's life. Women know intuitively how to function in a marriage and most men struggle to figure it out. Rutgers University researchers found that marital bliss is "strongly associated with whether or not the wife in the relationship is happy," proving the saying, "happy wife, happy life." The following are my "lucky seven" suggested minimum daily requirements for highly effective husbands:

1. Take initiative
2. Stay calm
3. Be a gentleman: say please, open doors, ladies first, be a mensch
4. Practice good grooming
5. Do guy chores: take out the trash, make the bed, bus the dishes, pick up your stuff

6. Be a handyman: basic repairs, change lightbulbs, maintain the cars, act as IT Manager
7. Take a few Jewish classes each week so inspired words are always on your lips

It's strange how these simple, chivalrous behaviors ignite the firmament of our spouse's universe. And now, my Torah-inspired tips for both parties in a rockin' good marriage:

1. Uplift your spouse: the word for a married person is "*nesuin*," which comes from the root "to lift." We lift our spouse with words of praise, moral support and acts of service. Every interaction is an opportunity for uplift.
2. Anticipate needs: look out for one another, figure out one's partner's "love language," divide and conquer but always be prepared to shoulder the burden if need be. Encourage nights out with the guys (or girls) to maintain friendships and give each other space.
3. Bring joy: if not you, then who? Serve as a consistent source of joy for your spouse, fill the relationship with laughter, sweet surprises, emotional and physical delight.
4. Be vulnerable: married people are partners, a team. Don't be a martyr or a solo artist. Be available, honest and real. Share your self. Invest in common denominator activites. We toast with the word, "*l'chaim*." It doesn't mean "to life," it means, "to lives." Open-hearted humans flourish with trust and fidelity in a mutually supportive relationship.
5. Choose battles: criticize privately and gently, only after bestowing praise. Wait for the right time for confrontation, never lay it on during the first hour of seeing one another.
6. Don't hold grudges: apologize quickly and meaningfully, don't let issues fester, don't keep lists of infractions, forgive and forget.
7. Commit to using the *mikvah*: the laws of family purity are the single most effective guarantee of lots of anniversaries. Study them, perform them with discipline and reap the benefits of a monthly honeymoon, a holy family and happiness ever after.

The institution of marriage is a divine gift. The *sheva brachot* are the secret to success for the Jewish future and for the world. May we readily perceive God's presence each time we pause to appreciate the gift of sevens and other "random" love songs from the Creator. May we be a source of abundant joy in our spouse's world. May the Jewish People eternally merit hearing "the voice of joy and the voice of gladness: the voice of the groom and the voice of the bride." (Yirmiyahu/Jeremiah 33:11)

THE FOUR QUESTIONS

1. Which of the many "sevens" in Judaism are the most meaningful to you and why?

2. What is the glue that binds the *Sheva Brachot* together (i.e., what do they share in common)?

3. How would you describe the "sevens" and "eights" of your life, the natural and the spiritual realms?

4. Why does God set up lifelong monogamous relationships as the ideal?

Bumps Along the Road: The Other Lifecycle Events

♫ DEAR OLD DAD ♫

joyjud.com/m/dod

I am your daddy and I love you
You are my very own dream come true
I've never seen someone quite as cute
As my little boy in his birthday suit
There's no one who loves taking care of you
As your dear old dad

You are my baby and I'm your dad
I'll show you the best time that you've ever had
There are so many things that I want to do
To travel this beautiful world with you
There's no one who loves taking care of you
As your dear old dad

How I love you
Want to hug you and kiss you all day
Wherever you wander you can always be sure
That I'm never far away

Cause I am your daddy and I love you
And I'm sure your mom feels the same way I do
So don't let her know that we made this deal
This one little secret be sure to conceal
That your very best friend in the world you feel
Is your dear old dad

Everybody knows about the famous lifecycle events: *bris, simchat bat*, Bar/Bat Mitzvah, marriage and funerals. All cultures commemorate rites of passage. Young adults in the USA look forward to graduations, sweet sixteens, getting a driver's license, and the Holy Grail, reaching drinking age. As a parent I've noticed a few other rarely discussed transitions.

The first is when children start nursery school. For some parents this is a tremendous relief—they get a few extra hours to go back to sleep or do errands. For me it was traumatic. I run a recording studio behind our house and young Max would co-engineer with me. He would man his own mixing console, paint, draw and scribble and crawl around looking for bugs to torture. I loved providing his entertainment, education and nutrition. Then that terrible day arrived. I grabbed my camera and shot pictures as he confidently strode down our street with his oversized yarmulke and new backpack. His mom drove him to the beginning of his seventeen years of incarceration and I lay down on the couch and wept.

I worried Max would be subjected to the reign of terror of underpaid, overworked teachers, brutal peer pressure, teasing and bullies. But I was wrong. He was ecstatic when he came home that day, bubbling over with an enthusiastic report of all the new experiences. I fished for information regarding any mistreatment or how badly he might have missed hanging out with me. Nope. I remember Max sharing a work of art he created, and my wife telling me to get over it.

The next underreported milestone is becoming "reproductively irrelevant." I always wanted lots of kids and believed a big brood meant that one was a real parent. Also, a favorite *rebbetzin* (rabbi's wife) used to lecture on the importance of having large families to undo the damage of Hitler's taking 1.5 million of our *kinderlach*. I loved the sweet adventure and mystery of pregnancy and birth (easy for me, the man in the family, to say). I tried to participate in everything, from birth coaching to burping and changing diapers. I treasured my duty of dispensing the milk my wife would laboriously pump.

After Sarah, our third child was born, my wife made it clear the "store was closed." She was quite finished going through the trauma of pregnancy, childbirth and miscarriages. She gently encouraged me to accept the gift of three children and the completion of our family. I must admit I had trouble moving on. To this day I find myself going straight for whichever babies are within reach and regaling them with baby songs, in spite of the pronounced distress of my embarrassed children. I am secretly envious of the stroller set, nostalgic for the days of portable children who don't say no.

I knew I needed some help to make this inner ache go away and scheduled an appointment with my rabbi. I don't remember his exact advice but it was something like, "Man up, move on and count your blessings," or something like that. I bear him no malice—he is a righteous man with better things to do, like counseling childless couples. I eventually got used to the idea that intimacy had nothing to do with reproduction. I also had to get used to the return of my wife's cycle and the need to separate for twelve days of each month.

The next lifecycle event came on the heels of our last child becoming a Bat Mitzvah. I was convinced this final *simcha* meant I was officially a senior citizen. Also, Sarah turning twelve meant her brother Max was a senior in high school. Yes, my friends, the empty nest phase was approaching. We shepherded Max through SATs, college applications and researching *yeshivot* for his gap year in Israel. This was all very exciting for Max and a bit heartbreaking for me. I realized he wouldn't be with us for Pesach, High Holidays or Chanukah. We wouldn't enjoy his brief appearance at dinner every night. And his brother Jesse would soon follow in his footsteps. I know I should have been stoic and matter of fact about this transition. But I leave any semblance of stoicism for my wife, who wears the pants in the family (actually I wear the pants, but she tells me which pair).

More of these mini-milestones are on the way: a completely empty nest, menopause, college graduations, our children's weddings (God willing!), grandparenthood and avoiding senility. No one prepares you for this adventure when you are a teen and think you are going to live forever. The only constant in life is change. Thankfully, I get to ride this roller coaster with a great spouse and profound spiritual guidance. The alternative to a holy, purpose-driven life is self-medication, isolation or depression, responses I endeavor to keep at bay on a daily basis.

Just know that if I ever beeline for your babies, I mean no harm. I'm a perpetual kid and a loving dad trying to get a fix of the dreamy feeling of an infant falling asleep on my shoulder. You might find me in *shul* with a newborn on my lap, clutching my *tzitzit* and drooling on my suit, laughing as I sing "*Swinging,*" "*Pony Boy*" and "*Run Away.*" I know my wife shares my desire that our offspring do the "be fruitful and multiply" mitzvah sooner than later so we can enjoy what my parents consider the ultimate pleasure: becoming a grandparent. May we enter our golden years with health and love for each other, filled with the wisdom that only comes from surviving these bittersweet bumps along the road.

THE FOUR QUESTIONS

1. What micro-milestones have been important in your life?

2. How has Judaism helped you deal with challenging times?

3. What personal rituals have you developed to help you cope with the transitions?

4. If you have an "empty nest," what are methods that you have undertaken to keep the marriage strong?

Engage the Dying of the Light: Caring for Aging Parents and Beyond

♫ HEY PAPA ♫

joyjud.com/m/hpp

Hey papa, hold me closely
Where is the light in your eyes
You gave of your heart so completely
Now time is movin' on
That fire you had is gone
Damned if I just let you slip away
Is it too late?

Hey papa, don't be angry
How long can you hold it inside
Do you remember the time
Life was carefree
And now your shoulder's hurtin'

Like you're the only one to bear this burden
Damned if I just let you slip away
There's no going back to yesterday
But there's today and tomorrow

Hey papa, tell me where you're going
Are you thinking about that final ride
You sacrificed so completely
As sure as I love you
We'll survive this time too
Damned if I just let you slip away
There's no going back to yesterday
But there's today and tomorrow

My late father-in-law was a music lover who regularly attended the L.A. Philharmonic, L.A. Opera and musicals at the Pantages Theater. He and his wife traveled the globe so frequently that we were never sure if they were on another trip when we couldn't reach them at home. At the age of eighty-four he went to the hospital complaining of stomach pain. The doctor wasn't sure how to alleviate his symptom but since his blood pressure was low, he ordered an emergency pacemaker installation. The procedure was scheduled for the next morning. By that afternoon, my sweet papa was comatose in the recovery room, having suffered a significant stroke. The doctor botched the surgery, attaching the lead wire to his vein instead of an artery and sending the resulting clots mainlining into poor Grandpapa's brain. The hospital staff couldn't find the missing three liters of blood they replaced with a transfusion. Needless to say, we switched hospitals, found the missing blood in his chest cavity, had the unnecessary pacemaker removed and began the long road to recovery.

Instead of dwelling in his comfortable home in Marina Del Rey, Grandpapa became a resident of the dementia ward in a nearby senior home. He still had his sense of humor and could play a tango on the piano, but he lived in a fog with no recollection from one moment to the next, no concept of time, no idea of our family details or why he had been confined to this lockdown facility. I spent many an afternoon challenging his recall and regaling the residents with old time favorites at the piano. They may have lost their capacity for the lyrics but never faltered in recalling melodies so deeply embedded in their cerebella. Grandpapa would lead the charge, smiling and singing with radiant, palpable joy.

After two years of limbo, Grandpapa finally succumbed to leukemia. Thankfully, his discomfort was minimal and a day before he died he was able to hold my hand and tell me how much he loved me. My wife showed me a disturbing video of him from later that day, moaning and miserable. That night I felt a distinct impulse NOT to include him in my *refa'eynu* (healing) prayer. A few paragraphs later, in *sh'ma koleynu*, I prayed instead that he be relieved from suffering. I heard a voice in my ear stating, *when?* My automatic reply was, "Tonight." I felt an immediate sense of guilt for making such a callous statement. And then a sense of shock when I learned he left the world that night.

When my own father had back surgery, he shopped around to nearly every top orthopedic surgeon in L.A. until he found one willing to cut into his ailing eighty-five-year-old frame and repair three levels of his lumbar vertebrae. We were overjoyed to see him recover from the spine operation but soon thereafter he needed a knee replacement. Oy vey! For all his health issues, he still maintains his Dodger and Laker season tickets, trades on the stock market and teaches a monthly Jewish history class. But his pleasure in life is sharply curtailed in what seems to be a cruel downward spiral of Job-like proportions.

Why must we endure end-of-life agony? Why must our loved ones witness our demise? According to the *Midrash*, the symptoms of old age are due to the prayers of our forefather Avraham. He and his son Yitzchak looked so alike they were indistinguishable. Avraham *davened* for God to introduce gray hair and senior moments to differentiate the aged from the sprightly. I'm sure his beautiful wife Sarah was thrilled when she woke up wrinkled. The sages suggest Avraham initiated aging so people might learn the important lesson of respecting elders. At least we can say there's a consolation prize to losing our ability to play tennis and surf. Thanks to Avraham, we know who we need to honor, an important lesson in our youth-driven culture.

God causes us to value our precious time by limiting the amount we have. Just like absolute power corrupts absolutely, an endless supply of time might cause us to take it for granted and ironically, cripple our ability to get anything done. The importance of gratitude for this finite asset trumps the value of longevity. Furthermore, since youthful vigor is fleeting, God created a scenario where we have to suck the marrow out of every life experience while we're mobile. That's why we have this uniquely human quality of having regrets. As we discussed, Jewish tradition refers to a dead person as a "*niftar*," meaning relieved from duty. We must seize the day while we're "on duty," while we <u>can</u> perform mitzvot. Why be couch potatoes when at some point most of us will wind up couch bound? In one of the ski movies I scored, narrator-producer Warren Miller exhorted the audience to get out and ski or, "You'll just be another year older when you do."

Perhaps we witness the demise of our loved ones in order to promote real service and not lip service. After all, honoring parents made the top ten-commandment countdown. Is there a better way to demonstrate respect than caring for the parents who lovingly provided for our needs during childhood? The mitzvah of visiting the sick is not for the sick…it's for those doing the visiting. In other words, it's for us to empathize with suffering, reclaim our humanity, feel vulnerable and give. We can't "outsource" the care that we give to ailing loved ones. When bedridden relatives and friends need us, human compassion transitions from the ephemeral to the actual; "the thought counts" is replaced by meaningful action.

Many of us are entirely focused on our careers or studies and find it difficult to carve out time for the acute needs of community or loved ones. When we do get called upon, the subconscious reaction is usually, "what a damn inconvenience!" God throws these footballs in our lap so we get off the treadmill for long enough to reassess our true goals. Is it "he who dies with the most toys wins" or are we here to genuinely love and support one another? This is the time to shout, "*Hineni!*" When I am vacillating between making the visit or passing the buck, I stop to think about what might be said when I am eulogized: did I pump out yet another arrangement for a client's album or was I responsive to those in need. In hindsight, it's easy to prioritize…pervasive *nachas* results when I reflect on my heroic, caring mitzvot.

Another crucial question: do we want to wait until our friends or relatives are in the hospital before we spend time with them and say how we feel?

The gift of a large extended family means my aging parents have brothers, sisters and cousins who are my beloved uncles and aunts. Shira and I are looking at this now octogenarian generation and realizing we have entered a period of our lives that will be marked by funerals. These will be gut-wrenching slashes in the fabric of our universe. Now that the elders are increasingly immobile and ornery, we are less likely to schedule Father's Day softball games or Chanukah parties. But getting together is more important than ever! After one of our power walks, Shira and I were relaxing on a park bench watching the neighborhood children play. We discussed how we will soon be the *alter kakers* (old-timers) in the family line. Maybe we are already there! We are also aware that we'll likely be the ones responsible for keeping the extended family together for Jewish occasions. My own cousins and their kids are so busy, many are intermarried, nearly all have become twice-a-year Jews in spite of their parents' attempts to keep them connected. We have to go out of our way to make sure there are family parties and our Shabbat and holiday tables are filled not only with local friends but our easily overlooked relatives.

One of my Potomac, MD pals received a treasured gift from her grandfather who received it from his grandfather. It's the Keeper of the Flame award, a beautiful crystal rendition of a torch with the name of the "keeper" in each generation engraved for posterity. Since she is the one who makes the big *Seder* each year and sends out birthday cards to everyone, she earned a spot on the coveted trophy. The toughest job often falls on the keeper's shoulders: upon the loss of a loved one, it's usually up to this family hero to supervise funeral plans and deal with the estate.

Jewish burial is a time to respect the dead and respect *halacha*. We have a 3500-year-old tradition concerning proper treatment of the body, burial and mourning. A corpse retains holiness and must be treated with utmost care until it is buried. The local *Chevra Kadisha* (Holy Society) ensures there is a constant *shomer* (guard) with the body and performs the *tahara* (ritual washing and dressing of the body in a simple, white shroud). Let them handle the details—this is not a time to innovate. Jews avoid autopsies at all cost; they are considered a desecration of the sacred body and injurious to the newly departed soul. We're not into open caskets, embalming or fancy funerals. We do believe in organ donation as long as there is a direct transference to a needy human. Make sure you have a competent rabbi in your life so you can make these tough decisions with confidence.

Ideally, burial happens immediately. Until interment, the immediate family retains the status of *onan*, focused only on getting the *niftar* properly buried. Because of this, the *onan* has most of the typical prohibitions of mourners and is exempt from all positive commandments, even making blessings over food, saying the *Sh'ma* or putting on *tefillin*. This is not the time for spiritual pursuits and shouldn't be unduly lengthened. Burial on the same day is considered meritorious, but sometimes the funeral must be delayed a day or two if the death is on Shabbat or a holiday or to allow for out-of-town relatives to attend.

A note on cremation: According to National Funeral Directors Association statistics, due to rising funeral costs, half of Americans choose cremation and in the next decade that number will rise to 70%. Assimilation has created a trend of Jews choosing cremation. This would have been unthinkable a generation ago. Jews going to crematoria? No thanks! Jewish law maintains cremation is an irreversible violation of the *niftar* and when chosen voluntarily, it voids the option for mourners to sit *shiva* or say *Kaddish*. Yes, it's that serious. More non-Orthodox mortuaries are making cremation an attractive alternative to the high cost of burial. This is a trend I hope readers of "The Joy of Judaism" will take an activist role to resist. It's also a good reason to leave end-of-life directives for loved ones. Prearranged details alleviate difficult decisions and interfamily discord. This in itself is an invaluable legacy.

The Jewish approach to (*aveylut*) mourning is an ancient system paralleling the findings of modern day psychiatric grief research. *Shiva* isn't just for Orthodox Jews—this is a period to rely on the wisdom of tradition, to be open to the guidance of a *halachic* expert. We mourn heavy and hard initially and then ease back into life over a set time. The stages include: the aforementioned period of *oninut* between death and burial when despite the mourners' despair, they must make funeral arrangements. Then there is the post-burial period of *shiva* for seven days of intense grief when the mourner stays in the house, wears a rent garment (that's torn, not a rental!), refrains from grooming, wears non-leather shoes, sits on a low stool and keeps all the mirrors covered. Mourners typically receive visitors and host a *minyan* for daily services. If they are capable, *aveylim* (mourners) lead the *davening* so they can maximize opportunities for the recitation of *Kaddish*. The repetition of the refrain, "*Y'hei Sh'mey Rabah…*" (May God's great name be blessed forever) allows the mourner to discern that losing their loved one is part of the master plan.

Visitors to a house of mourning must remember it's inappropriate to greet one another or make small talk. It's not a party. After the *minyan,* one should sit for a while and allow the *avel* to initiate conversation, which is ideally about cherished memories of the loved one.

On the seventh day of *shiva*, the mourners "get up" following the *Shacharit* service. They change out of their rent clothing and leave the confinement of the home to walk around the block. This ceremonial reentry into the world of the living expresses the mourners' choice to remain alive, active and engaged with society. The heaviness of loss lingers for the next three weeks, until the thirtieth day, aptly called *shloshim*. When one loses a spouse, child or sibling, *shloshim* marks the end of the official mourning period. For a parent, however, a full twelve months of solemnity is observed. The rabbis aren't necessarily saying mourning for parents is more difficult than the loss of a spouse or child, God forbid. Parents are singled out because they are deserving of the ultimate honor as a result of giving birth, raising, educating and transmitting values to their offspring. And paying for it! Those in *avelut* for a parent say *Kaddish* for eleven months and refrain from attending celebrations for a full year, until the first *yahrzeit* (death anniversary) of the parent.

I live in the land of smoke and mirrors, otherwise known as Tinseltown or La La Land. Hollywood is all about the façade. Here, illness and death is hidden, spoken about in hushed tones and clever euphemisms. When I walk down Rodeo or Beverly Drive, I marvel at carefully stretched grandmothers teetering on stiletto heels, bedecked in colorful neck scarves and oversized sunglasses. Who are they fooling? Many of these folks will die in mansions, surrounded by paid caretakers. God forbid they become a burden or anyone witnesses their degradation. Friends and relatives only hear of their demise after the funeral is announced. The community is denied the opportunity to help, to visit or pray on their behalf. Some insist on privacy to keep away "ambulance chasers" hungry for donations—ironic since the end of life is actually the ideal time to open the gates of generosity to worthy causes.

Remaining present with the inevitability of death keeps us humble. We can never fully complete the task. There is always more to learn and experience. How can we leave this world a better place? Ideally, we prioritize estate planning before the need arises. Hopefully that plan benefits multiple charities with which we were involved. It's hard to grasp that in spite of efforts to the contrary, we can't take it with us when we go. Billionaire Edward Reichman was a giant in *tzedakah* and left two wills for his family, one to be opened upon his death and the other to be opened at *shloshim*. The first stipulated all the standard details and added that he wished to be buried in his favorite socks. The *Chevra Kadisha* refused to do so and regardless of the amount of pressure applied, no rabbi would step forward to override them. Alas, even with all his power and influence, Mr. Reichman was buried in a simple shroud, barefoot, just like all Jews, according to tradition. Thirty days later, the second will was opened. It said, "My dear children, by now you must have buried me without my socks. I wanted you to truly understand that a man can have all the money in the world, but in the end, he can't even take along a pair of socks."

On one of my trips to Israel, I had the great fortune to meet legendary Starbucks founder Howard Schultz. During his whirlwind tour, he came to Aish HaTorah to teach rabbis about the art of franchising and I got to sit in on the sessions. After one of the meetings, he and a few other businessmen were brought to Meah She'arim to get blessings from *tzadikim*. Rabbi Noson Tzvi Finkel, zt"l, was then head of Mir Yeshiva and took the time to meet with them. He asked, "Who can tell me what the lesson of the Holocaust is?" The bashful executives muttered various reasons until the rabbi told them the story of his survival in Auschwitz. "Only one person was given a blanket for every six…he had to decide, am I going to push the blanket to the other people or am I going to pull it toward myself to stay warm? It was during this defining moment that we learned the power of the human spirit, because we pushed the blanket to five others. Take your blanket. Take it back to America and push it to five other people."

We are born wholly dependent on others and most of us leave the same way. Pain opens doors to prayer, to relationship, to compassion. Shira and I grapple with seeing our once superhero parents become frail. Soon it will be our turn. I hope our kids witness us treating our own folks with love and patience and will respond in kind when we are in need. I hope we merit becoming seniors who are worthy of *kavod* (respect), emotionally healthy and not too crotchety. At this time when our kids are becoming independent, our parents are at the stage where they are becoming needy. God continues to shower us with the gift of being needed! Soon we'll have grandchildren hungry for attention, God willing.

Witnessing my dad's decline is fueling my mid-life crisis. This crisis is exacerbated by the huge hole in my being since my oldest kids left the nest. It manifests itself in an incessant drive to engage in my favorite intensely physical outdoor experiences. I know in my heart that I won't be able to do these high-impact activities forever. I still skateboard and regularly haunt Pico Blvd. on my "man scooter." During one international concert-intensive quarter, I took dozens of hikes in five different countries, enjoyed scuba expeditions in Cabo San Lucas, Maui and the Red Sea, and mountain bike rides in Jerusalem and Cappadocia, Turkey. At the end of this period, I flew my college-age sons from Yeshiva University in New York to Colorado for a ski trip in Vail. No time for breaks; we carried lunch in our pockets and ate on the high speed lifts, bagging over 200,000 vertical feet in five days. I grew up on skis, raced on a team in high school, and hit the slopes nearly every winter weekend of my four years at the University of Colorado. Now I have my two boys flying with me, first run to last run. Big *nachas!* I know I'm nuts, but I believe my rabid participation in action sports and thrashing about the mosh pit at rock concerts is better than taking out a loan for a new Corvette.

One of my studio clients objected to having my kids burst in the room with their urgent needs. My studio is behind my home and my children grew up with a sense of entitlement, entering anytime they desired. To maintain a professional work environment, I enacted a strict policy prohibiting their visits any time this particular man was present. All went well until my father showed up one afternoon. I was mortified that he barged in mid-session, sat on the couch and told us in graphic detail about his gastrointestinal issues. We let him vent and I ushered him out as soon as I could do so in a respectful manner. I then apologized profusely to my impatient client, promising to take those wasted minutes "off the clock." He replied tearfully, "Sam, you never have to apologize for having your father visit. What would I give to have my dad back, to have him come to my office for even a moment, to give me love and express support for my undertakings?"

In spite of his maladies, my father says he wants to come with me on my concert tours. Daddy, I'm so sorry. I wish you could join me on my adventures. I should have invited you when you were able. I want you to be out of pain and mobile. I'm so lucky I have had a loving, supportive, concerned dad for my half century on this earth. I'm frustrated my prayers for your well-being seem fruitless. I value your wisdom, your perspective and your newfound love of impressive four syllable words. Keep fighting that good fight, Papa! Rage against the dying of the light! I remember the demise of your own mother, how you just wanted to hold her hand in the hospital and not let her go. Daddy, I love you so much. I don't want to let you go.

Teenagers individuate, becoming rebellious, taciturn or worse. This allows parents to stop clinging and throw them out of the house so they can get on to their futures in college. Individuation is a force of nature that is ennervating but is also predictable and normal. Similarly, God give us a gradually degrading body so at the end of the story we are ready to leave it behind.

This world is not the end of the journey. It is but a corridor on the way to a brilliant future of our own making, thanks to the acts of kindness and service to God we accomplish while in this temporal form. The "dying of the light" is all part of God's plan. The light of this world pales in comparison to the supernal light beyond. According to the Talmud, for the righteous, the soul leaving the body is like a kiss or a "hair being drawn from milk." May we go "gentle into that good night." God is good. Life is good. I say rage not…let us <u>engage</u> the dying of the light.

THE FOUR QUESTIONS

1. What do you do to remind yourself to enjoy every minute of your life?

2. How can you carve time for those in need?

3. What have you learned through caring for the infirm?

4. What helps you deal with the finality of life?

PART EIGHT

Organized Religion: Navigating Jewish Institutions

IN THIS SECTION:

Toward Loving-kindness: The Holiest Shul in Town 235

Finding a Rabbi: Asey L'cha Rav 239

In Search of Jewish Unity: The Family Portrait 246

Can I Get a Witness? A Tachlis Twelve-Step Program ...251

Jews in the Pews: Hillel and Holy Chutzpah 258

Chabad: The Closest Thing to Judaism 264

The Biennial: The Good, the Bad and the Plenary 267

Nurturing Jewish Educators: NewCAJE OutRAJE 271

Self-Hating Jews: Terror at the GA 274

Jewish in America: The United States of Israel 278

OVERVIEW

Jewish practice is designed for group interaction. We come into this world alone and leave the same way, but in between we have to learn to play well with others. The focus of any given Shabbat meal, *Seder*, or *Kiddush* at a synagogue is the shmoozing. Your family, friends and community are not ancillary to your life—they are your life! Some say, "You can choose your friends but not your family." Remember *b'chira?* We are "choosing beings." Our families need us to choose them. Even when they get on our nerves, the solution is not to retreat into isolation. Negotiating the onslaught of varied personalities is how we achieve our deepest pleasure and growth.

Avraham, the first Jew, inadvertently invented the concept of a *minyan* (praying with a quorum). While arguing with God to permit the survival of the righteous in the doomed city of Sodom, Avraham gave up his plea when there were less than ten candidates. According to our sages, when praying with fewer than ten individuals, we are each scrutinized according to our own merit. When we have ten or more, the collective merit of the cohort is judged. Even the intimate act of speaking with God is best achieved with a *chevra* (group of friends).

One of the great gifts of North American Jewish life is having multiple denominations from which to choose. We have more movements than just Reform, Conservative and Orthodox. There is also Renewal, Humanist, Reconstructionist and Traditional. Even within Orthodoxy there are many subdivisions: Chassidic, Yeshivish, Centrist, Modern, Open and of course, Hippy-Carlebachian. *Pirkei Avot* (4:1) states: "Who is wise? He who learns from all men." Those with a confident Joy of Judaism have a comfort factor among Jews of all stripes. I consider it a tremendous privilege to work in all these circles and appreciate the beauty and opportunity within each one. Wherever there are Jews, you will find me!

I believe joining a *shul* of some sort is crucial. Camraderie and communal commitment are irreplaceable ingredients in the Joy of Judaism cookbook. But affiliation doesn't get us off the hook of personal growth. We can't relegate our divine relationship to rabbis or assume the "regulars" will complete the *minyan*. We have to show up! And regardless of denomination, we must endeavor to make up for shortcomings in our own spiritual practice. Our individual expansion is the rising tide lifting all boats.

This section opens with perhaps the most crucial aspect of our innate drive to aggregate: the responsibility to provide a safety net for those less fortunate. I describe the importance of finding a personal rabbi and suggest how to choose a synagogue best suited for one's idiosyncrasies. Interdenominational relations are touched upon to clarify the commonalities and conflicts between the major Jewish movements. I offer ideas for attracting the often missing demographic of singles and young couples, increasing volunteerism and achieving the elusive goal of Jewish unity. I do a bit of ranting regarding Jewish infighting and the chronic undervaluing of our educators and lastly, salute the grand experiment of religious tolerance in the United States of America. Happy *shul* shopping!

Toward Loving-kindness: The Holiest Shul in Town

♫ AL SHLOSHA D'VARIM ♫

joyjud.com/m/asd

On three things stands the world	*On three things stands the world*
Not on two	*On Torah and avodah*
On three things, not on four	*There must be one thing more*
Stands the world	*Acts of kindness everyday*
Stands the world	*Will insure the world won't sway*
Al shlosha d'varim...	*Al shlosha d'varim...*

I often refer to the maxim of the Kotzker Rebbe: "Where is God? Wherever you let God in." As I have mentioned in previous chapters, when we make space in our busy lives, open our hearts and keep our egos in check, Godliness fills our being. It's an automatic response to creating a vacuum. A corollary to the "Where is God" question: God is wherever people are in need. The Torah is replete with thirty-six iterations of God looking out for the orphan and widow, the poor, the stranger. Think about times you have experienced dire personal need. For many of us, perilous moments are religious moments. The popular expression, "There is no atheist in a foxhole" was coined during World War Two. This isn't just a cute aphorism—according to a Cornell University study, soldiers' reliance on prayer rises from 32% to 74% as battle intensifies.

An oft overlooked byproduct of affiliation is direct contact with needy individuals. In a car-centric city like L.A., it's feasible to go straight from one's home garage to the garage at work and never interact with strangers. This isn't the case when interfacing with a tight-knit Jewish community. For some, daily life is a battlefield. A morning *minyan* I frequent is next to Sova, a kosher food pantry serving those of all faiths. Many poor and homeless in the area connect with charitable individuals by trolling the daily *minyanim* where the penitent are primed to give. Attendance at our local *shuls* can be an expensive prospect when so many seek handouts at any given service. Sometimes I must remind myself that the seeming interruptions in my *tefilla* are actually the *ikar* (primary point) of my attendance. I feel blessed I can help and endeavor to have plenty of singles on hand. Perhaps more important than the cash is the chance to look the recipient in the eye, offer a warm smile and words of blessing.

One of my favorite haunts in Pico-Robertson is the famous Happy Minyan. Anytime

I'm feeling particularly beaten by my week and dancing into Shabbas is the only way to stay awake, this musical *minyan* is the best address. Cantor Yehuda Solomon's *davening* is deeply inspired, David Sacks and Rabbi Tzvi Freeman's *divrei Torah* are captivating and the singing is unparalleled. At the conclusion of services one Saturday, the packed house circled the smorgasbord tables, waiting impatiently for the recitation of *Kiddush*, ready to pounce on the *cholent* (traditional Shabbat stew) at the sound of amen. Since this was *Shabbat M'varchim*, the special Shabbas when we bless the imminent new month and take the catering up a notch, a delectable buffet was on display. I stayed until the end, schmoozing with friends old and new, eating my fill of cold cuts and kugel and leading the singing. I made note of the pecking order: those with other places to go for lunch shake a few hands and leave. The cool cats and well-to-do have a nosh and trickle out soon thereafter. The people left are the simple folk, the holy brothers and sisters who depend on the food served for their meal that day. Pico-Robertson is blessed with over forty synagogues in the 'hood. The Happy Minyan is a refuge for those who don't quite fit the mold in the other places, including those who can't contribute financially, have been through a recent divorce, are handicapped or psychologically challenged, or even living out of their cars. And that is why the Happy Minyan is, for me, the holiest *shul* in town.

When we reflect on the holy things we have done, the list probably doesn't include attending synagogue fundraisers or High Holiday services. It's more likely our divine connection was maximized while helping a special needs kid with homework, working in a soup kitchen or visiting the sick. I can think of instances when I stayed up all night with friends in the emergency room. Or shared tears with those who lost a loved one. Once, when I was filling up my gas tank on a cold Los Angeles night (yes, we get a few of them each year), a tall, African American woman in a threadbare dress asked to wash my windows. They didn't need washing but I gladly gave her a few bucks to do her thing. When I returned home, I told my wife how sad I felt that this lady was out there on such a cold night. My wife's response was unflinching: "Then bring her a jacket!" D'oh! Such a revelation! I grabbed a down trench coat and drove back to the gas station. Seeing the smile on this lovely woman's face when I gave her my jacket was a holy moment I will never forget.

Back in my twenties, I didn't do the synagogue thing but I did find a way to give back in a manner that truly brought holiness into my life. I remember seeing a Jewish Big Brothers brochure with a friend of mine pictured on the cover. I thought, "If Phil could do that, I can too!" I'm a big kid at heart with love to share. I didn't have millions to donate to Jewish causes but I did have some time on my hands. After a six-month vetting process, I became a "Big" and got matched with an adorable eleven-year-old who is still my buddy twenty years later. Can you imagine my *nachas* when he asked me to serve as best man at his wedding?

The following biblical milestones demonstrate the importance of serving God through caring for the less fortunate: The first comes from *Parashat Vayera* when Avraham was sitting at the entrance of his tent just after his circumcision. A *brit milah* is hard on an eight-day-old infant—imagine a self-induced *bris* on a ninety-year-old! And yet the *Midrash* teaches that Avraham was out there in the stifling heat waiting earnestly for guests he could serve. God arranged the extraordinary temperature so visitors wouldn't bother him, but Avraham persisted despite the discomfort. While he waited, God appeared in order to "visit the sick" and Avraham was able to fulfill his lifelong dream of rapturous divine communication. Suddenly three angels disguised as travelers appeared. Amazingly, Avraham interrupted this blissful revelation to greet them. One might think it was a tremendous chutzpah to put God "on hold." However, according to David Sacks, Avraham wasn't interrupting God—by serving the guests he was <u>deepening</u> the conversation. Caring for God's creations trumps revelation since we are taking emulating God from theoretical to practical.

Another example of the importance of mastering compassion is the jarring juxtaposition of the Torah portions *Yitro* and *Mishpatim*. *Yitro* features smoke, fire, earthquakes, ear-splitting *shofar* blasts and the gift of the Torah to several million Israelites assembled at Mt. Sinai. The text then takes a seeming left turn into the *Mishpatim* chapters, which outline no less than fifty-three laws pertaining to the maintenance of a just society. In Judaism there is no distinction between one's "religious" life and how one conducts business. Awe and wonder sit side by side with day-to-day ethics. We can't work hard, study Torah and get honored at synagogue only to mistreat employees, fudge taxes and ignore the tribulations of the homeless. A primary goal of *Mishpatim* is to drive home the *ikar* of *Halacha*: the protection of the weak from the strong in society. Rabbi Warren Goldstein, Chief Rabbi of South Africa, emphasizes that the root of our legal system is the "vulnerability principle:" the law exists to protect those who would perish in a system of natural law or "might makes right." Therefore, it makes sense that the portion right after Revelation opens with the treatment of the most defenseless member of society, the slave. Jews were the first to espouse women's rights, employee rights and freedom from tyranny. If protecting the vulnerable is our raison d'etre, every interaction with the needy becomes an opportunity to bolster one's eternal legacy.

Judaism discourages monasticism as a spiritual goal. We are encouraged to actively seek human connection, even if it leads to friction, even with folks whom we would not typically befriend or whom we find infuriating. Rabbi David Aaron explains that "having more" isn't the key to happiness. The key is "being more," and the key to "being more" is "serving more." The Happy Minyan may be chaotic and chronically underfinanced, but the joy of exuberant service to God and others vanquishes the occasional discord. True holiness springs from diversity, from engagement in the trenches of heated interaction, from the mastery of techniques to attain harmony.

A great place for holy interaction is the gym. I belong to L.A. Fitness, an enormous, frenetic space where those of all ages, races and creeds gather to stay in shape. Once, I overheard my son's friend comment that my gym is "too crowded and totally ghetto." I, too, get annoyed with the multitudes when I have to wait for machines or can't find a place to stretch. But I have a completely different outlook on this physical fitness melting pot. This may sound strange, but when I first board the elliptical trainer, I make a point of <u>not</u> diving right into my magazine or music. I use the vantage point to marvel at the amazing variety of human shapes and sizes surrounding me, sending love in each direction. I try to connect with the unspoken story in every face. Rather than glaring at the obese with judgement, I mentally cheer them on and credit their gumption. Rather than thinking, *what are these elderly folks doing here*, I honor their perseverance. I greet the staff by name, I pray for the healing of those striving to recover from injury and offer a friendly smile to those who seem lonely.

We find a crucial formula for healthy communal interplay in *Pirkei Avot* (2:1). The world stands on the triad of Torah study, service (prayer) and acts of loving-kindness. Three legs are the minimum to offer sturdy support, like a camera tripod. Remove one and it collapses. Why are these three attributes essential to societal structure? Without Torah, one might have a great connection with God and humanity but have no vision of the divine pathway, the personal and societal benefit of the exacting performance of mitzvot. Without service to God, one could be a learned, kind-hearted individual who knows the depths of Torah but doesn't anchor them in faith, much like a secular academic. Finally, without acts of loving-kindness, we have a learned individual showing up regularly to synagogue who is too preoccupied with lofty thoughts to say hello to a stranger or interrupt a busy schedule to help a troubled friend. Note that the third leg of the tripod is <u>acts</u> of loving-kindness, not "nice thoughts" about loving-kindness.

Keep this triadic formula in mind when choosing a synagogue. We must demand from our *kehilla kedosha* (holy community) an ethic of kindness both within and without, demonstrating concrete action rather than lip service. Torah study must involve the whole congregation and not just the Religious School. No well-meaning individual can be excluded. The *davening* must be powerful and real, not watered down, mumbled or burdened with pomp and circumstance. Lastly, communal compassion must be shared locally, within the Jewish community and globally, aiding those of all faiths.

One of my favorite rabbis in L.A., Rabbi Nachum Braverman, described a time he tried initiating romance with his wife. He approached her in the kitchen and whispered, "Oh Emunah, I love you." She responded, "Nachum, will you take out the trash?" Clearly they have different "love languages." Emunah responds more to acts of service than words of affirmation. Rabbi Braverman recommends the best way to jumpstart any relationship is to give repeatedly and even unreasonably to the other person, in their preferred "language." A corollary: if one is feeling down, start giving to others and happiness will rally. Esteemable acts generate self-esteem. Jewish affiliation offers a clear path to societal and personal *shefa* (abundance) and is a virtual guarantee of the Joy of Judaism.

God has given us the gift of an unfinished world with enormous problems. Deepening our partnership with God by engaging in *Tikkun Olam* is the source of the most profound satisfaction in life. Perhaps God's statement in Genesis, "Let us make man," is a call to action for all of humanity. We have to create the world we want to inhabit. The highest use of the gift of our free choice is acting Godly: overcoming selfishness and choosing to help others, especially the weak and marginalized. These holy moments will be the ones on replay when we get to the next world. Where is God? Wherever we let God in <u>and</u> whenever we let others in. May we open a space in our hearts so that we are flooded with heavenly inspiration to give. May the illumination generated by our generosity shine brilliantly unto all the nations.

THE FOUR QUESTIONS

1. What are the most important factors in your choice of a community?

2. In what ways do you/can you learn Torah on a daily basis?

3. How can you make *avodah* (service to God) practical in your everyday life?

4. What acts of loving-kindness can you increase in your life?

Torah · Prophets · Nigun · Pesach · Teshuva · Wedding
Holiness · Brachot · Diaspora · Bris Milah · Simcha · Halacha · Bracson · Holidays
Israel · Mikveh · Prayer · Moshiach · Tefillin · Shabbat · Community · Torah · Prophets
Teshuva · Weddings · Spirituality · Holiness · Brachot · Diaspora · Bris Milah
Halacha · Bracson · Holidays · Bar Mitzvah · Tell · Israel · Mitzvah · Prayer · Moshiach
Shabbat · Community · Torah · Prophets · Nigun · Pesach · Teshuva · Weddings · Spirituality
Diaspora · Bris Milah · Simcha · Holidays · Bar Mitzvah

Finding a Rabbi: Asey L'cha Rav

♫ ASEY L'CHA RAV ♫

joyjud.com/m/alr

*You know that you're not going to be right
every time*

Sooner or later you step across the line

*You might need a guide just to let you
know*

Which is the way that you ought to go

Asey l'chah rav, uk'neh l'chah chaver

Vehevey dan et kol ha'adam l'chaf z'choot

Get yourself a teacher

Earn yourself a friend

Judge all people charitably

Our fathers recommend

Chovah al kol adam

*There are gonna be times when you're
feeling all alone*

*You're gonna need someone to call up on
the phone*

*Someone whose friendship is tried and
true*

Someone who just wants the best for you

I n *Pirkei Avot* (1:6), the *Mishnah* recommends we engage in a diligent search to "make" a rabbi. We shouldn't just accept whomever is available, rather, we must invest heart and soul in this crucial effort. For many of us, the moment of making this connection is when our spiritual ascent launches.

Kirk Douglas was in his seventies when he survived a helicopter crash. At this time, his memoirs were being compiled by a capable editor who was converting to Judaism. Kirk wrote, "I was in the hospital with my back almost broken…I was thinking, why am I alive?" His editor advised him to take his spiritual questions to her rabbi in Jerusalem, Rabbi David Aaron. In Rabbi Aaron, Kirk found an honest, humble teacher who could expertly communicate the essentials of Jewish thought. Kirk had dismissed his faith around the time of his Bar Mitzvah and yet remained a staunch defender of Jewish ideals and "always fasted on Yom Kippur." While in Israel learning with Rabbi Aaron, he realized he was foolish to grow so distant from his heritage based on an eighth grader's understanding of theology. He poured into daily text study and grew to love the enthusiastic celebration of Shabbat. The rabbi advised that upon his return to L.A., he find equally enthusiastic Jews with whom he could spend the Sabbath, and thankfully, my name was mentioned.

Yes, I got to marvel at that dimpled chin for many a celebratory Shabbat meal. I loved seeing Kirk, born Issur Danielovich, come alive while discovering his birthright of Torah wisdom. I did my best to feed his ravenous hunger for Jewish connection. We prayed, ate delicious meals and sang into the night and he became a fan of my music. Can you imagine my reaction when he called to brag that he learned *Modeh Ani* from my song or how he played my *Oseh Shalom* for anyone who would listen? At one point he mentioned he was ready for more Sam Glaser music. I admitted that I broke the bank on my last album and would have to wait a while to record the plethora of new songs in my inventory. He responded, "Maybe I can help out," and promptly wrote a check for the full amount. The result was my third Jewish album, the sixteen-song "Across the River" modelled after Elton John's "Goodbye Yellow Brick Road." Released in 1997, it helped launch my first fifty-city annual tour, a schedule that I have maintained ever since. Thank you, Issur D.

Kirk Douglas went on to have a second Bar Mitzvah at eighty-three, wrote several books about his heritage, built a movie theater at Aish Jerusalem and sponsored the construction of several playgrounds in Israel. All this because he met his rabbi!

Every Jew needs to have someone they call "my rabbi." Someone with whom they can relate, someone with whom the buck stops, whose advice they respect and "hold by." We can blame our rabbi, for example, "My rabbi told me this is what I have to do," until we're ready to initiate our own momentum. Rabbis are good for more than weddings and funerals, or as they say in the business, "hatch, match and dispatch." I've heard it said, "a good rabbi comforts the afflicted and afflicts the comfortable." At times in our lives we may be in either situation, and our rabbi must have the sensitivity to know how to respond in each instance. Effective rabbis gently coax us onto a path of growth. They introduce us to mitzvah options and help us inculcate a Jewish *weltanschauung*. Rabbis connect us with our history—they are a link to the written Torah and embody the oral, less structured Torah that accommodates modernity and the idiosyncrasies of the individual.

Ideally, we allow our rabbi to be the arbiter of Torah philosophy and best practices, a guide to a lifetime of spiritual commitment. In the secular realm, we have to figure out the game of life on our own. Most settle for a mix and match theology and hedge bets with whatever combination seems advantageous at the moment. Jews aren't truth seekers—we're truth finders. Life begins when we apply the truth of Torah to our day-to-day lives. Having a foot in many doors means eventually we have no legs on which we can stand. Choosing a path requires closing doors. The term "decide" has the root "cide" from the Latin *caedere*, to kill. in other words, we have to kill off philosophical options in order to commit to one. 3500 years of great rabbis (and Jewish mothers) can't be wrong! Take a chance on Judaism! Some go their whole lives trying to keep all options on the table. Emotionally mature people make a decision to excise indecision. They understand that chronic commitment issues wreak havoc on relationships, employment and spiritual progress.

God springs into action to help us realize our dreams as soon as we close the loop and commit to the calling of our *pintele yid*. Taking the plunge down the Jewish "rabbit hole" is scary, but our tour through this wonderland can be curated with personalized rabbinic wisdom. In the words of singer George Michael, "I gotta have faith, faith, faith."

Our newfound rabbi will have spent years training in the craft of spiritual and pedagogical leadership and deserves the utmost respect. They are the latest in a chain of scholars going back to Sinai. The top geniuses among the People of the Book have invested countless lifetimes parsing our texts for ultimate truth and understanding. In every academic discipline, those on the forefront valiantly pursue ultimate answers but hit humiliating dead ends. Think of those specializing in alchemy, blood-letting, flat-earth geography. Not so with Judaism. Our paradigm has never shifted. Our 3500 years of research has been dedicated to Torah with unwavering dedication and focus. What a miracle that our esteemed rabbinic leaders are still guiding us today.

Rabbis have to wear many hats. They are often the chief fundraisers for their organizations. They have to shmooze with both the power players and the meek, spreading love to seniors, soccer moms and second graders. They represent the synagogue in the greater Jewish community and also among the clergy of other faiths. They are the top dogs in the synagogue corporate structure and interface with the educational, administrative and governing teams. Rabbis are often authors of inspiring text and are counted upon as orators to express that text with originality and spontaneity. Rabbis are also the pastoral leaders of the congregation, dispensing words of solace in times of individual, communal and international strife. It's not a job for the faint of heart!

Rabbis are subject to intense scrutiny and can't help but ruffle feathers. They have to guide the community on a path of wisdom and growth and take care not to leave constituents behind. Rabbis don't get time off. Even when they are enjoying a vacation, congregants expect them to remain at their beck and call. Rabbis don't experience the essential weekly release of Shabbat to the same degree as the laity. In fact, the Sabbath and holidays are the times they are most in demand! Their family relationships can suffer as a result. The rabbi's kids are the subject of hyper-focus by the community. Rabbi's spouses are also on the hot seat, criticized if they don't become part of synagogue life, or conversely if they are too involved. Said spouses often become unpaid employees of the synagogue, like it or not.

Furthermore, rabbis must walk a consistent path of holiness and grace in public and in private. This is especially challenging in an era of pervasive political correctness and ubiquitous cell phone-camera-social media devices. There is no *t'shuva* for rabbis. Rabbis falling short of immense ethical expectations are left to crash and burn. They cannot "kiss and make up." Their transgressions are discussed with a hush and a wagging finger or worse, exposed on the pages of the local paper for all to enjoy. When any given rabbi blows it, their contracts are promptly voided. They are shipped off to another locale or must leave the rabbinate in shame.

When shopping for a rabbi, there are several factors to consider. First and foremost, one must find the rabbi inspiring. Of course, inspiration is totally subjective, so one's choice of a rabbi may differ from his or her spouse. Particularly applicable to clergy is Teddy Roosevelt's line, "Nobody cares how much you know until they know how much you care." Our rabbi should be humble and approachable, exuding concern and making us feel like an important part of the synagogue family, even if we're not a top donor. Rabbis should be fluent in the language of both the Judaic and secular world. After all, that's where we live and they must grasp what we are going through. Most importantly, our rabbi needs the chutzpah to nudge us to grow. Rabbis have to get us out of complacency, help us take on spiritual challenges and try new mitzvot. Our rabbi should give us impetus to say *hineni*, calling on us to make a verifiable difference for our family, synagogue and world.

Where can we find this dream rabbi? For many of us, it's a moot point. We live where we live and only have so many local options. That's OK. Remarkably, this is an era when we can affiliate with our local congregation but look to another more distant rabbi for

Torah guidance. We have the miracle of high-speed Internet and nearly free long distance phone calls. Finding a rabbi in one's hometown is best, but if that doesn't work out, it's time to employ a rabbinic search engine! All the gifts of 24/7 Jewish living can be ours. Ask any Judaically committed friends where they get their inspiration. Join Partners in Torah. Attend Jewish conventions. Read books and articles by influential rabbis—certainly some will resonate. Many of these authors, even the famous ones, will welcome a relationship. While it's best to have one official rabbi, in the absence of that ideal candidate, we can subdivide our spiritual guidance. Whatever it takes to get us on a sanctified path and stick with it.

When I was getting started in Jewish music, I was offered a wonderful job as Music Director of Continuing Education at AJU (American Jewish University). My responsibilities included supervising the arts curriculum, booking the talent for thirty shows each year in their five-hundred-seat theater and leading Elderhostel programs. I felt I was able to have a tremendous impact reaching multiple age groups and the schedule dovetailed perfectly with my studio business and concert tour. Word got out in the Orthodox world that I had accepted this position. To my dismay, as a result, some suggested I no longer be considered for a High Holiday cantorial post at a certain Orthodox synagogue. I consulted many rabbis to get feedback. None grasped the outreach opportunities this AJU job offered and defended the principles of the "establishment." None, however, except former *Rosh Yeshiva* of Ohr Sameach Jerusalem, Rabbi Natan Lopes Cardozo. His response? "By virtue of the fact that you may touch even one *neshama*, you MUST work there." Alas, I had found my rabbi!

In the early '50s, Rabbi Shlomo Carlebach, then an acolyte of the Lubavitch Rebbe, was told by Chabad that he could no longer entertain mixed audiences. Having seen the effect of his music on the college kids in Washington Park, Manhattan, Reb Shlomo realized he could no longer abide by the confines of this organization. He is reported as saying, "Worrying about such details is like giving a cardiac patient a manicure." In other words, the Jewish People are hemorrhaging, and in his opinion, the urgency of outreach trumps certain *chumras* (stringincies). I was comforted by this story early in my career—it offered corroboration for my resolve to take my music and mission to any audience that would have me.

There are both treasures and obstacles in all the Jewish denominations. When shopping amongst rabbis, don't accept a denominational ceiling to growth. If they utter, "well, we don't have to do this because we are _____ Jews," run for the exit. The right answer is: "Here are the mitzvot, go for it!" Our rabbi's heart and gumption matter more than where they got *smicha* (rabbinic ordination). Our rabbi must be wise <u>and</u> intuitive, in other words, not just book-smart, intellectual. I am proud to work with Reform through Chassidic institutions and I can verify that all denominations have something crucial to offer the *k'lal* (whole group). That's why there are twelve tribes in our ancient heritage...as the Talmud says, "these and these are the words of the Living God." At a minimum, our rabbi must exemplify God-consciousness, holy living and teach the importance of mitzvot. Their patient guidance allows us to maintain growth, balance and enthusiasm.

When seeking a rabbi, note which of their communities offer the greatest degree of warmth and friendship. The crucial role of community cannot be overstated. Rabbi Hillel states, "*Al tifrosh min hatzibur*" (*Pirkei Avot* 2:5), don't distance yourself from the community. As I mention in the parenting section, a Jewish community sets certain expectations of all members and therefore the parents don't have to work quite as hard to educate their progeny. It's much easier to thrive in mitzvot when it's simply the way everyone lives. To go it alone can be harsh and is certainly less fulfilling. Online is not optimal; even the coolest Mac cannot substitute for a flesh and blood *chevra* (peer group). Society, the media, economic stress and our base inclinations exert a strong downward influence on our spiritual ascent—much like running up a downward escalator. Growth requires never standing still. As frail humans, we may not have sufficient resolve to progress on our own and can use a bit of peer pressure to stay engaged. Moving to the epicenter of a Jewish community can make all the difference. Those in smaller towns can find (or build) *minyans* of like-minded individuals, study on the Internet and travel periodically to Torah centers. It's possible we may surpass the level of observance of our peers. It takes heroic effort to stay in growth mode when those around us remain in the comfort zone. Remember: no pain, no gain! And also, remember to share the love and never be judgmental.

A final note: we <u>all</u> can serve as someone's rabbi! A Chassidic saying states, "If you only know *aleph*, teach *aleph*." We don't need ordination to influence friends and family. According to the Lubavitch Rebbe, "The pauper is also obligated [to give *tzedakah*], for even the most impoverished person can find a way to help his fellow pauper. The same applies to spiritual charity. There is no man or woman in Israel who cannot, in some way, influence his or her fellow Jews and bring them closer to God." When we hear an inspirational thought, it's selfish to horde it. We must fight the inclination telling us, *no one wants to hear me carry on about this spiritual stuff. They might laugh at me! Who am I to teach anyone?* One's Torah insight might propel others to initiate their own spiritual quest. Or not. Some will be ready to hear it, some don't yet have the vessel to contain such treasures. The key is patience and timing. The following examples illustrate the challenge of reaching others with Judaism's message.

I stopped doing gigs on Shabbat in 1991. In addition to my own band, I was a member of a popular Motown tribute act called The Hitmen. We typically did three-night stands at clubs and resorts around Southern California. I began sending in a substitute keyboard player for the Friday night portion of the weekend. The head of the band, also Jewish, cornered me one Saturday Night and said, "Glaser, what's up on Fridays?" I finally admitted my newfound Judaic predilection and begged his tolerance of my new circumstances. I explained the joy and tranquility that the observance of Shabbat added to my life and suggested he give it a try. He responded by promptly kicking me out of the band, saying, "If I'm Jewish and showing up on Fridays, so are you!" Fast-forward a decade: my Jewish career blossomed and I could call my own shots in terms of bookings on Shabbat. One of my Shabbaton weekends brought me to Houston, the city to which my old bandleader had moved. He was now excited about integrating in the local community and asked me to stick by his side for the entirety of the sacred day to help him observe it fully.

Another tale: one frigid December, I traveled with my brother Yom Tov from L.A. to the Canadian border in search of perfect surf. At the time, he was a junior at UC Santa Barbara, majoring in geography and spending most free moments in the ocean. We planned to hit every famous break along the West Coast, sleeping at friend's homes and videotaping our exploits. We packed his truck with our boards, wetsuits and munchies and began our north-bound odyssey. On the road, we sang along to favorite albums and debated philosophy, my own viewpoints having been shaped by my recent experience in yeshiva. At the time, Yom Tov leaned toward moral relativism and anti-establishment anarchism.

The waves grew in stature over the course of a week of amazing sessions—by the time we hit San Francisco, they were triple-overhead and the water was a mind-numbing fifty-five degrees. With the Golden Gate in the background, Ocean Beach was storm-lashed and chaotic. It looked utterly forbidding but Yom Tov was determined to paddle out. How could I leave my brother alone? I had no choice but to accompany him to ensure he survived the experience. I was glad I did—we dropped in on several of these memorable monsters until the wind chill and absolute exhaustion forced us back to shore.

We surfed as far north as Arcata, CA, where we decided the icy dawn patrol would be our last. A few days later, we arrived in Portland to find the L.A. Lakers scheduled to play the Portland Trailblazers. We were stoked to score cheap seats but felt unremitting animosity due to our allegiance to the victorious Lakers. After the game, we set up camp on couches at a friend's house, accepting his offer of a midnight visit to hot springs in a nearby forest. We drove over an hour on a moonless night until we arrived at the trailhead. We then hiked a few miles in pitch darkness, aided by the light of a single penlight flashlight. I was reluctant to put my trust in this tiny device, knowing if it faltered we'd be spending the night in the woods. Sharp branches threatened our straining eyes; a single misstep would send us plummeting down the muddy slope. As we neared the baths, we heard screaming in the forest. The screams grew louder as we approached—a woman had remained in the tubs too long and got lost trying to find her way in the night. We were thrilled to offer her solace but informed her she would have to wait until we had our fill of soaking.

Under a spectacular canopy of stars, we relaxed for hours in the nearly scalding water, pausing from time to time to add buckets of cooler water to make the temperature tolerable. I spoke of miracles, angels and the universality of Torah. I mentioned my belief that the God Who controls everything guided us on this journey in order to aid the lost hiker. This woman then described the lifestyle of a community of aliens dwelling in Mount Shasta. She believed wholeheartedly that they lived a highly advanced life in a series of tunnels and had much to teach humanity. Yom Tov and our hippie hosts discussed the impossibility of absolute values in a world with multiple faiths and perspectives. Indeed, organized religion was seen as the source of all evil.

Years later, after Yom Tov "found" Hashem in Jerusalem, he chided me for withholding my gleanings from yeshiva. After I stopped laughing, I reminded him of our many all-night sessions debating the truth of Torah—clearly he wasn't ready for the information, even with his propensity to intuit matters of the spirit. Of course, when the time <u>was</u> right, his passion for humankind was redirected within a Jewish worldview and he became an esteemed Jewish leader, touching the lives of untold thousands. Soon thereafter, Baruch Hashem, my brother Aharon followed in his footsteps.

The moral of these stories? Find a *rav*, listen to your *rav* and become a *rav*. As your *emunah* develops, bravely share the light with those in the dark. Growing in Judaism brings new responsibilities—we accept the mantle of leadership when we seek mastery. *Pirkei Avot* (4:6) explains Torah study isn't merely an academic exercise, we must learn in order to do and teach. And like Hashem is endlessly patient with us, be patient with your *talmidim* (students), respecting their unique path. A maxim in outreach: it's hardest to influence those closest to you. Go easy on friends and family; the best technique is silently serving as a visible, concerned, righteous role model.

Choosing a rabbi is the single most important step in initiating a powerful Jewish journey, second only to finding a great spouse. I want to take this moment to thank my *rav* of over thirty years, Rabbi Moshe Cohen, for all the wisdom and kindness he has shared with our family. I'm grateful to him and all my teachers for inspiring me to explore my heritage and share the perpetual feast of the *Shulchan Aruch*, the "set table" of Jewish life.

THE FOUR QUESTIONS

1. Do you feel ready for another step in your Jewish growth?

2. What would <u>you</u> look for in a rabbi that would allow you to feel a strong connection?

3. Who are rabbis that have inspired you in the past?

4. How can you serve as a "rabbi" to others in your life?

In Search of Jewish Unity: The Family Portrait

♫ ONE BIG HAPPY FAMILY ♫

joyjud.com/m/ohf

We are one big happy family together
We are one big happy family
Beneath the morning sun
No matter where the road may lead
Or which way the wind blows
Forever will this family be one

Together forever
Together we will always be
Together forever
One big happy family are we

I was mortified by the 2013 videos of *Charedim* (strictly Orthodox Jews) taunting school children in Beit Shemesh. I didn't see them until I was asked to participate in the production of a new song composed as a response of Reform Jewry. I immediately watched the plethora of YouTube versions of the incidents and had a visceral reaction of nausea. I had to ask myself: *obviously this is horrible, but why is it having such a profound impact on me?*

This publicity disaster for Orthodox Jewry helped me realize that my dedication to bringing our people together is more than skin deep. My parents made unity an essential part of my upbringing and clearly it has played a central role in my choice of career. Situations stoking Jewish divisiveness damage the cool core of my being. There's something unspeakably disturbing in blatant, public hatred for fellow Jews. Spitting on children? Throwing rocks? Disrupting a peaceful house of learning? This is my people? What can we do?

I did some research and discovered the culprits were members of a fringe group disconnected from the 99% of decent *mensches* in Beit Shemesh. Still, I couldn't shake the blues. While discussing my feelings with Shira, she directed my attention to a portrait taken at one of our Glaser family reunions. She recommended I analyze our unique clan and expound on our vast differences in observance combined with our unbreakable, loving bond. Thanks Shira, for reminding me that if we can all get along in our microcosm, perhaps there is hope for our diverse people.

Allow me to take you on a tour of adults seated in this portrait, from oldest to youngest. My dad, seated on the couch, is looking somewhat haggard thanks to the sixteen grandchildren invading his peaceful Pacific Palisades, CA home for the week of Sukkot. He was raised in a depression-era Bronx family and moved to L.A. while he was a teenager. After completing L.A. High School, he rebelled and joined the army instead of going to college. He then took over a division of his dad's garment company and built it into a multi-brand success story. My dad had a Modern Orthodox upbringing but eventually joined one of the largest Conservative synagogues in L.A., Sinai Temple, the congregation in which I grew up. Nowadays he regularly *leins* (reads) the Torah for his local Chabad and actively engages in the passion of his retirement years: studying English literature and teaching Jewish history.

Next to him, with a baby on her lap, is my beloved mom, who was able to cook for this whole crew and keep a smile on her face, most of the time. She grew up in a staunchly liberal Reform household in Sacramento. Her dad, Bill Berman, blew the *shofar* at their temple on Rosh Hashana and led epic *Seders* for all of us happy grandkids. Her mom, Zetta, founded the local Hadassah chapter. Thanks to my mom's love of Israeli folk dancing, we had a continuous stream of *sabras* (native Israelis) visiting our home. These contacts provided us with scores of hosts while on trips to the Holy Land and a comfort level with folk dancing that would get us through many an *Oneg Shabbat* (post services gathering on Friday nights). Thanks to the influence of her newly *frum* sons, my mom became a founding member of her local Chabad. Her famously open home is one of the few in the area in which even the rabbis agree that the *kashrut* can be trusted. Yes, that's a *sheitl* (wig) on her head.

Then there is me and Shira. We both came from an observance-free singlehood knowing eventually we wanted community in our lives. We fell in love with the Pico-Robertson neighborhood where family life is the rule rather than the beachside exception. Our children are a spicy mix of my Romanian and Lithuanian background and Shira's Italian and Argentine roots; they are worldly, Modern Orthodox and hip.

My brother Aharon, seated on the far left, is a campus outreach rabbi influenced by the teachings of Rabbi Nachman of Breslov. He transitioned from his secular life working as a sports-car-driving real estate developer into a humble teacher of Torah with an emphasis on psychology. At the time of this shot, he and his wife Dena led an outreach organization for twenty-something singles near Toronto, where they lived with their two daughters, Penina and Batsheva. Rabbi Aharon is living proof that you can have Orthodox *s'micha* and still look cool in jeans.

Next brother, on the far right, is Yom Tov. I guess it's appropriate that he's sitting on the far right. He and his wife Leah are *Ba'al T'shuva* Chassidim, with Leah from a steadfastly secular New England family. They are raising their eight amazing kids near Meah She'arim in Jerusalem and have dedicated their lives to loving the Jewish people with Torah, song and microbrew beer. It's no wonder my brothers and I straddle the fence between Chassidic and *Litvak* world views. On my mom's side, we are straight-laced Lithuanians, and on my dad's, descendants of devotees of the Vishnitzer Rebbe.

Finally, when this photo was taken, my youngest brother Joey and his wife Jennifer were raising their three children in a suburb of San Diego. These rambunctious kids are a potent mix of Glaser/Berman genes and Jennifer's Dutch and Indonesian beauty. They send their kids to a Reform Hebrew school and belong to both Reform and Conservative synagogues. They have a beautiful Shabbat ceremony in their home every Friday night, build an epic *sukkah* in their suburban backyard and serve as role models for their fortunate friends.

In spite of our many differences, our family finds common ground and makes a point of expressing our love for one another. Yes, there are frustrating moments like dealing with degrees of *kashrut* on Pesach and accepted skirt length. Certain cousins hug the opposite sex; others can't be touched. We have to negotiate how to attend extended family *simchas* when they fall on Shabbat, but we always go. The cousins may come from three countries and dress differently but perceive they are one family. Jennifer told me her kids went into mourning when their Chassidic cousins returned to Israel after this reunion. We know that together we are strong and have far more in common than those picayune details that divide us.

Does this sound familiar? This is the story of the Jewish people. We are truly an extended family.

My dad has a recurring mantra: he wants his four boys to get along. Any time we are bickering or if any of us is in need, he gets on the phone and prods us to call and check in with the relevant brother. He is a fan of intervention and has taught the value of facing issues and not sweeping our pain under the rug. I intuit that God feels the same way with God's own children. Our internal strife as a people creates disunity in the heavens. Out of the millions of Jews at Sinai, only a few thousand *Erev Rav* (mixed multitudes of Egyptians who chose to join the Exodus) participated in the sin of the *Egel Hazahav* (Golden Calf). Still, we were punished collectively and still bear the burden to this day. We have to look out for all who consider themselves a part of our flock, even those with whom we don't agree or barely tolerate. The Talmud states, *Kol Yisrael arevim zeh bazeh* (All Jews are responsible for one another). Want to impress the Almighty? Get the Jewish People on the same page, not just tolerating each other but looking out for and loving one another.

We must present a united front not only to gentiles but also to unaffiliated Jews looking for excuses to defend their apathy. The world judges God by watching the Jews. As they say, "Jews are news." We are held to a higher standard, whether we like it or not. Even if the term makes us uneasy, we are stuck with the designation of Chosen People. Chosen to take a stand against injustice, chosen to serve as the world's conscience, chosen to witness God's hand guiding human history. We glorify God's name by loving each other and judging "to the side of merit." Let us focus on each other's attributes and not the faults. God knows we have plenty of faults.

The following is an *achdut* (unity) builder I use in my *tefillot* (prayers), based on the well-known *Alyenu* and *Sh'ma* prayers. Thankfully, these prayers are essentially identical in the *siddurim* (prayer books) of all denominations. At the end of *Aleynu*, we mention our desire that God's name become one. In other words, at this juncture, God's name (or reputation) isn't one! Our world is filled with bickering among the Reform, Conservative and Orthodox movements, Israel versus Diaspora, Jew versus gentile. Atheists, pantheists and pagans abound. Every day there are acts of violence and terror in God's name. Clearly, we have plenty of work to do. In contrast to the message of *Aleynu*, the *Sh'ma* requires we cover our eyes and state aloud that God is one. Isn't this a contradiction? Of course God is one, it's just that humanity doesn't always perceive it.

Here's the exercise: when saying the *Sh'ma*, take a moment to live in a perfected world where *Tikkun Olam*, the goal of the *Aleynu* prayer, has been realized. Don't just imagine this reality...actually live in it. Close your eyes and listen to your breath as you nurture every syllable of those six words. Don't rush into the "*V'ahavta*" paragraph. Use that silent space in between to enter a Godly realm beyond time. When our eyes are open they are flooded with evidence of duality—light/dark, high/low, us/them. When we keep them shut, even for a few moments, we can sample the elixir of true oneness.

Neuroanatomist Dr. Jill Bolte Taylor described her debilitating stroke on a popular Ted Talk. She entered a soul realm when her common-sense, methodical right hemisphere detached from her spiritually-connected left hemisphere. She felt "enormous and expansive, like a genie liberated from a bottle...like a great whale gliding through the sea of silent euphoria." As she lay in the hospital she thought, "There's no way I would ever be able to squeeze the enormousness of myself back inside this tiny little body." My friends, we are huge, unlimited, united. This is the space we enter each time we say the *Sh'ma*. This is our unique aura, our *ohr hamakif*, a surrounding of light through which all blessing shining from above must pass. As Sting says, "We are spirits in the material world." The key is remaining in this space of unity as we merge with society, serving as a force of *achdut* amidst the insanity foisted upon us by dissention and diatribe, polemics and provocation.

Mirroring the diversity of Jewish people, the Glaser family is a diverse tapestry of colorful personalities. The backside of any tapestry is a chaotic jumble of clashing threads and random knots. Like any family, we have our share of knots. The media, in its effort to be newsworthy and controversial, directs our communal gaze at the unraveling of the fabric of life. Our job as holy individuals is to focus attention on God's view of the tapestry, the smoothly presented work of art that is our national destiny. As Rabbi Shlomo Carlebach said, "Bring right and left together and you get music, the sound of clapping." Yes, there must be recrimination for those in Beit Shemesh or anyone who chooses to destroy our treasured unity. But at the same time, we can make it our personal responsibility to tie more knots, weave more patterns and repair the jagged masterpiece.

A true *Charedi*, one who "trembles at the word of God," exudes wisdom and calm, where the inner *neshama* is at parity with outside appearances. Righteousness is determined by refinement in action and thought, not in the display of long black coats and beards. Let our generation be known as holy unifiers, those who create a heaven on earth, a feast of life grounded in tradition and filled with love and compassion. This is the Judaism in our grasp. This is the Judaism beyond denominations. Let us become the role models who will inspire our children and our children's children. May the genuine love the Glaser family shares serve as a beacon of harmony to our extended family throughout the four corners of the earth.

THE FOUR QUESTIONS

1. Do you feel comfortable with those who are more observant than you? Why or why not?

2. Do you feel comfortable with those who are less observant that you? Why or why not?

3. How can you help promote unity in your community?

4. Have you had interactions with *Charedim*? Describe your experience. How can you transform any feelings of negativity?

Can I Get a Witness? A Tachlis Twelve-Step Program

When I walk beside You
There's a certain confidence I feel
A power unmistakable
It seems there isn't anything
That's far beyond my reach

I've always been a dreamer
There've been times when I almost lost my mind
I've got big plans if You're with me
It may feel like slow motion

But we're closer everyday

You give me trust and understanding
You give me hope when hope is gone
When it seems the doors are closing
You give me the will to carry on

You got this special way to calm me
When I need to ease my mind
But the single greatest gift I'll ever see
Is that You believe in me

Someone pulled me aside at a recent Shabbaton and asked about my *tzitzit*. He said, "I noticed your fringes…there must be a story here." I told him about my gradual process in mitzvot and he responded, "That sounds great, but how do you know where to stop?" "Stop," I replied, "why stop? We're talking about a relationship with God, the Creator of Heaven and Earth…I'm in all the way!" Hopefully, at some point in our ascent we are ready to pull out all the stops. Therefore, I have enhanced the Organized Judaism section with an overview of what taking it "all the way" might require.

As I progressed in observance I learned about a certain threshold considered the "minimum daily requirement" in the service of the Almighty. This threshold is the common bond with all those in the traditional community. Before recent history there was no such thing as Reform, Conservative and Orthodox. For millennia, the *tachlis* (bottom line) understanding of "making it" in Jewish life involved basic observance in three main areas: Shabbat, *kashrut* and *taharat mishpacha* (family purity). Taking on these primary categories of *halacha* offer one a comfort level in any community worldwide. Just to clarify, one is just as Jewish without taking on the "Big Three." But until we obtain a certain achievement level within these areas, according to Maimonides, we stand on the outside of "normative" Judaism and cannot even serve as a witness in Jewish court or at a wedding.

During one of my Israel tours, I had the opportunity to appear on the Tuesday Night Live TV show, broadcast from Jerusalem. I performed a set of my songs with my brother Yom Tov, backed by a hand-picked local band. We finished our set with a rowdy encore of Shlomo Carlebach classics and got the crowd dancing through the theater. As is his custom, my brother showed up in full Chassidic garb, *shtreimel* (fur hat), satin coat and all. Following our performance, the host interviewed us and while looking us up and down asked, "I know you both got into your Judaism in your twenties. I see your modern clothes and then I see your brother's. What happened?" I responded, "Well, I got to first base, and Yom Tov hit a home run." I thought it was a clever answer. Shira disagreed. After the show she chided me for denigrating my own achievement in spiritual growth, as if one's outfit indicates degrees of holiness.

Clearly I had committed the mistake of judging a book by its cover. My response to the TV host demonstrated my subconscious feelings of inadequacy in my learning, feelings of intimidation by the "black hat" crowd, or what my mom might describe as an imposter complex. My wife helped me recognize that every individual is on a personal trajectory and may or may not wind up looking like a Jerusalem Chassid. Vive la différence! There are infinite ways to shine as a Jew. And my way is no better or worse than anyone else's in this extended family.

My friend David Suissa comments that for most of us, religious life means we decide, "That's not what I do" and then defend that stance religiously. Some argue, "Why try a mitzvah if it makes me a hypocrite for not sticking with it?" Our personal Joy of Judaism is immeasurably amplified each time we up our game. Be a hypocrite once in a while! Our Torah accomplishments may bring us to levels of observance that freak out or annoy peers. That's OK. Why not choose to be the one in your community who is basking in spiritual abundance? Some fear becoming a clone or being pushed into a cult. Some see the uniform of observant Jews as oppressive and withdraw in revulsion.

I may not resonate with my brother's outfit but I recognize the importance of the *kedusha* such garb implies. Most newcomers to Torah take on the outfit of their local *shul*, but not because they are trying to fit in. They just don't want their old way of dress to mark them as an outsider and thereby interfere with their growth. Chassidim wear what they wear not to imitate Polish noblemen; they are emulating the regal clothing of the founder of Chassidism, the Baal Shem Tov. "*Yeshivish*" types wear the garb of American businessmen in the fifties. They want to stand before God dressed for success, at all times. Many holy hippie friends in Jerusalem and beyond weat colorful, lightweight, befringed caftans as per our Mideast ancestors. I thrive as a jeans and t-shirt Modern Orthodox L.A. guy. All of the above Jews take it up a notch come Shabbat and holidays. I wear my best suits but avoid black and white in order to add some color to the *minyan*. I'm concerned newcomers might enter and worry they are the only ones with non-conformist outfits.

One friend who is integrating into our community claims he is "sarcastically Jewish," in other words, he is into the kitsch and culture but isn't ready to dive into the 24/7 well of holiness. He'll wear Jewish-themed T-shirts with tongue-in-cheek graphics but not a *kippah*, and saves doing mitzvot for Shabbat. Rabbi Shlomo Schwartz, zt"l (AKA Schwartzie) said,

"God counts only the mitzvahs you do, not the ones you don't." We can be a holy brother or sister all week!

Personal transformation seminars emphasize the need to be "unreasonable." We are always coming up with <u>reasons</u> to avoid growth, to stay in a comfort zone. To be unreasonable means we catch ourselves every time we invent another <u>reason</u> for saying no to life. We can't let the outfits, hair covering requirements or whatever other excuses hold us back from reaching our full potential as 24/7, dedicated Jews. In my song, Across the River, the lyric welcomes the listener, "Come with me across the river, far across the great divide." The Big Three <u>is</u> the "great divide." As Jews, we are called upon to transcend comfort and convenience and venture into the realm of holy accomplishment. Remember the movie "Yes Man?" Jim Carrey plays a character stuck in negative thinking who learns the power of the affirmative. When it's time to try on a mitzvah, just say yes, man!

Can I Have a Witness?

The Chabad rabbi of hipster haven Berkeley, CA has seen every variation of Jewish practice. One weekend, Rabbi Yehuda Ferris was looking for a witness at a wedding he was conducting in the idyllic coastal town of Saulsalito. The couple had purchased a beautiful kosher *ketubah* (marriage contract) stipulating the date of the event in indelible ink. Just before the ceremony, the rabbi was panicking since the sun was setting and he couldn't find Sabbath observant Jews in the crowd to serve as witnesses. If he didn't find one by sundown (the end of the Jewish calendar day), the *ketubah* would need to be rewritten, in other words, there could be no *kiddushin* (marriage) that day. Two witnesses must sign on the dotted line and the rabbi counted as one. The first witness presented by the groom didn't know how to write his name in Hebrew—not a good sign. The rabbi asked a single question: "Do you walk to the synagogue on Shabbat?" The guy answered, "Yes, sometimes." Strike one. Then another candidate was presented, then another. The same dialog, the same answer. With minutes to spare, the *rav* noticed a Sephardic guy in the crowd. From experience, the rabbi knew it was possible to nudge Sephardim into observance. They are typically deeply respectful of rabbinic authority and have God-fearing relatives. With Ashkenazim, *t'shuva* is more an uphill battle. Rabbi Ferris cornered this unwitting guy and queried: "Is your older brother religious?" "Yes," he responded, unsure where this was going. "I need you to be a witness. Will you become *shomer* Shabbat?" "OK," he replied. As simple as that!

Orthodox *gerim* (converts) are required to take on the Big Three before dunking in the *mikvah*. The rabbis maintain it makes no sense to take on the commitment to join the Jewish People if one plans to transgress afterwards. It's like taking the drivers test but telling the clerk at the DMV that you plan to run stop signs. We believe all good folks go to heaven—gentiles need not undertake our rigorous lifestyle to ensure salvation. The demands on converts are formidable. Rabbis simply want to ensure they're serious before they take the plunge. Potential converts must live within a mile of the synagogue. If dating a Jew, their Jewish spouse must also attend classes. They have to fully disavow their religious past and survive the ire of their relatives. They have to learn a mountain of information and apply the teachings to their lives. But then they enter the *mikvah* and emerge miraculously as full-fledged members of our ancient tribe. They are reborn, counting Avraham and Sarah as their parents. Conversion is sacred and private. *Halacha* states we don't opress a convert by reminding them from whence they came. According to the Talmud, "In the place where the *ba'al t'shuva* stands, a *tzadik* cannot stand." Neither can hold a candle to the heroism of a convert.

One rabbi friend who has mentored several *gerim* asks them a single question once they have fulfilled the educational requirements to convert: "Is the shirt blue?" In other words, "Are you *shomer* mitzvot?" It's a plain question, like the color of one's garment. Yes, or no. Not, "Well I only eat non-kosher when we're on vacation," or "I keep Shabbat but not every one of the holidays." Jews-by-birth have a legacy that potential Jews-by-choice envy. How ironic that we can ignore the Big Three mitzvot and remain just as Jewish as the Chief Rabbi. Potential Orthodox converts do not have that luxury. If you were born Jewish, treasure your legacy! Own it! Hopefully at some point you will reach this critical juncture in your spiritual growth. Is the shirt blue?

The best way to get tight with tradition is to go to yeshiva. There are *yeshivot* for Jews of all stripes. A recent phenomenon in Jewish history is the existence of *yeshivot* for those with little or no background in *halachic* Judaism. When one is surrounded by Torah study, kosher meals and great leadership (and enough time to take it all in) spiritual growth is inevitable. *Ba'alei t'shuva* (those who return to tradition) are a rare breed since the temptation to capitulate to material concerns is so great. Usually, the fortitude required to take on the Big Three is born out of a positive yeshiva experience. Once folks enter this pantheon of accomplishment, they need mentors to coach their reentry into post-yeshiva life, much like someone sinking in quicksand needs a savior standing on solid ground.

Hopefully, freshly minted *ba'alei t'shuva* don't just run with the pack of their black and white Orthodox peers. They can use their colorful past to shake up the *frum* world, sharing their special gift of freshness and enthusiasm for divine service.

At the end of every Friday night service, the congregation sings a special paragraph in unison. Right after the *Amidah,* the cantor leads *"Vay'chulu,"* the same passage from *B'reishit* (2:1-3) found in the *Kiddush.* Since observing Shabbat is considered a mitzvah in the category of *edut* (witness—see the *Halacha* chapter for details), this passage depicting the first Sabbath must be recited by a <u>pair</u> of witnesses. If one takes too long praying the *Amidah* and misses saying this paragraph with the *minyan,* at least one other person should be sought to join in. That someone has to be a kosher witness. Think of the *nachas* in your grasp…the witness can be you!

A Twelve-Step Program to Reach the Big Three

The following lists detail my progression into mitzvah observance. These steps are not set in stone; the process is different for everyone. The third list pertains to the laws of family purity so it's primarily for married folks. Each level is cumulative, in other words, by the end of the list one has taken on all prior steps. Every step is meritorious, even miraculous! My choice of twelve steps alludes to the popular program to achieve sobriety, which is also a challenging, incremental effort requiring divine assistance to realize.

The *halachic* status of permanence is conferred when any given event transpires three times. By repeating a mitzvah with intention, like taking on any of the aforementioned Big Three, one "acquires" the mitzvah. This is called establishing a *chazakah*, from the root *chazak*, meaning strong or solid. Three legs form a tripod, three strands form a rope, three links form a chain. According to Talmudic real estate law, occupancy for three years creates a *chazakah*. If one keeps three full Shabbatot with intent, that person is *shomer* Shabbat. Therefore, the unparalleled personal transformation afforded by Sabbath observance is only three weekends away! There is so much at stake, not only in our own lives but for all humanity.

Imagine a world with a universal, God-focused day of rest. Let us all light the way—Reform, Conservative and Orthodox bonding together, presenting a collective wisdom offering on behalf of the Jewish People. The *Midrash* states that *geula* (redemption) will come as soon as all Jews keep just one Shabbat. *Tikkun Olam* really is in our grasp!

    One of my favorite scenes in the rock and roll spoof "Spinal Tap" is guitarist Nigel Tufnel's demonstration of his favorite Marshall amp. Normal amps go up to a maximum volume of ten. Nigel's has been customized to go to eleven. Rob Reiner, the narrator asks him, "Why not just make ten the top number?" Nigel's deadpan response: "It goes to eleven." I mention this because although these lists go to twelve, EVERY step along the way is meritorious. And in most Jewish communities, if you can take it at least to eleven, you qualify as a kosher witness.

Kashrut

1.   Abstain from all pork or shellfish (any sea creatures that don't have fins and scales).

2.   Abstain from eating red meat in non-kosher restaurants. For me, this meant I was ordering chicken sandwiches rather than burgers at fast food joints.

3.   Abstain from eating fowl in non-kosher restaurants.

4.   Avoid overtly combining milk and meat in a single meal or dish.

5.   Only buy food for the home with kosher ingredients.

6.   Make the proper *b'racha* (blessing) <u>before</u> eating.

7.   Wait to eat *chalavi* (milk-based) foods when you are *fleishig* (having eaten meat). The length is between one and six hours...ask your rabbi. Sorry, most Ashkenazim are stuck with six.

8.   Only buy food with a reliable *hechsher* (kosher symbol), including wine and grape juice.

9.   Make the proper *b'racha achrona* (blessing <u>after</u> eating).

10. *Kasher* (make kosher) your kitchen: Get separate plates, utensils and pots and pans for meat and milk meals, immerse them in *mikvah keilim* (ritual bath) before use, *kasher* countertops, oven, microwave.

11. Only eat out in kosher or strictly vegetarian/vegan restaurants.

12. Only eat out in kosher restaurants.

Shabbat

1.   Light candles eighteen minutes before sundown (especially women).

2.   Share a weekly Friday night dinner with the brief table ceremony including *Shalom Aleichem, Eishet Chayil*, blessing children, ceremonial hand washing and *motzi* over the bread.

3.   Attend the synagogue on Friday night for *Mincha-Ma'ariv* services before dinner.

4.   Attend a Shabbat lunch on a regular basis.

5.   Go to the synagogue for Saturday morning services, enjoy *Kiddush* at the synagogue

before lunch.

6. Stop driving and working on Friday night by candlelighting time.

7. Consciously prepare for the Sabbath all week with food shopping, cooking, inviting guests, preparing *divrei* Torah, etc. If you aren't hosting, let others know you need a meal—don't be bashful!

8. Incorporate the Saturday Afternoon *Mincha*, *Seudah Shlishit* (Third Meal), *Ma'ariv* and *Havdalah* service.

9. Study the thirty-nine *melachot* (prohibitions of Shabbat) and relevant subcategories.

10. No driving at all on Shabbat, get a regular place to stay for Shabbat in your 'hood within a mile of the synagogue.

11. Take on a full twenty-five-hour rest from any *melacha* (proscribed acts of creation) on Shabbat <u>and</u> *Chagim* (holidays). This includes both days of two-day holidays.

12. On Saturday evening add a *Melava Malka seudah* (a festive meal to figuratively escort the Shabbat Queen).

Taharat Mishpacha

1. Recognize that sex is a private, holy act, a mitzvah that must be cherished and nurtured.

2. No relations during menstruation (usually five days).

3. No physical contact during menstruation.

4. No relations for full *niddah* period (which includes an additional seven "clean" days after menstruation ends)

5. Prepare for *mikvah* (immersion in ritual bath) before relations resume.

6. Separate beds in the bedroom during this period.

7. No physical contact at all during this period.

8. Avoid sexy content in conversation, movies, TV during this period.

9. Avoid sharing food, eating from the same plate, passing things directly to one another during this period.

10. Use of a *bedikah* (inspection) cloth to ascertain that clean is really clean, and sharing it with a competent authority if uncertain.

11. Become *Shomer negiah* (guarding touch in terms of limiting contact with opposite sex other than immediate family) <u>within one's Jewish community</u> and observe laws of *yichud* (avoiding isolation with the opposite gender who is not an immediate relative).

12. Completely *shomer negiah* in all circumstances.

These three categories can be summed up into daily, weekly and monthly commitments to God, respectively. *Kashrut* is perhaps the most formidable when considering how often we stuff our faces. It is also the most divisive since it becomes challenging to entertain clients or dine with friends at an old favorite bistro. However, keeping kosher is the most effective method for clearing up clogged celestial pipelines. There is truth to the adage, "You are what you eat." Tasty as the dish may appear, we must find the inner resolve to refuse anything sabotaging *shefa* in our quest for the Joy of Judaism.

There's another name for a witness. It's "*yirat shamayim*," someone with awe of heaven. The ultimate compliment one might make about another Jew is that he or she is a *yirat shamayim*. The Talmud limits God's omnipotence: "All is in the hands of heaven except the awe of heaven." Becoming a witness is the ultimate personal choice. It cannot be forced upon us by God or anyone else. That would be duress. Taking on the Big Three is formidable but not insurmountable. The rewards flow in this world and the next. But we don't do it for the reward. Moshe sums up Hashem's foremost desire for the Chosen People in this sentence from Deuteronomy (10:12): "And now, Israel, what does God, your God, demand of you? Only to have awe of God, to walk in all God's ways and to love God, and to serve God with all your heart and soul." Awe comes first. God is AWE-some! Having awe implies recognizing God cares about each one of us and mitzvot matter. Once we really get God's majesty, walking in God's way is the only way. These fundamental commandments keep us in tune with all creation, opening a channel to truly love Hashem with heart, soul and might.

THE FOUR QUESTIONS

1. Every journey begins with the first step. Are you ready to take the next step?

2. Look at the steps on the Kashrut list—where are you? Can you try the next step for a month?

3. Look at the steps on the Shabbat list—where are you? Can you try the next step for a month?

4. Look at the steps on the Taharat Mishpacha list—where are you? Can you try the next step for a month?

Jews in the Pews: Hillel and Holy Chutzpah

♫ EYES ARE OPEN ♫

by Neshama Carlebach and Sam Glaser

joyjud.com/m/eao

I got up early so I could taste the day
The air was sweet
The sky so bright
No room for pain
It is clear that I am free to walk with You
Just outside I found a world
Where everything's new

My eyes are open, hitor'ri, hitor'ri
Don't let me go back to sleep
Eyes are open, ki va oreych kumi ori
Lift my heart so I can see

My eyes are open, uri uri shir dabeyri
I am in Your hands

I took a journey through my day to day
A place I'd never been
A thousand times before
It is clear that I am home within Your arms
Stand by me as I reach for the highest star

And I know You have plans for me
I know I'm not forgotten
No matter what may come, I will go on

What was the most heartbreaking finding in the Pew Research Center's 2013 Portrait of Jewish Americans? The majority of today's young Jews are not even exposed to opportunities presented by affiliation. The last ties to tradition are fraying thanks to multiple generations of assimilation. There is little nostalgia for the old country or guilt associated with disappointing parents. The Holocaust is seen as a drag and Israel a source of embarrassment. Jews on the fringe are an endangered species and the challenge of our generation is to identify with the pathos of this tragedy, fight complacency and endeavor to bring them back.

The statistic sending organized Judaism into a frenzy: over a third of Jews age thirty-three and younger, the American Jewish future, are claiming they are Jewish with no religion. They have a vague sense they are part of an elite and afflicted ancient cult and are predisposed to enjoy matzah ball soup. Thanks to the widespread acceptance of Jews in the greater culture, most have a sense of Jewish pride. But the net result of that acceptance is 4/5ths of these "non-religious" Jews will marry out of the faith. This unfortunate leap in assimilation started its exponential rise in the the 1970s. Now, fifty years and a two generations later, the floodgates are open. For those immersed in the Joy of Judaism, seeing our youth raised without basic Jewish values is a source of grave consternation. We feel the loss of Jewish potential viscerally. What will happen to our demographics in the greater American culture? Who will support Jewish non-profits in the future? Who will our teachers teach? Who will fill the pews of our mega-synagogues? No wonder this study has the Jewish world reeling.

Two of my friends, Richard Horowitz and Antony Gordon, extrapolated this 2013 Pew data on a grid entitled, "Will Your Grandchildren Be Jewish?" Their findings were widely published and portray a harsh reality for non-Orthodox movements. Yes, there is value to afternoon Hebrew school and Jewish summer camp, but in the long run, the toll of intermarriage and apathy ravages the numbers of Reform and Conservative adherents by the third and fourth generation. Given current trends, out of a sample of one hundred Jews, by the fourth generation there are fifty-two Jews left in the Conservative movement, thirteen in the Reform and four amongst those considering themselves secular. In contrast, in Orthodox camps, there are 337 Centrist Orthodox Jews and 3,400 *Charedi* Jews. Unless something dramatic changes, current ratios of observance will flip-flop. Today, nearly a third of Jews younger than eighteen live in Orthodox households. No one is excited about this victory in Orthodox camps. This is not a contest. These statistics expose the tragedy of today's velvet genocide, a Holocaust in which we are being loved to death by our host culture.

I'd like to offer a few ideas for righting this foundering ship: engendering "holy chutzpah" in our Jewish leaders and strengthening youth initiatives like Hillel on campus.

In my office, we feel a sense of urgency that the programs I offer are maximally effective. Every *neshama* I'm able to impact is precious. A reviewer once referred to my concerts as "musical triage for Jewish youth." Most organizations hire me, pay a deposit and then we don't hear from them until they request my travel information a few weeks before the show. We strive to help our clients to be self-sufficient in marketing my events by making all the relevant materials available online. Conversely, some venues keep our phones ringing, working with us to help "get out the vote." These organizations realize they must strive to gain consensus, for example, establishing committees for the sake of getting more people involved in the planning and having local adult and kids' choirs learn my material to join me for the finale. They may honor a few dignitaries, include a raffle or Chinese auction and beseech local businesses to advertise in a printed program. They promote links to my videos, send buses to senior homes to bring in the elderly and have teens run the intermission concession and pass out programs. They ask the community to participate in an online vote regarding which workshop I present during my Shabbaton, arrange for multiple individuals to drive and feed me and give out honors in advance for opening the ark and being called to the Torah. Furthermore, they request I include the local cantor(s) for a song, invite brave teen instrumentalists to sit in and have my music playing "on hold" when people call the synagogue. Can you see the strategy here? My event has become a command performance for every last man, woman and child!

In short, Jewish leaders need "holy chutzpah." They galvanize the community by making requests, giving individuals the chance to answer with "*Hineni.*" Holy chutzpah is the key to effective *Kol Nidrei* appeals, coordinating membership drives, outreach to the unaffiliated, initiating artist-in-residence programs, planning banquets, even recruiting folks for a *minyan*. Synagogues with "holy chutzpah clergy" are typically busy beehives of activity, with all ages constantly coming and going, more like community centers than cold, corporate auditoria.

Once, I co-officiated with a young rabbi who had just begun his first full-time position. He was a capable speaker, practiced what he preached in terms of living a Jewish life and connected with the community in compassionate pastoral moments. I didn't want to ruffle any feathers, but before I left town I felt compelled to share my holy chutzpah theory with this well-meaning but somewhat milquetoast clergyman. His community is aging and suffers from the "running for the exits" tendency of the younger set. I believe all those inspired sermons and moments of tenderness will be ineffective in stemming this tide unless he finds the inner resolve to get under people's skin with unmitigated holy chutzpah. I encouraged him to invent programming to empower the full range of congregants, to chase after ex-members, singles and young families with communal, even secular activities and not to spend an extra minute in his office when he can be meeting his constituents "where they live." In short, to get past the fear of rejection and find ways to empower every Jew he meets. Unfortunately, he didn't agree this was part of his job detail.

Holy chutzpah can transform communities in unexpected ways. One morning, my movie producer friend, Lou Rudolph, joined one of our communal rabbis on a fundraising trip to the offices of famed bodybuilding entrepreneur, Joe Weider. Lou came to provide moral support—the rabbi was hoping for a $100,000 donation for the new Aish Center in Jerusalem. They presented a colorful brochure illustrating the possibility of creating "Weider Hall" within the edifice. As the rabbi began to suggest the amount he was hoping for, Lou hit his leg under the table and interrupted, saying, "And for you, Joe, to have this incredible honor, the price is only $1,000,000." Joe agreed! Lou embodied the truism: to sell, one must believe in the product. He intuited the potential of this meeting. And he possessed the holy chutzpah to close the deal.

The "holy" aspect of holy chutzpah is based on the much overlooked but crucial role of Jewish leadership: to connect Jewish souls to their primeval drive to seek Godliness and grapple with the 613 commandments. Mitzvot are oxygen to the *neshama*. They are the skeleton supporting the body of Judaism. There is no continuity or survival without them, regardless of denomination. When an interviewer asks me where I've seen evidence of flourishing communities, I point out those synagogues where the leadership has laser-like focus on making mitzvot a priority. One case in point is Temple Emanuel in Greensboro, NC, a Reform congregation where I have performed several times and have found an especially united, dedicated community. I asked Rabbi Fred Guttman to reveal his secret. He replied, "It's simple: I just get the congregation to take on mitzvot and build from there."

Making mitzvot the priority requires clergy and synagogue leaders who respect *halacha*, or as the term indicates, "walk the talk." It requires ample education budgets allotted for children's programming and increasing the chance for true "informed choice" for the adults. It requires a real relationship with congregants and gentle, private encouragement when any given individual is far from from the path. What harm could there be in nudging members to try *kashrut*, to make Shabbat and holidays sacred in the traditional sense, to marry within the tribe and be fruitful and multiply? We have to model love for all things Jewish and remember that despite evidence to the contrary, our kids and students do care what we think. We can all look back on our lives and acknowledge the times a mentor steered us on the right track. Jews have a soul-level "right track." Our divine mission is worthy of aggressive marketing and we must nurture leaders who are "holy chutzpah black belts."

The other crucial area of emphasis is reinvigorating organizations like Hillel and other Jewish programming for our endangered tribes-people under thirty. I love working on college campuses and have experienced some of the peak moments of my career jamming with rowdy students. Well funded Hillels are key to enhancing Jewish life on campus for those lucky enough to have had a Jewish day school education. They are the last chance of engagement for those who haven't. Since the 11th commandment for American Jews is "thou shalt go to college," a reinvigorated Hillel and programs like JAM, JLIC, Aish on Campus and Chabad can impact nearly the entire target market.

Once, I led a Shabbaton for the Hillel of Lafayette College, a top fifty liberal arts school in the rolling hills of Easton, PA. I was joined by a passionate, self-selected cadre of Jewish students from all over the country. It was my second visit to this particular Hillel and our 27-hour experience included spirited *davening, divrei Torah*, communal meals and my workshop "Jewish Perspective of the Afterlife." After *Havdalah*, a rowdy concert ensued where many students got into the act. I felt I was able to have a profound impact during my short stay—imagine if they had the budget to provide similar programming every weekend. According to the Hillel website, 94% of active members say being Jewish will "continue to be important" to them after graduation. Is there any question where benefactors should be directing funds?

One caveat: I'm concerned the Pew study demonstrates that "continue to be important" is not enough to give these young people the gift of Jewish grandchildren. Nor is the amazing Birthright Israel trip or the multitudes of great Jewish summer camps dotting our countryside. While these programs are valuable and utterly worthy of support, the question is whether they open the door to a life of Jewish commitment, in other words, a life of mitzvot. Hillel Shabbatons, Camp Ramah, USY and NFTY will succeed only to the degree that Jewish leadership pursues holy chutzpah growth opportunities with each individual. When these young people are called upon, the framework on which they base their Jewish choices must include not only adventure travel and falafel but also an opportunity to consider a traditional Jewish *derech* (path). Only with the option of encountering beautifully portrayed observant life is there true pluralism.

Effective Hillels must boldly expose students to the full array of Jewish lifestyles and endeavor to get them out of their comfort zone. All movements deserve to be portrayed proficiently, with kindness and respect. I have sat through many a class where the Orthodox are spoken of with disdain or as the butt of jokes. I've witnessed Talmud study where teachers purposely choose passages to make traditional Judaism look ridiculous. Non-Orthodox educators must make supernal effort to avoid bias and barb-throwing from a position of defensiveness or anger. They may rationalize that Orthodoxy is quick to criticize liberal Judaism. The future of Judaism should outweigh the temptation to succumb to such pettiness.

Some argue that students coming to Hillel events are from varying backgrounds and therefore must be catered to with kid gloves so as to not offend those with less Jewish education. No! Our national Hillel rabbis and interns must take their personal practice up a notch. As I've seen at every Hillel function that I've had the pleasure to lead, the students will rise to the occasion. They are hungry for Torah. They need role models living a mitzvah-filled Jewish life with style and a sense of fun. They want their programming to include not only talks on Jewish history, Israel and the Holocaust, but on the Jewish soul, deep text study and personal growth through Torah. They know they're about to enter the abyss of the job market and are interested in our tradition's secrets to success. Like most Jewish events, food is the primary magnet to attract these "starving students." But once they are present for the (hopefully kosher) meal, we must also feed their appetite for spiritual transformation, offering them invaluable tools they can use to navigate the turbulent waters of life.

You may be thinking: *well, that's what organizations like JLIC and Aish are for.* Actually, I'm talking about reaching kids who have never heard of those institutions. The 100,000 Jewish freshmen entering the collegiate system each year deserve a fighting chance to lead committed Jewish lives. Let Hillel be the crown jewel of the U.S. Jewish charity effort. Our kids can get an academic angle on Judaism from their professors. It's up to Hillel to touch their souls.

Students inspired by Jewish programming possess a bulwark against the spiritual vacuum of our melting pot society. We can arm them with a love of Shabbat, an appreciation of *kashrut*, basic *davening* skills, a sense of pride in their uniqueness and perhaps most importantly, a repertoire of Jewish music! We must also arm them with an unabashedly pro-Israel outlook so they can counter the forces of evil in the form of BDS and rabid anti-Israel student groups. At a minimum, I suggest lifting the national Hillel observance level to Camp Ramah standards. Some Hillels I have visited have uber-liberal leadership, leaving students interested in tradition to find their own way. The priority for the disbursement of funds for Hillel programming is ensuring there is an observant, Zionist co-director at each Hillel House. Will students be brainwashed by sampling *halachic* Judaism? Of course not! Most will likely go back to their communities and familiar synagogues…but at least they will be literate and aware of their options. Most importantly, they will look to Judaism for answers when they face life challenges and transitions.

When I attended L.A.'s Brandeis Collegiate Institute (BCI) in the 1980s, it was run by three powerful Orthodox leaders: Dennis Prager, Joseph Telushkin and Pinchas Pelli. The music sessions were led by accomplished arranger/publisher Velvel Pasternak, also Orthodox. This primarily Conservative movement-funded institution had wise leaders who understood the importance of emphasizing intensive Jewish living, at least for the precious month when camp was in session. Some of my alumni friends took on mitzvot and moved to Pico-Robertson, which then gave me my first Shabbat invitations when I started considering the Sabbath as a weekly option.

Fast-forward twenty years, when I had the great fortune to serve as Musical Director of the institute. I loved the sublime, mountainous setting and did my part to fill the air with sweet music. The program had a remarkable impact on all who attended. There was one fundamental difference: the intensity of kosher Jewish immersion got diluted thanks to a multicultural, anything-goes philosophy. *Davening* was now optional, the leadership was too politically correct to apply holy chutzpah and instead of the whole community taking on *halachic* Shabbat observance (as we did in my day), there were many non-Shabbat-appropriate activities offered. The *mashgiach* (kosher supervisor) was told to stay in the kitchen and prohibited from making presentations to the students…God forbid he might influence someone! This is pluralism? BCI can do better. Hillel can do better.

The urgency of this effort to enrich the Jewish life of our young people cannot be overstated. It must be ratified in partnership with all denominations. Some may argue that Orthodox Jews don't need to get involved with the continuity efforts of the greater Jewish community, as if they are immune to assimilation. I can state from experience that they, too, are badly in need of an injection of renewal and joy. I know of countless *frum* parents who are losing sleep over their kids' faltering connection to *Yiddishkeit*, especially during the college years. Some believe encouraging mitzvah observance is outside the purview of Reform Judaism. To wit: "The (1999) Pittsburgh Principles assert that each Reform Jew has the right, indeed the obligation, to enter into dialogue with the mitzvot…affirming a mitzvah, declaring one is not ready yet to accept it, or even rejecting it. But the dialogue must precede the decision, or it is not really a decision."

Conservative Judaism wins the prize in the Pew reports of Jewish organizational hemorrhage. The Conservative movement was my beloved home throughout my life and the number one source of my concert bookings. Some Conservative institutions are thriving but I find it heartbreaking to see nearly empty mega-synagogues and skeletal religious schools in many of the cities I visit. Accomodating modernity with *halachic* authenticity is a winning formula as long as the *halacha* is authentic. I'm hopeful the new breed of rabbinic graduates eschew the ivory tower-academic rabbinic model and instead incorporate a wide-eyed sense of amazement with Hashem and a willingness to share it. Many Conservative rabbis model *halachic* life but are unwilling to offer *halachic* education or *tochacha* (criticism) to increasingly secular congregants for fear of appearing pushy or damaging relationships with the board. Our youth need Torah guidance! Why aren't the incredible introductory texts on my Suggested Reading List found in most Reform and Conservative libraries? In the Hebrew school where I grew up, all I knew about two-thousand years of rabbinic Judaism was stories of the idiots in the "Wise Men of Chelm" books. This is criminal! Some parents won't send their kids to an Orthodox-run camp, yeshiva or Israel program for fear they will get "brainwashed." That's right: their kids will get excited about Shabbat, study and family values. And then what?

All our factions are in need of healing and any movements' success is a victory for the Jewish People. We all occupy different branches of the same tree, an *Eitz Chayim*, a Tree of Life. When our leadership has the guts to engage in holy chutzpah, I'm confident we will rise up and say, *"Hineni!"* When we support programs nurturing every age group with the basics of Jewish literacy, our out of kilter orbit will stabilize. We can foment a lasting love for our heritage with substantial resources devoted to inspiring young adults, making the decision to raise a Jewish family a no-brainer. Subsidized Jewish day school education wouldn't hurt either! Let us spend our hard-earned *tzedakah* not on further Pew exposés of our demise, but on programs with proven efficacy in stemming the tide of assimilation. With resolve, sagacity and a healthy dose of holy chutzpah, we will once again see Jews in the Pews.

THE FOUR QUESTIONS

1. Have you ever used holy chutzpah for the benefit of your community?

2. How can you apply holy chutzpah in your personal life?

3. Is there a young adult among your contacts that you could strive to inspire?

4. What Jewish literacy programs can you support?

Chabad: The Closest Thing to Judaism

♫ LOVE TO UNDERSTAND ♫

by Sam Glaser and Julie Silver

joyjud.com/m/ltu

What is this sweetness, completeness
Or am I dreaming
Are we together or are we apart
For just a moment's sensation
A celebration
But I open up my eyes

Stand here in my shoes
I'll walk right beside you
Now that we're face to face
We see love and understanding
I'd love to understand

So we are scattered
What matters is everything in between
You know it's love that moves us along
Must we be rivals, survival
We can achieve
If you open up your heart

Stand up I need you
I think you need me too so
Why do we argue
We need love and understanding
I'd love to understand

How many times has Chabad come to my rescue with a kosher meal, a place to stay for Shabbat or a *minyan*? Thanks to Chabad I have "secular" friends who can quote *chassidut* (Chassidic teachings). Chabad *shlichim* (emissaries) live to share the Joy of Judaism and increase the study of Torah and performance of mitzvot. We may find ourselves in a fast-paced, high-tech world, generations removed from the *shtetl*, but we can always find a bowl of hot chicken soup or *lulav* to shake with an adopted Chabad *bubbie* and *zaydie*. Just after my parents started to keep kosher (a miracle I thought might never transpire), they moved to Pacific Palisades, a decidedly kosher-free zone. I feared they'd never make it without a community to support their revamped lifestyle. Lo and behold, that very year a new Chabad rabbi, Zushe Cunin and his growing family set up shop in their neighborhood. My parents were welcomed as founding members of this fledgling chapter which is now a full-blown *shul* brimming with Jewish life.

My own children have grown up at Aish HaTorah on Pico Boulevard. They crawled the carpeting, hid under my *tallis*, ditched childcare and eventually had their Bar Mitzvahs in our intimate Jerusalem stone-trimmed sanctuary. When it was my daughter Sarah's turn to step up to the podium, she used her newly found womanhood to assert she would ONLY have her Bat Mitzvah at my parents' Chabad. She claimed that it was where she truly felt at home. Given the approachability of the rabbis and *rebbetzins*, the relaxed environment and the reliably delicious lunch after services, I don't blame her.

Chabad is here for everyone. They make no distinction between levels of observance, income or color of one's skin. They just want to help Jews do Judaism. Chabad isn't here to brainwash. Nor do they encourage congregants to drop former affiliations. While at the Reform Biennial, I learned that due to Chabad's ethic of radical inclusion, more Reform Jews attend Friday night services at Chabad than their own temples. Chabad is ubiquitous, with over 3,500 institutions in eighty-five countries. I think I've been to half of them! I sent my twenty-one-year-old son on a solo Eurail adventure over the summer, much like the trip I made at his age. I knew he had good survival instincts and the character to get the most out of the experience. I arranged a frenetic twenty-city-in-six-weeks itinerary and managed to find Chabad Shabbat hosting in every relevant place he visited. Paris, Prague, Copenhagen, Geneva, Florence…even Munich, where the Chabad House overlooks Hitler's home, *y'mach sh'mo* (may his name be obliterated).

My positive experiences with Chabad are too numerous to mention but I'll offer one notable anecdote. I regularly attend a Reform rabbinic convention which is cleverly scheduled each January in Vail, Colorado. I have grown to love this bunch of learned ski addicts. We study Torah for an hour in the morning, ski all day and then meet for *Mincha* and more learning when the lifts close. What better way to combine my love of Judaism with my favorite sport? During one of the conferences, I was fortunate to stay at a relative's condominium that was equipped with a piano. I figured I'd share the good fortune with my dear rabbi friends, so I invited them to gather for songs and snacks one of the nights. I scrambled back to the condo after a very intense day of shredding the back bowls (search YouTube: Sam Glaser in Vail) and discovered the local grocery store had just closed. Now I had a serious problem. My friends were on their way within the hour. I had no car, no libations and no knowledge of another market in the area.

I suddenly realized where to go for help. The previous year I had performed a concert in Aspen, sponsored by the local Reform community in conjunction with Chabad. That Chabad rabbi had a brother who was setting up shop in Vail. I looked up this brother, someone I had never met in my life. When I called to beg this newly minted rabbi for the immediate delivery of wine, sodas and snacks, he responded without hesitation, "I'll be right over!" A smorgasbord of munchies appeared within twenty minutes, just before the group of rabbis arrived. This well-meaning *Chabadnik* wouldn't accept any money—he didn't want to diminish his mitzvah of kindness to strangers.

When my guests arrived, we sang favorite camp songs and offered toasts. I noticed the rabbi wasn't quite ready to leave and wanted to offer a word of Torah. I realized it might be a bit awkward but thought *what could be the harm?* I introduced Rabbi Mintz to the crew, he spoke about the *parasha shavua* (Torah portion of the week) for a few minutes and said goodbye. A furious convention leader then escorted me into a bedroom. "How dare you invite a Chabad rabbi to speak to us! This whole *kumzitz* was a setup so you could get that man here!"

This attitude reflects a resounding theme I have heard during my travels, for example: Chabad steals members from neighboring congregations, they brown-nose the rich or are steeped in misguided messianism. Let me state for the record that these Reform and Conservative rabbis and cantors are some of my dearest friends, entirely dedicated to their holy work and wear their love for Judaism on their sleeve. Nevertheless, comments slip out like, "Oh, Chabad—the closest religion to Judaism!" Or, "those #*&^s just opened down the street so they could siphon off our membership!" First the dig and then, "But they do great work."

After enough of these ripostes I was concerned this diatribe was a universal mantra. That was until I led a Chanukah Shabbaton in Jacsksonville, FL where I met Rabbi Gary Perras. He is a veteran Conservative rabbi and surprisingly, hanging in his office is a formidable portrait of the Lubavitcher Rebbe. He explained his perspective as we lit Chanukah candles together. Rabbi Perras was the only rabbi to welcome Chabad to Jacksonville when other Jewish institutions were attempting to prevent them from getting settled. He argues that one can't "steal" members…they vote with their feet and many crave the spiritual nourishment that Chabad provides. When his congregants opt for Chabad, he considers it a success story: they will be more likely to keep kosher and marry a Jew. He stated, "My job isn't to retain members, it's to get people into Judaism."

One year, I was nominated a "Jewish Community Hero" in the national Jewish Federation-sponsored online campaign. I hadn't heard about this news until friends who had read the announcement wished me *mazel tov* (congratulations) as I walked the streets of my neighborhood. When I checked the website to see who else was nominated, I discovered the majority chosen were *Chabadniks*. A Conservative rabbi friend called to offer help in getting out the vote since a $25,000 prize was offered. When I mentioned the skewed presence of *Lubavitchers* (the town in Russia where Chabad originated) in the running, he responded, "Well, that's because they have the time to be out in the streets with the people. They run to visit the sick, counsel addicts and *kasher* kitchens, while I'm stuck behind a desk with budgets and board meetings." When I asked if it was possible to sort out his priorities, he gave me a long list of reasons why that couldn't happen. He then ranted about Chabad's free Hebrew school and how it was wreaking havoc on his own synagogue's membership policies. This sounds a lot like a Yellow Taxi vs. Uber-style disruption. At best, it is forcing Reform and Conservative leaders to innovate. At worst, it encourages damaging *lashon harah*, evil speech.

I salute Chabad for loving us without judgment, for serving as examples of unflappable Jewish commitment and profound self-sacrifice. What a miracle we can find a spiritual Jewish home in our own neighborhoods and around the world. Thank you, Chabad, for helping us keep our eye on the goal of redemption. Let us make this a generation where our *achdut* serves to create a world where God's name is truly one.

(In case you were wondering, this chapter marks the end of the inclusion of The Four Questions).

The Biennial: The Good, the Bad and the Plenary

♫ HINEY MA TOV ♫

joyjud.com/m/hmt

Walking together down this winding road
Looking back to see how far we've gone
It's the most amazing view
To think somehow we made it through
And managed still to keep the power on

Working together on our future
Knowing we stand on common ground
We're only going to hear the call
When it's all for one and one for all
When we spread a little kindness all around
Hiney ma tov uma na'im...

Now is the time for building bridges
Founded on tolerance and love
Let our generation be
The light that every nation sees
United by our trust in God above
Hiney ma tov uma na'im...

Imagine the magical sound
As we sang with one voice
Stronger and stronger
We never will wander alone

I began one of my annual Chanukah roadtrips at the sparkling new Gaylord National Convention Center in Washington DC. This mega-hotel easily housed the six thousand delegates of the Reform Biennial. Is there a special prayer for so many Jews sleeping under one roof? I have performed at several Biennials, but this one felt special, perhaps because we were in the nation's capital. It ran like a well-oiled machine with a record number of participants and myriad opportunities for study, conducting the business of the movement and power schmoozing. An impressive array of my musical peers were on hand to add a creative touch to the proceedings and the well stocked exhibit hall of Judaica from around the world was a shopper's delight. I couldn't walk more than a few feet without being embraced by the leadership and clergy of synagogues where I have performed over the years. The Reform movement has been a beloved home for me and has made my music a part of its worship and education curricula. Half my gigs are in Reform institutions. Can you feel the love in the room? Multiplied by 6000?

  There were two highlights of the conference for me. One was the climax of my friend Craig Taubman's standing-room-only concert when he invited me to the stage to lead a slow, spiritual version of *Ma'oz Tzur*. It takes a big man to share the spotlight with another artist. For me, it was a moment of redemption. Earlier that day, my own concert was scheduled during a major plenary session and therefore attendance was light. It happened to be my birthday and I was questioning the wisdom of accepting the Biennial invitation rather than celebrating with my family. Having this chance to contribute to the intense *ruach* (spirit) of a packed house gave me (and hopefully the audience) a powerful uplift. At the conclusion of the song, Craig mentioned that a certain conference participant had pressing medical needs. He borrowed the guitarist's baseball cap, placed it center stage and announced that the audience was going to come forward and make a miracle happen. Blame it on peer pressure or the addictive spirit of giving: that sweaty hat overflowed with bills within five minutes.

  The other highlight was a pair of amazing late night jams. I had just finished a midnight hour-and-a-half *kumzitz* in one of the concert halls, during which I led a continuous medley of all tunes Jewish, Beatles and Broadway for a happy crowd of insomniac conventioneers. Afterwards, with little strength remaining after such a long day, I lumbered through the cavernous lobby on the way back to my room. There I saw a group of immensely talented young songleaders who had just been kicked out of the lobby bar following "last call." We started singing in the main atrium and were promptly encouraged to find somewhere else to make noise. I dragged them back to the stage where my *kumzitz* had recently concluded and we began a few hours of sharing new musical creations with one another. Every musician had a keyboard, guitar or percussion in hand and lent their voices to one another's songs as we went around the circle. The collaboration was organic, the degree of mutual respect was palpable.

  Most of these musicians are part of the *Hava Nashira* songleader community, a crown jewel of the Reform movement. Each summer, over three hundred singers and instrumentalists gather in rural Wisconsin to talk shop and share techniques. Most importantly, they come to SING! Four days of song sharing, open mic sessions, group singing, Shabbat singing, *kumzitz* singing, vocal and guitar instruction…it's a wonder these songleaders don't lose their voices before starting their jobs at the URJ (Union for Reform Judaism) camps. I'm accustomed to serving as the official musician in any gathering. Imagine my joy in this rustic, lakeside camp setting where <u>everyone</u> is a musician! Most importantly for me, attending *Hava Nashira* fills me with a sense of optimism. Thanks to the emphasis of music in Reform spirituality, ecstatic Judaism is very much alive. It may not be easy to make a buck for these young artists, but in spite of the harsh economics of today's music business, there is a huge future for contemporary Jewish music.

  Plenary sessions at Biennial can be inspiring or a grind. Imagine attending several three-hour banquets per day…and you don't even get the tepid chicken dinner. That year, President Obama, Eric Cantor, Ehud Barak and Natan Sharansky held court. I've been to enough Biennials and Jewish Federation General Assembly conferences to predict the exact script of each of these speeches. The politicians impress the audience with teleprompter readings of exactly what the constituent population wants to hear, pausing at preset moments for rousing applause, posing for a snapshot with the movement leaders and then running to a waiting helicopter. Yes, it's exciting to be in the room with the political giants of the day. But the succession of humorless sound bites left me wishing for a left turn, a bit of levity, a novel idea. The rest of the plenary sessions were chock full of congratulations for incoming or outgoing movement executives, showcasing cutting-edge programming and waiting for malfunctioning videos. No one was forcing me to be there. I attend the plenaries because I deeply want to learn about innovations, to be inspired, to feel hopeful for this largest movement on the American Jewish scene.

A few issues tainted this otherwise perfectly run Jewish love fest. As discussed in the Jews in the Pews chapter, real pluralism tolerates and engages all aspects of the spectrum of the Jewish people. I found many speakers to be defensive, taking a stand against tradition and using the word Reform to excess. In other words, rather than just say, I'm a Jew, the phrase continuously repeated was, "Since I'm a Reform Jew," "As Reform Jews we…" or, "I am proud to be a <u>Reform</u> Jew." Can't we just be proud to be Jews first and foremost? Many speakers missed the chance to inspire attendees with the *nachas* of belonging to the greater whole of our glorious people.

This idea of pluralism also must take into account the presence of Reform Jews with right wing leanings. I heard closet conservatives whispering amongst themselves in fear of political backlash. Several of my conservative Reform friends have learned to self-censor any right-wing viewpoints on social media and the pulpit or risk being ostracized by peers. The AIPAC meet and greet was nearly empty in spite of the free cocktails. Applause for Republican Congressman Eric Cantor was guarded. Have we lost our souls in a stew of political correctness? Where is the famous Reform openness and tolerance here?

While I'm venting, when I asked if there were provisions for kosher meals, the few provided had been sold out in advance of the conference. No kosher deli booth among the multitude of dining options, nothing with a *hechsher* (kosher certification) for the many exhibitors and attendees who might appreciate such a concession. I lived on store-bought bagels and salad for the duration of the conference. Over Shabbat, if attendees wanted to eat, they had to handle their cash. Cell phones, the ultimate "day-of-rest killer" were ubiquitous. I heard lots of speeches about outreach… would it hurt to have some outreach directed towards those on the traditional end of the spectrum?

I know some of my readers are saying, "You idiot! Go to the Young Israel convention next time!" But that's missing the point. I have seen in my short career the exodus of my generation from Jewish life, and the next generation's circumstance is even more dire. A URJ youth director explained how 80% of Reform kids leave Judaism after Bar/Bat Mitzvah. Gone. For good. One of the conference speakers reported that only 15% of those indentifying as Reform have any involvement in organized Jewish life. More than half say they have not attended a synagogue within the past year and cannot read Hebrew. As I've said before, more than gimmick-laden trips or political posturing, our youth need the guidance of Torah and the skeletal system of mitzvot on which to hang the flesh of their spiritual lives. A Reform movement that emphasizes these fundamentals within the panorama of Jewish options will attract American youth hungry for authenticity. We must all support one another; any failure of the Reform movement is the failure of Judaism.

I was brought up attending Reform's NFTY (National Federation of Temple Youth) activities and was nurtured by the incredible camaraderie, music and spirit. Reform Jews are amongst the most dynamic, open-hearted, innovative and passionate of our people. Now is the time to step toward the center with vibrant educational programs expressing enthusiasm for, rather than fear of, tradition. I know personally of the power of Reform camping, prayer, social justice. I am amazed by the new generation of teens and twenty-something leaders, educators and musicians. Let's get this generation hip to "old-school" Judaism, giving them tools to have a full Shabbat every week, to rejoice in the majesty of the holidays, to see that *tefillin* are cool and that opting for pork sliders and shrimp hand rolls is opting out.

The departing leader of the movement, Rabbi Eric Yoffie, gave a fascinating presidential sermon on Shabbat. Much to his surprise, his daughter Adina has become Modern Orthodox. He said the following:

"When I look at Adina, I see someone who has put God and Torah at the center of her life. In her high school days, she would often challenge me. Judaism is of transcendent importance or it is not, she would say. And if you don't believe in your gut that Judaism matters to an existing God, why bother? Do I regret her religious choices? Absolutely not. She has chosen a path that I would not choose, but it is a worthy path. We continue our discussions, which are both vigorous and loving. And every time we do so, I think about the need to respect religious approaches other than my own. This is a subject on which I need reminding, from time to time. I am a combative person; I see myself as a defender of Reform Judaism; I am quick to offer a fierce defense of my liberal principles. But sitting across from my daughter and knowing the thoughtfulness of her convictions, it is respect that I feel and express; and I remind myself to stress the authenticity of my beliefs rather than what I may see as the shortcomings of hers. This above all is what I have learned from my daughter: that if we hope to engage our children, we will need to provide those answers—answers that are religiously compelling and intellectually engaging, as well as authentically Reform…this means making it clear that as Reform Jews, there are things that God expects of us. This means saying that ritual opens us to the sacred and gives structure to the holy. This means affirming our belief that if ritual dies, Judaism dies; it is only a matter of time. This means proclaiming that Shabbat is a God-given duty, even as we know that there are many, many ways for a Jew to fulfill that duty."

May Rabbi Yoffie's wisdom permeate liberal Judaism. Let us give our kids real "informed choice" and let the chips fall where they may. Let us open the gates of tolerance to all branches of Judaism and not just to LGBTQs and the intermarried. Let Reform clergy adhere to a life of mitzvot with enthusiasm, serving as role models for congregants hungry for spiritual leadership. If any movement in Judaism is going to make radical changes, it will be Reform. They have done so repeatedly as they have shifted to a Zionist platform and evolved from Classical Reform to a movement that adopted the latest batch of tradition-infused Ten Principles. The terse Union Prayer Book has been replaced by the Chassidic-inspired Mishkan T'filah *siddur*. It may be too late for the millions who have chosen to disengage from the mission of the Chosen People. But for those incredible young musicians who were singing late into the night of their love for God, let's give them a fighting chance at having Jewish progeny. Is it fair only Rabbi Yoffie be assured of such a luxury?

Nurturing Jewish Educators: NewCAJE OutRAJE

♫ TREE OF LIFE ♫

joyjud.com/m/tol

Let the Torah be our light
Please make our future bright
And let Your spirit dwell within us
As Your message we proclaim
Our voices praise Your Name
The Tree of Life will guide us

Kohanecha yilb'shu tzedek
V'chasidecha y'raneynu
Ki lekach tov natati lachem
Torati al ta'azovu

Eitz Chayim hi lamachazikim ba...

Each summer I attend the NewCAJE conference, the incarnation of the now defunct Coalition for Advancement in Jewish Education. One year, we gathered at the American Hebrew Academy campus in steamy, midsummer Greensboro, NC for five days of celebration, study and connection. I offered a ninety-minute workshop each day for dedicated teachers hungry for the information. I enjoyed the chance to hear both the veterans in Jewish music and the "up and coming" talent in concert. I attended lectures from master teachers, lost myself in tall tales spun by spellbinding storytellers and listened in wonderment to a fifty-voice choir that formed over the course of the conference. And every night, from midnight till 3am, I helped lead a motley crew of singers gathered in *"kumzitz mafia"* jam sessions of outrageous proportions.

My own concert was on closing night. What a gift to sing for a standing-room-only house that knew every lyric of my songs. I asked to keep the houselights up so I could see the joy visible on the faces of the veteran "CAJE-*niks*" whom I've grown to love, who have faithfully supported me on this multiple-decade odyssey as a Jewish performer-composer. These are the community leaders who rally to bring me to their congregations, who cherish my albums, who share my music with their peers and students. Many of them met me when I was single and over the course of twenty-five-plus CAJE conferences have followed my journey through engagement, marriage and becoming a father of three. Scarcely a CAJE meal goes by without having to break out pictures of my family.

I met one of my heroes, Debbie Friedman, at my first CAJE in 1992. I had sung her songs as a kid at camp and now I had the chance to share the stage with her. It just as well could have been Paul McCartney. Well, almost. That year, shining songstress Julie Silver and I were the new artists debuting on the big USC stage. Just before my set, with over two thousand in attendance, the power went out in the expansive theater. Nothing but emergency lights and acoustic instruments were functioning. Regardless, organizers Craig Taubman and Doug Cotler pushed me out on the stage to do my set unamplified. It was a tough break but the experience gave me an indelible memory of panic, frustration and eventually triumph. Only sax, piano, drums and acoustic guitar were audible behind my straining vocals. No one seemed to mind! I gave out a four-song demo cassette of my first Jewish tunes to everyone in the audience and subsequently started getting invitations to perform out of town. Amazing!

My favorite aspect of this conference is its emphasis on pluralism. Reform, Conservative and Orthodox learn, dine and sing together under one roof. For most of us, it's the ONLY time we experience such harmony and tolerance. *Pirkei Avot* (4:1) describes a wise person as one who learns from everyone. Only at CAJE do I really see this precept in full bloom. CAJE is nothing less than a microcosm of a world redeemed. Everyone is a bit uncomfortable and everyone grows. In the safe space of one's own movement, it's easy to say, "We're all in this together." But CAJE isn't the Biennial or OU conference. It's a true spiritual coalition, where all the colorful members of the tribe have something to add.

I credit CAJE for making me a Jewish educator. Each year I challenge myself to research and present new workshops on revelant Jewish subjects. These become the courses I deliver on my Shabbatons and artist-in-residence programs. Thanks to CAJE, I have nearly fifty topics listed on my website ready to go. CAJE is a benchmark in my year, the start of my touring season and a good excuse to finish new recordings and sheet music collections so I have them shrink-wrapped for this eager market. CAJE is not only for teachers; administrators, rabbis, cantors, composers, storytellers and artists are all nurtured by this special week of sharing, study and song. Perhaps the most compelling reason they return is the camaraderie. What a gift to belong to such an esteemed, generous family.

Sadly, teachers are usually on the low end of the socio-economic totem pole. Those charged with ushering the youngest generation into the fold rarely can afford to live in the neighborhoods of the synagogues they serve. CAJE gives these righteous individuals a chance for recognition and appreciation. Some chastise the organization, saying it's nothing more than adult Jewish summer camp. But if summer camp is the "great white hope" for Jewish kids, then why can't the teachers of our students have their moment in the sun?

Now I'm going to get on my soapbox. In March of 2009, CAJE went bankrupt. It was half a million dollars in debt and the international Jewish community let it fail. True, this was in the aftermath of the great recession and Madoff scandal. CAJE had too much overhead and the principals should have screamed louder for help. But for a infinitesimal percentage of the total given to Jewish causes, CAJE could have been revived. Individual benefactors donate millions to sponsor operas, university buildings and MRI machines. Who will take a stand for Jewish education? Where are our knights in shining armor?

At any given CAJE conference, many presenters are neophytes in their field. Where else will they have the chance to hone their craft in such a compassionate milieu? Israeli educators like Rav Yosef Liebowitz come because CAJE-niks are the best market for his online learning programs. Judaica suppliers and booksellers flock to merchandise their wares at the expo, attracted by a captive audience who will likely share their products with friends back home. If not for CAJE, Joel Grishaver might not have his flourishing Torah Aura publishing company, Nancy Katz wouldn't be covering the country in painted silk and Bruce David's amazing stained glass would not grace so many sanctuaries.

NewCAJE emerged out of the ashes in 2010. Thanks to the gumption of CAJE veterans like Cherie Koller-Fox, the conference is wobbling on new legs. Recently Cherie was overjoyed that a $9,000 matching grant was established. She's counting on underpaid teachers to come up with funds to keep this dream alive. My friends, NewCAJE needs $900,000 to revitalize this movement. $9,000? Oy! Where are the Jewish Federations of North America? How about a nationwide Bureau of Jewish Education allotment to this cause? Teachers used to have a source of funds from their synagogue or day school for annual enrichment programs. Professional development is a cost of doing business! Why are these monies disappearing? Benefactors must be solicited to cover the conference costs for the educators at their home institutions. NewCAJE giving opportunities (with naming rights) abound! One could subsidize the young leadership program, college program, new teacher recognition, veteran teacher awards, childcare, evening entertainment or fine arts.

I finished my Greensboro NewCAJE concert with a rendition of Debbie Friedman's "T'filat Haderech" song. It's the very melody I spontaneously sang with my fellow musicians at her funeral. It is the song I chose to sing at the Los Angeles commemoration of her *shloshim*. Now it's a heartfelt memorial on my "Power of the Soul" album. I brought instrumental tracks of my band playing this tune and set up high quality stereo mics to record the NewCAJE audience on the final chorus. If you listen to the track you will experience the love shared by this amazing group of educators. Hear how much we need and support each other. Hear the sound of Jewish unity. May NewCAJE continue to rally and raise awareness of the urgency of excellence in Jewish education.

Terror at the General Assembly Conference

♫ ONE HAND, ONE HEART ♫

joyjud.com/m/ohh

*Sometimes you need a friend to share the
sadness
Sometimes it seems that no one understands
All the lies cannot disguise
The rage and anger building up
So tired you feel like giving up
From out of the depths
You reach for a helping hand*

*When there's pain we all cry
When there's death we all die inside
With one hand and one heart we reach for
You*

*Sometimes a light can only shine in darkness
Sometimes the darkness never seems to end
How many lifetimes snatched away
Before we see the break of day
With all of our hearts we try to understand*

*One is the heart that beats within my people
One is the reason why
Ten thousand miles between me and my
brothers
Reading yesterday's news
And another voice inside me dies*

O nce in a while I am gifted with what I call a "trifecta" on the road. That is to say, I perform on any given trip for synagogues of all the major Jewish denominations. One such week, I had the fortune to cap off a city-per-day binge when I landed in New Orleans for the Jewish Federation's annual General Assembly conference (GA). I started in New Jersey where I led the *davening* and *ruach* (spirited music) for the Aish HaTorah Partners Conference, a gathering of 750 black-hatted rabbis and their friends from around the world. Then to New York where my brother Yom Tov and I entertained Chassidim in Boro Park, followed by St. Louis where I worked with three Jewish day schools and led a Shabbaton and concert at the University City synagogue. Then I traveled to perform at the stately Touro Synagogue of New Orleans, a historic Reform landmark, and from there, I sang for the Conservative to Modern Orthodox crowd at a New Orleans Hebrew Day School fundraiser. I get sublime satisfaction that my career allows me to sing for all Jews, wherever they may be, hopefully cajoling my audiences into deeper connection with each other, with Israel and their Creator.

The destruction of Hurricane Katrina was still very much in the forefront of NOLA consciousness, with an emphasis on rebirth and civic pride. My friend Rob Steinberg, who put me up (and put up with me), was a DJ at the local classic jazz station, WWOZ. That makes him a definitive authority on the hottest musicians in town and the clubs they haunt, to which we hopped nightly. I'm not sure if the locals were sober enough to notice that during the GA, every third guy wore a *kippah.*

Over four thousand business-attired Jewish Federation delegates wandered the vast square footage of the Sheraton and Marriott hotels downtown. From the vast exhibit hall to the ad hoc kosher deli in one of the ballrooms, there was an old friend around every corner. The GA is the Super Bowl of Jewish geography! I have been a supporter of the Federation since my childhood. My parents were active donors and as a kid, I would help man the phones on Super Sunday. In my single years, the Metropolitan Leadership Development Group became my monthly networking "hang" and I trained to solicit big gifts. I believe contributing to one's local Federation is non-optional. It is the address for the widest variety of needy in any given town and among the biggest benefactors to Israel. I may not agree with all the choices of allocations, but I won't throw the "baby out with the bathwater." As I said in the Asey L'cha Rav chapter, the *Mishna* proscribes us from distancing ourselves from community. Cutting the Federation out of one's *tzedakah* allocation violates this principle.

Just like the Reform Biennial, one of the highlights of the GA is experiencing the plenary sessions which feature the world's most prestigious speakers. I was particularly excited to hear Benjamin Netanyahu and managed to find a friend with an extra seat in the front row. The myriad opening speakers were so uplifting that the Prime Minister's talk seemed anticlimactic. One young man, Moises Lemor, inspired us with his saga of growing up in a Zionist family in Peru, making *aliyah* (emigrating to Israel) solo and serving proudly in the IDF. I was brought to tears by a young Hungarian woman who learned she was Jewish as a fifteen-year-old at her father's funeral. One comment in particular touched me deeply: upon discovering her heritage, she took the opportunity to "unwrap Judaism like a treasure." It made me wonder if we should purposefully deny American Jewish kids any connection with their heritage until they are mature enough to value it.

The hopeful messages soon gave way to an "Ever-dying People" (as opposed to eternal) dissertation from Netanyahu. He bemoaned the Iranian nuclear threat, the advancing trend of the de-legitimization of Israel and the difficulty of negotiating peace with a partner that will not recognize the Jewish state. He pointed to the failure of Herzl's tenuous dream that Israel's rebirth would end anti-Semitism. My smile soon diminished and I descended into a catatonic state of "bad news overload."

Then the terror began. A young woman just a few rows behind me stood up and chanted, "The settlements delegitimize Israel." She continued to scream this mantra while robust African-American guards dragged her a few hundred yards to the back exit. The other four hecklers timed their nefarious attack with every-five-minute precision. The honored leader of the Jewish people could only stand in silence and frustration. The crowd attempted to drown out the perpetrators with screams of their own, exacerbating the damage. No bombs went off, but I felt like my insides were turned to jelly. These hecklers weren't Palestinians; they were young, idealistic <u>Jews</u> with the willingness to deliver this ultimate "low blow" to the proceedings. I've never witnessed a better excuse to deploy a Taser. We can be our own worst enemy.

After the speech, I hung my head low and limped out of the imposing ballroom. I spoke of my shock to one of my peers on the Jewish music circuit. He responded, "While I didn't like the interruptions, I'm glad the kids had their moment of protest." Yes, I felt very alone. The Arabs we can handle. But threats from within? I recalled the peculiar "*V'lmalshinim*" paragraph in our *Sh'moneh Esrei* prayer. Composed as the nineteenth blessing of an eighteen-blessing suite, it pinpoints the dire threat of Jews who act as informers, who endanger the well being of the nation and corrode the integrity of the common heart we share. Yes, at times the Jewish State is deserving of criticism, but to actively sow the seeds of Jew hatred amongst our enemies is folly. Internal strife is the only thing that can bring us down. "Blessed are You, Hashem, Who breaks enemies and humbles wanton sinners."

BDS (Boycott, Divest, Sanction) is a particularly troubling front in the propaganda war against Israel. A nefarious tactic of the movement is threatening top-name artists and ensembles booked to perform in Israel. No, it is not the brainchild of Neo-Nazis. BDS was founded by Ofer Neiman and his fellow Israeli saboteurs. They protest publicly, picket concerts and launch campaigns on the web to intimidate acts into cancelling appearances. The Israeli government refers to this internal mischief as "cultural terrorism." Rock stars who dare not risk upsetting legions of politically-correct fans are quick to cancel. There have even been anonymous threats against the artists' children! We like to blame misguided singers like Pink Floyd's Roger Waters, but Ofer and his friends are truly the instigators of this disaster. They are emboldening radicals plotting our death, throwing kerosene on the flames of scorching public opinion and causing irreparable dissention from within.

We live in a time of acute polarization. The Holocaust taught that doing nothing, just standing idly by, places one in partnership with the perpetrators. Elton John, Rihanna, Rod Stewart, Metallica and Ozzy Osborne broke the boycott and performed in Israel anyway. That makes me want to go out and buy some heavy metal. Elvis Costello, Annie Lennox and Lorde cancelled. Red Shoes, Sweet Dreams and Royals will never sound as good to me. Arab-Israeli singer Nasreen Qadri described the destructiveness of BDS best: "It's counter-productive and only hurting those who wish to promote peace…this approach is hurting me as an Muslim Arab woman…those who call for boycott are only trying to divide us, to shut down the music. I will not be part of that." Jews and gentiles alike can take a stand against BDS on social media and by visiting Israel, buying Israeli products and supporting organizations like AIPAC and Stand With Us. We must boycott any organizations that would boycott us. Any assault on Israel is an assault against the Jewish People.

I'm reminded of the old joke about two elderly Jewish men on a park bench. While one is reading the Jerusalem Post, he notices his friend is captivated by an radical Arabic newspaper. "How can you do that?" he cried. His friend replied, "You read about Jews being persecuted, attacked, assimilated. I read that Jews own the banks, control the media and rule the world!"

In the macro sense, Israel is brow beaten in the worldwide media and faces dire threats from its nefarious neighbors and from within. In the micro realm, however, there is room for celebration. Jewish Federations continue to lift the needy from poverty to self sufficiency. They serve as a miraculous safety net for frail seniors, Holocaust survivors, immigrants and those with special needs. Amazing organizations are galvanizing young Jews: Birthright, Ramah, Aish, Chabad, JAM, Hasbara, NFTY, Nefesh B'Nefesh, Jewish Rock Radio. Witness the strength of the Internet to unite and inform those who defend Israel. Want to regain the feeling that anything is possible for the Jewish People? Don't look to CNN or the New York Times. Avoid AP and Reuters. Instead, try researching Jewish Community Heroes, the accomplishments of the Joint Distribution Committee, IDF field hospitals, Tomchei Shabbas, Jewish Life Television, Israeli High Tech.

My takeaway from the GA? When we are united, no obstacle is insurmountable. I pray for robust health for Jewish Federations nationwide and for their leadership to direct funding judiciously. The priority should be programs inspiring Jewish unity. Together we can defeat any enemy. We can turn terror into honor, dissonance into harmony, hopelessness into promise. We gave the world Hatikvah, the hope. And God willing, soon, we will give the world peace.

Jewish in America: The United States of Israel

♫ WE ARE AMERICA ♫

joyjud.com/m/waa

From sea to shining sea, united we remain
Grateful to the ones who stand for freedom
To show their sacrifice wasn't made in vain
The gift they gave will never be forgotten

We are America, America
Looking out for one another
Standing tall with all those
Who defend the stars and stripes
We are America, America
We are all sisters and brothers
We'll sing till every nation
Every person on this planet lives in peace

Our grandparents were dreamers
Who came from far and near
Searching for justice and equality
Where one could stake a claim
Raise a family without fear
Where courage and humanity will never disappear

O beautiful for spacious skies
For amber waves of grain
For purple mountain majesties
United we remain

Most American Jews are conflicted about Christmas but believe Thanksgiving is for everyone. We love turkey and stuffing and resonate with the concept of gratitude. Jews celebrate Thanksgiving everyday. Interestingly, both turkey and the act of giving thanks are called "*hodu*" in Hebrew. Thanks to the wisdom of the authors of the constitution, Jews were given a sanctuary where they could flourish in freedom. We are living proof of the power of free markets, access to education and social mobility. My Grandpa Sam came to this country as a penniless teenager from a one-horse town in Transylvania. He built a thriving business and in the next generation his three sons rose to prominence: a successful graduate from Harvard Law, a garment industry tycoon and an attorney/opera impresario. God bless America! As remarkable as our family saga is, we are certainly not alone. The following is a discussion of the symbiotic relationship between the Land of the Free and the People of the Book.

It was my eleven-year-old daughter Sarah's turn to join me on one of my tours. In between my shows in the Mainline and Yardley suburbs of Philly, we spent the days enjoying kid-friendly, educational outings. The thing to do in the City of Brotherly Love is run the Rocky Steps, visit Independence Hall and for kosher consumers, dine at the kosher vegan Chinese eatery downtown. We didn't expect to be embraced by Judaic icons everywhere we turned. I explained to Sarah how the Liberty Bell quotes our Torah, "Proclaim liberty throughout all the land…" (*Vayikra*/Leviticus 25:10), but the full scope of the Jewish contribution to America only became apparent after visiting two prominent tourist traps in the center of town. The high-tech Constitution Center credits Jewish ideology in guiding the vision of our founding fathers. These were deeply religious men who took their cues from the Bible and even considered making Hebrew the national tongue. Upon seeing my *kippah,* some tourists stated: "We love the Jewish people" or "We stand with Israel." Of course, the Jews that stopped us asked, "Oh, do you know 'so and so' from Sherman Oaks?" We saw exhibits highlighting prominent Jews in government and those who helped build the economy or promote civil rights. I could see the pride in Sarah's fifth-grade eyes as she witnessed evidence of her heritage in this beautifully realized testimony to our American democratic experiment.

Across the street stands the sparkling new National Museum of American Jewish History. It's a stunning 100,000 square foot, five story, state-of-the-art *nachas* factory for members of the tribe. We began the panoramic historical journey on the fourth floor, which is set in the mid-1600s, and worked our way down to the modern day on the ground floor. There we pondered Irving Berlin's piano, Sandy Koufax's mitt and Spielberg's filmography. This multimedia exploration of Jewish accomplishment will hopefully overturn ignorance-based anti-Semitism thanks to the portrayal of the selfless contributions of Jewish leaders and the degree Judaism has informed American values.

Several months later, I had the thrill of introducing my family to the State of Virginia, one of my favorite stomping grounds. I had just begun a new gig leading High Holidays in the lively vacation destination of Virginia Beach. Rosh Hashana weekend coincided with the annual end-of-summer Neptune Festival. Each day we walked the mile from our oceanfront condo to *shul* along an epic beach boardwalk art festival featuring multiple live rock bands. Scores of food stands beckoned with *treif* delights. My *shtetl*-raised kids remarked, "so much food and nothing's kosher?" I promised them that if we just *davened* hard enough we would find something we could eat. We got into a huddle next to the dog adoption booth, composed a spontaneous prayer for sustenance and then continued through the array of po' boy, kettle corn and funnel cake purveyors. Sure enough, at the end of grub row we found a Sabra booth where handsome young Israelis danced to Mid-East disco while distributing free hummus and pita chips—Halleluyah!

With a week to wander the countryside before Yom Kippur, we explored Colonial Williamsburg and then continued north through Richmond to our friend's home in Potomac, Maryland. For kids from L.A. where "really old stuff" is from the 1960s, visiting these 1700s neighborhoods was quite a treat. In advance of the trip, I assembled an overflowing itinerary and booked "E-ticket" Washington D.C. highlights with the help of my congressman, Henry Waxman. We secured tours of the galleries of Senate, Congress and the Supreme Court, plus a "never tell me the odds" moment: we won the lottery to obtain a rare pass into the White House where we enjoyed a personal tour from the resident Marines and played with the Obamas' adorable Portuguese Water Dog, Bo. It's no mystery why the celebrity canine comes when he is called ("*bo*" means come in Hebrew). Following that adventure, my best buddy

Chuck hooked us up with his brother Mike Sparks, a captain in the Navy, who welcomed us to peruse the inner-sanctum of the Pentagon.

One cannot visit D.C. without viewing the venerable monuments: we marveled at the Lincoln, Jefferson, Washington, WWII and Vietnam memorials and gawked at the enormous statue of Martin Luther King the week of its public unveiling. Yes, we got to know the underground Metro very well. Finally, we powered the museums: Holocaust, National Gallery, American Art, Portrait Gallery, National Sculpture Garden, Natural History and last but not least, our favorite, the Spy Museum. No, I'm not exaggerating—we did it all! We went bowling, shopped in trendy Georgetown, visited Chinatown, toured the historic 6th and I Synagogue and hiked in Great Falls National Park, all in five whirlwind days.

I'm reporting this travelogue to my dear readers not so you pity my exhausted children, but to highlight the Jewish presence in our nation's capital. One obvious landmark is the National Museum of the Holocaust, perhaps the most compelling testimony to the horror of Nazism in North America. This museum isn't hidden in a JCC. It's one of the nineteen official Smithsonian museums and 90% of attendees are gentile. Not only are we free to pursue our faith in this country; by locating the museum on the imposing central mall, it clarifies we occupy a place of honor and prestige. We sleep better knowing our host country stands with us saying, "Never again!" The Smithsonian art galleries feature Chagall and Modigliani right up there with the Monets and Renoirs. We watched senators in action and my kids noted that the two representatives from our state are proud Jewish women. By chance (is it ever really chance?) during our half hour in the Congressional gallery, the bill on the floor was an attempt by L.A. big business to do away with Clean Air Act provisions. It was being challenged by our own M.O.T. (member of the tribe), Congressman Waxman. Even the Spy Museum highlighted tales of the *Mossad* and displays describing the ignominious sagas of Jonathan Pollard and Ethel and Julius Rosenberg. A few blocks from the Lincoln Memorial lies perhaps the most important Jewish site of all: Eli's Restaurant, a glatt kosher eatery where we rested our tired feet and feasted every night before heading back to Potomac.

Over the past two centuries, the Jewish people have led lives of unprecedented blessing in the Golden Medina. We have struggled for acceptance, marched for tolerance and enjoyed breakthroughs in every field. The Jews are perhaps the best evidence of the potential of the cherished American value of freedom. Given the chance, Jews manage to excel in every vocation, from Broadway to boxing, garments to gambling, physics to physique. For the past century, Jewish Hollywood has defined the American Dream and exported that mythology to a world hungry for hope. Our innate financial aptitude has guided American economics. We even compose classic Christmas carols!

I pray we baffle demographers predicting our demise by initiating a renaissance in our beloved home away from Homeland. May a renewed focus on the Joy of Judaism encourage American Jews to affiliate, propagate and engage in mitzvot, having fun in the process. No need to reinvent the wheel. We already have the formula for survival…we just need to reread our notes. God willing the United States, by adopting our mission statement, will share our divine mandate as a light unto nations.

PART NINE

Raising Jewish Kids

IN THIS SECTION:

Love and Marriage 283

Early Childhood: Telescope Parenting 286

Day School: The Key to Continuity 291

Reward and Punishment: The Gift of a Reprimand 295

The Teenage Years: Better Run Away 299

Keeping Consistency Constant 304

Kids on Meds: Mood-Altering Drugs 308

A Love Letter to my College-Bound Son 311

Dear YULA Graduates: A Commencement Speech 316

The Baby and the Bathwater 319

OVERVIEW

This section is a guide to using the tools of Judaism to build the leaders of tomorrow. We will discuss the importance of the institution of marriage, surviving early childhood and tangling with teenagers on the cusp of college. I highlight the importance of Jewish day school education, rigorous but loving discipline, consistency in parenting and the dilemma of placing kids on meds. Lastly, I discuss the process of individuation and techniques for launching successful, well-balanced Jewish young adults into the fray of modern society. Regardless whether one is pre or post-childrearing, or totally uninterested in little people, I believe the following chapters will entertain with Torah insights and an assortment of adventures featuring this one man's occasionally dysfunctional family.

The last three chapters of this section are missives to my three children. One may notice a progression from one to the next. The letter to Max is filled with optimism, extolling the opportunities awaiting him in Israel and life in general. Jesse's chapter is actually a speech I wrote to deliver at his high school graduation ceremony. It is filled with caveats since I had witnessed the challenges facing Max and his peers upon returning from their gap year. Some were catapulted into dedicated observance by a powerful yeshiva or seminary experience. Some met their *basheret* (destined mate) or opted to start their adult lives as newly minted Israeli citizens. But many broke their parents' hearts as their ties to *Yiddishkeit* withered when encountering American college life, secular peers and the job market.

My letter to Sarah was the last chapter written for "The Joy of Judaism." It came at a time I saw some of my sons' *chevra* go from indifference to animosity toward tradition. I noticed a trend of adhering to the confines of negative mitzvot in order to fit in with the community, coupled with the wholesale abandonment of positive mitzvot like prayer, *tefillin* and study. Setting aside mobile phones on Shabbat and holidays seems to be a particularly challenging hurdle. I'm confident many of these formerly-*frum* twenty-somethings will make it back. As they age, they will have spiritual awakenings, especially when they want to give their own children the gift of family-focused Shabbat and Yom Tovim.

The likelihood of their return is proportional to the amount of joy in their upbringing. The daily blessing we recite for Torah study asks God to make it sweet in our mouths. Those raised with sweetness will share it, those with bitter memories will spare their offspring the *tsuris* (pain). Our Modern Orthodox youth's diminishing commitment has a silver lining: it makes parents' prayers more intense and lessens our propensity to develop smug, self-satified attitudes. In a perfect world, dotting the i's and crossing the t's in Jewish observance is the antidote to apathy and the guarantor of Jewish grandchildren. I'm discovering, however, that it's not a perfect world, there is no magic bullet and each individual must find his or her own way.

Love and Marriage

Baby, I've been thinking
The time is really right
You are on my mind each morning
And in my dreams at night

I could write it in a letter
And attach it to a ring
But I'd feel so much more comfortable
If I simply try to sing

The rest of my life
From now until the end of my days

I want the rest of my life
The rest of my life to start right away

Guess I'm ready for my future
To follow through with this romance
Just to think of being without you
Well, I don't want to take the chance

Now the bridge is long and narrow
And the water will be wide
But there ain't no river I can't cross
If you are by my side

I believe having children is the greatest gift available to humankind. Both the pain and pleasure involved in the effort is life's sweetest music. Shira and I gawk in amazement at our robust college-age kids. Where did these full-sized people come from? Our three blessings, Max, Jesse and Sarah, are the net result of decades of guidance, love and obsession. We want the *nachas* of childrearing for all young Jewish people and the entire world.

One might think that babies are endangered species. Not so much in our neighborhood where most *shuls* sport jam-packed stroller parking lots. In most other cities I visit, however, infants are in short supply. Synagogues are merging, religious schools are sparsely attended and only a few B'nai Mitzvah are celebrated each year. College grads raised in suburbia move to the big city and don't return. Before long, the median age in suburban pews pushes into AARP territory.

Growing up in L.A., I noted that few of my peers got married before their mid-thirties. The ones who did get hitched waited a while until they were "ready" to have children. Couldn't they hear the ticking crescendo of that biological clock? Many had to resort to heroics to facilitate conception. American men tend to stretch their myopic, self-absorbed teenage-hood into middle age. Most of my musician friends never married and if they did, chose to remain childless. The U.S. is approaching Europe's ambivalence towards traditional marriage and risks reaching a birthrate so low that it cannot sustain society as we know it. We're choosing convenience over custody, belongings over babies.

I recognize that the current challenges to starting a family are unprecedented. According to author Simon Sinek, millennials are entitled, impatient and addicted to instant gratification. Many lack married parents as role models and forgo organized religion. While my generation enjoyed a 90% marriage rate, Time Magazine reports that for millennials, the rate will drop to 70%. They are coming of age in an economy offering high rates of employment but unprecedented "underemployment," where workers with skills are stuck in low paying, temporary jobs. I can still hear my father saying that a man needs a steady income before endeavoring to start a family. Now that "steady incomes" are increasingly elusive for young adults, it's no wonder marriage gets postponed indefinitely. A Gallup Poll indicates only 9% say they <u>don't</u> want to get married and cite lack of an economic foundation as the primary barrier. Getting married used to be the beginning of adulthood. Now it's seen as the capstone of adulthood, to be endeavored only when one is "set." I hear newlyweds blame the economy as a primary reason for limiting family size. Maybe we should publicize the proverb, "Babies bring their own bread."

Getting married young is a great idea when both parties are mature and aware of life goals. I have noticed that Israeli kids reach this milestone nearly a decade before their American counterparts. Whereas Israelis endure the reality check of mandatory conscription and daily threats on the borders, Americans have things comparatively easy. Shira reminds me that neither of us were emotionally ready to meet one another until our late twenties. Once in the community, however, we found powerful examples of tight-knit families. We saw firsthand how 24/7 affiliation offers hands-on support and ancient strategies to keep marriages strong. Taking on a Torah-guided life is perhaps the most effective way to give new couples common goals, goals that are eternal, nurturing and meaningful.

Some of my friends are perpetually single and happy. Most, however, long to have someone to witness their lives, with whom they can celebrate milestones and grow old. Some have intense regret they didn't close the deal when they had periods of romance. They were too busy, unsettled or didn't want to reward their parents for years of guilt. Interestingly, the Talmudic passage recommending teaching kids to swim also stresses that a parent's duty is getting them married. This point seems to be lost on adherents of all denominations except perhaps *Charedim* who still engage in arranging *shidduchim* (matchmaking). Getting nudged by parents who are hoping for grandchildren is a good thing!

I had very little marital direction from my parents or the Conservative movement. My dad encouraged me to sow my wild oats and relish in the pursuit. He also gave me that aforementioned advice that I find so destructive: to wait until I had a steady income before seriously dating. I didn't have the marriage word in my vocabulary until I was nearly thirty. Young couples in our community take the exciting ride of starting careers during their early twenties, but they share the adventure with their *bashert* (destined mate) and bring multiple offspring into the world in the process. The "Princeton Mom" Susan Patton made headlines by claiming that women should spend seventy-five percent of their time in college looking for a man. Soon they will be unleashed on the job market and singles scene and will not enjoy the same unpretentious setting in which they can commune with such a large, captive audience of eligible mates.

If Jewish parents can accept their role of nudge-in-chief, our prone-to-suggestion offspring will be more likely to marry. As it stands now, most kids spend a post-college decade drifting in and out of multiple relationships. Precious time is wasted, hearts are broken and scar tissue develops. We certainly aren't motivated to maturity or commitment by secular society. Our media portrays marital commitment as frightening, foolhardy or for wimps who don't have the backbone to go it alone. Interestingly, the words religious and obligation share the Latin root, LIG. Lig refers to connection, like ligament, connective tissue. Parents in all denominations can inspire children to be reLIGious Jews, <u>connecting</u> with the mission and future of the Jewish People by marrying within the faith. What could be the harm in a Jewish Federation campaign encouraging our youth to marry Jews, with incentive to do so before the age of twenty-five? Our survival is predicated on doing whatever it takes to inspire the creation of joyful Jewish families.

The data may illustrate demographic disaster in the Liberal streams of Judaism, but the Orthodox movement is also facing tremendous challenges. Increasing numbers of marriages end in divorce. There is a *shiddach* (match) crisis, primarily among Jewish women. The cost of *frum* family life is prohibitive. The pressure to conform in *Charedi* society is intense, with marriage-related paranoia at the top of the list. My fifteen-year-old Israeli nephew was lamenting about having to change schools. I asked him if he was nervous about going to a new environment. He responded that he wasn't worried for himself, he just felt bad for the other boys in this school who felt like "damaged fruit." Even at fifteen, his fellow students were aware this "lesser" academy could damage their ability to find good *shidduchim*.

Marriage isn't for everyone. I have friends with significant personality problems and/or addictions who got married in an attempt to be less miserable. Some had children for the same reason. This phenomenon doesn't bode well for the next generation. Those prone to violence, abusive acts, addictions or uncontrolled anger must take radical measures to mitigate their own pathology before attempting the monumental task of childrearing. A prerequisite to parenting is robust emotional <u>and</u> physical health. We owe it to our kids to model healthy behaviors by way of example, like sobriety, altruism, eating right and staying in shape. Part of responsible parenting is realizing that one's vices affect everybody. Personal integrity is sacrificed when one's essence is split into a public angel and a private deviate. That's pure poison to the soul and a destroyer of the Joy of Judaism. And what happens if those "closed doors" accidentally open? Oy vey.

The Talmud describes a *chazzan* (cantor) based on the acronym of the word: he must be capable, with vision (*chozeh*), mature (*zakan*, bearded) and married (*nesui*). No, I'm not insisting cantors need beards. I point this out because, according to our sages, marriage and childrearing are the ultimate training course for the profession and by extension, any profession of import. Married men learn to put spouse and children first, gain humility and tame their wild ways. According to an Institute on Aging study, society benefits, and the men benefit: single men have six times the probability of being incarcerated, they are less connected to their parents and siblings and they make 25% less income than married counterparts. Married men and women are more likely to rate their health as excellent than singles of the same age. Smoking rates are nearly double for singles, and mortality rates are significantly higher. To summarize, parents who love their kids should get them married!

Jews aren't Jews based on belief. If we were, we could opt into Christianity or Buddism on a whim and leave Judaism behind. With Jews it's not so simple. We are a People, a Nation. We're Jewish because we have Jewish mothers or because we convert. We need more Jewish mothers! May we put marriage and childrearing at the forefront of our agenda, astounding those predicting our demise.

Kedushah • Tefillah • Shabbat • Community • Torah • Prophets • Aliyah • Pesach • Teshuva • Weddi
Spirituality • Holiness • Emunah • Diaspora • Bris Milah • Simcha • Halacha • Bitachon • Holiday
Covenant • Tribe • Israel • Mitzvot • Prayer • Mashiach • Rabbis • Shabbat • Community • Torah • Prop
Aliyah • Pesach • Teshuva • Wedding • Spirituality • Holiness • Emunah • Diaspora • Bris Mil
Simcha • Halacha • Bitachon • Covenant • Bar Mitzvah • Tribe • Israel • Mitzvot • Prayer • Mashia
Rabbis • Shabbat • Community • Torah • Prophets • Aliyah • Pesach • Teshuva • Wedding • Spiri

Early Childhood: Telescope Parenting

♫ PRECIOUS ANGEL ♫

joyjud.com/m/pca

Precious angel close your eyes
The moon will sing you a lullaby
Long past time to say goodnight
Dreaming till the morning light
Oh, oh, oh, precious angel

Precious angel close your eyes
The wind is going to whisper a lullaby
Make a wish and sail away

Gently toward another day
Oh, oh, oh, precious angel

Rest your weary head inside my
rocking arms
Oh, my angel, you don't need to weep I
am going to hold you
And keep you safe from harm
Let your body drift off to sleep

"What to Expect When You're Expecting" was our dog-eared bible for the first few years of child-rearing. Soon thereafter, my wife and I let the instinct developed from our own upbringing take over, much thanks to the great role models we had in our own parents. When our kids started speaking after about a year, they told us what they needed and we no longer had to run back to the book with every crying jag. We seem to have done all right. Our kids are in good physical and emotional shape, get along well with others and make schoolwork a priority, thank God. Once in a while we panicked, usually because one of our children fell off the minimum line of the development chart or because there was a playground bully on the loose. We had to learn about tough love to get them to sleep through the night and to survive trips to the store where they wanted everything in sight. But most of the time we've had overwhelming *nachas*. Bringing up our children has been the most fulfilling, awe-inspiring part of our lives.

I practice telescope parenting. When my kids were younger, I loved watching them run around in public and got great amusement observing their antics. I let them pick the agenda on the outing, interact with whomever they fancied and climb or explore at will. This worked great on hikes, at the beach, visiting museums or shopping malls, where they could safely wander and express themselves. It was always interesting to see who was charmed by their personalities, who would initiate conversation and who would look around for the irresponsible guardian who set the kids loose.

I wanted my kids to feel the world was safe so they would develop a sense of confidence and learn to make good judgment calls. Of course, I could only be anonymous until they would run back into my arms or if there was a need to intercede. In the meantime, I could witness their innocence and exuberance, something improbable had I imposed claustrophobic supervision like the shrill overhead rotors of a typical helicopter parent.

Telescope parenting requires giving children the spiritual space to make their own decisions. All parents engage in such activities as toilet, hygiene and manners training but most importantly, we are teaching our kids to make good choices. Shira and I discovered it was better for both parties to offer a choice rather than a command, for example, "Would you like to go to bed now or in ten minutes?" As human beings with free choice, kids crave the opportunity to make their own decisions. By offering a few alternatives, we keep the response in the realm of our preference. Allowing children to make choices also requires that they live with the consequences of bad decisions. "Are you sure you won't put on sunscreen for our day at the beach? I don't want to see you get sunburned!" When they couldn't sleep that night because their shoulders were fried, they put up much less of a fight the next time. (We called it "sunscream" because that is what our kids usually did when we applied it). With our teens, we used cash flow to make our point: they paid for their own luxuries and they knew they had to cover any damage to our property. Of course there are times when offering kids options isn't going to work and one must lay down the law. Hopefully they intuit the difference since they usually do get a choice; when none is presented, there must be a good reason.

A telescope parent empowers children to take on graduated levels of responsibility. They must be allowed to fail, to try out their own wings and deal with the consequences. But then their accomplishments are their own, they can relish in personal victories and the inevitable confidence boost. Telescope parents treat their children as adults-in-training. We raised our children with adult-level conversation since they could talk. No baby language or silly accents. We appreciated the power of words and were precise with the phrasing of admonitions. When sending our kids out into the world, we avoided grandmotherly warnings like, "Wear a jacket or you'll catch a cold," or, "Don't go that way or you'll fall." In other words, we chose our words carefully to avoid unconsciously placing a curse on their heads.

Rabbi Shlomo Wolbe, parenting expert and one of the luminaries of the *mussar* movement, describes the importance of helping a child develop independence. *Chinuch* (education) is the root of the word Chanukah. Light is a metaphor for wisdom and understanding—think of the "lightbulb" going off in one's head. Just like Chanukah is the festival of lights, so, too, is education the process of lighting up the world of a child. Once children achieve a modicum of understanding, the parent must withdraw their own flame, the heat of smothering supervision. This gives children the chance to initiate their own momentum, eventually becoming lifelong seekers of knowledge. Rabbi Wolbe compares proper *chinuch* to the kindling of the menorah in the Beit Hamikdash. He points to Rashi's comment on *Bamidbar* /Numbers 8:2 regarding the lighting of the menorah: the pilot torch must be held in place until the flames rise independently. Rabbi Wolbe concludes, "A parent must ignite the soul his child until the flames of love for Torah rise on their own."

Helicopter parenting typically results in parents transmitting their own fear and anxiety to their unwitting progeny. Parenting expert Dr. Deborah Gilboa reports that the very consequences such parents are trying to prevent are the best teachers of life lessons, lessons that could have made the overprotected kid into a *mensch*. Children accustomed to having needs micromanaged expect to always get their way and develop a sense of entitlement. By "protecting" their children's self esteem, helicopter parents send the message *my mom doesn't trust me to do this on my own* and therefore the child's confidence actually plummets. Such kids may graduate high school with undeveloped life skills since their parents are compelled to do everything for them. According to a University of Mary Washington study, over-parenting is associated with <u>higher</u> levels of child anxiety and depression. While all cultures have their Helicopter Parents, I'm guessing the Jewish People have cornered the market.

My parents were quite the opposite of helicopter parents. My brothers and I are amazed we survived our childhood. We were on the longest leash imaginable. The bus would drop us off from public school a block away and we would go right home, or not. We had a plethora of friends throughout the neighborhood, we considered the nearby Santa Monica Mountains our personal playground and had an undeveloped gully to explore right across the street. Yom Tov and I consider ourselves founders of L.A. mountain biking. We flew down the local trails on our improvised dirt bikes well before the first offical mountain bike was built in 1978. I ripped off the fenders and kickstand of my Schwinn Stingray, added knobby tires and covered the shiny royal blue finish with beige house paint so that it wouldn't look too pretty. We were "latchkey kids" before the phrase was coined. Actually, our front door was always open. Our mom didn't have a job but was the busiest lady in Brentwood and my dad often worked late and travelled overseas. Our home served as the local watering hole for our gang; the neighbors felt comfortable raiding our ample pantry and all were welcome in our pool or front yard for football games. Somehow we survived without cell phones, computers or parents curating our play dates.

As a teen, board-om was my antidote to boredom. Skateboards, surfboards, bodyboards and in the winter, my greatest thrill, strapping a pair of boards underneath a pair of trusted ski boots. I never excelled at team sports, preferring the individual expression and blissful speed offered by boards and bikes of all shapes and sizes. I was emphatic that my children graduate from riding Razor scooters to real skateboards. I pushed them, literally and figuratively, into the waves at our local Santa Monica beaches. I taught them to ski between my legs. Part of any action sport is the calculated risk of injury, and there were several times I incurred Shira's wrath when I'd bring a kid home with scraped up knees. But my children grew up learning to "go for it," a lesson I hope they took to heart.

There are caveats to telescope parenting. Kids fall down and must learn how to get back up. They get muddy, wet and sticky. They may wander too far for comfort and must be chased down. From time to time, I inadvertently exposed our precious offspring to troubled individuals. Our best outings included learning about fishing from those who fish for their supper on the Santa Monica pier or discovering how things work from construction workers. My kids witnessed the ills of drug abuse by riding bikes amongst the homeless on the Venice boardwalk and negotiating with heroin-damaged hippies selling homemade jewelry. Our adult children have had fender benders, parking tickets, F's on report cards and shattered expectations. We live in a homogenous neighborhood and they attended schools where every last kid was Jewish. I felt compelled to expose them to the melting pot of society so that they would fall in love with humanity and become open hearted to differences.

I choose to live in a world of honesty and security. That doesn't mean I leave my wallet out at the shopping mall or my car unlocked in funky neighborhoods. But when we go to the beach, we set up camp with our towels and snacks and leave them unguarded for hours while we bodyboard and explore. I let strangers borrow my iPhone. Bikes sometimes stay overnight on the front lawn. I trust vendors on Ebay and Craigslist. Acting with cavalier naiveté can backfire of course. But I'd rather take a hit once in a while than live in a state of paranoia. I want my kids to feel they are off the leash, making their own (age appropriate) decisions and trusting their fellow man. I emphasize that ninety-nine percent of the people they will meet are nice and strangers are just friends they haven't yet met. Yes, from time to time they might encounter the evil one percent, God forbid, but in the meantime they feel safe and happy in a world of goodness.

I also taught my children to be aware of danger, to trust their sixth sense and act on it. In the made-up bedtime tales I spun nearly every night, I included sagas of surviving natural disasters, stampedes at crowded sporting events and finding out that the person you thought you could beat up had a concealed weapon. Having a sense of openness and wonderment need not include being a sucker. Should they meet a member of that evil one percent, they must realize this is not someone with whom they should hang out and if pursued, to run fast. By exposing them to occasional unsavory types I gave them a taste of what that sixth sense might feel like. The aforementioned tractate of Talmud recommending parents teach kids how to swim is a *mashal* (example) for parents to teach navigating the stormy seas of life: how to "watch their butt" in dangerous situations and "kick butt" when they must. With two boys at Yeshiva University in the Washington Heights neighborhood of New York City, having street smarts is a skill they are putting to good use.

Parents never stop influencing their children. They watch our every move and store the data in a seldom seen, long-term databank, accessed periodically over the course of their lifetimes. They may profess indifference to our demands but they care very much what we think. We had billboards in our neighborhood stating: "Parents, the Anti-Drug." This campaign implores moms and dads to have heart-to-heart conversations about life matters even if they believe their children will ignore them. Even as a middle-age dad, I care about what my parents think! In a subconscious way, I still want to please them. Parental guidance is crucial to support the natural development of conscience in the child, especially when they are teenagers. Dennis Prager states that children are born selfish and narcissistic and it's up to parents to teach them goodness and ethical behavior. We certainly can't rely upon public schools for values education.

Telescope parents recognize there is no sense in trying to shield children from the vicissitudes of life. Shira and I didn't hesitate to involve the family in discussing adult matters. Our kids were aware when cash flow was tight but they also observed that it didn't vanquish our *shalom bayit* (peace in the home). Tough subjects like mortality, divorce, reproduction and business ethics were openly discussed. I brought my kids to *shiva minyanim* (services to pay respect for the deceased) throughout their lives so they learned to perceive the preciousness of time and the importance of cherishing their loved ones. I taught honesty by ensuring they witnessed me returning money to cashiers when I received too much change. I was careful to pay full price admission to Disneyland for my ten-year-old; he knew he was too old for the child ticket and getting him to lie would have unraveled years of integrity training.

Shira and I believe we are constantly modeling how to treat one's spouse and hope these unspoken lessons result in successful relationships for our offspring. We are candid with our unabashed love for one another. As I mentioned, I get down on my knee and gaze lovingly at my wife every Friday night when I sing *Aishet Chayil* (the traditional salute to a virtuous wife), even though it embarrasses the kids. We attempt to resolve conflicts peacefully and don't let sharp word exchanges escalate. Our weekly date nights demonstrate that people who love each other make time for each other. We never engage in *lashon harah* (slander) about one another to anyone, especially our kids. One Shabbas we had a guest who kept affectionately dissing her humble husband throughout the meal. Each time, my daughter would shoot me a look indicating, "I know that's not OK!"

A final thought: practicing telescope parenting better prepares parents for the inevitable empty nest syndrome. Such parents have created a strategic distance from their children and have given them confidence to stand on their own. Parents must nurture their own individuality, avoiding the trap of defining themselves solely as mom or dad. Helicopter parents describe empty nest separation as excruciating and feel a sense of abandonment. Telescope parents certainly miss their kids but are thrilled they are functioning on their own and will eventually be off the payroll. Such parents may suggest career options but don't impose their own bias or try to shoehorn the kids into a mold. They offer a sturdy set of life tools and allow their offspring to discover themselves. They serve as living examples of refined emotional intelligence, helping kids become other-focused and excited about stewardship. They teach that adulthood is when one no longer has to "win" in every interaction—we win the game of life when we help others win.

Our children are gifts from the Creator, on loan, entrusted to our care for only a few short years. We do our best to endow them with all the wisdom and blessings we can muster so they can formulate and pursue their unique paths. Until, of course, they have too much laundry, and then they can come running home.

Day School: The Key to Continuity

Get your bod out of your bed
Put a smile on that sleepy head
Throw your legs over the side
Pretty soon you're hitting your stride

Wash your hands, wash your face
Brush your teeth all over place
Slip on a shirt, stretch on a sock
Before you know it you're ready to rock
Morning time again...

Eat some breakfast, give it a crunch
Finish your homework
Pack up your lunch
Get your backpack ready to go
Looks like you're the star of the show

Brush your hair, you're looking great
Get in the car, don't be late
Sit at your desk, pull out your pen
When the day is done we'll do it again

Parents concerned with Jewish continuity send their offspring to Jewish day school. In our community, it's not considered optional. A Jewish day school education is the ultimate weapon to fight assimilation and create a confident, informed Jewish identity. Like any private school option, Jewish day schools are costly. But that financial sacrifice in the short term engenders ultimate *nachas* in the long term. For those intent on maximizing their family's Joy of Judaism, day school is the best gift they can offer.

According to the PEJE (Partnership for Excellence in Jewish Education), day school is the best insurance that youth will engage in Jewish activities, show support for Israel, become Jewish leaders and raise their own connected kids. A less discussed attribute is the "trickle up" effect. Parents denied a Jewish education get the benefit of sweet Jewish songs and words of Torah on their kids' lips each Shabbat. They pick up Hebrew when assisting children with homework and get drawn into text study. Day school education emphasizes Judaism as a full-time gig. It's not an "add on" to one's busy life like soccer practice and favorite TV shows. Relegating Jewish education to an afternoon or two a week underlines the "add on" aspect. Hebrew School is certainly better than nothing at all, but in my experience, many kids are turned off rather than turned on. Most retain only a vague memory of precepts accumulated until puberty and live with this rudimentary, adolescent outlook for the rest of their days.

Our neighborhood is blessed with over a dozen fine educational institutions and our experience has been overwhelmingly positive. When I would ask my kids how their day went, the usual reply was, "Great!" Our daughter Sarah was regularly awarded best *davener* and helped to guide her class with heartfelt *kavanah*. Our middle son Jesse had a tight knit *chevra* of considerate schoolmates who gathered in driveways around the 'hood to shoot hoops with kippot clipped to their hyperactive heads. Our oldest son Max surpassed me in his ability to take apart a text; one year he read Homer's Odyssey AND tractate Kiddushin. Priceless *nachas*!

Of course, priceless *nachas* has a cost. The primary roadblock to universal day school access is economic. When middle class families must choose between having a roof over their heads or Jewish education, day school loses. The sad joke in our neighborhood: "Day school tuition: the best form of birth control." "Sophie's Choice" of our generation? Which kid to take out of school for lack of finances.

Established Jewish communities need only look to the old world Eastern European model of universal fundraising to make education attainable. Even the smallest *shtetl* supported the *mikvah*, the *shul* and the *cheder* (classroom). The Chicago Jewish community established the Kehilla Fund, which collects monthly donations from families of all levels of income. According to the Fund's website, "Communal funding of education is an obligation based on Jewish law. Furthermore, it is a moral responsibility of the greatest urgency. In Talmudic times, the great sage, Yehoshua Ben Gamla instituted a system of communal funding for Jewish day schools, and every Jewish community since that time has sustained a communal education system. It is only today, in the most prosperous Jewish community of all time, that Jewish families lack the communal support to educate their children."

Also in Chicago, businessman George Hanus created the "Five Percent Mandate," encouraging families to earmark five percent of their estate towards the cause. This pool of scholarship monies supplements the budgets of institutions of all denominations, making the Jewish day school option feasible for any Chicago family. These tuition-aided kids eventually become Jewishly-committed parents who send their children to day schools… entire generations of windy city Jews have been transformed by this remarkable undertaking.

I live in a community graced with fabulous wealth. There are few homes west of Downtown L.A. worth less than a million dollars. We have the Broads, Sterlings and Resnicks bequeathing art galleries and concert halls. Jewish rock stars, actors and producers are ensconced in Bel Air and Brentwood mansions. Mega malls and new home communities built by Jewish developers line our freeways; Jewish hedge fund managers, doctors and lawyers dominate the professional scene. Who will be the one to light the fire of our citywide superfund?

Modeling Jewish Commitment

The long-term success of a Jewish education is proportional to the degree parents model a love for Judaism. Day school isn't a magic bullet. Many kids within the system opt out during college years and beyond. No movement is exempt; even the Orthodox see increasing numbers of their offspring steering for the secular rather than sacred when choosing their own lifestyles. A concerned father asked the Kotzker Rebbe how he could get his kids to be devoted to Torah. The rebbe answered, "If you really want them to do this, then you yourself must spend time over the Torah, and they will do as you do. Otherwise they will not devote themselves to the Torah, but only <u>tell</u> their children to do it. And so it will go on." In other words, if we model commitment, we get commitment; if we model lip service, we get lip service. We are more likely to pass on the legacy of our actions than our philosophy.

Parents must demonstrate Joy of Judaism even if they don't feel it. Our sages suggest taking on mitzvot "*lo lishma bo lishma*" (not for the sake of heaven becomes for the sake of heaven). Go ahead…start for the wrong reasons. It all works out in the end. Make sure your kids catch you in the act of doing Jewish stuff. Mine grew up seeing me *daven* three times a day. They knew they were welcome to join me but couldn't interrupt this sacred time. I study Torah publicly in our well-trafficked kitchen. I share interesting Torah tidbits I've discovered at the dinner table. I dress up for Shabbas, even if it's "just the family." Most importantly, I don't assume my kids are getting Judaism by osmosis and I keep the subject of continuity on the table. Emphasizing continuity requires that kids witness their parents' commitment to Jewish life. How many parents with only the faintest traces of observance take umbrage at their child's choice of a gentile spouse? Is that fair? Enthusiastic, lifelong affiliation is predicated on being incubated in a loving, actively Jewish home.

Customizing Jewish Education

In *Mishlei* (Proverbs 22:6), King Solomon states, "Educate a child according to his way, even when he grows old he will not turn away from it." Some kids are aural learners and some are kinesthetic. Some are great at science and some prefer creative writing. Some can't sit still for any subject! There are many ways to touch the *neshama* within the realm of Torah. A crucial part of raising Jewish kids is helping them find their specific channel and reassuring them that their way is ideal. Day school parents must be prepared to supplement beyond the standard Talmud-based curriculum for those kids who don't have a *Gemara Kup* (a head for learning Talmud). Make sure your institution educates in all modalities and covers subjects like prayer, spirituality, prophets and mysticism. The "why" of Judaism must inform the dissemination of every subject. A well-rounded, inspiring curriculum dovetailing with the student's strengths is the key to raising a lifelong learner.

One of my superstar Jewish leader friends, Lori Palatnik, inspires Jewish kids by inspiring their mothers. Her remarkable mission is based on encouraging non-Orthodox moms with children still at home to fire up their Jewish connections. She took it upon herself to figure how to get these lucky ladies on nearly all-expenses-paid, action-packed Momentum trips to Israel. Thus far, this one woman's effort has succeeded in raising funds to send over fifteen thousand women on this life-changing Jewish Women's Rennaisance Program (JWRP). You can go too! I have helped to conduct recharging weekends for the alumni and I marvel at the passion of this once disenfranchised group. Countless children are now being nurtured in Jewish educational settings as a result. When kids see their parents making Judaism a lifelong priority, continuity programming is built into their everyday life experience.

Getting Off the Fence

For those parents unsure whether day school is worth it, trust me, IT IS! For those forced to do the public or homeschool thing due to financial limitations, join me in my quest to raise awareness of our plight by circulating this chapter and expressing your frustrations to your community leaders. If you're a benefactor motivated to donate, operators are standing by at your local Bureau of Jewish Education. For day school parents in the trenches, innovate, take on that extra job and pray for God's help. As Whitney Houston says, "I believe the children are our future...teach them well and let them lead the way!" Let me close with a selection of quotes about the efficacy of a day school education:

"Day school education is still the most effective way to create serious, committed Jews. There is a categorical difference between a child who has been educated through twelfth grade in a Jewish day school and one who has not. Every Jewish educator and honest layperson sees this immediately. The leaders of the future American Jewish community will emerge from those who have been blessed with this schooling."
—Eugene Korn, Adjunct Professor of Jewish Thought, Seton Hall University

"80% of adults with six or more years of day school training are married within the faith to another Jewish adult. By contrast, the recent Pew study showed intermarriage among non-orthodox Jews soaring above 70%"
—Kohelet Foundation

"These extra hours of Jewish studies mean that students in Jewish day schools receive extra mental stimulation such as analyzing texts, discussing ethics, studying a second or third language, and developing organizational skills."
—Joel Hoffman

"Being Jewish Very Important? A 'yes' response: day school (7-12 years) 64%, no Jewish education 36%."
—UJC Report on the National Jewish Population Survey 2000-2001

"Reinforcement at home, Hebrew School and frequent visits to Temple cannot make up for, or come close to, the level of engagement and knowledge imbued in Jewish day school students."
—Bestselling author Alina Adams

"Day school is the best place for a young Jewish person to gain Jewish cultural literacy. There are lots of places where you can gain a Jewish identity, but in terms of cultural literacy—reading, writing, developing a comfort with Jewish texts—Jewish day schools are the best places."
—Carol Ingall, Forward

"(Learning to question) fosters leadership, highlights our responsibility to act, and safeguards the freedoms we so value. Jewish schools encourage asking questions and a quest for deeper understanding. If leadership and critical thinking are important to you, a Jewish school is the right choice to make."
—Edgar Bronfman

"70% of participants at Hillel events at Northwestern University were graduates of Jewish day schools"
—Partnership for Excellence in Jewish Education

Reward and Punishment: The Gift of a Reprimand

♫ STILL MY DADDY ♫

joyjud.com/m/smd

You hear him leaving the driveway
Ten of nine
For the last forty years
He's been right on time

Sometimes he didn't make it home
Till you went off to bed
And though you felt alone
At least he made it home

He couldn't help with your homework
He had too much to do
But sometimes after you finished
He would read it through
You didn't want to interrupt
But at times you couldn't wait

And though he made you mad
He was still your dad

He is still my daddy
He's the only one I own
He is still my daddy
Guess I don't want to change him after all

Once he made up his mind
It did no good to fight
You didn't ask his opinion
But he was always right
He taught you not to give up hope
How to take it till the end
And though it may seem grim
You are a lot like him

J ews believe in a loving God Who is rooting for every individual's spiritual growth. Our liturgy is filled with constant reminders of God's love and our prayers and rituals offer myriad opportunities for returning God's grace with grateful service. On the other hand, our texts are rife with descriptions of disastrous cause and effect chain reactions resulting from arrogance, indifference and infidelity. God's love includes challenging us with real life responses to our choices. The secret of true love is tough love, the presence of consequences. But it all starts with love.

People joke that Jews have cornered the market on guilt. Common knowledge dictates that Christianity is a religion of love while Jews are more in touch with the "fear" side of the love-fear continuum. Please note that this book isn't called "The Guilt of Judaism!"

I'm a big fan of the "love" side. I serve God as a partner rather than overlord. Fear or awe is a crucial part of the equation, however. Awe infers an awareness of respect, power and a sense of wonder.

The *Sh'ma* sums up our aspiration to find balance between awe and love. The opening declaration uses two words for God, *Adonai* and *Eloheinu*. The former signifies love-femininity-mercy and the latter awe-masculinity-judgment. We then assert God's oneness, clarifying that both energies originate from the same source, but with mercy as the emphasis (*Adonai echad*). The balancing act continues with the rest of the prayer: the *V'ahavta* asserts the power of love and the next paragraph deals with reward and punishment, or perhaps more accurately, cause and effect. Peace and harmony dwells side by side with judgment and reprimand.

Children have a tough time appreciating the gift of a reprimand. Parents have a tough time doling them out. We'd rather be friends with our kids than parents to our kids. We selfishly don't want to disrupt a meal, spoil an outing or cancel a vacation. But if we're not going to be the parent, who is? One Sunday, when Max was fifteen, he woke up in a dreadful mood. He emerged from his room with a sullen expression and heaped insult on each family member. I reluctantly had to draw the line when he slammed his brother Jesse's laptop on his fingers. The punishment? His lifeline to the world, a new cell phone, was promptly snatched away and hidden. This didn't bode well for the outing we had planned that day. Max ensured all of us suffered until he was having too much fun on his bike to remember his resentment.

Our kids go berserk when we reprimand them. Sometimes it's fun to video their reactions. Tempting as it might be, I don't post the tantrums on Facebook. Thankfully, our kids are usually considerate of others and know when they are crossing the line. They have also learned when to steer clear of their mother just by reading the look on her face. But when we have to lay down the law, we let them freak out in their room during the requisite "time out." Strangely, afterwards they are especially sweet and loving. I think they intuit that structure in their lives is crucial for them to flourish. If Jesse smashed Max's fingers in the computer, Max would expect swift justice. They have learned from their Beverly Hills peers that those who are spoiled rotten turn out just that way: rotten.

Parents must be prepared to punish, but only as a last resort. Better to have rewards and positive reinforcement doled out in a calm, unruffled manner. Maintaining tranquility in the heat of battle requires that parents have an arsenal of anger management techniques like reframing and deep breathing. We must be the adult in the situation! Rabbi Shlomo Wolbe describes children's two mutually exclusive modes: learning, characterized by a relaxed state that facilitates real change, and obedience, a nervous and rebellious state inhibiting real change. Punishment may seem effective initially, but it flips children from learning mode into obedience mode, stifling long term improvement. A vicious cycle results from frequent punishment since harsher measures must be imposed, further stunting the internal growth needed to effect long term change. Calmly dispensed reprimands teach children methods to handle their own anger with peers and eventually, with their own families.

In the book, "In Forest Fields," Rabbi Shalom Arush urges us to feel gratitude for the trials we face, because in the long run, *tzuris* (problems) brings us closer to the Almighty. Judaism maintains that God only does things for our good. Part of God's role as *Avinu Malkeinu* (Our Father and King) requires dispensing love in the form of discipline or rebuke (wait till your father gets home)! Just like I had to take away Max's phone to make my point, so, too, does God give us pause for thought when it's necessary to re-orient our actions. The setback is a gift. By intervening, I show my son love. To ignore the problem would be cruel. Richard Bach sums it up in his brilliant book, *Illusions*: "To love someone unconditionally is not to care who they are or what they do. Unconditional love, on the surface, looks the same as indifference."

Sometimes our parents' love can take on strange forms. My folks are a daily presence in my life and their involvement is welcome and cherished. My father has taken upon himself the job of worrying for me. It's quite a relief I don't have to worry for myself since my dad does such a good job of it. Many of our conversations evolve from small talk about day-to-day matters to an analysis of all the problems in my life. It took me years to understand that my father isn't trying to wreck my good mood. He shows his love by ensuring I remain focused on what needs doing for my family. His broken record repetition of the uncertainty of my finances or the burden of sending my kids to private school is the way he communicates love, hidden in the "garment" of worry.

How many parents show their love in the "garment" of screaming, paranoia or nagging? My mom still admonishes that I might break a finger while skiing or skateboarding. "And then what?" she adds accusingly. She still reminds me to take my jacket because it might get cold. I love it! Some only see the silver lining of their parents' love after they have left the earth. I often refer to my song "Still My Daddy" from my "Fatherhood" album when I feel like bucking the onslaught of paternal judgment. I must consciously remind myself that my parents' caveats and tantrums represent their abiding affection.

God's reprimands may appear in the form of soul-crushing setbacks like financial disasters, illness and breakups, God forbid. Of course, it is difficult to appreciate a loving Universe when one is in the depths of despair. Overly helpful friends may advise that God only tests those whom God loves. Some might explain how God is counting on us to grow. In the thick fog of despondency, we are typically blind to the opportunities impregnating any so-called "reversal of fortune." Our appreciation of God's hand within the reprimand is directly proportional to the health of our divine relationship. For those oblivious to God's presence, setbacks are just bad luck. Sometimes it takes an enlightened guide to coach us out of the trough, to "lift our eyes" to a vision of healing, consolation and even victory. We must be that coach for our vulnerable children.

Connor Cochran, a columnist for Keyboard Magazine who became a musical collaborator of mine, wrote about a "five-year plan." According to him, one cannot judge divine reprimands until five years have transpired. In other words, feel the pain, rally and get over it. Don't overanalyze. Usually, a light shines on the inner purpose for any given "darkness" in life, thanks to the healing power of time and the gift of perspective.

One memorable day, I braved the L.A. drizzle to take my family to the book signing of a young woman who was diagnosed with ovarian cancer as a twenty-year-old. As soon as she was able to transcend the sense of victimhood, cancer gave her the incentive to take life seriously and the awareness she could counsel those in similar straits. The audience was overjoyed to hear that eight years after her lifesaving surgery, she gave birth to healthy twins. Her sister donated the eggs and thanks to the miracle of in vitro fertilization, she and her husband are parents of darling daughters. At the nadir of her struggle I can't imagine she would have uttered the words she said today: "I'm grateful for my cancer." Clearly, patience is essential to interpreting our holy reprimands. It may even take years, but likely a silver lining will appear.

We don't ask for tests; we don't seek problems. They do a perfectly good job finding us. At one point I broke my foot while playing kickball in the street with my kids. Determined to make it to home plate under pressure, I rounded third at high speed and blammo! I survived the ignominy of being pushed in a wheelchair on the Sabbath, barely mastered crutches, and had my low back go out due to the imbalance of walking around in a Frankenstein boot. Thank God, I eventually recovered and gained a new sense of appreciation for my mobility. I became more sympathetic to those in wheelchairs, to all who suffer with inadequate access, crumbling sidewalks and gaping potholes. Only afterwards did I recognize God's immense kindness: my injury transpired during the only six-week window in my schedule when I didn't have to get on an airplane and tour.

I still remember the first hike with my boys shortly after my foot healed. Boy, did I smell the roses. Just twenty minutes from our home, we encountered a mystical canyon where we saw ducks, geese, doves, quail, lizards and turtles. We sampled wild grapes amidst a fragrant forest of eucalyptus and then dined by a picturesque lake on Jeff's Gourmet chicken cilantro sausages with hearts of romaine, smeared with Caesar dressing, accompanied by a side of seasoned fries. With every breath of fresh air I sang praises to the Almighty for the ability to walk and engage the sweet sensations of this magnificent world. Life is so good.

Max eventually recovered from having his cell phone confiscated. He experienced real consequences for his irresponsible behavior. Subconsciously, he realized his parents love him enough to do something seemingly odious for his own good. The Ten Commandments are divided into two tablets, one side detailing responsibilities between us and God and the other side, our interpersonal human relations. Surprisingly, the law of respecting parents is on the God side. The reason? Appreciating our parents' love (and their tough love) is a stepping-stone to appreciating God's love. The gift of a reprimand served to bring me closer with my son, and the two of us closer to Hashem.

Tefillin • Shabbat • Community • Torah • Prophets • Niggun • Pesach • Teshuva • Wedding
...city • Holiness • Emunah • Diaspora • Brit Milah • Simcha • Halacha • Birchon • Holidays •...
...ah • Tallit • Jewry • Mikvah • Prayer • Moshiach • Identity • Shabbat • Community • Torah • Prophets
...an • Pesach • Teshuva • Weddings • Spirituality • Holiness • Emunah • Diaspora • Brit Milah
...h • Halacha • Birchon • Holidays • Baal Kriyah • Tallit • Jewry • Mikvah • Prayer • Moshiach
...ity • Shabbat • Community • Torah • Prophets • Niggun • Pesach • Teshuva • Weddings • Spiritual...

The Teenage Years: Better Run Away

♫ RUN AWAY ♫

joyjud.com/m/ray

You can try to hide but I will find you
There's no escaping from my charms
If you're quick you might just trick me, oh yeah
If you're slow I'll have you in my arms
So now what do you say, can you make a getaway
The time has come to play...
Better run away (before I grab you)
Run away before I grab you

You can try to fool me with distractions
You can try to catch me unaware
Just when you assume I am sleeping
I'll fly so fast you haven't got a prayer
It could be your lucky day, the chase is underway
The time has come to play...
Better run away (before I grab you)
Run away before I grab you

I love to watch our quiet street come alive when I *daven Shacharit* on our front porch, bound in my *tefillin*, enveloped in my *tallit* and connected to the Source of all creation. Our next-door neighbors have two adorable kids, the oldest a loquacious blonde with a favorite game. I watch him try, often successfully, to run away from his house and down the street while his panicked nanny chases him and screams epithets in Spanish. Every day he gets a little farther and she screams a little louder.

My brothers and I did a similar thing with our dad. We'd stand in front of his oversized leather easy chair and he'd trap us between his knees whispering, "Run away!" We'd wait for the trap to open and before we could charge out of his grasp, he'd grab us with his enormous hands and whisk us back where we started. Every third or fourth time we'd actually escape, sometimes with too much velocity, and crash to the floor. We'd pick ourselves up, stop laughing and try again.

Of course, I performed the same shenanigans with my own precious offspring. When they grew bigger, I made an art form out of chasing them around the house. Any "Soap Soup" fans know our game of "Run Away (Before I Grab You)" as memorialized in the song by the same name. When I caught them, I would emit a primordial growl as I prepared to devour them limb from limb. Then I would freeze and count, "five, four, three, two, RUN," thereby giving them time to escape. As they grew older and could outrun me, I devised a corollary to the game called Anger Bottle. I would drink most of the water out of a twelve-ounce plastic bottle and then huck it at them with all my might. I would leave just enough liquid to serve as ballast so it would scare the pants off them as it struck the wall where their heads were moments before. I hurled insults in my best Pirate tongue and we'd run until we were too sweaty or until someone got hurt. Neighborhood kids still come over asking me to terrorize them with my handy bottle of Evian.

I'm describing the evolution of this chase because the rules have shifted once again. After high school, our kids ran away from home. As far from their parents as they could get. They didn't quite cut the cord completely. We're still paying the bills. But they ventured to the Middle East and beyond and their flesh and blood presence was replaced by an occasional, ephemeral text or call. I, too, left home at seventeen. I was fiercely independent and confident, with a love for travel and the great outdoors. I blithely left my three brothers and dear parents to deal with the impact of my disappearance from the family dynamic. I was busy with Berklee College of Music in Boston, new friends and summer piano jobs in Montana and Greece. I never stopped loving and appreciating my *mishpacha*, but I only connected with postcards from the road. When my son Max was sixteen, we already felt the gravity of his imminent departure. We started a countdown to his senior year and watched him mature into an independent citizen of the world as he left for a year and half in Israel and then college in New York.

During his teenage years, Max started hiding, creating his own sense of self away from the shadow cast by his doting parents. In a song from my "Fatherhood" album written for him, I have a line summing up this new chapter: "I could hold your hand in front of all your friends, then I became an idiot." This new dynamic meant that when Max welcomed his gang over every Shabbat afternoon, he'd hint not too subtly I find my own friends to play with. His million-dollar smile was reserved for his peers and if I wanted a conversation, I had to bribe him with a fancy meal in a restaurant or force him on an outing. Thanks to his always buzzing cell phone, I rarely had his full attention. I tried to teach him not to text while in a conversation with a live human. He would attempt to comply until an "important" message came through.

Jesse, son number two, was affectionate and demonstrative well into his mid-teens. He was as easygoing as Max was willful, never too busy to join me for a hike or a walk around the block. He reassured us that as a rich doctor he would build us a guesthouse for our retirement on his expansive property. This dynamic also changed. Around the age of sixteen, on our way to a family friend's Bar Mitzvah, Jesse warned us that we were not allowed to dance. Max chimed in, "don't even talk." Thankfully Sarah was still willing to party with us on the dance floor while her brothers cowered in shame. Soon she, too, entered the dreaded individuation stage with a passion and left us in the dust, feeble and unneeded.

My kids used to clamor for bedtime stories. They would fight over who got to have me in which room. As I mentioned, I made up the narratives every night from scratch; fully realized adventures, mysteries, business sagas, tales of spiritual rendezvous. They would each give me two random nouns which I incorporated into the story line. I accepted this challenge to keep their curiosity piqued throughout the dozen minutes of drama. I owed them a dollar if I forgot their word and rarely messed up. Max stopped asking for stories when he hit fifteen. No longer would he volunteer words to be included in the tale and at one point, during the spinning of an especially intricate yarn, I caught him underneath his covers wearing his headphones. Like clockwork, the age of fifteen was also the bedtime ritual cutoff for the other two kids. Thanks to my mother's insistence, I started recording the stories back in 2007. When my youngest turned fifteen in 2014, the fountain ran dry, but not before over 1200 tales filled the inventory. Fodder for my grandkids, I suppose.

Back when all three kids lived under our roof, I had an epiphany during a camping trip in awe-inspiring Kings Canyon, CA. I hiked with dear friends along a wild river on a blue-sky day, occasionally soaking in glimmering pools replete with fallen sequoia diving boards. After a few hours of sunning and strolling, we felt at one with the flow, physically and mentally relaxed, hearts open. That is, until I reinjured my leg while frolicking in the shallows. Thankfully, I was able to cool it down in the current while my friends commiserated with me. A maddening series of questions coiled in my brain: *how would I get back to our campsite? How long would it take to heal? Why now? Why me?*

A few weeks earlier I had pulled a calf muscle while skateboarding with Max. After watching the X Games athletes compete at L.A.'s Staples Center, Max and I did some freestyle on our own, soaring down the slopes of an urban parking garage. We slalomed multiple laps down a dozen stories, employing the elevator as our chairlift. I challenged my boy, shouting, "Go for it, Max!" Toward the end of our adventure, I felt my leg suddenly spasm in an agonizing split second—a deep muscle pull that took weeks to heal.

One of my friends mentioned that revisiting the same trauma may indicate there's still a lesson to learn. I never thought much about my calf strain—these things just happen, right? She patiently prodded me to share what was weighing on my mind. After listing my pressing business concerns, I hit the mother lode: I was grappling with Max's imminent departure to college. How was my injured calf connected to this transition in my life?

Shira and I were coming to terms with the realization that there would soon be a vacant chair at our dinner table. Then another kid would leave, then another. We were anticipating the silence of the empty nest, and my reaction was to greedily hold on to each moment. I was taking more photos than ever, packing in memorable activities and filling my son's head with advice.

As I dipped my hand into the river, water poured through the cracks between my fingers and continued its inevitable descent. In an instant, clarity washed over me. I blurted out, "I'm trying to hold onto my kids like I'm trying to hold onto this water." I was hopelessly attempting to stop the flow of time. I sobbed tears of sadness and then relief as I acknowledged the pain I had been carrying inside. Perhaps the physical contraction in my calf was metaphorically representing the emotional contraction of holding onto my children. Remarkably, once I acknowledged the connection, the discomfort slowly subsided.

Our children are leaving to spend time in Israel, go to college, find jobs, marry and propagate the species, God willing. That's what we want! Parents are like archers, pulling back the bow with all our strength and launching our treasured offspring into the fray, using the best aim we can muster. Then they are flying. Separating from us. Soaring. They will follow their own voice, make their mark on the world, stand on their own two feet. Hopefully, they are perched on our proverbial shoulders with as expansive a view as we can provide. Perhaps, at a time of indecision, they will hear an inner voice saying, "Go for it!"

To stop the circle of life from spinning is like trying to dam up a rushing river. One can pile stones in a Sisyphean rage…or go with the flow. Since that day in Kings Canyon, I recognize that resisting change broadcasts a message of insecurity: *I don't have what I need, I'm living in fear, I'm desperate.* Holding on to the past creates subliminal tension; imagine a tightly clenched fist like Rodin's "The Thinker," calcified in a defensive pose. Our sages teach us to be "supple like the river reed." A dry, brittle twig will break under pressure. Instead, we can remain fluid, open and available. Peaceful and joyful. Just like the Kings River as it descends effortlessly towards the Pacific.

Our community has a proven technique to prod even recalcitrant homebodies out of the nest. The treasured Modern Orthodox custom is to send high school grads on a "gap-year" study trip in Israel before starting college. Thanks to peer pressure and financial aid, nearly everyone gets their first taste of life away from the folks while in the safe haven of a yeshiva or seminary. Most of them take to their new found independence like a raptor released. If they can navigate Israel, hopefully going to college afterwards is a piece of cake.

Sometimes it takes a crisis to get the kids to venture out of the nest. Especially when the nest is extra cushy. In 1990, my father's garment manufacturing company went bankrupt. This forty-year enterprise was my dad's raison d'être and losing it ruptured our family's security bubble. It's likely that several of his four sons would have gone into the business—my dad created a division of the company for each of us to run. Instead, after working for my dad for five intense and enlightening years, I helped close the doors by supervising the sale of our inventory. I went back to being a full-time musician and fell in love with my Judaism, eventually marrying these two passions in this unusual career of mine. Two of my brothers became popular rabbis and the other brother is a respected lawyer. Since the bankruptcy, we haven't had the silver spoon in our mouths, which I think is a good thing. We've had to fight for every last nickel and have learned the value of hard work and perseverance.

The Talmud's advice to parents of children reaching adulthood is teaching them a trade. Initiating children into the world of honest work and helping them marshall their aptitudes is seen as mandatory in Judaism. Adam was commanded to work and guard the Garden of Eden, not to recline in a lounge chair drinking mai-tais. He was soon expelled from Paradise into an imperfect, unfinished world where he had to "work by the sweat of his brow." Once the Israelites arrived in the Promised Land, we transitioned from enjoying *manna* from heaven to engaging in backbreaking labor to cultivate our crops. God created a system where our sense of accomplishment is based on our ability to earn cash in order to eat. The pressure of fiscal survival forces emotional and intellectual growth. God rewards our effort with spiritual currency: career satisfaction, our unique talents, our lifespan and the gift of friends and family. Shira and I pray our children inherit the work ethic we have modelled and eventually wean themselves from the open tap of our generosity. *Halevai!* (it should be!)

Hopefully, our children move out of our homes but not our lives, and then God willing, grandchildren will follow! We are toasting our newfound liberty…we just took our first vacation as a couple in recent memory. Admittedly, it's hard to replace the heady sensation of always being in demand when the kids competed for our attention. I also miss the youthful tumult filling our household when my kid's friends would crowd their bedrooms. I wish I had a freeze frame or at least a slow motion button on the video of my life. I believe our offsprings' disappearance from our daily dynamic teaches that the only constant in life is change and perhaps, prepares us for loss in general.

The best "empty nest" survival tip is to nurture activities shared by both spouses. I recall when my first girlfriend's father became an ornithology buff. I said, "Gerry, are you really so excited about watching birds?" He replied, "Birds are fine. I became a birdwatcher because my wife took an interest. Get it, Sam?" Couples must get creative to find common goals other than childrearing. This is the ideal time to pursue dormant bucket list items. Our spouses might not be enthuisiastic about all our preferred activities. That's fine…sometimes we have to go it alone. We come into this world alone and leave alone. While every moment with those we love is a blessing, a relationship with our Creator is the deepest wellspring of joy. Everything else is a bonus. The Joy of Judaism doesn't require outside stimulus. We are treasured children of the Almighty, actors on a stage where cohorts enter and exit, leaving us alone with God for the curtain call.

I'd like to offer a blessing to parents everywhere: "those that sow in tears will reap with joy" (*Tehillim* 126:5). May all those years of heroic effort be amply rewarded. Show overflowing love to your children and maximize precious opportunities to be together. Do it while you can. Remember that even the challenging times with teenagers are precious. Take your spouse out on a regular date night so when the house empties out, you remember what one another looks like. Embrace the change of seasons, grow with the flow, let go and let God. In the immortal words of James Taylor, "Shower the people you love with love, show them the way that you feel, things are going to work out fine if you only will."

Keeping Consistency Constant

Tell me papa what have I done
I haven't been much of a son
I thought I had just what it takes
And now it seems that I'm the only one
Tell me papa just who I am
I've tried to be so many things
I've heard the music in my heart
And now I know just why the caged bird
sings

Help me come unfrozen, tell me I was chosen
Papa, hold me like you used to hold me

Tightly to your chest
Tell me papa, tell me papa

I don't want to disappear
Who will remember I was here
Each day I think I'll get my break
Then I'm lookin' at another year
Hey there, daddy, look at me
I'm climbing up another tree
I'm going highest on this swing
I just want you to be proud of me

Two key factors have kept us sane while raising the next generation of Jewish kids: involving God in the process and striving for consistency in our parenting effort.

We leave the heavy lifting to God. What we eat, how we treat others and what we do on Shabbat and holidays isn't something we have to negotiate. We have a priceless 3500-year-old tradition offering precise guidelines on maximizing life and minimizing drama. We treat God as a member of the family, hearing us, helping us, loving us. The words *B'ezrat Hashem* (with God's help) and *Baruch Hashem* (Blessed or Thank God) are constantly on our lips. The kids see us not only respecting *halacha* (Jewish law) but also maximizing *hidur* mitzvah, taking our observance up a notch by beautifying the details. We appreciate that the genius of Judaism is revealed within seemingly picayune details and we embrace, rather than obsess about, the supposed limitations of religious life. *Frumkeit* doesn't take us out of society. We can pursue free-time activities, hobbies and vacations <u>and</u> keep our spirituality intact. We serve our children a banquet of mitzvah opportunities on a buffet of real life examples rather than through lectures. Our efforts to raise mensches is greatly assisted by our tight-knit community where love of Torah and a natural adherence to mitzvot is the norm.

Our kids learned the laws of *kavod* (respect) for parents in day school, including those basic "how-tos" taught for millennia, for example, not to sit in our chairs without permission or to anticipate our thirst by offering us a drink. Obtaining *kavod* doesn't require emotional distance; our children sense we are teammates and do whatever we can for them within our means. We rely on Torah, God's instructions for life, for the parenting basics.

The other factor around which Shira and I have rallied is consistency. We try to always be available for our kids, cheering them on, going to bat for them at school, giving them an attentive ear, encouraging self-expression. We try to be consistent with our discipline, not tolerating their abuse of one another, wasting time or rudeness. Back in carpool days, when we said we'd be at the corner to pick them up, we would show up promptly, give or take a few minutes. Much thanks to my overachieving wife, dinner was on the table for a family sit-down every night. We rarely had to police their actions or resort to punishments other than occasional time outs and groundings. When the ground rules in our mostly peaceful household were broken, our kids immediately sensed the placid order of their micro-universe was altered. Yes, they could have kept pushing or nudging or driving us crazy, but why do that? It didn't get them anywhere.

We consistently temper criticism with unconditional love. As hard as it is to have a meeting of the minds, Shira and I dispense justice in tandem and resist attempts to play one parent against the other. We strive to enforce immediate consequences in response to errant behavior. As described in the Gift of a Reprimand chapter, living with consequences prepares children for the real world, and not delivering them in the name of "kindness" is really cruelty. Our parenting style isn't "disciplinarian." Just disciplined.

A household with consistency as a foundation sets up children for a lifetime of achievement. As an example, all three of our kids took lessons on their respective musical instruments and were required to practice regularly if they wanted to continue. Thankfully they became quite competent, Max on guitar, Jesse on sax and Sarah, who fills our household with the sounds of Chopin, Beethoven and Debussy, on the piano. We encouraged them to choose trustworthy friends and avoid those who ran hot or cold based on ever-mutating peer popularity contests. We modeled follow-through and expected them to meet the obligations they had taken on. I resonate with the Torah's teaching regarding the construction of the holy *aron* (ark). It was made of acacia wood and lined with gold leaf on the outside <u>and</u> the inside. Wood symbolizes solidity: we shouldn't try to shape the Torah to match our lives, but instead shape our lives to match Torah. And why waste precious gold on the inside? Because consistency isn't just an outward attribute; a true *tzadik* (righteous person) is golden on the inside and the outside. When kids learn to be consistent, they become better sons and daughters as well as better employees, employers and most importantly, spouses.

Consistency is important for couples of all ages. My wife and I regularly reflect on the *chassan* and *kallah* classes we enjoyed as newlyweds. As Shira eloquently states in the women's ritual chapter, Torah wisdom suggests husbands make spouses the queen of the household, and women must radiate sincere respect for their husbands. Thriving marriages are those where the couple is consistent in managing these behaviors. Guys must remember that when our wives are berating us, it's really God communicating through them. Bearing this in mind, snapping back or criticizing makes no sense. While women may "wear the pants" in the family and especially if they are the primary breadwinner, they must avoid henpecking or belittling and instead make husbands feel venerated. And not just on Father's

Day. Anyone can be a *tzadik* for a minute or two. Consistent, proactive adulation keeps marriages strong.

Another piece of advice I received as a neophyte groom regarded setting a consistent standard during the first year of marriage. This included pitching in around the house as well as setting aside time to bond spiritually and physically. During that *shana rishona* (first year of marriage), we adhered to the sensible custom of minimizing outside distractions in order to develop the deepest attention and passion. The true aphrodisiac in a loving relationship is consistency; honesty and reliability build real trust and foster intimacy. Establishing this fundamental connection allows one's spouse to feel secure that the pattern of love and duty is not going to diminish. My rabbi also recommended not firing on all cylinders at the starting line if I couldn't maintain the pace.

Similarly, those growing in Judaism must strive for observance they can maintain and not burn out. Yes, we all need to be learning and growing; good enough is the enemy of greatness. But not all at once. Most wise teachers suggest a gradual path so growth remains consistent and practical. It's hard to take someone seriously who jumps from eating Big Macs into a *glatt* kosher ascetic the next day. Ideally, spouses striving in Torah take baby steps to ensure their spiritual development brings them together as a couple rather than apart, *chas v'shalom* (God forbid). We know many couples where one spouse (usually the husband) took off like a race horse, leaving the other feeling abandoned or inept. Just like we build marital intimacy with consistency, so, too, do we bond with the Creator of the Universe. Our sages debate which is the most important pasuk of the Torah. The winner, according to the Midrash, is *Sh'mot*/Exodus 29:39, regarding the twice a day *Tamid* (always) offering in the Temple. Seasonal devotion to God is great, but Jewish survivial is predicated on daily, continuous, consistent commitment. Consistency with one's service to God is the very engine of the relationship; after all, God created the spiritual attributes of fidelity, integrity and patience and responds in kind to our faithfulness.

My father had a mantra: don't be a quitter. God forbid we ever quit anything or we would have to endure his accusing finger pointing at us as he uttered, "Quitter!" Sometimes one must cut losses and stop throwing good money after bad. But rarely do we look back and state, "Wow, I'm glad I quit that." This has been one of our quintessential challenges as parents. We have watched our kids take on various sports and hobbies, some requiring substantial investment, only to abandon them weeks later. We blame their short attention span on smartphone ownership. Their pastimes are either "instant satisfaction" or nonexistent. I mentioned this parenting dilemma to one of my buddies, Saul Blinkoff, a director and animator with Disney. He told me that he fears for this impetuous generation, claiming most lack a work ethic and have little concept of the discipline required to accumulate the essential "10,000 hours" of experience. The drama of childrearing is enough to make any parent religious: it triggers continuous prayer that children survive their future relationships and careers.

One of the key aspects of The Possible You seminar is distinguishing *emes* from *sheker* (truth from falsehood), in terms of our relationships with God, one another and ourselves. When we are consistent, we bring truth into the world. When we break our word, we bring falsehood. The goal of the seminar is harnessing the power of the word, creating reality with our declarations and maintaining this new reality with steadfast consistency. This isn't a recipe for all-consuming guilt every time we are running late, just something to keep in mind in case of a lapse. One can restore *emes* to the world by apologizing, re-committing to a new goal and moving on. The prophet Shmuel says, "*Netzach Yisrael lo yishaker*," usually translated as, "The Jewish People are eternal." A better translation is "the eternity of Israel is intact because we don't deceive." Our relationship with God is unbreakable when our word is our bond. As parents, teaching our children the value of their word and of maintaining a "good name" is priority number one.

We all have areas in which we are inconsistent. We can thank our ever powerful *yetzer harah* (evil inclination) for tripping us up in the areas we most need consistency. As discussed in the *Middot* chapter, our shortcomings typically involve the very traits necessary for accomplishing our *tafkid* (personal task) in life. This primal force jeopardizes our life goals so we have a sense of accomplishment for vanquishing it. The million dollar question is: how can we conquer the *yetzer harah* and create more consistency in our lives? The key is threefold: once we identify things that make us procrastinate, give us cold sweats or get us addicted, set small, manageable goals in writing and tackle them one by one. Too big a mountain and we'll never climb it. Secondly, bring God into the picture. For example, when I have a creative roadblock, I ask God for the music or insight needed before I go to sleep. I am rarely let down. Some folks feel funny praying on their own behalf. Of course you should pray for your own well-being! Establish a small goal and ask for God's help in achieving it, in the same language you would use asking a friend to do you a favor. Finally, reward yourself for being consistent. For me, chocolate ice cream is a great perk. In fact, I think I'll have some right now as a reward for getting this chapter written.

There are so many lessons we can learn from that simple *Modeh Ani* sentence we utter upon awakening: "I am grateful to You, living and eternal King, Who <u>consistently</u> returns my soul with abundant compassion." Consistency is God's gift to us. That way we can busy ourselves with Facebook while our lungs breathe, blood circulates and food digests. Every morning on this spectacular planet is a miracle. *Modeh Ani* reminds us not to leave our beds without acknowledging our miraculous lives are sustained by God's quiet consistency. Perhaps the best way to emulate the Creator is with an emphasis on bringing the same consistency to our interactions with our children, spouses and everyone we meet.

Kids on Meds:
Mood-Altering Drugs

♫ ONE DAY AT A TIME ♫

joyjud.com/m/odt

It's happening again, I'm blown by the wind
It keeps coming 'round like some unwanted friend
At times I'm feeling so damn strong
I could carry the whole world
But other times I cannot lift a finger

Climb back aboard the program
Time for your curtain call
Once you fall off the wagon
Somehow you must recall
One day at a time

It never sleeps, it dwells in my dreams
I'm wearing a smile for you but inside I scream
At times I think I've kicked it
Like it's gone away for good
Then suddenly I find I'm starting over

Climb back aboard the program
Time for your curtain call
Once you fall off the wagon
You can redeem your soul
One day at a time

For many years I have taught an L.A.-based class called Seasons of Joy. Every week, a wonderful group of Jews-by-birth and potential Jews-by-choice join me for an overview of the Torah portion of the week, basic Jewish law and tips for ecstatic Jewish living. Since this course satisfies the educational demands of the L.A. *Beit Din* (conversion court), attendance by the Jewish future spouses of conversion candidates is compulsory. One thirty-something Jewish woman who frequented the class would often ask questions having little to do with the topic at hand. She tested my patience as I struggled to keep to our detailed curriculum in my precious hour-and-a-half. She would ask about angels, the soul or the afterlife and reacted with authority to my answers. In private conversations, I learned she could hear and see angels and was in a constant dialog with her spiritual guides. Her intuitions were at parity with Kabbalistic teachings and I recognized she had a degree of vision denied the rest of us.

One afternoon I was visiting a Judaica store in our 'hood to restock my CDs. The 613 Mitzvah Store was always a great place to schmooze with those shopping for books and ritual objects and was one of the best outlets for my music. I usually made a few sales each time I stopped in. One day, this aforementioned student of mine saw me helping a newcomer pick out a *mezuzah*. As we pondered the various options, I joked, "Someone bought me one of these boxes, but the instructions were in Hebrew so I threw them out." I described the content of those "instructions" and remarkably, when I picked up a scroll off the counter, I could feel a tangible energy in the parchment. I explained that a holy Jew devoted himself to the detailed calligraphy of the sacred text, giving a kosher scroll tremendous spiritual power. Soon, everyone within earshot wanted to touch the parchment; whereas not everyone felt the same rush, when my student held it, she reacted like she was mainlining heroin.

Over time, this woman's statements grew more bizarre and she developed a tic. Her flower-child dress and observations of auras were scaring away others in the class. On my rabbi's advice, I asked her not to make any more off-topic comments. I later found out she had been banned from many *shuls* and classes around the neighborhood. When she no longer showed up, I frequently wondered about her well-being.

One Shabbas years later, I saw her sitting at a bus stop. She was calm, the tic gone, her speech slow and measured. She explained she started taking medication to allow her to live a "normal" life, sublimating her gift so she could function in society. I pondered her dilemma as I walked away.

George Gershwin was famously hyperactive. Unlike his mellow older brother Ira, George couldn't sit still and got in trouble for fighting, theft and playing hooky. He medicated himself with music: "Studying the piano made a good boy out of a bad one, it took the piano to tone me down." One must wonder if we would be hearing Summertime and Rhapsody in Blue had he been subdued by pharmaceuticals. At a recent Earth, Wind and Fire concert, my wife and I marveled at the energy of the legendary band, particularly bass virtuoso Verdine White. He grooves with unparalleled intensity every night—and he's in his senior years! Shira turned to me and commented, "Can you imagine if his parents had put him on Ritalin as a kid?" Are we medicating our future Verdine Whites and George Gershwins into submission? Placing all our precious square peg offspring in round holes, thanks to the miracle of modern medicine?

Our oldest son Max gave me permission to disclose that he required ADHD meds to survive school. His teachers insisted he was not "available for learning" and after a few agonizing years of indecision, we finally opted to take the plunge and feed him narcotics. We tried homeopathics, neurolinguistic programming and multiple therapies, to no avail. Thankfully, Max is a success story in a situation traumatizing so many families. Meds gave him the ability to concentrate, minimized his tendency to distract peers and made him more docile with his siblings. When I saw the drugs were helping him develop a sense of confidence, replacing his despondence with a can-do attitude, I became a believer. I must admit I preferred him un-medicated during our outings—I got a kick out of his spontaneity and enhanced sense of humor. Now in his twenties, he has weaned himself off the meds, resorting to them only when he has a crucial need to buckle down and study. Unfortunately, he feels he lost some of his unique sparkle, as if the decade of meds contributed to a permanent dampening of his ebullient personality.

Many of my loved ones have opted to medicate themselves out of experiencing life's highs and lows. I'm not preaching against the use of Prozac and Xanax for the clinically depressed or anxious. I wonder, however, if our national addiction is burying the source of malaise and eliminating the challenging but rather rewarding work of personal growth. One in four women in my age bracket take powerful antidepressants. Nearly 20% of boys are diagnosed with ADHD. Is this normal? Should we be researching issues with diet, food additives and device-based distraction? How about alternative teaching methods? Music therapy? Anything?

A note on modern self-medication: medical marijuana is now legal in the majority of states and every year more are permitting recreational use. I'm not sure increasing access is a great idea. Currently, the level of THC, the active ingredient, has reached hallucinatory proportions. Proponents argue that it is safer than booze and less addictive. Tell that to my hapless, "wake-and-bake" stoner friends. The urge to indulge isn't as acute as a heroin or meth addiction (*I must have it now or I will murder someone*), but millions of Americans are acquiescing to a daily hazy, lazy realm of indolence, dulled by pot's happy glow. Frequent consumption wreaks havoc on decisiveness, follow through and memory. Many lose motivation, jobs and relationships as a result. According to the National Survey of Drug Use and Health, one in six who start indulging when they are teenagers will become addicted. Pot is a proven gateway drug; addicts are three times more likely to get hooked on harder stuff. I consider marijuana today's "opiate of the masses." There are a dozen dispensaries within a few miles of my home. Public schools, private schools, yeshivas…all are facing this invasion of students' developing minds. Legalization doesn't mean it has become harmless. Pot can offer creative expanse, relaxation and has proven medical benefits for certain ailments. But its call is a nefarious siren song and I urge anyone with addiction issues to get professional help before they crash the well-tended vessel of their lives on the rocks.

Regarding life's many illicit temptations, David Sacks offers great advice for standing one's ground. By definition, a line is a series of discreet, individual points, creating the illusion of a solid entity. Each moment is a new "now." We can always pivot in a new direction. We carry within us the DNA of those who left Egypt for the uncharted, barren desert. Just when we began the journey, Moshe was told to reverse his course. It must have made no sense at the time, but we obeyed and enshrined the ability to turn around for time immemorial. On your way to the refrigerator for another snack when on a diet? Reaching for a bottle or a bong? About to get lost in salacious websites? We can turn around! That's true freedom, the inner teaching of the Exodus.

I realize this former student of mine required intervention. Without meds it's unlikely we would have had a cohesive conversation on that Shabbas. Still, she is one of the few I have met who possess such a degree of "knowing," with the ability to potentially guide others to share her vision. Three times a day we pour our hearts out in prayer—how often are we really connecting? How rare and valuable is accurate rebuke? How often do we meet someone who can look right into our eyes and perceive our soul, giving us a crucial message we need to hear?

In a world bereft of spirituality, perhaps the antidote is to find insightful mentors to sensitize us to heavenly messages, to the presence of angels in our lives. Rabbi Shlomo Carlebach used to say that we have to take moments of personal ecstasy and bring them into our service of God. The idea is to summon a favorite holy memory and inject it into everyday prayer. This requires moments of personal ecstasy, unmedicated highs and lows! Let us strive to maintain a state of wonder, to nurture our childlike perception of the world with awe and delight. Let us get high on life without requiring artificial mood enhancement. Let us deftly ride the waves of everyday ups and downs and always remember the Solomonic advice, "This too shall pass." Should you meet someone like my enlightened student, no matter how zany the interaction, don't dismiss her as a hippie freak, but instead take a few minutes to receive her insight before moving on to the "important stuff" in your busy day.

A Love Letter to My College-Bound Son

♫ YOU'RE ON YOUR OWN ♫

joyjud.com/m/oyo

Yesterday I carried you around the block
Searching for bluebirds
Waiting for the day that you would start to talk
And your first word was in Spanish
Now 30,000 pictures later
You've still got that smile
Welcome to your world

You're standing tall
You got your own point of view
Don't need no one doin' you any favors
You hear the call, you got your own attitude
No more cryin' for mama to save ya

I spent every day preparing
For this treacherous time
And there's one thing that I got to say
You're on your own
But never alone

Yesterday I taught you how to swing a bat
And play the piano
I could hold your hand in front of all your friends
Then I became an idiot
Now you're sure your birthday present
Should be my old car
That's why I kept it clean

In 2013 my wife and I were preparing for a momentous change in our lives—the departure of our son Max for his gap year in Israel. I wrote him this letter, which he gave me permission to share.

Dear Max,

I just booked our summer family vacation in Lake Tahoe. This jewel of the spectacular Sierras features world-class mountain biking, hiking and water skiing. We're going to do everything! As excited as I am, I can't help but be a bit melancholic. I have had the great gift of being your dad for the past eighteen years. You are a superstar kid who has given me and your mom nothing but *nachas*. You are entering your college years with so much enthusiasm and readiness to take on the world. I believe in you, Max. There's nothing you can't do.

So yes, it's our last vacation with all of us together for a while. Soon we'll have our last family dinner, our last Shabbat, a rockin' graduation party and then you'll be off to the

Holy Land. What a gift to have a year in Israel before college kicks off. Dreamy. I think some parents of teens are ready to see their kids hit the road. I'm not one of those parents. I love being with you. Many of my fondest memories are the times we've had together. We've had crazy adventures, deep musical connections, intriguing conversations. I have great joy serving as your music teacher and watching you grow both in Jazz Ensemble and the Recording Technology class. I feel close to your friends and enjoy when the gang comes over every Shabbat afternoon. I get chills watching your mom look at you with unfathomable love in her eyes.

Everyone who has met you only has great things to say about you. That's a pretty rare thing. I've never seen leadership ability like yours. You've had it all your life. You are comfortable in any situation, with any age group. When you joined me on my concert tours, you instantly connected with the synagogue youth regardless of location or denomination. Your teachers and rabbis rave about you. On our annual Pesach programs, Mom and I marvel at how the entourage gravitates to you and how when you move on, they move too!

You are so at ease with yourself and remarkably, you wear your confidence without pushing anyone down. Working the crowd without having to be the joker, troublemaker or scammer. Clearly you have garnished only the good stuff from your devious dad. Other than driving too fast. You are sweet and gentle with young kids and are a beloved cousin, counselor and mentor. You are so sensitive with the "specially-abled." You are totally there for your four loving grandparents. You are a wizard on the guitar and on the computer, capable at just about anything you try. You have gotten school wired, improving every subsequent report card and busting out nearly straight As your senior year. Do you see a certain trajectory here?

And now you're off to the Promised Land. It is a wild, wonderful place. A place where holiness is flowing in the very air you breathe. The opportunity for connection is so powerful and present. You will be in a stimulating growth environment with rabbis and peers who will support you in your spiritual flight. Starting your post-high school educational and professional life with Jewish fundamentals makes so much sense. After all, whether you become a hedge fund manager, psychologist or rock guitarist, you will have a serious foundation in place. I first got turned on in Israel when I was just a bit older than you. I was ready to do big things in my life and my heart was open. It may be hard to believe, but you will become even more open as you put teenage angst, L.A. hype and living with your parents behind you. Yes, you can spend the year partying, but if you can find the discipline, you will come out of this period supercharged, with a passion to maximize every moment. You will become more creative, productive and the master of your destiny.

I'm happy you have Uncle Yom Tov and Aunt Leah and their eight kids to hang out with on a regular basis. Please bond deeply with all of your cousins. They love you so much. They have been deprived of having you in their life and deserve to get their fill of you. I know they will see what a towering *mensch* you are. I'm getting weepy as I write this. I'm so proud of you, Max. I love you so much. You are a credit to our family, a living testimony that mom and I did a pretty good job. You are an extension of us to the world. We will be living vicariously through your adventures. Please keep us posted!

You are already a powerful ambassador for the Jewish People. Everyone who sees your *kippah* feels your good vibe and gains respect for the heritage you represent. Do you understand what an intense *Kiddush Hashem* (sanctification of God's name) that is? You will likely ramp up your commitment in Israel. It's true many "flip out" (become more Observant), but not just on the surface. You feel God's presence so clearly through your learning and holy lifestyle that you would never do anything to mess it up. You perform mitzvot not because your parents or rabbis have expectations. The motivation comes from an outpouring of intense love for Hashem. The relationship becomes palpable. Why would you ever blow off your best friend in the Universe? You will be driven by unspeakable gratitude for your life and everyone you meet will be deeply attracted by the light you radiate. Yes, you! This simple but profound *d'veykus* (connection) with Hashem transforms mitzvot from burdensome to joyous, from feeling bored to feeling like your soul is on fire.

You also know from your hyperactive father that Judaism doesn't mean you have to sit on your butt and study all day. Judaism means you are out in the world, spreading light. Yes, we're an Orthodox family, but we ski and surf and travel and drink in everything that life has to offer. Except non-kosher wine, of course. I give you permission to get on a bus to Eilat the moment your *neshama* (soul) says you need a break. Learn to scuba dive, take some hikes and play beach volleyball—hopefully as captain of the YULA Volleyball Team you have some skills to show the Israelis. When you have a *l'chaim,* please have a round for your old dad back in L.A.—and have a designated driver.

I hope you get to the Old City often. Catch as many *minyanim* (services) at the *Kotel* (Western Wall) as you can. It's the center of the universe! Try your hand at bargaining in the Arab *shuk*. You'll get a kick out of your Uncle Yom Tov's daily lecture at Aish, in a spectacular room overlooking the Temple Mount. He catches major air on his mountain bike as he flies down the Arab Quarter steps. He arrives at his class out of breath and addresses an unusual group of hippies, Harvard grads, seminary girls and visiting grandparents with an unscripted flow of whatever is on his mind. Anyone can come to his talk and it would give him great *nachas* to see you there. Our yeshiva, Aish HaTorah, has become the number one outreach address in the world and aish.com is the biggest Jewish website on the web. I'm not saying you should ditch your program in Mevaseret Tziyon, but I hope you can wander the *Rovah* (Jewish Quarter) and get to know all my rabbi friends who will be overjoyed to meet you.

Speaking of Aish, as you know we've been members of Aish L.A. since you were born. There are plenty of other synagogues we attend, but Aish is our home. It's where you crawled around every Shabbat, where you boys celebrated your Bar Mitzvahs, where you went to teen *minyan* and helped run childcare. You're going to discover it's more than just a *shul*. It's a movement. You're a part of it whether you realize it or not. You have seen me and your mother dedicate much of our time, money and effort toward ensuring every Jew we meet has the chance to get excited about Judaism. It's why you've had strangers at a good percentage of your Shabbat meals. It's why I leave you to go on the road every other weekend. We love sharing our heritage and it breaks our heart when our fellow Jews throw it away.

In my secular upbringing, I was raised with a devotion to Israel and the Jewish People but had no experience keeping kosher, *davening* (praying) or respecting Jewish law. It's sad when you think about it. We had no idea what we were missing. Can you imagine your life without *sukkah* hopping? Partying up and down Pico on Purim? Surrounding yourself in the twenty-five hour feast that is Shabbat? We didn't even know how to say the *Sh'moneh Esrei* (central Jewish prayer). Worse yet, we didn't have clarity on God's presence in our lives and the power of Torah to help us keep our act together. Thank God, both Mom and I had great parents who gave us plenty of love and values. But we floated in a "what is this life all about" mystery zone and explored the cultures of the world to find answers. Yes, there are lots of interesting answers out there, but none are as compelling as the powerful truths in our own texts. You can use your time in Israel to bone up on the answers to fundamental questions your fellow Jews will inevitably ask you. I just want to remind you that we have Aish to thank for jumpstarting our process and encouraging us to share the wealth of *Yiddishkeit* with others.

Not to overdo the accolades for our *shul* but I think it's important to point out that the outreach revolution began with one man, Rav Noah Weinberg, zt"l, who had a vision and would not be defeated. Several times he tried and failed to establish *yeshivot* for the unaffiliated. I think Aish is number seven. King Solomon in Proverbs tells us that the righteous fall seven times but always get back up. Thanks to Rav Noah's tenacity, the world today is a different place. Please learn from his example, Max. The sky is the limit. Dream big. Get back up when you fail. Depression is not an option. Know with perfect clarity that Hashem is with you. The days we have on this planet are too few to waste feeling sorry for yourself. Your face and your mood are public property—don't pollute the world with a scowl. Rav Noah always offered encouragement to everyone and fought with grace until the end of his days. Keep the good attitude, keep the faith, keep smiling and the world will smile with you.

In your studies, you'll find there is no divide between your spiritual life and material life. We can make money in a holy way. We ski at the speed of sound because it excites and refreshes us, body and soul. We eat only after we thank God for the miracle of our food. We are intimate with our wives and as a result, deepen our marital bonds and bring holy children into the world. Living in the realm of Torah doesn't make you a recluse or weird. You have a gift you can share with Jews of all stripes. You have a gift you can share with all nations. They don't need us to try so hard to be like them. They are blessed by blessing us. Those whom you meet throughout your life will be fascinated by your story, by the things making you different. In this politically correct world no one is allowed to "dis" people because they are different. We can use that to our advantage. We can be the best Jews we can be, living in the world, interacting and influencing and serving as a *Kiddush Hashem*, perhaps the highest of all mitzvot. Along the way you may meet some people who are not so excited about Jews. You don't have to be so excited about them either.

I'm telling you all this so you have perspective of where you are going. This trip you are taking is not just for you or your family. Your learning is for *K'lal Yisrael* (the Jewish People), for those martyrs who perished in the Holocaust and other times of persecution, for those who don't know how to learn. God willing, this journey will empower you to become a great Jewish man, a spiritual leader encouraging others to reach their potential, helping to bring back our disenfranchised brothers and sisters. You truly acquire knowledge when you are able to teach a particular subject. I hope you learn in order to teach. It's selfish to be complacent, to be self-satisfied while there are so many disconnected Jews with little concept of the priceless diamonds in their grasp. I'm not telling you to join any particular *shul* or movement. I'm just saying you have a very unusual family and you have inevitably inherited a similar passion. Yes, you are going to Israel to study, travel, party and make lifelong friends. You are also going there to get a sense of the importance of your life's mission, beyond just earning a living and raising a family. It's your turn now, my beautiful son. I pray that you'll use your vast abilities to be a hero for the Jewish people, for all humankind.

So, my dear Max, there's my *shpiel*. There are some other things I want to discuss— we'll save them for the next soak in the Jacuzzi. Please try to break away from the computer to have a few more jams, *oshkibunis* (walks) and conversations with me. I treasure every minute we have together. Your friends will come and go over the course of your life…your family is forever. Make these few months meaningful. Hug your mom frequently. Try to imagine a world where she's not cooking for you, driving you everywhere, feeding your friends, doing your laundry, making you ice chai just the way you like it. Start listing all the things she gives you and see where the resulting burst of gratitude leads you.

Please try to show love to your sister. She needs you. She needs your hugs and your compassion. She is going to miss you so much. She will be crying tears of grief when she doesn't have you around. You may think she'll be fine but I know the gravity of your departure will profoundly affect her. You have this precious time to leave an impression. Regarding your brother Jesse, you already know that he adores you, looks up to you and so values your companionship. You guys are best friends, thank God. OK, I'm crying again. Jesse may not be able to express the intense bond he shares with you, but trust me, it informs his being. You have created big shoes for him to fill. You have set the bar high. Give him love and honor. Build him up and avoid words that tear him down. May you always take pleasure in his success and may he always celebrate yours.

I love you Max, Ze'ev Dov ben Shmuel, my *pidyon haben*, my beautiful, capable, precious son.

Love, Dad

Dear YULA Graduates: A Commencement Speech

♫ THE END OF THE LINE ♫

joyjud.com/m/eol

A few millennia ago	The merit of generations
The words were carved in stone	Binds our people to the text
The single greatest gift mankind would ever see	Our ancestors have given their lives
In Your image were we cast	For the right to say a prayer
Not to ever be alone	So how is it we're gonna pass
And You gave us a working world	The blessing to the next
To show Your love eternally	When most of us cannot recall
	The reason we should care
Given the precious connection	
We have the opportunity	Quietly stand on the sidelines
Passing it on or we will lose it forever	Slowly we throw it away
Look into our people, take a little time	Watching our birthright disappearing forever
To be a new beginning or the end of the line	Look into our people, look into our mission
	Don't deny our children our beautiful tradition

The following is a commencement speech I prepared for my son Jesse's graduation from Yeshiva University of Los Angeles high school, class of 2015. Jesse is a sensitive, studious and focused young man. Thanks to his supernal discipline, his gym workout and diet have shaped a body and attitude of Olympian proportions. He has a great sense of humor and a beautiful smile, much thanks to a small fortune spent on orthodontia. At the time of the writing of this book, he switched from a pre-med major to studying accounting. Whatever he does, he will do it with excellence and precision. He will always be my cuddly, blond buddy, no matter how buff he gets. Jesse, we love and cherish you.

Dear YULA Graduates,
It gives me great *nachas* to stand here with you today. I have watched many of you grow up, either as your music teacher at Hillel or YULA, or as you have befriended my own children, one of whom, Jesse Glaser, is wearing a cap and gown today. Some of you are thinking this ceremony is not a big deal. Some are here because your parents made you show up. Some want to lose the gowns and toss the hats and cut right to the party.

I want to clarify that graduating YULA is, in fact, a big deal. Graduates of this legendary institution have gone on to remarkable careers in business, science, law and medicine, becoming powerful leaders in their communities. Some have even become teachers and rabbis! Most importantly, they have done so as proud Modern Orthodox Jews, fully aware of the presence of God, cherishing every mitzvah, seizing opportunities for *chesed*. Because they interface with society at large, they touch countless others with whom they interact. It doesn't matter so much what you choose as your career as it does whether you are being a *Kiddush Hashem*, one who is sanctifying God's name everyday.

At this point in your lives, you may not feel that serving God is priority number one. This is the peak of a period in your lives where you are doing the very normal teen activity called individuation. You are likely rebelling in your own unique way, distancing yourself from parents and teachers. You may be worrying about what everyone thinks about you, wondering what you are going to do with your life and struggling with a toxic combination of angst and *shpilkes* (impatience). Leaving your parents and siblings isn't easy but it's necessary if you're going to stand on your own. Believe it or not, your occasional ungrateful or even obnoxious behavior is a crucial function of your pituitary gland. It serves to make your adoring parents want to throw you out of the house.

What's next for you is the greatest, most exciting ride of your lives. How totally amazing to share this moment on the edge with you. You may detect a hint of jealousy when you tell people your age. You are in the prime of your lives, filled with optimism, ready to change the world. Most of you will be spending a year studying in Israel. That's the best place to be an open-minded, adventurous Jewish teen, learning about spirituality and how to survive waiting in line with Israelis. This is a magical time when you are on your own, yet still have your folks helping with the bills and offering advice, even if you pay no attention. People go to Paris and Italy to learn about food and art and to Jerusalem to learn about God. It's said the air makes you wise and access to God is a "local phone call." Around a quarter of you are going straight to college. *Mazel tov* on getting accepted. I will be *davening* for your souls.

You see, one of the problems with individuation is that Hashem can get thrown off the bus. Separating from your parents is a good thing. Separating from Hashem is not. Remember the song from kindergarten? Hashem is everywhere! Loving you, giving you breath, keeping your body functioning, arranging all the unique circumstances in your life. Hashem gave us our awesome Torah that is the deepest source of wisdom, insight and self-help advice in the universe. *Torat Emet*—the Torah is truth. Our Christian and Muslim friends appreciate that the Torah is indisputable and so, perhaps reluctantly, incorporate it in their own traditions. Torah is the key to our eternity. Every mitzvah is a once-in-a-lifetime chance to make that particular moment holy. *Kedoshim T'hiyu*…be holy. That's our mission statement. So don't run from Hashem. It just doesn't make sense.

As you leave YULA, you will be responsible to nurture this relationship. A relationship is as strong as the weakest partner. If I think you are my best friend but you only call me back once a month, we have a once-a-month relationship. God loves us so much—we will always be the weakest partner. Your *rebbeim* and teachers have presented a profound 3000-year-old system to keep this relationship on fire. Are you sick of the *Shmoneh Esrei*? From now on, no one is going to make you say it. Find those *tefillin* annoying? Well, now you can just leave them in the bag. Or you can choose life. You can choose to bring gratitude into your every day with a blessing over everything that goes in your mouth. You can act as Hashem's partner in creating the world by perceiving the impact you have in your *tefillah*. You can hear

Hashem's patient voice in every word of Torah you learn. You can touch everyone you meet by serving as an example of what it means to be a fully invested Jew. You can have the soul satisfaction of initiating this relationship of your own volition, as an adult. Hashem is ready to provide miracles for you, to make your life amazing, to hear your requests in your prayers and make those dreams come true.

Observant Jews recognize that while we are engrossed in material concerns, we are simultaneously separate, spiritual. You have learned techniques in school, *shul* and home to maximize both worlds. Modern Orthodox Jews have a particularly challenging path: we don't eschew all connections with secular culture and the Internet. We understand we have to be "in the world" in order to be a light unto nations. Whether you realize it or not, you are all Jewish leaders! People will see how you act and judge all Jews accordingly. For the rest of your life, you will be explaining your dietary habits, your *kippah*, your dress and why you have to leave work early on Fridays. It's not easy to walk on this tightrope and maintain your footing. In college, the balance gets even trickier with academic mentors preaching secularism and even anti-Israel sentiments. That's why today is a big deal. Your parents have spent a small fortune to put you in an environment like YULA, one empowering you with our eternal traditions, providing access to our priceless formula to stay on track and excel in life.

Here's another reason why today is a big deal. Look around at your graduating class. These people are your brothers and sisters. You have a lifelong connection with one another, a deeper bond than you'll make with your future college buddies and business peers. All those demanding teachers, issues with the administration, school trips to Israel and Poland, sports and other extra-curricular activities have served as the glue to connect you. What you have with each other is real *achdut* (brother/sisterhood). *Achdut* is precious. Our Temple was destroyed because of lack of *achdut*. The restoration of *achdut* brings us closer to our redemption. Invest in your YULA friends. Treasure them. Count on them. Some of your peers left YULA early to go straight to City College or wherever. They missed out on this opportunity. Take a moment to be grateful for the circumstances allowing you to make it all the way. You got a real diploma and not a High School Equivalency Certificate. Most importantly, you got *achdut*.

Finally, I urge you to keep your Judaism fresh. Judaism is a lot of work. It can get tiring and repetitive. It can be expensive. If you keep a minimum daily requirement in your lives, like morning *tefillah*, learning *parashat hashavua* (the Torah portion of the week) and *kashrut*, you'll establish a solid connection on which you can build and know when you are slipping. You have spent the past twelve years growing into bona fide YULA graduates. Don't lose it! If you can't find the internal motivation, do it for the wrong reasons. Do it for your parents. Do it for your rabbis and teachers. Do it for your unborn children. Do it for the six million. Even if you're not positive God exists, do it just in case God does exist! You've probably heard the *Gemara*, "*lo lishma ba lishma*" (not for its own sake becomes for its own sake). In other words, "Just Do It!"

So, my friends, thanks for your attention. Please continue to give your parents and teachers *nachas*. Choose life. Live to the fullest. Be true to yourself. Learn to balance "You-ish" AND Jewish. That is the unbeatable combination that will guarantee you success in every part of your life. The YULA Class of 2015 is a stunning, shining group of remarkable young people who will make the world a better place. This world needs your help in a big way. Stand proudly, YULA graduates, and know you carry with you the hope of your families and the Nation of Israel for a brighter future for all humankind.

The Baby and the Bathwater

Oh I wanna hold her
How long since I told her
How I love my Sarah
She's my little lady
She just drives me crazy
Oh, I love my Sarah

Oh, she knows I'll do anything to please
Head to toe, she's got me on my knees
Watch my baby groovin'
She just keeps me movin'
Dancin' with my Sarah

Right on the money
She's my little honey
Hand in hand with Sarah

Oh, she knows I'm floating on a breeze
As we grow, her love is all I need
She's my little treasure
She is such a pleasure
No one's quite like Sarah
We're just chasin' bubbles
Getting into troubles
Laughing with my Sarah

A letter written to our daughter Sarah when she left for her gap year in Israel

Dear Sarah,
Our house is so quiet. More than any of your siblings, you make your presence known. We no longer hear your mellifluous piano playing ringing through the halls. We miss the sound of your turntable cranking out your favorite vinyl through that tinny speaker while your myriad friends giggle in your room. Mostly, we miss you. Your five-foot-eight-inches of sweetness, passion, humor and intensity. I have come to realize that writing "The Joy of Judaism" has been an exercise to prepare myself for this day. This very quiet day.

Fatherhood is a strange thing. You search high and low for the ideal spouse, one who will light up your days and ignite your nights. One who has the qualities you wish to impart on your yet-to-be-conceived children. One who will be responsible with your credit cards, yet knows how to have a good time. You get engaged and then married—at least a year of high drama and expense. Then you pray God gives you the gift of precious children to raise. If you are lucky, you get to usher souls into this world, with little faces that look a bit like you. You share your wisdom, life lessons and bad jokes along the way. You spend every last hard-earned dollar and minute of the day providing for their food, clothing, shelter and education. You invest heart and soul into building the relationship, getting so close they become the best part of your being. Then eighteen years into the process, just when they are moving past teen angst and can relate to you as a functioning, spiritual, grateful adult…they leave.

What?

Don't worry. Mom and I are doing fine. We just got back from our awesome twenty-fifth anniversary European cruise. We endured long flights, tight deadlines, packed itineraries and humid weather…and no fights! We are so deeply in love. We cherish our time together and look out for one another. When we started out in our marriage, some people advised us not to work together in my business. We ignored them and created a partnership where we learned to complement each other's strengths. What a gift to have most of our meals together. And now that it's just the two of us, you kids aren't eating my leftovers. I love staring into her eyes, getting her advice, sharing whatever experiences I've had or Torah I've learned that day. I feel so blessed. I pray you also find someone who cherishes you so much.

You were totally primed for your gap year in Israel. You were ready to leave behind the pettiness and games of high school life. You have been studying *Mishlei* and *Pirkei Avot* on your own, hungry for learning. You have a cosmic connection with our Homeland. This is your eighth trip in your brief eighteen years on this planet. I will never forget the journey you took when you were eleven. You had fallen in love with the country on our family trips and then your best friend, Sarah Hulkower, moved there. At the time, you were making remarkably detailed beaded jewelry for family and friends. I encouraged you to bring the inventory to sell at my concerts. At some shows, receipts from your sales exceeded those from my CDs! Soon you accumulated enough profit to buy yourself a plane ticket. You flew alone, across the world and spent a happy summer having Israeli adventures with your dearest friend. Now you have an entire year to soak up the sunshine and spirituality with an awesome group of young ladies at Machon Mayan in Ashdod, your chosen seminary. Somehow you will survive without your mom's cooking. Good luck.

The big challenge to your spirituality will commence upon your return, should you choose to return. As you have witnessed with your older friends, holding on to the uniquely powerful Israel experience is not easy. We love our hometown and sweet community, but it is a far cry from Jerusalem. Back in L.A., one is beset by a whole new set of role models—rappers, DJs, athletes and movie stars. Illicit nightlife. Drugs. A culture that laughs at modesty. The language of holiness to which you've grown accustomed is replaced by the parlance of the street. The memory of your honored teachers fades and you can't imagine how you survived such ascetic conditions. You will be making your own decisions and relishing in your independence, so parental advice will be intolerable. Life in the big-city-USA fast lane is alluring and exciting. Unfortunately, it can also be toxic to Jewish values. Even Superman can't bathe in kryptonite.

Gap year alumni have the tendency to "throw the baby out with the bathwater." Society tells us Orthodoxy is politically incorrect. It can be painted as intolerant, exclusionary, discriminatory, cruel. Observance feels like a drag and any excuse to drop it is tempting. The excuses these days are numerous. Long dresses on hot days? You got to be kidding. Can't eat with friends in whatever restaurant? Can't go to a music festival because it requires breaking Shabbat? Soon you have found plenty of reasons to let your hard-earned spirituality drain down the tubes. The precious baby goes down with the proverbial bathwater. Suddenly, you are rationalizing it's imperative to use your phone on Shabbat, our dietary laws are way too strict and who has time for Torah study? Some insist they were brainwashed in Israel and rather than be nurtured by the experience, allow the memory to fade like a winter sunset.

Then there's laziness. It's hard enough to study, get a job, maintain a social life. Who has time for mitzvot? No one is supervising you anymore. Many of your twenty-something peers will be staying up all night, sleeping past noon, mindlessly staring into screens, taking minimal course loads in college...in other words, avoiding reality. Some hold on to the Jewish basics but drop the "inconvenient stuff." This doesn't work—it's those inconvenient details that make Jewish life amazing. Remember *Pirkei Avot*, "According to the effort is the reward?" Our tendency toward laziness is exacerbated by substance abuse. Everyone is smoking pot these days; it's the new normal. Ever try to get a stoner to motivate? How about binge drinking in a perpetual pregame? How can one focus on personal growth in a city where something amazing is happening every single night?

So these are the challenges facing you when you get back. They are formidable. What's the secret to success? Just remember the "baby with the bathwater" image. Your precious *neshama* is like a baby. It requires protection, nurturing, breastfeeding. It won't survive on the streets. I've heard it said that *emunah* is like breakfast. You need breakfast every day. You can't say, "Well, I had breakfast on Monday—I'm good for the week." Similarly, we need to build *emunah* every day. Never take your *emunah* for granted. It's fragile, easily damaged. Your Jewish education must be referenced constantly. You have to say *Modeh Ani* when you wake up. You have to *daven* daily. You have to say *Sh'ma* every night. You have to learn Torah regularly. You have to go out of your way to make Shabbat and *chagim* amazing. In terms of the "bathwater" part of the image, bathwater will get dirty. Life is messy. That's normal. There are going to be hard times, there are going to be things in observance that bother you, you will get lazy. Taking a bath means getting in the water, in other words, mixing with society, living in the world. But when you open the drain, protect your baby—it's your baby!

Once I met with a cantor friend, one of the veteran *chazzanim* in the business. He was lamenting the sad state of *Yiddishkeit* in his Conservative synagogue. He described the kids in the Hebrew school as *chutzpadik* and unreachable, their parents as utterly ignorant of their heritage and the situation growing worse with each generation. He explained that he got into the Conservative movement because it was supposed to be the "American stamp on Orthodoxy." But then it started to split from tradition little by little. He compared the split to "two rails of train tracks that aren't perfectly parallel. At first they are just a bit off. But after a hundred miles, each track is in a different state." I'm not telling you this story to criticize the Conservative movement, God forbid. I just want you understand that any investment you make in your Judaism really does matter. You are at the crossroads. Your decisions affect multiple generations. They affect your parents and siblings, your friends at school and the workplace. Mom and I have done our best to give you the tools to stay "on track," both in Judaism and in quality of life. Now it's up to you to choose a direction. You are not just choosing for yourself, you're choosing for your great-grandchildren. Of course, we will always love you, whatever you choose.

You have so many remarkable traits. You are a born leader. You are exceptionally compassionate. You are selflessly dedicated to your friends and family. You are a proud, influential Jew. You are sharp, organized, entrepreneurial and motivated. You are vastly talented and creative. We are fascinated by you and love watching you grow. We *daven* for your success in seminary and beyond. You give us so much *nachas*. May you continue to go from strength to strength. I love you, my darling daughter, up to Hashem!

Love, Dad

PART TEN

The Music of the Soul

This section is dedicated by
SHMUEL AND LYNN BAR-LEV

Sammy, since early childhood, your orderly collections of rocks, shells, art and of course, music, demonstrate a unique, wondrous and worldly curiosity. Over the years, your focus has been in four vast areas—music, Judaism, family and fun! Your scholarly, loving and inquisitive approach to Torah study has shaped the mensch you are. Your uncanny ability to joyously engage every person in every musical performance or lecture you offer is magical. Your devotion to the Jewish People and your family, friends and community has made you a man admired around the world. We envision The Joy of Judaism becoming an important part of of every Jewish family's library, handed down l'dor vador. Mazel tov!

IN THIS SECTION:

Music in Judaism: In Search of the Tenth Song 325

The Making of a Musician..330

Deepening the Experience: Ode to the 8-Track 336

Legacy: The Yellow Violin.. 339

Mentors: Losing Debbie 342

Shabbat Tent: The Treasure of the High Sierra 347

Musical Thunder from Down Under 354

Coda: The Secret of Six 358

OVERVIEW

Alas, you have made it to the last section of the book! Thanks for sticking with me on this Jewish joyride. By now, you realize I see the world with a musician's eyes. I'm excited to write about my journey in my profession and its juxtaposition with spirituality. As you've read so far, this book is quite personal, so how can I write a memoir of sorts and not include a part of my life shaping my existence and giving me purpose every day?

Music has a powerful role in Judaism and for many, is a primary point of connection. I'm gainfully employed because few things unite Jewish audiences as effectively as spiritual Jewish music, and as we have discussed, unity is a core value that we ignore at our peril. Music bridges nations, generations and denominations. Furthermore, music keeps us young and nurtures us as we age. It touches us in the depths of our soul. Our musical memories are among our most formative. I have performed in many a senior home where the ONLY thing to reach the folks in the dementia ward is a favorite tune. Familiar melodies can transport us to the very time and place we first heard them, evoking whatever emotions and visuals we associate with the scene.

In the chapters that follow, I describe my own musical evolution and discuss music as a transmitter of values, music in history and the current renaissance in contemporary Jewish music. I relate to the oft-quoted phrase, "Talking about music is like dancing about architecture." I get queasy anytime someone tries to neatly wrap my music in a genre-specific bow. There is no quantity of spoken words that can communicate as profoundly as a short snippet of music—but I'm going to give it a try in the next several chapters.

One might think that someone engaged in music all day would prefer the solace of silence when off duty. Not me! Music is my vocation and avocation. I love great music of all styles performed by dedicated musicians. I can't get enough. I hope my enthusiasm for the arts is contagious. Rather than another movie this weekend, maybe check if there are worthy musicians playing in your town. Arena concerts are great but don't forget the small clubs— that's where you can congratulate the players in between sets and get to know your fellow music fans.

Any inspired melody is truly the melody of our Creator, channeled through the hopefully humble soul of God's musicians. May we all hear the music of creation and sing the song of our redemption speedily in our day.

Music in Judaism: In Search of the Tenth Song

♫ WHAT WILL YOU LEAVE BEHIND ♫

joyjud.com/m/wlb

It's the death of sincerity
Searching your memories to market pork and beans
It's a rape of the melody
Refining divine inspiration for prime-time TV
The best of intentions
Will not keep the food on the table
But nobody mentions
The food that is for your soul

Waiting for the day
When you'll have it your way
The time you plan to find

No, there is no second chance
When you're done with your dance
What will you leave behind

It's the end of humanity
Tomorrow's Picasso is working 9 to 5
Don't deny it's insanity
The landfills are brimming with packaging sublime
A nursery school student
Can rival a modern museum
While artists more prudent
Are rendering cans of beer

I'm writing this chapter in Colorado, having just performed an outdoor concert for the Denver Jewish Experience. The day was bright and sunny and I seemed to know every other person in the audience. By gathering in an expansive park, the organizers managed to avoid any one synagogue's fiefdom and hosted families from all denominations. There was no need to bring my own band—I recruited a variety of talented local friends who have accompanied me over the years. I added a pair of gifted Latin percussionists from a local church who volunteered their time to express support for the Jewish community.

I feel a sense of homecoming every time I visit the Mile High City. I return at least once a year to give concerts and visit my alma mater, University of Colorado, Boulder. I opted to extend this trip a few days to see friends and hike. What a thrill to enjoy blue sky days on the trail, relive memories on campus and visit the "youngsters" who now inhabit my fraternity house. I enjoyed meals with old pals, jammed with hippies on the Pearl Street Mall and lodged in a creative friend's imaginative canyon home.

One morning I chose to sleep in, pray leisurely and do some much-needed yoga. My regimen becomes even more crucial on the road since I am enduring cramped airline seats and beds of varying quality. Colorado was my third tour stop of the week, and it was long past time for me to get on the mat. As I did my downward dog, crescent and pigeon poses, I was listening to an album by one of my favorite singer-songwriter-bassists, Richard Page. The music filled me with inexplicable, indescribable joy. I knew every phrase and sang unabashedly in my friend's empty home. Why does this album make me so happy? I could say the same about so many of the thousands of albums in my collection. Why do they have such an impact on my psyche? How is it possible to anticipate every beat and every lyric? Why is music so directly connected to my sense of well-being? How do these ephemeral sound waves transform my workout from drudgery to a celebration?

Here's what I deduced on that sweet, sweaty morning: familiar music graces established neural templates in the deepest storage troves of our memory. The first time we hear any given piece, the sound traces a path in our brain, much like grooves on an LP. The next time we hear those notes, we have a vague recall of where the rhythms fall. And by the tenth or hundredth time we hear that same music, every lyric, each kick drum and hi-hat, every guitar lick and violin flourish, all the counterpoint and harmony, oozes like dripping honey along ever more sophisticated synaptic paths. Our favorite recordings actually become a part of our physiology, remaining predictable and reassuring in an ever-changing world.

We have a limited window of opportunity to establish deep connections with the genres we consider to be OUR music. Our brains are infinitely more malleable when we are young. Just as it's easier for kids to learn a foreign language or to pick up a new accent, the same is true when learning a musical instrument or building repertoire. Those neural receptors "calcify" with age; the musical input we receive from birth until we're in our early twenties is rendered most profoundly in our gray matter. For the rest of our lives, the impact of new music pales in comparison. Much like when high school seniors view incoming ninth graders with disdain and claim the student body is going downhill, we grow intolerant of the latest hits. For most of us, by our mid-twenties, we recoil in horror at the latest "noise" on the radio.

Now that I've hit my fifties, it takes a really amazing album to penetrate my consciousness. I do listen to Top 40 radio to stay current for my studio work and to humor my kids who switch it on as soon as we're in the car. But it remains "my kids' music." I often find new songs resonating because they mine a retro vein from the "old days." Keeping up with the trends is essential in my business—in the immortal words of John Lennon, "Either you grow with music or music outgrows you." Another reason we may find it a challenge to incorporate new music later in life is because we have so much input filling our brains by adulthood. Not only is there less cranial storage space for new stimuli—by our late twenties, we start losing neurons and by sixty, our brains actually shrink. Paul McCartney's album released at the advanced age of (When I'm) sixty-four was cleverly entitled, "Memory Almost Full."

I took advantage of my children's youthful synapses by strategically feeding them a steady diet of my musical heroes from rock to jazz to classical. I experience unbounded mirth when they call me from college to rave about a "new" favorite band from the seventies. I turned Max on to my favorite instrumental jazz band, Pat Metheny Group, when he was a pre-schooler. He listened intently to half the album and then asked in a tiny voice, "Daddy, when are they going to start singing?" To this day music serves as a primary bonding mechanism with all my kids. Now that Max is back in L.A. after his stint at Yeshiva University in New York, we hit a jazz club every week. Jesse, a sax player, prefers Stevie Wonder, Billy Joel and Earth Wind and Fire; I spoil my classical pianist Sarah with outings to Beethoven, Bach and Brahms (and occasionally, Bieber).

Music is perhaps the best medium for the dissemination of universal values. According to author Georgia Cates, "Music is what feelings sound like." At its core, music wields a cross-cultural element of truth. That's why a hit in Sweden can also rise up the charts in countries around the globe. Movie scores enhance emotional engagement and allow audiences to suspend disbelief. Studios may dub in foreign languages but the scores serve their purpose worldwide. Imagine hearing a major arpeggio played by the organist at a major league baseball game. The crowd can't help but yell, "Charge!" Contrast that with the suspenseful two notes of the "Jaws" theme; they slowly crescendo and accelerate and our teeth clench as we dread an impending shark attack, even on dry land! Regardless of our age, education or birthplace, we can describe a tune as happy or sad, suspenseful or romantic.

We are currently witnessing the explosion in popularity of the multi-day music festival. Our youth are discovering oneness, peace and loving-kindness not in places of worship but in carefully manicured, colorful settings where music is the common language and catalyst for unity. At a U2 concert several years ago, a message appeared on the gigantic video screen imploring fans to take out their cell phones. Within moments, the arena was bathed in a surreal Android glow as the audience swayed in time with the messianic-tinged song, "One." We were then instructed to text our names to a certain number. Immediately, the room went dark but everyone's face lit up as they quickly texted. Finally, at the climax of the song, while 25,000 people were jumping ecstatically singing in unison, "One love, one blood, one life," our projected names cascaded like alphabetic confetti across the stadium walls. I still get chills thinking about it.

For the Jewish People, religious life without music is unthinkable. Some say beer is proof that God loves humanity. I prefer Kurt Vonnegut's take: "Music is, to me, proof of the existence of God." Jews see music as the catalyst of Creation. The Big Bang is summed up in the first line of Genesis, beginning with the word *B'reishit*. According to the Dzikover Rebbe (Rabbi Yidele Horowitz, 1905-1989), *B'reishit* can be rearranged to spell *Shirat Aleph Beit*, the song of the alphabet. In other words, every aspect of the universe is continuously sung into being. Our *Tanach* (Bible) is replete with epic songs punctuating the narrative. Jubal, inventor of the first instruments, is one of the few key characters mentioned in the first ten generations of humankind. The patriarchs composed while in the fields with their livestock—Jewish tradition maintains King David was "hearing" their songs as he composed his Psalms. Our prophets of yore required music to enter a transcendent realm and hear God's voice. Vast orchestras accompanied the service in the Temple. *Perek Shira* is a gorgeous text indexing the songs of all creation found throughout *Tanach*. From the stars, sun and moon to the rivers and seas, from fruit and trees to the birds and bees, all sing to Hashem.

What is the origin of this music coming to me almost nightly? How is my subconscious creating a soundtrack for my dreams? Is it an amalgam of all the melodies I processed that day? Am I hearing remnants of biblical melodies in the ether? After an extended wedding ceremony in the Old City of Jerusalem, I had the rare opportunity to spend an hour in *yechidus* (one on one) with Rabbi Shlomo Carlebach. For years I had served as his West Coast keyboardist and relished any time I was able to spend in his presence. Underneath the arch of the Churva Synagogue ruins, he spoke of my music and how it moved him. He told me I possessed a tremendous gift and a *mamash* (hugely) enormous responsibility to share it. He then warned that I had to be prepared for when the *Mashiach* would come to me and say, "Sam, how did you know all my *nigunim*?" Of course, Reb Shlomo always knew the right words to say…can you imagine a more powerful charge for a young composer? I was told that when he left this world at the tender age of sixty-nine, he was on an airplane bound for the next gig with my "Shira" album in his Walkman.

Music in Prayer

When we sing our prayers, we transform our worship from lethargy to ecstasy, from stasis to action and commitment. Find a *shul* where they sing! The *nusach* (traditional melody) of prayer is so beautifully detailed that one could conceivably travel by time machine to any service in history and know if it's a weekday, Shabbat or a holiday, if it's morning, afternoon or evening and whether the congregation is Sephardic or Ashkenaz. Let's ensure the neural pathways of our children are engraved by magnificent Mosaic music!

Specific tropes accompany the public reading of our Torah and prophetic writings. These musical symbols add color and even commentary to the black and white text. We even have a melody for Torah study. The revelation of Torah to the millions assembled at Sinai was marked by an unprecedented concert spectacular, featuring mass synesthesia where we "heard" the sights and "saw" the sounds. According to the *Midrash*, the Jews were so blown away by Revelation that they died and required resuscitation. One thought is the holy music of the angels was so extraordinary they <u>chose</u> to leave their mortal bodies.

In the past several hundred years we have inherited the rich tradition of Chassidic *nigunim*, or wordless melodies, gifts of *tzadikim* (righteous people) allowing for the deepest spiritual connections without lyrics getting in the way of the sentiment. Lacking Hebrew fluency? Just sing, "*Aye dee di di dee.*"

According to the Maharal of Prague (Judah Loew ben Bezalel, 1512-1609), music serves the threefold purpose of the creation of humankind: to develop a connection with the divine in the form of prayer, to connect us with one another and to connect us with our own souls. The gift of music is one of the best examples of the majesty of our *neshamot* (souls). Human ability to compose masterworks is a miracle that baffles evolutionists. The apex of human achievement resides in the expression of our limitless soul. According to Rabbi Benjamin Blech, we don't go to the symphony to hear horsehair scraping on catgut! Music helps us appreciate that the physical realm exists primarily to give structure to the spiritual. Another function of music is to give us a unique sense of the dimension of time. Music requires time to unfold and develop, one note requires the next to complete a musical phrase. We can only enjoy it in the present but it requires the past for context and draws us into a glorious future. Music makes time fly! We also gain an appreciation of eternity through music. Think of great symphonies and operas, John Coltrane's bebop or The Beatles' Sgt. Pepper—gifted composers capture indescribable profundity from beyond; their accomplishments never die.

Some folks can't abide by my new settings of liturgy, preferring the "traditional" melodies. I, too, enjoy the old favorites but I can point to King David as the source for engaging in "*shir chadash l'Adonai*," (singing a new song for God). New music communicates vitality and excitement and keeps ritual from becoming stagnant. As one of my favorite composers, Gustav Mahler, puts it, "Tradition is tending the flame, not worshipping the ashes." When I'm asked if I perform "originals" or "covers," I reply that no one really writes originals. Composition is a more accurate term since all composers stand on the shoulders of those who have come before. However, each unique way of combining notes, rhythm and harmony brings freshness to life. Remarkably, even with millions of songs on Spotify, we can still be surprised by a new creation. New music is crucial to the Jewish concept of redemption. The Talmud teaches that King Chizkiyahu was destined to be *Mashiach* (the Messiah) but was deemed unworthy because he couldn't sing. According to Rabbi Nathan Lopes Cardozo: "Judaism can't be passed on without a song and a smile."

The *Midrash* describes ten primary songs featured in *Tanach*. Nine have already been sung, such as *Az Yashir*, the spontaneous outpouring of prophetic music sung by the masses at the splitting of the sea. We also have Moshe Rabeynu's final song, *Ha'azinu*, as well as songs by Devorah, Hannah and Kings David and Shlomo. One song has yet to be written, awaiting a future date "when the redeemed ones leave exile." This is the Tenth Song for which we are yearning. I have a feeling it's ready for download—can you hear it yet?

It is a tremendous privilege to channel God's music and share it wherever I travel. The best part of my day is the occasional note from a listener describing how they were moved by one of my albums. What a gift! And yet, I can't claim credit—I have God to thank for the inception of my compositions and the tenacity to make them public. May God bless all of us with a holy life filled with sweetness and harmony. And may we soon merit singing the Tenth Song of creation together in Jerusalem.

The Making of a Musician

♫ ALONE (WRITTEN AT AGE SEVEN) ♫

joyjud.com/m/aln

Alone is when you have time to spare
And do not have anyone to play with or
share
Alone is being lonely
Having nothing to do
Feeling sad and fearful
Uncomfortable and blue

While other people are talking
Really having fun
You feel so embarrassed
You feel you want to run
Without any friends
Till the very end

I am a musician. It makes me smile just typing those words.

Working as a musician is like trying to run a marathon. Every mile, your body tells you to stop. Quitting is the reasonable thing to do. Conversations with cousins and uncles frequently include the question, "But Sammy, how long can you do this?" When hearing yet another stellar local jazz band, I must quell the subconscious mantra *look how amazing these guys play…and you call yourself a musician?* For half a century I have been fighting this internal and external dialog and somehow, I can audaciously claim I am a bona fide full-time, successful musician. Here's how it happened.

All musicians have a beloved relative or formative teacher who helped them spread their musical wings. I'm grateful to my parents for creating a space where I could pursue my dreams. Crucial for my survival was the family rule: "Sam can sing." I sang all the time. Still do. It drove my brothers crazy. I put myself to sleep every night bouncing my head on my pillow and gnashing my teeth to the groove in my head. It freaked out my parents and they sought medical help. I sang through meal times, on car rides, in the bathtub. I sang along with the classical pieces I played on the piano. Legend has it I started harmonizing when I was three. My folks defended my tuneful quirk and would not allow anyone to silence it.

Around that age they took me to see my favorite musical, Fiddler on the Roof. During the pregnant pause after the line, "Then you love me?" I filled in the gap in my best toddler soprano, "I suppose I do."

By age seven, I was writing songs. My third grade teacher asked the class to write a poetic ode to a color, much like those in the book "Hailstones and Halibut Bones." My poems always had music attached to them. I thought that was normal. I started with Black, moved onto Yellow and then wrote a song about my loneliness. Other themes followed: the scourge of air pollution, the allure of the ocean and a song about the joyful chaos of living with three little brothers. My mom, a talented singer and pianist, marveled at my first poem, Black, and must have intuited its lyrical rhythm. Having no idea that it was already a song, she sat at the piano attempting to put it to music. I scampered up next to her exclaiming, "Mom, that's not how it goes!"

I have music coming down from both sides of the family. My maternal grandmother Zetta was the family pianist and grandfather Bill (Ze'ev Dov, for whom my oldest son is named) was a gifted violinist and violist and played with the Sacramento Philharmonic. His brother Reuben played oboe and bassoon for the Minnesota Orchestra. My mom and her three siblings are all musicians. She's a pianist but picked up the guitar so we could do gigs together when I was a preteen. She earned her music degree at UC Berkeley and UCLA, sang with the L.A. Master Chorale and performed all over L.A. with her professional singing group, Collage. She still meets weekly with pianist friends to hammer out classical music for four hands on the pair of grand pianos in her living room.

My dad plays the trumpet. He also comes from a musical family where one brother, Jerry, sang opera and the other, Herb, is a jazz pianist. My Grandpa Sam, for whom I'm named, didn't like my dad's choice of instrument and he was forced to practice in the closet. All his pent up passion for that brassy sound exploded anytime we had a family occasion. He sent everyone in the room ducking for cover as he played "My Yiddeshe Mama" or a big band favorite. At age eighty-eight he is still playing! Dad taught me a lifelong lesson: never give up. He modeled his own advice as a master salesman in his garment manufacturing company. Thanks to my dad, I have a love for horns and the entrepreneurial spirit to persist in my chosen career.

As described in the TGIF chapter, Friday Night in my household meant Shabbat. Even though we rarely went to the synagogue and didn't keep kosher, Shabbat dinner was non-negotiable. It consisted of candlelighting, *Eishet Chayil* (we would riff on an English translation) and *Kiddush*. My dad would give us a blessing, the very same priestly benediction I offer my children and hope they will say to their children. My mom, an incredible cook, would serve delicious, predictable food for her family and guests. Then, like clockwork, we'd move en masse to the Steinway in the music room and sing every song in the book. These days, my observance level doesn't allow me to play the piano on Shabbat, but luckily for me, singing is always encouraged so we enjoy music in our home everyday.

My primary motivation to master the piano was due to my desperation to make the hammers of the piano jump and get everyone singing just like my mom. Those seminal songs of my childhood became the influences resonating in every note I compose. Great Songs of the 60s by Milt Okun. Rodgers and Hart to Rodgers and Hammerstein. Fiddler, Hair, The Me Nobody Knows, A Chorus Line. Cole Porter, George Gershwin, Carole King, Simon and Garfunkel. The Beatles Complete. The Fireside Book of Folk Songs. My Songs We Sing album series borrows its title from the classic Jewish songbook of the same name. Back then,

I didn't even realize I was coming up with counterpoint or using dynamics. I loved to sit next to my mom on the piano bench embroidered by my Grandma Zetta, carefully following the notes so I could turn pages at the right moment, harmonizing until I was hoarse.

The summer after third grade, we moved to Brentwood. For my dad, it was a big statement to move to a sizeable house in a fancy neighborhood. For my mom, it meant more space to keep clean. For me, it meant my own room and interesting new neighbors. OJ Simpson and Fred MacMurray lived nearby. Caesar Romero once picked me up off the pavement after a bike crash. Just across our backyard fence lived John Densmore, drummer for The Doors. I can't describe the feeling I had when I first heard Stevie Wonder's Talking Book album coming through the bushes, loud. When Superstition played, my knees went weak. That groove, that horn section! How did he get the piano to do that? I ran inside and filled the Steinway with notebook paper and paper clips to simulate a Clavinet sound. Can you imagine my mom's shock when she eventually sat down to play?

When I was ten years old, following a month at my beloved Camp Ramah, my dad sent me to Tony Trabert's Tennis Camp. Dad's ultimate goal was to make tennis players out of his four boys. Any self-respecting Jewish kid had to know how to handle a racket and as an A-rated player, Dad wanted us to give him a good game. I was placed in the lame group and only once did Tony stoop to teach us personally. A few nights each week we had disco night. Super cool! This was the summer of Elton John's "Crocodile Rock," The Doobies "Listen to the Music" and "Take it Easy" by the Eagles. Rock and Roll was awesome but I was even more blown away by Tower of Power's "You Got to Funkifize." I think it's due to my dad's attempt to make a tennis player out of me that I discovered funk. Soon I was hooked on Earth, Wind and Fire, War and Marvin Gaye. This was the early seventies—I wore tight bell-bottoms, tie dye shirts and imagined myself to have serious swagger.

My mom purchased season tickets to nearly every symphonic, choral and opera event available. This was a veritable gold mine for me since my brothers had little interest in such culture. While I loved going to Laker and Dodger games with my sports fan dad, I was happiest accompanying my mom for these elegant evenings of sublime music. My own concerts with the L.A. Jewish Symphony have fulfilled the dream of that little kid in the suit sitting in row E, soaking in every note of the L.A. Philharmonic's eclectic repertoire.

My musical influences were also shaped by my mom's cousin, Lynn Berman, now Bar-lev, who I thought of as my aunt. Lynnie turned me on to the world of jazz with front row seats to Les McCann, McCoy Tyner and Herbie Hancock, among others. She always had super-cool jazz on her stereo. Aunt Lynnie also encouraged my love of art; she worked with some of the most brilliant artists and graphic designers on the planet and they became my buddies. It's thanks to her that I can glance at a canvas at any given museum and guess the artist. She gave me my first taste of being published by using one of my early songs called "This World" as a holiday card for her design firm. The silver gloss panel featured the lyrics in my own hand, signed at the bottom: "Sammy Glaser, age 7. May this child's dreams be realized by all mankind."

When I was eleven, Aunt Lynnie took me into a recording studio and hired a professional guitarist so I could record my first fourteen-song album. I can still see the walls of that studio in my mind—I had found nirvana. She recently reminded me that I was totally copacetic in these sessions…until the guitarist tried a groove or a chord voicing that didn't jive with my vision. For my Bar Mitzvah, Lynnie had all of those songs beautifully transcribed and bound in a book that I treasure to this day. Take note: the best gifts are thought out, unique and clarify we really know the recipient. We can make a huge impact on young people with our praise and love—they don't have to be our own kids. Thanks Auntie Lynnie...I love you forever!

Mom pushed me hard during my Bar Mitzvah year. She took me to lessons in Torah trope with the Sinai Temple organist, Aryell Cohen and made me practice daily. Cantor Joseph Gole took an interest in my budding ability to interpret liturgy and invited me into his *Shacharit* Choir every Saturday morning. I learned to chant the entirety of Shabbat and holiday services as well as Torah and *Haftorah* trope. I remember my mom saying, "Sam, if you work this hard at everything in your life, there is NOTHING you can't do."

The next year, the Concert Choir at Paul Revere Jr. High held auditions to find a male and female delegate to a citywide vocal competition. My folks exulted when I was chosen to represent the school. We went through my repertoire and opted for *Every Valley Shall Be Exalted* from Handel's Messiah. I had no problem with the range or long runs—I was still a boy soprano and my breath control and ability to project was likely due to the need to sing over the din of my piano playing. My mom rehearsed with me and *shlepped* me to the final tribunal. I won the first prize male vocalist in the L.A. City Schools and had the award presented by my hero, conductor Zubin Mehta, at the L.A. Music Center. Best $100 of my life.

High school got off to a rocky start. In ninth grade, as a senior in Jr. High, I was on top of the world. Tenth grade, not so much. I had a delayed adolescence and was now surrounded by hordes of larger, hairier guys. I was tortured by Algebra but a natural at Biology. I loved my enthusiastic Spanish teacher, Mrs. Mednick and became a Spanish major, largely because it was so easy—I grew up in a Spanish-as-a-second-language home. I had a tough-as-nails English teacher who gave me a C but taught me to write. Thanks you, Mrs. Mary Redclay, for not letting me take any shortcuts! I eventually found my way to the Palisades Madrigals, the top shelf vocal ensemble in school. Yes, we spent much of our time singing Christmas repertoire, but the arrangements were inspiring and the choir room became my second home.

That year, thanks to my Aunt Lynnie's connection with pawnshop owner Darryl Kaplan in San Francisco, I purchased my first electric keyboard. I lugged that beasty Yamaha Electone to rehearsals with my new high school band. We covered Led Zeppelin, Doors, Queen and Cars tunes and I got the gig because I could hit the high notes and play keys at the same time. I was in polyphonic paradise thanks to the ability to endlessly sustain notes on this organ and spent hours in my room holding down the keys. My rock and roll piano chops were coming to fruition thanks to the aid of piano teacher David Kaminer, who liberated me from the constraints of Beethoven and Chopin. He also introduced me to the Fender Rhodes and soon I saved enough for my first Suitcase 88.

In eleventh grade, I noticed my buddy Brian Hance was getting a lot better than me. I got on the waiting list to study with his piano teacher, Dick Fister (yes, I'm serious). As soon as he worked me into his schedule, he would show up at my house, request a scotch on the rocks and teach me jazz. He taught me the standards, how to comp, how to voice chords and most importantly, how to get solos out of my head and into my fingers. Mr. Fister was the entertainer at a piano bar in Santa Monica called The Round Table. Whenever he needed a night off, he would send me in as a sub...a smooth-faced sixteen-year-old playing Stella by Starlight amidst a cacophony of smoking divorcees. They would put bread in my jar and joke, "Sam, what are you doing here?"

When I graduated Palisades High, I went straight to Berklee College of Music in Boston. I was a long-haired, seventeen-year-old wannabe rock star. I learned how to sneak into every jazz club and concert hall and negotiated the byways of the historic city with a combination of my trusty skateboard and the T subway. I had the time of my life partying with my uber-talented peers in the dorms, joining the jams in the maze of rehearsal rooms and studying with the likes of Mike Metheny and Gary Burton. I spent my free time trying to figure out the keyboard parts to Dixie Dregs, Weather Report and Billy Cobham tunes. Every few weeks my progressive jazz band would perform at clambakes and fraternity parties along the Massachusettes and New Hampshire coast. I somehow schlepped my enormous Rhodes, Yamaha organ and Arp Odyssey in taxi cabs!

Eventually, I felt the clarion call of the wilderness, namely Boulder, Colorado. I fancied myself a renaissance man and wanted to study subjects other than orchestrating and ear training. Mostly, though, I wanted to attend a school that had girls, fraternities and skiing, all of which were absent at Berklee. My dad was thrilled because it meant I might go to the business school and study accounting. For four years I pulled off a double major in business and voice, which required twenty plus units per semester. In spite of the workload, I became an active member of Chi Psi fraternity, summited several 14,000 foot peaks with the hiking club, skied most winter weekends and supervised the apparel sponsorship of the Coors International Bicycle Classic. Thanks to my ability to tickle the ivories, my summers were spent in piano bars in Glacier National Park and the Greek isle of Hydra. My wanderlust was insatiable...during this five-year period I managed to travel around the world three times. One of these expeditions included a hundred amazing days circumnavigating the globe on Semester at Sea, where I performed with my shipboard band, The Tune Officials.

Over the course of my Boulder years, I danced a schizophrenic ballet of musical genres. Freshman year, I joined a heavy metal band called Castlerock, sophomore year, a jazz-fusion quintet called Open Flight, then as a junior I bécame a proud member of a New Wave band called Early Man. I was absolutely positive each of these bands was going to make it to the top of the charts. As a voice major in a classical music-focused school, I had to study opera and prepare arias in multiple languages for voice juries each semester, adjudicated by my demanding professors. I met all the cool cats in the local live music scene, had my first taste of working as a studio musician and got to perform in ski resort music halls throughout the state. I initiated my first "all Sam Glaser music" band in my senior year, The Third Wave. One of our first gigs in Denver was at the Rainbow Club; a few weeks later I got to see a little known band called U2 play the same stage. At this point, I realized I functioned better in a dictatorship than a democracy. I was able to call the shots, hire and fire players and make the financial investment in recording my own music. To this day, the only investments that have paid off for me are those where I have backed my own career.

Post-graduation, I moved back to L.A. and opened my first recording studio, a compact but elegant facility right by the airport, hence the name LAX Records. My music partner Chuck Sparks and I purchased, rented and borrowed the minimal gear necessary to make multi-track records and in spite of our lack of experience, somehow turned out decent sounding music. We moved into a beachside townhouse in Playa del Rey in order to be closer to work and the surf. Most importantly, I now had a hideaway where I could indulge my predilection for music and technology around the clock and no one could make me turn down the volume. I felt blessed to live in a city where creatives from around the world gathered to make dreams come true. Before long, those top musicians I looked up to as a kid became my friends and peers. I got to boss them around in marathon studio sessions for albums I was producing and performed with them in nightclubs like The Roxy, The Whisky, The Troubadour, At My Place and Madame Wongs.

Around this time, my sightreading skills came in handy when the baritone chair opened up in the Temple Emanuel of Beverly Hills High Holiday octet. It paid well and offered me my first professional Jewish music opportunity as an adult. I sang with them for eight years and the best part of the job was learning the craft of *chazzanut* from master musician, Cantor Baruch Cohen. Subsequently, I studied with him privately until I felt ready to enter the field on my own. I'm grateful to him every time I lead a Shabbat or Holiday service—I have been gainfully employed as an itinerant *chazzan* for thirty years.

That's my story. I'm still singing my songs in syngagogues and concert halls and recording my music. My primary employment when I'm not on the road is music production for a wide variety of clients. Every day is different. To date I have scored countless cues for film, TV, radio, games and apps. I've written half a dozen musicals and published multiple songbooks and lyric collections. The albums I produce for my loyal customers stretch my creative muscles, keep my world-class musicians working and the artists become part of my extended family. I get to see the world while performing in an average of fifty cities a year. That's over 1000 shows (and 1000 times I've sung "Hineni"). Best of all, the new songs haunting my dreams eventually find an audience with you, my dear readers.

So yes, with a little help from my friends, I am a musician. Thank God.

Deepening the Experience: Ode to the 8-Track

♫ MY FAMILY VACATION ♫

joyjud.com/m/mfv

C'mon kids we're going on vacation
Gather in the car
We're gonna travel this great nation
C'mon get those shoes upon your feet
Make sure you use the bathroom
Well before you take your seat
Oh, how much I love my family vacation

How many more minutes till we're there
How many more minutes
Until we can leave our chair
How many more minutes till we're done
How many more minutes
Until we can have some fun

Daddy, can we stop to get a drink
Daddy, we're so bored
We just got nothing left to think
Daddy, will you play some rock n' roll
How far can we push you
Till you start to lose control

Mommy, I am feelin' kinda crummy
All those pickles gave me
Such a tickle in my tummy
Daddy this is much more than a hunch
Open up the window or I'm gonna lose my lunch

A certain piece of dubious technology served a critical function for those growing up in suburban America during the 60s. As you drove down the freeways, if you wanted to hear your favorite songs, you needed an 8-track tape player in the dash. A clunky cassette about the size of six iPhones held about forty minutes of music in spectacular stereo. There were a few caveats. There was no way to rewind. And at certain points, a metallic piece of tape signaled the tape head to switch tracks. That meant a moment of somber silence and then a clickety-clack, sometimes right in the middle of your favorite song. It wasn't ideal but it was certainly more graceful than trying to operate a turntable when changing lanes.

Three times a year, our family would pile into our nine-passenger Oldsmobile Vista Cruiser station wagon equipped with skylights, a 450cc V8 and a trusty tape deck. On our way to Lake Tahoe, Arizona or Colorado we would sing at the top of our lungs with our favorite thirty-two 8-track tapes. That's all that fit in the black vinyl carrying case and that's all the portable music we owned. The cassettes were pricey and fragile. We had several Beatles albums, War, Tower of Power, Carole King, Roberta Flack, Joni Mitchell, The Temptations, Shostakovich, Beethoven and assorted musicals. This vehicle was handed down to me when I left for the University of Colorado, Boulder. A favorite collegiate pastime on snowy nights was stuffing the car with a dozen friends from the dorms, cranking up the aforementioned albums and doing donuts in the nearby Safeway parking lot.

A few years back, I had an epiphany while attending a L.A. Philharmonic concert. One sunny Sunday morning, I was knee deep in over thirty arrangements for the half dozen albums I was juggling for clients. I was about to embark on twenty hours of background vocal sessions with some of the finest singing specialists I know. These sessions aren't cheap to run and I wanted to make sure every song was ready to go with all the vocal parts, lyrics and recording templates prepared. Midday, I glanced at my calendar and was reminded that the L.A. Phil was presenting a matinee of Beethoven's 5th at 2:00 pm. One voice in my head said, *Sam, just buckle down and get these charts done.* The victorious voice said, *you deserve a break today!* I hadn't experienced this immortal masterpiece in years and I couldn't pass up the pleasure of hearing it performed by one of the greatest orchestras in the world, in Disney Hall, one of the greatest concert halls ever constructed.

No, I didn't have tickets. There are always seats. I have a maxim particularly relevant in an entertainment town like L.A.: if you don't go, you don't get in the show. In other words, "If you build it, he will come." While milling about the box office, I found someone with an extra ticket and was treated to a few hours of symphonic bliss. Third row center. Gustavo Dudamel conducting. Beethoven affects me in a visceral way. It's not just that I share my birthday with the great composer—I know every last passage of his major works intimately and during the concert I had to force myself not to conduct. I was even ready for that measure mid-movement when the family 8-track tape would clunk as it switched to the next section.

Here's the epiphany—I grew up getting to know certain pieces of music intimately. The relationship with every groove of my records or the clunk of my 8-tracks creates unmistakable magic when we reunite. Repetition and commitment deepen the experience, and deep experiences are what we want out of life.

After the concert, I wandered Downtown L.A. feeling uplifted, recharged and filled with possibilities. Rather than go right back to work (OK, now I was really procrastinating), I crossed the street and visited the Museum of Contemporary Art. What a collection! The most compelling (and valuable) pieces of art are those where creators limited themselves to a certain medium and theme. Rothko's rectangles of sultry color, Jackson Pollack's monochrome splatters, Jasper John's maps and flags. Depth and commitment, once again.

My children, on the other hand, have grown up with unrefined chaos in the form of millions of YouTube videos, Spotify, SoundCloud and Apple Music. All geared for a three-minute attention span. Unlimited songs and videos for free, forever. And thousands more appearing daily. It's impossible to keep up with what's new and knowing what's hot is increasingly irrelevant. There will be something hotter in a few hours. This infinite cornucopia of media is entirely taken for granted. With the landscape changing so radically, there is scarce opportunity to make even superficial connections. Other than my own music, which my kids were coerced to enjoy by growing up in our home, their musical predilections are fickle and fleeting. The repercussions are significant. Do they process relationships the same way? Instant satisfaction online does not translate well in "meat-space." A great conversation takes hours to nurture before it reaches revelatory territory. It's the same with friendships, professional experience and reputations. There is no quick fix for the test of time.

In the early days of the music business, engineers and producers were forced to master the confines of technological limitations, unleashing breathtaking creativity to realize their musical vision. During my time at Berklee College of Music, I tried to coax radio-ready recording out of my primitive Tascam Portastudio. Trying to compress my musical vision into the confines of those noisy cassette tapes proved futile, but the exercise allowed me to envision a future when memory and track count limitations would cease to exist. Years before the first Mac came out in 1984, I sketched out details of a recording system where unlimited computer speed and storage would permit the miraculous layering of tracks and access to sounds we enjoy today. I had faith in Moore's law, which forecast the exponential rise of computing power, allowing me to enjoy such treats as a masterfully sampled, hundred gigabyte concert grand piano stored on a tiny thumb drive. I'm glad I was alive for the past forty years of the digital revolution—it gave me a great appreciation for the astounding abilities we have at our disposal. It also taught me to push boundaries, forging credible creations in spite of technological confinement.

Rabbi Nathan Lopes Cardozo comments on the essential difference between Beethoven and Bach: Bach was a dutiful adherent to the "rules" of music in his days. In spite of his discipline we hear vast creativity within the constraints of the Baroque construct. Beethoven, on the other hand, broke with the accepted rules. He liberated music much the way the Beatles rescued rock and roll from the sugar-coated doo-wop of the 50s. Not to dis ol' Ludwig V, but there is a certain power in Bach's approach. Cardozo quotes the philosopher Goethe stating, "In limitation does the master really prove himself and it is only the law which can provide us with freedom."

Over the millennia, the Jewish People has perfected the art of finding the greatest freedom within the margins of biblical injunctions. Just like learning a musical instrument takes tremendous discipline, learning to maximize the 613 Commandments takes a lifetime of study. Mitzvot compel us to transcend intellectual pursuits in order to master the instrument of the soul. We endeavor the "yoke of Heaven" and like Bach, compress our creativity, deepen our context and explode in our human potential.

Sixty years ago, the 8-track tape arrived on the scene in order to make music portable. A product of a simpler time, it allowed us to intensify our experience with the few dozen "deserted island" albums we couldn't live without. It sowed the seeds for further miraculous innovations allowing us to keep our music close at hand. Now, in my pocket I carry a compass, chronograph, multiple feature films, a siddur, Bible, Talmud, GPS, word processor, camera, newspaper, web-browser, games, flashlight and a jukebox. Yes, it's a phone too. Funny how with 20,000 songs, I still listen to the same thirty-two albums. I have thousands of Facebook friends but I still call a select few with the big issues. I love having choices. I don't want to go back to my 8-track repertoire. But I'll take my friendships deep, my food slow-cooked and my soul a'rockin in the bosom of Abraham.

Legacy: The Yellow Violin

♫ A MILLION BUTTERFLIES ♫

joyjud.com/m/amb

I never saw a butterfly until today
I mean, I saw them flying 'round
But never quite like what I saw today
These butterflies were different
Made of paper, paint and glue
Telling us a story, a story sad and true

The butterfly upon the wall
Can't fly away
Colored orange and lavender
It's here to stay
But paint more than a million
You've got something to say
Oh butterfly, please fly away

Children are unlimited, ready to surprise
Children are impossible
The smile of mischief hiding in their eyes
These children are different
And they're looking at you
Will you tell the story
Of all that they went through

I never saw a butterfly until today
The voices of the Holocaust
Sounded like an ocean far away
Perhaps if the sun's tears would sing
Against a white stone...

Flemington, New Jersey was stop number one on my three week August concert tour. Half of the buildings in this Delaware River town are on the Register of Historic Places. Masterfully restored nineteenth-century Victorians resplendent with sumptuous flower boxes line each side of the main boulevard. This is not just another exit on the turnpike— its claim to fame is the immense Greek Revival courthouse built in 1828, the site of the Lindbergh "Trial of the Century." I was staying in a quaint bed and breakfast just a block away. Mild summer weather made for beautiful walks with congregants who volunteered to accompany my explorations. The Jewish community had been primed on my music and the Shabbat prayers and meals were nothing short of ecstatic. All these niceties have little to do with what made this event so special. Here's the story:

In 1925, Chaskel Frand and his wife and kids left Dubiecko, Poland for the "Golden Medina," armed with his sole source of income, a violin. He had to bid farewell to his extended family of musicians, the Frand Klezmorim. Packed in his violin case was the handwritten music they performed for weddings and for such visiting dignitaries as the Belzer and Bluzher Rebbes. Tragically, after the war, Chaskel was anguished to discover that all his relatives had perished at the hands of the Nazis.

In 1955, Chaskel decided to move to Israel so the imminent arrival of the Messiah wouldn't require that his bones roll all the way from New York (yes, the rolling of the bones is a part of Jewish tradition). At the airport, he learned he was only allowed one carry-on item. His daughter convinced him to choose his *tallis* and *tefillin* over the violin—he could buy another instrument in Israel. He reluctantly handed it to her and she stashed it in her basement for the next several years. At one point, a cousin came to visit from California. He had just started playing the violin and requested his grandfather's instrument. Eventually, the violin floated from house to house and much of the Frand sheet music portfolio wound up framed and hung in the homes of various relatives.

Fast forward to 1996. My dear friend Sharon Brooks, Chaskel's granddaughter, had a five-year-old daughter who wanted to learn violin. Sharon tracked down Chaskel's instrument and had it sent to New Jersey. It was in such a state of disrepair she had to splurge to have it restored. When word got out that the violin was back in use, relatives sent Sharon the Frand music so the priceless pieces could be played once again on the family heirloom.

In 2009, Sharon made a trip to Dubiecko to explore her roots. Even though Jews made up over half the town's population before the war, there was no sign of their presence. The Jewish cemetery was in shambles and the mass grave unmarked. Nazis had used ancient Jewish headstones to pave a road. In a moment of inspiration, she realized how to make "lemonade out of lemons:" The recovered music of the Frand Klezmorim would be the very vehicle to restore the cemetery and honor the memories of her ancestors.

Upon her return, Sharon called to ask my opinion regarding what to do with this portfolio. She sent me copies and I worked my way through the arrangements, soon recognizing the uniqueness of this treasure trove. I recommended she have them professionally transcribed so they could be performed by a modern ensemble and we discussed the logistics of throwing a debut concert as a fundraiser. Before long, she hired klezmer flutist Adrianne Greenbaum to create usable charts out of the Frand ensemble's hieroglyphics and we put a concert date on the books.

After much preparation, the big weekend arrived. Whereas many *shuls* have a completely different crowd between Friday night and Saturday services, the entire community came out for every aspect of the Shabbaton. We found capable klezmer musicians to fill out the band for the Saturday night concert and I hired one of my favorite studio drummers from New York. After a set of my songs, we presented the melodious and quite complex klezmer from the Frand catalogue. This Eastern European folk music is not intended to be listened to in a passive manner; Adrianne enthusiastically led the audience in various dances and we jammed late into the night while everyone sang along.

Thousands of dollars were raised to restore the cemetery. New music was launched in the klezmer world. The JCC of Flemington enjoyed a Shabbaton they would not soon forget. I felt blessed to have a role in this incredible saga.

I received this email from my new flutist friend: "I'm not so good with words, I'm afraid. What I want to say is that you brought such vitality to the meaning of Shabbat, with such feelings of being grateful, of what is truly important. You manage to transcend, to explore the meanings in everyday life and not make it hokey or phony. You are the real thing.

You speak with such honesty and your conviction reaches out so very simply to others who aren't yet convinced there is value to taking time off. That was your biggest message: Stop. There is a time to stop and great value to stopping. If God can stop, why not us little folk? You gave such a gift to the Frand family and to klezmer in general. Thanks for an amazing weekend of spirit and song."

I asked Sharon Brooks to fact-check this chapter and she responded with the following: "Sam, you asked me a question I never thought about before. What if my grandfather was able to bring the violin to Israel? Would this music have this new life, this revival of spirit? Perhaps what seemed like such an injustice back then was a part of the master plan. Maybe the time wasn't right. This violin, this music was, like Moses I suppose, never intended to enter the land of Israel."

Sharon's "what if" question led to one of my own. According to family legend, my grandfather Sam was a rabble-rouser in his youth. In his teenage years in Glod, Romania, he accrued gambling debts and had to skip town. He wandered the Carpathian Mountains, wound up at the Black Sea and befriended a nice Jewish girl. He convinced her family to allow him to join them on the voyage to Hamburg to catch a New York bound ship. Much like my shenanigans without my passport (noted in the Bitachon chapter), in 1921 my grandpa managed to slip into the United States without paperwork. During one of my N.Y. tours, I took my son Max to Ellis Island and scoured the records for our relative's names. Officially, Sam Glaser never made it!

My "what if" question: what if Grandpa Sam wasn't a gambler? Would he have made it to the Golden Medina to sell neckties on a pushcart on Orchard Street, eventually ramping up to a large manufacturing operation? Or would he have been extricated from Glod and carted to Auschwitz with the rest of his family? I never understood why my relatives were passive when the Nazis came for them. One year, after an Israel tour, I traveled by train, plane and automobile to access his one-horse town in Transylvania and find out for myself. As I stood there on the porch of the two-bedroom home where my grandpa lived with his ten brothers and sisters, a local elder in peasant garb spotted me from a block away. He walked right up to me and said "Glahzer!" Yes, all of us Glasers have a certain look. And this man, who used to play with my beloved aunts and uncles, was curious who survived the war. It's a shockingly short list. I realized the war was my rural ancestor's introduction to the twentieth century. Could they have fought back with pitchforks? Thank God Grandpa Sam played cards.

Every note played on the Frand violin is miraculous. Its presence in the world is a simple statement of rebuke to the nations that yearn for our destruction. The Nazis are gone. Never again will we wear the yellow star of shame. Let the melodies of the Frand Klezmorim ring up to the heavens; I'm sure these joyful cadences have the angels dancing.

Mentors:
Losing Debbie

♫ SHINE A NEW LIGHT ♫

joyjud.com/m/snl

I need a hero, I need a guide
Who will I turn to when I need to cry
You're with us forever, as big as the sky
As bright as the first light of creation
Your presence lets me fly
How on earth can we say goodbye

I picture you walking right by my side
Dream of you dancing with angels in flight
You are my hero and I'm not alone
As close as the next breath in my body

The image in my mind
Can I hope as dear a friend to find

Shine a new light, shine a new light
Shine a new light across the sky
So tomorrow will dawn

As bright as a new star in the twilight
The shimmer in my eye
Suddenly I know that you're alright
Shine a new light...

In 2010, I was invited to present at Limmud UK. This revolutionary British organization was celebrating its 30th anniversary and Debbie Friedman and I were the US-based musicians honored with an invitation. Limmud UK is the foremost Jewish learning conference worldwide; 3500 lay people of all denominations spend the last week of December engrossed in Torah study and Jewish culture at the University of Warwick. This explosive grass-roots phenomenon has now spread to over eighty cities worldwide. I have performed at US, European and Australian versions of the conference and love seeing Jewish unity fully lived rather than merely theoretical.

When I accepted the invitation, I didn't anticipate my November and December would be booked to the hilt. Twenty cities in two months is enough to make any grown man long ardently for his family, bed and wardrobe. After a ten-day East Coast marathon I had a three-day turnaround in L.A. and then boarded the ten-hour transatlantic flight. British Airways managed to sell every seat on the gargantuan 747. I was seated next to a Jewish filmmaker from Brussels named Michael Goldstein. Large world, well managed: we had friends in common and discussed the arts until he fell asleep on my shoulder. In spite of my discomfort, I managed to close my eyes, eventually awakening to a view of monochromatic, snow-laden, patchwork fields framed by indigo seas. A four-day blizzard shut down Heathrow and thankfully, it had just reopened that morning. Once on the ground, we had a two-hour wait for a two-hour bus ride. I took solace in the fact that at least I'd be able to spend quality time with Debbie.

Debbie Friedman is considered the matriarch of Jewish folk music. She started out as a camp songleader and flourished as a composer, setting liturgy to melodies of stunning sweetness and simplicity. She had a special knack for incorporating English into the prayers and creating educator-friendly material that resonated with all ages. As a young artist I was able to glean so much from her craft. We bonded over the course of twenty years of gigs and conferences when we were both on the bill. I loved her *yiddeshe neshama*, musical genius and incessant jokes. Best of all were the jams with just the two of us at her Upper West Side Manhattan apartment where I sat at her Steinway and she strummed her never-quite-in-tune guitar.

Debbie usually had protective fans smothering her with affection, ensuring she didn't overdo it. This time, she was totally in the mix, teaching, singing in the ad hoc choir, performing and hanging out at the inevitable jams until the wee hours. Several nights in a row, well past three in the morning, insomniac musicians huddled in the lounge with guitars, dumbeks and tambourines. Thanks to the miracle of ubiquitous Internet access, anytime we couldn't remember the lyrics, someone was ready with an iPad linked to the right words. Typically, I am thrust into a leadership role at these *kumzitzes* in order to manage segues and land in ideal singing keys. At Limmud, however, the leadership was shared by a dozen song leading masters. Sometimes Debbie would start something and the choice of the next tune would pass organically to another person. We enjoyed an unspoken clarity regarding when to move on to a new number and over a four-hour period covered just about every contemporary genre.

I taught a different workshop each day of the conference and even managed to attend a few classes offered by my favorite scholars. The highlight was Dr. Raphael Zarum's three-part series scrutinizing the normally tepid subject of combining meat and milk. Several artists were in need of keyboard backup so I had to schedule rehearsals to run their sets. I found I could keep up my frenetic pace as long as I saved my java jolt for mid-afternoon. The best moments at Limmud were the cracks between formal events when I made new friends and enjoyed spontaneous reunions with peers. How remarkable to visit a frigid island 8,000 miles from home and see so many familiar faces.

Debbie's last official concert was everything her fans wanted. All the hits, the crowd singing with abandon, tears aplenty at her epic ballads. Her voice was frail but she still hit the notes. Her patter was spot on and her trademark issues with guitar tuning created several comedic moments. Our beloved EJ Cohen was "on hand" to interpret both Debbie's and my shows with her flowing, bi-lingual sign language. Debbie asked that no one video, photograph or post on Facebook. Just to be present, to be with her. Of course, she sang *Mi Shebeirach* (healing prayer) for us and then us for her. Little did we know.

The next night, Debbie came to my concert with a black eye. She was walking with a tortured gait after having slipped on the ice. When temperatures dip below freezing, London fog turns into icy mist, coating the sidewalks with a treacherous layer of thin ice. I was elated she showed up—she had every excuse not to come. The highlight for me was hearing the British audiences sing along with my songs in a cockney accent. After the show, I managed to sell nearly all my CDs and then hung out at the mosh pit of a bar scene with the young folks.

I saw Debbie sitting there alone and available. Alone? This never would have happened at any of the seventeen CAJE conferences I did with her. We spoke of her new music and her tale of woe caring for her ailing mother. We brainstormed about projects we might do together now that she had moved to Southern California to be close to her mom.

Over two thousand people crammed into the auditorium for the closing gala. Many numbers featured a capable ad hoc choir assembled over the course of the week. Following my "Hineni" song, conductor extraordinaire Stephen Glass presented a moving musical tribute to Limmud, sung by the choir and featuring Debbie and me on the opening verses. She held my hand throughout the number and at its conclusion, gave me a warm, maternal smile I will never forget. I realize we make an odd couple for a number of reasons. But we are truly singing the same song, fully engaged in getting our fellow Jews invested in a relationship with a loving God.

I returned to L.A. after a full week of near all-nighters. My throat felt like high grit sandpaper from the singing, teaching, schmoozing and experiments with the eclectic beers on tap. Thrashed is the best word I can think of. At my first Shabbas meal back in L.A., my healer friend Hal Krevoy, who refers to me as his "joy coach," suggested I do a full week liver cleanse. I took him up on it. No carbohydrates, soda, caffeine, Advil, meat, booze, etc. I usually get back to work after my kids go to bed. I found myself exhausted at 10:00 pm. If this trip to the ice planet Hoth took such a toll on me, imagine what it did to my delicate friend Debbie. Tragically, she contracted pneumonia and didn't have the resources to fight it. The entire Jewish world (at least the non-Orthodox affiliated segment) held prayer vigils and sing-alongs to appeal to the Creator of the Universe to give Debbie another chance. But this was to be her time. Reform leader Jerry Kaye's Facebook post delivered the impossible news simply and finally.

Heartbreak. Tears. Shock. Disbelief. Sadness. Then all of them over again and all together. The condolences and memories poured in on Facebook, Jewish music blogs and email. I called peers just to hear their voices and get perspective. I was overbooked in the studio that week and it was hard to focus on my work. I posted these feelings at the height of my grief:

"I'm broken hearted. Our dear friend, mentor and spiritual *ima* (mother) has left the world. I can't imagine what a beautiful, holy place she is in right now. How many of us did she touch with her sweetness, with her direct channel to the angels? I will always sing for her and with her wherever I go. Everything I do I think, *wow…Debbie can't do that now*. I'm stoic and then crying again. I just reminded my kids which songs she wrote and then broke down again. I'm still not sure what losing Debbie means. I don't think any of us know. We lost her on *Parashat Beshalach,* Shabbat *Shira*. Without a doubt she's dancing with Miriam. The seas are splitting. She parted the waters for all Jewish performers. She showed us our potential. She taught us how to open the hearts of our audiences to hear God's music, how the concert or song session was not about us in the limelight, but about lifting the spirits of everyone in the room, getting them to sing and connect. Last week I got to sing with her, to hold her hand, share her smile. What a gift."

Debbie and I came from different worlds, different coasts, different theologies. She often made jokes about my move to Orthodoxy. The only people who check if I am wearing *tzitzit* are one of my Aish rabbis, Craig Taubman and Debbie Friedman. I realized the impetus for my sorrow was the impact of the loss of a mentor. Debbie was one of the few other artists who worked at her Jewish music full time, without a "day gig." When I was trying so hard to break into the business with my first release, she already had eight albums in Tara Music's Top 50. She showed me what was possible in my life. Moreover, she used her position to create opportunities for other composers and song leaders. She was the master and we were her students. She proved there were no barriers to entry; not gender, sexual preference, handicap or level of education. What mattered most was talent and tenacity and getting ourselves out of the way so God could speak through us.

Like a great Shlomo Carlebach tune, Debbie's songs connect immediately, resurfacing every time we are innocently eating a *latke*, planting a tree or teaching the *aleph-bet*. I didn't always get it. I remember when Debbie was leading a song session on the last night of the 1993 CAJE conference. I was thinking, *this kumbaya nonsense has got to stop…it's time to rock!* Her accompanist, Carol Rivel reminds me how I nearly knocked her off the piano bench in an effort to get the party started. Yes, it was only my second season in the Jewish music business and I was rash and impetuous. I didn't always appreciate the magic of Debbie's soothing music and the power of its simplicity, especially at a time when I thought rowdiness should prevail. I'm still embarrassed!

A few years ago, I was dining with Debbie in her Upper West Side apartment. We sang and schmoozed and spoke of hopes and fears. Even brilliant Debbie could feel vulnerable and question if she was making a difference. I admitted I was living on the edge… three kids in private school and a considerable mortgage riding on the back of a sole-wage-earner-musician dad. I shared how all my relatives thought I was nuts for choosing my field. She said, "Sam, if times are ever tight and you need help, I will be there for you. I will give you half the money I get in my gigs to help you out." I laughed at her gesture and she looked at me with dire seriousness. "Sam, I'm not kidding. You need to be doing what you are doing. And I will be there when you call on me."

I sobbed continuously throughout her funeral. It's the music that gets to me. Every song had me reaching for more Kleenex. Yes, I wanted to be one of those chosen to sing. But I'm not sure I could have found my voice through the tears. It was shocking to see the Collings guitar I had played just a week before resting on her casket. We had to be reminded that this ceremony was not for the musicians or the Reform movement; it was really for Debbie's immediate family grieving in the front row. The audience was a who's who in Jewish music. Sad that it took the loss of a peer to get us together.

I will never forget the graveside service. A thousand people came to the memorial and only a few hundred continued on to the interment. The Jewish custom of mourners shoveling dirt to fill the grave is ingenious. We bury our dead. It's so final and real. We sang her songs as we shoveled. I cried with her mother and sister. The three of them were a team and now they lost their captain. We formed a line to comfort the mourners and then everybody left. Except the musicians. No one told us to stay. I can only speak for myself. I couldn't leave her. I stood half-paralyzed as I contemplated a world without her. I deliberately avoided petty conversation so I could focus on the moment and perceive her liberated *neshama*. When I came to, I looked around and I saw a dozen of my fellow musicians standing in random places on the grass in the golden light of the setting sun. Wordlessly, we all started coming into a circle around her *kever* (grave). We joined hands, swayed and sobbed. Wow.

As I drove home, a powerful determination swept over me. I could not settle for mediocrity in my life, in my career. I had to force open the gates of possibility for Jewish music and the Jewish people, to reach all nations with our message of hope, prayer and sanctity. Mortality descended on my complacency like a tidal wave. How many years do I have left to change the world? To sing, perform, record, travel? What if I died in the middle of my current projects? They would never see the light of day. My many albums have been a defense against feelings of insignificance. But it's not enough to just put out albums. I must use my music as a means to take a stand for all Jewish people and our allies. I must help all my brothers and sisters connect enthusiastically to the wonders of our tradition. I must open the financial barriers that limit my fellow musician's expression and stifle this renaissance. Music is a gateway to transcendence and unity between nations. Debbie Friedman started the fire and I must do my part to turn this flame into a conflagration.

Debbie, thank you for setting the stage, for taking the lead, for teaching us, for striving through your pain to inspire us. Thanks for tolerating me and loving me. Thanks for your amazing songs that continue to change the world. Most importantly, thanks for singing with me and being my friend. I miss you so much.

Shabbat Tent:
The Treasure of the High Sierra

♫ CALIFORNIA ♫

joyjud.com/m/cal

Rollin' all along on the interstate
I'm in search of the American dream
I got my sights set on the sunset
I've seen what becomes of those who wait
I was lookin' just like the rest
I started to see the dreamer in me
Settle for second best

So I'm gone, off to the Golden Gate
By the Pacific blue
Me and the Golden State

We got a rendezvous
I'm gonna stake my claim in California

Rollin' past the fields of blazing wheat
And then I crossed the Continental Divide
Oh, it's so hard to leave the Rockies
I know my life won't be complete
Until I lay myself on the sand
With the waves a-crashin' at my feet
And my destiny in my hand
So I'm gone...

I have a new music discovery. It's called the High Sierra Music Festival and I am convinced it is the ultimate musical indulgence on the planet. Sports fans have the World Series and the Super Bowl. For us classic rockers, High Sierra, taking place each 4th of July weekend in Northern California, is the Holy Grail. I've been to plenty of single day rock, R&B or jazz festivals from which I return home with a smile on my lips and my ears ringing. But this festival is a binge of another dimension: a captive audience of 10,000 fans gathers to hear over fifty top-notch bands for four days, 'round the clock. The whole motley crew camps together at the picturesque Quincy Fairgrounds, replete with grassy meadows and towering pines. It's co-curated by my friend Dave Margulies, a nice Jewish boy who REALLY knows quality music. The common denominator between featured acts is a proven track record, years on the road, virtuoso musicianship, upbeat tunes and a cross-genre sensibility. No Top 40, DJs or Tribute Bands need apply. Sideshow distractions include yoga on the hour, a kids' play area, Frisbee, hula-hoops, slacklining, impromptu campsite concerts and a delicious public swimming pool. Incredible alpine hikes are just down the road. And did I mention fifty of the hottest touring acts in the world?

My excuse to dedicate the long weekend to music materialized thanks to an unusual set of circumstances. I was hired by Rabbi Yonah Bookstein to lead the music at their annual High Sierra Shabbat Tent (shabbattent.com) program. The staff provides a welcome refuge from the din and heat at summer festivals by offering free kosher munchies, cold drinks, Shabbat meals, jam sessions and prayer services to anyone in need. For me, July 4th typically involves a command performance at my parents' home in Pacific Palisades. Their *shul* has a gala BBQ overlooking the parade route followed by beachside fireworks at my alma mater, Palisades High School. That summer, my mom was in Israel visiting my brother's family. My boys were counselors at Moshava summer camp in Wisconsin and my wife and daughter made plans to visit my brother Joey's family in San Diego. High Sierra here I come!

I'd like to share my experience at this event to extoll this unique Shabbat Tent method of Jewish outreach, salute the new generation of insanely talented musicians and explore the power of music to promote unity.

I arrived at this party-in-progress feeling disoriented and alone. By midday Thursday, most folks had set up camp and the bands were already jamming. Just inside the entrance, I found the Shabbat Tent and was overjoyed to see familiar faces. Thankfully, Rabbi Yonah had already set up my tent in order to save the space. He gave me a hearty hug and lent a hand getting my stuff to the campsite. It was late afternoon and the heat had abated somewhat— now it was only ninety degrees inside my tent. I inflated my air mattress, made the bed, unpacked my gear and then escaped the sauna to hear the first band of the thirty or so I would eventually audition. The three main outdoor venues employed cascading schedules to allow rowdy overachievers like me to see nearly every act. There were also three indoor spaces hosting specialty concerts and "artist playshops." Add to this campsite jams, childrens' shows and my Shabbat Tent concerts…total music overload!

The opening night headliner was Robert Plant and his new band, the Sensational Space Shifters. I was prepared for a self-indulgent, esoteric bluegrass set, but instead Plant rewarded the stoked crowd with bombastic renditions of classic Led Zeppelin songs. I stood transfixed at the power that he held in his grasp: he could woo the crowd with a sweet new ballad or create an immediate frenzy with the first measure of a standard like Black Dog or Whole Lotta Love. In spite of the impact of the performance, I was not entirely present and felt alone in the darkness. Halfway through the set, I met a group of festival clothing vendors who had abandoned their booths along the perimeter of the field in order to rush the stage. I bonded deeply with them and managed to enter the headspace of the sweaty, happy mob. If you can't beat 'em, join 'em.

After the show, my new friends walked me back to their colorful booth filled with brilliant handmade batik clothing. The multitude of vendors had created their own private community—their booths linked up in the rear, forming an extended living room replete with hammocks, lounge chairs, tie-dyed tapestries, dining tables and ample food and drink. Clearly, these folks made this annual four-day pilgrimage both for fun and profit.

I met my old friend Rob Steinberg for the official after hours shows. He was the first to bring this festival to my consciousness and served as a patient guide throughout. High Sierra costs around $260 for the four days of music, camping and fun. Late night shows (11:30 pm-4:00 am) cost extra, about $25 per venue. There were two amazing lineups to choose from and both had sold out. I was relieved that Rob had a few tickets set aside in his name. He introduced me to a rowdy bunch of veteran High Sierra aficionados and we all enjoyed the talents of bluegrass headliners Leftover Salmon and party bands Pimps of Joytime and Orgone. The guys asked if I would consider bringing my wife next time. I pondered the past twenty-four hours. None of the venues had chairs. My boogers turned black from dust inhalation. The days were torrid, with precious little shade and no air conditioning. We camped with thousands of other people in close proximity and the bathrooms were blocks away. With lines for the stalls. And mosquitoes. Thursday night there was a five-foot space on one side of my tent, allowing me to enter along the dense corridor of tents from the nearby path. By Friday midday, another half dozen tents had filled the aisle—now access required shimmying through a rainbow forest of ripstop nylon. During the first night, my queen-size air mattress sprang a leak, leaving me with a thin yoga mat to cushion my fifty-year-old bones from the uneven ground below. I lay there imagining my wife sharing this yoga mat with me after a day of travel, crowds, heat and inebriated uberfans. Better to do this one on my own.

I got to sleep at 4:30 am and had the gift of a private concert right outside my tent at 6:00 am when one of the late night revelers decided to practice his guitar. I recognize this scenario sounds nightmarish—but it's all part of the experience. I tried to get back to sleep with the aid of earplugs, but by 7:30 am the tent got so hot I had to flee. I figured I'd take a nap in order to get through the day and still be dancing late night. But where would I nap? Now I understood why I saw countless people throughout the fairgrounds passed out on the grass, in hammocks, and some, in the dust on the edges of the concert venues. Remarkably, no one bothered these people, save for the occasional Samaritan moving them to safety. In spite of arduous conditions, everyone was smiling, behaving peacefully and looking out for one another.

Perhaps I thrive in this extrovert's paradise because it is a microcosm of the perfected world paradigm anticipated by the Jewish People for millennia. Of course, for many, the peace and harmony is drug-induced, but somehow, 10,000 individuals of all faiths, ages and income brackets manage to get along famously. The emphasis is on how much one can share, rather than the selfish nature of city life. One inter-act MC announced, "There are no strangers at High Sierra—the people next to you are just best friends that you haven't yet met." This statement resonated deeply with me. Since my high school days, I strive to leave anyone with whom I interact feeling a bit better for the interaction. Perhaps it's because I felt so left out and disenfranchised those years. All of us are vulnerable and insecure in some way. With so much negativity and judgement in the world, we can be the friendly face in the crowd. Some might say a Shabbat Tent at a "hippie rock festival" is an oxymoron. I think it makes perfect sense. What better way to reach people where they are at, demonstrating the innate Jewish trait of *chesed* and inspiring them in the process? Hopefully, the good vibes experienced during the event translate into acts of kindness "paid forward" when revelers return to their real lives.

I searched the fairgrounds for a good place to *daven*. Certainly there must be an isolated tree and some shade! My efforts to find solitude in this maze of humanity proved fruitless, so I strapped up in the middle of the empty Vaudeville tent. I was one of only two people wearing a *kippah* at this festival. The other was Rabbi Yonah, and he stuck mostly to the confines of the Shabbat Tent, leaving me as the official wandering Jew. I lost count of how many people "outed" themselves as members of the tribe. One family of wild-eyed stoners watched me praying and sure enough, the longhaired patriarch introduced himself as a Jewish pot farmer from Northern California. Another woman and her daughter Shaina were fascinated with my *shuckling*. They had never seen *tefillin* and had all sorts of questions. I walked them over to the Shabbat Tent and they became regulars. If only for connecting with this one family, the whole Shabbat Tent experiment was worth it.

I swapped my *tallis* bag for my yoga mat and headed out to the main lawn for an hour of Hatha yoga with a hundred new friends. Some didn't have mats but still participated even though their sticky bodies were getting covered with dirt. Our transcendent leaders were a Jewish couple from San Francisco who tag-teamed over the course of the vigorous hour-plus workout. That afternoon, I played long distance Frisbee with tattooed teenagers in between four incredible concerts: the first was guitar slinging Scott Pemberton, a vastly innovative player with radical, unorthodox technique. Then I gyrated to virtuoso folk-rock-dance bands The Tumbleweed Wanderers and The Revivalists. I'm easy to find at any given festival—I always wind my way to eighth row center so I can be in the epicenter of the action and enjoy optimal stereo imaging. My last show before Shabbat was neophyte pop act, Houndmouth. This youthful quartet of "easy on the eye" musicians was having a tough time winning over the ambivalent crowd. The initial bias against these seeming pretty boy (and girl) posers disappeared in the light of their excellent material, great vocals and competent musicianship. I have never seen a band overcome indifference to this degree—by the final songs the audience was SCREAMING for more.

I emerged from a swim and shower at the local pool, relieved to be cleansed of the layers of dust and sunscreen. I donned my Shabbas whites and returned for Friday night services at the Shabbat Tent with a smile on my face. I led a musical session consisting of common denominator Jewish folk songs and was joined by about a hundred people who were swaying arm in arm. Since it was well before candlelighting, I was able to use my keyboard with several friends backing me on guitar and percussion. Rabbi Yonah did his best to get everyone into the magic of Shabbat in spite of our manic surroundings. We ate a delicious dinner prepared by Rebbetzin Rachel and staff while hearing the stories from those individuals who were having their first experience with the Jewish Sabbath. Hosting this varied crowd of guests of all faiths created an uncanny Avraham and Sarah-style biblical ambience. With the tent open on all four sides to anyone who wanted to enter, the staff interfaced with a diverse group who in all likelihood would not be celebrating Shabbat. Just as we finished dinner, the nightly High Sierra parade passed by the tent, pausing at our doorway to engage our crowd in a wild dance led by colorful Cirque du Soleil-style performers on stilts and an ad hoc twenty-piece drum corps. When official candlelighting time arrived, the staff and I *davened* a proper *Kabbalat Shabbat* and *Ma'ariv* filled with song and soul.

The following day we enjoyed a quiet *Shacharit* in the Shabbat Tent as the tireless *rebbetzin* prepared a delicious lunch. The bands hadn't yet started up and most revelers were sleeping in. Among those who opted to relax in our beanbag chairs was an Alabama-based band called Earth Noodle. I invited them in, offered them food and coaxed them into joining me in singing a cappella spirituals. The Shabbat Tent folks were the first Jewish people they had ever met—how awesome their first impression of Jews was of such giving, happy people. The afternoon was filled with more camaraderie and music and when three stars appeared, I fired up my keyboard and led *Havdalah* for the *chevra*. I kept the music flowing as we lit the candle and smelled the spices, accompanied by an enthusiastic Rabbi Yonah on congas.

In attendance at *Havdalah* was festival founder, Dave Margulies. He commented how much he appreciated Shabbat Tent and promised we would have an even higher profile the following year. He doled out backstage passes to the Vaudeville venue, allowing the whole Shabbat Tent staff to enjoy Lee Field and the Expressions' electrifying Motown set from the side of the stage. As I was leaving for the show, a family that missed *Havdalah* insisted I walk with them back to their RV to sing for the rest of their group. Next to their vehicle, several high school musicians were engaged in an amplified jam session. How could I lead the service amidst the din? I tried another tactic: when they played a blues number, I simply chanted the *Havdalah* prayer to their chord progression and grooved everyone along to a *shavua tov*.

Late night I met Rob once again, this time for the funk of Jelly Bread and the progressive rock jamming of Moe. These seasoned musicians put in overtime with incendiary, non-improvised dueling guitar solos, tight-as-nails breakdowns and a three-pronged lead vocal attack. At 3:00 am, I walked over to Mineral Hall for a mellow acoustic set with San Francisco-based Naked Soul. The focus and connection was palpable and the fifty or so late night fans felt blessed to be in the presence of these gifted artists. Once again I had to force myself to bed in spite of my exhaustion.

On Sunday, I was determined to get up early and hit the trail. I had printed out the directions to explore Gold Lake, recommended online as the nicest hike in this region. I drove about fifteen miles out of town to a well-banked dirt road that gained about 2000 feet of elevation as it wound through an old growth coniferous forest. It terminated at a dusty, neglected campground by the partially drained Silver Lake. I slathered on sunscreen and started up a two-mile trail traversing a ridge with breathtaking views on either side. Finally, I spied my destination below, a pristine, circular, aqua-blue body of water surrounded by spectacular granite cliffs. I dove into the liquid glass, swam to the center of the lake, floated on my back and meditated on the azure sky. A few lone clouds slid silently across the astral plane like slow motion floats in a parade. The few families present soon departed, leaving me alone to sunbathe, do yoga and sing along with my own echo. High Sierra splendor.

I drove back to the fairgrounds and the melee of bodies, heat and the pulsating beat, grateful for my morning respite. I started with concerts by David Mayfield, Anders Osborne and jazz giant John Scofield. Then I joined the annual Guitarmageddon jam, a festival tradition where top guitarists from the various bands relish in 70s hard rock glory. The head-banging audience pumped their fists in the air to Stones, Journey and Zeppelin standards. Following the funky folk of Fruition, I square danced to my new favorite bluegrass band, the Infamous Stringdusters (I didn't realize I had a favorite bluegrass band!) Next up were the Barr Brothers and Thievery Corporation. Towards the end of the day, during a set by Brooklyn-based dance band Rubblebucket, the lead singer jumped into the pit, firing the crowd into a frenzy. Soon the horn section followed suit and were lifted upon the shoulders of their rabid fans, never missing a beat. At one point, the singer grabbed me and a few others and guided us up the enormous subwoofers to groove with the band on the grandstand stage. Crazy!

Just before the evening set of reggae heroes Steel Pulse, I realized I was out of gas. Nothing left. I had long since passed the second-wind mark. One of my neighbors broke out an Emergen-C packet, which I downed with a double espresso ice coffee and a pair of Advil. That got me dancing again in the VIP section for one of the tightest reggae shows I had ever seen. I befriended the overheated folks behind me who were pressed up against the barrier fence. I took initiative and surprised them with a tray laden with free backstage refreshments to slake their thirst. I could see the joy in their eyes as they were revived by the gift. Following a fortuitous backstage hang with the band, I ran to the front row to cheer on Moe. Their stellar set featured many luminaries from other acts who were watching from the wings.

Tired as I was, I decided to splurge for the late night Greyboy Allstars-Moksha show. I danced with new friends gathered from this four-day marathon where I befriended music lovers at every venue. Somehow I remembered nearly everyone's names, a phenomenon I don't always accomplish. I usually try to hyperfocus when introduced, employing a mnemonic reminder to connect names to faces. I also repeat the new name a few times in conversation. Still, these techniques don't always work. I believe my recall was enhanced by the mission of Shabbat Tent, serving as a "light onto nations," broadcasting a compassionate Jewish presence in this alpine love fest. When I lead Shabbaton weekends, I strive to "get" everyone I meet. I felt similarly present in this euphonious extravaganza.

There were markedly fewer people still awake at 4:00 am on the last night. I wandered the nearly deserted fairgrounds back to Shabbat Tent where a few staffers gathered around a smoldering grill. They were preparing leftover meat for the ride home and I helped them by gobbling down some perfectly spiced hamburgers, thrilled to have my first taste of meat over the weekend.

After a few hours of sleep, I forced myself to wake up so I could pack up my tent before the sun got too stifling. I made sure to leave my campsite in zero-impact condition and schlepped my gear a few blocks to the fairground entrance. After a quick breakfast and earnest goodbyes at the Shabbat Tent, I loaded up my trusty rental Hyundai and headed to the final rendezvous of this Northern California journey, Lassen Volcanic National Park. My demeanor had changed fundamentally since the first day of the trip. Now I was suntanned, relaxed and buzzing with new friendships and musical discoveries. My nearly new vehicle smoothly negotiated the winding mountain roads as verdant vistas unfolded around every corner. A brief hour and a half later I was at the entrance to this striking high alpine environment for the first time in my life. While it doesn't compare to Yosemite and Kings Canyon to the south, this park is a prime destination, with unusual hikes and a volatile history. After watching a film on park history and plate tectonics, I left the headquarters for a quick seven-hour hiking tour. The ranger told me to expect a one-hour drive through the park and then another two hours back to Reno airport, plus whatever side trips I took. I crammed in visits to the popular bubbling springs and mud holes of Bumpass Hell (yes, that's the real name) plus a hike to spectacular Kings Creek Falls.

On my way back to the airport, I sensed I was running a bit late. I started to panic each time I was caught behind motorhomes on the curvy two-lane road. By the time I got to the northern park entrance, I had exactly two hours to make it to the the latest check-in time. I fretted when I saw that I still had over one hundred fifty miles to drive, much of it on isolated mountain roads. As my iPhone cascaded through the alphabet in my music library, I sped through gorgeous Sierra forest and then down to the arid flats toward Reno. At the first sign of civilization, I stopped to splash water on my face and down a double Frappuccino. With about forty minutes to go before my flight, I pulled up to the airport and sprinted with my suitcase to make the bag check cutoff. I then burned rubber out of the airport to a miracle gas station a few blocks away. I ditched my car at the rental return, ran across the driveway with my overloaded carry-on bags, slipped through security and to my gate where I *davened Mincha.* I boarded the plane just as they were closing the door and plunked down in my window seat. I watched the sun set over the golden Sierras as we floated to the lights of L.A., returning exhausted and content into the arms of my ever-loving wife.

I'm thankful to Rabbi Yonah and his staff for their selfless commitment to bringing an "out and proud" Judaism to music festivals across the US. I'm especially grateful to the benefactors of Shabbat Tent for allowing me to participate in the mitzvah of radical hospitality. Kudos to the High Sierra artists, staff and vendors for nurturing this epic festival.

They have succeeded in creating an extended 10,000-member family that continues to share light and love year round. *Baruch Hashem* for the gift of music, mountains and new friends. Hope you can join us for some California hospitality next year!

Kiddush • Tefilla • Shabbat • Community • Torah • Prophets • Sage • Pessah • Teshuva • Wedding • Rituals • Holidays • Entangle • Diaspora • Brit Milah • Simcha • Halacha • Bracha • Holidays • Seder • Israel • Mikveh • Pessah • Mashiach • Tehilla • Shabbat • Community • Torah • Prophets • Sages • Pessah • Teshuva • Wedding • Spirituality • Holidays • Brain Plus • Diaspora • Brit Milah • Simcha • Bracha • Mezuza • Bar Mitzvah • Elite • Israel • Mikveh • Present Mashiach • Shabbat • Community • Torah • Prophets • Sinai • Reserve • Teshuva • Wedding • Spirituality

The Jewish Music Manifesto

♫ SONG FOR SHLOMO ♫

joyjud.com/m/sfs

Are you listening, if you can hear me now
I want to thank you for the chance
To sing a couple songs together
Are you listening, can I tell you how you made
This dark and lonely place
Seem a little sweeter
Than before you came to share the view
That only you could see

And I will not give up hope
Cause I know that hope is always there
And I will not hold back my love
You showed me that love is everywhere
I just think about the times we had

Are you listening, now that you're gone

I've got to wonder who can take your place
To remind us why we're singing
Are you listening
Ten thousand arms cannot embrace me
Like a single kiss
The love that you we're giving
Seemed to know no earthly bounds
You always found the words to say

You helped me learn to cry
You told me that I was beautiful
You showed me a paradise
Hiding within every soul
I just think about the times we had
And my troubles don't seem quite so bad
We're so lucky to have loved you

Shlomo Carlebach and Debbie Friedman started something big. These composer-performers wrote music from their hearts and delivered it directly to the people. They didn't go to conservatories to get degrees in composition or spend years at cantorial school. Their inspired melodies were accompanied by simple guitar chords and sweet, non-operatic voices. Constantly on the road, they captivated audiences around the world with optimistic, post-Holocaust exuberance. Erica Jong said, "Everyone has talent. What is rare is the courage to follow the talent to the dark place where it leads." Shlomo and Debbie courageously shone the way for all subsequent Jewish performers, but it was a place of the holiest, most brilliant light.

Their music was not klezmer, the schizophrenic happy-sad party music of the Ashkenazi old world. Nor was it weighty like their predecessors Louis Lewandowski or

Ernest Bloch. It didn't poke fun at tradition or lament *shtetl* life like Yiddish Theater or Allan Sherman. It wasn't yet another repackaging of Israeli hits born from the legacy of war. This was genuine American Jewish music, made for the people, by the people, rooted in the radical belief that Judaism is a religion of life and celebration. Shlomo and Debbie are the unsung founders of North American Contemporary Jewish Music (CJM). CJM is performed by individuals flourishing in a land offering unprecedented tranquility, success and freedom. These songs are the unprecedented byproduct of modern Jewish history: the well-adjusted Jew.

I grew up with Reb Shlomo's songs since my family regularly attended the touring Chassidic Song Festivals. We owned all the LPs. These shows provided the soundtrack of American Jewry, and Shlomo was the most prolific composer featured. Our Glaser Bar Mitzvahs and weddings were attended by our venerated Holocaust-survivor uncles, Moishe and Shloime, who taught us even more of his songs. Can you imagine my thrill back in 1990 when I was first asked to accompany this superstar rabbi? I got the gigs because I was a Jewish keyboard player with a good ear who already knew his tunes and was willing to work for the stipend of *divrei Torah* (words of Torah). I was privileged to perform with him for five years and was continuously intrigued by the majesty of his deceptively simple melodies. Reb Shlomo was effusive about my music and piano playing and once in a while, would blow me away with a phone call out of the blue. He always knew what to say, exactly what I needed to hear at that moment. Regardless of what mistakes he made in his personal life, Carlebach's influence on Judaism and Jewish music is unquestionable.

Thousands of young Jews flocked to Shlomo's and Debbie's concerts and memorized their songs. Their material became the "standards" taught in summer camps and Hebrew schools. Over the decades, the very institutions mocking these seminal figures found themselves enraptured by their melodies. Their music captured the ebullient mood of Jewish youth and then those young people matriculated into positions of power and made CJM normative. The next generation of Jewish musicians, myself included, saw them in the limelight and realized, "YES…this is what we want to do!" This included the likes of Craig Taubman, Julie Silver, Dan Nichols and Rick Recht, groups like Kol Beseder, Safam, Blue Fringe and Moshav Band. These artists were compelled to record music exceeding the production quality of their mentors while carrying the same message of the spirit. Their success has encouraged the current generation to innovate by combining hip hop, worldbeat, rock and reggae with clever beat-boxing, looping and generous helpings of studio magic.

The current renaissance has launched a treasure trove of new material from countless young artists. Among the Jewish music industry summits are such conferences as NewCAJE, Hava Nashira and the Reform Biennial, where songwriters perform their latest creations into the night. Jewish Rock Radio is a popular iPhone app and there are hundreds of Jewish stations on Internet radio. The annual Songleader Boot Camp offers three days of training in the art form to hundreds of young singers and composers. The main CJM online outlet, Oysongs. com, boasts thousands of songs available for download as well as the matching sheet music. "*Jefe*, would you say we have a plethora?"

And yet, all is not rosy, even for us rose-colored lens musicians. The global music business is imperiled and Jewish music has its unique *tzuris* (troubles). Like all musicians, we pay our bills by virtue of our live bookings and sales of our music. Unfortunately, cultural arts events are on the chopping block due to the disappearing budgets of shrinking synagogues and JCCs. As *shuls* merge, many are forced to eliminate cantors and songleaders, leaving the transmission of the Jewish arts in the hands of whichever parent volunteer can play guitar or wield a paintbrush. Our precious children are growing up with limited awareness of their cultural history, their repertoire of music is stunted and access to Jewish musical role models is rare. And that's for the kids who ARE affiliated, who actually show up to the synagogue once in a while and attend Jewish summer camps.

A primary issue with our industry is the wholesale abandonment of the physical delivery of music. Young consumers don't own CD players and have never paid for music. Their iPhones hold thousands of songs "gifted" from friends or "found" on the Internet, and unlimited streaming fills in the gaps. It's a great era to be a music consumer and a lousy one to be a provider. Music ownership is utterly obsolete. Brick and mortar record shops are a quaint memory. In the Jewish world, this trend is manifest in the disappearance of Judaica stores, and for the hearty survivors, the elimination of the music department. Nearly all Jewish music distribution companies are gone and the remaining few are earning so little, it's easier to walk away than sell their beleaguered enterprises.

A silver lining amidst the high-tech storm clouds is the possibility for widespread dissemination of our products via streaming outlets like Apple Music, YouTube, Facebook and Spotify. Like never before, we can get the word out about new projects, share behind the scenes adventures and concert footage with fans. We no longer must endure the tyranny of record labels or distributors dictating marketing moves. That said, revenues from streaming are abysmal. I used to tell studio clients they had to sell around 1,000 CDs to break even on production costs. That was based on the $15 per album they could typically charge and represented an annual sales goal the average working musician could fathom. The new models have emasculated the long form album, in which musicians had a dozen or so songs to make their artistic statements. With the advent of "album killer" iTunes, the breakeven point required selling over 50,000 singles. Today, on demand streaming of millions of songs means fans never have to spend a nickel. Spotify and other services became the "iTunes killer." They have little transparency in their operations and claim to pay the artist roughly .004 cents per stream. That's right: 1,000 listens and we can *almost* buy a latte at Starbucks.

I have some ideas to brighten the future. My plan is to revitalize the Jewish Music Commission, a dormant non-profit I served as Executive Director for nearly a decade. I will locate like-minded benefactors who appreciate the musical gifts of Rabbi Shlomo Carlebach and Debbie Friedman and the revolution they inspired. In addition to supporting hospitals and the hungry, we need to keep our cultural aspirations alive. Under a single umbrella, we will create a collection of entities lifting the profile of Jewish music, providing publicity, enhancing composing, recording and performance opportunities and offering recognition for accomplishments. A renaissance in the arts is within our grasp! Among the flagship programs will be:

- The Jammies: A Jewish version of Grammy Awards, recognizing acheivment in categories such as CJM, cantorial, klezmer, children's and instrumental music
- The American Jewish Song Festival: a reboot of the popular competition that invited songwriters around the country to compose Jewish-themed music
- The Max Helfman Institute for Excellence in Jewish Music: weekend and week-long seminars inspiring new and established composers to enhance their craft
- Album Production Scholarships: awarded to the most promising young artists
- Jewish Music Teacher of the Year: annual award recognizing excellence in music education

- Jewish Music Royalty Multiplier: a fund boosting documented streaming royalties of accredited CJM composers
- Music for Worship Commissions: a clearinghouse for synagogues to connect with established composers to create customized pieces
- Collaboration: financial support and cross-pollination with organizations like the L.A. Jewish Symphony, Zamir Chorale, Shalshelet, Cantorial Programs and NewCAJE
- Jewish Music Commission Concert Series: finance and logistics support for live music productions, debuts, coffee house performances, large and small ensemble events
- Milken Archive of CJM: create a multi-album series of the best of CJM, much like the existing archives of contemporary classical works

Insightful, well-produced Jewish music is the most powerful, accessible expression of our heritage. Every dollar invested in the arts yields exponential returns. During an L.A. visit, former Chief Rabbi of the UK, Lord Jonathan Sacks told me, "Sam, more than we need sermons, we need your music to unite our people. You have the unique ability to take what has been and breathe new life into it. While Torah stays the same, music must change. We need your new music, your *shir chadash*, to keep Judaism alive." Rabbi Sacks understands the crucial role played by CJM. I consider it my personal responsibility to enlighten Jewish benefactors regarding this *nachas* enhancing, tax deductible opportunity.

Rabbi Sacks included two songs I recorded on his "Israel at 60" anniversary album. CDs were gifted to over 260,000 families throughout Europe. I reached Rabbi Sacks initially because I was invited to play a high profile UK event based on the word-of-mouth publicity from certain American performances. I got those gigs because I had a viable business composing, recording and performing Jewish music. How could a young artist make such an impression these days? I am grateful I have been able to make a living with my music. I think the next generation of talented Jewish musicians deserves the same chance.

Shortly after Rabbi Carlebach died, I went to Israel to perform a few concerts and a wedding. The last night of my journey, I convinced my friend, playwright Joyce Klein, to accompany me to Shlomo's *kever* (gravesite) at the Har Menuchot cemetery. She was reluctant to be in a cemetery after midnight under an eerie full moon but relented when I explained this was my last opportunity of the trip. We carefully followed the directions I had been given but our search proved fruitless. After I strolled yet another row of graves in the darkness, I realized I had to throw in the towel. I returned to Joyce who was now waiting in the car and asked for another five minutes to *daven* the *Ma'ariv* service and pray for divine insight. During the *Sh'ma Koleynu* section, I paused to ask God to help me intuit the location of the grave. At that very moment, I opened my eyes and saw a flicker of light in the distance. It was the moon reflecting on the glass bookcase over Shlomo's tombstone. I thanked God for the vision, finished my *tefillah* and walked directly to the *kever*.

I reverently placed a rock on the headstone, sang his songs and prayed for an *aliyah* for his *neshama*. I worded a simple prayer asking for Shlomo's help to intervene with God on my behalf in order to elevate the CJM revolution he started. I then asked for a blessing to continue making a living singing my own songs and inspiring God's children. This may sound strange, but I heard Shlomo's voice state emphatically: "You don't need it!"

Thanks to Shlomo and Debbie for their incredible music, for striving against all odds, for giving CJM artists a dream and a career path. Should anyone desire a founding role in the reboot of the Commission, please contact me at sam@samglaser.com.

Qoshech • Tefillin • Shabbat • Community • Torah • Prophets • Niggun • Pesach • Teshuva • Wedding • Matchday • Holiness • Catnalal • Diaspora • Bar Mitah • Simcha • Halacha • Biachen • Holidays • Torah • Torah • Israel • Mitzvas • Prayer • Mashiach • Tetullin • Shabbat • Community • Torah • Sing • sigon • Pesach • Teluva • Weddings • Spirituality • Holmes • Tentin • Diaspora • Bar M • hacha • Bhacha • Brachen • Holidays • Bar Mazvali • Italia • Israel • Mitzvas • Prayer • Moshin • Bible • Shabbat • Community • Torah • Prophets • Niggun • Pesach • Teshuva • Weddings • Spirit • Halacha • Holidays • Tong • xxvate xxi • xxxxxx xxx xxxx xxxxx xxxx xxxxx xxxxxx • Bar Mitva

Coda:
The Secret of Six

♫ I HAD A GOOD TIME ♫

joyjud.com/m/hgt

Is there any law against me having too much fun

Cause I'm havin' a hell of a time

Is someone gonna grab me when the day is done

And throw me in jail

Baby I'm feelin' like a 747

30,000 miles from the ground

Waitin' for an angel to kick me out of heaven

For smilin' too much

When the day is done I wanna say

I had a good time

Is there anybody out there that's feelin' it too

I say we form a team

Let's go some place where they got beer and food

And the music is loud

Nothin's gonna stop me from feelin' this way

You can lock the door and bury the key

Take away everything I own

I will still have me

Mazel tov! You made it to the seventieth and final chapter of "The Joy of Judaism." Thank you for sharing this adventure with me. Hopefully by now you consider yourself part of the Glaser family. Our clan is casual, welcoming and friendly. Be in touch! I teach weekly classes in L.A., travel every other weekend for concerts and speaking engagements and lead transformational seminars. I help make musical dreams come true in my state-of-the-art recording studio, Glaser Musicworks. I also offer Joy Coaching: personalized meetings with corporate groups, individuals, couples or families to enhance relationships, careers and spiritual connections, via Skype or in my L.A. studio. Sign up for my monthly newsletter at samglaser.com. Certainly we can find a way to rendevous.

Why stop the book at seventy chapters? Well, according to my editor, this book is already too long! The other reason, as you may have surmised by now, is that I love the connection of numbers and Torah. Torah, in macro-terms, is the blueprint of the universe. The Creator of physics gave us math as the language of reality, the bedrock of our cosmos. Since seven represents the natural world, seventy represents the expanded, full potential of any given aspect of the world. For example, the *Midrash* states there are seventy "faces" or perspectives in Torah, in other words, lots of ways to interact with the truth of our texts—they are not monolithic. At the time of the Tower of Babel, the world was divided into seventy root nations and languages. Thanks to Avraham Avinu, the Jewish Nation was given the gift of seventy biblical holy days to celebrate each year (fifty-two Sabbaths plus eighteen festival days). Two generations later, the seventy members of Jacob's family descended to Egypt. There were seventy elders given prophecy when we wandered in the desert, seventy judges on the Great *Sanhedrin* (Supreme Court) and our first exile (Babylonian) lasted seventy years. How could I stop at sixty-nine in this encyclopedic text? Hence, the completion of the puzzle with chapter seventy, the coda.

In terms of music, a coda is a featured addendum, a final addition to the basic structure of a song. Consider, for example, the frantic last few minutes of Beethoven's Ninth Symphony. Great rock codas include the "Na, na, na" section of The Beatles' "Hey Jude," the heavy metal conclusion of Queen's "Bohemian Rhapsody" or the instrumental jam finishing off Eric Clapton's "Layla." To cap off "The Joy of Judaism," even though it's in the music section of the book, I offer techniques from our tradition to remain focused on our mission. We've come so far together—now we have to hold on to the inspiration. Below I offer several lists of important tips; four are from our texts and one is my own summary.

Each list has six items. Yes, another significant number! What is the secret of six? According to the famous Passover song, One is Hashem, two are the tablets, three are the forefathers, four are the matriarchs and five are the books of Torah. Six are the books of the *Mishna*. The difference between Torah and *Mishna*? The Torah is the formal, written word of God, through the pen of Moshe Rabbeinu. Six represents the Oral Torah, the compendium of explanations given to Moshe on Sinai. The six orders of the tersely worded *Mishna* are the foundational kernels of law expounded upon in our Talmud. Therefore, six represents humankind, our free will contribution to the world of knowledge, our partnership in creation with the Creator of the Universe.

Humans are the only creatures blessed with walking the tightrope between the sacred and profane. We are represented by the sixth letter in the alphabet, the *vav*. In Hebrew, a *vav* is a hook or connector, symbolizing our unique ability to bridge Heaven and earth. Our instruction manual enabling us to aspire to greatness, the Torah, was given to us on the sixth day of the month of *Sivan*. Humanity was formed on the sixth day of Creation. We have six days each week to strive for greatness and on the seventh, we turn the reigns back to Hashem. It makes sense, therefore, that the lists guiding our ascent have six entries. These lists are the antidotes to amnesia, the keys to the castle, time-tested techniques to keep Hashem in our lives. They beg memorization so they can be referred to at moments of strength and weakness, joy and sorrow, temptation and triumph. Imagine each item as the corners of the six-pointed Jewish star, the *Magen David,* with yourself in the middle. Ready?

The Six Constant Mitzvot

The first list is the *Sheish Mitzvot Temidiot* (Six Constant Mitzvot). Whereas some mitzvot are time-bound, like shaking a *lulav* on Sukkot or making *Kiddush* on Shabbat, these six can be observed 24/7. *Chazal* (our sages) recommend these *D'oraita* (directly from the Written Torah) commandments remain in our thoughts always:

1. Know there is a God
"I am Hashem your God who brought you out of Egypt." (*Sh'mot* 20:2)
This mitzvah is derived from the first of the Ten Commandments, to <u>know</u> (not just believe) God exists. God created the universe and stuck around to supervise and maintain it. God

is continuously involved in our personal lives. It's up to each of us to fully investigate the evidence so we are unequivocally convinced God's presence is absolutely real. Then we have to take that knowledge on the road, living our lives accordingly and sharing the good news.

2. Don't believe in any other gods

"Do not recognize any other gods in My Presence." (*Sh'mot* 20:3)

God is everywhere! There is no power except God. Not your boss, not your parents, not even the president of the USA. While we're not driven to worship statues and planets like our ancestors, we are prone to place our faith in technology, government, fame and fortune. Don't do it!

3. Know God is One

"Hear, Israel, Hashem is our God, Hashem is One." (*D'varim* 6:4)

We must keep the lesson of the *Sh'ma* in our hearts and minds constantly. Not only must we utter this six-word formula twice a day, morning and night—we must constantly keep in mind the essential lesson of God's uniqueness and unity. If God is all that exists, then we are "inside" God, a part of God, a figment of God's imagination. God created time and space and is therefore beyond time and space. God is indivisible; we don't hold by a "Trinity" or a competitor to God like Satan. Satan (or the evil inclination) works for God! Our constant *kavanah:* God is right here, right now, always.

4. Love God

"You shall love Hashem your God with all your heart, with all your soul, and with all your ability." (*D'varim* 6:5)

This is the first line of the *V'ahavta* paragraph, recited after the *Sh'ma*. If we appreciate God is the source of everything and nothing is owed to us, all of our gifts inspire immense gratitude and love. Loving God with our *me'odecha* (might or ability) can be translated as loving God with our "very." Everyone has a different "very." It's that special thing we do, our *tafkid* (life task), our purpose on this planet. We can constantly use our unique talents to love God.

5. Be in awe of God

"You must revere Hashem your God and serve God." (*D'varim* 10:20)

A constant awareness of God's presence results in a perpetual state of awe. God is awesome! Revering (or fearing, as *yirah* is often translated) implies we understand actions have consequences. We know that challenging the law of gravity is foolish—Judaism teaches that spiritual realities are just as real. This constant mitzvah keeps us on the right track, knowing God (think success coach and not cruel overlord) is lovingly aware of our every move.

6. Don't stray after your desires

"Don't follow your heart or your eyes, after which you can go astray." (*Bamidbar* 15:39)

We must keep our eye on the goal and not get distracted by emotional (heart) or physical (eye) temptations. We continuously are besieged by obstacles derailing our Joy of Judaism. This constant mitzvah urges us to learn what these traps look and feel like and when tempted, to rely on our pure soul and concerned Creator to help us choose life.

Next time you're stuck in line, review these six constant mitzvot! A handy acronym to memorize them: **FLOOKS**—Fear, Love, One, Other, Know, Stray

The Six Remembrances

In many *siddurim*, at the conclusion of *Shacharit*, there's a list of the *Sheish Z'chirot*, the six mitzvot which, according to the Torah, we are commanded to always remember. By the time I'm done with *Aleynu* and the *Shir Shel Yom* (Song of the Day), I already have my *tefillin* off and I'm very ready for breakfast. This is the time, however, that a review of the Six Remembrances is recommended. Remembering key events in our past ensures the Jewish future.

1. The Exodus from Egypt

"Remember the day when you left Egypt all the days of your life." (*D'varim* 16:3)

This mitzvah is typically fulfilled morning and night in the recitation of the third paragraph of the Sh'ma. The Artscroll Siddur has a note reminding the reader to concentrate on our redemption at this point so we perform this crucial mitzvah with *kavanah*. This remembrance made the first spot on the list because keeping it top of mind is crucial to our gratitude to God. God loved us and redeemed us then and still is doing so every day.

2. Receiving the Torah at Sinai

"Be careful and guard yourself so that you do not forget the things that your eyes have seen… the day you stood before Hashem your God at Sinai." (*D'varim* 4:9-10)

God chose us, saved us from slavery and brought us into the desert in order to give us the Torah at Mount Sinai, the climax of human history. The Torah is our greatest gift, our most precious inheritance. "Turn it and turn it again, for all is in it." (*Pirkei Avot* 5:22) Over two million people witnessed this event and made sure to share the drama with subsequent generations in perpetuity. Our sages tell us we were there too. Holding onto this remembrance is the key to a life of gratitude and amazement.

3. Amalek's attack

"Remember what Amalek did to you on the journey when you left Egypt…you must erase the memory of Amalek from beneath heaven. Do not forget." (*D'varim* 25:17-19)

Jews have enemies. Anti-Semitism is the world's oldest hatred. It began with Amalek and has continued in various pernicious forms to the present day. We must remain vigilant. We can never rest on our laurels. Until *Mashiach* comes, we can never assume that our efforts to make peace will pacify this vile, irrational force.

4. The making of the Golden Calf

"Remember and do not forget how you angered Hashem, your God, in the desert." (*D'varim* 9:7)

We were at the top of our game, standing proudly at Sinai just after having crossed the *Yam Suf* (Reed Sea). God wiped out the Egyptian army and we were about to receive the Ten Commandments. Then due to poor calculations, we lost faith, assumed our leader Moshe was dead and built an idol to worship. We were so close to victory! The lesson? When we're at the cusp of greatness, we're in the most danger of falling. As they say, "The bigger they are, the harder they fall." Some call this syndrome fear of success. I can relate: I used to be an avid tennis player and as soon as I thought the set was "in the bag," I would choke. As Jews, we must go for greatness, filled with confidence in our heritage. That said, when approaching our goals, we must remain humble and grounded, never arrogant or cocky.

5. Miriam's punishment

"Remember what Hashem your God did to Miriam on the journey when you left Egypt." (*D'varim* 24:9)

Miriam was Moshe's big sister, a great prophetess and a leader of the Jewish People. Even she was vulnerable to the snare of *lashon harah* (gossip) and as a result, contracted the spiritual disease of *tzara'at* (poorly translated as leprosy). How much more do we regular folks need to guard our tongues, ensuring our words sow harmony and not discord? Sticks and stones can break my bones and names can hurt me. The Talmud teaches embarrassing someone is like shedding blood. It's that serious. This remembrance helps us exercise care regarding our power to bring blessing or curse to the world. *Sh'mirat halashon* (guarding one's tongue) is the foundation stone of Jewish unity.

6. Celebrating Shabbat

"Remember Shabbat to make it holy." (*Sh'mot* 20:8)

The final remembrance is the key to continuous Jewish connection. But isn't Shabbat only once a week? As we have discussed, the mitzvah to remember the Sabbath can be done daily. Setting aside special food or outfits, inviting guests, planning the festive meals...all can be done *lichvod Shabbas*, for the honor of the Sabbath. Make Shabbat the center of the week rather than the finish line. Shabbat is a taste of *Olam Habah*, the world to come. This remembrance reminds us we can live there all the time, experiencing heaven on earth.

The formula to summarize/memorize the remembrances: **MEGASS**—Miriam, Egypt, Golden, Amalek, Sinai, Shabbat

The Six Questions We'll Be Asked When Arriving in Heaven

After one hundred and twenty amazing years on earth, we will arrive in Heaven and face a tribunal. Our entrance exam, according to the Talmud, consists of six crucial questions. We've discussed a few of them in the preceding chapters. Now, as superstar alumni of the Joy of Judaism, we have to master the whole list! Each item parallels one of the six orders of the Mishna. Each demonstrates reaching a lofty level of emotional maturity and going beyond the call of duty in our life's work. The idea is to nail all six before we meet our Maker.

1. Did we do business with honesty and integrity?

Did we cheat in secret assuming no one would know any better? Were we afraid of public shame but uncaring about God's perspective? Were we givers or takers? Were we exacting with our calculations? Did we nurture our employees?

2. Did we set aside fixed times for studying Torah?

Did we recognize the benefit of regular Torah study? Did we live a disciplined life with emphasis given to matters of the spirit? Were we dedicated to personal growth? Did we share the sweetness of Torah?

3. Did we participate in the commandment to be fruitful and multiply?

Did we see ourselves as links in an ongoing chain of humanity? Did we become selfless through the experience of child-rearing? Did we assist others in their efforts to marry and propogate the species?

4. Did we anxiously await the redemption?
Did we have an optimistic outlook on life? Did we live only for the moment or prepare for the future? Did we engage in *Tikkun Olam*? Did we place our faith in God to better our lot?

5. Did we engage in the pursuit of wisdom?
Were we absorbed with mindless time wasters or endeavor growth? Did we ask questions and seek answers? Did we challenge the status quo? Did we share the knowledge we gained? Did we nurture a broad intellectual curiosity? We may be prohibited from studying Torah in the bathroom but we can still pursue wisdom; my stall is equipped with the latest Wired, Electronic Musician, National Geographic and Mix magazines.

6. Did we have awe of Heaven?
Did we have an awareness of God in our everyday lives? Did we appreciate God's amazing world? Did we recognize God's exacting *middah k'neged middah* (measure for measure) judgement of our efforts?

We are lucky—our Teacher has given us the test questions in advance. Here's a way to keep them top of mind so we can answer confidently in the affirmative when the great day arrives: **WHARFS**—Wisdom, Honesty, Awe, Redemption, Fruitful, Study

Sam's Six Suggestions for Jewish Joy
Reviewing the previous lists have kept Jews connected for generations. The following are my own suggestions to supplement the Constant Mitzvot and Remembrances and bring joy to one's life every day.

1. Fun: have a good time! Do the things you love with the ones you love, and if no one is available or interested, do them yourself.

2. Stay Balanced: devote ample attention to personal needs <u>and</u> keep your family, community and world close to your heart. Keep growth in Torah manageable by taking baby steps. Stay in shape. Ensure *middot* (character traits) never get extreme.

3. Relationships: invest deeply in primary relationships. Love God, cherish friends and relatives and anticipate their needs. If married, maintain emotional and physical fidelity, if a parent, nurture children with your presence.

4. Affiliate: find a rabbi, shul and community and stick with them, showing up at least once a week. Dedicate both time and resources to communal service.

5. *Tzedakah*: give 10% of net income as a minimum, and give with a smile. With beggars, share words of encouragement <u>and</u> cash, grateful you have the chance to do a mitzvah. Give time by volunteering to assist the needy and offering your unique abilities pro bono.

6. Courage: live your Judaism fearlessly! Stay on a path of growth and as you ascend, don't worry about what the neighbors think. Learn in order to teach, act with holy chutzpah

and boldly seize every mitzvah opportunity.

Mnemonic device: **CRAFTS**—Courage, Relationships, Affiliate, Fun, Tzedakah, Stay Balanced

The Six Results of Not Learning Torah

We've discussed the importance of learning Torah at length. Rashi offers a fascinating list of steps (in his commentary on *Vayikra*/Leviticus 26:15) resulting from the cessation of incorporating Torah wisdom into one's life. Picture the Dead Sea, the lowest place on earth. It is rapidly drying up, losing about three feet of depth annually. Satellite pictures from 1972 until the present day portray a body of water on its way to becoming the Dead Pond. Thanks to prodigious dams and agriculture upstream, the Jordan River, which used to be a torrent, has been reduced to a trickle. Just like any body of water needs inflow, so, too, do Jews require a steady input of Torah to keep our connection to the Joy of Judaism. Rashi's list is a premonition of the period when Jewish immigrants flooded North America. Tragically, many of our ancestors "threw their *tefillin* overboard" when entering the New York harbor. In their quest to fit in as Americans, they replaced *limudei kodesh* (Torah studies) with secular academics, farmed out spirituality to clergy and washed their hands of "old world" ritual. The rest is history. According to Rashi, if Jews stop learning Torah, the progression is as follows:

1. They don't fulfill the commandments
2. They despise those who do
3. They hate the Sages
4. They prevent others from fulfilling the commandments
5. They deny the authenticity of the commandments
6. They deny the omnipotence of God

Oy vey…so that's how we got here! It's up to all of us to reclaim Torah study and joyful Jewish living, reversing the descent of our holy community. Five minutes each day can avert this severe decree. Get a good *Chumash*, find a *chevrusa* (learning partner), attend a weekly class, read Jewish blogs, listen to lectures on tape, whatever it takes, for God's sake!

The bottom line to the Joy of Judaism: enjoy the process. Let any perceived offenses or grudges roll off your back. Open your heart to all humans. See the miracle in everyone you meet. Be an expression of gratitude. Connect with God's emissaries. Let music feed your soul. Don't just love—live in love, surround yourself with love, bask in God's love.

Shira and I have had the opportunity to throw many *sheva brachot* celebrations after the weddings of dear friends. At one of these events, the groom asked all assembled to offer marital wisdom. Many delivered lengthy sermons chock full of helpful tips. When it was my turn, I somewhat flippantly suggested, "Have a good time." Months later, when the couple came to our home for Shabbat, they gave me the gift of a Mickey Mouse watch with a card stating, "To Sam, may you always have a good time." I appreciated the sentiment and realized that having fun, while not sounding very serious, sums up the recipe for Jewish joy. My friends, may you go from strength to strength, celebrating your Creator, your extended community and your extraordinary legacy. And don't forget to have a good time.

APPENDIX

IN THIS SECTION:

Dedications 366

Hebrew Alphabet and Gematria 372

Biblical Chronology 373

Holiday Calendar 374

Reading List/Sources 375

Music that Moves Me 377

Discography 380

Tour Schedules 389

Glossary 396

About the Author 406

Dedications

Dedications

The Joy of Judaism is dedicated by
CHESTON AND LARA MIZEL

In memory of Shirley Frysh (Sarah bat Avraham), a woman whose love of Torah and life knew no bounds.

The Joy of Judaism is dedicated by
DR. NOREEN GREEN AND DR. IAN DREW OF THE LOS ANGELES JEWISH SYMPHONY

La'y'hudim haita ora v'simcha, v'sason vikar (For the Jews there was light, gladness, joy and honor). With love, for the words and music that you have shared with us over the years.

oshiach • Tehilim • Shabbat • Community • Torah • Prophets • Nigun • Pesach • Teshuva • Wealth
rituality • Holiness • Emunah • Diaspora • Brit Milah • Simcha • Halacha • Bitachon • Holidays
israel • Tallit • Israel • Mikvah • Prayer • Moshiach 6 • Tehilim • Shabbat • Community • Torah • Pro
gun • Pesach • Teshuva • Weddings • Spirituality • Holiness • Emunah • Diaspora • Brit M
lah • Halacha • Bitachon • Holidays • Bar Mitzvah • Tallit • Israel • Mikvah • Prayer • Moshi
Gun • Shabbat • Community • Torah • Prophets • Nigun • Pesach • Teshuva • Weddings • Spirit
uality • Diaspora • Community • Halacha • Bitachon • Holidays • Bar Mitzvah • Brit Milah
Israel • Israel • Mikvah • Prayer • Moshiach 6 • Tehilim • Shabbat • Community • Torah • Pro

Dedications

The Joy of Judaism is dedicated by
JEFF AND SHAWNI ASTROF

*Fifteen years ago Sam helped to ignite the rocket
booster that took our Judaism to another level. His
spark continues to glow in us as our family continues
to grow physically and spiritually. May this book help
to ignite many more souls the way it did for us.*

The Joy of Judaism is dedicated by
BARBARA AND HAL CRANE

*It is our hope that Sam's infectious enthusiasm for
Judaism inspire even more people to connect to the
Joy of Judaism. In memory of parents Jack Crane
(Yakov ben Feivel HaLevi) and Fae Crane (Feigel bat
Mordechai Hirsh), and in honor of our daughters
Shoshana Natt (Shoshana Chaya bat Tzvi HaLevi)
and Joelle Kanter (Yael Davi bat Tzvi HaLevi), their
husbands Brett Natt (Yitzhak ben Yakov) and Andrew
Kanter (Avraham ben Yoel), and our grandsons Jaden
Brody Natt (Meir Yonah ben Yitzhak), Alex Shawn
Natt (Sasson Eitan ben Yitzhak) and Bennett Ezra
Kanter (Baruch Ezra ben Avraham).*

Dedications

The Joy of Judaism is dedicated by
THEO, DEB, TERVOR, JUSTIN AND LAUREN BRANDT-SARIF

We cherish our long lasting friendship with your family. You embody all that is joyful about connecting with Judaism. Your music elevates and speaks to our hearts. May you go from strength to strength and continue to inspire others with your holy work for many years to come.

The Joy of Judaism is dedicated by
EZRA AND LAUREN KEST

Dedicated to all those who pursue the beauty and truth of Judaism—may you be strong in your pursuit

Dedications

The Joy of Judaism is dedicated by
THE GLASER FAMILY

*In memory of Seymour (Sy) Glaser,
who lived a life of decency*

The Joy of Judaism is dedicated by
NORMAN AND NANCY LIPOFF

In honor of Nancy, my wife, best friend and adviser

Dedications

The Joy of Judaism is dedicated by
EDWARD SLATKIN

The Joy of Judaism is dedicated by
CYNTHIA AND MICHAEL LEBOWITZ

*May the love of Hashem and the joy of Torah in
Sam's songs and teachings be an inspiration to our
grandsons Zack and Isaac Lebowitz*

Hebrew Alphabet and Gematria

	Book Print		Block	Script	
Silent letter	א	Aleph	א	lc	1
B as in **B**oy V as in **V**ine	בּ ב	Bet Vet	בּ ב	ב ב	2
G as in **G**irl	ג	Gimmel	ג	c	3
D as in **D**oor	ד	Dalet	ד	ד	4
H as in **H**ouse	ה	Hay	ה	ה	5
V as in **V**ine	ו	Vav	ו	l	6
Z as in **Z**ebra	ז	Zayin	ז	5	7
CH as in Ba**CH**	ח	Chet	ח	ח	8
T as in **T**all	ט	Tet	ט	6	9
Y as in **Y**es	י	Yud	י	'	10
K as in **K**itty CH as in Ba**CH**	כּ כ	Kaf Chaf	כּ כ	כּ כ	20
L as in **L**ook	ל	Lamed	ל	ƒ	30
M as in **M**oon	מ ם	Mem	מ ם	N ρ	40
N as in **N**ow	נ ן	Nun	נ ן	J ן	50
S as in **S**un	ס	Samech	ס	O	60
Silent letter	ע	Ayin	ע	γ	70
P as in **P**ark F as in **F**ood	פּ ף פ ף	Pay Fay	פּ ף פ ף	ə ƒ ə ƒ	80
TS as in Nu**TS**	צ ץ	Tsade	צ ץ	3 ƒ	90
K as in **K**itty	ק	Kuf	ק	ק	100
R as in **R**obin	ר	Resh	ר	ר	200
SH as in **SH**e S as in **S**un	שׁ שׂ	Shin Sin	שׁ שׂ	e e	300
T as in **T**all	ת	Tav	ת	ת	400

Vowels

X̲ **a** as in y**a**cht	פַּתַח patach
X̳ **a** as in y**a**cht	קָמַץ kamats
X̣ **ee** as in b**ee**	חִירֶק chirek
X̤ **ay** as in h**ay**	צֵרֵי tsere
X̱ **e** as in b**e**d	סֶגוֹל segol
וֹX or Ẋ **o** as in r**ow**	חוֹלֶם cholem
X̦ **oo** as in p**oo**l	קֻבּוּץ kibuts
וּX **oo** as in p**oo**l	שׁוּרֶק shurek
X̡ **o** as in r**ow**	חֲטָף קָמַץ chataf kamats
X̤ silent/short sound	שְׁוָא sheva

EKS Publishing Co.
PO Box 9750
Berkeley, CA 94709

Phone: 877-7-HEBREW
877-743-2739
Fax: 510-251-9102
Email: orders@ekspublishing.com

EB324 © 2010 EKS Publishing Co.

Biblical Chronology

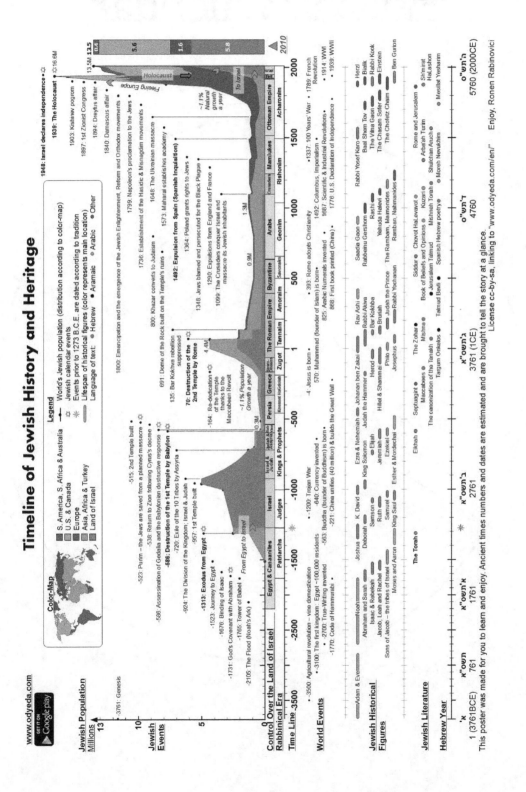

Holiday Calendar

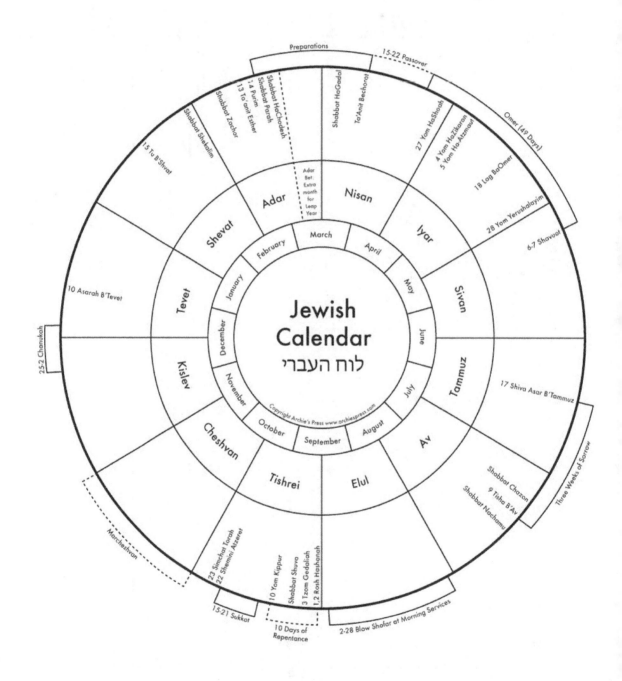

Reading List/Sources

The following books are among those I feel are crucial for any English language Jewish library. These are the cherished authors whose texts and lectures inform my writing and my life. As a start, I recommend purchasing a quality *Chumash* (Torah with commentary) to peruse each morning, and for bedtime reading, pick book below, read the description on Amazon and splurge. As my rabbi says, "You're always safer with a *sefer* (Jewish book)."

Don't have the time to read? Well, as an experiment for one short month, cut off Netflix, avoid the Internet, cancel the newspaper and forego Stephen King. New vistas for stimulating Torah study will materialize! For those interested in procuring an instant Jewish library, simply present this list to the local Jewish bookstore and bring plenty of money. In the meantime, most of these authors have lectures and texts online. Ideally, you can find a *chevrusa* (learning partner) who will help choose the reading material and nudge you to keep the date with your heritage.

Please note that the majority of these authors are rabbis. Essential references from Artscroll Publications include the Stone *Chumash*, *Chumash* with Rashi, *Kitzur Shulchan Aruch*, *The Prophets* and various holiday guides. Chabad has two excellent *Chumashim* I enjoy: The Gutnick Edition and the expanded Wisnefsky version. Let me also plug the indispensable Artscroll *siddur* and *machzor* (High Holiday prayer book) which includes modern translations, commentary, excellent typography and full instructions for the neophyte, and is available in an interlinear or transliterated version. I use the Ashkenaz Interlinear everyday and love it.

Pick a book and open your mind. *Talmud Torah k'neged kulam* (The study of Torah is equivalent to all the other mitzvot). Keep me posted on your favorites!

David Aaron — *Endless Light, Seeing God, Secret Life of God, Living a Joyous Life*

Yitzchok Adlerstein — *Be'er Hag'dolah, Nesivos Shalom*

Nachum Amsel — *Encyclopedia of Jewish Values*

Shimon Apisdorf — *The Rosh Hashanah/Yom Kippur Survival Kit, The Passover Survival Kit, Chanukah: Eight Nights of Light, Judaism in a Nutshell Series*

Shalom Arush — *The Garden of Emunah, The Garden of Peace, In Forest Fields*

David Baum — *Non-Orthodox Jew's Guide to Orthodox Jews*

Benjamin Blech — *Understanding Judaism, Idiot's Guides to Judaism, If God is Good, Secrets of Hebrew Words, Taking Stock*

Nachum Braverman — *The Death of Cupid, The Bible for the Curious and Clueless*

Moshe A. Braun — *The Sfas Emes*

Nathan Lopes Cardozo — *Between Silence and Speech, The Written and the Oral Torah, Judaism On Trial, Thoughts to Ponder, For the Love of Israel, Jewish Law as Rebellion*

Shlomo Carlebach — *Holy Brother, Shlomo's Stories, Torah Commentary, Life, Mission and Legacy*

Baruch Chait — *39 Avot Melacha of Shabbat, Haggadah, Incredible Voyage to Middos*

Avraham Chill — *The Minhagim, The Mitzvot*

Eric Coopersmith — *The Eye of the Needle*

Nechemia Coopersmith and Shraga Simmons — *Rabbi Noah Weinberg's 48 Ways to Wisdom, Wisdom for Living, Heaven and Earth, Like Water on a Rock*

Eliyahu Dessler — *Strive for Truth, On the Parsha*

Hayim Donin — *To Be a Jew, To Pray as a Jew*

Aharon Feldman — *The River, the Kettle and the Bird, The Juggler and the King*

Yissoscher Frand — *In Print, On the Parsha, Too Little Too Late*

Tzvi Freeman — *Bringing Heaven Down to Earth, Heaven Exposed, Haggadah*

Avraham Greenbaum/Rabbi Nachman — *Advice, Under the Table, The Universal Torah*

Ari Kahn — *Explorations, Emanations, Echoes of Eden*

Aryeh Kaplan — *Anthology I & II, Reader, The Living Torah, The Living Nach, The Infinite Light, Jewish Meditation*

Lawrence Kelemen — *Permission to Believe, Permission to Receive, To Kindle a Soul*

Yitzchok Kirzner — *The Art of Jewish Prayer*

Eliyahu Kitov — *Book of Our Heritage, The Jewish Home*

Avraham Isaak Kook — *The Lights of Penitence*

Moshe Chaim Luzatto — *The Way of God, The Path of the Just, The Way of Reason*

Gila Manolson — *The Magic Touch*

Tom Meyer — *Five Levels of the Soul*

Michael Munk — *The Wisdom of the Hebrew Alphabet*

Zelig Pliskin — *Growth Through Torah, My Father, My King, Anger*

Simcha Raz — *The Sayings of Menachem Mendel of Kotsk*

YY Rubinstein — *Refuas Halev, Jewish Life and Jewish Laughter*

Kalonymus Kalman Shapira — *The Holy Fire, To Heal the Soul, A Student's Obligation*

Matisyahu Soloman — *With Hearts Full of Faith*

Menachem Mendel Shneerson — *Torah Studies, Toward a Meaningful Life, Bringing Heaven to Earth*

Akiva Tatz — *Living Inspired, Letters to a Buddhist Jew, Worldmask, Will, Freedom and Destiny, Thinking Jewish Teenager's Guide, As Dawn Ends the Night*

Ezriel Tauber — *Choose Life, I Shall Not Want, Darkness Before Dawn, As in Heaven, So on Earth*

Avraham Twerski — *Living Each Day, On Spirituality, Happiness and the Human Spirit*

Berel Wein — *Echoes of Glory, Herald of Destiny, Triumph of Survival, Faith and Fate*

Matis Weinberg — *Frameworks, Patterns in Time*

Noah Weinberg — *What the Angel Taught You*

Herman Wouk — *This is My God*

Music that Moves Me

Enjoy this "Deserted Island" list of my all time musical favorites. You can catch me on any given flight, driving L.A. freeways or bombing ski runs while cranking up these timeless tunes. For me, great music is survival. Once upon a time, friends would gather on a couch and audition a new album while scrutinizing the cover art and allowing their imaginations to soar. If you don't have a vintage Marantz receiver and Infinity speakers, don't fret. An off-the-shelf smartphone and headphones sound great. Take time to focus on the miracle of music: stifle conversation, close your eyes and ensure it is loud enough to have impact. Give me fidelity or give me silence!

Each of these artists produce consistently excellent releases, such that one could reach into their vast catalogs at random and pull out a winner. These artists make albums—not just singles. I endeavor to see these acts every time they tour in my area. I recognize that the opportunity to hear them live is rare and is guaranteed to induce a state of aural bliss. They are listed alphabetically; no ranking is implied. The astute listener will hear many an unconscious tip of the hat in many a melody, cadence or production of mine. The final list features session musicians who are regulars in my studio. In addition to my own material, I have had the privilege of producing over a hundred full-length albums for clients; this list acknowledges many of the awesome players who get the parts off the page and into your ears. I'm grateful to them for their immense talent, amazing work ethic and plentiful good vibes.

I cut each list off at fifteen. Fifteen is the number representing completion, fullness. For example, the full moon is on the fifteenth of each month, there are fifteen parts in the Passover *Seder* and one had to ascend fifteen steps to reach the Holy Temple in Jerusalem. Stopping at fifteen means lots of my favorite players got left off the list. With few exceptions, all these musicians recorded from the sixties through the eighties. That's <u>my</u> music. These artists were fortunate to enjoy the financial boon of surviving several formats, requiring that their ardent fans repurchase multiple times, first vinyl, then cassettes, then CDs. Of course, now all are available for free on streaming sites. Great for the consumer! (For the artist, not quite as great…we will overcome.) Happy listening.

UK Rock Bands

1. The Beatles
2. The Clash
3. Coldplay
4. Crowded House
5. Genesis
6. Led Zeppelin
7. Pink Floyd
8. The Police
9. Queen
10. The Rolling Stones
11. Tears for Fears
12. The Who
13. U2
14. UK
15. Yes

US Rock Bands

1. Aerosmith
2. Bon Jovi
3. Boston
4. Crosby, Stills, Nash and Young
5. The Dixie Dregs
6. The Doobie Brothers
7. The Doors
8. The Eagles
9. Fleetwood Mac
10. Heart
11. Journey
12. Kansas
13. Steely Dan
14. Toto
15. Van Halen

R&B Acts

1. James Brown
2. Earth, Wind & Fire
3. Marvin Gaye
4. Whitney Houston
5. KC and the Sunshine Band
6. Kool and the Gang
7. Michael Jackson
8. Bruno Mars
9. The Ohio Players
10. Prince
11. Seal
12. The Temptations
13. Justin Timberlake
14. Tower of Power
15. War

Singer/Songwriters (Male)

1. David Bowie
2. Thomas Dolby
3. Peter Gabriel
4. Bruce Hornsby
5. Joe Jackson
6. Billy Joel
7. Elton John
8. Kenny Loggins
9. Paul McCartney
10. Michael Ruff
11. Paul Simon
12. Bruce Springsteen
13. Sting
14. James Taylor
15. Stevie Wonder

Singer/Songwriters (Female)

1. Adele
2. Shawn Colvin
3. Sheryl Crow
4. Aretha Franklin
5. Chrissie Hynde
6. Rickie Lee Jones
7. Janis Joplin
8. Carole King
9. Lady Gaga
10. Annie Lennox
11. Joni Mitchell
12. Alanis Morisette
13. Pink
14. Bonnie Raitt
15. Carly Simon

Jazz Bands

1. Brecker Brothers
2. Chick Corea Electric Band
3. El Trio
4. Fourplay
5. Karizma
6. Gipsy Kings
7. The Manhattan Transfer
8. Pat Metheny Group
9. Return to Forever
10. The Rippingtons
11. Snarky Puppy
12. Spyro Gyra
13. Strunz and Farah
14. Weather Report
15. Yellowjackets

Jam Bands

1. The California Honeydrops
2. Galactic
3. Lettuce
4. Lotus
5. The Main Squeeze
6. moe.
7. Orgone
8. Phish
9. Pigeons Playing Ping Pong
10. The String Cheese Incident
11. TAUK

12. Tedeschi Trucks
13. Turkuaz
14. Twiddle
15. Umphrey's McGee

Keyboardists
1. David Benoit
2. Billy Childs
3. Chick Corea
4. George Duke
5. Keith Emerson
6. Russell Ferrante
7. Dave Grusin
8. Herbie Hancock
9. Corey Henry
10. T Lavitz
11. Ramsey Lewis
12. Jeff Lorber
13. Lyle Mays
14. Jordan Rudess
15. Dave Stewart

Guitarists
1. Ritchie Blackmore
2. Marc Bonilla
3. Larry Carlton
4. Eric Clapton
5. The Edge
6. Dave Gilmour
7. Jimi Hendrix
8. Eric Johnson
9. Kerry Livgren
10. Brian May
11. Pat Metheny
12. Lee Ritenour
13. Steve Morse
14. Carlos Santana
15. Stevie Ray Vaughn

Drummers
1. Terry Bozzio

2. Bill Bruford
3. Vinnie Coliuta
4. Phil Collins
5. Stewart Copeland
6. Phil Ehart
7. Steve Gadd
8. Omar Hakim
9. Manu Katche
10. Abe Laboriel, Jr.
11. Simon Phillips
12. Jeff Porcaro
13. Antonio Sanchez
14. Steve Smith
15. Dave Weckl

Bass Players
1. Jeff Berlin
2. Richard Bona
3. Stanley Clarke
4. Andrew Gouche
5. Jimmy Haslip
6. James Jamerson
7. Abe Laboriel
8. Graham Maby
9. Marcus Miller
10. Jaco Pastorius
11. John Patitucci
12. Steve Rodby
13. Leland Sklar
14. Chris Squire
15. Verdine White

Horns
1. John Coltrane
2. Miles Davis
3. Brandon Fields
4. Dizzy Gillespie
5. Freddie Hubbard
6. Dave Koz
7. Eric Marienthal
8. Wynton Marsalis

9. Branford Marsalis
10. Bob Mintzer
11. Charlie Parker
12. James Pankow
13. Chris Potter
14. David Sanborn
15. Trombone Shorty

Classical Composers
1. Bach
2. Beethoven
3. Bernstein
4. Brahms
5. Chopin
6. Copeland
7. Debussy
8. Gershwin
9. Mahler
10. Mozart
11. Puccini
12. Rachmaninoff
13. Shostakovich
14. Richard Strauss
15. Verdi

Glaser Musicworks Players
1. Charlie Bisharat
2. Cassio Duarte
3. Mat Gurman
4. James Harrah
5. Joey Heredia
6. Dave Hill
7. Dave Hooper
8. Jake Jacobs
9. Michael Lington
10. Michael Nelson
11. Larry Steen
12. Lee Thornberg
13. Jerry Watts
14. Toshi Yanagi
15. Leah Zeger

Discography

Yes, I want you to own all my albums! They are like my children. Each took about a year of full-time work to write, produce, record and mix. Each is truly a labor of love, and all the effort I expend is amply rewarded when you enjoy them, hopefully in glorious stereo on quality speakers or headphones. The long form album is my artform of choice. In the twelve to fifteen songs therein, I get to tell a story, express my deepest feelings, teach and hopefully inspire. I've written thousands of songs…only a select few make the cut to actually get recorded. Here's the list from 1989 to the present. I love hearing how they are received—thanks for letting me know!

Excerpted from the liner notes of the Sony/JMG release *Inspired: Best of Sam Glaser*:

I will never forget the first time I heard Sam Glaser. It was the summer of 1993 at the annual CAJE Conference San Antonio, Texas. Sam was at the piano belting out an absolutely make-your-jaw-drop tune called, Hineni. I don't think I had been that excited about a song since the first time I heard Rosalita. I bought the Hineni album, couldn't wait to get it home to my wife, and Sam Glaser's music has been a part of our lives ever since. Sure, it's tempting to compare Sam to this or that great artist, but frankly, that misses the point. We have an ancient tradition that says, "Words that emanate from the heart, touch the heart." And that is what this music is all about—Sam Glaser's music always goes right to the heart.

There are certain experiences in life, certain moments, for which mere words are inadequate. You know what you want to convey but the words in your mind just seem to fall flat. That's where an exceptionally rare kind of music steps in. Every once in a while we are blessed with a musician who is able to take our thoughts, our yearnings, our tears, our smiles—and the deepest rumblings of our souls—and weave them together into a melody. Into a form of expression that is at once inspiring, motivating, haunting, illuminating, and even fun. That's Sam Glaser. Through strikingly sincere lyrics and profoundly inspired music, Sam Glaser is able to take us on a journey to a place that is often hidden, always beautiful, and never quite what you expect it to be. Sam, like all of us, is on a journey. It's our good fortune that through his music he shares a bit of his journey with us, and in so doing, enriches our own.

You want music to cruise down the highway with and belt out every word as you go? Music that will fill your spirit with a fresh, intense sense of optimism? Music that will make you feel like anything is possible? Music that will make you want to reclaim your deepest self, your awesome potential? Then do what I did in San Antonio, start with Hineni and then go right on listening. On a personal note, I want to thank Sam. Over a decade ago my wife said, "Why don't you just call him and tell him how much we love his music." And so I did. Since then, beyond the music, I've come to know Sam Glaser the person and all I can say is this: through his music, this guy is sharing his deepest self with all of us, and once you hear the music, you will be glad he did. Thanks Sam.

—**SHIMON APISDORF**, award-winning author and founder of the Jewish Literacy Foundation

1989: MIDNIGHT AT THE BALL

On Sam Glaser's first full-length album, finely crafted pop-jazz settings combine with lyrics describing shrinking resources and a hope for a new world order. Recorded on eight-track ½" tape, "Midnight at the Ball" pushed the boundaries for a self-produced release, relying on Sam's early adoption of MIDI technology. Sam's Thursday Night Band performed this material at such notable L.A. clubs as The Whisky, Roxy, Madame Wongs and Lingerie. Their once-a-month stand at At My Place in Santa Monica earned them the Thursday Night Band moniker. To date, Chuck Sparks has mixed and Dave Hooper has hit the drums for nearly every Glaser release. Guitar wunderkind George K created the guitar atmospheres and backup vocals feature Greg Walker from Santana, Michael Lennon from Venice and Sam's long time soprano ally Michael Ian Elias. Midnight's opening track, *I Had a Good Time* became the theme for Warren Miller Sports Television, *Comrades* celebrated the fall of the Iron Curtain and *Where Are You Now* raised awareness of the war in Central America.

1991: TIME OUT

"Time Out" is a grooving collection of songs describing dating frustration and relationships gone wrong. The final track features a duet with fitness junkie and record biz executive Marcia Fassino, the woman that Sam would wed a few years later. This crisp production reveals the coalescing of Sam's studio skills, maturing songwriting and the blessing of the first affordable sixteen-track tape machines. Noted funk bass player Freddie Flewellyn replaced Latin master Edgie Sierra in the Thursday Night Band lineup. "Time Out" also marked the start of Sam's lifelong friendship with musician/artist Ramiro Fauve who sang backup vocals and whose graphic talents have given all of Sam's products their unique and professional look.

1992: HINENI

"Hineni" is Glaser's first Jewish album and became one of the best-selling Jewish albums of the year. Songs such as *Shabbas*, *Pitchu Li* and the title track have since become standards at synagogues, camps and Jewish households worldwide. It features the guitar work of Bruce Burger (AKA RebbeSoul), drummer Chuck Sparks and sax great Michael Lington who has played on nearly every subsequent Glaser album. Sam composed the title track for a Capitol Records release to benefit Operation Exodus, helping raise the funds for Russian Jews to immigrate to Israel. It also became a hit for popular performer, Craig Taubman. Several of the songs were written during the Center for Jewish Culture and Creativity's month-long creative institute in Jerusalem. "Hineni" debuted at the CAJE conference (Coalition for Advancement in Jewish Education) and launched Sam's first concert tour of the Jewish world.

1993: SHIRA

"Shira" is a collection of love songs composed for Sam's beloved wife-to-be Marcia, AKA Shira, over the course of their two-year relationship. Released shortly after their August 1993 wedding, Shira tracks the ups and downs shared by countless couples on their way to the *chuppah* (marriage canopy). "Shira" features versatile bass player Larry Steen and percussion wizard Cassio Duarte, who have played on nearly every Sam Glaser release to follow.

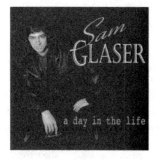

1994: A DAY IN THE LIFE

"A Day in the Life" is a deeply inspired collection of songs illuminating the beauty of Jewish prayer. This album features the acoustic and electric guitar playing of Mat Gurman; his unique sound and impeccable technique would become a permanent presence in Sam's concerts and future albums, cementing the band membership to date. Horn arrangements are by Tonight Show trumpeter Lee Thornberg and string arrangements by maestro Lucas Richman. One can hear generations of Jewish triumph, joy and pain in these songs influenced by Sam's newfound immersion in the ancient texts. Over a half dozen Jewish hits resulted from this effort including *Modeh Ani, Oseh Shalom, V'ha'er Eyneynu, Learnin' Machine* and the Holocaust-themed *Born to Remember.*

1995: LULLABIES AND JITTERBUGS

"Lullabies and Jitterbugs" is Sam Glaser's first kids' album. Its release corresponds with his son Max's first year on the planet; Lullabies was composed on the job trying to pacify his young charge. This release is ideal for new parents and their lucky offspring while getting used to one another. Six of the songs are for playtime and six for bedtime, with one bonus instrumental track to put on repeat mode until Jr. is really out. The styles range from Broadway to big band, marches to tender ballads and all the songs are filled with love and humor.

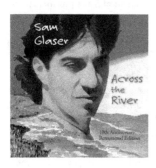

1997: ACROSS THE RIVER

Sam's third Jewish album celebrates the course of the Jewish year with moving songs about major holidays and lifecycle events. He promoted this album in the fifty-city One Hand/One Heart tour across the globe in '98/99. Generously sponsored by Kirk Douglas, "Across the River" was modeled after Elton John's "Goodbye Yellow Brick Road," employing the same sixteen-song, double-album concept and a piece of original art for every number, painted by Sam's mom, Harriet Glaser. ATR was one of the first Glaser Musicworks Studio releases, having been recorded in Sam's new state-of-the-art studio built behind his home. ATR ushered several "standards" into the Jewish world including the title track, *Blessing, Asher Bara, Yisrael Shelanu* and *One Hand One Heart.*

1999: KOL BAMIDBAR — A VOICE IN THE DESERT

"Kol Bamidbar" is a musical theater "Journey Through the Five Books of Moses." This studio soundtrack album features thirteen songs tracing Jewish history through the stories of the Torah. Sam recorded this memorable "edutainment" music with his band and the Kol Bamidbar Childrens Choir culled from several school choirs in the L.A. area. Each year Sam supplements his concert schedule with large-scale performances of this interactive musical with afternoon and day school students nationwide. The libretto was penned by Emmy-winning writer David Sacks and informative classroom activity guides deepen the learning experience. This musical launched the popular songs *Letter in the Torah, Unbreakable Soul, Uv'nei Yerushalayim, The Seven Days* and *The Bat Mitzvah Song.*

2001: THE SONGS WE SING

"The Songs We Sing" features Sam and his band performing classic songs in the Jewish repertoire. The innovative arrangements and state-of-the-art production give new life to these standards that have been enjoyed for decades. A perennial bestseller in the catalogue, SWS was recorded live in the studio, without a click track and without strict form. Additional guitars and vocals were overdubbed but the essential roots of the sound are raw and unpremeditated. Guest drummer and dear friend Jake Jacobs gave his all to his parts just after having completed the *shiva* period for his father; it is to him that the album is dedicated. Selections include *Adon Olam, Erev Shel Shoshanim, Bashana Haba'a, Kol Ha'olam Kulo* and *Yerushalyim Shel Zahav.*

2002: THE BRIDGE

"The Bridge" is a jubilant collection of fifteen upbeat Glaser compositions celebrating the unifying themes that bind the Jewish people. Sponsored by Israel's Common Denominator organization, it was featured in unity concerts over the course of 2002/2003 where many communities accepted the challenge to involve at least three synagogues across denominational lines. Finally freed from the limitations of tape, "The Bridge" stretches Glaser's musical vision unencumbered by track counts and mixdown limitations. With six-part horn arrangements and the playing of famed violinist Charlie Bisharat, "The Bridge" features *In Israel*, which became a theme song for the Nefesh b'Nefesh Israel aliyah program, and hits *Al Shlosha D'varim, Od Yishama, Hallelu* and *Adon Olam.*

2002: O/SEE WHAT YOU WANT

"O/See What You Want" (O stands for Origins) is a concept album co-composed and produced by Sam and his buddy Ramiro Fauve. Speaking to the heart and the conscience, O's hypnotic music and lyrics convey a world vision of hope and love for humanity. While not a Jewish album per se, O is a deeply spiritual musical experience, drawing from progressive and alternative rock styles and indulging the senses with inviting textures. Given the interconnected quality of the songs and message, the album is best enjoyed in a continuous, uninterrupted seventy-minute span. O features Ramiro on acoustic guitar and lead vocals (and state-of-the-art graphics), Sam on keyboards, keyboard bass and background vocals and legendary session players Toshi Yanagi on guitar, Russ Miller on drums and Charlie Bisharat on violin.

2002: CHASHMAL

Sam's other side project of the year was a Jewish "boy band" called "Chashmal," meaning electricity in Hebrew. Imagine four Jewish singers with strap-on keyboards, plus guitar and drums, fancy outfits and ambitious choreography. "Chashmal" features original Jewish music with an electronica edge that is guaranteed to lift one to greater simcha. Composed, produced and arranged by Sam Glaser and Naftali Finkel, with vocals by Sam Glaser, Michael Ian Elias and Brad Schachter.

2003: PRESENCE

Glaser's 2003 releases feature a pair of albums on the softer, more spiritual side. These fifteen introspective Sam Glaser compositions are based on the themes of the High Holidays and the month of Tishrei. With rich orchestrations and immaculate production, highlights of "Presence" include *Believe in Me,* which became a regional hit on Christian radio, plus *Achat Sho'alti, Take Me As I Am, Tree of Life* and *Shehecheyanu.* "Presence" is the album that Sam often recommends when approached by new fans at the merchandise table.

2003: EDGE OF LIGHT

On "Edge of Light," Sam Glaser and concert pianist Sha-Rone Kushnir explore twelve of Sam's most evocative ballads from his first four albums. The music truly soars in this intimate, classical-cum-new age improvisational piano/vocal setting. A bonus piano-only album is included in the package and is ideal for meditation, massage and healing.

2003: SAM GLASER LIVE AT THE ALEX

With over 120 gifted performers on the stage, Sam Glaser delivered this ambitious concert before an enthusiastic crowd at the historic Alex Theater in Los Angeles. Conducted by Dr. Noreen Green, the acclaimed L.A. Jewish Symphony integrated seamlessly with Glaser's eight-piece band, an adult choir and the Kol Bamidbar Children's Choir. This event was produced by the Valley Alliance of Jewish Federations and featured twenty of Sam Glaser's hits from his first decade in Jewish music. The concert was professionally recorded by orchestral producer/engineer Michael Stern and mixed and mastered at Glaser Musicworks.

2004: SOAP SOUP

"Soap Soup" is a witty kids' album featuring twenty new Sam Glaser songs for children and their families. This acclaimed recording won the John Lennon Songwriting Competition and such awards as Parent's Choice, the National Association of Parenting Publications and the International Songwriting Competition. "Soap Soup" touches upon themes that make kids laugh and sing in their daily lives, highlighting such activities as eating ice cream, birthday parties, visiting the zoo, taking baths and family vacations. Released as a labor of love for his three children, "Soap Soup" has become one of Sam's most popular albums. Top songs are *Family Vacation, Ice Cream, Sarah, Trip to the Zoo* and *Hummingbird.*

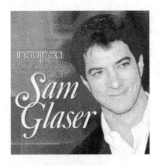

2005: INSPIRED/BEST OF SAM GLASER

Sam's "Greatest Hits" collection has eighteen of the most requested songs from his various Jewish albums. Sam is one of the first artists signed by Jewish Music Group, a division of Sony Music seeking to bring Contemporary Jewish Music into the mainstream. This album represents their first collaborative release and serves as a launching point for new fans into Sam's catalog. It also features the Bababanewz Magazine commissioned *Hatikvah* recorded in Techno style, and an updated, orchestrated version of Sam's first hit, *Hineni*.

2006: NIGUN/VOICE OF THE SOUL

"Nigun/Voice of the Soul" is a collection of nineteen spirited *nigunim* (songs without words) featuring a co-production effort with acclaimed world-beat guitarist RebbeSoul. Almost all the songs are penned by Glaser, with a few classics included to round out the festive collection. This novel combination of klezmer, reggae and world music styles is enhanced by noted country music bassist Chad Watson, hip hop drummer Paul Allen and klezmer kings Leo Chelyapov and Ruben Berci. Guest vocalists include members of such notable Jewish bands as Moshav, Soulfarm, Blue Fringe, Gershon Veroba and Beatachon. One can't keep still when listening and it's almost impossible not to sing along.

2007: SAM GLASER'S ROCKIN' CHANUKAH REVUE

"Sam Glaser's Rockin' Chanukah Revue" is a wild musical adventure celebrating this favorite of family holidays. Sam and his original band are joined by a variety of guest musicians and a children's choir from Harkham Hillel Academy. The Revue features a mix of clever parodies, traditional Chanukah hits and Sam Glaser originals. This album injects fresh energy and meaning into the traditional Chanukah fare with twenty songs guaranteed to rock all ages. Many songs have become part of Sam's concerts year-round including *Maccabee, Latkes* and the bonus track, *My Sukkah's on Fire*. Distributed by Sony/JMG, the album was the recipient of the Parent's Choice award. The project launched Jewish Life Television's "Sam Glaser's Rockin' Chanukah Special."

2008: HALLEL

Sam Glaser's "Hallel" is a jubilant musical experience expressing humankind's ultimate joy and deepest gratitude. "Hallel" incorporates the full text of the Hallel Service, which is the climax of the prayers on most Jewish holidays. The Psalms of King David take on a new life within these sophisticated, interconnected rock/worldbeat settings. The innovative arrangements feature Sam and his eight-piece band, strings, adult and childrens' choirs and an array of guest vocalists.

2010: THE SONGS WE SING, VOLUME 2

Two years in the making, "The Songs We Sing, Vol. 2" is the follow up to the bestselling 2000 release, "The Songs We Sing." Volume Two includes contemporary versions of twenty-eight classics of Jewish music on a double-length album featuring Sam, his full band and guest vocalists. These are the common denominator songs beloved by Jews everywhere, each ingeniously arranged within two-song medleys. SWS2 utilizes the same lineup as SWS1, a group of world-class musicians who have made a career out of interpreting Jewish music. The release of this album marks Sam's "chai" year; a memorable eighteen years of touring to over a thousand venues throughout the Jewish world.

2011: FATHERHOOD

"Fatherhood" is a compilation of moving songs about fathers, parenting, families and lifecycles. It features eleven of Sam's new compositions that are among the most heartfelt of his career, and four classic cover tunes: Neil Young's *Old Man*, country hit *Butterfly Wings*, Harry Chapin's *Cats in the Cradle* and the Temptation's *Papa was a Rolling Stone*. New additions to the band for this album are bassist Jerry Watts and Huey Lewis and Herbie Hancock alum, guitarist James Harrah. Sam donated a portion of the proceeds to the Diabetes Research Institute and dedicated the album to his beloved father.

2012: THE PROMISE

Sam Glaser's "The Promise" is an uplifting musical celebration of the gift of the Land of Israel. It explores the love affair with the Promised Land through the biblical period, two millennia of exile and the recent miraculous years of *aliyah* (return). "The Promise" features Sam's top-notch band of L.A.-based musicians, gifted guest vocalists and a children's choir. It hit the airwaves with songs *Inside of Yerushalayim, Mezuza, Dancing in Jerusalem, Hatikvah* and the title track. The *Simple Song for Israel* and *Dancing in Jerusalem* videos are Sam's first million-hits-plus videos. "The Promise" offers lovers of Israel a hopeful message of the future of the Jewish Homeland and the eternal quest for peace.

2014: TOWARDS THE DAWN

"Towards the Dawn" picks up where the first "Edge of Light" album left off: over seventy minutes of powerful renditions of Sam Glaser's most moving songs in a bold pop/classical/jazz setting, featuring concert pianist Sha-Rone Kushnir, virtuoso violinist Leah Zeger and Mike McGuffey on trumpet and flugelhorn. Using Hebrew lyrics from Jewish liturgy and the Psalms together with his incisive English interpretations, "Towards the Dawn" is a profound sonic journey of the mind and spirit.

2016: STAGES: 25TH ANNIVERSARY TRIBUTE ALBUM

"Stages" is a thirty-two song, double CD tribute album of the best of Sam Glaser's music performed by America's favorite Jewish artists. Published by Behrman House, the largest provider of teaching materials for religious and day schools, this collection highlights Sam's vast repertoire of uplifting, spiritual music composed during his twenty-five-year career traveling the globe in concert. Includes performances by Gershon Veroba, Julie Silver, Noah Aronson, Moshav, Todd Herzog, Taylor Dayne, Dov Rosenblatt, Ari Herstand and many others.

2018: HATIKVAH THE MUSICAL

"Hatikvah the Musical" is a contemporary musical theater program expressing the historical, geographical and spiritual connection of the Jewish people to Israel. Day school and religious school students co-star with Sam while learning about the unique relationship between the Jewish People and the Land. This upbeat soundtrack recording includes all the songs from the eighty-minute show performed by Sam's dynamic band and featuring a group of top L.A. kids on background vocals. The libretto was penned by Emmy Award-winning writer David Sacks and the package includes an engaging Classroom Activity Guide.

2019: THE POWER OF THE SOUL

The Power of the Soul is a collection of new Sam Glaser songs describing the triumph of the eternal human soul. Complementing Sam's originals are classic "soul" songs including Debbie Friedman's *Tefilat Haderech*, *The Miser* by Moshe Yess and *Nafshi* by Yehuda Glantz. This heartfelt, smoothly produced album speaks to the heart and touches the neshama.

2019: THE SONGS WE SING, VOL. 3/DANCE

Completing "The Songs We Sing" trilogy, this album features nearly eighty minutes of Sam's amazing band performing wild Jewish dance sets. These continuous, rambunctious horas combine world beat, klezmer and pop to make any *simcha* come alive. Includes an *Ashkenaz Wedding Hora*, a *B'nai Mitzvah Hora*, a *Middle-East Hora* and *Israeli Folk Dance Medley*.

2019: A GLASER FAMILY SHABBAT EXPERIENCE

The "Shabbat Experience" is the first of five new albums dedicated to the celebration of the weekly Sabbath. Sam and his extended family make special music at the Shabbat and holiday table. This sweet recording features Jewish music typically sung at celebratory meals. It includes the blessings over wine and bread, the *Birkat Hamazon*, and typical *z'mirot* and folk songs. Accompanied by concert grand piano and starring Sam, his parents, children and sibling's families on vocals.

2020: SAM GLASER'S KOMPLETELY KLEZMER SHABBAT

Sam partnered with famed New Orleans ensemble, the Panorama Jazz Band to record this uplifting klezmer Kabbalat Shabbat service. Intended to be performed with full ensemble for services in the spring and summer when Shabbat enters later in the day, this music guarantees a Shabbat of ecstatic joy. The full liturgy of the service is set with well known Jewish folk tunes and klezmer classics, executed with technical grace and enthusiasm by world-class NOLA musicians.

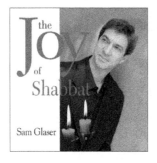

2020: THE JOY OF SHABBAT

"The Joy of Shabbat" is Sam's first album of original Shabbat songs. These all new compositions express the depths of the beauty Shabbat liturgy combined with Sam's English "Midrash" interpretations. Over a dozen tunes are meticulously recorded with Sam and his top-notch band, featuring live horns, strings and talented guest vocalists.

2021: THE GREATEST HITS OF SHABBAT

Sam's Shabbat-inspired greatest hits culled from his thirty Jewish albums, presented together for the first time.

2021: INSPIRED 2/BEST OF SAM GLASER 2006-2021

Sam's second "Greatest Hit" collection includes the eighteen top songs from the dozen albums released since 2005's JMC/Sony Music Inspired Vol. 1.

2021: THE BA'AL TEFILLA TUTORIAL PROJECT

A web-based recording project featuring a number of cantors singing Shabbat and holiday liturgy to allow laypeople to learn to lead. Sam offers a standard Ashkenaz *nusach* (prayer melody) and a Shlomo Carlebach *nusach*, and several guest cantors add their own unique voices.

sam glaser in concert
presence
tour 2003

Aspen, CO
Austin, TX
Baltimore, MD
Bethlehem, PA
Cancun, Mexico
Chicago, IL
Cleveland, OH
Costa Mesa, CA
Denver, CO
Erie, PA
Flint, MI
Fresno, CA
Hempstead, NY
Herndon, VA
Johnson City, TN
King Of Prussia, PA
La Jolla, CA
Laguna Niguel, CA
London, England
Los Angeles, CA
Melrose Park, PA
Metuchen, NJ
New York, NY
N. Miami Beach, FL
Northbrook, IL
Philadelphia, PA
Phoenix, AZ
Puerto Plata, D. Rep.
Raleigh, NC
Reading, PA
Reno, NV
San Diego, CA
Stoughton, MA
Vail, CO
Ventnor, NJ
West Bloomfield, MI
West Palm Beach, FL
Westchester, NY
Winston-Salem, NC
Youngstown, OH

NEW CD!
Soap Soup

Tour Schedules

Where's ~~Waldo~~ Sam? My "doctorate" in Jewish life comes from years of travel to communities around the globe. I have performed at synagogues of all denominations, JCCs, schools and concert halls in about fifty cities annually since my first worldwide tour in 1997. Below is a sample of the institutions that allowed me to share my music and teach over the years. I am grateful to all of them for giving me the chance to express my art and connect with their constituents. Thanks to my family for tolerating my every-other-weekend absence and thanks to my amazing staff for keeping the connections smooth and the gigs coming in. Thanks also to the airlines, hotels and rental car companies making my wanderings possible…I haven't missed a show yet, thank God!

2016 ROCK YOUR LIFE TOUR

Jan 10, 2016, Private Event, Palos Verdes, CA
Jan 17 Private Event, Denver, CO
Jan 22-24 Shabbat Shira, Beth Tzedec, Toronto, Canada
Jan 25 Tu Bishvat Concert, Cabo San Lucas Chabad, Mexico
Feb 14 Private Event, Maui, HI
Mar 2-14 Israel Concert Tour
Mar 16 Ulus Jewish Academy Concert, Istanbul, Turkey
Mar 24 Purim, Private Event, LA, CA
Apr 8-9 Shabbaton, Wallingford, PA
Apr 10 Beth Sholom Congregation, Elkins Park, PA
Apr 22-30 Worldwide Kosher Passover, Lake Las Vegas, NV
Jun 1-5 Hava Nashira Institute, Oconomowoc, WI
Jun 9 Board of Rabbis Shavuot concert and workshop, Phoenix, AZ
Jun 29 Reno Jewish Community Concert, Reno, NV
Jun 30-Jul 4 High Sierra Music Festival Shabbat Tent, Quincy, CA
Jul 31-Aug 3 NewCAJE Conference, Naperville, IL
Aug 21 Private Event, Beverly Hills, CA
Sep 4 Private Event, Malibu, CA
Sep 16-17 Ahavat Torah Shabbaton, Stoughton, MA
Sep 18 Manchester, NH Jewish Federation Concert
Sep 23-25 Bnai Israel S'lichot Shabbaton, Gainesville, FL
Sep 25am Temple Shir Shalom School Concert, Gainesville, FL
Sep 25pm Concert, Chabad of Ocala and The Villages, FL
Oct 2-4 Rosh Hashana, Ner Simcha, Agoura Hills, CA
Oct 11-12 Yom Kippur, Ner Simcha, Agoura Hills, CA
Oct 20 Sukkot Concert, Private Event, LA, CA
Oct 23 Sukkot Concert, Temple Israel of Hollywood, Hollywood, CA
Oct 31 JAM on Campus, USCB, Santa Barbara, CA
Nov 4-5 Shabbaton, Chabad of Potomac, Potomac, MD
Nov 6 Concert at B'nai Shalom, Olney, MD
Nov 7 Concert and Workshop, Homecrest House, Silver Springs, MD
Nov 9 Teen Concert at B'nai Shalom, Olney, MD
Nov 10 Yeshiva University, NY, NY
Nov 11-12 Congregation Sons of Israel Shabbaton, Manalapan, NJ
Nov 13am Family Concert, Adas Israel Congregation, Washington, DC
Nov 13pm Community Concert, Lancaster, PA
Nov 19 Carlebach Tribute, Happy Minyan, LA, CA
Dec 2-3 Shabbaton Congregation Beth El, Fairfield, CT
Dec 3 Concert, Rodeph Shalom, Bridgeport, CT
Dec 4 Religious School concert, B'nai Torah, Trumbull, CT
Dec 4 PJ Library Concert, Jewish Federation, Bridgeport, CT
Dec 14 Concert, Beth Torah, Miami
Dec 15 Private Event, Boca Raton, FL
Dec 16 School Concert, Congregtation B'nai Israel, Boca Raton, FL
Dec 16-17 Temple Beth Am, Margate, FL Shabbaton
Dec 18am Concert, Bet Shira, Miami, FL

Dec 18pm Private Event, Aventura, FL
Dec 25 Concert, Chabad of South Orlando, Orlando, FL
Dec 26 Concert, Chabad of Palm Coast, FL
Dec 27 Concert, Chabad of St. Petersburg, FL
Dec 28 Concert and Fireworks, Calabasas Commons, Calabasas, CA

2015

Jan 9, 2015 JWI Shabbaton, The Jewish Experience, Denver, CO
Jan 10 Services and Cholent Cookoff, BMH-BJ, Denver, CO
Jan 10 7pm Havdalah Concert, The Jewish Experience, Denver, CO
Jan 11 10:30am Kids Concert, Lowry Elementary School, Denver, CO
Jan 13 Synagogue of the Summit Concert, Frisco, CO
Jan 15 Jewish Community Center Concert, Vail, CO
Feb 8 Shearith Israel Concert, Dallas, TX
Feb 20-22 JWI Shabbaton, LA, CA
Feb 22 Wisdom Tribe Ted Talks, LA, CA
Mar 5 Purim Concert, Private Event, Hancock Park, CA
Mar 6-8 Congregation Ahavath Israel Shabbaton and Concert, Kingston, NY
Mar 13 Jewish Day School Concert, Allentown, PA
Mar 13-14 Temple Beth El Shabbaton, Allentown, PA
Mar 14 JCC Community Concert, Allentown, PA
Mar 15 Children's Choral Zimriyah/Concert, Allentown, PA
Mar 16 Shalshelet High School Workshop, Allentown, PA
Mar 22 Private Event, Pacific Palisades, CA
Apr 3-12 Worldwide Kosher Passover, Lake Las Vegas, NV
May 11 Rooftop Concert, Beth Am, Los Angeles, CA
May 17am Concert, Kol Tikvah, Lake Norman, NC
May 17pm Concert, Beth Meyer, Raleigh, NC
May 20 Aish LA Banquet, Beverly Hills, CA
May 28 Concert, Social Dashboard, LA, CA
May 31 Private Event, Long Beach, CA
Jun 3 Concert, Yeshiva of LA, LA, CA
Jun 26-28 Limmud Bay Area, Sonoma, CA
Jun 28 Private Event, Beverly Hills, CA
Jul 1 Concert, Mosaic Law, Sacramento, CA
Jul 2-5 High Sierra Music Festival Shabbaton, Quincy, CA
Jul 25 Tisha B'Av Program, Aish HaTorah, LA, CA
Aug 2-5 NewCAJE Hartford, CT
Aug 7-8 Shabbaton, Ahavath Torah, Stoughton, MA
Aug 9 Sharon, MA, Private Event
Aug 16 Private Event, La Jolla, CA
Aug 23 Private Event, Calabasas, CA
Aug 26 Private Event, Beech Mountain, NC
Aug 28-29 Beth Israel Shabbaton, Asheville, NC
Aug 29 Beth HaTephila Concert, Asheville, NC
Aug 30 Concert, Jewish Experience, Denver, CO

Sep 13-15 Rosh Hashana, Beth El, Yardley, PA
Sep 22 Yom Kippur, Beth El, Yardley, PA
Sep 27 Private Event, Santa Monica, CA
Oct 4 Temple Israel of Hollywood, Hollywood, CA
Oct 23-24 Agudas Israel, Ottowa, Canada
Nov 23 Heritage School, Longmeadow, MA
Nov 23-24 Shabbaton, Con'g B'nai Torah, Longmeadow, MA
Nov 25 Hatikvah the Musical, Springfield, MA

2014 TOWARDS THE DAWN TOUR
Jan 16-27 Israel Concert Tour
Jan 22 Concert, Modiin
Jan 23 Concert, Shaarei Mevaseret Tziyon
Jan 25 Simchat Shlomo Banquet, Talpiyot
Jan 29 Taste of CAJE, UCLA, LA, CA
Feb 3 Women of Amit Concert, Beverly Hills, CA
Feb 10 Ponevez Yeshiva Banquet, Beverly Hills, CA
Feb 16-18 The Possible You Seminar, Los Angeles, CA
Feb 21-22 Congregation Ner Tamid Shabbaton, Henderson, NV
Feb 28-Mar2 Jewlicious Festival/Shabbaton, Long Beach, CA
Mar 12 Pico-Robertson Community Concert, Morry's, LA, CA
Mar 14 Chabad of Beverlywood Shabbaton, LA, CA
Mar 16 Purim Concert, Ventnor, NJ
Mar 17-27 Israel Concert Tour
Mar 30 Young Israel-Aish Banquet, Las Vegas, NV
Apr 5 Private Event Pella A Cappella, LA, CA
Apr 6 Private Event, Beverly Hills, CA
Apr 13 Private Event, Simi Valley, CA
Apr 14-22 Passover Program, Worldwide Kosher, Henderson, NV
May 4 Pella A Cappella, Beth Jacob, Beverly Hills, CA
May 18 Kansas City Lag B'omer Concert, Overland Park, KS
Jun 3-16 Australia Tour
Jun 3 Tikun L'eil Shavuot, North Shore Temple, Chatswood
Jun 6-7 Shabbat, Great Synagogue, Sydney
Jun 7-9 Artist in Residence, Aus Jewish Choral Festival, Sydney
Jun 11 Workshop/Concert, Masada College, St Ives
Jun 12 Concert, Emanuel School, Galston, New South Wales
Jun 13am Workshop, Mt Sinai College, Maroubra
Jun 13-14 Shabbaton, Central Synagogue, Sydney
Jun 15 Yom Limmud, Concert and Workshops, Sydney
Jul 4-5 Shabbaton, Congregation Bet Shalom, Tucson, AZ
Jul 6 Private Event, Sherman Oaks, CA
Jul 11 Ohr Zarua Shabbaton, LA, CA
Jul 19 Shabbaton, Chabad of Los Feliz, Los Feliz, CA
Jul 30 Stand With Us, Saban Theater, Beverly Hills, CA
Aug 10-13 NewCAJE Conference, UCLA, LA, CA
Aug 31 Private Event, Calabasas, CA
Aug 31pm Private Event, Cheviot Hills, CA
Sep 1 Private Event, Hollywood, CA
Sep 19-20 Selichot Shabbaton, Selichot, Beth El, Norfolk, VA
Sep 24-26 Rosh Hashana, Virginia Beach, VA
Sep 27 Private Event, Virginia Beach, VA
Oct 3-4 Yom Kippur, Virginia Beach, VA
Oct 12 LAJ Sukkot Concert, Hancock Park, CA
Oct 15 Temple Israel of Hollywood, Hollywood, CA
Oct 29 Private Party, Pacific Palisades, CA
Nov 8 Shlomo Carlebach Tribute, LA, CA
Nov 14-15 Aish Partners Shabbaton, Stamford, CT
Nov 16-20 Possible You, Toronto, Ontario
Nov 21-22, Shabbaton, Torah Links, Marlboro, NJ
Nov 22 Concert, Pardes Shlomo, Brooklyn, NY
Nov 23-27 Possible You, Brooklyn, NY
Dec 5 Teacher Appreciation, Beth El, Bethesda, MD
Dec 6 Beth El Hebrew Congregation, Alexandria, VA
Dec 17am Chanukah Concert, Berman Academy, Rockville, MD
Dec 17pm Chanukah Concert Chizuk Amuno, Baltimore, MD

Dec 18 J Fed of San Antonio Chanukah Concert, San Antonio, TX
Dec 19-20 Chanukah Shabbaton, Rimon Center, East Windsor, NJ
Dec 21 Chanukah Concert, Chabad of Stonybrook, NY
Dec 22 Hebrew Home, Rockville, MD
Dec 23 Chanukah Concert, YULA, LA, CA

2013 THE PROMISE TOUR
Jan 4, 2013 LA Jewish Experience, LA, CA
Jan 13 Private Event, Marina del Rey, CA
Jan 27 Concert, Temple Emanuel, Honolulu, HI
Feb 1 Agnon School Workshops, Cleveland, OH
Feb 1-2 Shabbaton Shaarey Tikvah, Cleveland, OH
Feb 3am Park Synagogue Workshops, Cleveland, OH
Feb3pm Agnon School Concert, Cleveland, OH
Feb 9-11 The Possible You Seminar, LA, CA
Feb 17 Yom Limmud, J Fed of Houston, Houston, TX
Feb 23 Purim Concert, Temple Beth Am, LA, CA
Mar 3 Private Event, Brentwood, CA
Mar 8-9 Jewlicious Festival, Queen Mary, Long Beach, CA
Mar 17-19 The Possible You Seminar, LA, CA
Mar 25-Apr 2 Worldwide Kosher Passover, Henderson, NV
Apr 27 Lag B'omer Concert, Aish/Young Israel, Las Vegas, NV
Apr 28am Chabad of CA Lag B'omer Festival, LA, CA
Apr 28pm Private Event, Beverly Hills, CA
May 1 Tikva Odessa fundraiser, London, England
May 5 Temple Shalom Kol Bamidbar Concert, Naples, FL
May 7 Aish Banquet, Beverly Hills, CA
May 17-18 Shabbaton, Ormand Beach, FL
May 22 YULA Jazz Ensemble Concert, LA, CA
Jun 23 Private Event, Beverly Hills, CA
Jul 4-7 Shabbat Tent, Jewlicious, Quincy, CA
Jul 21 Private Event, Palos Verdes, CA
Jul 28 Chabad of Berkshires Concert, Lenox, MA
Jul 29-31 NewCAJE, Dudley, MA
Jul 31 Ahavath Torah, Stoughton, MA
Aug 3am Chabad of Laguna Beach
Aug 3pm Private Event, Laguna Beach, CA
Aug 16-17 Temple Bat Yam, Lake Tahoe, CA
Aug 25am Private Event, Westlake VIllage, CA
Aug 25pm Private Event, Brentwood, CA
Aug 31 Slichot Concert, The Pico Union, LA, CA
Sep 4-6 Rosh Hashana, Virginia Beach, VA
Sep 13-14 Yom Kippur, Virginia Beach, VA
Sep 24 Jewlicious Sukkot Jam, LA, CA
Sep 25 Private Event, Temple Israel of Hollywood, CA
Oct 6 Private Event, Cabo San Lucas, Mexico
Oct 12 Private Event, Young Israel North Miami, Miami, FL
Oct 13 Community Concert, Beth El, Ormand Beach, FL
Oct 18-19 Lafayette College Hillel Shabbaton, Easton, PA
Oct 19 Community Concert, Easton, PA
Oct 20 Private Event, Bethlehem, PA
Oct 27 Private Event, Malibu, CA
Nov 3 Community Concert, Baton Rouge, LA
Nov 4-5 New Orleans, LA
Nov 6 Workshops and Concert Birmingham, AL
Nov 9 Private Event, Nashville, TN
Nov 10 Community Concert, Chatanooga, TN
Nov 15 Hebrew Home Concert, Rockville, MD
Nov 15-16 Chabad of Potomac, MD Shabbaton
Nov 16 Bethesda Jewish Cong'n Chanukah Concert
Nov 17am Congregation Beth Shalom, Wilmington, DE
Nov 17 Bnai Tikvah Chanukah Concert, North Brunswick, NJ
Nov 18 Possible You Seminar, Monsey, NY
Nov 19 Washington Hebrew Cong'n Concert, Potomac, MD
Nov 20 Washington Hebrew Cong'n Concert, Washington DC
Nov 22-23 Rimon Center Shabbaton, East Windsor, NJ
Nov 23 Shaarei Emeth Concert, Manalapan, NJ
Nov 24am Con'g B'nai Israel, Emerson, NJ

Nov 24 Workshop and Concert, JCC of Rockland County, NY
Nov 29-30 Shabbaton, Congregation Bnai Israel, Tustin, CA
Dec 3 Beth El Chanukah Concert, Berkeley, CA
Dec 4 Congregation Etz Chaim Chanukah concert, Palo Alto, CA
Dec 5 Brandeis Hillel Day School, Marin County, CA
Dec 6-7 Beth David, Kol Emeth Shabbaton, Saratoga, CA
Dec 11-13 URJ Biennial, Concert and Workshops, San Diego, CA
Dec 22 Private Event, LA, CA
Dec 28 Happy Minyan Shlomo Tribute Concert, LA, CA

2012
Feb 8, 2012 Kol Ami, Tu Bishvat Concert, Salt Lake City, UT
Feb 11 Young Israel of Upper West Side, NY
Feb 12 UJA Concert, Huntington, NY
Feb 24-25 Jewlicious Festival, Long Beach, CA
Mar 2-3 Pacific Jewish Center Shabbaton, Venice, CA
Mar 7 Erev Purim concert, Marietta, GA
Mar 8 Purim Day Concert, Chabad of Metarie, LA
Mar 9-10 Shabbaton Chabad of Uptown NOLA, LA
Mar 10-11 Limmud NOLA, New Orleans, LA
Mar 18 Private Event, Boca Raton, FL
Mar 19 Temple Beth Emeth, Cooper City, FL
Mar 19 Combined Miami Area Hebrew High Schools Workshop
Mar 23-24 Shabbaton, Beth Emeth, Cooper City, FL
Mar 25 Concert, Ormand Beach, FL
Mar 25pm Concert, Bnai Aviv, Weston, FL
Mar 26 Yiddish Club Concert, Boynton Beach, FL
Apr 6-14 Passover, Worldwide Kosher, Las Vegas, NV
Apr 26 Israel Under the Stars, Boca Raton, FL
Apr 27 Shabbaton, Randloph/Stoughton MA
Apr 29 Concert, Tom's River, NJ
May 9-10 Lag B'omer Concerts, Menorah Park, Cleveland, OH
May 11 Leo Baeck Day School Concert, Toronto, Ontario
May 11-12 Shabbaton, Adas Israel, Hamilton, Ontario!
May 13 Holy Blossom Temple, Toronto, Ontario
May 13pm Concert, Hamilton, Ontario
May 14 Associated Day School, Toronto
May 16 JET Organization, Ottowa, Canada
May 18 Hebrew Home Concerts, Rockville, MD
May 18-19 Aish DC Shabbaton, Rockville, MD
May 20am Temple Shalom school concert, Chevy Chase, M D
May 20pm Private Party, Westwood, CA
Jun 27 Aloni Tribute Concert, Valley Beth Shalom, Encino, CA
Jul 13 Etta Israel Concert, LA, CA
Aug 3-4 Shabbaton, FJCC, Flemington, NJ
Aug 5-8 NewCAJE, Montclair, NJ
Aug 10 JCC of Boca Concert, Boca Raton, FL
Aug 10-11 Shabbaton, Boca Raton Synagogue
Aug 11, Private Event, Boca Raton
Aug 12 National Anthem, Marlins baseball game, Miami, FL
Aug 17-19 Shabbaton, Jewlicious Summerfest, Simi Valley, CA
Aug 19 Private Event, Beverly Hills, CA
Aug 26 LA Jewish Symphony, Ford Theater, LA, CA
Sep 16-18 Rosh Hashana, Temple Emanuel, Virginia Beach, VA
Sep 23 Community Concert, Beth El, Norfolk, VA
Sep 25-26 Yom Kippur, Virginia Beach, VA
Oct 4 JConnect Sukkah Bash, LA, CA
Oct 7 Temple Israel of Hollywood, Hollywood, CA
Oct 9 Chabad of Pacific Palisades, PPalisades, CA
Oct 11 Private Party, Beverly Hills, CA
Nov 18am Private Event, Universal City, CA
Nov 18 Private Event, Westlake, CA
Nov 25-27 Possible You Seminar, Brooklyn, NY
Nov 30 Congregation of Moses Shabbaton, Kalamazoo, MI
Dec 2am Cong'n Shaarey Zedek School Concert, E. Lansing, MI
Dec 2 Adat Shalom Synagogue, Farmington Hills, MI
Dec 3-4 Possible You Seminar, Beverly Hills, CA
Dec 7-8 Chanukah Shabbaton, Temple Sinai, Worcester, MA
Dec 9 Temple Israel, Sharon, MA
Dec 10 LA Jewish Symphony Fundraiser, Encino, CA
Dec 12 Private Event, Beverly Hills, CA
Dec 13 Cedars Sinai A Cappella Chanukah Concert, LA, CA
Dec 14-15 Chanukah Shabbaton, Rimon Center, E. Windsor, NJ
Dec 16 Congregation Neve Shalom, Metuchen, NJ

2011 THE CHAI TOUR
Jan 7-8, 2011 Beth Jacob, Beverly Hills, LA
Jan 16 Private Event, Beverly Hills, CA
Jan 18 Jewish Chaplains Conference, Scottsdale, AZ
Jan 30 Concert, Temple Emanu-el, Honolulu, HI
Feb 4-5 Ohr Zarua Shabbaton, LA, CA
Feb 13 D. Friedman Tribute, Valley Beth Shalom, Encino, CA
Feb 20-21 Limmud LA, Costa Mesa, CA
Mar 8 Har HaMishpacha, Steamboat Springs, CO
Mar 11 Pressman Academy Concert, LA, CA
Mar 18-19 Purim Shabbaton, Beth El, Yardley, PA
Mar 20 Purim Concert/Seudah, Aish Philly ,Mainline, PA
Apr 10 Private Event, Beverly Hills, CA
Apr 17 Wilshire Blvd Temple, LA, CA
Apr 18-27 Passover with Worldwide Kosher, Lake Las Vegas, NV
May 5 Beth Shalom Concert, Santa Clarita, CA
May 12 Yom Ha'atz, Pasadena Jewish Temple, Pasadena, CA
May 13 Ohr Zarua Shabbaton, LA, CA
May 17 Aish HaTorah West Coast Banquet, Beverly Hills, CA
May 22 am Private Event, Beverly Hills, CA
May 22 Kol Bamidbar Concert, Sinai Temple, LA, CA
May 29 Private Event, Beverly Hills, CA
Jun 1 Kol Bamidbar, Temple Menorah, Redondo Beach, CA
Jun 3-4 Shabbaton, Ohel Moed, W. Bloomfield, MI
Jun 5 Congregation Beth Shalom, Oak Park, MI
Jun 12 Private Event, Beverly Hills, CA
Jun 20 Concert, Jewish Discovery Center, Scranton, PA
Jun 26 Private Event, Brentwood, CA
Jun 30 Private Event, Ft. Worth, TX
Jul 1-2 Noahide Nations Conference Concert, Dallas, TX
Jul 3 Private Event, Beverly Hills, CA
Jul 8-9 Mussaf, Chabad of Downtown, Vancouver, Canada
Jul 22 Ohr Zarua Shabbaton, LA, CA
Jul 29-30 Private Event, San Diego, CA
Jul 31-Aug 3 NewCAJE conference, Greensboro, NC
Aug 21, Private Event, Beverly Hills, CA
Aug 26 Etz Chaim, Marietta, GA
Sep 28-30 Rosh Hashana, Temple Emanuel, Virginia Beach, VA
Oct 1 Concert, Temple Emanuel, Virginia Beach, VA
Oct 7-8 Yom Kippur, Temple Emanuel, Virginia Beach, VA
Oct 16 am Sukkot Concert RAJE LA, Los Angeles, CA
Oct 16 pm Sukkot Concert, Maayon Yisroel, Los Angeles, CA
Nov 5 Kol Sason A Cappella, Century City, CA
Nov 5pm Private Party, Beverly Hills, CA
Nov 13 Hadassah of Nashville, TN
Nov 18-19 Shabbaton, Cong'n B'nai Israel, Tustin, CA
Nov 20 Private Event, Seal Beach
Dec 1-4 Aish Partners Conf, Stamford, CT
Dec 4 am Marlboro Jewish Center Religious School Concert
Dec 9-10 Private Event, Tucson, AZ
Dec 11 Or Chadash Concert, Tucson, AZ
Dec 14-15 URJ Biennial, Washington DC
Dec 16 Beth Shalom Shabbaon, Potomac, MD
Dec 17 Chabad of Potomac, Potomac, MD
Dec 17 PM Hebrew Home Concert, Rockville, MD
Dec 18 Temple Beth Shalom, Arnold, MD
Dec 19 Temple Isaiah, Fulton, MD
Dec 21 Chanukah Concert, Syracuse, NY
Dec 22 Chanukah Concert, Temple Beth El, Rochester, NY
Dec 23 Aish HaTorah, LA, CA
Dec 26 Pacific Jewish Center, Venice, CA

2010

Jan 8, 2010 Ohr Zarua, Los Angeles, CA
Jan 26 Cabo Jewish Center, Cabo San Lucas, Mexico
Feb 5-6 Barack Hebrew Academy Shabbaton, Bryn Mawr, PA
Feb 13 Limmud LA, Costa Mesa, CA
Feb 14am Private Event, Beverly Hills, CA
Feb 19-21 Congregation Bnai Israel Shabbaton, Boca Raton, FL
Feb 21 JEC Palm Beach County Educators Conference, FL
Feb 21 pm Broadway on the Bima Cantors Concert, Kendall, FL
Feb 26-27 Purim Shabbaton Rimon Center, E. Windsor, NJ
Feb 28 Congregation Beth Shalom, Wilmington, DE
Feb 28 pm Aish HaTorah Philly Purim Concert, Philadelphia, PA
Mar 6 Private Event, Beverly Hills, CA
Mar 13 Sam and YT Glaser Concert, Kol Rina, Jerusalem, Israel
Mar 15 Private Event, Jerusalem, Israel
Mar 21am Temple Kol Emeth Community Concert, Marietta, GA
Mar 21pm J Federation of Chattanooga Concert, TN
Mar 26 Cantor in Residence, Beth Am, LA, CA
Mar 29 Worldwide Kosher Passover Seder, Palm Springs, CA
Apr 1 Passover Concert, Riviera Hotel, Palm Springs, CA
Apr 25 Yom Ha'Atzma'ut Concert, J. Federation, SLC, UT
Apr 25 American Friends of Israel Concert, Stansbury Park, UT
Apr 30 Kabbalat Shabbat, Beth Abraham Jacob, Albany, NY
May 2am Kol Bamidbar, Beth Emeth Congregation, Albany, NY
May 2pm Yom HaAtzma'ut Concert, Carlebach Shul, NY, NY
May 3rd, Cantors Assembly Concert, NY, NY
May 11 Aish HaTorah Banquet, Beverly Hills, CA
Jun 9 LA Womens Choir Concert, LA, CA
Jun 13 Tiferet Israel, Dallas, TX
Jun 17 Private Event, LA, CA
Jun 19 Father's Day Council of Tucson Gala Concert, Tucson, AZ
Jun 20 Congregation Anshei Israel, Tucson, AZ
Jul 8 Concert, Brandeis Barding Institute, Simi Valley, CA
Jul 11 Private Event, LA, CA
Jun 18 Ohr Zarua, LA, CA
Jun 19 Private Event, LA, CA
Aug 1 Private Event, Beverly Hills, CA
Aug 8 Private Event, Vancouver, BC
Sep 8-10 Rosh Hashana, Beth El, La Jolla, CA
Sep 17-18 Yom Kippur, Beth El, La Jolla, CA
Oct 3 Jewish County Fair Concert, Malibu, CA
Oct 10 Private Event, Valley Village, CA
Oct 23 Shabbaton, Beth Jacob, Beverly Hills, CA
Oct 26 Yavneh Academy Concert, LA, CA
Nov 4-6 Aish Partners Conference, E. Brunswick, NJ
Nov 7, B'derech Concert, Boro Park, NY
Nov 8-9 GA Conference, New Orleans, LA
Nov 10 am New Orleans Jewish Day School Concert, New Orleans, LA
Nov 10 pm Touro Synagogue Community Concert, New Orleans, LA
Nov 11 Private Event, University City, MO
Nov 12, am Block Yeshiva, St Louis, MO
Nov 12, pm Epstein Academy, St. Louis, MO
Nov 12-13 U City Shul Shabbaton, St. Louis, MO
Nov 14 Private Event, St. Louis, MO
Nov 15 Emek Academy Concert, Van Nuys, CA
Dec 1 Chanukah Concert, Beth Torah, Miami, FL
Dec 2 Meyer Academy, West Palm Beach, FL
Dec 3-4 Shabbaton - Chabad and Young Israel of Potomac, Potomac, MD
Dec 4 Chanukah Concert, Jewish Federation of Howard County, MD
Dec 5 am Chanukah Concert, Beth El, Baltimore, MD
Dec 5 pm Bnai Shalom Chanukah Concert, Olney, MD
Dec 7 Princeton Jewish Center, Princeton, NJ
Dec 8 Chanukah Concert, Monsey, NY
Dec 10-12 Shabbaton Temple Emanuel, Pittsburgh, PA
Dec 12 Conejo Jewish Federation Concert, Thousand Oaks, CA
Dec 15-17 Valley Beth Shalom Kol Bamidbar Concerts, Encino, CA
Dec 19 Dix Hills Jewish Center, Dix Hills, NY
Dec 24-25 Limmud Shabbaton, Coventry, UK
Dec 26-30 Limmud, Coventry, UK

2009 ATTITUDE OF GRATITUDE TOUR

Jan 10 Stand With Us Rally for IDF/Gaza, Westwood, CA
Jan 21 Kauai Jewish Community Concert, Kauai, HI
Jan 25 Temple Emanu-El Concert, Honolulu, HI
Jan 29 Private Event, San Diego, CA
Jan 30-31 Shabbaton, Beth El, La Jolla, CA
Feb 13 Private Event, Beverly Hills, CA
Feb 14-16 Concert/workshops, Limmud LA, Costa Mesa, CA
Feb 18 Concert with Yom Tov Glaser, Monsey, NY
Feb 20-21 Shabbaton, Beth El, La Jolla, CA
Feb 22 Private Event, Westwood, CA
Mar 6-8 Kahal Yosef Shabbaton/Kol Bamidbar, Charleston, SC
Mar 9 Congregation Mikve Israel Purim Concert, Savannah, GA
Mar10 Purim Concert, Congregation Etz Chayim, 1000 Oaks, CA
Mar 22, Private Event, LA, CA
Apr 9-15 Passover Retreat, Riviera Resort, Palm Springs, CA
Apr 28 Yom HaAtzmaut Concert, Peoria, IL
Apr 29 Congregation Beth Judea, Long Grove, IL
May 17am Temple Israel, Stockton, CA
May 17pm Peninsula Sinai Congregation, Foster City, CA
May 19 Jewish Community Night, Dodger Stadium, LA, CA
May 20 Aish HaTorah Banquet, Beverly Hills, CA
May 27 Jewish Academy Sponsors Dinner, San Diego, CA
May 28 San Diego Jewish Academy Concert, San Diego, CA
Jun 19-20 Private Event, Tucson, AZ
Jun 21am Congregation Ohr Chadash, Tucson, AZ
Jun 28 Temple Beth Tikvah, Fullerton, CA
Jul 5 Private Event, Beverly Hills, CA
Jul 8-10 Camp Gan Israel Artist in Residence
Jul 12 Jewish Federation of the Berkshires, Pittsfield, MA
Aug 7-8 Shabbaton, JCC of Flemington NJ
Aug 9 Concert, Mid Atlantic Educators Conf, Baltimore, MD
Aug 10-12 Workshops, Educators Conference, Baltimore, MD
Aug 14-16 Shabbaton, The Jewish Experience, Denver, CO
Aug 27 Happy Minyan Banquet, LA, CA
Aug 30 Private Event, LA, CA
Sep 6 Private Event, Disney Hall, LA, CA
Sep 12 Slichot Concert, Beth El, La Jolla CA
Sep 18-20 Rosh Hashana, Beth El, La Jolla, CA
Sep 28 Yom Kippur, Beth El, La Jolla, CA
Oct 23-24 Beth Torah Shabbaton, N. Miami Beach, FL
Oct 25 am Bnai Torah Congregation Concert, Boca Raton, FL
Oct 25 Educators Conference, West Palm Beach,FL
Oct 25 Concert, JCC of Greater Palm Beaches, W Palm Beach, FL
Nov 7 Private Event, Boston, MA
Nov 8 1:30pm Temple Reyim, Newton, MA
Nov 8 6pm JCC of the North Shore Concert, Marblehead, MA
Nov 11 JMC Community Concert, VBS, Encino, CA
Nov 21 Private Event, Beverly Hills, CA
Nov 28 Private Event, Encino, CA
Nov 29 Private Event, LA, CA
Dec 11-12 Temple Israel Chanukah Shabbaton, Winter Springs, FL
Dec 20 Private Event, Malibu, CA
Dec 27 Private Event, LA, CA

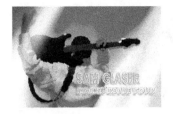 

2008 ROCKIN' REVUE TOUR
Jan 6-9, ONEG Conference, Snowmass, CO
Jan 10 Aspen Jewish Community Concert, Aspen, CO
Jan 13 Community Concert, El Paso, TX
Jan 14 Shalhevet Banquet, Beverly Hills, CA
Jan 20 Private Event, Newport Beach, CA
Jan 22 Tu Bish'vat Concert, Kauai, HI
Feb 8 Hebrew Day School Scholar in Residence, Phoenix, AZ
Feb 8-9 Congregation Beth El Shabbaton, Phoenix, AZ
Feb 10 Anshei Israel Concert, Tucson, AZ
Feb 17 Private Event, Irvine, CA
Mar 16 Jewish Music Festival, Ormand Beach, FL
Mar 21 Congregation Etz Chayim Purim Concert
Mar 22 Private Event, Los Angeles, CA
Mar 23 Private Event, Los Angeles, CA
Apr 22 Dead Sea Music Festival, Israel
Apr 22 Tuesday Night Live, Jerusalem
Apr 23 Jerusalem Crowne Plaza
Apr 24 Israel Center, Jerusalem
May 2-3 Congregation Beth El Sanctuary Dedication, La Jolla, CA
May 4 Temple Israel Concert, Canton, OH
May 5-7 Menorah Park Artist in Residence, Cleveland, OH
May 7 pm JCC of Akron, OH Yom HaAtzmaut Celebration
May 8 Yom HaAtzmaut Community Concert, Cleveland OH
Jun 1 Jewzapalooza Concert, JCC, Austin, TX
Jun 8 Shavuot Scholar in Residence, B'nai David, LA, CA
Jun 29 Artist in Residence, Camp Gan Israel, Running Springs, CA
Jul 8 Camp Ramah Artist in Residence, Ojai, CA
Jul 11-12 Brandeis Bardin Shabbaton, Simi Valley, CA
Jul 16 Hadassah National Convention, LA, CA
Aug 5 Camp Ramah Artist in Residence, Ojai, CA
Aug 8-13 CAJE Conference, Burlington, VT
Aug 13-14 Land of Israel Conference, Sandy, UT
Aug 17 Private Event, Beverly Hills, CA
Aug 24 Private Event, Rancho Palos Verdes, CA
Aug 31 Private Event, LA, CA
Sep 1 Private Event, Manalapan, NJ
Sep 12 Shabbaton, Beth El, La Jolla
Sep 18-21 San Antonio Community Shabbaton, TX
Sep 21 Jewish Fed'n of Greater Ft Worth Concert, Ft Worth, TX
Sep 26 Shabbaton, Beth El, La Jolla
Sep 27 S'lichot Community Concert, Beth El, La Jolla, CA
Oct 10, Shabbaton, Beth El, La Jolla, CA
Oct 19 Aish LA Sukkot Concert, LA, CA
Oct 25 Temple Emanuel Concert, Cleveland, OH
Oct 26 Temple Emanuel of South Hills, Pittsburgh, PA
Oct 29 Private Event, Los Angeles, CA
Nov 2 Jacksonville, FL JCC Concert, Jacksonville, FL
Nov 14 Shabbaton, Beth El, La Jolla, CA
Nov 15 Private Event, Del Mar, CA
Nov 16 Tifereth Israel Religious School Concert, San Diego, CA
Nov 28 Shabbaton, Beth El, La Jolla, CA
Dec 5-6 Temple Beth Torah Shabbaton, Tamarac, FL
Dec 7 Private Event, Boca Raton, FL
Dec 11 Youth Educator Workshop, Detroit, MI
Dec 12 Shabbaton, Aish Southfield, Detroit, MI
Dec 13 Concert, Shaarey Zedeck, Southfield, MI
Dec 14 Sunday School Workshop, Shaarey Zedeck, Southfield, MI
Dec 14 Jewish Fed'n of Flint, Flint, MI
Dec 15 White House Chanukah Party, Washington, DC
Dec 21 Chabad Chankah Concert, Santa Monica, CA
Dec 26-27 Shabbaton, Beth El, La Jolla, CA
Dec 27 Chanukah Concert, Beth El, La Jolla, CA
Dec 28 Chanukah Party, Aish HaTorah, LA, CA

2007 VOICE OF THE SOUL TOUR
Jan 3, Hillel Banquet, Beverly Hills, CA
Jan 7-10 ONEG Conference, Vail, CO
Jan 11 Jewish Federation of San Antonio, TX
Jan 14 Private Event, Los Angeles, CA
Jan 14 RAVSAK Conference, Los Angeles, CA
Jan 16 Jewish Chaplains Conference, Redondo Beach, CA
Jan 27 American Zionists of Hawaii, Honolulu, HI
Feb 1 Private Event, St. Louis, MO
Feb 2 Soloman Schechter Day School Tu B'shevat Concert
Feb 2 Shabbaton, Sha'arei Chesed, St. Louis, MO
Feb 4 Temple Israel Family Concert, St. Louis, MO
Feb 18 Private Event, Beverly Hills, CA
Feb 25 Private Event, Boca Raton, FL
Feb 26 Donna Klein Hebrew Academy Concert, Boca Raton, FL
Mar 2-3 Emanuel Synagogue Shabbaton, Oklahoma City, OK
Mar 4 Temple Israel and Bnai Emunah School Concert, Tulsa, OK
Mar 6 Jonathan Pollard Benefit, The Joint, LA, CA
Mar 10 Private Event, Laguna Beach, CA
Mar 18 Private Event, Nessa Synagogue, Los Angeles, CA
Mar 23-24 Aish HaTorah Shabbaton, Toronto, Canada
Mar 25 Benefit Concert, Toronto
Mar 29 Pre-LA Kings game concert, Staples Center, LA, CA
Apr 2-11 Worldwide Kosher Passover, Hyatt Newport Beach, CA
Apr 5 Chol Hamo'ed concert, Hyatt Newport Beach, CA
Apr 24 Yom HaAtzmaut, J Fed of Boca Raton, FL
Apr 27/28 Shabbaton Temple Beth Emet, Cooper City, FL
Apr 29 Beth Torah Concert, N. Miami, FL
May 6 Temple Beth Emeth, Albany, NY
May 9 Aish HaTorah Banquet, LA, CA
May 27 Private Event, LA, CA
Jun 10 B'nai David Banquet, Beverly Hills, CA
Jun 12 Hillel Graduation, Beverly Hills, CA
July 29 Jewish Federation of the Berkshires, Pittsfield, MA
Aug 3 Private Event, St. Louis, MO
Aug 3-8 CAJE, St. Louis, MO
Aug 12-16 Artist in Residence, Maccabee Artsfest, Deal, NJ
August 26 Pasadena Jewish Temple, Pasadena, CA
Sep 2 Private Event, LA, CA
Sep 8 Beth El Slichot Concert, La Jolla, CA
Sep 9 Neveh Shalom Teachers Conf. and Concert, Portland, OR
Sep 10 Seattle Hebrew Academy, Seattle, WA
Sep 12-15 Rosh Hashanna Services, La Jolla, CA
Sep 21-22 Yom Kippur Services, La Jolla, CA
Oct 12-14 Shabbaton, Beth Am, Randolph, MA
Oct 26-27 Bethesda Jewish Cong. Shabbaton, Bethesda, MD
Oct 28pm Beth Emeth Book Fair Concert, Herndon, VA
Oct 29 Day School Concert, Silver Spring, MD
Nov 8 Chanukah Concert, Nessa Synagogue, Beverly Hills, CA
Nov 11 Temple Gan Elohim Concert, Glendale, AZ
Nov 17 Carlebach Yahrzeit Concert, LA, CA
Nov 22 Private Event, LA, CA
Nov 27 LA Jewish Symphony Concert, Encino, CA
Dec 2 University Synagogue Chanukah Concert, Brentwood, CA
Dec 9 Chanukah Concert Pasadena Jewish Center, Pasadena, CA
Dec 9 Chanukah Concert 1-4pm, Chabad of Agoura, CA
Dec 13 URJ Biennial Concert, San Diego, CA
Dec 16 Hillel Banquet, Beverly Hills, CA
Dec 23 Private Event, LA, CA
Dec 30 Private Event, Universal City, CA

2006 UNBREAKABLE SOUL TOUR

Jan 8-11 ONEG Conference, Park City, UT
Jan 9 Har Shalom Concert, Park City, UT
Jan 15 Private event, Los Angeles, CA
Jan 20-22 Congregation Brith Shalom Shabbaton, Bellaire, TX
Jan 23 Austin Jewish Community Day School, Austin, TX
Jan 25 Beth Evergreen, Evergreen, CO
Feb 4 Private Event, LA, CA
Feb 5 Private Event, La Jolla, CA
Feb 7 LA Jewish Symphony, Valley Beth Shalom, Encino, CA
Feb 10-11 Religious Zionist Shabbaton, Bloomington, IL
Feb 12 Congregation Solel School concert, Highland Park, IL
Feb 12 Congregation Eitz Chayim evening concert, Lombard, IL
Mar 5 Purim Festival, Magic Mountain, Valencia, CA
Mar 6 LA BJE Early Education Conference, Woodland Hills, CA
Mar 12am Bnai Israel Concert, Sacramento, CA
Mar 12 Private Event, Santa Monica, CA
Mar 14 Purim Concert, Jacksonville, FL
Mar 19 Private Event, LA, CA
Mar 25 Etta Israel Shabbaton, Valley Village, CA
Mar 30 Temple Shalom Concert, Aberdeen, NJ
Mar 31 Shabbaton, Shir Chadash, Metarie, LA
Apr 1-2 New Orleans Int'l Jewish Music Fest, New Orleans, LA
Apr 7-9 NFTY Shabbaton, Jackson, MS
Apr 12-21 Pesach Program, World Wide Kosher, Monterey, CA
May 7 Los Angeles Israel Celebration, Woodley Park, Encino, CA
May 18 Associated Hebrew School, Toronto
May 21 Orange County JCC Yom Ha'atzma'ut, Irvine, CA
May 28th Private Event, Marina Del Rey, CA
Jun 3 Private Event, LA, CA
Jun 6 Aish HaTorah Banquet, Beverly Hills, CA
Jun 11 Private Event, Los Angeles, CA
Jun 18 Private Event, San Diego, CA
Jun 20 CCAR '06 Conference, San Diego, CA
Jun 22 Private Event, Beverly Hills, CA
Jun 23 Isralight Shabbaton, Beverly Hills, CA
Jul 23 Dedication, Friedman Center of Los Angeles, LA, CA
Aug 4-10 CAJE Concerts/workshops, Durham, NC
Sep 10 Private Event, Brentwood, CA
Sep 16 Slichot Concert Beth El, La Jolla CA
Sep 22-24 Rosh Hashana, La Jolla, CA
Oct 1-2 Yom Kippur, La Jolla, CA
Oct 17 Private Event, Beverly Hills, CA
Oct 20am Hillel Day School, Tampa, FL
Oct 20 Kol Ami Shabbaton, Tampa, FL
Oct 21 Eisenstadt Memorial Concert, Tampa, FL
Oct 22 Congregation B'nai Torah, Ormand Beach, FL
Oct 28 Kol Ami Concert, Woodinville, WA
Oct 29 Private Event, Seattle, WA
Nov 2 Israel Bonds, Beverly Wilshire Hotel, Los Angeles, CA
Nov 12-15 General Assembly Conference, Los Angeles, CA
Nov 24 Shabbaton Young Israel, Harrison, NY
Nov 25 Agudath Shalom, Stamford, CT
Dec 3 Stand With Us Banquet, LA, CA
Dec 10 Aspen Jewish Community Concert, Aspen, CO
Dec 16 Chanukah Concert, JCC Metro West, Whippany, NJ
Dec 17 Sinai Temple, Springfield, MA
Dec 18pm Westboro JCC, Westboro, MA
Dec 19 Beth Am Chanukah Concert, Randolph, MA
Dec 20 Bnai Abraham and JRC Chanukah Concert, Beverly, MA
Dec 21 Jewish Fed of New Hampshire Concert, Manchester, NH
Dec 22 Chabad of Beverlywood Friday Night Light, LA, CA
Dec 26 Private Event, Bnai David, Los Angeles, CA

2005 PRESENCE TOUR

Jan 9-13 ONEG Conference, Snowmass, CO
Jan 14-15 Congregation Sons of Israel Shabbaton, Manalapan, NJ
Jan 16 Festival of Jewish Learning Concert, JCC of San Diego, CA
Feb 2 Hillel Academy Concert, Milwaukee, WI
Feb 3 Agudas Achim Concert, Iowa City, IA
Feb 4-5 Temple Brith Sholom Shabbaton, Springfield, IL
Feb 6 BJE of Chicago Kol Bamidbar Concert
Feb 14 LA Jewish Symphony, VBS, Sherman Oaks, CA
Feb 18-19 Temple Beth El Shabbaton, Charlotte, SC
Feb 20 Temple Emanuel Concert, Greensboro, NC
Feb 25-26 Temple Beth Israel Shabbaton, Fresno, CA
Mar 5 Private Event, LA, CA
Mar 23 Central Synagogue Purim Concert, NY, NY
Mar 23 Voices for Israel Concert, Town Hall, NY, NY
Mar 24 Purim Concert, Mogen David/Chai Center, LA, CA
Apr 3 Private Event, NY, NY
April 5 Aish HaTorah, Toronto, Ontario, Canada
Apr 10 Temple Beth Am, Seattle, WA
May 11 Buffalo JCC Yom Haatzmaut Concert, Buffalo, NY
May 12 Temple Beth David, Palm Beach Gardens, FL
May 13-14 Shabbaton, Young Israel of Greater Miami
May 15 Temple Beth Emet Concert, Cooper City, FL
May 17 Greenfield Day School Concert, Miami, FL
May 19 BJE Teachers Concert, Great Neck, NY
May 26 Lag B'Omer Concert, Beverly Hills, CA
May 28 Isralight Shabbaton, LA, CA
June 3-4 USY Shabbaton, Louisville, KY
June 7 Aish Banquet, LA, CA
July 2-3 Aish Young Leadership Shabbaton, SD, CA
July 3 Private Event, Bel Air, CA
Aug 2 Temple Menorah Concert, Redondo Beach, CA
Aug 15-18 CAJE, Seattle, WA
Aug 21 Anshe Torah Concert, Plano TX
Aug 27 Private Event, LA, CA
Aug 28 Teacher's Apprec. Concert, Akron, OH
Sept 4 Private Event, San Diego, CA
Sept 11 Concert for Katrina Victims, San Antonio, TX
Sept 18 Katrina Benefit, Westside Institutional Syn, NY, NY
Sep 24 Slichot Concert, Congregation Beth El, La Jolla, CA
Oct 4-13 High Holidays, Beth El, La Jolla, CA
Oct 21-22 Temple Beth Am Shabbaton, Randolph, MA
Oct 23 10am Tiferet Bet Israel Concert, Blue Bell, PA
Oct 23 12:30pm Aish HaTorah Sukkot Party, Philadelphia, PA
Oct 23 4pm Solomon Schechter Fundraiser, Toms River, NJ
Nov 1 Private Event, LA, CA
Nov 11-12 Shabbaton, Aish HaTorah, Toronto, Canada
Nov 12 Sephardic Kehilla Concert, Toronto, Canada
Nov 13 Bnai Israel, Rockville, MD
Nov 14 CE Smith Jewish Day School, Rockville, MD
Nov 19 Private Event, LA, CA
Nov 20 Concert, LA Hebrew High, Camp Ramah, CA
Dec 4 Temple Sinai Concert, Roslyn, NY
Dec 7 Workshop, Ahi Ezer Yeshiva, Flatbush, NY
Dec 8 Middlesex JCC Chanukah Concert, Edison, NJ
Dec 8-10 Aish HaTorah Partner's Conference, Stamford, CT
Dec 11 Conservative Synagogue Concert, Westport, CT
Dec 15 Private Function, La Jolla, CA
Dec 17 Ner Tamid Concert, Poway, CA
Dec 18 Private Function, Beverly Hills, CA
Dec 25 JCC of Scottsdale, Scottsdale, AZ
Dec 27 Calabasas Shul Chanukah, Calabasas, CA
Dec 28 Chabad of Hollywood, Hollywood, CA
Dec 31 Private Function, W. Hollywood, CA

inspire
awaken
rekindle
hope

sam glaser in concert

the bridge tour

2003-2004 THE BRIDGE TOUR

2004

Jan 9-11 Ahavath Torah Scholar In Residence, Stoughton, MA
Jan 11 Temple Sinai Concert, Denver, CO
Jan 12-14 Oneg Conference, Vail, CO
Jan 15 Aspen Jewish Congregation, CO
Jan 16-17 Young Israel of Greater Miami Shabbaton, Miami, FL
Jan 18-19 Center For Jewish Ed Conference, W. Palm Beach, FL
Jan 20-22 Club Kosher Concert, Puerto Plata, Dominican Republic
Jan 31 Private Event, Beverly Hills, CA
Feb 25 Aish HaTorah Singles Speakers Series
Feb 27-28 Shabbaton, Beth Shalom Concert, Northbook, IL
Feb 29 Congregation Beth Shalom Kol Bamidbar, Northbook, IL
Mar 6 Happy Minyan Purim Concert, LA, CA
Mar 26-27 Congregation Brith Shalom Shabbaton, Bethlehem, PA
Mar 28 Brith Achim concert, King of Prussia, PA
Mar 29 Community High School of Gratz, Phlladelphia, PA
Mar 30 Congregation Beth Judah Concert, Ventnor, NJ
Apr 8-14 Pesach Concerts, Club Kosher, Cancun, Mexico
Apr 25 Mainline Reform Sunday School, Wynnewood, PA
Apr 25 Yom HaAtzmaut Concert J Fed of Reading, PA
May 9 Westchester Jewish Center Lag B'Omer, Mamaroneck, NY
May 16 Beth Emet, Herndon, VA
May 17 JCC, Erie, PA
May 19 Yom Yerushalyim, Fuchs Mizrahi DS, Cleveland, OH
May 23-24 Kol Halev, Austin, TX
May 30 Private Event, Johnson City, TN
Jun 8 Aish HaTorah West Coast Banquet, LA, CA
Jun 10 Private Event, LA, CA
Jun 27-29 CAJE Early Childhood, Hofstra University, NY
Jul 4 Private Event, San Diego, CA
Jul 13 Hadassah Convention, Phoenix, AZ
Aug 8 Private Event, San Diego, CA
Aug 9-10 Jerusalem Fund Retreat Concert, Laguna, CA
Aug 13-19 CAJE conference, Long Island, NY
Aug 29 Private Event, LA, CA
Sep 5 Private Event, Youngstown, OH
Sep 12 Private Event, LA, CA
Sep 16 Rosh Hashana, Beth El, La Jolla
Sep 25 Yom Kippur, Beth El, La Jolla
Oct 3 Chabad of Los Angeles Sukkot Celebration
Oct 15/16 Shabbaton, Young Israel, Cleveland, OH
Oct 17 Private Event, Cleveland, OH
Oct 23 Shlomo Carelbach Memorial Concert, LA, CA
Nov 3/4 Scholar in Residence, Brandeis, CA
Nov 10 East Meadow Jewish Center, E. Meadow, NY
Nov 10 Reconstructionist Synagogue of N. Shore, Plandome, NY
Nov 11 BJE, New York, NY
Nov 12-13 Community Shabbaton, London, England
Nov 14 Encounter Conference, London, England
Nov 21 B'nai Israel Concert, Tustin, CA
Dec 3/4 Community Shabbaton, Reno, NV
Dec 5 Orange County Chanukah Concert, Costa Mesa, CA
Dec 5 Stand With Us Concert, U of Judaism, L.A., CA
Dec. 7 San Diego Jewish Academy Chanukah Concert
Dec. 8 Aish Chanukah Party, LA, CA
Dec 9 Beth Sholom Chanukah Concert, Johnson City, TN
Dec 10-11 Temple Emanuel Shabbaton, Clemmons, NC
Dec 12 Raleigh, NC Community Concert
Dec 13 Temple Israel Chanukah Concert, W. Bloomfield, MI
Dec 14 Beth Israel, Flint, MI

2003

Jan 12 Salt Lake City JCC, Salt Lake City, UT
Jan 16 Temple Sinai, Denver, CO
Jan 17 Knesseth Beth Israel, Richmond, VA
Jan 18 Richmond JCC, Richmond, VA
Jan 19 Temple Sinai, Newport News, VA
Jan 20 JCC of Greater Orlando, Orlando, FL
Feb 1 Beth Ahm Israel, Hollywood, FL
Feb 2 Temple Shalom, Naples, FL
Feb 23 Private Event, Beverly Hills, CA
Mar 1 Sinai Temple, Milwaukee, WI
Mar 2 Milwaukee JCC, Whitefish Bay, WI
Mar 18 Purim Concert, Shaarei Tefilla, LA, CA
Mar 23 Jacksonville Jewish Center, Jacksonville, FL
Apr 4-5 Temple Emanuel, Tempe, AZ
Apr 6 Adat Ami, Las Vegas, NV
Apr 16-25 Worldwide Kosher Passover Program, Las Vegas, NV
Apr 27 Kahal Kadosh Beth Elohim, Charleston, SC
May 4 B'nai El Congregation, Frontenac, MO
May 5 Temple Isaiah, Stonybrook, NY
May 6 Har Shalom, Potomac, MD
May 7 Charles E Smith Day School, Rockville, MD
May 8 Merrimack Valley Jewish Federation, Laurel, MD
May 10 JCC Concert, Paramus, NJ
May 18 Private Event, Beverly Hills, CA
May 20 Private Event, LA, CA
May 30 Peninsula Sinai Congregation, Foster City, CA
Jun 7-21 Australia Concert Tour
    Yom Limmud Sydney
    Moriah College
    St. Ives School
    Masada College
    Temple Shalom, Surfers Paradise
    Community Concert, Brisbane
Jun 29 Private Event, Santa Monica, CA
Aug 1-6 CAJE, Ohio State University, Columbus, OH
Sep 9 S'lichot Concert, Beth El, La Jolla, CA
Sep 16-17 Rosh Hashana, Beth El, La Jolla, CA
Sep 25 Yom Kippur, Beth El, La Jolla, CA
Oct 3 Sukkot Concert, LA, CA
Oct 5 Sukkot Concert, Beverly Hills, CA
Oct 16-28 Israel Tour
    Hebrew University
    Aish HaTorah
    OU World Center
    Mayanot Yeshiva
Nov 1 Anshe Emeth Temple, New Brunswick, NJ
Nov 2 Agudas Israel, Caldwell, NJ
Nov 4 Young Israel, Harrison, NY
Nov 9 Private Event, Burbank, CA
Nov 15 Ner Tamid, Palos Verdes, CA
Nov 16 Private Event, N. Hollywood, CA
Nov 21-22 Shabbaton, Jerusalem Fund, Laguna Beach, CA
Nov 24 Chicago Torah Network, Chicago, IL
Dec 5-6 B'nai Aviv, Weston, FL
Dec 7 Segerstrom Hall Chanukah Concert, Irvine, CA
Dec 19-20 Community Shabbaton, Pleasanton, CA
Dec 21 Chabad of San Francisco, San Francisco, CA

Glossary

Achdut — Jewish unity

Akeyda — the binding (and near sacrifice) of Isaac on top of Mount Moriah

Aleynu — closing prayer declaring God's oneness and the hope for Tikkun Olam

Aliyah — emigration to Israel; referring to the divisions of the Torah portion into smaller subsections; calling someone up to read from the Torah

Alter Kaker — slang term for a senior citizen (Yiddish)

Am Kadosh — Holy Nation

Amidah — the standing prayer, the main part of any given prayer service

Amud — synagogue lectern from which clergy leads services; one side of a folio of Talmud

Arba Minim — the four species waved on Sukkot (palm, myrtle, willow, plus the citron/etrog)

Aseret Y'mei T'shuva — the Ten Days of Return from Rosh Hashana through Yom Kippur

Ashkenazi — a descendant of Jews from Eastern European communities

Ashrei — fortunate; alphabetic prayer of praise recited three times a day

Aufruf — celebration where a groom is called to the Torah on the Shabbat before his wedding (Yiddish)

Aveirot — sins, lit. to cross over (a moral boundary)

Avinu Malkeinu — "Our Father, Our King" prayer recited during High Holidays and fast days

Avodah — sacred work, service to God; prayer

B'chol Dor Vador — "in every generation," shorthand for the rabbinic obligation for all Jews to visualize themselves as having participated in the Exodus from Egypt

B'ezrat Hashem — with God's help

B'hatzlacha — much success (or good luck)

B'nai Yisrael — the Children of Israel

B'racha — a blessing

B'racha Achrona — blessing after food is eaten

B'reicha — a pool

B'reishit — "in the beginning;" Genesis, the first book of the Torah

B'tzelem Elokim — in God's image

Ba'al Tashchit — the commandment not to waste or destroy natural resources

Ba'alei T'shuva — "masters of return," those who have returned to the path of the Torah

Bachura — young woman

Badeken — ceremony where the groom veils the bride

Bamidbar — Numbers, the fourth of the Five Books of Moses, lit. "in the desert"

Baruch Hashem — Blessed is God, or thank God

Bashert — soulmate

Batim — boxes housing Mezuzah scrolls

Beit Din — Jewish court

Beit Hamikdash — Holy Temple

Beit Midrash — study hall

Bimah — pulpit

Birkat Hamazon — blessing after eating bread

Bitachon — acting on one's faith in God; in modern Hebrew, security

Bocher — young man; an unmarried male student

Brit milah (also bris) — circumcision ceremony

Chabad — a Chassidic sect of Judaism focused on Jewish outreach and spirituality

Chad Gadya — playful Passover song with deep symbolism; lit. "one small goat"

Chag Sameach — traditional Jewish holiday greeting; lit. "happy holiday"

Chai — life; also refers to the numerological value of eighteen

Chalav — milk

Challah — traditional braided bread made for Shabbat and holidays

Chametz — food that is prohibited on Passover; lit. "leaven"

Charedim — strictly Orthodox Jews, usually rejecting modern secular culture; lit. "those who tremble (in fear of God)"

Chas V'shalom — God forbid; lit. "completely disgraced"

Chassid — a follower of the Chassidic movement

Chassidim — plural form of Chasid

Chassidut — the teachings of Chassidic rabbis based in Jewish mysticism

Chatzot — midday or midnight according to rabbinic calculations

Chaya — life force; can also mean "animal"

Chazal — an acronym for "our sages, of blessed memory"

Chazzan — cantor

Cheder — classroom, elementary school for Charedi children

Chet — sin; lit. "missing the mark"

Chevra — peer group, any group of friends

Chevra Kadisha — Jewish mortuary, prepares body for burial, lit. "holy community"

Chevrusa — (or chevruta) learning partner

Chok — a Torah law that does not necessarily make logical sense, i.e., not eating shellfish

Cholent — traditional Shabbat stew, usually served at Shabbat lunch

Chiddush — an new interpretation; lit. "renewal"

Chinuch — education

Chiyuv — halachic obligation

Chol Hamo'ed — the intermediate four days of an eight day holiday when one is free to engage in activities prohibited on the first and last days of the festival

Chrein — horseradish, usually served with gefilte fish

Chumus — Middle Eastern chickpea spread

Chuppah — bridal canopy

Chutzpadik — with chutzpah, audacious

D'varim — Deuteronomy, the final of the Five Books of Moses, lit. "words"

D'veykus — deep connection with God, cleaving

Daf — a leaf (both sides of the page) of Talmud

Daf Yomi — the tradition of learning a daf of Talmud each day in conjunction with Jews worldwide, eventually finishing all tractates in seven and a half years

Daled Amos — biblical measurement equivalent to six feet; the distance one escorts guests

Daven — to pray (Yiddish)

Dayenu — Pesach song with theme of gratitude; lit. "it would have been enough"

Derech — path; commonly refers to the path of Torah

Derech Eretz — "the way of the land;" acting with civilized behavior

Emes — truth

Emunah — faith

Emunah P'shuta — simple faith

Eretz — the land, pertaining to Eretz Yisrael

Eruv — Shabbat boundary fence beyond which no object may be carried

Etrog — citron fruit essential to the rituals of Sukkot

Fleishig — a meat dish

Frum — observant of halacha (Yiddish)

G'zeirot — "fences," or rabbinic laws to prevent inadverdent transgression

Gam zeh l'tovah — for our ultimate benefit; lit. "this is also for good"

Ganze mishpacha — the whole family

Gashmius — materialism

Gedolim — Torah luminaries

Gemach — free loan society, i.e. for cash, strollers, wedding dresses, etc.

Gemara — rabbinic commentary on the Mishnah (oral tradition); lit. "the completion"

Gematria — numerical value of a Hebrew letter or word

Gerim — converts to Judaism (singular is "ger"), lit. "strangers"

Geulah — redemption

Gevurah — strength/discipline

Glatt — food with the strictest standard of kashrut, lit. smooth, referring to the butchered animal's lungs

Haftorah — selection from Nevi'im read on Shabbat and holidays

Hagbah — lifting of the Torah at the end of the public reading

Haggadah — book of Passover liturgy read during the Seder

Halacha — Jewish law as established by the rabbis

Halachic — of or relating to Jewish law

Halevai —it should be, if only (Aramaic)

Hallel — a series of Psalms sung on holidays describing national redemption, God's love for the Jewish People and how we reciprocate with partnership and gratitude.

Halleluyah — "praise the Lord"

Hamelech — "the King"; often used in reference to a prayer said on Rosh Hashana asserting God's Kingship

Hashem — title used in place of the ineffable four-letter name of God; lit. "the name"

Hatarat Nedarim — Nullification of Vows ceremony on Erev Rosh Hashana

Hatikvah — Israel's national anthem

Havdalah — the ceremony with which we commemorate the Sabbath's departure on Saturday night; lit. "the separation"

Hechsher — a mark on a product signifying it has been certified Kosher

Hesped — eulogy

Heter — a rabbinic leniency

Hillel — student organization on college campuses named for a great sage of the Mishnah

Hineni — an enthusiastic response to the call of a higher purpose; lit. "here I am"

Hodu — "thanksgiving" or "turkey" in Hebrew.

Ikar — central point

K'lalot — curses

K'hila — congregation

K'hila Kedosha — holy congregation

K'riya — ritual tearing of clothes upon a close relative's death

Kabbalah — a term referring to the body of Jewish mystical teachings; lit. "receiving tradition"

Kabbalist — one who possesses a masterful understanding of Kabbalah

Kaddish — Aramaic prayer exalting the Kingship of God; recited multiple times throughout every prayer service as well as at funerals, houses of mourning, and during the eleven-month period after the death of a close family member

Kaparot — pre-Yom Kippur atonement ceremony using cash or fowl

Kasher — to make something Kosher

Kasha — a difficult Halachic question

Kashrut — Kosher status

Kavod — respect

Kedusha — holiness; the central, interactive part of the cantor's repetition of the Amidah

Kedoshim t'hiyu — "you shall be holy", the mission statement of the Jewish people

Kedushin — the first stage of the Jewish wedding process in which the bride and groom "separate" themselves as a couple from all others

Ketuvim — the third part of Tanach after the Chumash and Nevi'im; lit. "writings"

Kever — grave

Ki heym chayeynu — expression used to stress the importance of the Mitzvot to the Jewish people; lit. "because they (the Mitzvot) are our very lives!"

Kibbutzniks — residents of a Kibbutz (Israeli commune)

Kiddush — sanctification of the day integral to the blessing over wine for Shabbat or a holiday; the festive snack served at synagogue following services

Kiddush Hashem — a sanctification of God's name; an action through which the beauty of Jewish values is put on display for all to see

Kinderlach — term of endearment for "children" (Yiddish)

Kinnot — the anguished poetry of suffering through the ages; read primarily on Tisha B'av

Kippah — Hebrew word for yarmulke, the skullcap worn by Jewish men

Kiruv — outreach; the act of bringing relatively uninvolved Jews closer to Judaism

Kittel — a white ceremonial robe worn by men for weddings, certain holidays and burial

Kiyor — the washbasin used by priests in the Mishkan

Klezmer — Ashkenazi folk music

Kodesh — holy

Kohanim — priests (also Cohanim, singular is Kohen)

Kotel — The Western Wall in Jerusalem, the only remnant of the Holy Temple foundation; the holiest religious site of the Jewish people

Kumzitz — a communal gathering to sing spiritual songs with musical accompaniment, often held around a campfire or in a dimly lit area

L'chaim — the traditional Jewish toast; lit. "to life!"

L'haniach — "to put on"; the key word in the blessing for putting on Tefillin (see below)

L'hitpalel — to pray; a reflexive verb, can be translated as to imagine or dream

L'sheim Shamayim — for the sake of heaven

L'shana haba'ah — final song at the end of the Seder and Yom Kippur services, "next year" (in Jerusalem)

Latkeh — potato pancake fried in oil; a traditional Chanukah treat

Lech L'cha — "go for yourself"; God's command to Avraham to travel to the land of Israel

Leil — the night of, as in Leil Seder, the night of the Seder

Levaya — funeral

Lichvod Shabbas — to honor the Sabbath

Limudei Kodesh — Torah studies

Litvak — Lithuanian-style

Lulav — the combined species of plants waved in conjunction with the Etrog for the rituals of Sukkot, also refers specifically to the palm frond

M'varchim — the Shabbat before Rosh Chodesh when we bless the upcoming new month

Ma yakar — how precious; the first few words of the prayer uttered while putting on the Tallis

Ma'ariv — the evening prayer, established by the patriarch Yaakov

Machmir — strict, especially in regards to matters of halacha

Machzor — a prayer book used for a specific holiday

Magen David — Jewish star: lit. Shield of David

Maykel — lenient, especially in regards to matters of halacha

Manna — an edible substance that God provided for the Israelites in the desert

Mashal — parable; example

Matzah — flat, crunchy, unleavened bread eaten on Passover

Mazel tov (or Mazal Tov) — Hebrew equivalent of "congratulations"; lit. "good luck"

Mechitza — room divider in Orthodox congregations to separate men's and women's sections

Megillah — scroll; refers to the story of Purim, or Megillat Esther; Other Megillot are

Ruth, Eicha (Lamentations), Kohelet (Ecclesiastes), Shir Hashirim (Song of Songs)

Melech — King

Mensch — an individual of exemplary character (Yiddish)

Menucha — rest

Mesorah — heritage, religious tradition

Mevatel — nullify

Mezuzah — scroll mounted on the doorposts of a Jewish home; contains the Sh'ma and V'ahavta (D'varim 6:4-9)

Midrash — the non-legal oral tradition, a collection of stories and wisdom teachings relating to Tanach

Mikvah — ritual bath

Milchig — a milk-based dish

Mishlei — the Proverbs of King Solomon, part of the Ketuvim (Writings) section of Tanach

Mishnah — the Torah's law-related oral tradition, passed down from Moses at Sinai through the generations, eventually compiled by Rabbi Yehuda HaNassi (189 CE)

Mincha — the afternoon prayer, established by the patriarch Yitzchak

Minyan — a group of ten assembled for prayer; an established prayer group

Mishpatim — Torah laws that make logical sense; i.e. thou shalt not kill

Mishkan — the Tabernacle, or the portable temple used for priestly service in the desert and up until the building of the first Temple in Jerusalem

Mishpacha — family

Mitzvot — commandments; the 613 Torah commandments, composed of 248 positive commandments (thou shalt) and 365 negative commandments (thou shalt not)

Modim — prayer in the Amidah (see above) offering thanks to God

Motza'ei Shabbat — Saturday Night

Muktzeh — any object not to be used/touched on Shabbat or holidays

Mussaf — additional prayer service for Shabbat and most holidays; lit. "that which is added"

Nachat (Nachas) — Jewish pride

Nazir — one who gave up grape products and haircuts in order to connect with God

Nechama — comfort

Nefesh — the basic life force, instinct, autonomic survival functions; the first of the five levels of the soul

Neshama — the generic Hebrew term for soul; the third level of the five levels of the soul

Netzach — eternity

Nevi'im — the books of Tanach after the Five Books of Moses, describing the period of the prophets; lit. "prophets"

Nusach — the unique, traditional melodies of prayer

Ohr Hamakif — aura, lit. "surrounding light"

Olam habah — the World that is Coming; the Jewish conception of heaven, the world as it will be in the Messianic era

Omanut — Hebrew word for "art," also used to refer to crafts done at children's camp

Omer — a measurement used during the Temple era for grains and dry goods, equal to about 3.64 liters; the daily offering of barley between Pesach and Shavuot

Oshkibunis — my Grandpa Bill's nonsense term for taking walks

P'sukei D'zimra — Psalms of Praise; collection of prayers providing emotional uplift and connection in the morning service; lit. "sung passages"

Parashat Hashavua — the Torah portion of the week

Pasuk — sentence; a verse of Tanach

Pesach —Passover

Peyot (Peyos) — the sidecurls of a man's hair that grow unchecked in accordance with the Torah's chok to "not round off the corners of your head"

Pidyon haben — the ceremony performed in order to redeem the firstborn son who is the property of God according to the Torah; lit. "redemption of the son"

Pinteleh yid — the Jewish pilot light that gets ignited when visiting Israel or hearing a great sermon, song or story; lit. "the spark of the Jew" (Yiddish)

Poskim — rabbis who answer halachic questions

Poskin — to rule in accordance with a Halachic dictate (see above)

Posul — not fit for ritual use

Pushke — tzedakah box (Yiddish)

Resha'im — evil people, plural of rasha

Rachamim — compassion

Ratzon — desire; will

Rebbe — a term of endearment applied to a rabbi; the head of a Chassidic sect

Rebbetzin — a rabbi's wife

Refa'eynu — shorthand for the blessing in the Amidah (see above) where we pray for God to heal us; lit. "heal us"

Rosh — the head, as in Rosh Yeshiva (head of a yeshiva) or Rosh Hashana (head of year)

Rosh Hashana — Jewish New Years; the first of Tishrei

Rova — the Jewish Quarter of the Old City

Ruach — the second of the five levels of the soul; great feeling and enthusiasm; lit. "wind"

Ruchnius — spirituality

S'fatai — my lips

S'firat Ha'omer — the forty-nine day period between the second day of Passover and Shavuot

S'lichot — penitential prayers said on fast days and during the High Holiday period

Sh'ma (Shema) — the quintessential prayer of Judaism, declaring God's oneness and uniqueness; lit. "hear"

Sh'moneh Esrei — alternate name for the Amidah; lit. "eighteen" in reference to the original Amidah being composed of eighteen blessings

Sh'mirat Halashon — Guarding one's tongue, not engaging in lashon hara

Sh'mitah — the seventh (Sabbatical) year when we let the land go fallow in Eretz Israel

Sh'mot — Exodus, the second of the Five Books of Moses, lit. "names"

Sh'varim — shofar sound in which three medium long blasts are blown

Sh'vil Hazahav — the balanced path; lit. "the golden path"

S'micha — rabbinical ordination; lit. "the leaning of the hands"

Sabras — refers to native—born Israelis, who are characteristically prickly on the outside and soft on the inside; lit. "prickly pear cactus"

Sandek — the person honored with holding the baby boy during the bris

Sanhedrin — the supreme court in Temple times, located adjacent to the Temple in Jerusalem

Schnorrer — a beggar or scrounger, one asking for charity

Seder — the succession of readings and rituals performed around the dinner table on the first and second night of Passover (first night only for residents of Israel); lit. "order"

Sefer — a book, typically referring to a holy book of Jewish teachings

Segula — a protective or benevolent charm or ritual, lit. "treasure"

Sephardi — Jews from Spanish, North African and Middle Eastern communities

Shacharit — the morning service established by the patriarch Abraham

Shalom Bayit — peace in the home

Shalosh Esrei Middot — Thirteen Attributes of God, part of prayers of S'lichot and holidays

Shana Rishona — the first year of marriage

Shana tova umetuka — traditional greeting used during Rosh Hashana and the days immediately following the holiday; lit. "a good and sweet new year"

Shavua tov — "have a good week," greeting after conclusion of Shabbat

Shavuot — the festival of "weeks" celebrating the giving of Torah; occurs the 6th of Sivan

Shefa — abundance

Shehakol — shorthand for the blessing recited over any food or drink that does not fall under the category of fruit, vegetable, baked goods, bread, or wine

Shehechyanu — a blessing over something new, ie. clothing or fruit, also said in the first night Kiddush of any given holiday

Sheker — falsehood

Shep nachas — to derive pride (Yiddish)

Sheish Mitzvot Temidiot — The Six Constant Mitzvot (see Coda chapter)

Sheish Z'chirot — The Six Remembrances (see Coda chapter)

Sheva brachot — the seven blessings recited under the chuppah; the festive meals during the week after a Jewish wedding

Shiva — week long intense mourning period and prayer gathering after burial

Shidduch — a marriage arranged by a matchmaker; also refers to the person with whom the match is being made

Shochet — one who performs ritual slaughter

Shofar — the ram's horn blown each day of Elul and on Rosh Hashanah

Shoftim — refers to the leaders of Israel during the period preceding the Davidic monarchy; lit. "judges"

Shomer — guarding, as in guarding Shabbat, mitzvot, or negiah (physical contact with opposite sex other than parent, child or spouse)

Shpilkes — impatience (Yiddish)

Shtetl — the insular Jewish village of "the old country"

Shtreimel — a fur hat worn by men of certain Chassidic sects (Yiddish)

Shuckling — ritual swaying of worshipers, from the Yiddish "to shake,"

Shuk — a Middle Eastern market

Shul — synagogue (Yiddish)

Shyla — question; Yiddish analogue of the Hebrew word "She'elah"

Siddur — prayer book

Siyum — celebratory completion of a holy book, i.e. a tractate of Talmud

Sofrim — scribes; singular is "sofer"

Sukkot (Succot) — 7 or 8 day festival of joy (depending on whether or not one lives in Israel) marking the ending of the harvest and culmination of the High Holiday season

Sukkah — the temporary dwelling we build and live in throughout the holiday of Sukkot

Sur meyrah v'asey tov — "run from evil and do good," T'hillim 34:14

T'ki'ah — the shofar sound in which one long blast is blown

T'ki'ah g'dola — the final extended blast of the shofar service; also the end of Yom Kippur

T'ruah — the shofar sound in which nine or more short, stacatto blasts are blown

T'shuva — repentance, the process of returning to God; lit. "return"

Tachanun — portion of the daily prayer service where one asks God's forgiveness

Tachlis — the bottom line, the heart of the matter

Tafkid — personal task or responsibility

Tahor — pure

Tahara — ritual washing of a Jewish corpse

Takanot — rabbinic decrees

Tallis — (or Tallit) prayer shawl

Tallit katan — the inner garment with four fringes worn under one's shirt

Tanach — complete Bible, composed of the Five Books of Moses, Nevi'im and Ketuvim

Tefillah — prayer

Tefillin — pair of black leather boxes containing the passages from Torah on parchment; one is strapped on the forehead, the other to the weaker bicep

Tehillim — the book of Psalms, part of the Ketuvim

Talleisim — plural form of Tallis

Tikkun Olam — the responsibility to fix the world; lit. "healing of the world"

Tinok — baby

Tish — a celebratory ceremonial meal, often accompanied by singing and dancing

Tisha B'Av — the Ninth of Av, annual fast day commemorating the destruction of both Temples and other tragedies befalling the Jewish people

Tishrei — the seventh month of the Jewish year containing the High Holidays

Tochacha — rebuke

Tofel — secondary

Treif — non-kosher food; also used colloquially to describe anything incongruous with a Torah lifestyle; lit. "unfit for use"

Tzara'at — a skin condition often mistranslated as leprosy, usually resulting from speaking lashon harah,

Tzedakah — charity; lit. "righteousness"

Tzitzit — the fringes attached to a four cornered garment to remind one of the Mitzvot; also used to describe the tallit katan, the inner garment

Tzniut — modesty or privacy

Tzuris — strife; Yiddish analogue of the Hebrew word "Tzarot"

Uman — the city in Ukraine where Rabbi Nachman of Breslov is buried

Upsherin — first haircut for boys on their third birthday (Yiddish)

V'ahavta — shorthand for the second paragraph of the complete Sh'ma reading, which is made up of four paragraphs; lit. "and you shall love"

Vaad — a rabbinic council or group

Vaiter — forward, as in moving on in the text when studying (Yiddish)

Vayikra — Leviticus, the third of the Five Books of Moses, lit. "And He called"

Vidui — portion of the daily Tachanun prayer and Yom Kippur prayers where one recites a "confession" of sins committed

Y'mach sh'mo — may his name be obliterated, a phrase used when referring to an archenemy of the Jews

Yam Suf — Reed Sea (often mistranslated as Red Sea), crossed by the Jews a week after leaving Egypt

Yarmulke — Yiddish word for kippah, the skullcap worn by Jewish men

Yahrzeit — anniversary of one's death

Yechida — to be alone with God; The fifth level of the five levels of the soul; the identification with the ultimate universal soul. Lit. "oneness"

Yehudim — Jews

Yeshiva — a place of Jewish learning with a Beit Midrash; lit. "sitting"

Yetzer harah — the evil inclination

Yetzer hatov — the good inclination

Yichud — to be alone with another, namely with one's spouse right after the chuppah

Yichus — direct connection to one's Judaically enlightened ancestry

Yidden — Jewish people, plural of Yid (Yiddish)

Yiddishkeit — Judaism (Yiddish)

Yisrael — Israel

Yitro — the Torah portion containing the Ten Commandments; named for Moses' father-in-law

Yizkor — the memorial service held on certain Jewish holidays

Yom Kippur — The Day of Atonement; the tenth of Tishrei

Yovel — the fiftieth "Jubilee" year after seven sh'mittah cycles

Z'rizut — alacrity; an intense readiness to perform God's will

Ziv Hashechina — the light of God

About the Author

Sam Glaser's soulful music has become part of the fabric of Jewish life in communities worldwide. Named one of the top ten Jewish performers in the U.S. by Moment magazine, Glaser is equally comfortable behind a grand piano in intimate solo concerts, leading his eight-piece band or headlining with full orchestra. While he typically performs in synagogues and Jewish Community Centers, he has appeared at such venues as L.A.'s Greek Theater, Gibson Amphitheater, Staples Center and Dodger Stadium as well as on Broadway and at the White House. He has traveled the world over in concert, from Sydney to London, Hong Kong to Istanbul. Glaser performs for a wide array of audiences of all faiths; his devoted fans in the Jewish world range from those in the Reform and Conservative movements to Modern Orthodox and Chassidim. He has performed at the foremost Jewish national conventions including General Assembly, Limmud, Central Conference of American Rabbis, Coalition for Advancement in Jewish Education, Cantors Assembly, American Conference of Cantors, Union for Reform Judaism's Biennial, Orthodox Union, Hadassah, American Jewish Outreach Professionals, Aish Partners Conference and the National Association of Temple Educators.

Glaser's compositions have enigmatic appeal; they are complex and catchy, wise and witty, youthful and seasoned. His best-selling Jewish albums include *The Promise, Hallel, Nigun/Voice of the Soul, Presence, The Bridge, A Day in the Life* and the award-winning children's musical *Kol Bamidbar*. He was one of the first artists signed by Sony/JMG Records, a Jewish music label that released *Inspired: Best of Sam Glaser* and *Sam Glaser's Rockin' Chanukah Revue*. Glaser's childrens' album *Soap Soup* won such awards as the John Lennon Songwriting Competition, Parents Choice, National Association of Parenting Publication and the

International Songwriting Competition. Sam's popular *The Songs We Sing* series updates the classics in the Jewish repertoire for a new generation. In addition to his twenty-five albums, he has published collections of lyrics and poetry, written six musicals and published multiple sheet music songbooks and an SATB choral book. In his cutting-edge recording studio, Glaser Musicworks, he produces albums for a variety of recording artists, music for apps and games and scores for Warner Brothers, PBS and Sports Channel networks.

Since 1997, Glaser has performed in an average of fifty cities a year. His energetic style and passionate delivery never fails to ignite the spirit of audiences of all sizes and age groups. Countless fans credit Glaser's music with their enhanced connection with God and the mission of the Jewish People. His annual tours frequently include performances throughout Israel, making him a unique ambassador for the Holy Land. He has performed outside of the Jewish world in churches of various denominations, family and executive retreats and events honoring Israel. In addition to his concerts, Glaser leads joyful living seminars, Scholar-in-Residence programs and Shabbatons where he is featured as performer, cantorial soloist and speaker. As an informed and committed Jew, Sam is able to speak from the heart and lead by example.

One of Sam Glaser's gifts is working with young people: he acted as director of the renowned Yad b'Yad Youth Theater Troupe, music specialist at Camp Ramah, music director for the JCC Maccabee Games and music director for the Brandeis Collegiate Institute. He frequents religious school retreats, NFTY, USY and NCSY youth conventions and collegiate Hillel Houses. Glaser has served as an enthusiastic music teacher at Harkham Hillel Hebrew Academy, Sinai Akiba Academy, Shalhevet and Yeshiva University High School of Los Angeles.

Glaser has emerged as one of the leaders of the Los Angeles music scene. For eight years, he was Executive Director of the Jewish Music Commission, an organization that commissions and produces major Jewish works. He has produced such events as the annual American Jewish Song Festival, American Jewish Idol and Taste of Kosher LA. For six years, Glaser acted as Music Coordinator for the Department of Continuing Education at American Jewish University where he supervised the music curriculum and directed the Cultural Arts Program. Currently, Glaser teaches Seasons of Joy, a weekly outreach/conversion class and leads The Possible You personal growth seminars.

Glaser has been composing, singing and tickling the ivories since the age of seven. He graduated the University of Colorado, Boulder with a Bachelor of Science in Business and a Minor in Music and supplemented his studies at Berklee College of Music in Boston and at the UCLA Film Scoring Program. He began his post-college career as a journalist writing for the Santa Monica Bay News, the L.A. Reader and the L.A. News and has worked as a photographer, sportswear manufacturer and sales manager. He is a life-long skier, body-boarder and mountain biker.

Glaser is active in NewCAJE, Aish HaTorah, The Happy Minyan, The Community Shul, The Jewish Music Commission, Chabad, Pico Shul, Brandeis-Bardin Institute, The Center for Jewish Culture and Creativity and Jewish Big Brothers. He is a seven time ASCAP Award winner, has been honored with the Jewish Big Brother Achievement Award and received the Power of One Award from Aish HaTorah/Young Israel for his significant impact on the Jewish world. He lives in the Pico-Robertson neighborhood of Los Angeles and devotes his life to his wife Shira and children Max, Jesse and Sarah.